D1521554

The Stratigraphy and Archaeology of VENTANA CAVE

— *Photo by Marc Gaede*

The Stratigraphy and Archaeology of VENTANA CAVE

EMIL W. HAURY

Collaborators

KIRK BRYAN

EDWIN H. COLBERT

NORMAN E. GABEL

CLARA LEE TANNER

T. E. BUEHRER

THE UNIVERSITY OF ARIZONA PRESS

Tucson, Arizona

Second printing 1975

THE UNIVERSITY OF ARIZONA PRESS

I.S.B.N.-0-8165-0536-5
L.C. No. 51-802

Preface 1975

A number of significant additions to the Ventana Cave story have been made since this book first appeared in 1950.

Foremost among these new insights are radiocarbon determinations established by a technique not available to us when the excavations were undertaken in the early 1940s. Thanks to Hayden's initiative, the C^{14} samples collected by him have produced the following results: charcoal from the Volcanic Debris Layer, 11,300 B.P. (9350 B.C.) ± 1200 (A-203, Damon and Long 1962); carbonate of bone from the Conglomerate Layer, 12,600 ± 600 B.P. (GX-1896); cement carbonate around bone, Conglomerate Layer, 7210 ± 240 B.P. (GX-1895). Susceptibility of exchange with carbonate dissolved in descending ground water renders the last date suspect.

Radiocarbon results convincingly support Kirk Bryan's early geologically based determinations that the minimum age of the oldest culture-bearing layer "... may be as late as 10,000 years ago" (p. 126). Furthermore, they are consistent with recent findings in southwestern Early Man sites.

The presence of *Equus occidentalis* Leidey as a contemporary of man in Ventana Cave has been further confirmed (Colbert, E. W., *The Kiva,* Vol. 29, No. 1, 1973).

In the light of recent discoveries in Southern Arizona, the basalt flake point imputed to be Folsomoid (p. 179–180) may be recognized as a local imitation of a Clovis point. The quartz point (p. 179), by material and technique, is also within the Llano tradition (Haury,

E. W., E. B. Sayles, and W. W. Wasley, *American Antiquity,* Vol. 25, No. 1, 1959), and therefore foreign to the desert lithic technology.

Extensive work in desert archaeology since 1950 has convinced Hayden that the Malpais horizon, deleted by Rogers (p. 193), should be restored as basal to the San Dieguito complex. Tool types attributed by Haury (p. 193) to San Dieguito I were actually those related to San Dieguito III, a regrettable and confusing error. The relationship of the initial human manifestation in Ventana Cave to the pan-western desert complexes and clarification of dating problems await Hayden's further treatment.

A review of plant remains in 1957 by Hugh Cutler has determined that *Cucurbita moschata* and *C. maxima,* discussed on page 165, were both *C. mixta.*

Ventana Cave has remained essentially unchanged since the excavations in 1941–1942 except in one respect. Regrettably, the uncontrolled curiosity of visitors has largely destroyed a demonstration block of the consolidated Volcanic Debris Layer left by us as an exhibit. Ventana Cave is listed in the National Register of Historic Places.

The availability once again of this long-out-of-print book has been made possible by the generosity of friends of the University of Arizona Press. They deserve the gratitude of an ever-widening circle of people who are interested in desert archaeology.

EMIL W. HAURY
JULIAN D. HAYDEN

Preface to the Original Edition

This report has grown out of anthropological studies on the Papago Indian Reservation, southern Arizona, inaugurated in 1938 by the Arizona State Museum and the Department of Anthropology, University of Arizona. It is in no sense an accounting of all work done in this area to date but specifically covers only the excavations in Ventana Cave. This project, carried through two successive seasons, from March 18 to May 27, 1941, and from February 5 to April 11, 1942, was made possible largely through two assignments of funds for labor from the Indian

Division of the Civilian Conservation Corps, allowing the employment of an average crew of ten native workmen. Overseers were paid from funds of the Department of Anthropology and the Arizona State Museum, and additional financial help was graciously given by Mr. and Mrs. Wetmore Hodges.

The deep, stratigraphically deposited layers of Ventana Cave, with their diversified human evidences, possess much of intrinsic interest and give us a truer glimpse of the archaeology of this marginal area than we have had heretofore. For the first time, too, light is shed on the nature of Hohokam perishable culture and, most important of all, the long inherent cultural sequence provides a working chronology which brings new information to bear on other culture complexes, particularly the pre-ceramic and pre-agricultural pattern of the lower Colorado River and California desert areas.

Every available opportunity since the excavations were brought to a close in April, 1942, has been spent in preparing this report. A frontal attack on the manifold problems posed by the cave has demanded a call for help from others, and it is now a pleasant task to acknowledge the able and unselfish assistance given by many people. Time-consuming jobs were cheerfully undertaken by various specialists when they themselves had little to gain, but whose contributions were essential to the understanding of these problems. Hence, any credit which this report may earn must be shared by all, from the Indian laborer to the specialist.

My first thanks go to the Papago Tribal Council, which at all times has maintained a most charitable and interested point of view toward our work. Without permission from this group we should not have been able to lay the original plans for archaeological studies in the Papago Reservation. Similarly, district councils and individuals, on whose land our work took us, have been most coöperative. From the Indian Service personnel, notably Superintendents T. B. Hall, Wade Head, and later Mrs. Head who succeeded him, we have received both encouragement and helpful suggestions. The administrative affairs of the CCC-ID were in the hands of Mr. Minton Nolan, to whom thanks are due for sparing us from many hours of clerical details. Mr. and Mrs. Alden Jones of Sells have given invaluable assistance in countless ways.

I am certain that due to their sympathetic understanding of the Papago, many obstacles were avoided which otherwise might have arisen during the course of our several projects.

To the Papago workmen, mostly recruited from the Ventana district, goes my admiration for sticking to a job which, at times, was anything but pleasant. They earned for themselves the reputation of being hard workers, of being interested in what we were doing, and of relating among themselves many things which amused them greatly—chiefly at our expense. Mr. Juan Xavier was helpful in our dealings with the Indians and he assisted also as foreman of the labor crew.

The immediate supervision of the field work in 1941 was in the hands of Mr. Wilfrid C. Bailey, then a graduate student in the Department of Anthropology, University of Arizona; and in 1942 this responsibility rested with Mr. Julian D. Hayden who has had wide field experience in Arizona and California. Contact between the field supervisors and myself was maintained as closely as teaching duties at the University would permit. These men ably organized the work, kept the necessary records, cared for the thousands of specimens, and often ingeniously solved the unending problems arising in cave work. Full recognition must be given to Mr. Hayden's keen powers of observation and for his sensitiveness to changes in the cave fill, all of which has made the reconstruction of events possible. His field notes and diagrams are a model of completeness and clarity, and have been drawn upon heavily in this report.

I feel a particular sense of debt to those who have collaborated directly in writing this report: Drs. Kirk Bryan, of Harvard University; Edwin H. Colbert, of the American Museum of Natural History; Norman E. Gabel, of Santa Barbara College; and Mrs. Clara Lee Tanner, of the University of Arizona. Authority has been imparted to special problems by each. Dr. Bryan's important section in the dating of the early cave deposits is the outgrowth of a first-hand study in January, 1942, and in it he has drawn on his wide experience in similar problems elsewhere.

Mr. Malcolm Rogers, of the San Diego Museum of Man, who is intimately acquainted with the difficult desert archaeology of the Southwest, was good enough to spend several days in the Papago Reservation with me searching for surface evidence of Early Man to amplify the cave's story. He also visited the excavations and later examined the collections in the laboratory, making many helpful suggestions. The correlation of the early Ventana lithic manifestations with the lower Colorado River complexes, Figure 117, was worked out jointly with him.

I also voice my appreciation to the following persons who have assisted in the ways indicated:

The late Dr. Glover M. Allen and his successor, Dr. Barbara Lawrence, Museum of Comparative Zoology, Harvard University, for identification of the abundant modern faunal remains; Dr. H. R. Hill, Los Angeles County Museum, identification of marine shells; Dr. Forrest Shreve, Tucson, who undertook the analysis of the plant remains; Dr. Edgar Anderson, St. Louis Botanical Gardens, for analysis of corn; Dr. Thomas W. Whitaker, Geneticist, U. S. Dept. of Agriculture, for identification of pumpkins; Dr. A. C. Whitford, Newburgh, N. Y., for identification of cordage fibers; Mr. Arthur Woodward, Los Angeles County Museum, for evaluating certain items of early historic white culture; and Dr. Joseph D. Aronson, then with the U.S. Indian Service, for x-rays of mummies. Mrs. Kate Peck Kent aided in the analysis of several complicated textile problems. Among the University's personnel, whom I have plagued constantly, must be mentioned Dr. T. F. Buehrer, who undertook the analysis of soil samples, the results of which are presented in the Appendix; Dr. A. B. Caster for the water analysis of the cave's spring; Dr. C. T. Vorhies* and Dr. L. P. Wehrle for animal and insect determinations; and Drs. R. A. Darrow and W. S. Phillips for help on certain botanical problems; mineralogical determinations were made by Mr. R. E. Heineman, formerly with the Arizona Bureau of Mines. Drs. F. W. Galbraith, E. D. Wilson, and E. H. McKee visited the cave in my company and offered useful information on geological problems.

To Mr. Oscar F. Davisson I owe thanks for modelling the bust of a male mummy in an effort to recapture the original features of this person. With war-time restriction on civilian aerial photography, the United States Army Air Corps willingly complied with a request for air photographs of the cave and environs, seen in Plates 1*a*, 2*b*, 3*a*, and 4. Mr. E. T. Nichols has kindly supplied the photograph used in Plate 1*b*,

* Deceased.

and Mr. Alfred A. Cohn supplied Plate 26*f*. Laboratory photographs are by Mr. E. B. Sayles, Curator of the Arizona State Museum.

Much of the drudgery connected with preparing the specimens has been done by students, and I desire especially to mention Mr. Charles Hewitt, who donated his services to this end for the better part of the summer of 1942. The brunt of the technical job of typing the manuscript and of setting up and checking the tables has fallen to my secretary, Mrs. Frances Slutes, and to Mrs. Joe Ben Wheat, who have worked uncomplainingly at this tedious task.

I am deeply grateful to Mrs. Slutes for having expertly guided the manuscript through the proof-reading and indexing stages, a heavy responsibility which she shouldered during my sabbatical leave from the University of Arizona.

A word as to the illustrations: The difficulty of photographing chipped tools predominantly in a near-black stone, and the war-time film shortage are responsible for the extensive use of line cuts. Lacking an artist, the undersigned was forced to prepare these to the best of his limited ability. A special effort was made to reproduce the specimens faithfully, frequently with the aid of a camera lucida, but it has not always been possible to translate the exact stony quality to paper. In the drawings with sections or edge views of stone implements chipped on one side, the section to right of the plan is oriented with unchipped face to left and in transverse sections, below plan, this face is down.

For the illustrations used in Figures 97, 98, 102–110 inclusive, 112 and 113, I am indebted to Mr. Barton Wright, student in the Department of Anthropology.

The facts revealed by the cave have been presented herein to the best ability of each co-author. But I will be the first to admit that this report leaves much to be desired. The complexity and extent of the subject has made it overly long and it has not been possible to satisfactorily explore many problems. Much has had to be glossed over. Some of the conclusions reached do not coincide with those presented by others, but we feel privileged to have viewed the picture from an unusually good vantage point.

Emil W. Haury

Contents

PART IV

PART VIII

APPENDIX

PLATES

TEXT FIGURES

TABLES

APPENDIX

PART I

Introduction

It has become customary in recent years for institutions to plan research which brings together a number of related and interdependent fields of learning and to extend these studies over some years of time. This mode of attack, it is felt, produces more in the long run than a number of small-scale and independent operations. In 1938, the Department of Anthropology of the University of Arizona and the Arizona State Museum jointly developed and embarked on such a program. Several circumstances influenced the choice of a major problem.

It was clear from the start that the locale of our work should be within easy reach of Tucson so as to cut down travelling time and expense. It was believed further that any studies undertaken should be carried out during the winter, or school year, when the maximum amount of assistance was available.

Two regions suggested themselves. The first was northern Mexico, and the second was Papagueria, lying west of Tucson principally north of the International Line and approximately coinciding with the area now set aside as the Papago Indian Reservation (Fig. 1). After weighing the advantages and resources of each area from an anthropological point of view, and keeping in mind ease of access, Papagueria was eventually decided upon.

The chief attraction of this area was its present day Indian population, the Papago, numbering approximately 7,000 members, and although several extended pieces of research had been done among these people,[1] there was still much to be learned about every phase of their culture. Archaeologically, the area had been inspected only by reconnaissances of the most preliminary sort. Work along this line, it was believed, would not only clear up the void which existed there in the archaeological studies of Arizona as a whole, but would also provide the basis and background for projected studies of the Papago as well as paving the way for archaeological studies in northern Mexico.

A resumé of the accomplishments of our varied interests follows:

Racial study:[2] 1938-39, by Norman E. Gabel, results presented as a doctoral dissertation, Harvard University, 1941.

Linguistic study: started in 1938 by William Kurath.[3]*

Ethnological studies: (1) Certain aspects of Papago music, 1941-43, by Jane Chesky, results presented as M.A. thesis, University of Arizona, 1943.

(2) An analysis of Papago basketry with emphasis on the recent developments, 1941-42, by Margaret Shreve, presented as M.A. thesis, University of Arizona, 1943.

(3) Collection of Papago folklore and mythology, 1930, and continuing, by Clara Lee Tanner.

(4) Collection of Papago material culture by the Arizona State Museum.

Archaeological studies: (1) Reconnaissance, 1938 and continuing.

(2) The excavation of a 14th century site, 1938-39, by Frederick H. Scantling; results offered as M.A. thesis, University of Arizona, 1940.[4]

★

1. M. L. Kissell, 1916; E. F. Castetter and R. M. Underhill, 1935; R. M. Underhill, 1939; E. F. Castetter and W. H. Bell, 1942; W. Kurath, 1945; A. Joseph, R. Spicer, and J. Chesky, 1946.

2. N. E. Gabel, 1949.

3. 1945.

4. F. H. Scantling, 1939.

*Deceased.

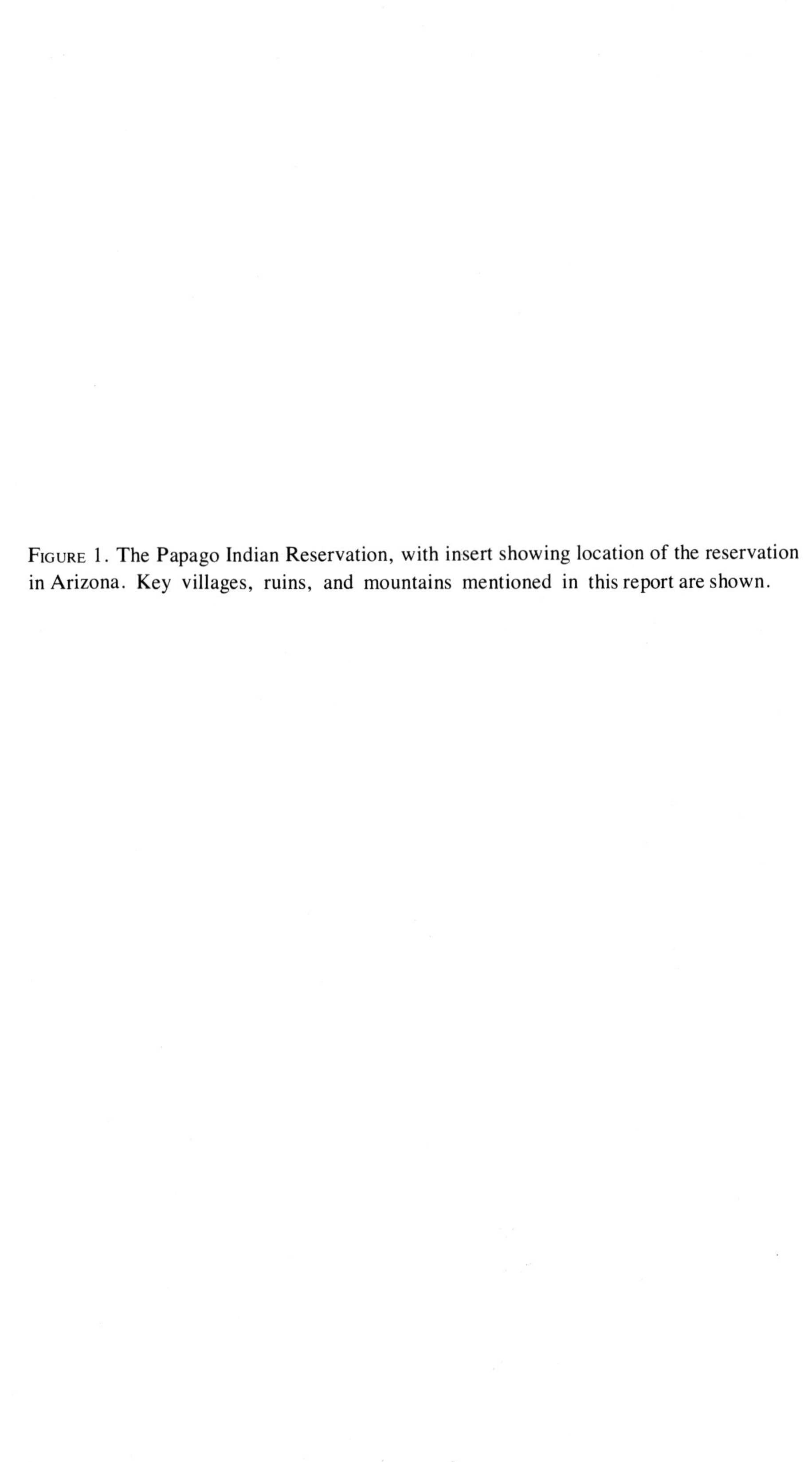

FIGURE 1. The Papago Indian Reservation, with insert showing location of the reservation in Arizona. Key villages, ruins, and mountains mentioned in this report are shown.

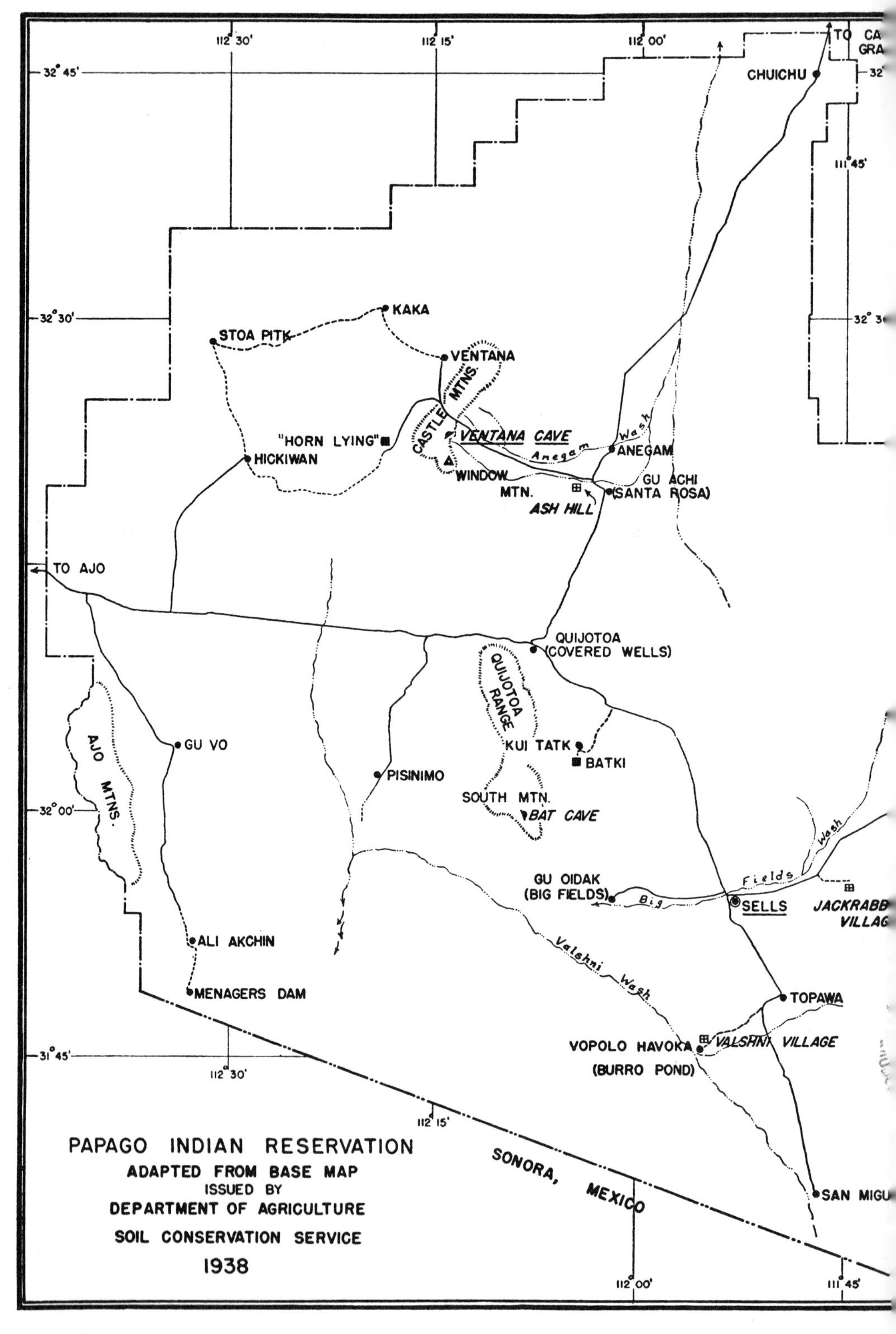

PAPAGO INDIAN RESERVATION
ADAPTED FROM BASE MAP
ISSUED BY
DEPARTMENT OF AGRICULTURE
SOIL CONSERVATION SERVICE
1938

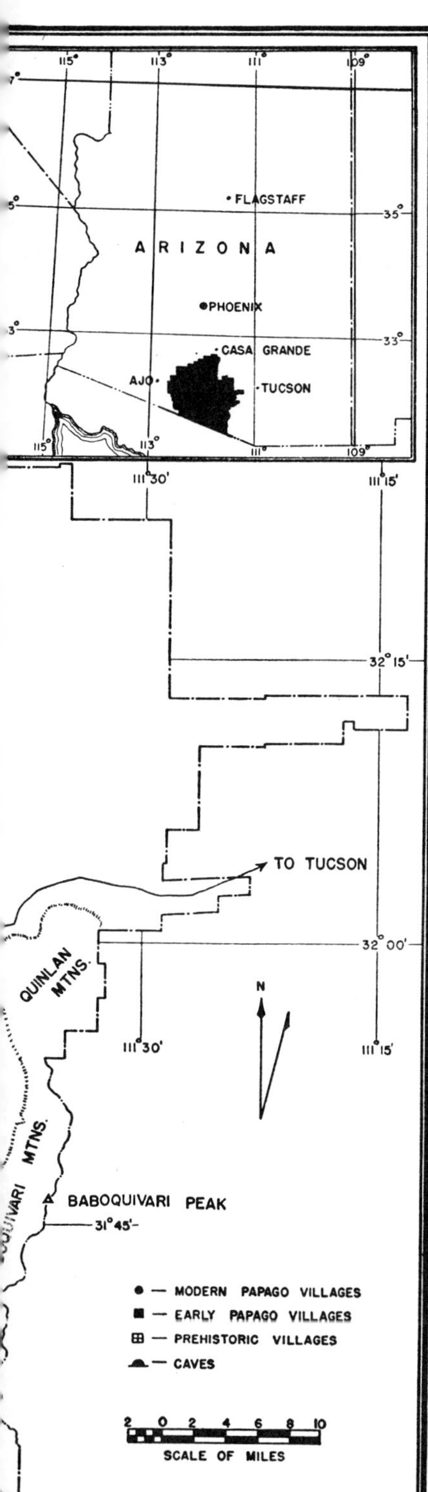

FIGURE 1. The Papago Indian Reservation, with insert showing location of the reservation in Arizona. Key villages, ruins, and mountains mentioned in this report are shown.

(3) The excavation of a pre-14th century site, 1939-40, by Arnold M. Withers; results offered as M.A. thesis, University of Arizona, 1941.[5]

(4) Additional testing in a second pre-14th century site and start of excavation of Ventana Cave, 1940-41, Wilfrid C. Bailey in charge.

(5) Completion of Ventana Cave, 1942, Julian D. Hayden in charge.

As this report is concerned with the results of the Ventana Cave excavations, now is not the time to dwell on further details of the above projects excepting those in the archaeological category.

SUMMARY OF THE ARCHAEOLOGY OF PAPAGUERIA

Southwestern Arizona and the adjoining territory in Sonora, Mexico, have been known since Spanish times as Papagueria. Today a large parcel of land, comprising about 2,775,000 acres, has been set aside as a reservation for the Papago Indians on the American side of the International Line (Fig. 1). Perhaps no part of the Southwest is so little known from the archaeological point of view. Largely responsible for this are the facts that, until recently, the country presented certain difficulties in transportation, and the existence of a general feeling that the archaeological resources of the area were extremely limited. As early as the 1880's, Bandelier, for example, during his historic pilgrimage through the Southwest, decided not to go into Papagueria because of the "gradual disappearance of aboriginal ruins in that direction."[6] Likewise, Lumholtz,[7] who made an extended traverse of Papagueria, mentioned only occasional archaeological remains. More recently Gladwin says "The impression one receives is that the archaeological remains are those of venturesome Hohokam groups which . . . . found the desert environment unfavourable, and withdrew."[8] Conse-

★

5. A. M. Withers, 1944.
6. A. F. Bandelier, 1892, pt. II, p. 472.
7. C. Lumholtz, 1912.
8. H. S. Gladwin, 1937, pp. 94-95; see also R. M. Underhill, 1939, pp. 5-13, for a summary of Papaguerian archaeology as of that time.

quently the area held no particular attraction for systematic work, especially since much more spectacular remains were available for study in northern Arizona and in neighboring states.

Shortly after the establishment of Gila Pueblo in 1928, the work of this institution focused attention on the middle and lower Gila River drainage and on Papagueria. This was followed by Sauer's and Brand's[9] work a few years later. Gila Pueblo's survey in the Papago area netted approximately seventy ruins which were used as a basis for a brief report.[10] The Gladwins at that time were interested primarily in uncovering traces of the migrations of the Hohokam who, it was thought, colonized the Gila Basin as a fully blown culture. While their study shed no light on this problem,[11] it did call attention to the presence of scattered ruins throughout the area.

From all of this preceeding work, limited as it was, and coupled with the survey and excavations conducted by the Arizona State Museum, a few general conclusions may be reached. Actually ruins are not particularly scarce, since it is impossible to go very far in any direction without stumbling across vestiges of early people. The impression entertained by Bandelier was largely inspired by the fact that what evidence existed was thinly spread out, standing in sharp contrast to the well-known pueblo ruins where the people lived in compact houses and where all debris was concentrated within the immediate area. The general economy of the Indians in Papagueria a thousand years ago could not have been much different from that of the Papago of today, namely, a *rancheria* type of life wherein the individual family homes, flimsy in nature, were scattered over wide areas. As a rule, this does not lead to vast midden accumulations or the piling up of architectural remains. There are, nevertheless, a number of ruins which show sizeable trash mounds reflecting a more concentrated village form, as has

★

9. C. Sauer and D. Brand, 1931. pp. 102-104.
10. W. and H. S. Gladwin, 1929.
11. *Op. cit.*, p. 133.

been noted by the Gladwins.[12] In addition, there are numerous other evidences of occupation, as, rock shelters, fortified hills,[13] canals, *charcos*,[14] and shrines.

With relatively few possibilities of studying stratified remains, the task of reconstructing the prehistory of Papagueria is a difficult one. On the whole, the archaeologist must be willing to expend much more time and money for what he gets than in most other areas. The first two seasons of intensive digging by the Arizona State Museum in what were considered very promising sites produced disappointingly small results; but these, nevertheless, were better than none at all.

The first of these ruins, known as the Jackrabbit Village, was excavated under the field supervision of Frederick H. Scantling from December 12, 1938, to March 28, 1939, with the aid of a CCC-ID grant from the Federal Government. This ruin is located seven miles east of Sells, and approximately four miles from the foothills of the Quinlan Mountains (Fig. 1). It occupied an area over 300 m. square and consisted of one large rectangular earthen inclosure and a great number of trash mounds ranging from nearly imperceptible elevations above the surrounding terrain to a mound somewhat over 2 m. in depth. In spite of the extent of this village, the excavations failed to reveal any change whatsoever in the culture within the period of occupancy. As a consequence only a single phase was defined.

The second village, known as the Valshni[15] Village, was excavated from November 7, 1939, to April 20, 1940, under another federal aid arrangement with Arnold M. Withers in charge. The Valshni Village is located fourteen miles southwest of Sells and one-half mile east of the modern Papago village of Vopolo Havoka (Burro Pond). It was spread out over an area approximately 200 x 275 m. and was recognizable by five conspicuous trash mounds having a depth range of about

★

12. *Op. cit.*, p. 117.
13. J. W. Hoover, 1941.
14. Reservoirs for impounding surface water.
15. Valshni is a Papago term meaning "wash" and refers to the large drainage flowing in a northwesterly direction a short distance west of the site. This the map makers have called Valshni Wash—actually meaning "wash-wash."

1 to 2 m. Examination of surface sherds from these mounds gave strong indications that several phases might be determined, none of which would duplicate the evidence thus far ascertained at the Jackrabbit Village.

Combining the results of these two enterprises, Scantling and Withers determined three consecutive phases, namely: Sells, Topawa, and Vamori, the latter being the oldest in the series. We may now proceed with the synopsis of these phases, drawn chiefly from the reports[16] of Scantling and Withers.

Sells Phase

Distribution in Space

Principally north of the International Boundary, east to the eastern flank of the Baboquivari Mountains, north approximately to the present limits of the Papago Reservation, and west to the Ajo Mountains.

Distribution in Time

Approximately A.D. 1250 to 1400, estimated on the basis of intrusive pottery of known age.

Excavated Sites

Jackrabbit Village (Ariz. DD:6:1) and Ash Hill (Ariz. Z: 12:5, Fig. 1).

Unexcavated Sites

Approximately 55 ruins of this phase have been visited. These are well distributed over the reservation with a concentration in the southeastern part.

Phase Determinants

Architecture— (a) Domestic structures built on surface, wattle, or wattle-and-daub construction, outline rectangular with rounded ends; 6.00 to 7.00 m. in length and about 3.00 m. wide; main roof supports near corners, no entrance passage, hearth near door, clay lined; door normally oriented to east and cen-

★

16. F. H. Scantling, 1939, 1940; A. M. Withers, 1941, 1944.

trally located in long side of house. (b) Massive adobe walled inclosures with no evidence of habitations within. Evidently walls were for retaining artificial fill in the construction of elevated platforms. (c) Large rectangular earthen inclosures, flimsy unit-habitations within. These are somewhat suggestive of the compound idea.

Disposal of the Dead—Inhumation, semi-flexed or extended, in shallow graves; no offerings; bodies covered with rocks.

Physical Type—No data.

Pottery— (a) Indigenous types (coil, paddle-and-anvil): 1. Tanque Verde Red-on-brown:[17] the principal painted ware of the phase; distribution extends through the Tucson area and into the San Pedro Valley, where it occurs both with and without Gila Polychrome of the Salado Culture; constitutes approximately 3 per cent of the pottery produced in the Jackrabbit Village. 2. Sells Red: a slipped and polished redware occurring principally as bowls with everted thickened rims, interiors not smudged; constitutes about 55 per cent of the ceramic complex. 3. Sells Plain: a thick non-micaceous ware representing about 42 per cent of all pottery made.

(b) Intrusive types: 1. Casa Grande Red-on-buff.[18] 2. Gila Polychrome (very rare).[19]

Miscellaneous Clay Objects—Hemispherical, top- and pulley-shaped spindle whorls in plain and red slipped polished finishes.

Stone—1. Metates: troughed, open one or both ends; basin-shaped, flat, rectangular, or oval. 2. Manos: loaf shaped, both single and double handed types; also an elongated and well shaped type with overhanging ends.[20] 3. Mortars and pestles. 4. Axes: short, both single and double bitted, three-quarter

★

17. I. Kelly, in preparation.

18. W. and H. S. Gladwin, 1933, pp. 22-24; E. W. Haury, 1945, pp. 51-63.

19. W. and H. S. Gladwin, 1930, pp. 6-7; E. W. Haury, 1945, pp. 63-80.

20. This unique form of mano has been reported heretofore at Chametla, Sinaloa, by I. Kelly, 1938, p. 61, and farther north at Guasave, Sinaloa, by G. F. Ekholm, 1942, p. 107. The Papaguerian examples may be indicative of southern contacts.

groove. 5. Arrow shaft polishers. 6. Rectangular or triangular thin flaked blades with ground edges, designed for mounting in a wooden haft for use draw knife fashion. 7. Miscellaneous: hoes, slate palettes (rare), effigy, rings, drills, projectile points, all occurring too infrequently to establish standard types.

Shell—Whole shell beads, pendants, bracelets, rings, trumpet (*Strombus galeatus*); shell products are rare.

Bone—Splinter awls.

Food—No data, but corn and beans by inference together with natural foods of the area. Irrigation practiced by use of canals which gathered rain runoff from gently sloping terrain.

Remarks

Ruins of the Sells Phase in Papagueria greatly outnumbered those of all other times. It is inferred from this that the area experienced its densest population, the present time included, during this stage of cultural development. The locale of the larger villages was often so selected as to be near precipitous hills which could be easily defended. In many instances these natural vantage points were further strengthened by the building of defense walls and revetments representing a gigantic outlay of labor and suggesting that the time was one of danger. The identity of the people who were threatening the natives of the area has not fully been determined, but possibly some significance may be read into the fact that the Sells Phase development coincided with the southerly and westerly expansion of the Salado Culture at about the beginning of the 14th century. Although these immigrants settled in numbers in the Phoenix-Casa Grande area and on the Santa Cruz at Tucson, they did not gain a foothold in Papagueria.

With no possibilities whatever of applying tree-ring dating to Sells Phase remains, the determination of the age must be based on the next best line of evidence, namely, intrusive pottery, the age of which is known. The dated types include Casa Grande Red-on-buff and Gila Polychrome, the former with a span of approximately A.D. 1200 to 1400, and the latter dating primarily from the 1300's. Neither of these types occurs in abundance anywhere in the area covered by our survey and contacts to the north and east were apparently not very strong. The presence of an occasional Gila Polychrome sherd in Sells Phase contexts tends to point to the 14th century as the probable age for the phase. This cross-dating is also borne out at the University Indian Ruin[21] east of Tucson, where the companion wares of this phase occur strongly associated with the pottery of the Salado Culture.

Topawa Phase

Distribution in Space

Limited principally to the central and southern part of the reservation.

Distribution in Time

About A.D. 1100 to 1250.

Excavated Sites

Valshni Village, (Ariz. DD:1:11, Fig. 1) and Ariz. DD:5:8.

Unexcavated Sites

Only a dozen or so additional ruins assignable to this phase have been found.

Phase Determinants

Architecture—Domestic structures on surface, or slightly excavated, wattle-and-daub construction. Form, generally rectangular; lengths from 9.20 to 10.50 m. and widths from 5.85 to 6.10 m. Hearths near entrance consist of clay-lined basins, rims flush with floor. Post hole pattern not well established; entrance oval covered vestibule, stepped in the deeper structures, usually oriented to the east. The adobe-walled and earthen inclosures of the Sells Phase are absent.

Disposal of the Dead—No data.

Physical Type—No data.

★

21. J. D. Hayden, MS.

Pottery—(a) Indigenous types (coil, paddle-and-anvil): 1. Topawa Red-on-brown: a derivative of Vamori Red-on-brown and an obvious forerunner of Tanque Verde Red-on-brown. Constitutes but 0.5 per cent of all pottery made. 2. Valshni Red: a prototype of Sells Red, usually lacking the thickened everted rim and comprising about 22 per cent of the ceramic output. 3. Sells Plain: indistinguishable from that of the Sells Phase, representing about 77 per cent of the local pottery.

(b) Intrusive types: 1. Sacaton Red-on-buff.[22] 2. Casa Grande Red-on-buff. 3. A single Black-on-white sherd from the Anasazi area, not precisely identifiable but close to Mesa Verde Black-on-white or Sosi Black-on-white.[23]

Miscellaneous Clay Objects—1. Specialized spindle whorls as in Sells Phase (rare). 2. Perforated pottery discs.

Stone—1. Metates: shallow basin type (very rare). 2. Manos: both unshaped and shaped rectangular types. 3. Projectile points (too few to establish standard type). 4. Miscellaneous items include rubbing stones, hammer stones, crude flaked blades, and disc beads which are not particularly definitive.

Shell—Whole shells, cut shells, pendants, and bracelets, all of distinct Hohokam complexion.

Bone—Splintered and sawed awls.

Food—No evidence of canal irrigation. Inferentially people were agricultural but scarcity of grinding tools and abundance of animal bones, mainly mountain sheep, suggest heavy dependence on native foods.

Remarks

Although the definition of the Topawa Phase must be regarded as far from complete, such evidence as we have allows us to place it culturally as an antecedent step of the Sells Phase and chronologically to a period of time comparable with the late Sedentary and early Classic of the Gila Basin. The dating must be regarded as an estimate but is based on the presence of

★

22. H. S. Gladwin, *et al.*, 1937, pp. 171-178.
23. H. S. Colton and L. L. Hargrave, 1937, pp. 211, 231.

pottery types and other traits, such as mosaic plaques, whose approximate age has been determined. The affiliation of the culture is distinctly Hohokam with, of course, some differences attributable to the marginal location of the culture.

Vamori Phase

Distribution in Space

Known only in the Valshni Village with possibly a slight showing in Ventana Cave.

Distribution in Time

Roughly A.D. 800 to 1100, an estimate founded on intrusive pottery.

Excavated Sites

Valshni Village (Ariz. DD:1:11, Fig. 1).

Unexcavated Sites

A few sites, probably of this horizon, have been recognized in the survey.

Phase Determinants

Architecture—Houses on surface or slightly excavated, variable in plan from oval to rectangular with rounded corners. Lengths from 6.20 to 8.40 m. and widths from 3.60 to 5.40 m. Entrances were normally oval but occasionally straight-sided, sometimes stepped. Hearths located near entrance, deep, somewhat irregular in outline with a lip rising above floor level. Post hole pattern not satisfactorily preserved. Orientation of entrance normally to east.

Disposal of Dead—No conclusive data but one inhumation, probably belonging to this phase, was found in the Valshni Village.[24]

★

24. Cremation was also practised as indicated by a plain ware jar with incinerated bones exposed in a small arroyo cutting through a site (Ariz. DD:2:7) located at the northwestern edge of the Quinlan Mountains. This village was dominantly of Sells Phase age but a portion of it, where the jar was found, is assignable to a Vamori Phase occupation. This association is further strengthened by the type of jar, quite common in the Vamori Phase but unknown in the Sells Phase.

Physical Type—No data. Burial too fragmentary for determination.

Pottery—(a) Indigenous types (coil, paddle-and-anvil): 1. Vamori Red-on-brown: This is the oldest indigenous painted pottery thus far identified in the southern part of the Papago Reservation and consists of crudely drawn simple linear and occasionally curvilinear patterns in red on a rough brown ware. Less than 2 per cent of the pottery found was of this type and it may be regarded, on typological grounds, as the forerunner of a somewhat more developed Topawa Red-on-brown. 2. Valshni Red: indistinguishable from that of the Topawa Phase except that it was much less commonly made (1.6 per cent). 3. Sells Plain: the same as in later phases but constituting approximately 96 per cent of the ceramic output.

(b) Intrusive types: 1. Santa Cruz Red-on-buff.[25] 2. Sacaton Red-on-buff. 3. Trincheras Purple-on-red.[26] 4. Trincheras Polychrome.[27] 5. Altar Polychrome.[28]

Miscellaneous Clay Objects—Unperforated and perforated potsherd discs.

Stone—1. Metates: slab or basin types (two specimens only). 2. Manos: mainly rectangular with thick loaf-shaped cross section. 3. Axes: short, single-bitted, three-quarter groove variety with ridges. 4. Projectile points (too few to express types). 5. Stone vessels. 6. Frog effigy palette. 7. Mosaic plaque with pseudo-cloissonné.[29]

Shell—Whole shell and cut shell pendants, disc and tubular beads, rings, and bracelets.

Bone—Splintered and sawed awls.

Food—Same as for the Topawa Phase.

★

25. H. S. Gladwin, *et al.*, 1937, pp. 179-185.

26. C. Sauer and D. Brand, 1931, pp. 107, 109; D. Brand, 1935, p. 299.

27. C. Sauer and D. Brand, 1931, pp. 109, 110; D. Brand, 1935, p. 300; also referred to as Nogales Polychrome, E. P. Clark, 1935, Pl. XXX.

28. A. M. Withers, 1941, pp. 42, 43.

29. Late or Sedentary Period type; H. S. Gladwin, *et al.*, 1937, pp. 130-134.

Remarks

The Vamori Phase clearly represents people at a relatively undeveloped level of culture, at least insofar as aesthetic accomplishments were concerned. The local potters were only beginning to paint their own wares, whereas they had access by trade to the sophisticated products of their near kin and neighbors, the Hohokam, and the southern authors of the Trincheras complex. One gains the impression from this that the Valshni Village occupants held an area marginal to these two centers and that they lagged ceramically and doubtless in other lines as well. This appears to have been due in large part to their isolation and to the uncongenial nature of their desert environment. On the whole the affiliation was with the Hohokam,[30] reflected by such items as village arrangement, the accumulation of large trash mounds in the village area, house types and the possession of stone vessels, palettes, three-quarter grooved axes, mosaic plaques, and shell work.

The assignment of the age of this phase to the 9th and 10th centuries rests on the identity of the above features with those of the Santa Cruz and Sacaton Phases at Snaketown and the preponderance of Gila Basin intrusive sherds dating from these phases.

DISCUSSION

The deficiencies in our knowledge of the cultural history of Papagueria is thrown into stark relief by the preceding outline. There are many gaps and a decided lack of concreteness is in evidence but at least we have a working basis and a point from which further studies may be made. Contributing to the difficulties of reconstructing history in the area concerned are: (1) a scarcity of vertically stratified sites such as we are accustomed to in the Gila Basin and in the Anasazi area, and (2) the culture was never so highly evolved as in the adjoining areas to the

★

30. A. M. Withers, 1941, pp. 79-83, does not agree with this interpretation, believing that the people of this phase may have been remnants of an old group, pressed between and influenced by the Hohokam to the north and the Trincheras culture to the south.

north, leaving fewer material assets behind it. This means that in order to establish sequences, heavy reliance must be placed on horizontal stratigraphy and typology and that fewer criteria for determining the steps in the reconstruction of the cultural picture are available. Precise dating is impossible as the tree-ring technique cannot be used because of the unavailability of proper woods. Ideas pertaining to a general correlation of the steps in the local development must be based, to a large extent, upon pottery types foreign to Papagueria but which have been placed chronologically in those areas where they were at home.

In spite of all these shortcomings it may be claimed that the three phases outlined represent nuances within a single culture and that the culture, therefore, was not transitory. Continuity is indicated in the mode of life, in fundamentally similar houses, in basically the same pottery differing from time to time only because of local evolutionary changes, and in links suggested by practically all of the minor arts and crafts.

Without endeavoring at this point to fully justify the following observation (see p. 546), similarity in the majority of characteristics between the archaeology of Papagueria and that of the Gila Basin indicates a basic relationship between the people of these two areas. Papagueria must certainly be counted within the Hohokam domain. A few significant differences are observable, largely accounted for by environment. In Papagueria the economy throughout the three phases appears to have been predominantly food-gathering with agriculture secondary, whereas the reverse was true among the Hohokam who occupied fertile river valleys with unlimited agricultural possibilities. The persistence into modern times of this same pattern among the Pima and Papago is clearly brought out by Castetter and Bell[31] in their recent study of the agricultural practices of these people. It may be pointed out, however, that in Papagueria there is some evidence of increased dependence on agriculture from the Vamori to the Sells Phases inclusive.

★

31. E. F. Castetter and W. H. Bell, 1942, pp. 56-59.

This is seen in the simple irrigation systems of the southern part of the reservation which are assignable to the 14th century, coinciding in time with the major development of canal irrigation during the Classic Period in the Gila and Salt River valleys.[32]

The pottery of the two areas although constructed by the same technique, i.e. coil, paddle-and-anvil, does not display a comparable pattern of development. During the Santa Cruz Phase, when the Hohokam of the Gila Basin were producing highly decorated pottery, having gone through a whole series of introductory stages, the Papaguerian people were just beginning to indulge in a few bold and not very successful experiments in painting pottery. Not until the Sells Phase or by about the 14th century, when they seemed to have been influenced to a large extent by the ceramics of the Tucson area, was any prominence achieved along this line.

Perhaps the outstanding difference between these two regions was in the manner of disposing of the dead, namely, the customary cremation of the Hohokam as opposed to earth burial among the people of Papagueria. This is particularly true for the Sells Phase, as there are suggestions that the difference will prove to be less extreme in the earlier phases. It is doubtful if such a conflict can be interpreted as a denial of the relationship advanced above, where a majority of other traits reflect a bond so strongly.

Until information to the contrary is forthcoming, the inhabitants of Papagueria from about A.D. 800 to 1400 may be labelled as the Desert People, or the Desert Branch of the Hohokam, as recognizably distinct from those of the fertile valleys, the River People or the River Branch. The temporal relationship manifested in the development of the Desert Branch with the sequences establishd for the Hohokam of the Gila Basin and the Tucson area is illustrated in Figure 2. It is evident that this can be no more than a very tentative reconstruction since the chronological controls are vague.

★

32. H. S. Gladwin, *et. al.*, 1937, p. 58.

The foregoing discussion does not preclude contact between Papagueria and the people of adjoining areas other than the Hohokam. During the Vamori and Topawa Phases, apart from the close bond which existed with the Hohokam, the connection seems to have been chiefly with the people of northern Sonora, authors of the Trincheras complex. It is worth noting that the boundary between these two cultures was approximately that followed by the International Line of today, a curious coincidence, especially since there are no natural barriers to determine such cultural limits.

Later during the Sells Phase the relationship between Papagueria and Gila Basin peoples seems to have been considerably diminished and strong contacts were established with the Tucson area, which harbored an extensive population judged to be close kinsmen.

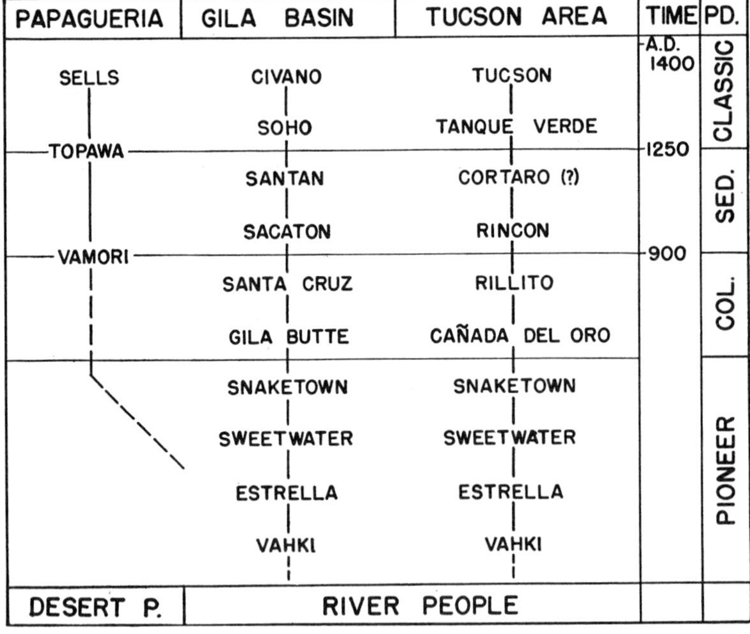

PAPAGUERIA
GILA BASIN
TUCSON AREA
TIME
PD.
A.D. 1400
SELLS
CIVANO
TUCSON
SOHO
TANQUE VERDE
CLASSIC
TOPAWA
1250
SANTAN
CORTARO (?)
SACATON
RINCON
SED.
VAMORI
900
SANTA CRUZ
RILLITO
GILA BUTTE
CAÑADA DEL ORO
COL.
SNAKETOWN
SNAKETOWN
SWEETWATER
SWEETWATER
ESTRELLA
ESTRELLA
VAHKI
VAHKI
PIONEER
DESERT P.
RIVER PEOPLE

FIGURE 2. Tentative correlation of Papaguerian phases with those of the Hohokam of the Gila Basin and Tucson area. Chronologies based on Snaketown and the Hodges' ruin (I. Kelly, MS)

The 14th century, as previously noted, was the time when the Salado people of puebloan extraction were pushing their frontiers in a southwesterly direction. Most of Papagueria appears to have been closed to them, probably because the local residents were unfriendly. Evidently minor contacts did exist, however, inasmuch as occasional Gila Polychrome sherds, a distinctive pottery type of the Salado people, do occur in the Jackrabbit Ruin and in Ventana Cave. What relationship there may have been to the Yuman people to the west has not been determined.

In a recent publication by Ekholm[33] a number of traits are described which represent important parallels in the archaeological remains of northern Sinaloa and those from the southern part of the present Papago Reservation. The latter are drawn principally from Sells Phase ruins, or from about the 14th century. Although the dating is not specific this appears to be within the time limits postulated for the Guasave Site. To mention a few of the parallels, attention should first be called to redware. Ekholm notes the fact[34] that northern Sinaloa and southern Sonora was the center of an excellent redware prior to what he calls the Aztatlan Complex. Sherds of this redware from Mexico, kindly submitted by Dr. Ekholm, when compared with Valshni Red of the Vamori and Topawa Phases are superficially almost indistinguishable. It may be logically suspected that the highly polished, hard redware from Papagueria, totally unlike that of the contemporary Hohokam, was related to and possibly derived from the redware complex farther south. By Sells Phase times there had been some divergence in the characteristics of this pottery in both areas so that Guasave Red from Sinaloa and Sells Red from Papagueria cannot be readily confused.

The Guasave Site yielded numerous clay spindle whorls, mostly of turbinate form.[35] Except for the fact that many of

★

33. C. F. Ekholm, 1942.
34. *Op. cit.*, pp. 75-77.
35. *Op. cit.*, pp. 87-88, Fig. 17.

these have incised decoration they closely resemble those associated in abundance in Sells Phase ruins. There can be no doubt that the spindle whorls of southern Arizona have a Mexican origin and at the present time the most likely source appears to be Sinaloa.

Among other traits worthy of mention Guasave shell work has a marked resemblance to that of the Hohokam, and a highly significant parallel is seen in the rare occurrence in Sells Phase ruins of a curious type of mano with overhanging ends, indicated by Ekholm to be the normal form for Guasave.[36] All of these clues to relationship sharpen the need for more extensive archaeological work, particularly in Sonora, if we are to understand the cultural links between Papagueria and northwest Mexico.

Throughout the Southwest one of the least known periods is the time immediately preceding the arrival of the Spanish explorers. The centuries from 1400 to 1700 are blank for the most part, even in those sections where there are existing Indian populations. So far this period has been most successfully bridged in northern Arizona by the work of the Peabody Museum[37] at Awatovi and in the ruins of the upper Rio Grande in New Mexico. One of the original objectives in the Papaguerian studies was to connect, if possible, the Papago Indians with the inhabitants of the ruins known to exist in their territory. The resumé just given of the archaeology of this area ends abruptly at about 1400 and at the conclusion of our second year's work we were faced with the need of finding sites assignable to this interim of 1400 to 1700 when the Papago Indians begin to figure in Spanish documents. Any conclusions as to relationship of the Papago with the ruins of the 14th century and earlier cannot be safely reached until the cultural pattern of this "dark age" has been determined. It should be pointed out that a similar hiatus exists in the archaeology of the Gila Basin, which has prevented linking the Pima directly with the Hohokam.

★

36. *Op. cit.,* p. 107.
37. J. O. Brew, 1941.

In the archaeological survey in the Papago area, encompassing something over 115 sites,[38] the majority of them were found to be of the Sells Phase vintage indicating that both the largest communities and numerically more of them were in existence during about the 14th century than at any other time. Some of the sites in the survey dated from still earlier phases and a few could be definitely assigned to historic Papago authorship. If any had been visited which fell within the period from 1400 to 1700 we had certainly not learned what to look for or what the criteria were for dating them. Consequently it became evident that the logical procedure was to work from the known to the unknown, *i. e.,* from sites known to be Papago, pushing the occupation back with the hope of establishing a connection with the latest prehistoric evidences as seen in the Sells Phase ruins.

Our first good documentation of the Papago comes from the diary of Father Eusebio Francisco Kino, who visited the region in the last decade of the 17th century. Among a number of places visited by him was a native village which he called Nuestra Senora de la Merced del Batki,[39] situated east of South-Mountain at the southern tip of the Quijotoa Range and approximately eight miles northwest of the present Papago Agency at Sells (Fig. 1). Kino reports that he was greeted in this village by more than two hundred people and that before his departure an additional three hundred Indians had come in from nearby points,[40] all of which indicated settlements of considerable proportions.

From the time of Kino's visit in the fall of 1698, Batki figured only in a minor way in the subsequent travels of Kino and his assistants. In about 1850 the village was overcome by a party of marauding Apaches who killed many of the Indians

★

38. That this is hardly an adequate sample is made clear by the ease with which additional sites may be found.

39. H. E. Bolton, 1936, p. 399. The name Batki, according to Alden W. Jones, is a corruption of the Papago name for the village Kui Tatk, brought about by poor phonetic translation from the Papago into Spanish by Kino, who was an Italian.

40. *Op. cit.,* p. 399.

and burned the houses,[41] thus effectively bringing to an end the occupation of Batki which, through documentary sources, we know to have been over 150 years in extent. After the Apache raid, most of the surviving Indians moved south and settled what is now known as Big Fields (Gu Oidak).

In laying out a course for future work it was evident that Batki might be a source of significant information. It was abandoned long enough ago so that the confusion resulting from recent inhabitation could be avoided; and it was a thriving and presumably prosperous village in 1698 permitting the assumption that it might even have had a respectable history prior to that date.

Through the help of Mr. Alden W. Jones, the ruins of Batki were located. They are, of course, well known to the local Papago, as the parents of many were born there. Among the indications supporting the identity of the place were: (1) burned houses, many with cremated bones of people killed or trapped in them,[42] (2) there was an absence of china, glass, and other trade goods of white origin,[43] (3) we recovered in the village area an iron lance blade of Spanish origin of 18th century date; and finally (4) there was present glazed pottery of Papago origin, but stimulated by early contact with the Spanish.

All of this strengthened the feeling that Batki would lend itself to archaeological work and, accordingly, plans were made to begin excavation. The necessary permission was obtained from the local Indians in addition to the permits already held. On March 3, 1941, actual digging began with Mr. Wilfrid C. Bailey in charge. Within the first hour a delegation of Papagos from Big Fields arrived saying that they had reconsidered the permission granted earlier and requesting that work cease

★

41. This event is recorded in a Papago calendar stick now in the possession of the Arizona State Museum. Many Papago children are reported to have been captured.

42. One account has it that the Papago placed those who were killed during the raid into the houses and set them afire.

43. Excepting glass beads reported by Mr. Arthur Woodward to date from about the middle of the 19th century.

at once. The principal reason given for this was that it was feared the malignant influences of the Apaches, now locked in the ruins of Batki, would be released by our work and that calamity would befall the residents of the reservation. We complied with the wishes of the Papagos, feeling that by further discussion and conference some workable plan might be developed. But two weeks of friendly arguing failed to produce any results and we were forced to abandon the project.

Again, through the assistance of Alden Jones, we were taken to another village called "Horn-Lying" located about twelve miles west of Santa Rosa (Fig. 1). It was reported to have been occupied during Kino's day and abandoned in 1880. The inspection of this site was disappointing since it was so excessively spread out and the culture so thin that it was believed digging could not be conducted profitably.

Enroute to "Horn-Lying" and not far from it, the road passed within a mile of a cave, visible when approaching the Castle Mountains from the east. Our visit to this cave was, in a sense, an answer to a prayer. The surface was littered with occupational debris, including scattered human bones, promising fruitful digging; and it came at a time when an *impasse* had been reached in the projected program. Plans were made at once to start work here and within a few days the crew of Papago laborers had been assembled for the job.

The preceding sketch outlines the work in Papagueria and presents the chain of circumstances leading to the excavation of Ventana Cave. It should be reiterated that Papagueria, instead of being an area penetrated periodically by people who were only to withdraw because of unfavorable living conditions, actually experienced permanent tenure and that, as a consequence, the area has archaeology in its own right, as is abundantly testified by the account in the following pages.

PART II

Ventana Cave

LOCATION AND ENVIRONMENT

The Papago country is in the Basin and Range Province of the United States. It is characterized by jagged and desolate mountain ranges of low altitude fringing broad and relatively flat alluvium-filled valleys. One of these ranges, located in the northwestern section, is known as the Castle Mountains (Fig. 1, Pl. 1*a*).[1] Like the rest, the axis trends roughly in a north-south direction having a length of approximately ten miles. From a five-mile breadth at the north end the chain tapers down at the south end to a series of hills separated by low passes. The range is of volcanic origin dating from Tertiary times and consists, for the most part, of agglomerates and complex basaltic flows. The violent processes of vulcanism seen here, coupled with subsequent erosion, have given these mountains a fantastic skyline of steep cliffs, turreted buttes, and domes, (Pl. 1*b*) which are the basis for the name. Added to this unreal range is Window Mountain (La Ventana) at the extreme southern tip, a hill approximately 150 m. high with two natural windows at the crest. The larger of these (Pl. 2*a*) is a prominent landmark of the re-

★

1. Extending from about Lat. 30°27′ N., Long. 112°11′ to 112°16′30″ W.

gion. The elevation of the range as a whole is inconspicuous, as the highest parts extend barely more than 200 m. above the alluvial plain.

Additional features of the Castle Mountains are the numerous niches, rock shelters, and cave-like hollows weathered out of the volcanic mass. The largest of these known at the present time in the whole range is the site of Ventana Cave (Pl. 2*b*).[2] It is situated[3] in the eastern face of a 300 m. long spur (Pl. 3*a*) which bears approximately north-northeast by south-southwest. This spur has a width of a little more than 100 m. and its crest is somewhat undulating, rising, on the average, 150 m. above the surrounding plain. With this height and relative narrow width, an abrupt rise is implied. Viewed from a distance, the ridge presents a slope-cliff profile, the lower half or slope rising at an angle of about 40° from the horizontal and composed chiefly of talus material, and the upper half consisting of a near-perpendicular cliff of massive basalt. The cave lies at the base of this cliff at a point where less talus has formed, due partly to the more resistant nature of the lava and because much of the waste rock has been carried away by gullying. The elevation above sea level at the cave floor is about 750 m. (2,460 feet).

From the cave an unobstructed view is had to the east and south of a vast lowland, broken by a succession of low mountain ranges, ending finally with the Baboquivari Mountains on the horizon sixty miles to the southeast. To the west and north, as seen from the top of Castle Mountains, this picture is repeated although on a less expansive scale.

The mountain ranges are not the barrier to travel one might suppose. Many of them are short and little more than islands in a generally flat terrain. Those ranges having some length are often broken by unsuspected passes and access to all parts of the territory could be had without difficulty. Scarcity of water was the real drawback to travel.

★

2. Arizona Z:12:5, Arizona State Museum Survey.

3. Township 12 South, Range 1 East, Section 14, northeast quarter; approximately ten miles west of the present Papago village of Santa Rosa (Gu Achi).

CLIMATE

Since a changing environment is reflected in the deposits of Ventana Cave, the climate and life of the area today should be examined in some detail. Excellent descriptions of the Papago country as a whole have already been given[4] and what follows here fits within the framework presented by others.

High temperatures, little precipitation, excessive evaporation, and a low relative humidity are the keynotes of the climate. As there are no weather stations nearer than thirty-five miles (Ajo), only approximations of temperature and rainfall for the Ventana district may be given. In Table 1,[5] mean annual temperatures are presented for stations to the west, north, and east of Ventana and ranging from thirty-five to eighty miles distant. With an elevation somewhat less than 750 m. (2,500 feet) above sea level a mean annual temperature for the Ventana area of about 65°, a mean maximum of about 80°, and a mean minimum of about 50° may be estimated.

TABLE 1

MEAN ANNUAL TEMPERATURES RECORDED AT SOUTHERN ARIZONA STATIONS

Station	*Elevation*	*Mean Annual Temperatures*		
		Max.	*Min.*	*Mean*
Ajo	1770	83.5	57.0	70.5
Gila Bend	737	89.3	54.1	71.7
Maricopa	1186			70.9
Phoenix	1108	83.7	55.6	69.7
Sacaton	1280	85.1	51.5	68.3
University of Arizona	2423	82.4	51.1	66.7

Extreme temperatures during the year are probably close to 115° and 20° and the diurnal range may be as high as 50°. The seasonal range is also great. The length of the growing season, computed on the basis of places of comparable altitudes[6] is about 245 days. Killing frosts may be expected by mid-November and continuing to mid-March.

The cave lies in a belt of Arizona receiving an average an-

★

4. K. Bryan, 1923, 1925*a*, pp. 29-53; E. F. Castetter and W. H. Bell, 1942, pp. 18, *et. seq.*

5. From H. V. Smith, 1930, Table V.

6. *Ibid.*, Table XI

nual rainfall varying from three to ten inches.[7] The figure for the cave area may be estimated at about seven to eight inches per year. This falls as rain, almost never as snow, about one-third coming during the general rains of the winter and the balance during the sharp thunder storms of late summer.

Dry land farming, under such low rainfall conditions, is next to impossible. Unless artificial means are introduced for concentrating water when it does fall and leading it to fields, or by selecting field sites where flood waters naturally spread out, agriculture cannot form the sole, or even an important, basis of economy.

Another effect of little precipitation is scarcity of surface water. Even the main drainage systems are dry except after heavy rain storms when they may run for a few hours, and natural rock tanks and springs are correspondingly scarce. Although Bryan[8] has shown that good water may be had by drilling relatively shallow wells, there is no evidence that the native population prior to Spanish times procured their water supply by this means. Population naturally gravitated to those favored localities where surface or spring water was present, or where flood waters could be impounded in artificial reservoirs. Ventana Cave was one of those places because it afforded the happy combination of shelter and a reliable spring.

Additional climatic factors may be briefly disposed of as follows: The high temperatures of the region, little cloudiness (possibly sunshine more than 85 per cent),[9] and low average wind velocity (6.3 miles per hour for Ajo, yearly average)[10] are largely responsible for a low relative humidity. At Ajo, humidity averages for the year from readings at 7:30 A. M. and 3:30 P. M. are 49.0 per cent and 29.3 per cent respectively, while at Tucson these are but slightly higher, 51.8 per cent and 31.1 per cent.[11] The relative atmospheric moisture at Ventana Cave

★

7. *Ibid.*, Fig. 6; T. D. Mallery, 1936, *a, b.*
8. K. Bryan, 1925*a.*
9. H. V. Smith, 1930, Fig. 11.
10. *Op. cit.*, Table XX.
11. *Op. cit.*, Table XVII.

thus may be expected to fall somewhere within these figures.

Although the cave is subject to strong gusts of wind from local eddying of air currents, there is no evidence that wind has measurably influenced the deposits within, except toward the very bottom where, even there, the effects were not pronounced.

FLORA

The southwestern third of Arizona is commonly designated as desert land. Specifically, it is a part of the Sonoran Desert. But unlike the popular conception of a treeless waste, an exotic and abundant plant life flourishes there. Even within the area, marked changes occur, dependent chiefly on soil differences, elevation, slope, rainfall, and temperatures. Consequently the Castle Mountains present a different vegetative cover than do the gentle alluvial slopes only a few miles distant.

In the immediate vicinity of the cave, particularly on top and on the ramparts of the spur, the floral structure is of the palo verde-cactus type.[12] The palo verde (*Cercidium microphylla*) is the outstanding tree, concentrated along the minor drainages, where chances for moisture are better. Some ironwood (*Olneya tesota*) and cat's-claw (*Acacia constricta*) also occur; but mesquite is lacking. There are numerous species of cacti, the sahuaro (*Cereus giganteus*), an important source of food, being dominant. It grows, in fact, at the very edge of the cave. Many forms of cholla and prickly pear (*Opuntia fulgida* and *O. engelmannii* chiefly), lend further character to the flora, as does also the ocotillo (*Fouquieria splendens*). Among the low shrubs, the resin plant (*Encelia farinosa*), dominates the landscape and in spring is heavily studded for an extended time with brilliant yellow flowers. The jojoba, or coffeeberry (*Simmondsia californica*), producing an edible seed, also falls in this class.

This covers only the most obvious plants of the cave environs, there being, of course, an infinite variety of others, all

★

12. A. A. Nichol, 1937, pp. 204-210.

of which combine in the springtime of favorable years to make the desert a spectacular flower garden.

Within two miles of the cave, to the east where the rocky slopes of the mountains give way to the alluvial plain of deep soil, the plant life undergoes a marked change. Here the creosote bush (*Larrea tridentata*) dominates[13] with an occasional sahuaro to break the monotony. Along the drainages, particularly in the lower portions of the valley, the mesquite (*Prosopis velutina*), mixed with ironwood and palo verde, form dense strings of growth.

From these two floral zones, the inhabitants of Ventana Cave gathered a surprising amount of plant foods, fibers for some of their woven products, and wood for implements and fuel. Significant changes have doubtless taken place in the plant environment within the time man has used the cave, but we have been unable to throw any light on the nature of these. Charcoal from the fossil-bearing zones proved to be so highly carbonized and with so little wood structure remaining that samples disintegrated to black powder long before reaching the colloidin for sectioning.[14]

FAUNA

The present animal population is probably much smaller than it was before firearms were introduced. Although the area is closed to white hunters, the Papagos depend extensively on their 22 calibre rifles for meat. The native workmen employed in the excavation of Ventana Cave obtained practically all of their fresh meat in this way.

No complete canvass of the animal life was made, but those animals most likely to be seen, or signs of them, are: bighorn sheep, a small band of them ranging through the Castle Mountains; desert mule deer; cottontail; jackrabbit; peccary (javelina); and a variety of rodents among which the pack rat and

★

13. *Ibid.*, 1937, pp. 210-211.

14. Examinations undertaken by Dr. Lyman H. Daugherty, San Jose State College, San Jose, California.

kangaroo rat are probably the most numerous. Antelope are reported[15] but none were seen by us. Predators include an occasional mountain lion, coyote, wildcat, and gray fox. Several species of skunks are also at home in the area.

Reptiles include at least two forms of the rattlesnake (diamond back and sidewinder) and the Gila Monster, the only venomous animals one is most likely to encounter. Horned toads, lizards, and the desert tortoise are fairly abundant.

Birds are not conspicuous save the Gambel's quail, vulture, raven, road runner, and hawks. Near the cave in a rock niche a pair of horned owls established their nest and a low hanging branch of a palo verde in front of the cave was the nesting place of a pair of Costa humming birds. A canyon wren was observed in the cave at times and doves, as well as quail, watered at the spring regularly in the late spring and early summer.

The animal bones recovered from the several layers of the cave, as discussed later, reflect highly interesting changes in fauna within the time man has inhabited the area. This is especially the case when the animal life of today is contrasted with that of a good many millennia ago.

In this brief sketch of the environment of Ventana Cave, a few aspects are worth emphasizing. At best this part of the Sonoran Desert is a difficult area for human occupation because of the low rainfall and high evaporation. These two factors limited the amount of surface water needed for agriculture and above all for random living. Hence, the unfailing but meager water of the spring in the cave created a miniature oasis, attracting people to it through the centuries as seen in the incomparably stratified debris left by them. What was lacking, of course, to make the location ideal, was fertile land close at hand and enough water from the spring to cultivate it. In favored localities at some distance from the cave, agriculture was possible on a small scale for those users of the place who were disposed to grow their food; but this could not form the sole, or perhaps even the main, basis of the economy. Compared with the still

★

15. K. Bryan, 1925*a*, p. 49.

more arid parts of the southwestern desert, the area provided considerable plant and animal resources which, with agriculture, made life possible. Exploitation of these was easy as there were no real barriers in the topography. But even with the development of some special methods for collecting, preparing, and storing natural foodstuff, the balance between success and failure to hold the area was doubtless a delicate one. This preoccupation with sustaining life and the mild desert climate combined to suppress a generally high advance in technology. The basic needs of food, clothing, and shelter were met, in most cases, in simple ways.

DESCRIPTION OF CAVE

The first general feature about Ventana Cave which should be made clear is the fact that, unlike Gypsum and Sandia Caves, it is not a deep cave. It has no extensive chambers and tunnels. On the contrary, it is actually a large rock shelter, only a portion of which begins to approach real cave conditions (Pl. 3*b*). Having a southeastern exposure, sunlight reaches most of it for longer or shorter periods some time during the morning, except in summer when the sun is high overhead. This means that the long axis of the shelter runs more or less parallel with the face of the cliff, not at right angles to it, and that, for most of the cave, the opening is as great as the overhanging cliff itself. Rain does not reach the habitable area below the cliff excepting the most exposed parts and then only during showers driven by high winds from the south.

The origin of the cave arises from a peculiar situation in the volcanic formations. As previously noted, it lies at the base of a resistant basalt cliff and at the top of the slope of rock waste forming the talus. Below the basalt and in front of what is now its near-perpendicular face, was a softer mass of agglomerate. This was more subject to the erosive powers of nature than the basalt and was worn away leaving the solid lava canopy.

The geologic events which seem to have taken place here

are:[16] (1) the accumulation and weak cementation of volcanic rubble into an agglomerate; (2) the weathering of the same to produce an undulating and debris-strewn surface; (3) the outpouring over the agglomerate from an undetermined source, of molten lava, cooling to a dense, purplish basalt; the lava flowing around and encasing the larger and more resistant elements of the agglomerate freed from the matrix by weathering; (4) tilting of the mass with a steep dip to the north, resulting in the situation sketched in Figure 3; (5) removal of the softer agglomerate by external erosive process, and above all, by the effects of waters percolating along the weak weathered material separating

★

16. Determined with the assistance of Dr. F. W. Galbraith, Department of Geology, University of Arizona.

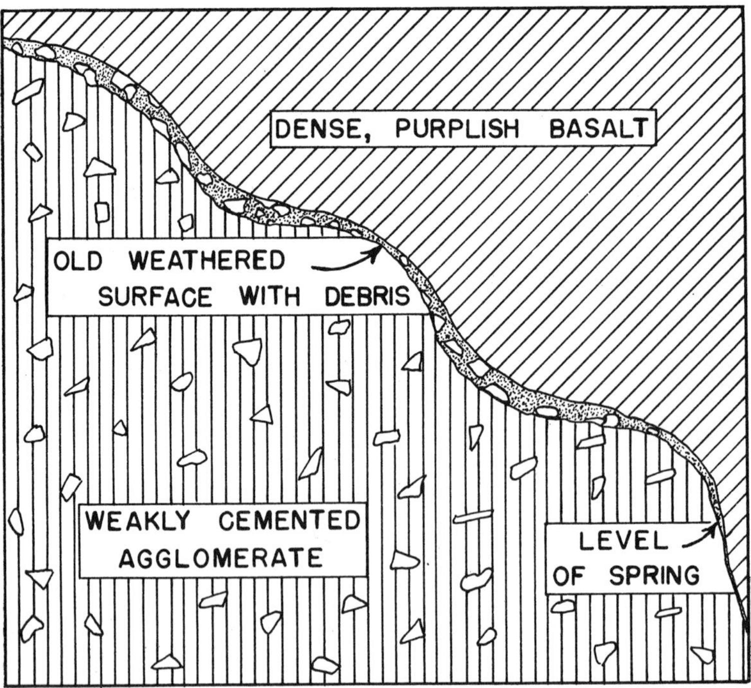

FIGURE 3. Cross section of the rock formations in which Ventana Cave had its origin. This shows the basalt overlying the agglomerate after tilting, separated by a weathered zone

Figure 4. Plan of the upper and lower units, showing the topography before excavation and the grid layout followed during the two seasons of digging.

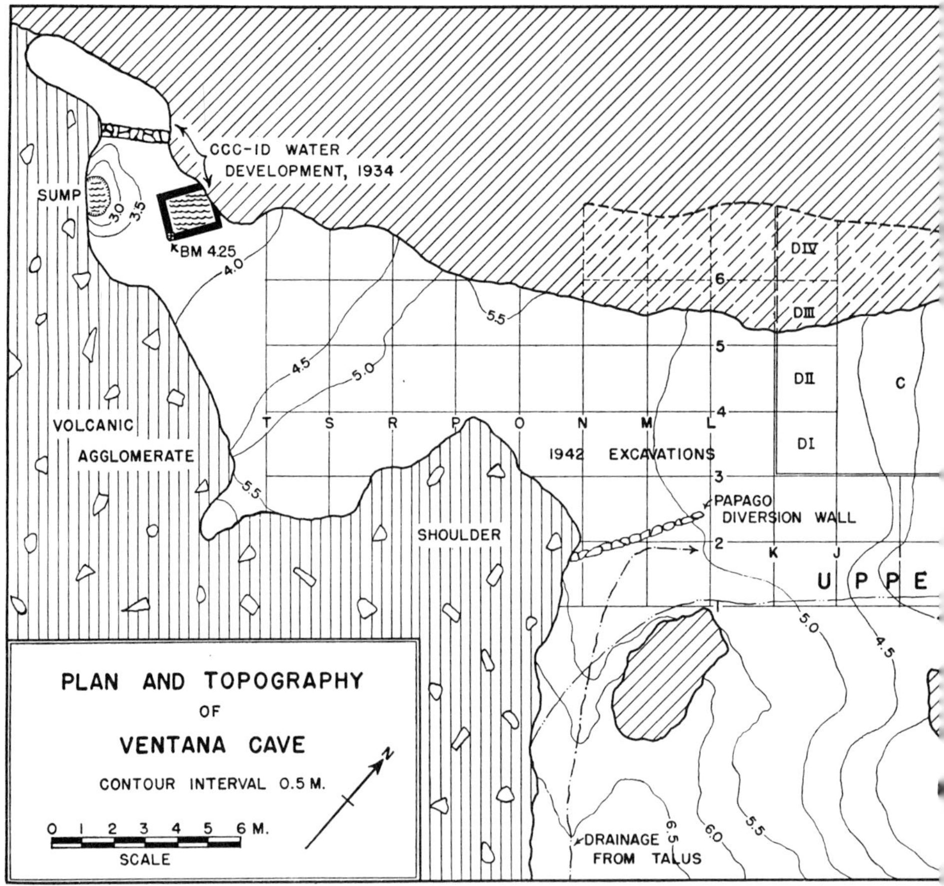

FIGURE 4. Plan of the upper and lower units, showing the topography before excavation and the grid layout followed during the two seasons of digging.

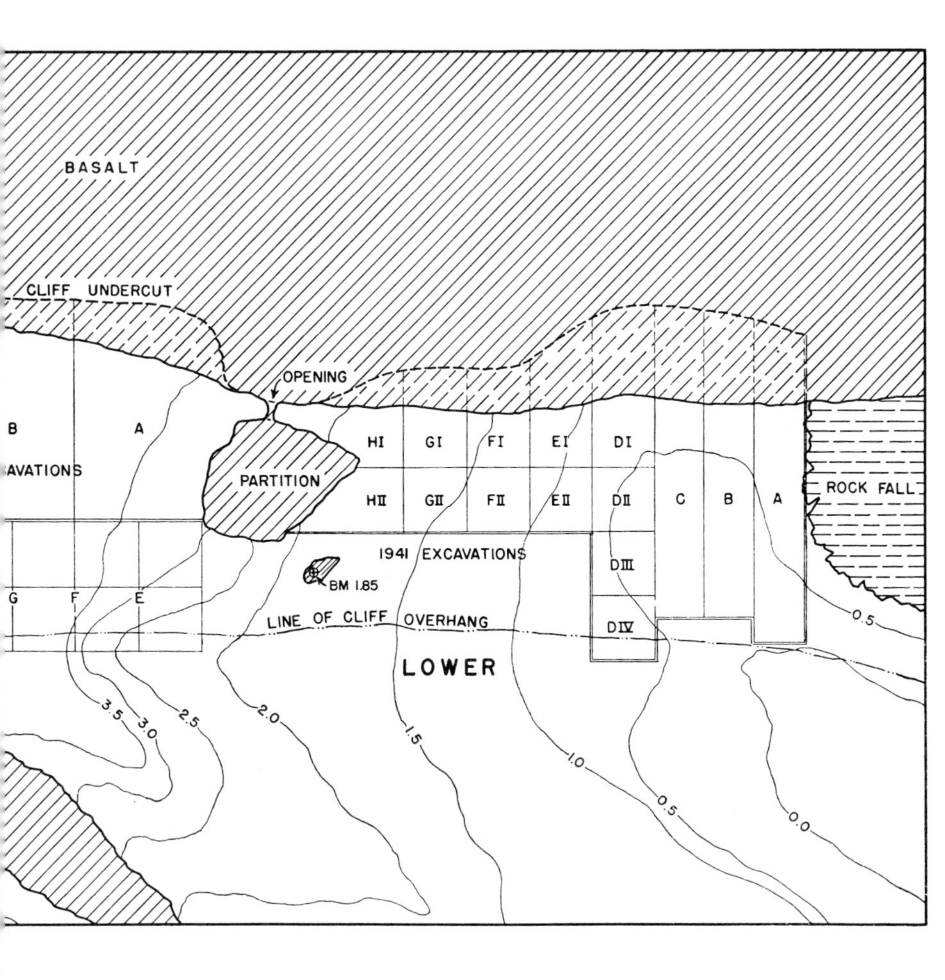
BASALT
CLIFF UNDERCUT
OPENING
B
A
AVATIONS
PARTITION
HI
GI
FI
EI
DI
HII
GII
FII
EII
DII
C
B
A
ROCK FALL
1941 EXCAVATIONS
DIII
BM 1.85
G
F
E
LINE OF CLIFF OVERHANG
DIV
0.5
LOWER
3.5
3.0
2.5
2.0
1.5
1.0
0.5
0.0

the agglomerate and the basalt, appearing at the cave floor as a spring. The southwestern end of the cave, the place of the spring's emergence, is the deepest part. Figure 4 brings out plainly the fact that the primary weathering followed the contact zone of the two rock types, making a crevice. Subsequently, moisture from the outside, and wind and temperature changes widened the crevice to the present proportions by reducing still further the agglomerate mass. That there has been relatively little erosion of the basalt is evidenced by the fact that assorted rock types, formerly loose on the weathered agglomerate surface, are still securely locked in the once molten under-surface of the basalt flow.

The overall length of the inhabited part of Ventana Cave is about 55 m., extending along an axis of northeast to southwest direction, and more or less parallel to the trend of the sheltering cliff. The area on which living was feasible varies from a width of about 6 m. at the northwest end, expanding to nearly 20 m. in the deeper southwestern end.

This area is divided naturally into two units by an erosive remnant of basalt designated as the partition. The northeastern segment has been termed the lower cave and the southwestern part, the upper cave (Fig. 4; Pls. 4 and 5). The partition has played an important role in the cave's history in that it prevented the early nature-laid deposits of the upper cave from extending also into the lower. It projects outward from the cliff to a distance of 4.50 m. and is about 4.75 m. wide, and highly irregular in outline. A curious feature is the thinning of the partition to little more than a rock curtain where it joins the cliff. Through this portion, erosive processes have made an oval opening about 1 x 1.50 m. in size, creating a small window within the cave. This was almost entirely filled with rubbish on both sides before excavation, and as work progressed it was revealed that the lower border of the opening lay approximately 1.50 m. above the rock floor of the cave. Further features prior to excavation are as follows:

The Lower Cave

From the partition to the northeastern end of the lower cave, where a rock fall and talus make use of the floor impossible, the length is 17 m. The area protected by the cliff has an average width of 6 m., beyond which vegetation grows and the level falls away rapidly. The rear wall rises steeply for a distance of about 35 m. at an angle of about 20° from the perpendicular. Figure 4 shows the habitable surface to have a gentle slope of 3 m. from southwest to northeast. When first seen by us, the surface was heavily littered with plant remains, bones, including some human, and the general trash of occupation. Except for one small area of disturbance, there had been no previous digging.

Fully cleared of its trash, the lower cave showed a rather sharp undercutting of the cliff, narrowing down sharply to meet the floor, thereby creating a horizontal crevice (Fig. 7). This was the result of mechanical weathering following the weak zone of contact between the basalt and agglomerate. It reached an extreme horizontal depth of 4 m.

The agglomerate floor over considerable areas was nearly horizontal but extremely pitted and near the partition it became very irregular.

The accumulated material in the lower cave was largely occupational debris. Finely shattered rock from the cliff above accounted for part of the fill toward the outer edge of the habitable area.

The Upper Cave

The length of the upper cave from partition to spring is about 35 m. Because the cliff veers somewhat to the south to rest finally on a mass of residual agglomerate, the floor assumes roughly a triangular shape (Fig. 4). From the overhang of the cliff back into the spring the depth is about 20 m., whereas the protected area at the partition is only 8 m. in width. The outermost edge of the cliff rises sharply as it turns to the south, creating a large and high-roofed opening into the deepest section (Pl. 4). Near the partition, the roof is much lower, in fact, so low that one could reach the rear wall only by crawling on hands and knees (Pl. 6*a*). Beginning at the partition the surface of the debris in the upper cave rose sharply and reached a maximum height of about 3.50 m. at mid-section above the unexcavated floor of the lower cave. Toward the spring, the contours dipped down slightly (Fig. 4), chiefly the result of the clearing out of debris during the water development program of CCC-ID. Like the lower cave the surface here was strewn with the debris of occupation and was broken only at two places by the probings of treasure seekers. The only artificial feature, apart from the trash and the spring development, consisted of a row of rocks laid roughly in a north-south direction from the southern outer edge of the cliff (Fig. 4). These rocks were laid up in recent years by Joe Thomas, a Papago Indian, to turn aside the water draining into the cave on rare occasions from the outside.

A ragged erosional remnant of the agglomerate juts into the upper cave from the south. This has been termed the shoulder. It effectively narrowed the cave at this point and provided a convenient work area for the cave inhabitants as indicated by a number of bedrock mortars.

The Spring

The spring, issuing as a small seepage from the basalt-agglomerate contact zone, is the only one for many miles around. In the survey of water resources of the Papago Reservation conducted by the Soil Conservation Service, this spring was designated as S-18. Originally the seepage was caught in an artificially dug sump approximately 2 m. in diameter and 1.15 m. deep from which the Indians, for countless generations, have been taking water. From January 8 to April 12, 1934, a small crew of men, under CCC-ID direction, endeavored to develop and increase the flow of water. A tunnel 4 m. long was driven through the agglomerate to enlarge the area of seepage and hasten the flow. The mouth of this opening was then partly walled up and the water collecting within the tunnel was piped to a cement-lined storage well just outside (Pl. 6*b*).

Although no verification can be offered for the following statement, it is doubtful if the source of this spring lies deep within the earth. More probably it derives its water from rain falling on the ridge above, a part of which filters down through the shattered and porous agglomerate and is forced out by the more impervious basalt. The storage capacity of the rock is obviously great and the rate at which the water percolates must be slow because the present flow of the spring, though small, appears to be constant regardless of how long the intervals between rains. The rate of seepage could not be readily determined but it is enough to maintain 1.45 m. of water in the concrete reservoir as well as a constant supply in the sump in spite of loss from evaporation and further seepage. Rains which fell during the course of our work produced no observable effect on the output of the spring. The permanency of this water was a prime asset to desert-dwelling people, for they could depend on it when all other sources had failed.

Since it can be shown that a substantial and permanent discharge flowed from this spring in former times, influencing to some extent the nature of the early cave deposits, a water analysis is in order.[17] The mineral constituents, expressed in parts per million, are as follows:

Carbonates	0
Bi-carbonates	146
Chlorides	79
Sulfates	trace
Nitrates	0
Calcium	40
Magnesium	17
Sodium	33
Total soluble salts	315

Compared with most well water this sample is very low in soluble salt content. The water temperature, taken December 29, 1942, was 57° Fahrenheit.

★

17. By Dr. A. B. Caster, Assistant Agricultural Chemist, Arizona Agricultural Experiment Station, University of Arizona.

Official U. S. Army Air Corps Photo

Tad Nichols Photo

PLATE 1

a (Upper). Air view of southern end of Castle Mountains showing location of Ventana Cave *(center)* and typical basin and range.

b (Lower). The Castle Mountains, looking north from the top of the spur in which Ventana Cave is located.

Official U. S. Army Air Corps Photo

PLATE 2

a (Upper). Window Mountain (La Ventana), a natural arch formed by erosion of volcanic formations. The cave is named after this feature.

b (Lower). Ventana Cave as seen from the air, looking southwest.

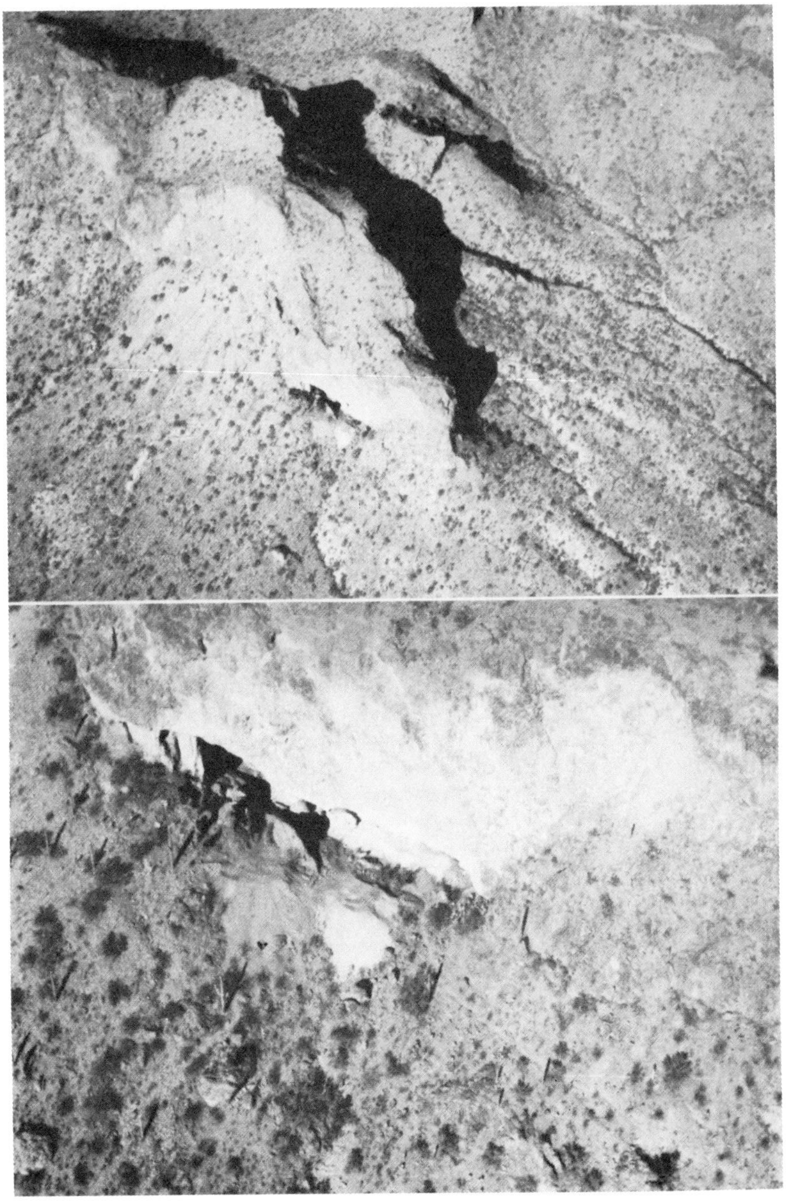

Official U. S. Army Air Corps Photo

PLATE 3

a (Upper). The long narrow spur with Ventana Cave near the right hand tip, seen from almost directly above.

b (Lower). Air view of cave clearly bringing out its shelter character. Deepest section is in upper left (black shadow). White dump is waste from the volcanic debris layer.

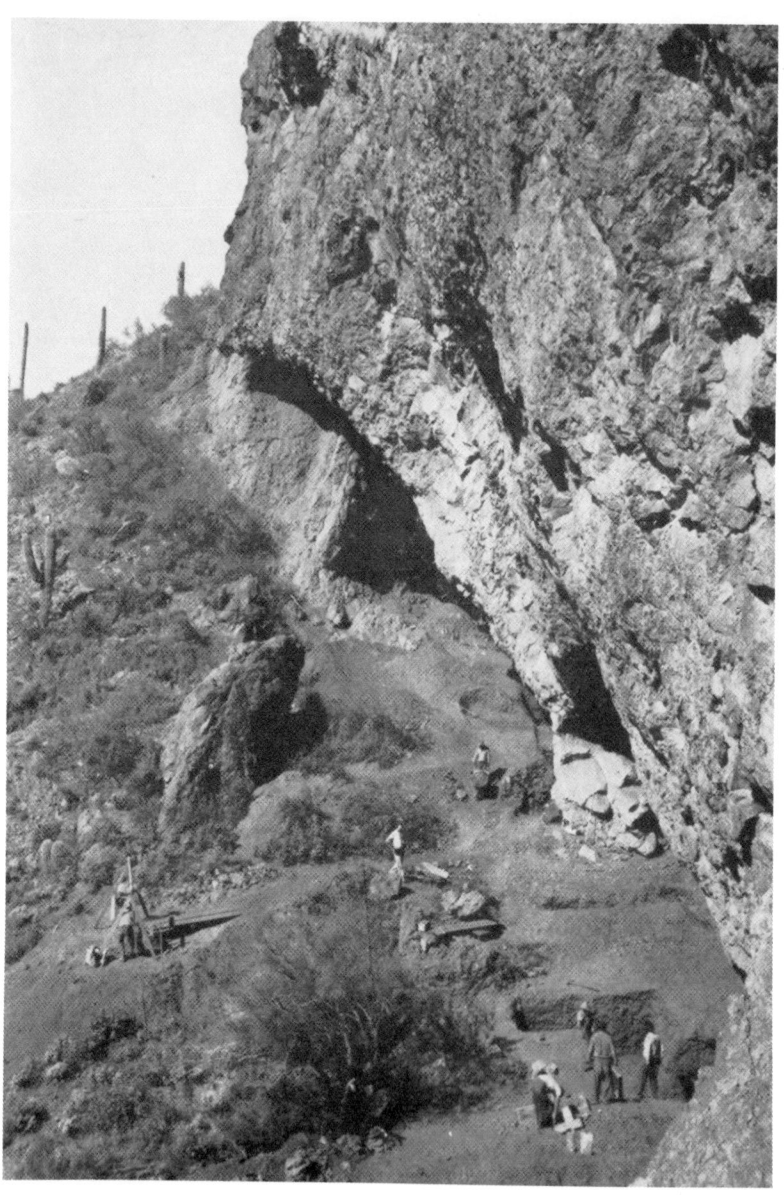

PLATE 4

Looking into Ventana Cave from the northeast. The partition (to right of man with wheelbarrow) divides the cave into the lower (lower right) and upper (center) units. Note talus following cliff to the outer edge of the shelter.

PLATE 5

The cave from the southwest, showing the full extent of the lower unit with partition (lower left) and the mouth of the upper unit (extreme lower left).

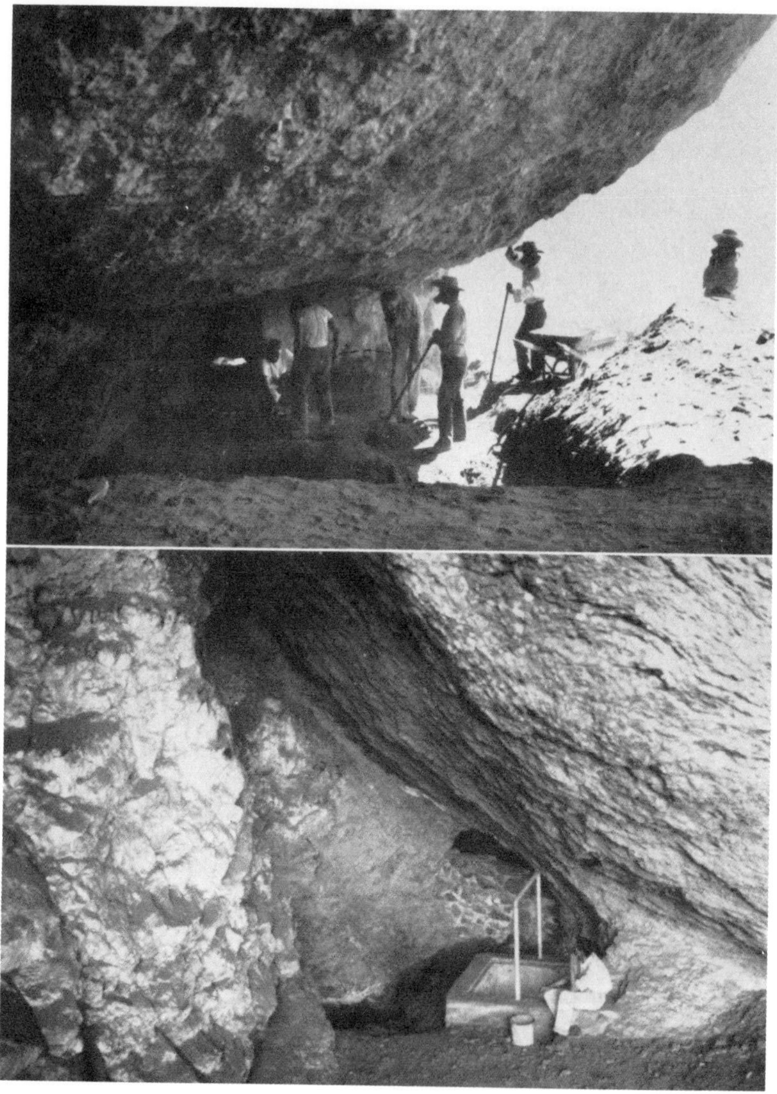

PLATE 6

a (Upper). Northeastern end of upper cave showing low flat roof. About 1 m. of debris has been removed. Top of opening in partition is barely visible.

b (Lower). The spring area of the upper cave. The water seeps out along the contact of the agglomerate (left) and the basalt (right). Walled tunnel and concrete reservoir are modern; dark spot to left is original sump dug by Indians in bedrock.

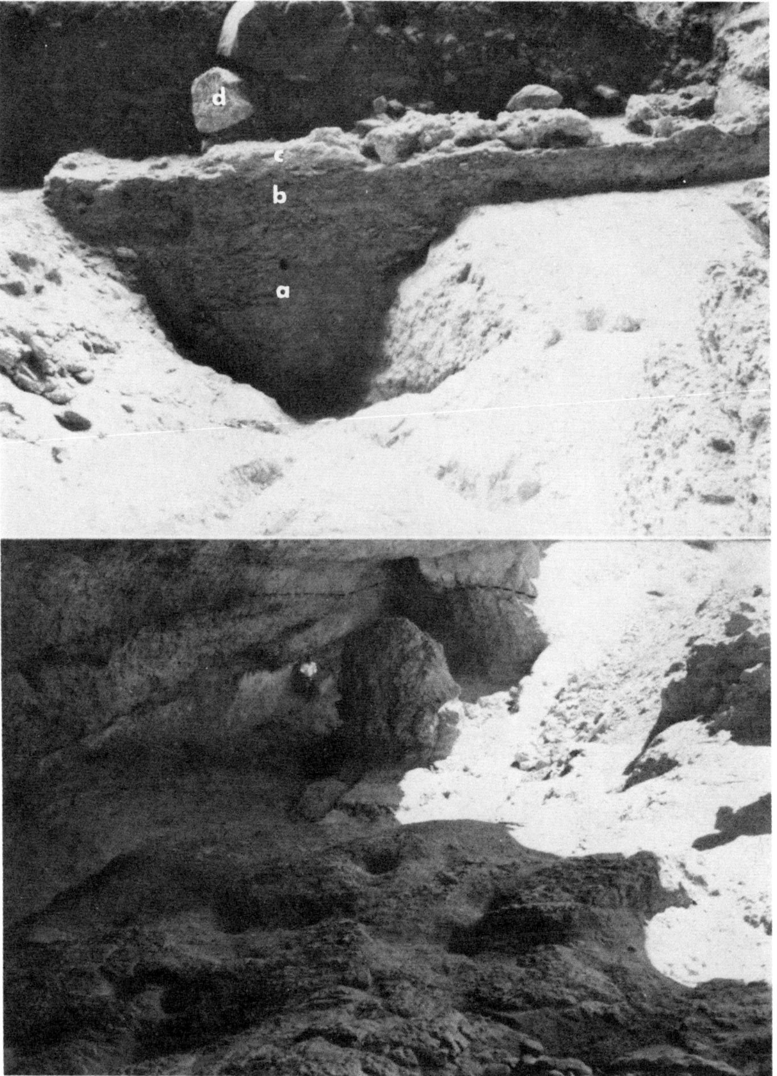

PLATE 7

a (Upper). The spillway as seen from the rear wall of the cave. Hardened silt and rock fill, *a;* conglomerate, *b,* considerably thinned down by erosion at this point; remnant of volcanic debris layer, *c;* fill from talus and rock scaled from cliff face above, *d.*

b (Lower). General view after excavation of upper cave from shoulder. Pillar shows up conspicuously. Opening in partition has been walled up (by us) to stop gusts of air. Dotted line indicates original height of trash. Note bedrock mortars in shoulder (foreground).

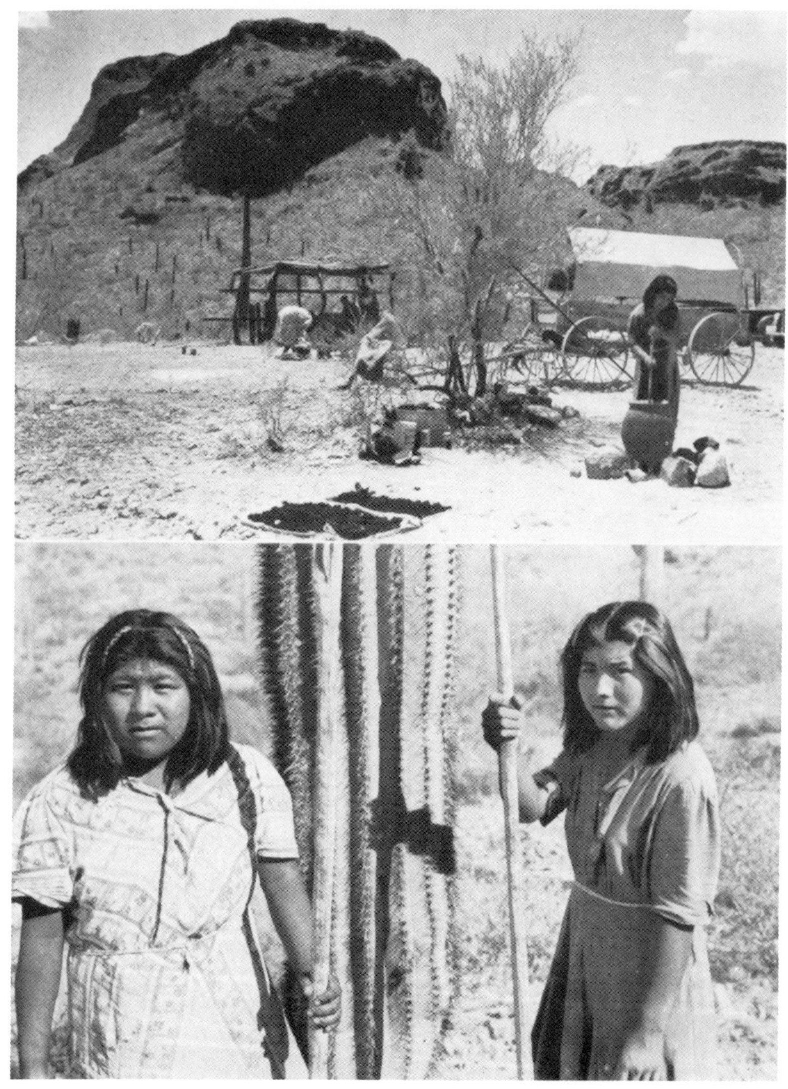

PLATE 8

a (Upper). Papago family encamped below Ventana Cave during sahuaro harvest, July 4, 1942. In earlier years the cave was used, giving both shelter and water. Girl stirs boiling sahuaro fruit and sahuaro seed (lower center) is spread out to dry. The ramada (left center) is the only permanent feature about the camp.

b (Lower). Ancestors of these two Papago girls formerly lived in Ventana Cave for a short time every year. Each holds long ribs from the sahuaro's skeleton, made into gathering sticks.

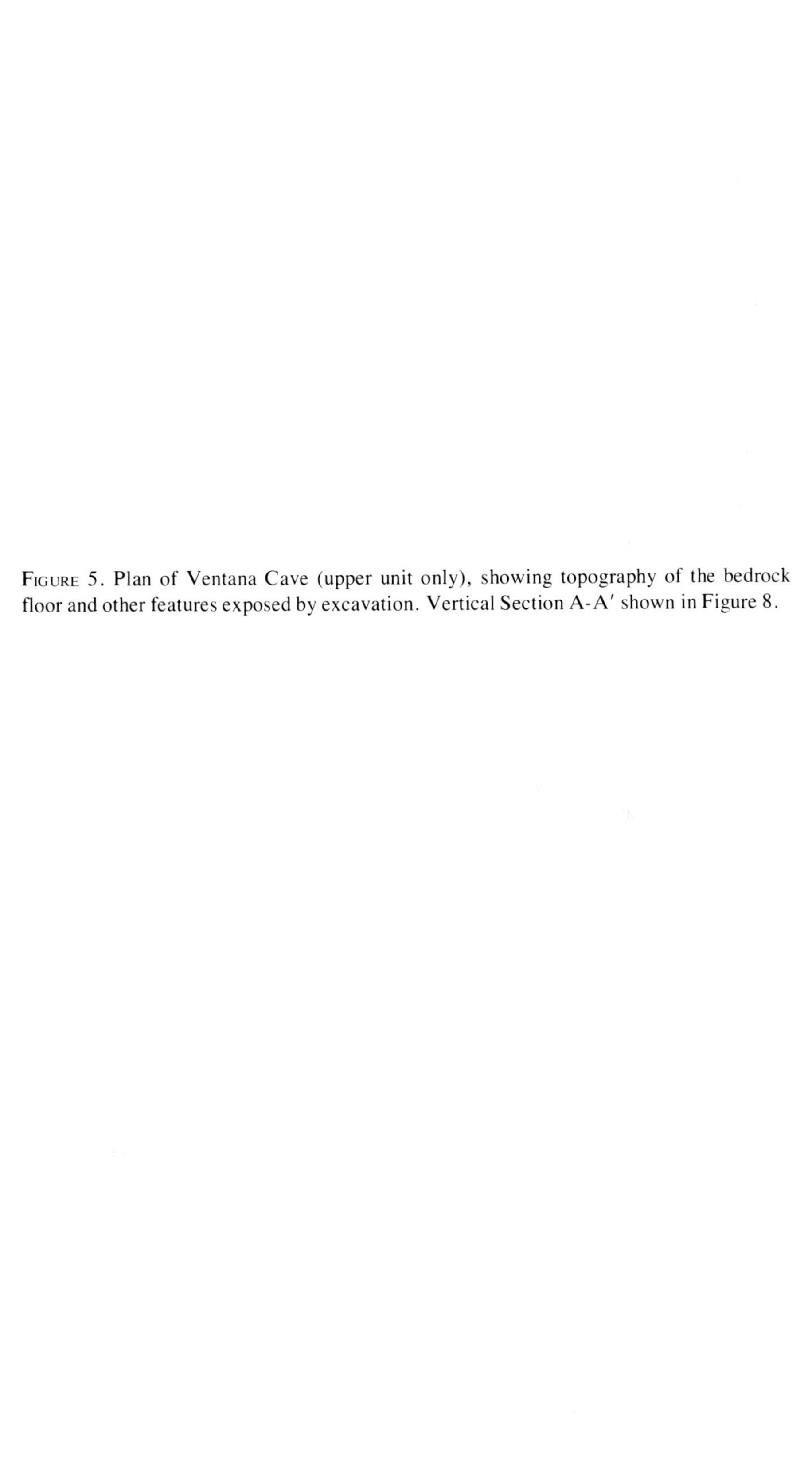

FIGURE 5. Plan of Ventana Cave (upper unit only), showing topography of the bedrock floor and other features exposed by excavation. Vertical Section A-A′ shown in Figure 8.

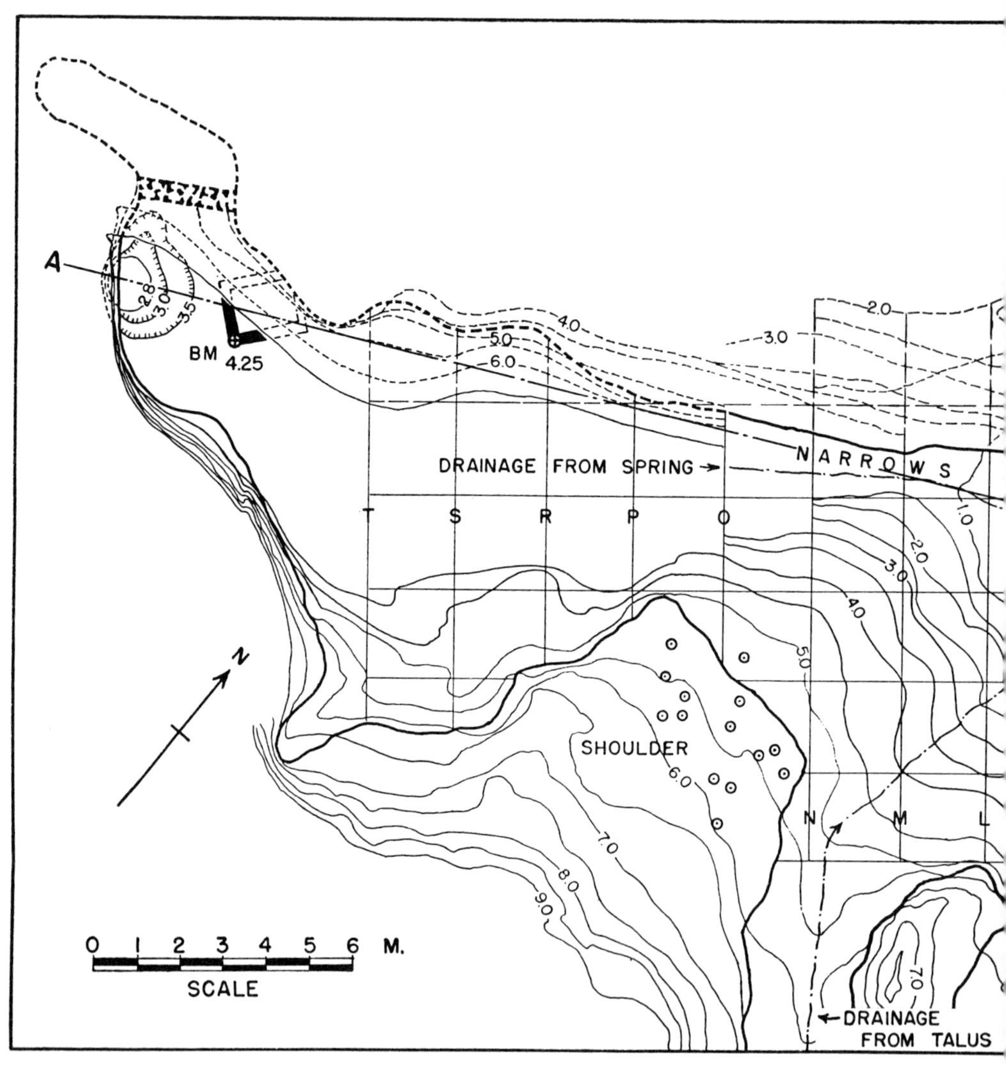

FIGURE 5. Plan of Ventana Cave (upper unit only), showing topography of the bedrock floor and other features exposed by excavation. Vertical Section A-A′ shown in Figure 8.

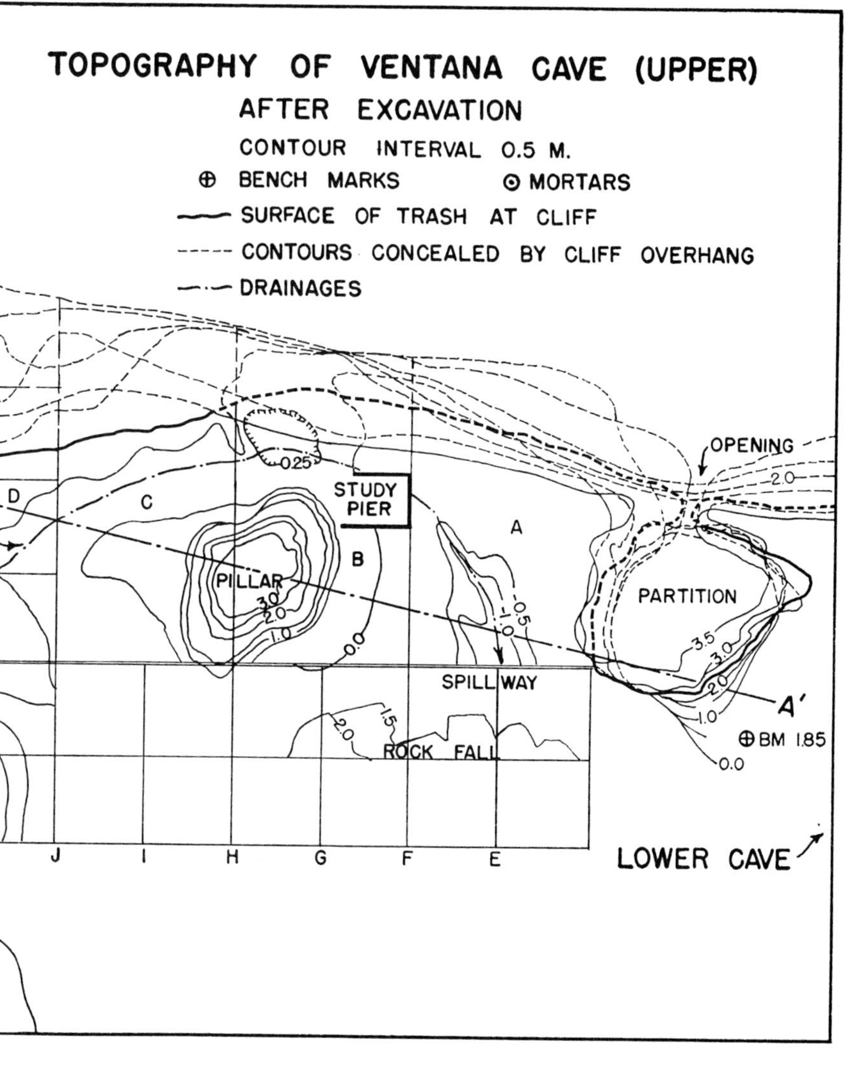

TOPOGRAPHY OF VENTANA CAVE (UPPER)
AFTER EXCAVATION
CONTOUR INTERVAL 0.5 M.
BENCH MARKS
MORTARS
SURFACE OF TRASH AT CLIFF
CONTOURS CONCEALED BY CLIFF OVERHANG
DRAINAGES
OPENING
2.0
0.25
STUDY PIER
D
C
A
B
PILLAR
3.0
2.0
1.0
0.0
0.5
1.0
PARTITION
3.5
3.0
2.0
1.0
0.0
A′
BM 1.85
SPILLWAY
1.5
2.0
ROCK FALL
K
J
I
H
G
F
E
LOWER CAVE

The nearly complete excavation of the upper cave revealed additional topographical features which should be considered before embarking on further discussions. The nature of these is clarified in Figure 5.

From the partition half way toward the spring and just above floor level the rear wall of the cave is sharply undercut to a maximum depth of nearly 3 m. (Pl. 12). This gave the cave an even greater depth of overhang than was first suspected and added a considerable amount of debris to the total which had to be removed.

Immediately west of the partition, the bedrock floor showed the beginnings of a drainage channel, scoured by water as it poured out of the cave. This has been called the spillway. It has a depth of approximately 1 m. at its outermost point as revealed by the excavations (Pl. 7*a*). The task of moving some 3 m. of overburden was considered too great to uncover the channel to its end, where it falls away abruptly toward the desert floor.

A few meters southwest of the spillway stands a rock mass somewhat elliptical in outline and with a rounded top, called the pillar (Pl. 7*b*). This is a remnant of the agglomerate and although it stands to a height of about 2.50 m., it was entirely covered by the debris and hence was not visible at the time the excavations were started.

The shoulder, previously referred to, extended well below the surface of the debris, dropping off sharply for 4 m. and levelling off to become the cave floor at about the 1.00 m. contour. Its northernmost edge came near the back wall creating a constriction in the cave at this point which we have called the narrows (Fig. 5). Although the general appearance of the shoulder is that of having been smoothed by erosion, it is rough and irregular locally, where large chunks of more resistant rock have been broken away from the soft matrix.

In Figure 4, drainage from the talus is shown as coming into the cave along the eastern margin of the shoulder where it has been turned aside by a Papago-built stone obstruction. As the excavation proceeded, it became evident that formerly this drainage was of sufficient force to erode a shallow channel through the east flank of the shoulder, dropping to the floor where it passed behind the pillar and out through the spillway (Fig. 5). The importance of this in the history of the cave will be dealt with later.

In the narrows portion of the cave lay a shallow channel in the bedrock scoured by the flow from the spring. It joined the talus drainage and was discharged at the spillway. This channel was not followed directly to the spring since some bulk of rubbish was left in place to safeguard the present meager water supply.

This briefly outlines the physical characters seen within the upper cave, and the rock remnants left by the erosive processes. Hayden, who had the opportunity to observe all of these features as they were exposed, aptly sums up the situation in his field notes as follows:

"It appears from the character of the cave and especially the features observed in the floor, that running water played the chief part in its formation. Water from the spring would not seem to have flowed in sufficient volume to have carved out the great cavity of the northeastern part of the upper cave, although this seepage may have been largely responsible for the formation of the southwestern portion. Runoff from the talus entered the cave over the shoulder, scouring widely between the shoulder and the pillar, sweeping around behind the pillar to strike against the partition and pouring outward to the east. This action cut the spillway, apparently into the edge of a declivity. The pillar shows the effects of cutting by swirling water, for it is markedly undercut on its west and north curves."

EXTERIOR FEATURES

A clear understanding of the natural events which influenced the deeper, and hence earlier, deposits cannot be gained without paying some attention to the immediate surroundings of the cave. Two features in particular must be noted, (a) the talus cone and its related drainage area, and (b) the water shed directly above the cave, emptying over the cliff in front of the southeastern or lower end of the upper cave.

The Talus Cone

A short distance beyond the southwestern end of the cave the volcanic cliff is gashed by a small canyon. The floor of this cleft rises steeply with frequent vertical steps making an ascent through it impossible. The water, responsible for cutting this canyon, is gathered in a relatively small drainage area on the southeastern face of the ridge near the crest. Concentrated in a single stream at the head of the canyon, it cascades down through the cleft leaving at the bottom, fanwise, its burden of coarse and fine material as its force is spent by a lessening of the gradient. This appears today as a talus cone of considerable size.

As viewed from the distance (Fig. 6) the right or north edge of this cone clings to the volcanic agglomerate cliff, its slope

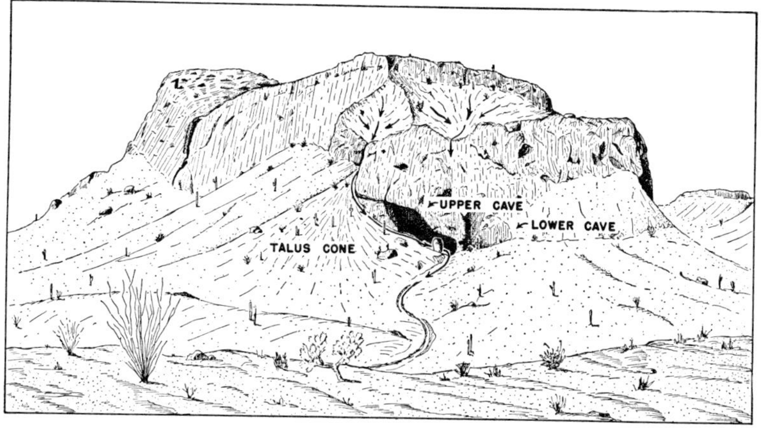

Figure 6. Looking northwest toward Ventana Cave, showing the relationship of the two parts of the cave to the drainages on top of the mountain and the talus cone to the west which have materially affected the character of the oldest deposits in the upper cave. Drawing represents cave before human occupancy and indicates how surface drainage from a small area on hill and from the talus flowed behind pillar through cave and out. Also note how upper basin discharges over cliff, falling directly on this channel

finally becoming one with the surface in the cave before excavations began. The apex of the cone is considerably above that of the surface of the cave fill (approximately 40 m.), so that water draining from the cone and properly directed would easily enter the cave. That this happens occasionally today is reported by Joe Thomas, whose family claims rights to the cave. Mention has already been made of the row of rocks placed by him to prevent the runoff from the talus during exceptionally heavy rains from flowing back into the cave to contaminate the spring. It was also observed that the scouring effect of occasional runoff has kept lichens from forming along the base of the cliff, although they occur abundantly just out of reach of the water. Flooding from this same source evidently has not been frequent in recent times, however, because no appreciable amount of rock waste had been introduced into the accumulation of human debris at this point, nor has the water arrived in sufficient amount to completely moisten the dry trash in that area, thereby decaying the perishable items of culture.

The talus cone appears to be well stabilized today and is thinly covered with vegetation. Sahuaro grow at random while palo verde and ironwood occur mainly along the shallow channels which wind their way through the boulder-strewn slope. In some places, where these channels have cut through the loose surface cover, cemented detrital material is exposed. The cementing agent is white, principally lime, and reminds one of the layer of consolidated volcanic debris in the cave.

From evidence that will be adduced later, the talus cone has changed materially since the arrival of man, its growth having directly affected the formations within the cave. Primarily because of its convex transverse surface, it forced some of the runoff to flow along the cliff, accounting in part for the initial scouring of the cave, and having been the source subsequently for both water and materials deposited within the cave. A combination of this effect with others still to be brought out, permits the logical explanation of the nature-made layers of the cave's stratigraphy.

The Upper Water Shed

Directly above the cave from the upper edge of the cliff and back to the crest of the ridge is an area of several acres extent with a slope of about 45° to the southeast (Fig. 6). Precipitation in this region drains off at a low place in the cliff which lies directly above the southeastern part of the upper cave and drops as a waterfall for about 45 m.

During our first season at Ventana Cave, in the late winter and spring of 1941, in spite of the fact that more moisture than usual fell in heavy and extended rains, never more than a mere trickle came over the cliff at this point. The following season, with normal winter rainfall, no water was observed to drain from this area. The small amount of waste rock at the foot of the fall, carried by the water from the area above, suggests that in recent times, this has been an insignificant source of material to build up the deposits at the outer edge of the cave. Also the cliff face directly behind the fall is shattered much more than elsewhere and, as a result of water seeping along the face, occasional pieces scale off. This action, too, appears to be stabilized today. But in earlier times, presumably when rainfall was greater, considerable amounts of debris accumulated as the combined result of waste carried from above and the spalling from the cliff. This was revealed by the excavation and is believed to have had a fundamental bearing on the origin of the early deposits.

It should be noted particularly that the water from above falls directly on the course of the drainage which passed through the cave, about at the outer end of the spillway channel in the bedrock floor. This was a happy coincidence. Otherwise the early history of the cave would have been much less clear and would probably not have preserved the all-important evidence of a period of moister climate. The discharge from the two systems combined at this point to form the most pronounced drainage channel to be found on the whole southeastern side of the ridge.

THE PAPAGO AND VENTANA CAVE

Thus far we have been concerned primarily with the natural setting and description of Ventana Cave. Before examining the contents, deposited by nature and man, the cave needs to be evaluated in terms of its present human setting. This will provide a convenient point of departure, particularly in the study of early cultures which found refuge in it.

Obviously, Ventana Cave has been known and used by the Papago Indians for a long time. Its attractions, water and shelter, would have been just as evident to them as to any other people. How long they have used it depends on whether or not one is willing to make the assumption that the late pre-Spanish inhabitants were the forerunners of the Papago. As I am not prepared to make such an assumption now, this discussion will be confined to the period since 1700, or since the first documentary evidence that the Papagos were in the country.

One of the principal native foods of the southern Arizona desert—important to this day in Papago economy—is the fruit of the giant cactus (*Cereus giganteus*).[18] This plant flourishes chiefly on the slopes and around the bases of the rugged volcanic mountain ranges. The Papago have long recognized family rights to the fruits in specified areas. Pilgrimages are made each year to these when the fruit ripens in late June and early July. The southeastern slope of the hill in which Ventana Cave is located has been the traditional collecting area for a family originally from Kaka, the descendants of which are now residing in the village of Ventana, about eight miles northwest of the cave. This brings Papagos to the vicinity of the cave yearly,[19] opening the way for some use of the cave even today. Since the extent of this use has a direct bearing on the story of the cave, the matter was looked into in some detail.

In the summer of 1942, the Joe Thomas family from Ven-

★

18. E. F. Castetter and W. H. Bell, 1937, pp. 7-27.

19. There are neither permanent residents in the immediate locality of the cave now nor have there been for a considerable time, judging from the absence of house ruins.

tana, consisting of seven members, began harvesting sahuaro fruit about July 1. A temporary camp was established below the cave, the chief structure being a 6-post flat-topped shade or ramada which was built some years ago (Pl. 8*a*). The attractions of the cave, according to Mr. Thomas, were its water supply and the protection it afforded against inclement weather and the blazing sun. But through the first week[20] of this season the cave had only been entered as a matter of curiosity, to see the extent of our final work there and to water a pair of mules. The domestic water supply was hauled from Ventana in gasoline drums, that water being preferred to the spring water in the cave. Mr. Thomas reported that, the year before, water was obtained from the cave but there was no actual living in it. This has doubtless been the case for at least a generation or more, as indicated by the informant and by the fact that the material culture assignable to Papago origin dates chiefly from the 19th century. Consequently we can rule out any appreciable effect of the Papagos' use of the cave since about 1900.

Before the turn of the century, particularly before the government developed wells, the Papago found the spring in Ventana Cave an unfailing source of water, no matter how extreme the drought. Mr. Thomas stated that his uncle's family, together with other families from Kaka, would move to the cave when the local water supply failed in late spring or early summer, and would reside there until the summer rains again filled the *charcos* or surface storage tanks. The story was also circulated by some of our Papago workmen that the Indians from Santa Rosa, ten miles to the east, depended on the cave's water when their supply was exhausted. In the case of the Kaka group, occupation of the cave might conceivably extend over as much as two to three months during which time there could accumulate considerable trash, given enough people (an estimate of how many people used the cave at any given time was not even attempted by the informant). But there was no great volume of trash of Papago origin. Sahuaro fruit hulls were the most

★

20. Harvesting sometimes continues through the month of July.

abundant vegetal remains and many of these came from the pre-Spanish debris. Recognizable Papago culture represents but a very small fraction of all items recovered.

Some accounts also had it that the cave was used as a refuge by the Papagos during Apache attacks in the area. Such occurrences were probably infrequent and the people never remained long. The conclusion is therefore reached that Papago occupancy was neither prolonged nor intense and that these Indians have not been responsible for any material addition to the gross depth of trash since 1700.

The Papago are known on occasion to bury their dead in caves and rock crevices.[21] On encountering numerous burials early in our excavations and realizing that the Papago had made some use of the cave, we were fearful that they would claim the dead as theirs, thereby forcing the abandonment of our work. At the end of the first week, some of our workmen who had been recruited from the Ventana district discussed the matter with their octogenarian leader, Pia Machita. His verdict was that he had no knowledge the Papago ever buried in the shelter and that it was "all right for us to dig them out." This attitude was also reflected by our workmen who showed little outward signs of concern over what we were doing. They assisted willingly in the uncovering of the burials and, with a little coaxing, helped in the transportation of the mummies down the trail to the camp. Mr. Thomas volunteered the information that as many times as he had been in the cave, he did not know any bodies were buried there. But, it will be recalled, on our first visit the presence of human bones on the surface was one of the clues which convinced us that the exploration of the cave would be worth while. Some of the mummies were practically at surface level, the toes and sandals of one (No. 9) having been scorched by a Papago fire.

To a limited extent, Ventana Cave enters the folklore and mythology of the Papago. It is little wonder that in naming the cave they recognize its most outstanding characteristic in one

★

21. R. M. Underhill, 1939, p. 188.

of the two names they use. This is *Chiu Vafia,* Spring Cave. The other is *Hewultki,* Whirlwind House.

Miss Jane Chesky, who, during the winter of 1941-42, was living at Santa Rosa and studying Papago music, heard of a song about the cave, originally sung by a man travelling across the desert. A literal translation of the words runs as follows:

> I am very thirsty. There is water over there; but it is a long way and I am very tired. Finally I reach the place and have a drink of water.

If the song actually refers to Ventana, which the informant emphatically claimed, it is but one more indication of the practical attitude the Papago have toward the cave.

The second name, *Hewultki,* stems from a more formal tale about the cave.[22] In the old days Wind lived in this cave. Wind did not like any but mesquite smoke and blew out fires of other wood.[23] Furthermore, there was a "wrong spot" in the cave near the spring and to build a fire there would set up a whirlwind which would "blow your head off." Two of our workmen camped in the cave in 1934 during a rainy spell and, forgetting, they built a fire of ironwood in the forbidden spot. The result of this transgression was as if "dynamite had been put in the fire." Coals were blown all over the cave, their blankets were burned and they had to run out in the rain. Then, one of them remembered that a particular stone, usually lying on the shoulder of the cave, if put in the fire, would extinguish it and stop the whirlwind.

There is doubtless some foundation for this belief as the eddying of wind and air currents was quickly recognized during the course of our work. Little dust devils continually travelled up and down the cave and over the dump. A fire in the "wrong spot" might easily set up a draft to give the story a basis. Concreteness of the idea is seen in the distribution of

★

22. Collected by Hayden.

23. It is interesting to note that no mesquite grows in the immediate area of the cave, although ironwood and palo verde are both available.

the wood ash in the inner part of the upper cave. One area about 2 m. square was practically ash free whereas nearby, said to be outside the "hexed" region, ash was abundant.

In the same range of mountains in which Ventana Cave is located there is another smaller cave called *Wihomki*. It was our hope to do some testing in this in 1942 in an effort to seek confirmation for our findings in Ventana. Permission to do so was denied by the Indians on the grounds that Lightning lived in this cave, that it was a sacred place and should not be touched. Incidental to this information we learned that Ventana Cave is the home of Thunder as well as Wind. Any qualms the Papago may have had about our work because of this were certainly not made known to us and as we were allowed to continue, it is evident that they did not consider the excavations would interfere in any way.[24]

It is not surprising in the light of the foregoing that there are some feelings about Ventana which border on the superstitious. Strange noises are sometimes heard issuing from it. One branch of the Joe Thomas family refused to collect sahuaro fruit in the vicinity of the cave during the 1942 harvest because of our excavations. During the early stages of the digging one of the native workers was sent up to the cave alone to clean out the mortar holes on the shoulder. He was frightened by the cave and bolstered his courage by whistling loudly. As soon as others joined him, all was well. Another workman, feeling indisposed, went up to the cave to sit in the sun. He heard quiet footsteps and the hum of machinery behind him. An inspection failed to show anything so he returned to his place in the sun. The sound of footsteps was heard again, and the man, becoming afraid, returned to his camp below. Evidently fear of the cave's mysterious forces is an individual matter, an emotion not experienced when a group of people go into it together.

Legend also has it that long ago a girl from Santa Rosa went to the cave for water and disappeared. Her jug was found at

★

24. C. Lumholtz, 1912, p. 111, noted that the Papago fear lightning, but are unafraid of thunder.

the water hole but no trace of her, or even her tracks, could be found. It was thought likely that she fell into the water hole. During our work in 1942, the school children from Santa Rosa were brought out to the cave and their first interest was to inspect the sump to find out if the girl could be seen in it.

The Apache are said to have shied away from Ventana Cave, particularly after a lone boy, who had been chased into it, turned and shot one of his pursuers with an arrow. Miss Chesky also heard a story circulated among the Indians that the cave was used as a hideaway by a Papago girl after her escape from an Apache war party which raided Batki about the middle of the 18th century. But it is clear that the cave in question was located north or east of Florence. Evidently in the retelling of the story the place of the incident has been transferred to Ventana.

It is appropriate at this point to consider an interesting but as yet unexplained feature of Ventana Cave. It was noticed from the start that the rear wall of the upper cave, particularly the innermost part near the spring, was liberally peppered with gray-colored daubs (Pl. 9*a*). These, it appeared, had been thrown as a soft material against the rough lava face where they stuck and dried. They range from about 40 to 85 mm. in diameter and extend from 2 m. above the surface of the cave fill upward on the wall for a height of about 15 m. where they are very numerous. Hayden estimated that some 30,000 daubs covered the cliff wall.

Our first question as to their meaning elicited the answer that when the Indians in the CCC crew worked on the spring, they had some mortar left over from the small masonry job of walling up the tunnel and that they threw handfuls of it against the wall. To check this story one of the daubs was removed and it did indeed prove to be mortar; but others had a slightly different appearance and the great number threw much doubt on this explanation. Additional examples were removed and they proved to be made consistently of a wood ash paste. Much to our surprise, many of them contained bits of textile. A few had string of both cotton and yucca fiber, and in still others were observed the quill-ends and downy parts of feathers. One encased a yucca quid, and practically all had minute pieces of charcoal and bone in the matrix. A good many of those examined had none of the above inclusions save such foreign substances which would naturally be picked up in gathering ash from the hearth (Pl. 9*b*, *a*). Of the two dozen or so pulled down with cloth imbedded in them, one had a small fragment of native spun and woven cotton textile (Pl. 9*b*, *b*), and all others contained bits of commercial cloth, mostly calico (Pl. 9*b*, *c*), of the type carried by the trading posts on the reservation in the late 19th century. This helped in fixing the recency or at least the late survival of this peculiar custom. The cloth fragments are in the form of narrow strips wadded up in the ash or running irregularly through the mass. In some cases the daubs must be broken to find the cloth, in others an end may be free. Obviously, all this sharpened our curiosity as to what they might mean. Many were so recent that the persons who put them there are probably still alive.

Further questioning brought strange and evasive responses. We were told by one informant that the Indians pitched them up with a pliable twig to hear the "plop" as the daubs struck the wall. Another said that long ago little people lived in the cave, that they put daubs of clay[25] and feathers on their arrows and shot them up "just for fun." Still another stated that eagle down and feathers were put in the daubs so that they would "look pretty" waving in the breeze.

All of these answers are charged with a naïveté which leaves much to be desired. It was felt that some of the oldsters from Kaka, who had likely been in the cave as youths, should be questioned. This Hayden did. The oldest man in a gathering, when asked about them, started to talk, then suddenly shrugged the whole matter off by saying that "unknown people used to do it." It is evident that those who know the answer have no intention of revealing it.

★

25. A daub of clay, fallen from the wall, was found in the 0.50 to 1 m. level of the trash, suggesting the custom may be fairly old.

There is tangible proof that feathers were occasionally imbedded in some daubs. One has a piece of yucca cord coming out of its center to which something had been tied, possibly a feather (Pl. 9*b*, *d*). Feathers may have been tied to the cloth also, as one informant stated, but in most cases this would have been impossible, and the cloth may be presumed to have helped in holding the ash together.

Ritual use of feathers among the Papago exists, as in the case of the four feather (eagle) wand used by medicine men, and also as parts of curative paraphernalia. But such usages cannot be cited logically in explaining the feathered daubs. They may have a votive significance, and again they may be one of those curious products of idleness. I have no explanation to offer. In any event, most, if not all of the daubs, can be credited to Papago origin.

Many of the rock paintings on the walls of both cave units were doubtless put there by the Papago. Since the problem presented by them is somewhat wider than is apparent at first, they will be considered in a separate section.

Attention is also called in another section of this report to the cultural items of the Papago and those objects of white manufacture which they brought into the cave.

PROCEDURE OF EXCAVATION

Fortunately the cave presented no such obstacles to excavation as were encountered by Harrington in Gypsum Cave or by Hibben in Sandia Cave. There was ample room in which to work and to dispose of the back dirt; the shelter was well lighted and for the most part, well ventilated. The solid cave roof eliminated the threat of rock falls except under the vertical face of the cliff which was mostly beyond the area of digging. There was no serious danger to the workmen of being caught in cave-ins of the debris. Dust, ever present in cave work, caused the most discomfort. As a safeguard against it, goggles and respirators were worn by the men. The absence of architectural features permitted the adoption of a straightforward and systematic stripping technique in removing the debris.

During the first season, several preliminary trenches were dug to determine the depth of trash and to give us some idea of the conditions which might be expected. Finding the debris to be deep, points of reference and a datum plane were established and the first areas (A in both cave units, Fig. 4) were laid out large, purposely, to provide working space for the diggers. A stripping technique was used, breaking the levels at 0.50 m. vertical intervals. Later, areas B and C were similarly dug, the excavations in both cave units proceeding simultaneously. In upper B, the vertical interval was reduced to 0.25 m. to determine if the previously used 0.50 m. depth might be too excessive and thereby cause loss of significant data. From this test and from general observations of others it became clear that the 0.50 m. interval could be used safely and all remaining digging was done on this basis.

Before the end of the 1941 season, the size of the test blocks was reduced to a 2 x 2 m. square. This was done to allow more precise comparisons, both horizontal and vertical, between smaller areas of the cave. The abundance of specimens made this small unit feasible. Any early irregularities in the cave fill, or disturbances causing mixture of culture of radically different ages, might thus be more readily detected.

It should be mentioned at this point that the arbitrary 0.50 m. vertical unit was applied only through the homogeneous midden, where visible signs of stratigraphy were almost entirely lacking. In the deep layers the natural lines of stratification were followed.

The first season saw the completion of the lower cave, and a fraction of the upper cave. The 1942 work followed the 2 x 2 m. square test scheme, although the numbering system was revised. The grid of coördinates was established to include the inner part of the upper cave and the area lying southwest of the previous year's work (Fig. 4).

Beginning at the outer edge and running toward the rear of the cave the southwest-northeast lines were numbered 1 through 7, while the intersecting coördinates were lettered from northeast to southwest, beginning with F near the partition and ending with T near the spring. Q was intentionally omitted to avoid possible confusion with O in labelling.

The designation of each square, or block, was determined by the letter and number of the intersecting lines at the southeast corner, as G2, L5, etc. Depths were indicated under these in terms of depth below surface and parenthetically relative to the datum plane, as $\frac{\text{G2}}{0.5-1.0(3.5-3.0)}$. This means that all specimens coming within any one test level in any one block were so labeled, excepting burials and special items which were more precisely located by triangulation from reference points. The bulk of material to be handled and richness of the deposit rendered any other system too costly and it is felt that little, if any, significant information was lost by the method adopted. Plate 10*a* illustrates the appearance of the fill in process of being tested by this procedure. Profiles of the test blocks on both axes were kept at from 2 to 4 m. intervals.

Altogether, somewhat more than 700 cubic meters of debris were handled. The most expedient system developed was to remove the material from each test level by wheelbarrow to the dump outside, thus eliminating the need to rehandle back-dirt and also reducing the dust in the cave itself. The wheelbarrows were emptied directly into a cradle screen (Pl. 10*b*) handled by two men who did the necessary shaking and the sorting of cultural remains. These were placed in sacks appropriately labelled and the larger tools, as manos and metates of which there were great numbers, were stacked in piles to await analysis.

The midden throughout was soft and could be shovelled without the use of a pick. The lower layers, however, particularly the volcanic debris and the conglomerate, had to be broken up forcibly before screening.

All test blocks, excepting a few near the spring (Fig. 8), were carried to bedrock. Thus approximately 95 per cent of the cave's deposits were removed to yield an almost complete sample. There is no reason to believe that the results obtained would have been appreciably changed by the addition of those specimens remaining in the unexcavated sections.

A small study pier of the deep consolidated layers was left standing near the pillar in the upper cave for the benefit of those who might wish to visit the cave in the future. The overburden of soft midden material could not be retained however desirable that would have been.

THE DEPOSITS

With all of the preliminary considerations out of the way, we are now in position to discuss the deposits in the cave, with particular respect to their nature and genesis. The internal features along with those described for the immediate environs of the cave must be drawn upon in full to explain the geological problems posed by the deposits.

Lower Cave

The stratigraphy of the lower cave was simple as compared with that of the upper unit and may be quickly disposed of. The reason for this is that the phenomena of sedimentation and erosion in the upper unit were blocked by the partition and hence prevented from reaching the lower section. Layers comparable to the conglomerate and volcanic debris of the upper cave were missing. The result was that most of the fill, having a maximum depth of only a little over 2 m., accumulated from man's use of the shelter. This appears to have begun at a time when the cave floor was still eroding or during a period of stability in the erosive process. In other words, human debris lay directly on the agglomerate floor.

Figure 7 shows three profiles of the lower cave, taken at right angles to the cliff. Fairly uniform conditions are indicated throughout, and four types of fill may be recognized:

A. *Dry Layer*

The surface deposit, usually deepest near the cliff (maximum 1.30 m.) and pinching out to a thin veneer toward the outside, was the only layer containing perishable materials. Since its formation it has not received enough moisture to decay the quantity of plant remains which made up a large part of the bulk, in spite of the fact that this portion of Ventana Cave was most exposed to the elements. Extensive churning of the layer was evident, much of it being due to the digging of the seventeen graves found in the lower cave. It is worth noting here, that, with few exceptions, pottery did not occur below the dry layer. This helps in defining it more or less as a cultural as well as a physical unit.

B. *Stony Layer*

Lying underneath the dry layer along the outer edge of the habitable area was a lens (maximum depth about 0.75 m.) com-

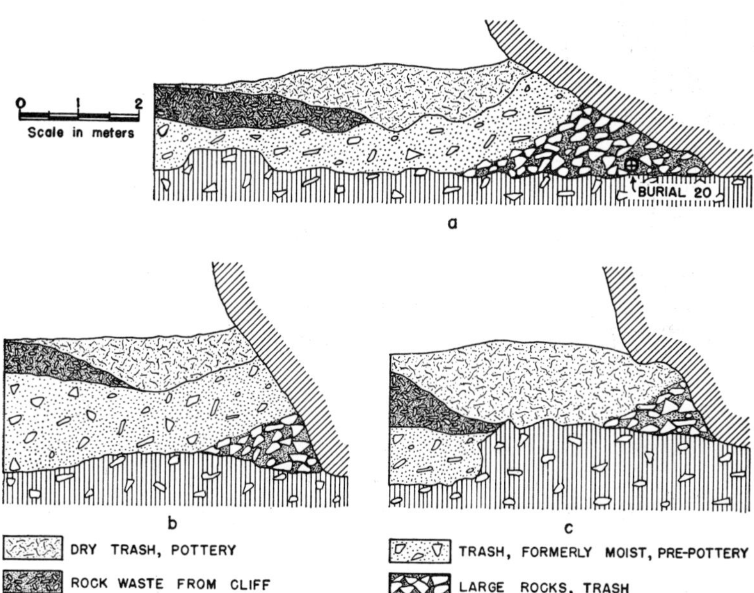

FIGURE 7. Profiles of the layers in the lower cave on northwest-southeast lines showing the northeast faces of test sections B, (*a*); F, (*b*); and H, (*c*)

posed chiefly of small rock flakes which have scaled off from the cliff above or fallen over the top. The concentration of this material directly under the greatest point of cliff overhang leaves no doubt as to its origin. It contained some culture, exclusive of perishable goods, but only enough to show that the lower shelter was in use at the time this deposit was collecting. The interesting feature is that there appears to have been a period of accelerated spalling of the cliff and possibly drift over it before the arrival of pottery and after the accumulation of the underlying debris.

C. *Pre-pottery Layer*

This is the zone which directly contacts the agglomerate bedrock. It varied considerably in thickness from 0.50 to 1.50 m. and was made up mostly of ashy soil and rocks, many of which were implements. The amount of rocks increased toward the outer limits of the tests, again within the range of cliff-fallen waste, and cultural items showed a proportionate decrease. Although dust-dry now, this layer at some previous time was moist, eliminating all recognizable organic matter. As the spring of the upper cave had no effect here, it may be assumed that the moisture needed to accomplish this came in from the outside, possibly at a time when there was more precipitation than today.

D. *Crevice Fill*

This should doubtless be regarded as a subdivision of the layer just described. For most of its length the horizontal crevice extending from floor level back under the cliff was too cramped for living purposes. But it became a handy place to dispose of large rocks and trash in general. As a consequence the composition of the crevice fill was heavy with angular rocks. There was no sharp line of separation between it and the pre-pottery layer and the assumption may be made that the two were contemporary. Only toward the southwestern end did any dry material appear under the overhang (Fig. 7*c*), and it is noteworthy that only here, too, was there any occurrence of pottery in the crevice, and this near the surface.

Attention is called to a fragmentary skull found just above the agglomerate floor near the deepest point of the crevice in Section B (Fig. 7*a*) which, from the nature of the stratigraphy, may be considered as dating from the pre-pottery period. (See p. 507).

In summing up the history of the lower cave, there is no reason to doubt that man and now extinct animals wandered through it in late glacial or early recent times, although there is no tangible proof of it as there was in the upper cave. In days when, presumably, more moisture fell, it would have been spurned in favor of the better shelter afforded by the upper unit. Subsequently, at a time corresponding to the formation of the oldest midden deposit of the upper cave, the lower unit evidently served as a permanent, or nearly so, place of abode. What perishable materials collected were soon decayed by moisture blown in during storms. At the same time large rocks which were in the way, trash, and even a burial, were crammed back in the crevice at the rear of the shelter. The duration of this earliest use is an unknown quantity. Then, either as the result of a purely local condition or as a response to some wider influence, rock waste from above formed a lens on top of the older debris toward the outer limits of the shelter. Man was making enough use of the place at this time so that some of his tools and waste became mixed with this deposit. The surface in the shelter was now more or less troughed longitudinally. The finer layer of debris centered in this trough and was characterized by its dryness, the presence of pottery and numerous burials. The Papago have added very little to the bulk of this layer and most of it can be assigned to an occupation dating before A. D. 1400.

Upper Cave

The maximum depth of culture-bearing deposits in the upper cave amounted to 4.50 m. (Pl. 11). This represents a greater depth of trash than is usually found in American caves. The deeper portion of the deposit revealed sharp stratigraphic layering, that is, beds possessing both geological and cultural aspects, while the upper debris was more homogeneous. These beds, or layers, will be considered in order from top to bottom.

A. *The Midden*

Approximately 80 per cent of the total cubic content of the cave was trash, the leavings of countless generations of man. This material was spread from the spring to the partition and from the cliff wall nearly to the line of cliff overhang. On physical characteristics, the midden may be subdivided into two zones, dry and moist.

The dry zone extended from the present surface to variable depths, reaching a maximum of about 1.25 m. near the pillar, and pinching down to nothing toward the spring (Fig. 8). In the region of the shoulder, particularly that area subjected to occasional flooding from the talus, the dry layer was thinnest (about 0.25 m.) because the water, sinking rapidly through the porous fill, dampened and decayed the deeper organic remains. But, as previously pointed out, moisture from this source since the trash formed has not been enough to completely destroy all perishable materials.

The composition of the dry layer included quantities of vegetal remains, mostly wastage of plants used for food or for other useful products; also worn out and discarded objects of all descriptions, as baskets, sandals, cloth, wood, bone, pottery, stone implements, bones of food animals, and a number of human burials. Hearths and ash beds also contributed to the bulk.

In the narrows, the surface reached its highest elevation, about 1.50 m. above the sump rim. This is evidently the section most recently occupied, as near the partition the rubbish had accumulated to within a meter of the cave roof rendering that area unusable (Fig. 8). Viewed in profile, faint slope lines were occasionally noticed, more often in the moist than in the dry zone. These lines, distinguished by ash and hard-packed layers, may be interpreted as surfaces of the trash in past times.

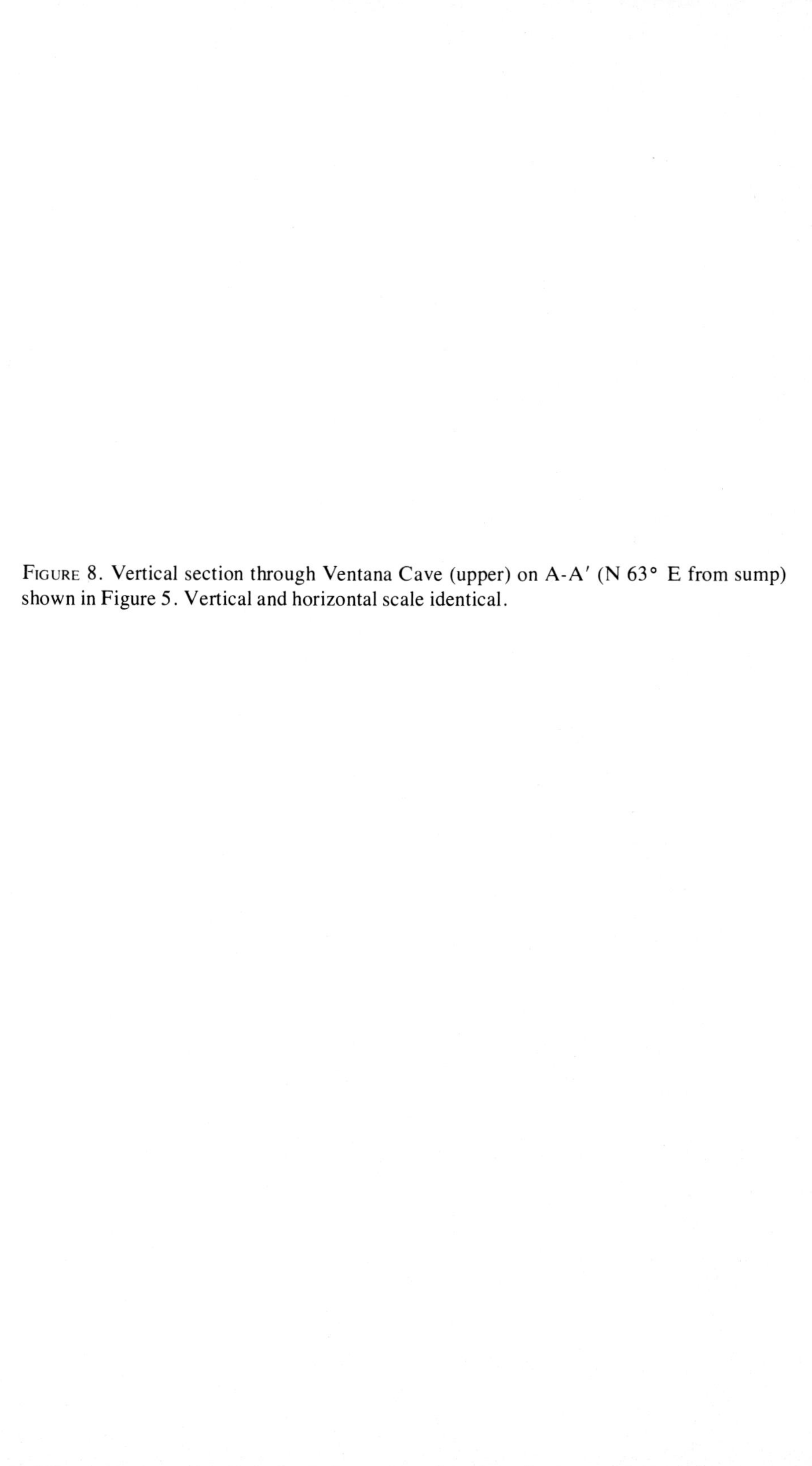

FIGURE 8. Vertical section through Ventana Cave (upper) on A-A′ (N 63° E from sump) shown in Figure 5. Vertical and horizontal scale identical.

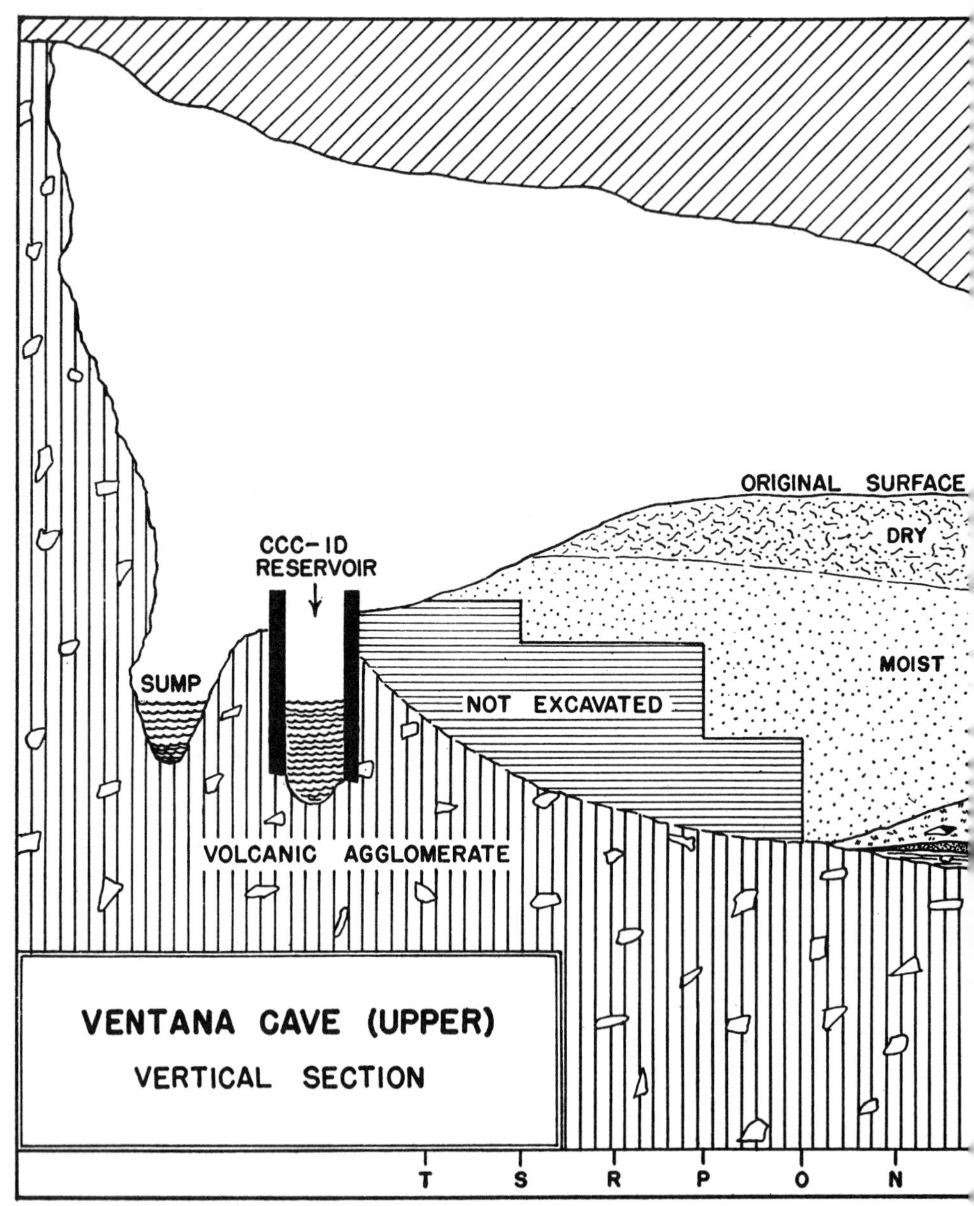

FIGURE 8. Vertical section through Ventana Cave (upper) on A-A′ (N 63° E from sump) shown in Figure 5. Vertical and horizontal scale identical.

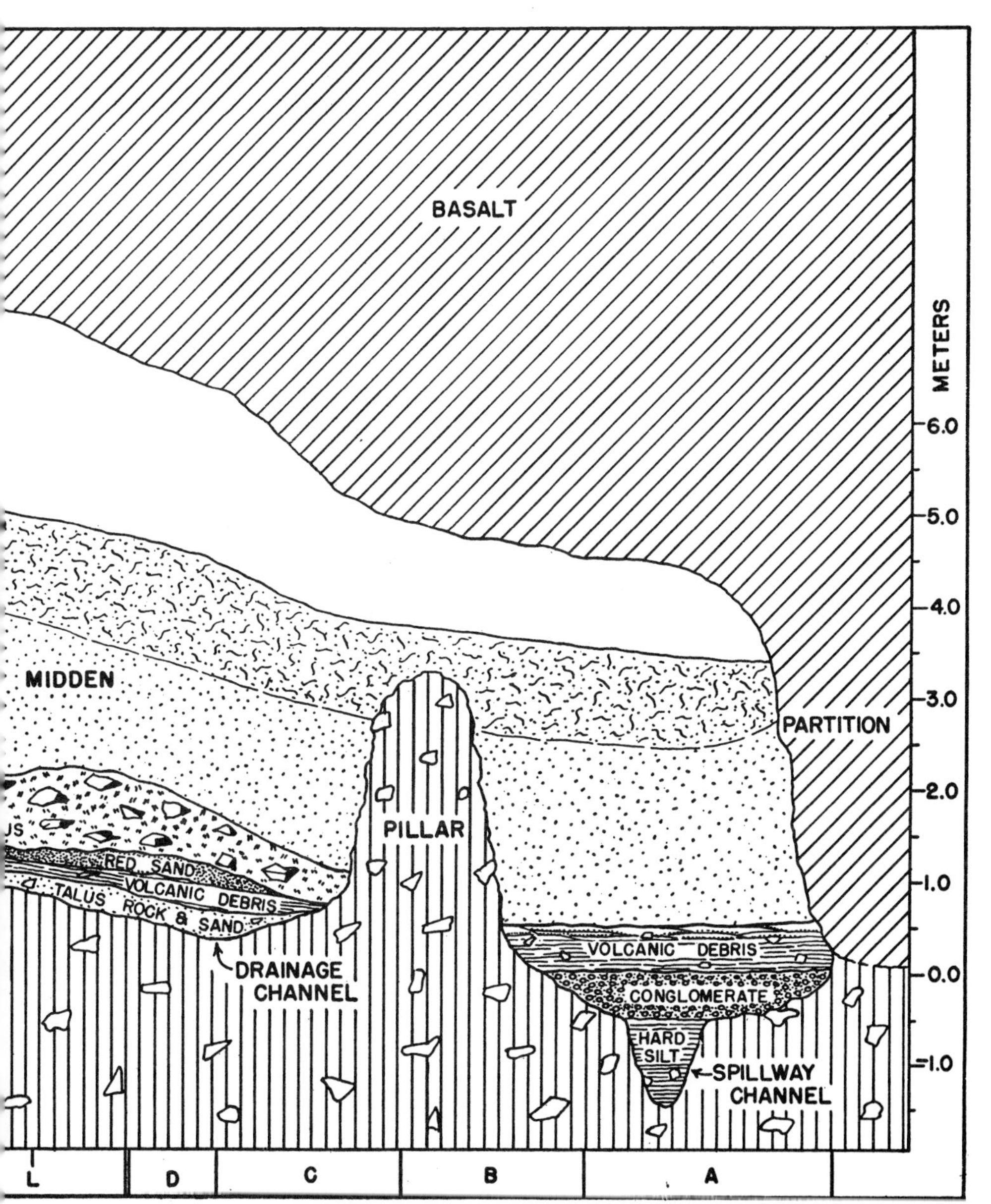

BASALT
METERS
6.0
5.0
4.0
3.0
2.0
1.0
0.0
-1.0
MIDDEN
PARTITION
PILLAR
US
RED SAND
VOLCANIC DEBRIS
TALUS ROCK & SAND
DRAINAGE CHANNEL
VOLCANIC DEBRIS
CONGLOMERATE
HARD SILT
SPILLWAY CHANNEL
L
D
C
B
A

They slope gently downward toward the rear wall of the cave (Fig. 9).

Along the cave's wall in the deeper section, for a width of about 2 m., the dry zone was barren of ash and hearths. Hayden suggests this area may have been reserved for sleeping and working. Also, on about the N coördinate in the narrows, the trash from the surface to about 0.50 m. down contained no ash beds whatever. This area coincides roughly with that portion of the cave in which fires were not to be built, according to the Papago.

Directly below the dry zone is the moist layer of the midden (Fig. 8; Pl. 12). In the narrows, and along the northern margin of the shoulder, it came to within 0.25 m. of the surface. Else-

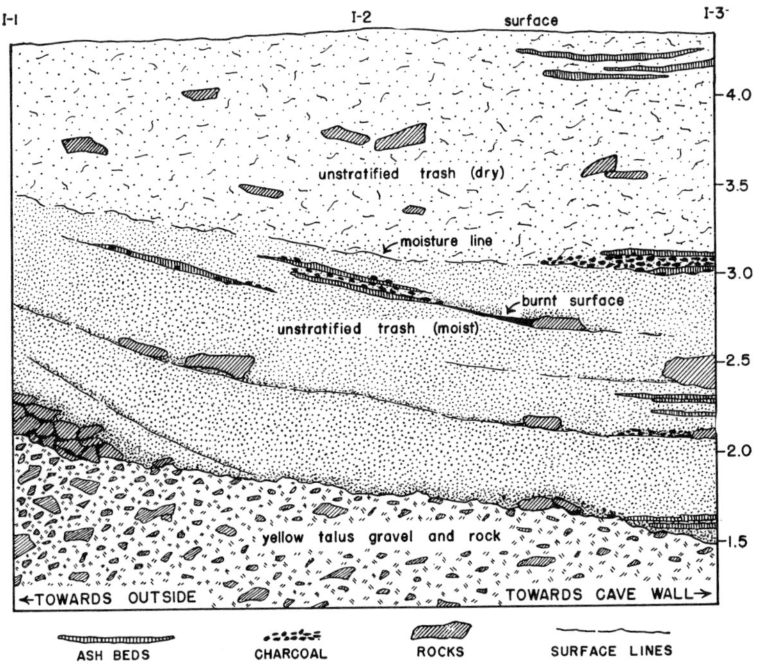

FIGURE 9. Profile of midden and upper zone of talus on the I co-ordinate, as seen from the northeast. This shows (1) the sloping character of the growing midden, high in front and low toward rear of cave, and (2) the midden resting on the irregular surface of the yellow zone of the talus

where it was topped by a heavier layer of dry material. The maximum thickness was about 3 m. near the pillar, the average being about 2.50 m. It was the thickest layer in the cave and also the richest in terms of imperishable implements. Pottery occurred only in the uppermost part and in some sections it was without pottery to the moisture line. This suggests that the difference between moist and dry rubbish did not represent a cultural boundary as well. In texture, it ranged from fine ash and soil to large rocks, most of which were metates; the color was grayish black and in most places this fill was very loose. Ash beds and hearths were fairly abundant.

Although designated the moist zone, in no sense was it wet. Vigorous shovelling would stir up some dust. Generally speaking, the northeast part of the cave was driest, the layer becoming slightly more moist on approaching the spring. It is obvious that, at one time, the layer held much more moisture than it does now, enough so that organic remains were completely destroyed. Previously it must have been somewhat thicker than when we found it, the destruction of the vegetal remains causing the debris to become denser and allowing the mass to settle.

During this process of decay, chemical elements derived from the organic matter were concentrated and redeposited as lenses and incrustations of crystalline form. Most of this was potassium nitrate (see p. 557). Bone and stone were often heavily encased with it and occasionally sizeable lumps appeared (Pl. 13).

As to the amount of water soluble salts present in both the dry and moist zones, a few observations may be made. Samples were submitted to Dr. T. F. Buehrer,[26] who kindly determined the results quantitatively as in Table 2.

Assuming that all levels tested had the same opportunity initially to acquire salts, the above figures suggest increasing moisture from top to bottom, or, the more the moisture, the greater the percentage of salts washed out. Except toward the

★

26. Head, Department of Agricultural Chemistry and Soils, University of Arizona.

TABLE 2
SOLUBLE SALTS

Layer	*Depth*	*Parts of salts per million of dry material*	*Percent of soluble salts on basis of dry material*	*Organic matter*
Midden	0.00-0.25 m. (dry)	83,000	8.30%	High
	0.75-1.00 m. (moist)	69,000	6.90%	Low
	3.00-3.25 m. (")	8,000	0.80%	Low
Volcanic debris	below 4.00 m.	1,690	0.17%	None

Partial results of analysis for soluble salts determined by electrical conductivity in midden and volcanic debris layers. Analysis by Dr. T. F. Buehrer. (See also Appendix). Samples from Upper Cave, D II.

base of the midden, moisture does not appear to have been excessive. In the volcanic debris layer, the situation was quite different, since that bed was water deposited and nearly all salts were flushed out. As the salt content of the moist midden zone was relatively high, indicative of low relative dampness, we may turn to the slow seepage from the spring as the main source of moisture, with the talus drainage providing a secondary source. Since the deepest parts of the moist midden yielded implements of the Amargosa II (Pinto-Gypsum) California and of the Chiricahua Stage of the Cochise Culture, a considerable lapse of time between now and then is indicated during which the spring drained just enough water to bring about the physical changes noted. And after some point in distant time, not easily determined, the seepage has not been enough to keep the whole bed damp. Furthermore, the trash laid down on top—the dry zone—perhaps within the last 1,500 or 2,000 years has not been affected by moisture at all from the spring.

In summary, it would appear, therefore, that in the light of more moisture in the layer formerly than today, and no moisture effect on the dry zone, the spring's output has steadily decreased during the period of midden formation. The importance of this in the whole picture will be seen when these facts are combined with the evidence of the spring's greater activity manifested in the still deeper beds.

Like the dry zone, the great bulk of material in the moist

midden must be attributed to the activities of man. The effect of natural forces, as wind, surface drainage from outside, rock falls, etc., may be largely discounted as of any consequence in its formation.

Viewing both zones of the midden there was no physical evidence, as a sterile layer, to indicate an interruption in the occupation throughout its accumulation. A cultural break does occur which may be dated as extending roughly from 1400 to well within historic times when there are identifiable Papago remains. With this exception, the more or less gradual transition of artifact types and complexes from one to another is highly suggestive of a continuity of occupation throughout the time of midden growth. The rate of accretion cannot be calculated accurately. The contained cultures, from Amargosa II and Chiricahua through San Pedro, Hohokam to Modern Papago, is indicative of a time interval to be reckoned in the thousands rather than in hundreds of years.

B. *Talus*

We now come to the first layer in the downward survey of the cave's stratigraphy formed primarily by nature. This is the talus wedge occurring in the central portion of the upper cave southwest of the pillar and just reaching into the narrows. Attention has already been called to the talus cone outside the cave to the southwest, its edge hugging the cliff and its slope meeting the surface in the cave before excavations began. During a particularly active period of talus formation, a tongue of this cone penetrated the cave around the northeastern curve of the shoulder, bringing in a considerable quantity of detritus. This varies from mud layers, gravelly lenses, to rocky areas, some individual rocks being as much as a ton's weight in size. Its thickness was, of course, variable, depending on where the measurements were made. On the profile shown in Figure 8, it reached a depth of about 1 m., thinning out from this point toward the wall, and becoming much thicker in the opposite direction, or toward the main mass of the cone itself.

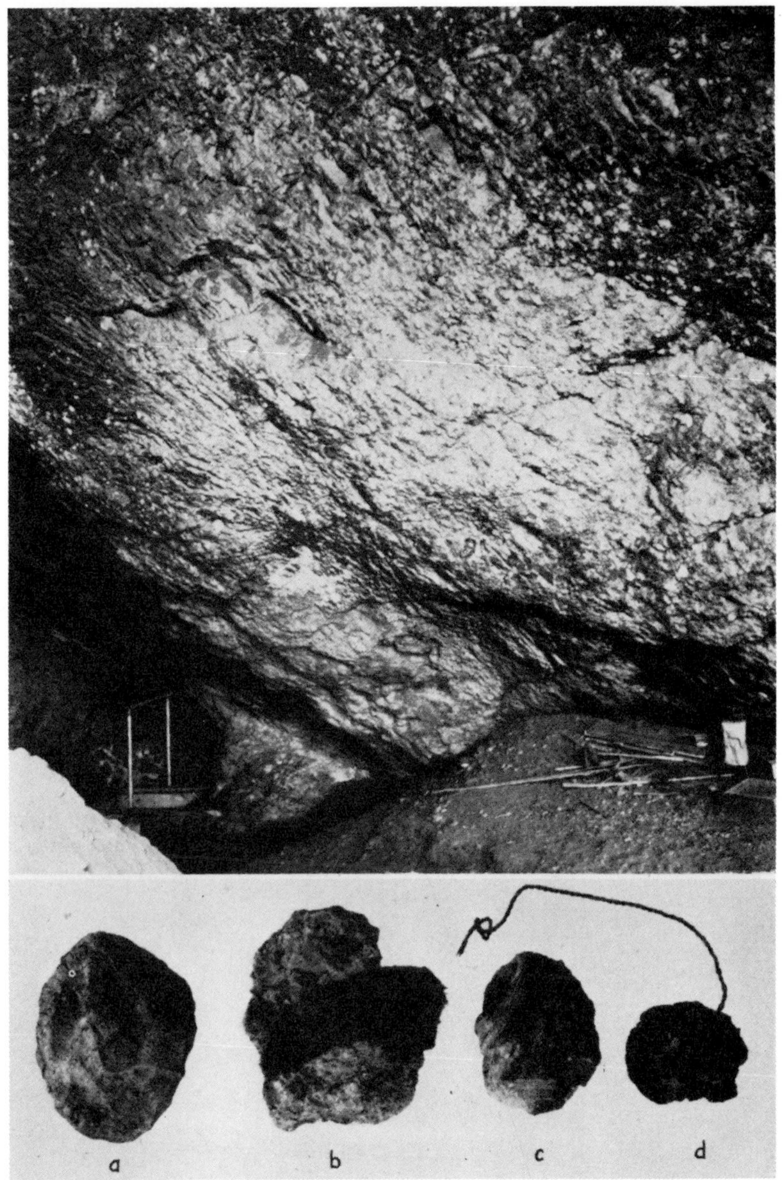

PLATE 9

a (Upper). Rear wall of Ventana Cave, near spring, heavily peppered with ash daubs.

b (Lower). Ash daubs from wall. Without inclusions, *a;* with native spun and woven cotton cloth (on under side), *b;* with recent (probably 50 years old) machine woven cloth, *c;* with yucca cord to which something had been attached, *d.* Diameter of *b,* 80 mm.

PLATE 10

a (Upper). The upper cave, central section, showing excavations in progress on the 0.50x2x2 m. testing system.

b (Lower). The cradle screen on dump used in sifting a large part of the seven hundred cubic meters of debris handled. Rock piles to left are implements from test levels. These were analyzed on the spot.

PLATE 11

General view of upper cave in pillar area, looking toward spring. Man at top stands on surface and man at extreme right is on bottom level of midden. Deposits in foreground are volcanic debris and conglomerate layers. The midden at this point had a maximum depth of 3.50 m.

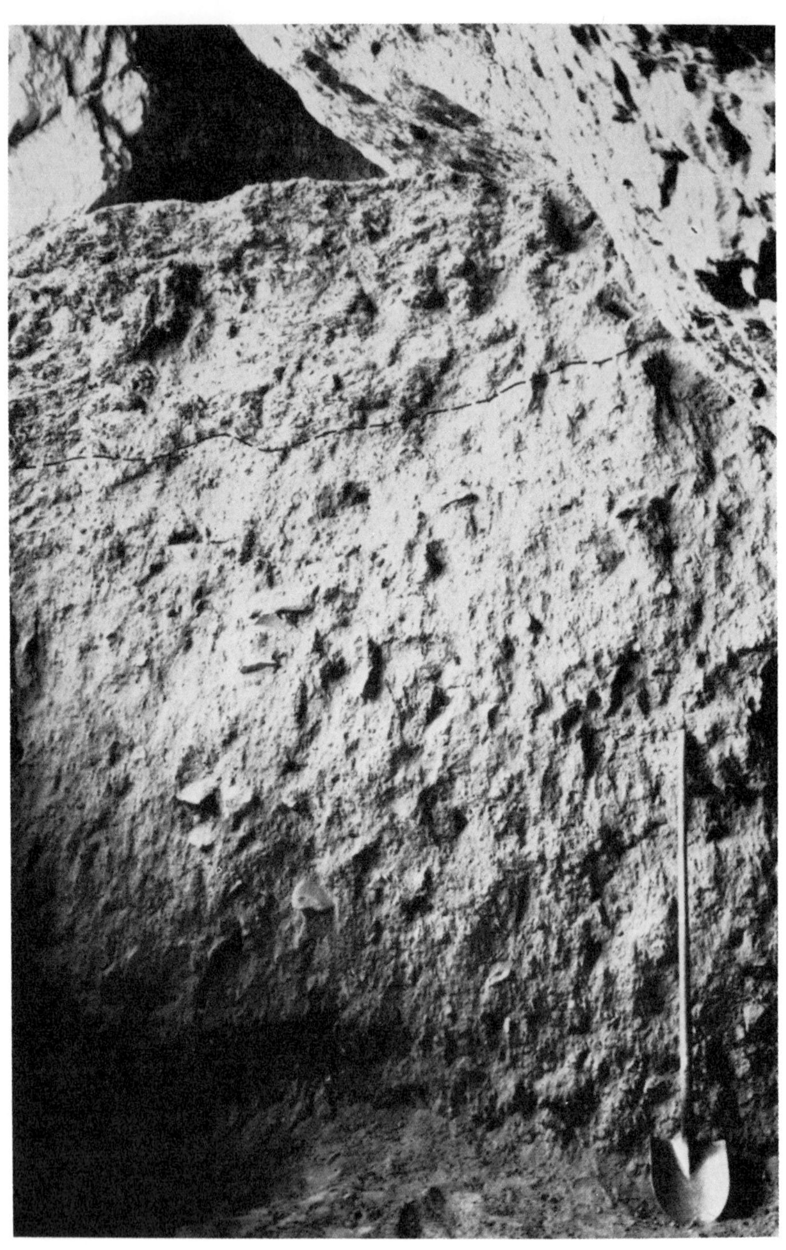

PLATE 12

Profile of midden in Ventana Cave (upper) taken near the pillar and looking toward spring. Dotted line indicates separation line between dry (above) and moist (below) zones.

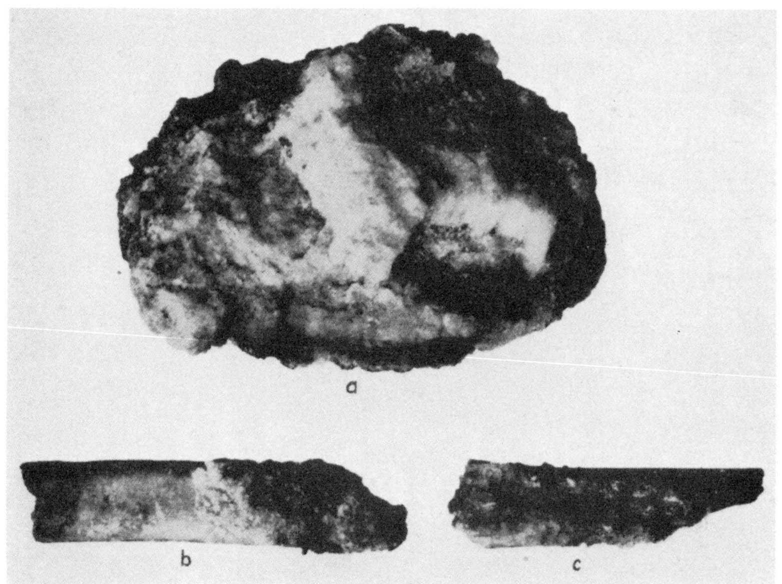

PLATE 13

Potassium nitrate from the moist zone of the midden. Heavy concentration on rock, *a*; incrusted bone, *b*, *c*. Length of *a*, 110 mm.

PLATE 14

a (Upper). Vertical section of J1-J2 from the northeast. Dotted line marks separation between midden (above) and yellowish talus (below). Note large rocks in exposure at left.

b (Lower). This picture, taken at right angles from the northwest to the one above, is looking toward the direction from which the talus came. The slope and texture of talus is evident. Attention is also called to the volcanic debris remnant (outlined) lying in the lee of the large rock, which protected it from complete removal by erosion.

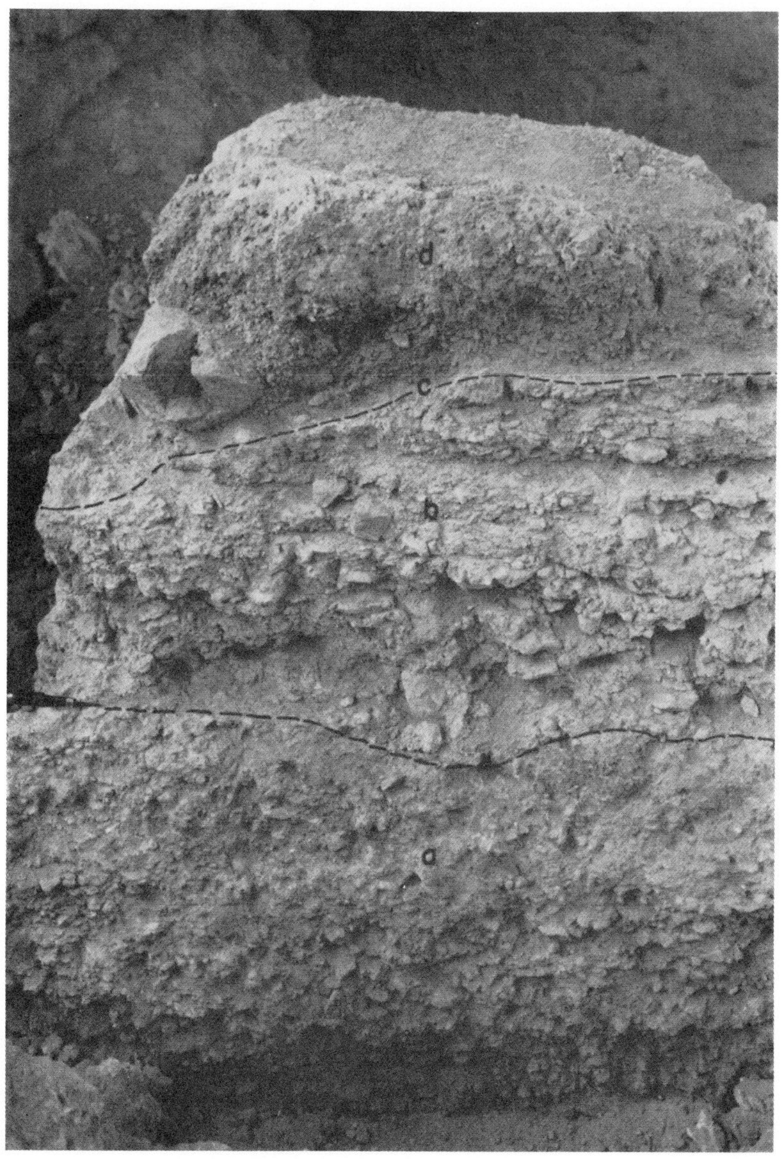

PLATE 15

Face of the cemented layers in Ventana Cave, showing, from bottom to top, the conglomerate, *a;* volcanic debris, *b;* the disconformity, *c;* and the base of the midden, *d.* The red sand was absent in the sequence here.

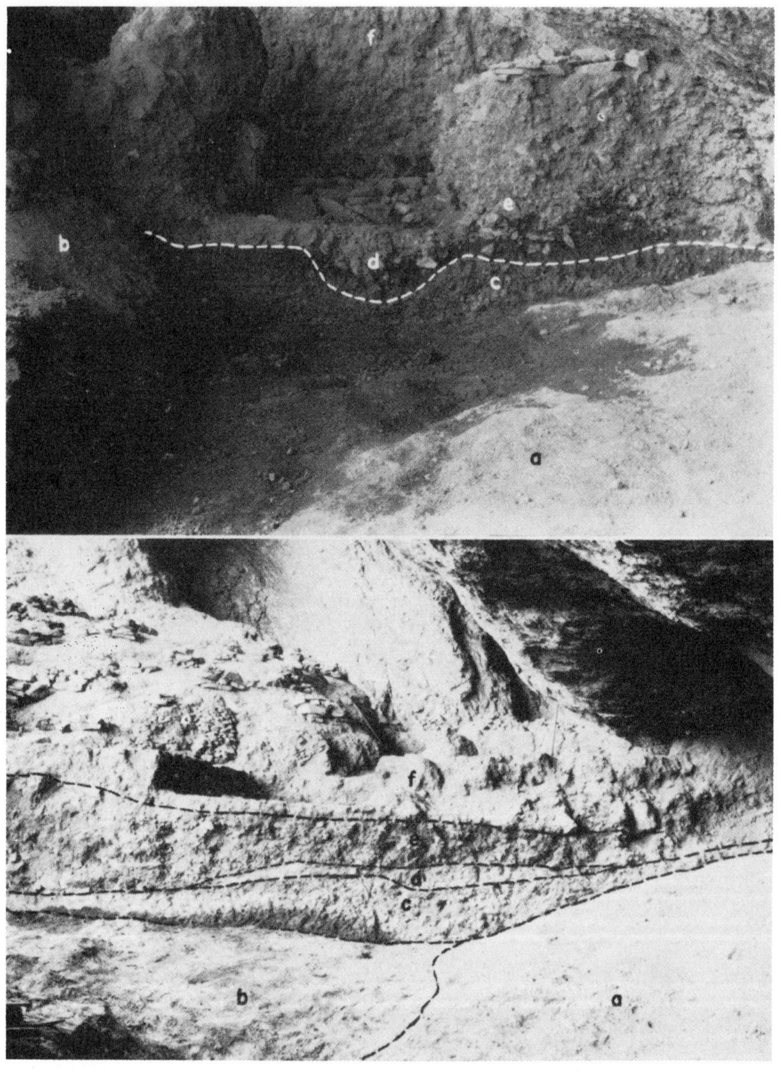

PLATE 16

a (Upper). The volcanic debris layer in the narrows, looking toward the spring. Bedrock, *a;* shoulder, *b;* volcanic debris, *c* (note fine laminations to left); rock-filled overflow channel from spring cut into volcanic debris, *d;* talus, *e;* midden, *f*. Dark stained area is present seepage from spring.

b (Lower). Section on K line looking toward spring, showing: bedrock, *a;* talus sand and rock, *b;* volcanic debris, *c* (note sharp dip to left where layer was planed down by water coming over shoulder to rear); red sand, *d;* talus, *e;* midden, *f*. Rock piles on shoulder are implements from various test sections awaiting analysis.

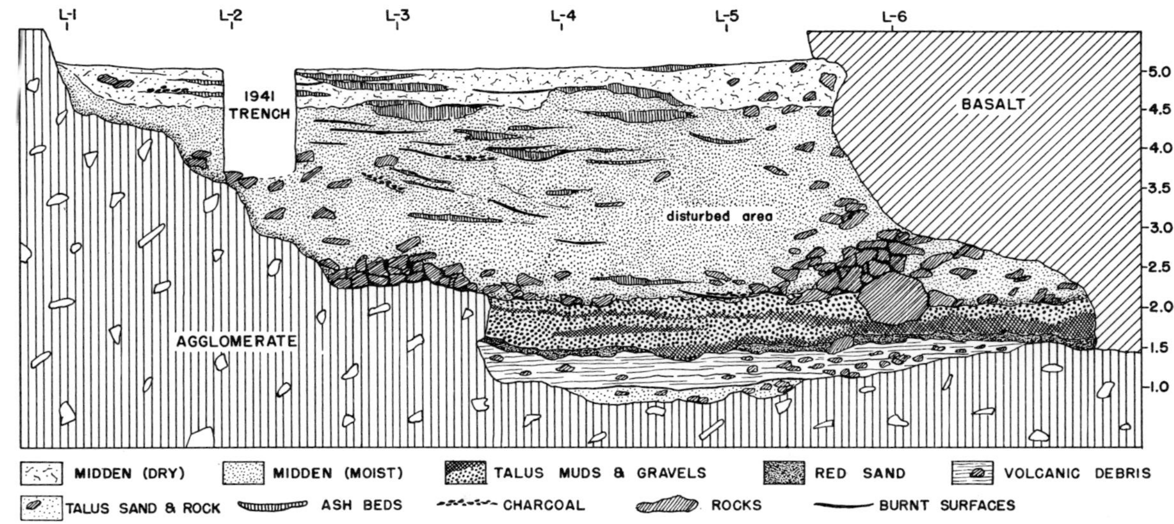

FIGURE 10. Profile of deposits on L line, as viewed from the northeast. Note particularly the talus which, at this point, consisted mostly of muds and gravels. Conglomerate not shown, as this section is out of pond area

Prior to the encroachment of the talus, the cave appears to have been subjected to flooding which materially reduced the thickness of some of the earlier beds. Possibly related to this flooding is a complex series of discontinuous deposits of a near-mud consistency intercalated with gravels, occurring most heavily in the lower end of the narrows (Fig. 10). The argument that these muds were linked with the talus advance is strengthened by the fact that lenses of similar material also overlay the detrital fringe in the same area. Their source was evidently the same as the detritus and the sorting of coarse and fine layers may be related in varying degrees to the intensity of flooding. Curiously, these mud layers were fairly well saturated with charcoal and rich in implements suggesting pauses in the flooding of sufficient length to allow such items to collect from camping.

After the formation of the first mud lenses, evidently the runoff from heavier rainfall moved in rock waste of grayish color, ranging from sand to sharp gravels to sizable angular rocks. This was capped by still more detritus, yellowish in color and, on the whole, coarser in nature (Pl. 14*a*, *b*; Fig. 9). It extended to and north of the pillar and, combined with rock shed from the cliff face above, added nearly 2 m. of material above the agglomerate cave floor in the spillway area.

A few hearths were found in and on the surface of the talus but it contained almost no artifacts or animal bones other than as mentioned above.

The advancing talus did not deny man the use of the cave, as both above and below the affected area habitation was quite possible. It may be concluded from the sparse culture in the talus that during its formation man was present, and that there was much traffic over it but no actual living on it. Simultaneously with its formation the oldest or deepest parts of the midden were doubtless accumulating.

The real cause for the advance of the talus is not easily determined. It may represent the culmination of purely local conditions, or it may be part of a more widespread cycle of accelerated erosion and hence faster deposition. It is certain, however, that water was the effective transporting agent and that the period of talus advance ended a long expanse of time during which nature measurably influenced the cave formations.

C. *Red Sand*

In sharp color and texture contrast to the talus was a layer of reddish-brown sand which lay beneath it (Fig. 8; Pl. 16*b*). This bed extended over almost the same area as the talus, *i. e.*, from the lower end of the narrows to within about 1 m. of the pillar and back to the cave wall. Its position thus, at the base of the shoulder, is an indication as to its source. It appears to have been deposited by the drainage coming off the talus along the cliff and over the shoulder, although Bryan believes it to be wind-derived.

This sand rested disconformably on the volcanic debris stratum below. Unlike the overlying talus, it was hardened appreciably by lime cementation, and its texture was fine, containing almost no large inclusions. There were no visible bedding seams. Much charcoal was present but no true ash beds or hearths; bones of modern animals were fairly abundant as were stone implements including projectile points of a distinctive type here assigned to the Ventana-Amargosa I Complex (Pl. 22). After deposition, this sand stratum was subjected to rather severe erosion which prevented the determination of its original depth. As exposed by the excavations, the maximum depth was 0.20 m. But the difference between the highest and lowest remnants suggests a possible former thickness of about 0.40 m. In the erosion of this bed some of the sand was redeposited as a thin layer over the volcanic debris layer between the pillar and the partition. As this underlies the midden accumulation here it is clear that the formation of the red sand and its subsequent erosion represent events transpiring before the growth of both talus and midden. It thus appears to reflect a time interval of some duration, a fact also borne out by the distinctiveness of the culture.

D. *Volcanic Debris*

It should be emphasized at the outset that the term volcanic debris, applied to the next deeper stratum in the sequence, does not refer to material resulting from a volcanic eruption. It does refer to material of ultimate volcanic origin, broken down by erosive processes outside the cave and carried into it by water.

This material extended over the entire lower half of the upper cave, from the narrows to the partition, completely encircling the pillar. In the narrows it was 0.50 m. in thickness on the average, increasing to 0.70 m. between the pillar and the cave wall. Between the pillar and partition the average thickness was about 0.50 m. but toward the outer edge, in the spillway region, it was present only as thin and fragmentary erosional remnants (Pl. 7*a*). It became evident as this layer was uncovered that a portion of it had been cut away and that what was left was only a sizeable residue.

Samples of the volcanic debris submitted to the Arizona Bureau of Mines[27] were reported on as follows:

> The rock has the general appearance of a tuff. It is composed of scattered fragments of several types of rock (including basalt, andesite, agglomerate chunks, and some stone foreign to the area, obviously brought in by man) cemented by calcium carbonate and silica. The carbonate may be dissolved out with hydrochloric acid and the remaining portion of the matrix becomes quite friable. Under the microscope this acid leached material is found to be definitely an ash of volcanic origin. The layer in question could be readily formed by the re-cementation of erosional material derived from the weathering of an original volcanic tuff or agglomerate. The amount of carbonate present would act as a secondary cement.

The rock inclusions varied in size from chunks weighing several pounds to minute chips. In areas of more finely distributed materials, the structure was isotropic. The layer was dry when excavated, except for a small area in the narrows, where it is now moistened by seepage from the spring. In color,

★

27. Analysis and report by Robert E. S. Heineman, Mineralogist.

the average tone was gray, but it varied locally from a light cream color to dark gray, depending chiefly on the relative absence or presence of charcoal.

The structure of the volcanic debris toward the bottom was generally dense and without bedding planes except for occasional short horizontal bands of lighter or darker material. On the whole, the larger rocks occurred in the lower part, grading to smaller inclusions above. Sometime during the period of its deposition the layer was eroded, producing an undulating and somewhat channelled surface. This was visible at several places. It probably represents no more than a purely local event and possibly one of no great duration in time. Sedimentation continued above it with bedding planes becoming much more prominent, especially in the area between the pillar and the partition. There the whole deposit was made up of dense laminae up to 50 mm. thick, giving the effect of weak cross-bedding. Between some of these uneven laminae were thin layers of uncemented yellowish sand which evidently had a wind-blown origin. These sand films disappeared toward the narrows where the volcanic debris appears to have been kept wet by spring seepage. Also in this area very thin laminae of finely sorted material seem to have been purely the result of overflow from the spring (Pl. 16*a*).

A qualitative chemical analysis of a sample of matrix made by Dr. T. F. Buehrer showed a low percentage of water soluble salts, as potassium nitrate, a condition sharply at variance with the moist midden above where potassium nitrate was plentiful. This means that there has been no downward infiltration of salt-charged moisture from the midden, and also that if any such salts were originally present, they were washed out by the abundance of water initially responsible for transporting the volcanic debris.

The spring water today contains but a small fraction of the elements present in waters which build up calcareous deposits, as travertine, or which carry in solution extensive amounts of calcium bicarbonate and deposits this when evaporating as calcium carbonate, commonly called caliche.[28] Consequently it is to be expected that water from the spring could not have precipitated any appreciable amounts of minerals during its long period of flowing. But, as will be shown later, travertine occurred in the early overflow channel of the spring and there was a calichified layer through which the spring ran near the spillway. Either the mineral content of the water was much higher at one time, thereby depositing the travertine in a relatively short time, or, if there has been no change in composition, the more likely alternative, the time element must be lengthened.

An interesting feature of this material is that, occasionally, highly fragmentary plant remains were preserved as carbonate replacements. It was noticed also that fine roots, similarly replaced, indicated the possibility of a former vegetative cover. Other extraneous materials included much charcoal, although no hearths as such; bones of animals, some of which are extinct; fragments of marine shells; and 90 man-made stone tools.

After the formation of the volcanic debris it was subjected to extensive erosion. An undetermined amount was washed out, producing a clearly defined disconformity (Pl. 15). A guess may be made that the 0.70 m. thickness of the layer west of the pillar represents its maximum thickness. Water, of course, was the agent which carried away the volcanic debris and left an undulating and channelled surface. But this water came from two separate sources: (1) the spring, which, during and after the formation of the debris, was flowing permanently. Evidence of this is seen best in the narrows where there was a channel carved into the debris (Pl. 16*a*). This channel later became filled with rocks rolling into it over the shoulder. Continued seepage of water heavily incrusted these rocks with travertine and lenses of the same material occurred along the drainage. As the spring runoff passed behind the pillar to leave the cave near the partition, it traversed practically the whole length of the volcanic debris layer and slow but continuous cutting fol-

★

28. J. F. Breazeale and H. V. Smith, 1930, p. 421.

lowed. (2) Violent flooding from the talus also had its effect. Evidence for it is seen in the remnants of debris on the leeward side of rocks (Pl. 14*b*) in the path of the talus drainage and the planing down of the layer, particularly toward the outer edge southeast and east of the pillar which was out of reach of the spring runoff (Pl. 7*a*).

This change in cycle from deposition to cutting is important in the history of the cave and represents the sharpest break in the whole sequence of deposits. In view of the marked changes outlined below, the interval of cutting, and before subsequent layers were put down, was a long period of time. The odds favor the idea that the phenomenon was related to a wide-spread climatic fluctuation rather than reflecting purely local conditions.

These changes, evident below and above the disconformity, are summarized in Table 3.

TABLE 3

PROPERTIES OF DEPOSITS BELOW AND ABOVE THE DISCONFORMITY

	Below	*Above*[29]	
		Red Sand	*Midden*
Origin	Primarily nature	Primarily nature	Man
Nature	Water deposited Cemented Light gray	Water (?) deposited Hardened Red	Camp refuse Soft Dark gray to black
Fauna	Extinct, plus some modern forms	Modern	Modern
Flora	?	?	Present forms
Culture	Ventana Complex	Ventana-Amargosa I	Chiricahua-Amargosa II

As previously stated, the volcanic debris layer was cemented by lime and silica. It could be removed only by vigorous picking and, particularly in the upper laminated portion, large chunks could be lifted which then had to be laboriously broken up. In areas where there was considerable admixture of char-

★

29. A division is necessary because both the red sand and the midden rested disconformably on the volcanic debris, the red sand having been limited in its area of distribution.

coal and trashy material, pieces could be crumbled by hand, while in areas of greater lime concentration the layer had a stony quality.

From the evidence at hand, it would appear that the actual cementing was more or less concurrent with deposition. The cutting of the spring channel and the general erosion of the layer was accomplished doubtless after hardening. The source for the cementing agents may be presumed to have been both from without and within the cave. Water running through the furrowed talus cone would pick up some lime which has cemented all but the thin cover of the talus. Also the spring, even with its low lime content, as shown by the analysis, would precipitate some of this mineral in the volcanic debris as it flowed over it. In favored spots, as in the narrows, travertine up to 40 mm. thick formed.

Fortunately, the hardening of the volcanic debris before the accumulation of overlying deposits eliminated the chance of later cultural materials becoming accidently included in it. Consequently, the human evidence locked in this layer may be confidently looked upon as representing a single time, as well as cultural, unit.

A word needs to be said about the fossil remains in the volcanic debris which are discussed in detail by Dr. Colbert in a later section. Throughout the layer, bones and teeth of animals occurred in abundance, but there were no whole skeletons or even articulated segments. All bone material was scattered and extensively broken up. This resulted most likely from the trampling of animals entering the cave for water and, more important, from man's activities, the dismembering of carcasses and splintering of bones for the marrow. Long bones were shattered, some fragments being very sharp and fresh looking while the ragged edges of others were extensively rounded and worn from being kicked and washed about on the cave floor. Preparation of the meat within the cave by man is indicated by the charring seen on some bones. The preserving qualities of the matrix were excellent and the bones did not suffer destruction during their long burial as a consequence. The degree of mineralization has not been determined accurately but most, if not all, organic matter has been lost. The bones are heavy, they have a decided ring when tapped and cling to the tongue.

A question which will inevitably be asked concerns the probability of redeposition. Did nature carry the bones from an older deposit into their present (and therefore younger) context in association with man's products? Such fossil remains would have needed to come from a layer like that immediately below, the conglomerate, if from within the cave, or from the talus slope if the penetration was from without. There is no evidence whatever of a fossil-bearing deposit in the cave higher than the level of the volcanic debris so that redeposition from such a source may be ruled out; further, as the volcanic debris completely covers the conglomerate and related talus sand and rock, also fossil-bearing, and shows clear-cut and unmolested lensing, there is no possibility of churning which might have brought bones from the conglomerate upward to become falsely associated with the later layer. To account for the bones as coming from the talus seems entirely out of the question. None were found in that part of it excavated. This area would have been most uncongenial to animal life then, as it is today, and least of all would the talus have been a place where bones would naturally collect in quantity. The only logical conclusion is that animals were attracted to the cave by its water and shelter where some doubtless died of natural causes and others were ambushed by man. Animal bones and man's tools became a part of the slowly accumulating cave deposits as reminders of contemporaneous existence.

E. *Conglomerate*

The layer just described rested on a conglomerate in the northeastern portion of the upper cave and a deposit of talus sand and rock in the central section. Both of these may be assumed to have been contemporaneously laid down but differing physically because of the peculiar topography within the cave.

Taking up the conglomerate first, we found it extending from the partition southwestwardly to the pillar. Its surface was more or less horizontal at 0.00 or the datum plane, and its maximum depth was 1.10 m. The bed was composed of well-rounded gravel, seldom exceeding 50 mm. in diameter, firmly lime-cemented in a silty matrix (Pl. 15). The predominant rock types of the gravel were basalt and other volcanics derived from the hill in which the cave has formed. Flattened pebbles lay horizontally. The color range of the bed was buff to pinkish and it was entirely dry. Partially mineralized animal bones and teeth were quite abundant. There were occasional charcoal bits and two doubtful artifacts occurred in the conglomerate near the surface level (p. 176). Some bedding was evident in the layer, caused by minor differences in concentration of coarse and fine material, and by reddish streaks, in all cases lying horizontally.

The conglomerate surface was rutted and pitted, probably the combined effect of physical erosion and the trampling of animals. An undetermined amount was obviously removed so that the depth recorded above does not represent the original depth. Over the spillway and toward the outer confines of the cave the conglomerate had been reduced to a thin layer (Pl. 7*a*) much in the same way as noted for the volcanic debris.

The conglomerate is not difficult to account for. Blocking of the spillway through which the flood and spring waters discharged would cause the water to back up over the area occupied by the conglomerate. The forces which were responsible for this obstruction were evidently two: (1) the extension of the talus fringe to the spillway area, elevating the terrain outside the cave, and (2) the dumping of waste rock directly over or in front of the spillway by the water emptying over the cliff from the upper drainage basin. The latter event was plainly recorded by a rock jam over the spillway, the crest of which was about on a level with the highest remaining conglomerate. Flow from the spring was evidently sufficient to maintain a permanent pool, and occasional flooding from the talus brought in the bulk of silt and rocks which, by the time they reached the pond area where the force of the flood was spent, consisted only of small units. These were then rounded in and along the edge of the pool by the combined action of solution and trampling under the hooves of animals watering there. Numerous animal bones and teeth imbedded in the matrix showed similar rounding.

How long the pool was extant, no one can say; but long enough for a minimum of 1.10 m. of conglomerate to form. Eventually the barrier was broken and water, unimpeded in its flow, scoured the conglomerate surface. Cementing of the bed probably took place as it dried out.

F. *Talus Sand and Rock*

As previously indicated, outside of the pool area toward the shoulder, the in-flowing talus drainage dumped large rocks, gravel, and sand which never reached the reservoir (Fig. 8). Like the conglomerate, this deposit lay beneath the volcanic debris. It represents, actually, a much earlier penetration of the cave by the talus than the one already recorded as being above the red sand layer.

Massive rocks, mixed with bedded sands and gravels, were heaviest between the pillar and the shoulder. Farther in the cave, small rocks and sand lay against the rising cave floor. Where visible, the bedding lines dropped from southeast to northwest, or coincident with the slope of the talus outside. The color of these materials was a reddish brown and all were hardened into a mass very resistant to the pick.

Only occasional animal bones were found in this member, rarely charcoal flecks, and there were no artifacts.

G. *Spillway Fill*

The initial obstruction of the cave drainage accounted for the filling up of the spillway channel with fine, dark brown silts. These had a clay-like quality near the bottom of the trough, becoming somewhat coarser higher up and mixed with angular blocks of basalt fallen from the cliff (Pl. 7*a*). Evidently a breach in the dam after the channel was filled allowed for some erosion of its surface but this was of such short duration that the channel was not washed clear again. No artifacts, charcoal, or animal bones were noted and the deposit has no particular significance in the picture except to complete the cycle of events.

RECAPITULATION

The examination of the deposits in Ventana Cave has been completed in reverse order of their formation. They need now to be reconstructed in order of occurrence. By referring simultaneously to Figures 11 and 12 for the main successive steps, a clear understanding of the events will be gained. These may be listed as follows:

1. Formation of cave. Spring flowing permanently, joined by intermittent water from talus, discharging through spillway. Talus slope gradually encroaching outlet area (Fig. 12, *1*).

2. Blocking of spillway by talus and rock waste coming over cliff.

3. Spillway fills rapidly with silt and rocks.

4. Brief piercing of dam, causing slight erosion of spillway fill.

5. Outlet again solidly blocked for longer period.

6. Formation of conglomerate in pool and talus sand and rock beyond pool area at foot of shoulder. Pond fed by spring, gravel and silt introduced by flooding from outside. Cave used as watering place by animals, including modern and extinct species, some dying and bones becoming part of bed. Evaporation concentrates calcium carbonate in pond area producing cementation of conglomerate (Fig. 12, *2*).

7. Dam broken again, pond drains, and surface becomes eroded. Spring continues to flow.

8. Weathered volcanics from outside introduced by flood-

ing, producing homogeneous zone at base, gradually becoming irregularly bedded with wind blown films between. Spring still flowing and cuts channel through growing volcanic debris. Bed solidified by calcium and silica. Animals (some extinct) and man both use cave (Fig. 12, *3*).

9. Long period during which volcanic debris was eroded, fauna became strictly modern, and cultural continuity was broken.

10. Accumulation of red sand by talus runoff. Man present. Spring discharge no longer sufficient to cut channel through sand (Fig. 12, *4*).

11. Erosion of sand and exposed area of volcanic debris.

12. Tongue of talus encroaches upon cave floor and covers

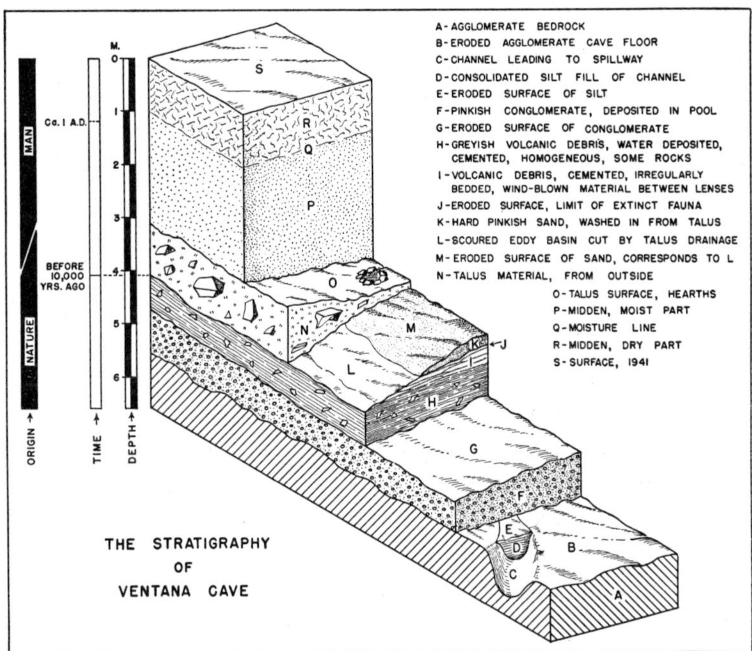

FIGURE 11. Profile of the deposits in Ventana Cave (upper). Depth scale shows average conditions. Talus sand and rock, deposited simultaneously with conglomerate, but on higher level, not shown

sand. Midden accumulating at sides from probably permanent occupation by man. Spring flow reduced to subterranean seepage (Fig. 12, *5*).

13. Midden accumulates over a long period of time, completely covering pillar and most of shoulder, raising trash level 2 m. above spring. Spring seepage with occasional drainage from outside dampens lower two-thirds of midden. Upper third always dry. Intensive occupation ends about A. D. 1400 (Fig. 12, *6*).

14. Papago use cave periodically in historic times, possibly also before. Stone diversion wall laid up within last twenty-five years.

15. Spring developed by CCC-ID, 1934.

This array of changing physical conditions, encompassing an implied long lapse of time, arouses much interest as to possible changes in climate and as to associated fauna, flora, and culture. The first of these interests is obviously a highly significant and specialized one, because if any sort of dating of the early beds is to be achieved, it must be done on the basis of a potential correlation with late Pleistocene or Early Recent climate. This is a task for a person competent in handling all the ramifications of the problem. Fortunately, Dr. Kirk Bryan, of Harvard University, with wide experience in dating Early Man, has collaborated and given us the benefit of his conclusions in the section following immediately. A few comments may be made by way of introducing his contribution.

Even to the uninitiated, the deposits in Ventana Cave reflect progressively drier conditions from early to late times, both as to the genesis of the layers and as to the output of the spring. The formation of the conglomerate and the volcanic debris layers, although distinct in make-up, and separated by a disconformity, are doubtless only phases of a single cycle. This diastem need not have been long. No beds comparable to these have been located outside the cave so that they are of purely local character and predetermined by the cave environment. But as

FIGURE 12. Plan of Ventana Cave (upper) at six successive stages. This should be viewed in conjunction with the stratigraphic section shown in Figure 11.

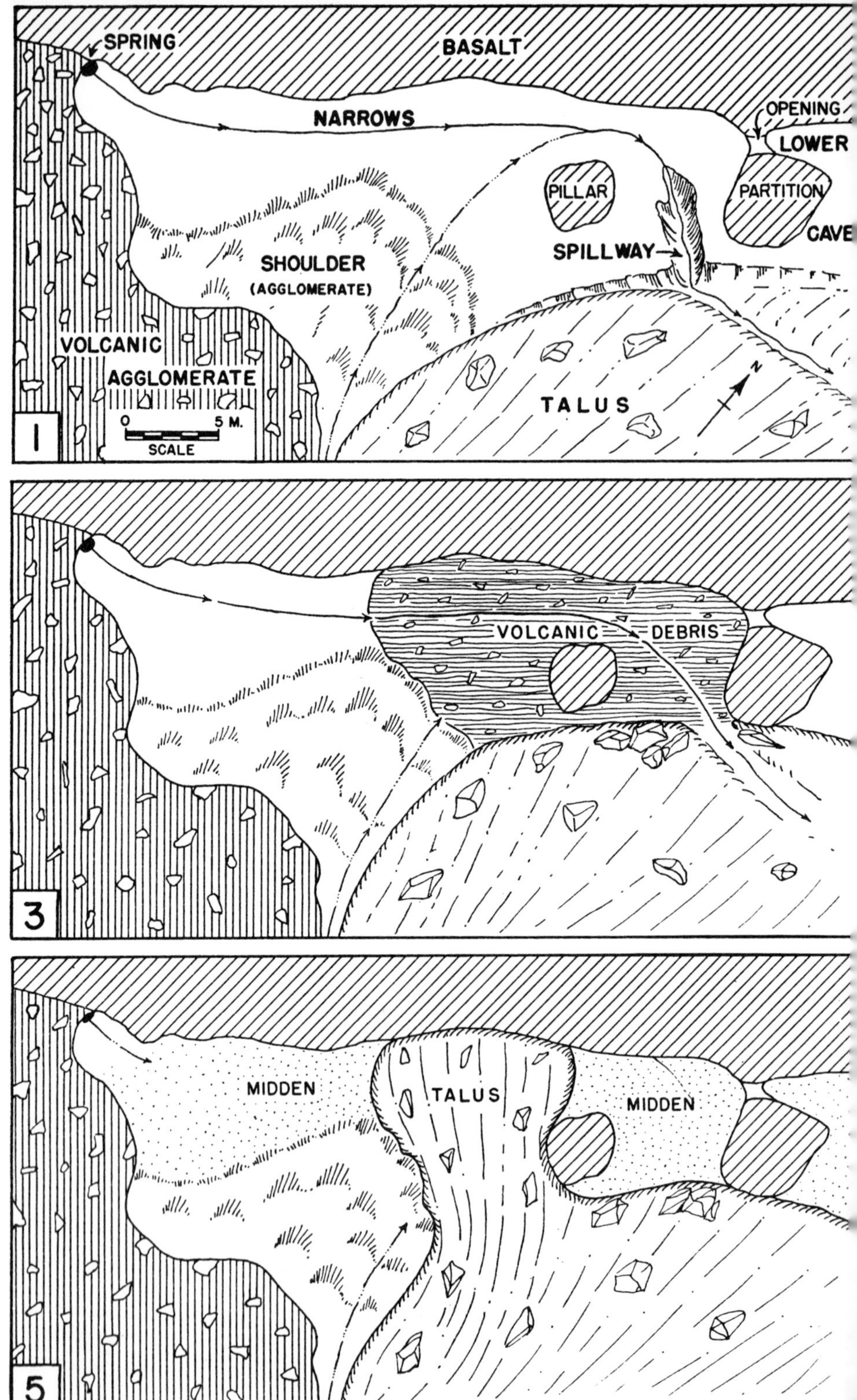

FIGURE 12. Plan of Ventana Cave (upper) at six successive stages. This should be viewed in conjunction with the stratigraphic section shown in Figure 11.

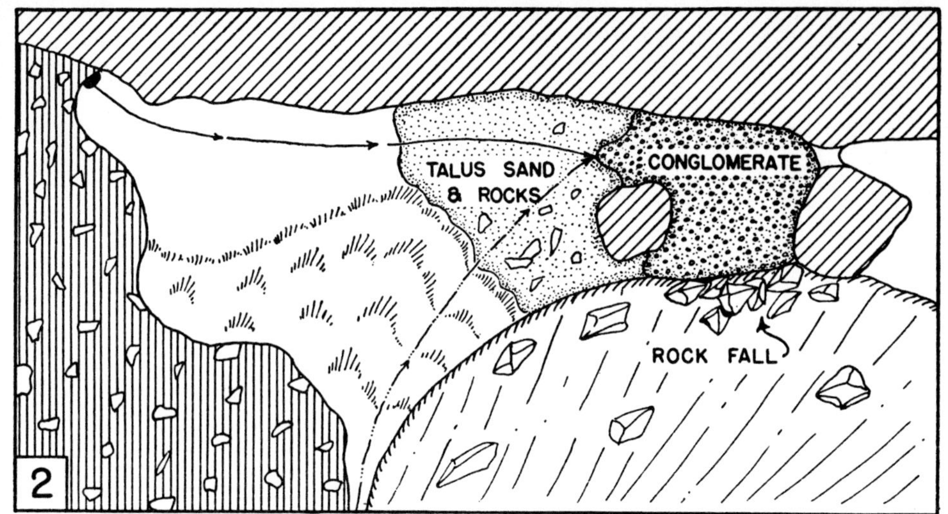
TALUS SAND & ROCKS
CONGLOMERATE
ROCK FALL
2

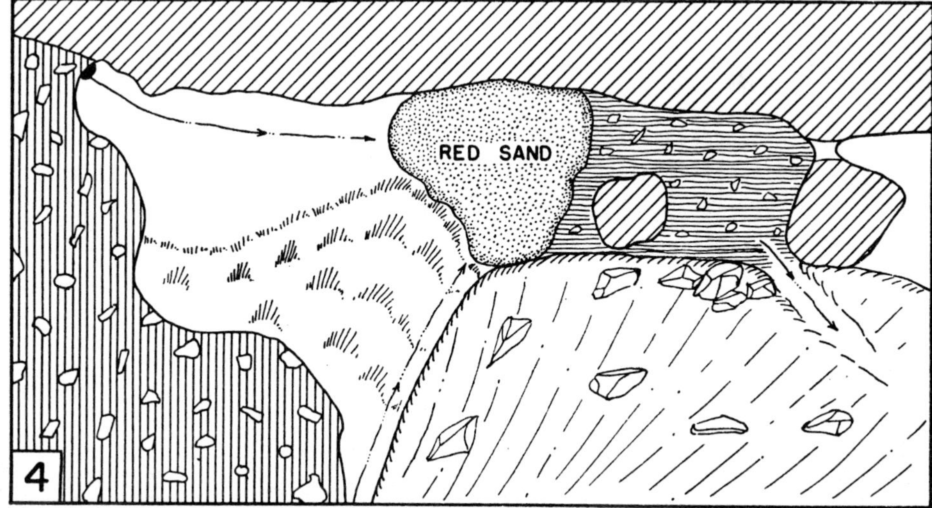
RED SAND
4

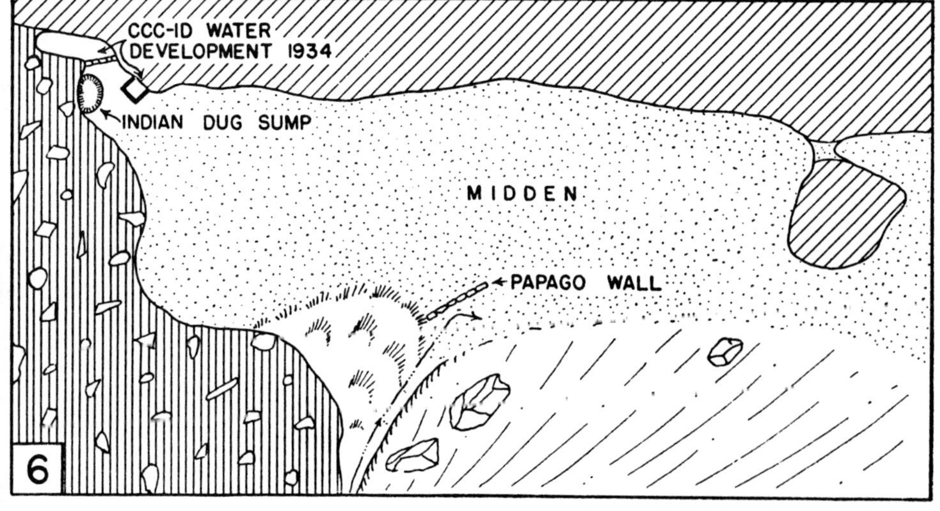
CCC-ID WATER DEVELOPMENT 1934
INDIAN DUG SUMP
MIDDEN
PAPAGO WALL
6

they had their origin outside the cave, and required water for transport and also as the solvent for cementing agents, climatic conditioning is implied. Supporting evidence for moister times is had in the faunal assemblage and especially the presence of such animals as the tapir. A similar trend of wet to increasing dryness to dry has also been noted for Gypsum Cave,[30] located some three hundred miles northwest of Ventana Cave, and for Sandia Cave,[31] near Albuquerque.

What stands in the way of clarifying this picture is our lack of knowledge of the alluvial chronology of the area. Events outside the cave cannot be directly correlated with those manifested in the cave. Deep arroyos, seen almost everywhere through the southwest, particularly of the kind which has made possible the determination of the Cochise Culture, are not to be found in Papagueria. Yet the deposits in Ventana Cave permit certain inferences as to what they are not and certain guesses as to what they may be in terms of age.

One or two additional aspects of the deposits need to be considered briefly. Foremost is the question of the possibility of mixed stratigraphy. What are the chances that faunal and cultural remains of one horizon accidently became lodged with those of another? For the nature-laid layers, the problem is rendered negligible by the early cementing. There was some slight evidence for a redistribution of the reddish sand and its artifacts, but not enough to cause any serious difficulty.

Disturbance in the soft midden, however, is a different matter. The activities of man himself, of rodents, the unequal settling of the trash could, and possibly did, cause some mixing. This may, in fact, account for our inability to draw hard and fast lines of distinction between the occurrence of culture types in the midden.

Another condition which might introduce confusion in the analysis of culture by the system adopted here are possible inequalities in level of the living surface. This was slowly rising

★

30. M. R. Harrington, 1933, p. 167.
31. F. C. Hibben and K. Bryan, 1941, p. 53, *et seq.*

during occupation because waste was disposed of underfoot. There is no evidence to suggest that any part of the upper cave was favored above others after trash had collected to the level where it covered the talus wedge. The probability is that along the longitudinal axis of the upper cave the level of the trash rose quite uniformly. There was some evidence in slight lines of stratification to show that, laterally, the surface was high in front and low toward the rear wall (Fig. 9), particularly in the area of the overhang between the pillar and the partition. A few sherds were found in the fill of this cliff recess where they were somewhat lower than elsewhere. But once again, it is doubtful if the resulting mixture from this dip is enough to nullify the general stratigraphic picture.

PART III

The Geology and Fossil Vertebrates of Ventana Cave

GEOLOGIC INTERPRETATION OF THE DEPOSITS[1]

Nature of the Problem

Analysis and correlation of the deposits of caves are interesting and difficult. Usually these deposits are neither directly connected with nor associated with any deposits outside of the cave. Conditions of the outside world, such as climate, may affect the deposits of caves and may even determine whether or not they will be formed. But these outside conditions are reflected within the cave solely by the physical character of cave deposits dependent on a complicated set of circumstances extending from the outside world to the interior through the mouth of the cave or through the rocks surrounding the cave. Direct observation of the processes which produced the cave deposits must be interpreted by a more or less elaborate chain of inferences. If this chain of inferences leads to conclusions appealing to our common sense as reasonable, they should be accepted as the best explanation of the known facts. Caves that have direct access to the outside world may be inhabited by man or animals. The record of occupation, in the form of animal fossils or of artifacts, provides a more direct chain of inferences as to the nature of the outside world and as to the time interval or inter-

★

1. By Kirk Bryan, Professor of Physiography, Harvard University, Cambridge, Mass.

vals at which the deposits were made. A comparison and correlation between the conclusions reached by these two chains of inferences provide a means of checking the validity of each of them. If the dual conclusions as to both time and circumstances are mutually compatible or similar, a still greater probability that the truth has been reached is attained. The validity of the results of a single investigation is, however, still uncertain by reason of the multiple possibilities inherent in the numerous inferences that are involved in the two lines or chains of inference. Confirmation can be reached only when future discoveries demonstrate that the predicted conditions, relations and chronology are valid in other caves near or far away, or in deposits of an entirely different origin.

Ventana Cave has been investigated with the foregoing difficulties in mind.[2] The geological facts are not numerous and have been largely brought to light by the extensive excavations recorded in the archaeological report by Professor Haury. The artifacts recovered in these excavations have also been analyzed by him. A sequence of cultural stages has been set up on the basis of this analysis, which leads to inferences as to the position in time of the cave deposits. The bones found in the excavations have been identified by Dr. Edwin H. Colbert and reported on in this volume. The bones provide the basis for further inferences as to chronology and also as to the contemporary vegetation and environment surrounding the cave.

The facts produced by excavation, and inferences therefrom, are set down in summary form in the following list as the basis of an analysis of the correlation of the deposits of Ventana Cave.

Summary of Facts and Simple Inferences Therefrom

The spring in Ventana Cave is determined in position by the rock structure. Its water supply is derived from local rainfall

★

2. The geologic investigation here recorded was made on Professor Haury's invitation in January, 1942. The cave was visited and a trip was also made to the Sulphur Spring Valley, for the study of the deposits in which the artifacts representing the Cochise Culture are found. The Arizona State Museum and Harvard University contributed to the necessary expense. To these organizations and to Professor Haury the author is grateful.

on the hill above, stored in the cracks of the rock and brought to the surface by a nearly vertical clayey seam. At the present time, the discharge is so small that no fluctuations can be detected. One cannot doubt that the water supply fluctuates with the quantity of the local rainfall and with its conservation from evaporation. Notable increase in flow of this spring is indicative of large increase in rainfall or low rates of evaporation on the hill above the cave and, therefore, in the adjacent countryside.

The cave deposits, as shown by excavation, consist of the following members from top to bottom:

	Meters	*Feet*
1. Dust and camp refuse, dry and containing undecomposed organic matter. Rests on lower deposits without sharp demarcation. Artifacts of pottery-using people	1.00	3
2. Dust, and camp refuse, slightly damp. No recognizable organic matter, crystalline potassium nitrate and bones of modern animals. Stone artifacts of Chiricahua and San Pedro Stages of the Cochise Culture and of the California Desert Cultures. Pottery only at absolute top	3.00	8
3. Coarse, largely uncemented, debris in limited area (talus); contains few bones of modern animals and artifacts. Rests on lower beds with erosional disconformity..............	0 to .75	0 to 1.80
4. Reddish-brown gritty sand, occurs only adjacent to shoulder. Strong erosional unconformity	0 to .25	0 to .80
5. a. Irregular plates of granular calcium carbonate separated by thin films of uncemented sand	0 to .17	0 to .50
b. Pulverulent tuffaceous silty sand with high lime content. Bone fragments of extinct animals: horse, jaguar, giant ground sloth, four-horned antelope, and tapir. Also chipped implements including one projectile point of Folsom aspect and a single grinding tool	0 to .33	0 to 1.00
(a and b are the Volcanic Debris Layer as used elsewhere in this report)		

6. a. Minutely bedded fine gravel, cemented by finely granular calcium carbonate (Conglomerate Layer). Rests on bedrock floor of upper cave	0 to .70	0 to 2.30
b. Channel deposit of restricted size consisting of coarse fragments of rocks embedded in a silt with a calcium carbonate cement. The cemented beds 5 and 6 range in thickness from 0.75 to 1.75 m	0 to 1.00	0 to 3.30

These facts and relationships brought out by the laborious and careful excavation of the cave, conducted by Professor Haury and his assistants and recounted in his report, remain to be explained from a geologic standpoint. The purely geologic analysis yields evidence for a series of events. These events would, however, be wholly isolated in time, as they are in space, except for the clues as to their position in the general chronology afforded by the contained fossils of animals and the relics of man.

The Cave and Its Water Supply

The Area

Ventana Cave lies ten miles west of Santa Rosa, a Papago village. It is eighty-five miles west of Tucson and seventy-five miles south of Phoenix, and thus lies well within the Papago Country, one of the largest desert areas of the United States. The Papago Country consists of broad open plains and detached mountains and mountainous areas.[3] The plains, locally called valleys, are drained by ephemeral streams which flow for a few hours or days after rain.

Santa Rosa lies in one of those broad valleys drained by Santa Rosa Wash, a tributary of the Santa Cruz River and thus of the Gila River. This wash begins near a broad divide that separates Santa Rosa from Cobabi Valley. The divide is called Sikul Himatk and lies between the Comobabi-Cobabi Mountains and the Pozo Blanco Mountains. West of Santa Rosa is a broad area of low mountains and hills lying east of the Castle

3. K. Bryan, 1925*a*.

Mountains and usually included under that name. The mountains and hills are separated from each other by plains slightly dissected by wet-weather streams. The topography is well illustrated by air photos (Plates 1 and 2). The cave lies in one of these groups of hills distinguished by a rock arch or window, the *ventana,* which gives its name to the hills and to the cave.

The mountains of the Papago country consist of rocks of four series, differing from each other in age and in general aspect. The oldest rocks are a crystalline basement of schist, gneiss, and granite, of pre-Cambrian age. These rocks are overlain by limestones and shale of Paleozoic and Mesozoic age. The limestone rocks have been largely removed and are now found in only a few localities, as in the Vekol Mountains. The next younger series consists of red shale and sandstone of Lower Cretaceous age, which occur in small areas and seldom form hills or mountains. Great intrusions of granite and, also, lava flows occurred in late Cretaceous or Eocene time. Some of the boldest mountains of the area are carved from the intrusive rocks of this category. Resting unconformably on these older rocks lie Tertiary rocks which are mostly great flows of andesite, basalt, and rhyolite in places underlain by conglomerate and interbedded with lenses of water-laid tuff. The Tertiary volcanics form great mesas, bold asymmetric mountains, and clumps of jagged hills. These uplands are carved from faulted blocks, as shown by the deformation of the once horizontal volcanic rocks. The broad basin-like valleys, such as Santa Rosa Valley, are downfaulted with respect to these mountain blocks.

The mountain blocks are largely in an advanced stage of dissection so that they consist of extensive, steep, sloping plains of erosion or pediments surmounted by isolated residual hills and small mountains. Ventana Cave lies in one of these isolated hills. The pediments are now dissected by little canyons 3 to 15 m. deep. Within the mountain blocks the plains, which from a distance appear smooth, are minutely rough. These little canyons fade out at the border of the broad basins and the streams spread widely in flood. Thus flood water is available for crops about the borders of the mountains and along the main channel-ways in the larger basins. Indian agriculture is dependent on this relation. During the summer rainy season, fields are planted in the basins and in a few of the broader valleys of the mountains. Water is available after rain in natural pools or charcos. Permanent water is available only at scattered springs and water holes in the mountain blocks.[4] Previous to the introduction of live-stock by the Spaniards, agriculture involved a seasonal migration from the winter home located near permanent water in the mountains to the summer home near the flood-water fields. Certain localities were, however, occupied only during the harvesting of wild fruits. As wild fruits were an important source of food, even among the agricultural people of this desert region, localities occupied during the wild fruit harvest were important places. It may easily be, as suggested by Professor Haury, that Ventana Cave has been such a locality.

Origin of the Cave

The cave lies in the southeastern face of a steep-sided butte, one of a number of ragged buttes and pinnacles that rise out of the surrounding brush-covered plains. The butte consists of a thick plate of andesite lava that overlies water-laid tuff and thin lava flows. These beds dip gently westward. The massive andesite of the butte is a single flow 75 to 100 m. thick. It consists of great blocks a hundred or so meters across, which were shoved forward as solid masses, after almost complete consolidation, with consequent tilting of the originally almost horizontal flow lines. This type of lava flow has been described and mapped in detail at the site of the Owyhee Dam, in Oregon.[5] The northeastern portion of the butte consists of one of these blocks. The flow lines are nearly vertical and the block is separated from a block forming the southwesterly portion of the butte by a seam of broken and decomposed lava .75 to 1.25 m. thick. This breccia was produced by the impact of the partly

★

4. *Ibid.*, p. 24.
5. K. Bryan, 1929.

consolidated blocks as they were shoved forward in the movement of the flow. Decomposition of this breccia and the production of clay appears to be due to later circulation of water.

The breccia zone has a curved trend from southwest to nearly north along the southeast face of the butte. It is also curved from a nearly vertical to a steep northwest dip at the base of the lava plate. Water, accumulated in the cracks and joints of the northern block, emerges at this seam in a small seep or spring. This flow of water has promoted weathering so as to influence the form of the butte. The steep eastern face parallels the breccia. It appears that the greater part of the southerly block has been removed by the intensified weathering promoted by this seepage of water. The cave is a mere hollowing out of the base of the cliff that otherwise parallels the seam.

The cave is divided into an upper and a lower portion by a narrow fin of andesite, the partition of Haury's description, which appears to be somewhat more resistant to weathering than the main mass of the lava. The two portions of the cave have, however, a common origin. Both are due to weathering at the base of a cliff induced by the emergence of water. The upper cave has been separated relatively recently from the lower and has since had a slightly different history.

As the sole water supply for the spring is the water which falls as rain on the relatively small area on the butte above the cave, the quantity of water emerging in the spring below must always have been regulated by climatic conditions. At present the local rainfall is small and infiltration into the cracks and crevices of the rock must be a very small portion of this meagre rainfall.

Professor Haury's diagram and cross-sections (Figs. 4 and 8) demonstrate that the size of the cave has increased very little during deposition of the cave deposits. A few blocks have fallen from the roof. The back wall of the cave gives evidence of slow wastage of the rock by decomposition and spalling. The rate of increase in size at present and during deposition of the cave deposits is, however, so small that the formation of the cave dates back to a more remote period. Presumably there was a time when the amount of water emerging in the spring was very much greater than now. The rock floor and the definite channelway shown in Figures 5 and 8 date back to this relatively remote period of strong flow of the spring—a period when, presumably, rainfall was much larger or evaporation so reduced that the quantity of water emerging in the spring was considerable. A colder climate, in which frost action would occur, would also promote effectively the retreat of the back wall of the cave.

Cave Deposits

The cave deposits consist of uncemented beds (1 and 2 of list on p. 77) and slightly to strongly cemented beds (3 to 6 of list on pp. 77-78). The uncemented beds occur in both the upper and lower cave. The cemented beds occur in a limited area of the upper cave only and are obviously older than the uncemented beds.

Lower Cemented Beds—The oldest of these beds (6b) is a mass of coarse rock fragments and silt, cemented with calcium carbonate. It occupies the channel in the bedrock floor, and is overlain by a minutely bedded fine gravel cemented by finely granular calcium carbonate to form a conglomerate (6a). This conglomerate extends over the eastern floor of the cave as a thin sheet. The pebbles are of andesite and similar to fragments found in the channel deposit except that they are smaller and more rounded.

The rounding of these pebbles is not due to wear but to solution and weathering. It must be supposed that there was once sufficient water so that the spring flowed from its point of issue through this area. The current rearranged and sorted the rock fragments. The fluctuations in volume of water from a small stream to a condition of almost no flow in dry seasons promoted their decomposition. During the annual periods of large flow the finer products of decomposition were removed. During the periods of low flow, evaporation of the water promoted the deposition of calcium carbonate. The fine-grained calcium carbonate is the type now deposited by spring waters under conditions of strong evaporation. These alternating processes of solution and evaporation would be possible if the flow of water fluctuated during the year from a strong flow in the wet seasons to a weak flow in the dry seasons and if this relation were maintained for an adequate length of time. Fossil bone occurred in this bed.

The cemented gravel is overlain by relatively loose and dusty, tuffaceous, silty sand with a high lime content (the Volcanic Debris Layer, 5*b*). This bed contains fossil bone and artifacts. It was deposited by the water flowing from the spring but obviously this water dried completely from time to time. The fine-grained, loose-textured material was brought in by wind or was washed in by flood-water. As shown in Haury's diagrams and explained by him, there is an alluvial debris cone on the south side of the upper cave. At present this cone has been built up so high that flood waters occasionally spill into the cave. This cone appears to have existed at the time when the lower cemented beds were deposited in the cave, and Bed 6a, the conglomerate, grades toward the south into a fan deposit. However, floods are not a necessary agent for the deposition of sand interbedded with the tuffaceous material or the ashy material, as wind drift from the slope eroded on tuffaceous beds just below the cave seems to be an adequate source of both the sand and the tuffaceous material in Bed 5b. The occupation of the cave by man at this time induced trampling of the slope below. Such disturbance of the ground is common to all sites of human occupation and leads to wind erosion. It is easy to infer that enough dust would be produced to provide the tuffaceous dust of Bed 5b.

Bed 5b is overlain by, and also grades upward into, a series of irregular plates of granular calcium carbonate separated from each other by films of uncemented brown sand, Bed 5a. This member is about 15 cm. thick. The plates of calcium carbonate are deposits of the spring water incorporating wind-blown sand.

Each plate is separated from the other by a thin and irregular film of this wind-blown sand. Obviously layer 5a is similar to layer 5b below in showing the presence of small quantities of water that evaporated completely again and again to form the calcareous plates. The brown sand was deposited by wind on areas in which no water flowed.

There is no essential difference in beds 5a and 5b except in the proportion of calcium carbonate deposited from evaporating spring water and in the size of their contained particles, which were brought in largely by wind action. The inference from their character is that the spring furnished less water than in the period represented by the underlying gravel of beds 6a and 6b, or the breccia of member 3.

Whereas, during the deposition of these earlier members, fine-grained material was washed out of the cave, at this later time part at least of the fine-grained material remained and was cemented in place by deposition of calcium carbonate. During the time represented by Bed 5b, the cave or the area just outside the cave was occupied by the people who left the artifacts. Obviously, also, the flow of water in the spring was decreasing and plates of calcium carbonate were being formed by evaporation of the spring water in more or less temporary pools.

The lower cemented beds of the upper cave (5 and 6) are separated from the upper beds by a marked erosional disconformity. How much material was removed during this period of erosion is not known, nor is it easy to visualize the agents of erosion. The lack of deposition of limey beds implies that the flow of water from the spring ceased. If the flow ceased entirely, the beds previously deposited would have been exposed to weathering and gradual erosion by beating rains widely spaced in time. Such dust and sand as might have been brought in by wind would have been removed by these rains. Broad open caves of similar dimensions, which have rock floors, exist in the region.[6] The lower cave had a bare bedrock floor at this time. In such caves, slow weathering of the rock walls and particularly

★

6. K. Bryan, 1925*a*, pp. 91-93.

the back wall goes on and the products of weathering, together with dust brought by wind, are periodically removed. Such caves are illustrative of the conditions under which the lower beds might have been eroded.

Overlying the lower cemented beds are two slightly cemented members, beds 3 and 4, which occupy relatively small areas. Bed 4 is a reddish-brown, gritty sand about 0-25 cm. thick. It appears to be a wind-derived material cemented with calcium carbonate.

A second partly cemented bed forms a wedge extending into the cave from the southeast (Bed 3). This bed consists of coarse angular debris which resembles the modern cone of debris that mantles the lower part of the cliff south of the cave. It appears to be an earlier extension of this cone. The cone appears to be a distinctly dry climate phenomenon. It is associated with the gulch south of the cave and is due to insufficient runoff to carry off the debris produced by weathering of the cliff. It contains a few bones of modern animals and artifacts.

The upper cave deposits (1 and 2) are loose and friable. They consist of wind-borne dust, fragments of rock that fell from the roof, and rocks and other debris including animal bones, brought in by human hands. The upper meter contains much organic matter; the lower 3 m. contain no visible material of this sort. In the lower zone crystalline potassium nitrate occurs. These two zones differ also in the type of artifacts found. The upper zone contains the debris of the camps of comparatively modern pottery-using Indians. The lower zone contains pottery only at the top, and, below, contains artifacts of earlier peoples. The bones of modern animals are found in both zones.

All this loose material has been accumulated during occupation and the extent of man's influence on local processes must be evaluated. The other known factor is the presence of the spring, which, at the present, has so small a flow that all the water is consumed by evaporation in the spring pool and by seepage into and evaporation from the surrounding ground. In fact, it is doubtful if a pool of water would exist if the Indians, and more recently the Indian Service, had not excavated holes in the bedrock floor. An additional fact is that on excavation during the winter season, the fill of the upper cave was slightly damp and certain zones damper than others. Obviously water was seeping through and evaporating from the fill. The loss of organic matter from the lower part of this upper fill and the crystallization of potassium nitrate would be promoted by an alternation from slightly damp to almost dry conditions. The movement of water from the spring into the fill presumably increased in wet seasons and decreased or ceased altogether in dry seasons.

At the present time, active wind work is not an important feature of the area around the cave. The climate is very dry, the vegetation is sparse and there is much wind. However, the area around the cave is a slightly dissected pediment—mostly bare rock or rock covered by coarse, water-laid debris. Loose material resulting from weathering is carried off by rains through numerous minor stream-ways entrenched in little canyons 3 to 10 m. deep. There is little wind-blown sand, but on windy days the sky is brassy with fine dust picked up through the region. Such dust might settle out of the air in a sheltered place such as Ventana Cave, but the fact that similar caves exist from which dust is removed as fast as it accumulates indicates that some special factor induced deposition by the wind in this cave. The use of the area as a camping place by primitives appears to be the special factor. The incorporation of organic wastes in soil prepares dust which, exposed to the wind by trampling of man and his animals, is such a noticeable characteristic of human habitations of all grades of cultural development. The slopes below the cave, being underlain by tuff, are particularly susceptible to degradation into dusts. Thus the bulk of the material incorporated in the upper loose and friable fill of the cave may be considered as induced by occupation, provided that the existence of the spring and a climate essentially like the present be assumed.

That fluctuations of climate have occurred during the

period of time covered by the deposition of this material is inferred on grounds discussed in a later section. The rate of accumulation of dust may have varied. The activity of the occupants of the cave has, however, arranged and rearranged the material so that any record of fluctuation in rate of accumulation has been lost.

Summary

1. The cave was formed when the rate of weathering and also of removal of material was greater than now. It dates back into Pleistocene time and may be the result of one or more humid and presumably colder periods whose record is not specifically recorded.

2. The lower cemented beds were deposited when the spring had a greater flow than at present and, therefore, when there was greater rainfall and presumably also less evaporation than at present. The flow of water appears to have decreased toward the end of deposition and the occupation by man seems, therefore, to have occurred toward the end of this comparatively wetter time interval. The antiquity of this time interval must be inferred largely from the contained artifacts and the vertebrate fossils.

3. The erosional unconformity between the upper and lower beds represents a considerable time interval when removal of material from the cave exceeded deposition. Such conditions are compatible with a much drier climate, one even drier than the present.

4. The upper beds were deposited under conditions of a relatively low flow of the spring and of occupation. The upper partly cemented beds 3 and 4 seem to be the work of flood and wind, and the presence of calcareous cement may indicate slightly humid conditions. Beds 1 and 2 appear to be largely man-induced and although they testify to relatively dry conditions, they do not give any indication of climatic fluctuations during the period of deposition.

Because of the lack of direct relation to any climatic rhythm, the antiquity of these beds must be inferred from the contained artifacts and vertebrate fossils, although the partly established alluvial chronology based on geologic and climatic evidence is a helpful aid.

Correlation with Glacial Chronology

General Statement

In the foregoing discussion, the intimate relation between the origin of the deposits of Ventana Cave and the rate of flow of the spring have been discussed. The flow of the spring depends on the local rainfall and on the conservation of this water. Thus the successive periods of increased or decreased flow are climatically controlled. The incidents of cave history that record these periods of varying rate of flow are climatic indicators.

If these indicators can be correctly interpreted, and if a complete climatic history of late geologic time were available, it would be possible to correlate definitely the cave history with the climatic history and arrive at the age of the cave deposits. The difficulties of interpretation of the cave history have already been emphasized. A sequence of episodes indicating a local climate varying from somewhat wetter to very much wetter than the present has been established. Some indication of a period drier than the present also exists. To evaluate this evidence in terms of general or world climate requires the use of numerous assumptions and much general argument supported only in part by other lines of evidence.

Unfortunately, there is no climatic history of late geologic time on which all students of the subject agree. The labor and thought devoted to this subject have been enormous. The conflicting evidence and honest differences in opinion as to the interpretation of the evidence prevent unanimity on the incidents and dates of the climatic history. It is generally admitted that the Pleistocene was marked by strong fluctuations in climate. The main outlines of the fluctuations in Europe have been fairly well established. That climatic fluctuations continue in diminishing degree into our time seems reasonable on general grounds, but many consider that the existing proofs are too conflicting and confusing to be usable. Admitting the difficulties in the use of climatic criteria, many scientists have contributed data on these later fluctuations which have been rigorously sifted and analyzed by Brooks,[7] who shows that climatic fluctuations within historic time must be accepted. However, the length of historic time varies in different areas. In Arizona, the first written record is the entrance of Coronado in 1540 A.D., and the first adequate descriptions of the country are those of Father Kino, whose explorations in Arizona began soon after 1687 and continued for several years. The earliest weather record is a complete year at Fort Defiance in 1853. The longest continuous record is that of Tucson, begun in the year 1867, so that fragmentary instrumental data extend back only ninety years.

However, there exists in Arizona a unique historical and climatic record in the rings of trees, both those living in forests and those cut for timbers by the ancient inhabitants. This record, gathered into the body of fact and inference known as dendrochronology, we owe to the ingenuity and perseverance of A. E. Douglass.[8]

The dates in this chronology have been carried back to 11 A.D. Also, a correlation between the tree-ring dates and archaeological events, particularly pottery types, has been made to approximately 400 A.D. The archaeological record with tree-ring dates is so precise for the past 1500 years that it may be considered as almost equivalent to an historic record.

The main dependence for time intervals prior to 1 A.D. lies in the glacial chronology with which various geologic events in the Southwest may be correlated. There are a number of dif-

★

7. C. E. P. Brooks, 1926.
8. A. E. Douglass, 1929, pp. 737-770; 1935.

ferences of opinion on these matters, and therefore an extensive review of the subject is here undertaken.

"Glacial" and "Pluvial" as Terms

The inquiring reader searching for geologic data on the antiquity of man encounters much difficulty in the confusion of terms used by different authors. Much of this confusion arises from the multiple meanings of the term "glacial." A glacier is a body of ice endowed with movement. It may be a great plate miles in diameter and then is called a continental ice sheet, or, if not too large, an ice cap. It may be a narrow tongue in a mountain valley and is then called a mountain, or better, a valley glacier. Ice of these types is "glacial." The land forms produced by the erosion or the deposition of such ice are "glacial forms." Thus there are "glacial" cirques and valleys, "glacial" moraines, outwash plains, deposits of boulders, clay, sand, etc. These usages of the adjective all derive naturally from the noun, glacier.

The most confusing usages have to do with time relationships. There is the "Glacial Period" or the Ice Age, a time interval extending some 500,000 to 1,000,000 years into the past, which was characterized by the formation of glaciers in areas now free of ice. The Ice Age is in marked contrast to the bulk of geologic time in its relatively low temperature. This period of time is also called the Pleistocene. The U. S. Geological Survey includes the Pleistocene and Recent in the Quaternary Period. In this usage, Recent is the vaguely bounded interval since the retreat of the last ice. Other authors consider that the Pleistocene includes the present. As no part of the period since the last ice advance has had a climate as warm as prevailed in pre-Pleistocene time, it is a fair statement that we still live under a Pleistocene climate. Within the Pleistocene there were at least four major intervals when ice formed and extended as great sheets into low latitudes and when extensive valley glaciers existed. These are the four "glacial" stages which were separated from each other by "interglacial" stages or intervals when the climate was as warm or warmer than the present. The Fourth Glacial, as hereafter explained in some detail, appears to have consisted of three major advances of the ice separated by intervals of mild climate more or less like the present. The periods of ice advance are considered to be substages and the times of ameliorated climate between them are referred to as "interstadial" intervals. Thus, "glacial" refers to the ice advance of a stage like the Fourth Glacial or any one of the substages in contrast to the relatively warm intervals of the interglacials or interstadials. But it will be noticed that the "Fourth Glacial stage" includes two periods of mild climate.

Confusion arises in attempts to distinguish the Last Glacial or the last substage of the Fourth Glacial stage from the present or from the Post-Glacial. Post-Glacial has a definite meaning in Europe, but in the United States it is frequently used for all the time since the melting of the glacial ice, of whatever substage, at the particular spot considered. In Europe, most geologists follow the Swedish definition and consider that Post-Glacial time begins at the instant when the melting Scandinavian ice sheet divided into two parts at a place called Ragunda. This definition confines Post-Glacial to the time when the glacial climate began to be modified into one like, but not precisely the same as, the present climate. As the climatic change occurred slightly before the separation at Regunda, some authorities wish to change the definition to this instant. Corresponding time in North America might be defined by the retreat of the melting ice sheet to some place in Ontario or Labrador, north of the Cochrane Moraine, but this locality is not now located. Under such a definition, it would be assumed that Post-Glacial time in North America is of the same length as in Scandinavia, or approximately 8700 years as measured by Lidén.[9]

Further confusion arises by reason of the use of "glacial" with respect to climate. It is obvious that the existing glaciers must require what is locally a "glacial" climate for their nourishment. But, presumably, the present climate of the Earth is

★

9. R. Lidén, 1913.

now not too much different from that in the past when glaciers were more extensive. The general climate of the Earth was then "glacial" but the present is not so warm as the interglacial time intervals. Furthermore, there is good reason for thinking that, during very long periods in the geologic past, the climate of the Earth was very considerably warmer than now and warmer than in the Interglacial stages. Brooks[10] discusses this question with acuteness, pointing to the finds of plant fossils of Carboniferous and of Early Tertiary age in the Arctic and also in the Antarctic which prove that at these remote time intervals temperate climates ruled at the poles. On this evidence, he presumes that in the Paleozoic and also in the Mesozoic and Early Tertiary there was no floating ice at the North Pole and no ice cap at the South Pole. With these considerations in mind, Brooks adopts Kerner-Marilaun's[11] term "acryogenic" (without ice) for these ancient periods of non-glacial climate. The whole of the Pleistocene and also the present would be a period characterized by ice at the poles or "cryogenic." The Late Pre-Cambrian and the Permian periods of earth history, which were also characterized by strong advances of glacial ice would also be considered cryogenic periods.

The difficulties of terminology become even more complicated when areas not covered by an ice advance are considered. Under current usage, during a glacial time interval such an area, if outside the ice margin, is "unglaciated." Lozinski[12] introduced the convenient term periglacial for the area immediately adjacent to the border of the Great Continental ice sheets, and also for the phenomena and the climate of this zone. Lozinski[13] and many others[14] have shown that severe frost and strong wind action are characteristic of this zone. The prevailing climate must have been peculiarly severe, much resembling, but also differing from, the present Arctic climates.

★

10. C. E. P. Brooks, 1926, 436 pp.
11. F. Kerner-Marilaun, 1930.
12. W. Lozinski, 1909.
13. *Ibid.*, 1933.
14. Paul Kessler, 1925; C. S. Denny, 1938.

At greater distances from the continental ice in areas that are in no sense "periglacial," other types of climatic changes are presumed to have taken place. In arid regions characterized by enclosed basins, lakes formed or had higher levels. These ancient lakes testify to increased rainfall or decreased evaporation or both. Many authors refer to these periods as "pluvial." However, "pluvial" implies greater rainfall or heavier rainfalls. Thus the term has an unfortunate connotation. It is entirely possible that during periods of ice advance, that is, the strictly "glacial" stages of the Pleistocene, increased rainfall actually took place in some of the present arid regions and also in the subtropical parts of the earth. However, most of the evidence of the climatic change, such as high lake levels, and fossil plants and animals, merely indicates a greater economy in the hydrologic cycle. Reduced evaporation from free water surfaces and reduced transpiration from plants such as might result from lowered temperatures, particularly in summer, would be effective in producing higher lake levels. A general increase in vegetative cover and a more sustained flow of streams and springs would also take place. To interpret the evidence so as to infer that these time intervals were "pluvial" implies too much; it is sufficient to say that they were relatively wetter.

The term "pluvial" as used by Antevs[15] has a still further connotation because a meteorologic theory is involved. According to this theory, set forth in his papers, the time of ice advance was a cold and dry period in western and particularly in southwestern United States until, on the recession of the ice, warmer and rainier conditions ensued. Therefore, lake levels did not rise until some time after the climax of each glacial advance. It is presumably true in Europe that the mere presence of an ice sheet over Scandinavia and the Baltic Sea and smaller ice caps in the British Isles would induce northerly winds, and that, as a result, northern and central Europe would be relatively cold and dry. Near the ice front the climate would be periglacial. Further south it would be of a cold and continental type or

★

15. E. Antevs, 1935, p. 310; 1937.

similar to the northern steppes of Russia. As the ice sheet melted away, winds from the Southwest would become dominant, and the present relatively warm and moist marine climate would prevail.

Antevs'[16] contention on the "pluvial" is summarized as follows: "There was probably one pluvial for each mountain glaciation. The pluvial culminations seem to have lagged slightly behind those of the adjacent glaciers."

The amount of this lag is discussed by him in several publications and constitutes an important element in his method of arriving at dates for deposits such as the Clovis "lake beds," containing the artifacts of man. The "lake beds" are correlated with extinct Lake Estancia which is held to have existed 10,000 years after the last culmination of the glaciers in the nearby Rocky Mountains. He sets this culmination at 25,000 years ago, and consequently the lake and the Clovis "lake beds" are given a date of about 15,000 years ago.

The analysis of meteorological changes in a glacial interval as used by Antevs cannot be applied without modifications. Southwestern United States lies to the south of the Rocky Mountains, a region in which the area of permanent ice, even during a glacial interval or a time of ice advance, was small. There were valley glaciers in the Rocky Mountains, but only a relatively small part of the mountain area was covered by ice and snow, particularly during the Fourth Glacial or Wisconsin stage.[17] The presumable climatic effect of these masses of ice would be to increase the southerly drift of the polar air masses. In the present-day winter when these mountains are more or less snow-covered, the polar air drifts south and cyclonic storms have paths much further south than in summer. Presumably the summer climate of the glacial intervals was somewhat like the present winter. The stronger rains that characterize the present summer on the plains of Texas and the higher plains and broad plateaus of New Mexico and eastern Arizona were

★

16. *Ibid.*, 1938, p. 176.
17. *Ibid.*, 1929, Map.

presumably much reduced. The belt of semi-monsoonal rainfall was pushed southward.

In the foregoing analysis, the summers of a period of ice advance are assumed to have been much like the present winters. The winters were presumably much colder than the present winters. Therefore, the total precipitation may have been slightly reduced, but relatively cool and cloudy weather more or less throughout the year would also have reduced evaporation and transpiration from plants. The effect would be to economize the water supply and increase the density of the vegetative cover. In Arizona, west of a line connecting Tucson and Flagstaff, the summer rains of the present time are relatively less important than farther east. In this zone, the small winter rainfall is the eastward extension of the winter or Etesian rains of California. Presumably the effect of glaciation in the mountains would be to extend the period of these rains into the summer. The relatively cool summers, with rain, would yield all the effects of an increase in rainfall although the total precipitation may not have increased and may have been smaller than at present.

On the basis of the foregoing analysis, Antevs' meteorological argument appears to be faulty. The "wet" intervals of the Southwest would correspond to the time intervals when glaciers were extended, that is, to glacial episodes. The "dry" periods began when the glacial ice had retreated far enough so that the present-day circulation of the air became dominant.

In 1941 Antevs abandoned the idea of lag. He stated:[18]

"The pluvial ages of the Southwest . . . were genetically related to the continental glaciations of northwestern North America. The moisture began to increase in the Southwest because evaporation diminished as a consequence of temperature lowering . . . Later precipitation increased . . . due to a southward migration of the Aleutian Low and of the paths of cyclonic storms. . . . The combined effect . . . resulted in

★

18. E. B. Sayles and E. Antevs, 1941, p. 40.

a culmination of the glaciers in the western mountains and of the lakes in the desert basins."

Thus he has abandoned the meteorological hypothesis which he originally used and now believes that the culminations of mountain glaciation and "pluvial" or moist periods in the Southwest are coincident. On this point there is no longer any controversy.

Even if pluvials and glaciations are coincident, the implications of the term "pluvial" are erroneous. These periods were not necessarily "rainier" nor did they have more violent rains than the present. Further, these periods were coincident in time with the "glacial" stages or intervals when the ice of continental ice sheets and valley glaciers was extended. They do not lag behind the "glacial" episodes as originally postulated by Antevs. The term "pluvial" is avoided in this report except when used in Antevs' sense previous to his paper of 1941. "Glacial" is used but so far as possible in self-explanatory sentences so that its numerous connotations may not be confusing to the reader. When used for a time interval, it refers to the period of advanced ice, that is, to the climax of a glaciation, and to a sufficient time both before and after the climax to include the interval of time when the climate was relatively cool and, therefore, "wet," that is, "glacial" rather than interglacial or interstadial.

The Glacial Period

As currently recognized, there were, during the Glacial Period, four great advances of the ice (Table 4). Many German authorities recognize minor ice advances near the close of the Third and Fourth Interglacials. They also hold that each of the three earlier glacial stages was marked by two ice advances.[19] These complications are not as yet proven to the satisfaction of all glacial geologists and, even if established, would not destroy the fundamental four-fold rhythm of the climatic fluctuations of the Pleistocene. As the deposits of Ventana Cave pertain to

★

19. W. Soergel, 1925.

the closing portion of the Fourth Glacial Stage, the chronological questions that might be raised with regard to the earlier glacial stages are not here discussed.

The Fourth Glacial Stage is the best known of the glacial stages as it is represented by the most extensive and best preserved deposits. It has, however, major chronological problems pertinent to the antiquity of Ventana Cave. The earlier students of this glaciation assumed that after an amelioration of climate in the Third Interglacial, or Sangamon, the ice advanced. In this advance there were halts and retreats of which the record has been mostly lost. The advance reached a climax

TABLE 4

SUBDIVISIONS OF THE GLACIAL PERIOD

<table>
<tr><th colspan="2">Short designation</th><th>Alps</th><th>North Germany</th><th>England</th><th>North America (Middle West)</th></tr>
<tr><td rowspan="5">Fourth Glacial</td><td>W_3</td><td>Würm III</td><td>Pomeranian</td><td>Scottish Readvance</td><td>Mankato</td></tr>
<tr><td>W_2/W_3</td><td>Laufen Schwankung</td><td></td><td></td><td>Two Creeks</td></tr>
<tr><td>W_2</td><td>Würm II</td><td>Weichsel</td><td>Hunstanton-Hessle (New Drift)</td><td>Tazewell-Cary</td></tr>
<tr><td>W_1/W_2</td><td></td><td></td><td></td><td>Peorian</td></tr>
<tr><td>W_1</td><td>Würm I</td><td>Warthe</td><td>Upper Chalky boulder clay (Old Drift)</td><td>Iowan</td></tr>
<tr><td colspan="2">Third Interglacial or W/R</td><td></td><td></td><td></td><td>Sangamon</td></tr>
<tr><td colspan="2">Third glacial or R</td><td>Riss</td><td>Saale</td><td>Great Chalky boulder clay</td><td>Illinoisan</td></tr>
<tr><td colspan="2">Second Interglacial or R/M</td><td></td><td></td><td></td><td>Yarmouth</td></tr>
<tr><td colspan="2">Second glacial or M</td><td>Mindel</td><td>Elster</td><td>North Sea Drift</td><td>Kansan</td></tr>
<tr><td colspan="2">First Interglacial or M/G</td><td></td><td></td><td></td><td>Aftonian</td></tr>
<tr><td colspan="2">First glacial or G</td><td>Günz</td><td>Elbe (?)</td><td>Later Crag deposits</td><td>Nebraskan</td></tr>
</table>

and thereafter there was a retreat marked by halts and readvances until the ice disappeared. This hypothesis was developed from an incomplete study of the deposits of the ice. In so far as climatic fluctuation was considered, it was assumed that climate deteriorated, *i. e.*, became colder from the relative warmth of the interglacial to the climax of ice advance and then ameliorated to the present.

That the Fourth Glacial, called Wisconsin in the United States, consisted of three distinct advances of the ice separated by periods of ameliorated climate or interstadial intervals, is a comparatively new idea. The subdivision as proposed is shown in Table 5 and also in more detail in Table 6. In North America, the generally current interpretation of the Fourth Glacial was proposed by Leverett[20] and slightly amended by Kay and Leighton.[21] It may be summarized. The main advance is the Tazewell, which was formerly called the Early Wisconsin. It overrode the earlier Iowan except in parts of the state of Illinois and Iowa. Accepting Kay's and Leighton's suggestion that the Iowan is the first advance of the Wisconsin, the Tazewell becomes the Middle Wisconsin, and the Iowan the Early Wisconsin. Following the Iowan advance, there was a retreat of the ice and a readvance to its maximum (the Tazewell), followed by a retreat and readvance of the ice (Cary). The Cary ice did not reach as far south as the Tazewell except in a few localities. There then followed a retreat and a readvance of the ice (Mankato). The first known advance of the Mankato was east of the Lake Superior Highlands (Lower Mankato or Valders), and it was followed by a more extensive movement west of the highlands. This is the Des Moines Lobe, which is the best studied portion of the Mankato advance. The eastern extension of the Mankato is thought to be the Port Huron morainal system which lies north of Lake Ontario and extends eastward to New York state. This moraine crosses to the south shore of Lake Erie

★

20. Frank Leverett, 1899.
21. G. M. Kay and M. M. Leighton, 1933.

Table 5

CORRELATIONS OF THE FOURTH GLACIAL STAGE

Short Designation	*Continental United States*	*North German Plain*	*Great Britain*	*Ireland*	*Alps*
		Post-Glacial & 1700 years	3rd Retreat	3rd Retreat	
W_4	Cochrane	Fennoscandian Moraine	Valley Glaciation	Valley Glaciation	
		Gotiglacial (Alleröd)	2nd Retreat	2nd Retreat	
W_3	Upper Mankato Lower Mankato	Pomeranian Moraine	Highland Glaciation (Scottish readvance)	Central Plains Moraines 1st Retreat	Würm III Bühl Stage
W_2/W_3	Two Creeks	Daniglacial	1st retreat		
W_2	Tazewell-Cary	Weichsel (Brandenburg Moraine)	New Drift to "York Line" (Hessle-Hunstanton)	Southern Irish End Moraine	Würm II
W_1/W_2	Peorian	Eem interglacial or interstadial			Laufen Oscillation
W_1	Iowan	Warthe (Flaming Moraine)	Old Drift (Upper chalky boulder clay)	Old Drift (Indurated boulder clay)	Würm I

at Buffalo but east of this point there is no general agreement as to its position.

Thus the usual viewpoint is that the Fourth Glacial consists of five advances: Iowan, Tazewell, Cary, Early Mankato (Valders), and Late Mankato (Des Moines Lobe), each separated from the other by retreats of the ice. Some authorities assume that Mankato is, in reality, only one advance and thus they have four advances. Antevs[22] has called attention to a later readvance represented by the Cochrane Moraine in western Ontario, which thus is the fifth or sixth.

Viewed from a climatic standpoint, a retreat and readvance of a continental ice sheet might take place by means of a slight weakening of the prevailing cold climate but without change to a climate like the present. On the other hand, the retreat of the ice sheet might be due to a greater fluctuation, bringing about a climate as mild or milder than the present. There is no question that the five advances, six including the Cochrane, occurred and that they were separated by retreats. The present differences of opinion in regard to the Fourth Glacial are concerned with the extent of climatic amelioration required by these retreats.

In the United States, the concept that, in the Fourth Glacial, important climatic change intervened between advances of the ice began with the recognition of the Iowan as a part of the first advance of the Wisconsin.[23] The Post-Iowan interval or Peorian is marked by very pronounced erosion during which much Iowan till was removed and valleys were cut. For many years the interval was considered an interglacial period and the erosion was attributed to stream work in an ameliorated climate. No evidence has been brought forward to indicate that this conclusion is incorrect. The Tazewell is separated from the Cary by a retreat of the ice front and a readvance. There is, however, no evidence of a marked climatic change in the Tazewell-Cary

★

22. E. Antevs, 1931.
23. G. M. Kay and M. M. Leighton, 1933.

interval although along river valleys there is conspicuous erosion.[24]

The description of the Two Creek forest bed lying between the Cary and Mankato (Valders) tills, by Wilson,[25] placed emphasis on the retreat following the Cary. The fivefold classification of Leverett or fourfold classification of others breaks into a threefold subdivision comparable to the newly devised European subdivision (Table 5). A strong influence on this view of the Wisconsin has been exerted by Antevs, who, as long ago as 1928, recognized the Tazewell, which was then regarded as the climax of the Wisconsin, as the equivalent of the Weichsel stage, of Germany, and the Mankato as the equivalent of the Pomeranian.

That retreat and readvance of the ice marked the intervals between the Iowan, Tazewell, Carey, Lower Mankato (Valders), and Upper Mankato has long been admitted. That there were genuine climatic ameliorations during two of these intervals is less perfectly established. The evidence is here briefly summarized.

The interstadial interval between the Iowan and the Tazewell has long been known as the Peorian. This term is also applied to a loess which has been usually regarded as interglacial (interstadial) and representative of the Iowan-Middle Wisconsin interval. It is now recognized that this loess overlies unweathered Iowan till. At Lisbon, Iowa, the loess is thick and its basal portion is unleached and calcareous[26] where it rests on unweathered Iowan till. In many places there is a line of pebbles at the top of the till and beneath the loess—the so-called pebble band. As Alden and Leighton point out, the pebble band is the residual coarse material left from wind erosion and rain wash on the till surface before the area was protected by loess. Presumably also frost action is involved in the formation of the pebble band, although this process is not mentioned by

★

24. W. E. Powers and George W. Ekblaw, 1940.
25. L. R. Wilson, 1932.
26. W. C. Alden and M. M. Leighton, 1917, pp. 156-157.

them. As they put it, ". . . The deposition of this loess followed almost immediately the recession of the front of the glacier which laid down the Iowan drift." There could have been no break in the prevailing cold climate, and, as suggested also by them, the winds were in part northerly or anticyclonic. Wilson[27] has recently described ventifacts from the "pebble band" in Wisconsin and thus confirmed the inference of strong winds and cold climate assumed by Alden and Leighton. In the Farm Creek section near Peoria, Illinois, the "Peorian," now called Iowan loess, is a blue-gray silt containing bits of moss and also larch twigs.[28] The presence of larch testifies to a cold climate such as now prevails on the northern border of the spruce forest. Presumably at the time when the silt was deposited by wind action, the area was a "taiga" covered by muskeg and scattered clumps of trees.

These facts make it evident that the loess was deposited in a cold climate during the beginning of retreat. It is, therefore, climatically a glacial and not an interglacial deposit. As pointed out by many modern authorities,[29] this and other loesses were dusts moved by the strong winds induced by the steepened temperature gradient from the ice-covered northern portions of the hemisphere to the equator. In part the winds were anticyclonic. The dusts were picked up on the broad beds of rivers carrying outwash from the ice and also from areas of recently exposed and still vegetation-free ground moraine.[30]

At the west end of the Farm Creek section, there is preserved at the top of the Iowan loess a humus-bearing soil of infantile development. Elsewhere the overriding of ice which deposited the Shelbyville (Tazewell) ice has removed this soil.[31] Leighton also records that a similar soil at the top of the Iowan loess is preserved beneath Tazewell till near Mackinaw, Illinois.

These infantile soils were developed in the ameliorated

★

27. L. R. Wilson, 1945.
28. M. M. Leighton, 1926.
29. F. L. Zeuner, 1945, and authorities cited.
30. See the recent rearguing of this point by W. H. Hobbs, 1943, and Andre Cailleux, 1942.
31. M. M. Leighton, 1931.

climate of the Iowa-Tazewell interval. Where the Iowan (Peorian) loess is exposed at the surface, it has a yellow or buff color and contains lime concretions in marked contrast to its blue-gray color where buried. These features must be considered as secondary phenomena gained after deposition. They are due to the advent of a mild interstadial or post-glacial climate when humus-bearing soils and solution of lime were the characteristic phenomena of the surface.[32] The Iowan (Peorian) loess extends far south of the limit of the Iown ice. It should be regarded as a strictly glacial phenomenon resulting from a glacial climate and from the activity of glacially-induced winds. As the production of material available to the wind was dependent on the existence of bare surfaces on outwash plains and on recently exposed till, the bulk of the loess was presumably deposited as retreat of the ice from its maximum began to expose such surfaces, and ceased as the glacial climate was modified and the glacially-induced winds ceased to blow.

Where the Iowan (Peorian) loess is overlain by later or Tazewell loess, the two are, in many places, indistinguishable. In other places, a soil zone has developed on the Iowan loess in the warm interstadial climate (post-Iowan-pre-Tazewell).[33] However, this soil zone is absent in places and difficult to trace. In practice, distinctions between the parts of a body of loess deposited in distinct episodes is frequently impossible.

That the Iowan-Tazewell interval was marked by a strong amelioration of climate is thus indicated by preserved infantile soils in critical sections and by scattered and discontinuous traces of a soil zone in the body of loess deposited south of the border of the ice. The sum of evidence is by no means as large as desirable.

During the Tazewell-Cary interval of retreat, very considerable erosion occurred in some places. At the contact between the Carey and Tazewell tills, there is no weathering or other evidence of mild climate before the advance of the Cary. The

★

32. See R. J. Russell, 1944, for an aberrant viewpoint.
33. A. L. Lugn, 1935, p. 167.

two advances of the ice seem to have occurred in one climatic period. The data on the leaching of tills from the most southerly Tazewell to the early Cary, (Bloomington Moraine) gathered by Thornbury,[34] indicate no great break in the time between these two ice advances. Thornbury's estimate of ten thousand years appears to be an exaggeration.

The Cary-Mankato period is, however, marked by a definite climatic amelioration. The evidence is found in northern Wisconsin where water-laid deposits containing stumps, logs, and plant debris, the Two Creeks forest bed, lie between the top of the Cary till and the overlying early Mankato till. These deposits, according to Wilson,[35] record the presence of a forest like that which now characterizes northern Minnesota and southern Manitoba. On this evidence the climate of the interstadial period between the Cary and Mankato must have been nearly as mild as that of the present.

Thwaites[36] holds that the Cary ice receded at least as far as the Straits of Mackinaw before the readvance of the Lower Mankato (Valders). Such a recession amounts to 120 miles to the north and 150 miles to the northeast from Two Creeks, in Manitowac County. He holds that the infantile soil development at Two Creeks and lack of soil at other contacts of the Lower Mankato (Valders) on the Cary testify to a short time interval. By implication, he holds that there was no important climatic change in the Cary-Mankato interval. However, he takes no account of the removal of such features by frost action in the belt of periglacial climate before the advancing Mankato ice and he minimizes the importance of the Two Creeks forest bed as evidence of a climate nearly as warm as that of the present.

The Upper Mankato (Des Moines Lobe) is represented by great looping moraines extending from North Dakota and Minnesota as far as Des Moines, Iowa. There is no evidence of a very long period of time nor of a climatic fluctuation of any

★

34. W. D. Thornbury, 1940.
35. L. R. Wilson, 1932.
36. F. T. Thwaites, 1943, p. 136.

moment between the lower and upper Mankato. The retreat of the Des Moines Lobe (Upper Mankato) is recorded by moraines and also by the history of glacial Lake Agassiz. There is no indication of a break in the prevailing cold climate. There was a readvance at Cochrane, Ontario, where a moraine was formed. According to Antevs,[37] renewed advance of the ice overrode previously deposited glacial lake clays and the retreat and readvance occupied about two thousand years. This episode of readvance is correlated by him with the Fennoscandian Moraine, of Sweden and Finland, which has a date of about ten thousand years ago.

The periods of climatic amelioration of Wisconsin time were (1) the Peorian or Iowan-Tazewell, W_1/W_2 and (2) the Cary-Lower Mankato, W_2/W_3. Such a threefold division of the Wisconsin in America corresponds to the subdivisions of the last ice age in Europe as shown in Table 5.

Deposits lying between the tills of the Warthe (Fläming Moraine) and the Weichsel (Brandenberg Moraine) represent the time interval between the first and second advance of the last ice. They have been described by Jessen and Milthers,[38] who have analyzed fresh water peats of this period by pollen analytical methods and conclude that the climate ameliorated to a climax with a summer temperature equal to that of the post-glacial optimum. There was also a marine invasion of the Eem Sea. They hold that this was a true interglacial period and, therefore, consider the Warthe as a part of the Third Glacial, much as the Iowan is attributed to the Illinoisan by Leverett. Others consider that the mildness of climate was not sufficiently prolonged and that the Warthe is the first advance of the Fourth Glacial.

In England the best section of deposits of the W_1/W_2 interval is at Kirmington Point on the Lincolnshire coast.[39]

According to Erdtmann[40] the peat contains the pollen of

★

37. E. Antevs, 1931.
38. K. Jessen and V. Milthers, 1928, p. 476.
39. Paul MacClintock, 1933, p. 1047.
40. J. P. T. Burchell, 1935.

SECTION AT KIRMINGTON PIT

	Feet
8. Weathered gravel	2
7. Hessle boulder clay (New Drift or W2)	0-1½
6. Sand and gravel	3
5. Silt and clay with marine shells	8
4. Peat	½
3. Clay with vegetation	1½
2. Rustry brown sand	3
1. Purple boulder clay (Old Drift or W1)	..

alder, birch, pine, spruce, oak, elm, lime, holly, ash (?), and hazel. A forest such as would grow in the present climate of Lincolnshire is indicated. The marine shells are those of the present day Baltic Sea. MacClintock also records the presence of soils at the top of the Old Drift till at Ipswich and at "The Travellers Rest" pit in Cambridge which could only have been formed in a long interval of mild climate. Movius[41] correlates with this interval deposits of the March-Mar submergence (also recorded in the marine bed at Kirmington) which consist of raised beaches and other deposits at many points in eastern England. They contain fossils indicating a temperate climate like the present or a little colder. He also summarizes less definite evidence from many localities in Great Britain and Ireland.

The climatic oscillation between the advance of the Brandenberg and Pomeranian ice in Europe is not definitely marked by plant-bearing beds. In England,[42] this interval is represented by peat at St. Bees, on the west coast, as recorded in the following section:

SECTION AT ST. BEES

Upper boulder clay (Scottish Readvance), W3
Peat contorted by override of ice
Sand
Gravel
Boulder clay (New Drift), W2

The peat contains a flora not unlike that of the region

★

41. Hallam L. Movius, Jr., 1942, pp. 33-40, 266-269.
42. *Op. cit.*, pp. 275-276.

today. At Holmpton, on the east coast, a peat bed containing a temperate flora overlies the Hessle (New Drift) boulder clay and is overlain by a bed with an Arctic flora. The peat is considered to be of the same age as the St. Bees peat and the Arctic bed represents the return to cold conditions coincident with the readvance of the Scottish Ice (W_3).

Correlation of Glacial Stages of the Southern Rocky Mountain Region

In 1940, Bryan and Ray presented a correlation of the substages of the last ice age in the southern Rocky Mountains with the continental ice of the Midwest and with Europe. In 1941, Ray published a very full account of the evidence and assigned a complete set of names to the substages in the southern Rocky Mountains. This correlation and the numerous substages of glaciation detected by Ray[43] are in striking contrast to the simple sequence of earlier workers, some of which are also shown in Table 6 and 7.

In the first comprehensive study of the glaciation of the western mountains, Blackwelder[44] recognized in the Sierra Nevada two Wisconsin stages of glaciation, the Tahoe and Tioga, with which he correlated similar twofold classifications by himself and others in the Basin and Range Province and in the Rocky Mountains. The Tahoe he correlated with the Iowan, but he did not commit himself as to whether the Tioga represented the Early or Late "Wisconsin." Antevs, however, on the assumption that the continental ice of the "Early Wisconsin," or Tazewell-Cary, had a less extension to the west than the Mankato, evolved the theory that the effective control of mountain glaciation in the West lies in the extent of continental ice in the Canadian Plains and in the northern Rockies, especially the Canadian Rockies. He, therefore, correlates the Tioga of Blackwelder with the Mankato.[45]

The contention that the Middle Wisconsin or Tazewell-

★

43. L. L. Ray, 1941.
44. E. Blackwelder, 1931.
45. E. B. Sayles and E. Antevs, 1941; E. Antevs, 1945.

TABLE 6

CORRELATION OF THE FOURTH GLACIAL STAGE ACCORDING TO VARIOUS AUTHORS

Short designation	*Byron & Ray*, 1940 *Ray*, 1941	*Mid-western Chronology*	*Blackwelder*, 1931*	*R. P. Sharp, San Francisco Mountain, Arizona*	*San Francisco Mountain, rearranged by K. Bryan*
W_5	Sprague			2 Pro-Talus Ramparts	2 Pro-Talus Ramparts
W_4	Long Draw	Cochrane		2 "Retreatal" Moraines	Moraine
	Erosion				
W_3	Corral Creek	Mankato (including Valders)		Later Wisconsin (Probably Mankato)	Moraine
W_2/W_3	Erosion	Two Creeks			
W_2	Home	Tazewell-Cary	Tioga		Moraine (Later Wisconsin of Sharp)
W_1/W_2	Erosion	Peorian			
W_1	Twin Lakes	Iowan	Tahoe	Iowan-Wisconsin	Moraine Iowan-Wisconsin

* Blackwelder's correlations of the California substages with phenomena in Wyoming and Montana are subject to revision.

Table 7

CORRELATION OF SUBSTAGES OF LAST GLACIATION IN THE SOUTHERN ROCKY MOUNTAINS

Short Designation	*J. T. Hack* 1943	*Ives Colorado,* 1942 *Slightly rearranged*	*Kesseli Sierra Nevada*	*Sharp Nevada,* 1938 *Rearranged by K. Bryan*	*Antevs et. al.* 1941	*Antevs et. al.* 1941 *Antevs,* 1945
W_5	Not found	Neva	Rock Streams or Double Moraine	Pro-Talus Ramparts		Later stages not discussed
W_4	Temple Lake Moraine	Monarch C	Rock Streams or Moraines (double)	Embankment Moraines		Corral Creek
W_3/W_4						
W_3	Big Sandy Opening Moraine	Monarch B Monarch A	Rock Streams or Moraines (with retreatal stages)	Irregular Moraines	Tioga	Home
W_2/W_3						
W_2	Lecke Ranch Moraine	Arapahoe A&B River	Later Moraines (one or two)	Angel Lake	Absent	
W_1/W_2						
W_1	Ice Advance	Stillwater	Earlier Moraines	Lamoille	Tahoe	

Cary substage is not represnted in the Great Plains of Canada cannot be supported. Bretz,[46] by a careful review of earlier work and his own field work, traces the Altamont Moraine, which he considers the equivalent of the Des Moines Lobe and Mankato substage, from a point north of Williston, North Dakota, northwestward to the 54th parallel of latitude, east of Edmonton, Alberta. West and southwest of this moraine, in Alberta and south to Montana, he recognizes a whole sequence of moraines. Near Edmonton, there are three moraines west of the Altamont and the most westerly, or Nuffield, "has as marked a development of steep morainal hills and of steep-sided undrained hollows among them as the Altamont. Topographically, both moraines are very youthful, comparable to Wisconsin moraines of the Great Lakes region in the United States."[47] Bretz does not state flatly that these features west of the Altamont represent the Tazewell-Cary stage, but he points out that they are in marked contrast to the glacial drift of Montana, which "rarely shows accentuated morainic topography and lacks undrained hollows almost entirely." Thus he implies: (1) that he agrees with Alden that most of the Montana drift is of the Iowan substage or possibly Illinoisan; (2) that most of Alberta is covered by drift of the Tazewell-Cary substage. Flint[48] states that the Iowan is much more extensively developed in South Dakota than heretofore recognized. There are two post-Iowan drifts which are both Mankato, or one may be in part pre-Mankato or Middle Wisconsin.

It is apparent that Antevs' viewpoint on the age of the tills in the northern plains is determined by his belief that the North American ice sheet was controlled by "centers." He holds that not only did movement take place from these centers, but each had a semi-independent existence, originating at different times and persisting for longer or shorter parts of each glaciation. Flint,[49] in a comprehensive discussion, points out that

★

46. J. Harlan Bretz, 1943.
47. J. Harlan Bretz, 1943, p. 34.
48. R. F. Flint, 1948.
49. R. F. Flint, 1943.

these centers are merely presumed to have existed by reason of striae of very late date in the retreat of the last ice. The centers were not fixed, but shifted in position as the last ice sheet shrank. Other centers not ordinarily considered also existed, such as the Newfoundland, New Brunswick, and the Gaspé. The Labradorian, Patrician, and Keewatin centers are presumed to have given rise to ice tongues that crossed into the United States, but Flint points out that this inference is not supported by the actual tracing of rock fragments from these centers, and all that can be said is that the ice tongues come from the general direction of the centers. Specifically, he rejects the interpretation of overlapping drift sheets by Leverett.[50] This theory, adopted with amplifications by Antevs,[51] assumes that centers arose and existed independently, and that in general the centers developed from east to west.

Flint holds that the formation of the ice sheet began by the formation of mountain glaciers in the highlands of Labrador and Baffin Land. The glaciers expanded into piedmont glaciers and into an extensive ice sheet by general westward growth under the influence of precipitation engendered by the passage of storms in the belt of prevailing westerlies. That the colder conditions provided greater opportunity for precipitation of "air masses moving northward, eastward, and northeastward from the Atlantic, Gulf, and Pacific," thus "the most active part of the ice should have been a broad marginal zone where relatively large accumulation induced relatively rapid flow." The centers of radial flow are regarded as phenomena of "some late part of Wisconsin time" and therefore, essentially phenomena of shrinkage. Flint points out that, during the retreat of the Lake Mankato ice, the so-called Keewatin and the so-called Labradorian (or perhaps Patrician) ice lobes were continuous, else Lake Agassiz would have lacked a northern shore and would have drained to Hudson Bay.[52]

★

50. Frank Leverett, 1932.
51. E. Antevs, 1934, 1938.
52. W. A. Johnston, 1935, p. 15.

Flint holds that the growth of the Cordilleran glaciers began with the oncoming of glacial conditions, that the glaciers were fed by the moist air from the Pacific. In the area of the Canadian Rockies, the maximum formation of ice occurred. There, also, the chief wastage occurred by reason of the steep slopes and the calving of icebergs into the sea. He holds that the moist air of the Pacific, in passing eastward over the mountains, was cooled, and on descending to the Canadian plains, was a drying wind so that precipitation east of the mountains was small and wastage of the ice large. In other words, the plains were in the shadow of the mountains then as now. His analysis of meteorological conditions is thus accordant with, although more generalized than, the general meteorological relations set forth above.

Sharp,[53] in a study of the Ruby-East Humboldt Range, redescribed the Lamoille and Angel Lake substages of glaciation, previously identified by Blackwelder,[54] and followed Blackwelder in correlating them with the Tahoe and Tioga substages. However, Sharp points out that there are, in certain canyons, obscure and irregular moraines above the Angel Lake moraines and "embankment" moraines at the mouths of certain cirques with pro-talus ramparts at the base of the cirque walls. Sharp did not discuss the age of these features, but if they are interpreted as representing separate and distinct ice advances according to the methods used in the southern Rocky Mountains, the arrangement shown in Table 4 would result.

Ives[55] has reinterpreted the glacial geology of the Monarch Valley, of Colorado, first studied by him some years previously. His sequence uses different names, but parallels closely the interpretation of Bryan and Ray.

Hack,[56] in a recent study of moraines and outwash plains in the Wind River Range, of Wyoming, failed to find a moraine corresponding to Blackwelder's Bull Lake (Tahoe) substage. He found scattered boulders below the first well-developed moraine

★

53. R. P. Sharp, 1938.
54. E. Blackwelder, 1931.
55. R. L. Ives, 1938.
56. John T. Hack, 1943.

and a high terrace which may be considered a representative of this stage. His Lecke Ranch, Big Sandy Opening, and Temple Lake moraines he considers correlative to the Home, Corral Creek, and Long Draw moraines of Colorado. The western slope of the Wind River Mountains is now under study by three geologists, Richmond, Moss, and Holmes, whose results will modify those of Blackwelder and Hack. They hold that the Bull Lake is Iowan and that the Middle Wisconsin and Mankato are both present.[57]

The recent study of San Francisco Mountain, Arizona, by Sharp[58] provides data on the area of glaciation nearest to Ventana Cave. San Francisco Mountain is a volcanic peak with a maximum elevation of 12,611 feet. The main glacial features are in the Interior Valley. The Iowan Glacier was four miles long and reached at its lower end an elevation of 8,500 feet, where it left strong moraines of which only the laterals and those east of the outwash plain are preserved. The next youngest glacier was 2¾ miles long and had its terminus at an elevation of 9,000 feet. A strong terminal moraine still exists. It is merely notched by erosion of the main stream of the canyon. In the canyon above this moraine there is outwash leading from a second moraine and just back of it a boulder filling. Two halts of the ice are indicated. In Doyle Canyon there are two moraines representing comparable stages. In the cirque at the head of the canyon there is a double pro-talus rampart well overgrown with trees. Sharp interprets his Iowan substage as equivalent to the Tahoe and the next moraine above as Tioga. Following Antevs, he believes that the Tioga is Mankato in age and that the upper moraines are merely recessional. This correlation is shown in Table 6 and in the next column the features described by Sharp are reassigned. In this interpretation, each moraine is assumed to represent a readvance of the ice after a retreat. The number and relative size of these advances are in accord with the substages recognized in the Rocky Mountains.

★

57. Oral communication.
58. R. P. Sharp, 1942.

Sharp admits that this interpretation is possible, but prefers Antevs' meteorological hypothesis, which holds that only during the first and third substages, when the continental ice was extended across the western plains of Canada and Montana, could glaciation exist in the western mountains. As shown above, the continental ice extended across the plains at all those substages.

As Blackwelder did not describe glacial features in the Sierra Nevada younger than the Tioga, Antevs' speculation was perhaps not unwarranted at the time it was first made. However, Kesseli,[59] in a discussion of the changes in the courses of flow of glaciers on the east flank of the Sierra Nevada, points out that the change in course took place after a long period of erosion, presumably associated with an interglacial or interstadial stage. It is obvious, from a comparison of his maps and photographs with those of Blackwelder, that he is considering an erosion interval between the Tahoe and Tioga substages. In some canyons, the Tioga substage is represented by one or more moraines and the Tioga stage also by double moraines. Kesseli makes no correlation with Blackwelder's named stages and says nothing of other stages. In another publication,[60] however, he presents a map of the Sherwin-Laurel Creek area, also shown in Figure 8 of his earlier paper. From a comparison of these two maps, it is obvious that on Laurel Creek there are moraines of the Tahoe and Tioga stages. Just above the Tioga moraines there is a strong morainal loop at an elevation of about 8,750 feet, which is breached by a narrow gorge and encloses seven recessional moraines. Higher up the canyon, at an elevation of about 9,500 feet, are two moraines close together and again at the cirque lip are two moraines. These features seem to represent at least three substages later than the Tioga. The bedrock of Laurel Canyon is largely metamorphic and in this canyon moraines were built. In Sherwin Canyon, the rock is granite and the later glaciers formed rock streams, each of which takes the place of a moraine and is interpreted by Kesseli as a moraine.

★

59. J. E. Kesseli, 1941*a*.
60. *Ibid.*, 1941*b*.

He mapped, in all, eight rock streams above the obvious Tioga moraines shown on his map of 1941. These features may easily represent three glacial advances later than the Tioga. Which rock streams are most closely related to each other, and which, therefore, should be assigned to single glacial substages, is not apparent from the map. The correlation of Kesseli's data with the chronology of the southern Rockies as shown in Table 7 is highly tentative and should be reviewed in the field. The data in themselves are extraordinarily valuable, for they demonstrate that Wisconsin glaciation in the Sierra Nevada was not a simple affair of two substages. It was, as might be expected in a region of relatively heavy precipitation, complex. The region may easily have been more sensitive to climatic fluctuation than the inland areas previously considered. Kesseli[61] makes the statement that he believes that there were five main glaciations. He may mean that these five were the McGee, Sherwin, Tahoe, and Tioga, previously recognized by Blackwelder, and one other —a later Wisconsin. If he means that there were five distinguishable advances in the Wisconsin, some of which were multiple, he is in complete accord with Bryan and Ray. Three of these advances, Tahoe, Tioga, and an unnamed stage, were separated by relatively long periods of almost complete deglaciation in the mountains. The fourth was a readvance during retreat from the third substage and the fifth deserves a separate discussion.

Matthes[62] has recently called attention to the "Little glaciation" or "Neoglaciation" by which he means the formation, advance, and retreat of mountain glaciers since the post-glacial warm period. He distinguishes between those existing glaciers which survived the warm period and those which were completely dissipated. Most of the glaciers which survived lie in the northern Rocky Mountains and in the Cascades, adjacent to the Pacific Coast. They lie in the areas that at present have, and presumably in the past had, the highest precipitation. In the southern Rocky Mountains and in the isolated ranges east of the

★

61. *Ibid.*, 1941*a*.
62. F. E. Matthes, 1939, 1940, and 1942.

Sierra Nevada, such glaciers were rare. In many locations the period of the "Little glaciation" was not sufficiently cold and the snowfall was inadequate to produce new glaciers. Permanent snowbanks were formed in cirques and over these snowbanks frost-loosened blocks rolled or slid to form pro-talus ramparts. These features form the principal evidence for the period of refrigeration that in many localities is the correlative of Matthes' "Little glaciation." This period was named by Ray[63] the Sprague glaciation, from a relatively recent moraine at the Sprague glacier that represents the maximum advance of the "Neoglaciation." Elsewhere in the southern Rockies this substage is represented by pro-talus ramparts: an older set covered with vegetation and a later set bare and somewhat younger. It may be that more than one period of refrigeration in post-glacial time may eventually be distinguished on the basis of these multiple pro-talus ramparts. At present, the recently deserted moraines in front of living glaciers, the minor moraines in cirques and the pro-talus ramparts, now identified, from many parts of the western mountains, indicate quite definitely at least one period of refrigeration which is post-glacial and presumably later than the post-glacial warm period.

In 1941, Antevs[64] took issue with Bryan and Ray[65] and correlated the Home Moraine of the Cache le Poudre Canyon, in Colorado, with the Mankato, and the Corral Creek Moraine with the Cochrane. In this correlation he ignored the existence of evidence for a pre-Home or Twin Lakes substage, and also the Long Draw and the Sprague substage.[66] In 1945, Antevs, in a lengthy review, places Ray's Twin Lakes (pre-Home) stage with the Durango, of the San Juan Mountains, and "Old moraine" remnants of the Rocky Mountain National Park[67] in a heretofore unrecognized glacial stage between the Illinoisan and the Iowan. He then correlates the Home with the Iowan,

★

63. L. L. Ray, 1941.
64. E. B. Sayles and E. Antevs, 1941, p. 41 and footnote.
65. K. Bryan and L. L. Ray, 1941.
66. L. L. Ray, 1941.
67. W. R. Jones and L. O. Quam, 1944.

and the Corral Creek stage with the Mankato in Table II, and on page 23 states that "In Table II, 6, 'Corral Creek or W3,' then a recessional substage of the last glaciation, should be replaced by Jones' and Quam's 'Upper Valley glaciation.'" He apparently overlooks the fact that Ray, in 1940, mapped Jones' and Quam's principal moraines, or "Upper Valley glaciation" as W3, so that whatever name is used the two are identical.

That moraines representing all the substages named by Ray exist can hardly be denied. Only the interpretation may be challenged. In the foregoing paragraphs, the evidence has been reviewed in part. It appears that the five substages of the southern Rocky Mountains have correlatives in northern Arizona, in Nevada, and in California, although the evidence described by various geologists has not heretofore been interpreted from this viewpoint. The main lack in the necessary body of proof for a correlation with the glacial sequence of the continental ice of the Middle West is in the lack of data on the later stages of mountain glaciation in northern Wyoming and Montana and in a detailed trace of the mountain glaciation into the continental glaciation of the northern Great Plains. Until this laborious task is completed, correlation must be made on a matching of events in number and in relative length. The correlation here advocated equates the three main substages, the Iowan, Tazewell-Cary, and Mankato, with the Twin Lakes (Tahoe), the Home (Tioga), and the Corral Creek. The principal readvance on the retreat from the Corral Creek is the Long Draw, and it is correlated with the Cochrane of Ontario, and its, as yet, unknown correlatives to the eastward.

The date of the Mankato substage and its European equivalent, the Pomeranian, has been discussed by Bryan and Ray[68] who accept Antevs' date of 25,000 years ago, but recognize that this figure is more or less nominal and subject to an unknown error which may reach 30 per cent. The recent emendation of this date to 23,000 years, as advocated by Antevs,[69] is based on

★

68. K. Bryan and L. L. Ray, 1940.
69. E. B. Sayles and E. Antevs, 1941, footnote, p. 41.

the contention that the Des Moines Lobe or Late Mankato of Iowa, with which he considers that the western mountain glaciation is alone correlatable, is somewhat younger than the Port Huron Moraine of the area east of Lake Michigan. The Port Huron Moraine is thought to be equivalent with an ice position at St. Johnsbury, Vermont, or north of that place near the Vermont-Quebec boundary. In fact, a definite trace through New York to the Connecticut River has yet to be made. Even if the facts and correlation used by Antevs are all correct, the error inherent in the method of arriving at a date for the last maximum of the Wisconsin, that is, W3, is so great that an emendation of two thousand years lies within a reasonable estimate of the error and has no significance

The Humid Period of Ventana Cave

As discussed on pages 82 to 87, the lower deposits of Ventana Cave were laid down under conditions of humidity which have not since recurred. When did this humid period occur? How shall it be fitted into the chronology heretofore reviewed?

The channelled floor of the cave seems to have been formed when there was a considerable flow of the spring. The overlying cemented gravels testify to a lesser, but still important, flow of water. The fine-grained limey layer in which the chipped artifacts are found (Bed 5) topped with alternating layers of lime crust and wind-blown sand, record a further decrease in the flow of the spring. The cemented lower beds may thus be interpreted as deposits of, and the consequence of, a period of decreasing flow of the spring. From a relatively large flow, the spring decreased to a flow little different from that of the present. As the flow of the spring depends on the precipitation which falls on the rock above and on its conservation, then this period of strong flow from the spring may be considered as one of relative local humidity. There may have been greater rainfall or less evaporation or both. Such periods are, according to the principles set forth earlier in this paper, coincident with periods of refrigeration when glaciers were advanced in the Rocky Mountains.

The deposits, in themselves, afford no criteria by which a decision might be reached as to which of the numerous episodes of glaciation in the Pleistocene is involved. It can be argued that one of the most recent glacial advances is the more probable, as otherwise the deposits would have been destroyed. Fortunately, Bed 5 contains artifacts including a point of Folsom aspect. As brought out by Professor Haury, some of the other artifacts are compatible with an assignment to the Folsom Complex. The Folsom Complex has been dated with some assurance as having been deposited just after the climax of the Corral Creek glaciation, which, as heretofore set forth, has a nominal date of 25,000± years ago.[70] However, the artifacts occur almost in the top of the beds which indicate the humid period. The spring was drying up and humidity was decreasing. The date, therefore, must lie some considerable time interval after the climax of the humid period and thus somewhat later than 25,000± years ago.

It is even possible that these upper parts of the cemented zone should correspond to the humid time of the Long Draw or W4 stage, with a date as late as ten thousand years ago. Such an attribution would require the assumption that the climatic fluctuation toward the warm and dry between W3 and W4 left no detectable traces in Ventana Cave. It seems preferable, therefore, to assign the artifacts and the vertebrate bones to the last stages of the Corral Creek or W3 glaciation, a date closer to 10,000 than to 25,000 years ago.

The Post-Humid Deposits

The hard, reddish-brown sand of Bed 4 and the talus breccia of Bed 3 are separated from the underlying beds by a considerable interval of erosion. Their calcareous cement testifies to a somewhat greater circulation of water than takes place at pres-

★

70. K. Bryan and L. L. Ray, 1940.

ent. They may therefore represent a recrudescence of moist conditions. The upper, uncemented beds are largely an accumulation by reason of occupation. They were laid down under conditions of moisture similar to those of the present.

To what time intervals should these beds be assigned? So far as the deposits in themselves are concerned, they might be assigned to any interval after the Corral Creek glaciation. Which interval depends on the time value to be assigned to the unconformity and therefore the erosional period which separates them from the lower beds and to the correlations that can be made by means of the contained fossils and artifacts. The discussion thus turns to the relative age of the complexes of artifacts which represent cultures. The complexes and inferred cultures are related to other complexes that have been found in alluvial deposits. The geologic relations of these alluvial beds is what is referred to as the alluvial chronology. This chronology is our only present basis for considering the age relations in the post-Corral Creek (Mankato) interval in the Southwest.

The Alluvial Chronology

General Statement

That the alluvial deposits forming the flood plains of the minor streams of the Southwest are divisible into units of differing age was discovered in 1924 and announced by Bryan in 1925. Since that time, information has been gradually accumulating. Wherever adequate field work has been done and the alluvium is sufficiently exposed, three alluvial formations are identifiable and the second of these formations is, in places, divisible into an older and a younger part. Data is accumulating to show that the erosional intervals separating these formations were marked by strong wind action and the accumulation of sand dunes. Our present knowledge of the alluvial sequence is herewith summarized briefly.

The Modern Arroyo

The alluvium of the minor valleys of the Southwest was in the process of being deposited at the time of first settlement. At that time, the streams had only minor and discontinuous channels. In floods they spread widely over the valley floors. About 1885, deep continuous arroyos began to form and are still forming and enlarging. These channels are so deep and wide that floods no longer top the banks so that the flood plains are relatively drier than before and are no longer being built up. The subdivisions of the alluvium are visible in the walls of these arroyos. It is obvious that the new arroyo is a successor to earlier arroyos of the same or even greater size. The valleys have been the sites of successive epi-cycles of erosion and refilling.

The dates at which the modern arroyos were cut can be determined by a variety of evidence. Much effort has been expended in determining the dates of cutting of arroyos on the numerous stream systems of the Southwest, as summarized by Bryan[71] and by Thornthwaite, Sharpe, and Dosch.[72] A controversy also exists as to whether the erosion of the arroyos is wholly due to over-grazing by domestic livestock or whether the present period of erosion is essentially climatic and the over-grazing is merely an added effect which timed a process about to begin. It is generally admitted that the cutting of the modern arroyo systems is broadly contemporary with the introduction of, and particularly the commercial exploitation of, cattle and sheep. Exceptions have, however, been noted in particular areas. To the writer, the over-grazing appears to have been merely a trigger pull which timed the explosive process that was imminent from climatic causes. The modern advocates of over-grazing as the sole cause of the cutting of the modern arroyos deny the existence of the alluvial sequence here summarized.[73] Hack[74] has, however, shown that the sequence is well displayed on Jeddito Wash, a tributary of Polacca Wash, in the Hopi Country of Arizona, and that part of the sequence is identified near the main road on Polacca Wash itself, about which the authors named above have written an elaborate report.

★

71. K. Bryan, 1925*b*.
72. C. W. Thornthwaite, C. F. S. Sharpe, and E. F. Dasch, 1942.
73. *Ibid.*
74. John T. Hack, 1942.

Regardless of the issue of the controversy on the origin of the modern arroyo, the alluvial sequence is identifiable in many localities in Arizona, New Mexico, and Texas.

The Older Alluvium or No. 1 Fill

The oldest alluvium in the minor valleys of the Southwest is usually slightly more compact than the younger formations. It contains soil horizons, swampy deposits, invertebrate shells or other evidence of deposition under slightly moister conditions. In many places it also contains the bones of mammoths, a circumstance in itself a testimony to some antiquity and to a generally denser vegetation than now obtains.

In the Big Bend, of Texas, the older alluvium contains extinct animals (mammoths and horses), and is called the Neville formation.[75] In northern Arizona it is called the Jeddito,[76] and elsewhere it has been described without a formational name. Usually no artifacts are found, but near Abilene, Texas, the Durst silt[77] contains artifacts. In the collections made by Dr. Cyrus N. Ray, are a mammoth bone, a mano, and a Folsomoid point from this formation. There is also an artifact resembling a drill. The "Gibson" points occur on and just below the unconformity at the top of the Durst.[78] According to Evans and Meade,[79] the upper part of their Tahoka formation is a correlate and contains extinct animals and Plainview points.

The association of this alluvium, the No. 1 fill of many reports, with extinct animals (mammoth and horse) implies that it was deposited in the last important time of wetter climate. It is presumably equivalent to the Corral Creek or third Wisconsin glaciations. The presence of the Plainview and other Folsom-like projectile points is to be expected.

On Whitewater Draw, Antevs[80] has described an alluvial deposit from which bones of mammoth, horse, camel, and other

★

75. C. C. Albritton, Jr., and K. Bryan, 1939.
76. John T. Hack, 1942.
77. M. M. Leighton, 1936.
78. J. Charles Kelley, 1947.
79. Glen L. Evans and G. E. Meade, 1945.
80. E. B. Sayles and E. Antevs, 1941.

extinct animals have been obtained. It also contains manos and metates, the main indication of human occupancy. These tools are attributed to the Sulphur Spring Stage of the Cochise Culture. The alluvium rests unconformably on reddish compact alluvium of presumed Pliocene age. It contains, in one locality, beds deposited in a pond, and the sands contain limonite. From this and other evidence, Antevs argues correctly that it was deposited at a time wetter than the present. Thus it corresponds to every particular with other deposits of the older alluvium or No. 1 fill.

The Intermediate Alluvium or No. 2 Fill

The older alluvium is overlain disconformably by a younger alluvial deposit, the intermediate or No. 2 fill. The streams cut great gullies or arroyos in the No. 1 fill and in many localities removed it completely. Extensive wind action is characteristic of this interval of erosion.

The intermediate alluvium was then deposited. It contains, in places, humic layers, but was deposited under drier conditions than the older alluvium and usually is relatively uncemented or weathered. It resembles closely the deposits of the modern streams and contains no bones of extinct animals.

In the Big Bend of Texas, it is called the Calamity formation,[81] and in the Hopi country, of Arizona,[82] the Tsegi formation. In both these areas there are localities in which it is divided into a younger and older portion by a disconformity. The two parts are so similar that on geologic criteria it is impossible to separate the older from the younger except under favorable circumstances. However, there seems to be little doubt that the intermediate alluvium or No. 2 fill is actually twofold. It represents two periods of alluviation separated by an interval of erosion.

In the Big Bend of Texas, Kelley, Campbell, and Lehmer[83] found artifacts of their Maravillas type on the disconformity be-

★

81. C. C. Albritton, Jr., and K. Bryan, 1939.
82. John T. Hack, 1942.
83. J. Charles Kelley, T. N. Campbell, and D. J. Lehmer, 1940.

tween the lower Calamity and Neville. Artifacts of the Santiago type occurred near the top of the lower Calamity. The San Jose Culture of central New Mexico occurs in a soil zone on old sand dunes correlatable with the erosion interval between the Neville and Calamity formations.[84] These stone cultures are similar, to the extent that projectiles have serrated edges.

In Whitewater Draw, an alluvial formation having a definite channel form overlies and is separated from the Sulphur Spring horizon by a disconformity. It contains manos and other artifacts attributed to the Chiricahua Stage of the Cochise Culture. Only seven projectile points are reported, two of which have serrated edges.

This formation corresponds in age and position to the lower Calamity and Tsegi formations. It is separated by a disconformity from an overlying formation which corresponds to the upper Calamity and Tsegi formations. A few artifacts are found which are correlated with the San Pedro Stage of the Cochise Culture largely represented elsewhere.

The Late Alluvium or No. 3 Fill

The youngest alluvium of Southwestern valleys lies in a channel eroded in the older beds. The channel is generally about the size and shape of the modern gulch or arroyo and the contained beds are loose and friable.

At Chaco Canyon, this channel deposit contains the latest pottery made at Pueblo Bonito. This pottery has a date of about 1200 A. D. and it is believed that the channel was cut about 1250 A. D. and filled by about 1400. In the Hopi country, a similar filled channel contains pottery and the formation is called the Naha. In the Big Bend, a similar filled channel is called the Kokernot. At Whitewater Draw, the so-called "upper silts" form part of a channel fill. They contain pottery made after 1100 A. D.

As previously shown by Bryan,[85] the available evidence in-

★

84. K. Bryan and F. T. McCann, 1943.
85. K. Bryan, 1941.

dictates that the erosion preceding the No. 3 fill occurred about 1250 to 1300 A. D. and corresponds to the dry time also recorded by tree rings. The fill was deposited in part before 1400 A. D. and continued to be deposited until the modern arroyos began to form. The excavation of these modern channels began about 1885 A. D. and continues to the present.

Relation of Ventana Cave to the Alluvial Chronology

The disconformity at the top of the lower cemented beds appears to correspond to the erosion of the No. 1 fill of the alluvial chronology. This erosion interval represents a dry period following the last glacial and thus corresponds to the warm interval known in Europe as the post-glacial optimum.

This warm interval appears to have been also dry in most of the United States and evidence for its existence has come forward from many sources. If it was coincident in time with that in Europe, it dates from 2500 B. C. to 5500 B. C. Beds 1 to 4, with their wealth of artifacts, would all be later than 2500 B. C. They would include equivalents of all the cultures of the Southwest which have been found associated with the No. 2 and No. 3 fills and with the erosional intervals between these deposits.

Only the slightly cemented materials of Bed 4 need cause hesitation in correlation. This bed represents the distal portion of a debris cone which may have extended into the cave during part of the erosional interval between No. 1 and No. 2 fills of the alluvial chronology. Under such an interpretation, the contained artifacts would be considerably older than those of the No. 2 fill. They might have an antiquity between B. C. 2500 and 5500, but a closer designation of age would at present be impossible.

Conclusion

According to the interpretation set forth above, the lower cemented beds (No. 5 and No. 6) of Ventana Cave were deposited during the last phases of the wet period coincident with the last glacial advance. They have a date after 25,000± years ago and may be as late as 10,000 years ago.

The overlying beds are separated from the lower beds by a marked disconformity representing strong erosion. This erosional interval corresponds to the similar erosion in stream valleys of the region between the No. 1 and No. 2 fills of the alluvial chronology. It was a dry and presumably warm interval equivalent to the post-glacial optimum of Europe and has a date from B. C. 2500 to 5500. The cemented Bed 4, although it overlies the unconformity, may, however, have been deposited during this erosional interval, and may thus have a date earlier than B. C. 2500.

However, Beds 1 to 3 are definitely younger than B. C. 2500 and cover the interval represented by the No. 2 and No. 3 fills of the alluvial chronology.

THE FOSSIL VERTEBRATES[86]

Introduction[87]

The prehistoric rock-shelter known as Ventana Cave was investigated by the Arizona State Museum as an archaeological problem, in line with the series of cavern and terrace studies that have been made in the southwestern portion of the United States by various institutions in recent years, all as a part of the large problem of Early Man in America. In the course of excavations at Ventana Cave, during which numerous artifacts were discovered at certain levels, a considerable number of fossilized mammal bones were found. These were carefully recorded as to levels and locations, and were systematically preserved. In December, 1941, Dr. Haury brought the fossils to New York and submitted them to the author for investigation.

★

86. By Edwin H. Colbert, The American Museum of Natural History and Columbia University, New York City.

87. The author is much indebted to Dr. Emil W. Haury, of the University of Arizona, in charge of the Ventana Cave project, and to Professor Kirk Bryan, of Harvard University, for advice on the field relationships of the fossils considered in this study.

While studies of these fossils were under way, a second field season at Ventana Cave was begun, in the spring of 1942, and additional fossil bones were found. These were shipped to The American Museum of Natural History to supplement the material of the previous year's operations.

With the combined materials at hand an attempt was made at their identification and interpretation, the results of which will be set forth in the present contribution.

It was immediately seen that these fossils might have some bearing upon the problem of dating the human occupation of Ventana Cave, and also upon the problem of the general environmental conditions that may have prevailed at the time of that occupation. This was dependent upon two sets of attributes, characteristic of the collection.

(a) In the first place, the fossils were found at two levels, one of which was antecedent to the period of human occupation, the other one of which was contemporaneous with the occupation of the shelter by primitive man.

(b) Secondly, the mammalian fossils from these two levels in Ventana Cave, as represented by the collection at hand, consist of certain forms which are similar to, if not identical with, modern animals living in this general region, and of other forms now extinct.

What is the significance of these two Ventana Cave assemblages, or faunas, when analyzed qualitatively, as to the types of animals present, and quantitatively, as to the relative numbers of each species present? What are the bearings of these mammals upon the date of the human occupation of Ventana Cave, and upon the environmental conditions prevailing at that time? An attempt to answer these questions will be made in the following report.

Stratigraphic Relationships of the Fossils

There is no need here to enter into a detailed description of the stratigraphy of Ventana Cave. This has been done fully by other authorities herein, to whose work the reader is referred.

It might be well, however, to recall that, in the Ventana Cave excavations, there are two horizons containing fossil bones, as mentioned above, and these are the only levels in the Ventana Complex of particular concern to us at this place. The relationships of the two horizons may be expressed as follows:

Cemented grayish volcanic debris	0.50± m.	Fossil bones	Tools suggesting Folsom and San Diegito Complexes
Pool-formed pinkish conglomerate	0.50+ m.	Fossil bones	No certain evidence of Man.

For the purposes of the present study, the fossils from the two horizons have been treated and analyzed as separate "faunas" in order that the assemblages of vertebrates living in two distinct chronologic periods might be compared with each other. It is recognized in doing this, that from a strictly zoological point of view, all the fossils at Ventana Cave may possibly represent a persistent unit fauna.

The Vertebrates Found in Ventana Cave

MAMMALIA

Lagomorpha

Leporidae

Lepus californicus Gray—Jackrabbit

Materials—Several maxillae and lower jaws; also a few bones of the post-cranial skeleton (Pl. 17, *b, c*).

Horizon—Volcanic debris.

Description—The lagomorph bones need no detailed description or discussion. These remains are closely comparable to the same elements in the modern jackrabbits of the species *Lepus californicus,* and for this reason the above designation is assigned to the fossil material. Naturally, upon the basis of these few bones, no attempt has been made to attach a subspecific designation to them, and the same holds true for other mammalian remains found at Ventana Cave.

Remarks—The jackrabbit at Ventana Cave has no particular significance, since these animals are found in this region at the present time. The presence of this hare in the cave materials would be an indication in favor of environmental conditions similar to those now prevailing in this vicinity.

Rodentia

Sciuridae

Cynomys ludovicianus (Ord)—Prairie Dog

Materials—A right maxilla with two cheek teeth (Pl. 17, *d*).

Horizon—Volcanic debris.

Description—The teeth of this specimen show the characteristic *Cynomys* pattern, and appear to be closely comparable to similar teeth in the modern *Cynomys ludovicianus.*

Remarks—As in the case of the jackrabbit, discussed above, the presence of prairie dog in the Ventana Cave fauna parallels the similar presence of this animal in southern Arizona at the present time. Thus this form gives no evidence for any significant difference in environmental conditions between the period at which Ventana Cave was used by Early Man and those prevailing in recent times.

Callospermophilus lateralis (Say)—Say's Ground Squirrel

Materials—A left mandibular ramus with the first two molars, and the last premolar in the process of eruption (Fig. 13); also the front portion of a left mandibular ramus.

Horizon—Conglomerate.

Description—The form and size of the teeth in the fossil show that this specimen may be placed in the genus *Callospermophilus.* The mandible itself is rather small, but since the last premolar is still in the alveolus it would seem evident that the small size of the jaw may be attributed to the juvenile character of the individual in question rather than to any distinction of taxonomic value.

It should be said, however, that there are certain differences in the teeth from any of the several subspecies of *Callospermophilus lateralis* now living in the southwestern portion of the United States. Thus, the teeth of the fossil are perhaps slightly smaller than is the case in most of the individuals of the recent *Callospermophilus lateralis,* yet these teeth are so much larger and of sufficient difference in form as to preclude any reference to *Citellus* or to *Ammospermophilus.* Perhaps the most noticeable difference between this fossil form and the recent Say's ground squirrel is in the proportions of the second lower molar, which in the extinct animal is distinctly narrower in relation to its length than is the case in the recent form. For instance, the length and width of the second lower molar in the extinct animal are virtually equal, whereas in the recent animal the width exceeds the length of the tooth by about one-fifth.

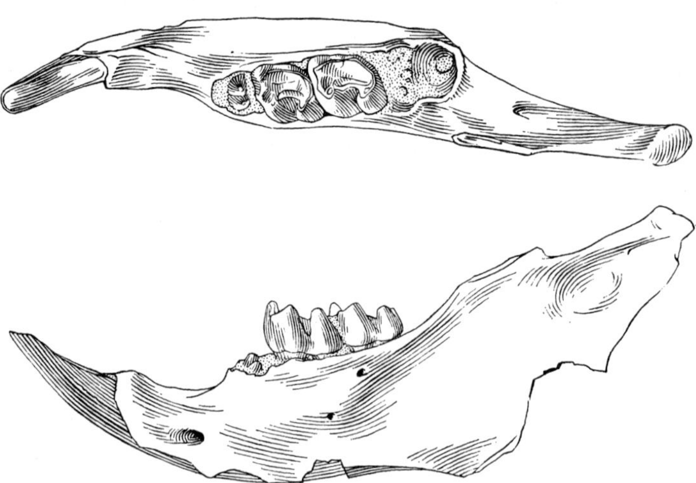

FIGURE 13. Left mandibular ramus of Say's Ground Squirrel, *Callospermophilus lateralis,* from Ventana Cave. Crown view above, external lateral view below. Four times natural size

Measurements and Ratios—

		Ventana Cave	*Callospermophilus lateralis* Recent, A. M. N. H. 72931
M_2	length	2.05 mm.	2.10 mm.
	width	2.10	2.50
Ratio	width/length	1.03	1.19

In view of these differences, there might be some reason for supposing that the ground squirrel from Ventana Cave represents a species distinct from any of the recent ground squirrels of this general type. And such may very probably be the case. But in view of the paucity of fossil material it is hereby proposed to regard the Ventana Cave material as identifiable under the name of *Callospermophilus lateralis.* For our purposes the specific identity of this animal is of no great consequence. The important thing is that at Ventana Cave there was, at the time the region was inhabited by Early Man, a ground squirrel of the *Callospermophilus* group. The implications of this fact are discussed below.

*Remarks—*The presence of Say's ground squirrel in the Ventana Cave fauna is interesting, since this animal does not now inhabit the southern portion of Arizona. In fact, its southernmost extension at the present time is limited by the Gila River, which flows across the state somewhat below its middle portion. Since *Callospermophilus* is primarily an animal of the open pine forests, living in the Transition zone, its presence at Ventana Cave would seem to indicate a wetter, and perhaps also a cooler environment than prevails at the present time.

Carnivora

Canidae

Canis dirus Leidy—Dire Wolf

*Materials—*A left upper first molar and a left upper second molar (Pl. 18, *i*).

*Horizon—*Conglomerate.

Description—The specimens listed above represent the presence of a very large wolf at Ventana Cave before and during the first occupancy of this site by Early Man. Because of the large size of these teeth, and because of certain structural characters shown by them, notably the limitation in the forward extension of the hypocone on the first molar—a character cited by Merriam as distinctive for the extinct dire wolf—the specimens are hereby referred to *Canis dirus*, or *Aenocyon dirus* of some authors.

Remarks—The presence of the dire wolf in Ventana Cave has no particular significance, either for the dating of the deposits or for an interpretation of environmental conditions existing at the time the fossils were being accumulated. Of course, we cannot make definite remarks as to the habits of an extinct species, but it is a pretty safe guess, judging from our knowledge of modern wolves, that the dire wolf was an adaptable animal, capable of living within a great range of environmental conditions. Its remains are found from Pennsylvania and Florida to California.

Canis latrans (Say) —Coyote

Materials—A right upper first molar (Pl. 18, *h*).

Horizon—Conglomerate.

Description—Nothing in particular needs to be said concerning this specimen, except that it is closely comparable to the modern *Canis latrans.*

Remarks—The presence of the coyote in the Ventana Cave fauna is not unexpected, since this animal lives at the present time in this region of Arizona.

Vulpes macrotis Merriam—Long-eared Kit Fox

Materials—Portion of a left maxilla with P^{2-4}; a right first upper molar; a left first lower molar (Pl. 17, *a*).

Horizon—Conglomerate.

Description—The teeth listed above are very small and delicate, and obviously indicate the presence of one of the smaller type of desert foxes in the Ventana Cave fauna. A careful comparison with the several recent species and subspecies would seem to show that these specimens are referable to *Vulpes macrotis*.

Remarks—This species is known at the present time in southern Arizona; therefore its presence at Ventana Cave would seem to indicate environmental conditions paralleling those of the present day.

Mustelidae

Taxidea taxus (Schreber)—Badger

Materials—A broken right maxilla with the fourth premolar and the first molar (Pl. 18, *j*).

Horizon—Volcanic debris.

Description—The specimen, although poorly preserved, shows clearly its close affinities to the modern badger of North America.

Remarks—The presence of a badger in the Ventana Cave fauna is of little significance, since this animal is widely spread through western North America at the present time, living in a variety of environments.

Felidae

Felis atrox Leidy—Extinct Jaguar

Materials—The blade of a right upper fourth premolar (Pl. 18, *g*), and a small portion of the anterior part of the tooth.

Horizon—Volcanic debris.

Description—The single fragment listed above is clearly representative of a very large felid in the Ventana Cave fauna. Because of the large size of this carnassial blade, and its close correspondence in form to the comparable feature in *Felis atrox*, the fossil under consideration is referred to this species.

Remarks—It is not surprising to find *Felis atrox* in the Ventana Cave fauna. The interesting and important fact concerning this fossil is that it comes from the ash layer, so that the animal was evidently a contemporary of Early Man in this portion of Arizona.

The presence of *Felis atrox* might favor the postulate of somewhat less desert-like conditions in this region than now exist. However, there is no certainty as to this point, and it may very well be that *Felis atrox* was capable of living in relatively dry surroundings.

Edentata

Megalonychidae

Nothrotherium shastense Sinclair–Ground Sloth

Materials–Three cheek teeth, two from the maxilla; the other, which is unworn, probably from the mandible. Also a median phalanx from the manus (Pl. 18, *f*) .

Horizon–Volcanic debris.

Description–Although the remains of sloth among the Ventana Cave fossils are scanty, they are sufficiently diagnostic as to leave no doubt regarding the presence of this interesting element in the fauna. These fossils represent a small gravigrade edentate, and because of their size and general form they are referred to *Nothrotherium shastense.*

Remarks–It is interesting to have this new record of an association of one of the extinct ground sloths with Early Man in North America. Since *Nothrotherium* at Ventana Cave is confined to the volcanic debris layer, there can be no doubt as to the contemporaneity of this animal with the first human inhabitants of the Southwest. On the other hand, such an association does not necessarily imply an unduly great age for the evidences of human occupation in this area, for we know that *Nothrotherium* was a very late survivor among the Pleistocene mammals now extinct. This is shown by the preservation of hair, ligaments and dried muscle tissue in certain ground sloths from the southwestern United States, especially the fine specimen of *Nothrotherium* described by Lull in 1929. In addition there might be mentioned the fairly numerous and comparatively fresh pieces of dung deposited by these animals, found in certain Southwestern caves.

A coprolite found in association with the specimen of *Nothrotherium shastense* which was described by Lull, was analyzed and the result of this analysis led that author to make the following remarks regarding the probable environment in which the sloth lived.

" 'In summary: The sloth apparently was feeding upon low-growing, hairy, desert-scrub vegetation, such as at present grows in the southwestern United States.' (From the statement of Professor Arthur J. Eames, who made the analysis of the food ball.)

"This would seem to imply as little climatic and vegetative change as topographic. . . . Our animal was evidently less particular (than the modern tree-sloths) and lived on such sustenance as the region afforded, except the cacti."[88]

All of which evidence points, of course, to the probability that the environmental conditions at Ventana Cave during the period with which we are concerned, were approximately parallel to those existing at the present time.

Perissodactyla

Tapiridae

Tapirus sp.—Tapir

Materials—Numerous fragments of teeth (Pl. 18, *d*), specifically thirteen from the conglomerate and eight from the volcanic debris layer. A metapodial?

Horizon—Conglomerate and volcanic debris.

Description—Although the tooth fragments are small, nevertheless they are quite diagnostic, and there is no doubt as to their assignment to the genus *Tapirus*. The metapodial is identified as questionably referable to *Tapirus*. It is possibly a right second metatarsal, but the lack of the distal epiphysis and the worn condition of the proximal facets make its certain assignment somewhat doubtful.

The fragmentary nature of the specimens precludes the possibility of a specific identification.

★ 88. Lull, R. S., 1929, Mem. Peabody Mus., Yale Univ., III, Pt. 2, p. 18.

Remarks—We see here, as in the case of the sloth, an animal now extinct (in this instance, only in North America) which extends through both the conglomerate and the volcanic debris layers. Therefore it was present in this section of the Southwest before and after the arrival of Early Man in the region.

The presence of tapir in Ventana Cave is perhaps the most perplexing problem of the entire faunal assemblage, a problem the significance of which will be more fully discussed below. Suffice it to say here that the tapir indicates fairly moist environmental conditions, if we base our judgment on a knowledge of the habits of modern tapirs, as well as upon the distribution of the Pleistocene tapirs of North America. Naturally this evidence as to the environmental conditions that existed during the early human occupation of Ventana Cave is in some conflict with the evidence afforded by many if not most of the other elements in the mammalian assemblage, the jackrabbit, prairie dog, coyote, horse, and antelope, all of which are definitely plains animals. It may well be that the association of tapir with these typical prairie mammals indicates a condition of grassy savannahs, of uplands cut by shallow wooded streams.

Equidae

Equus occidentalis Leidy—Horse

Materials—A large number of teeth and fragments of teeth (Pl. 18, *e*). Also certain other elements.

Horizon—Conglomerate and volcanic debris, with a preponderance of the material in the conglomerate layer. Thus there are about 163 identifiable teeth and tooth fragments in the conglomerate as against 23 such fossils in the volcanic debris.

Description—From the study of several specimens it is possible to get a fairly accurate idea as to the crown pattern of the upper cheek teeth of the Ventana Cave horse. This pattern may be characterized by the elongated protocone, the relatively simple fossette borders and the absence of a pli caballin. Because of the seeming simplicity of the crown pattern in the upper cheek teeth (Fig. 14), this horse is therefore referred to the species *Equus occidentalis.*

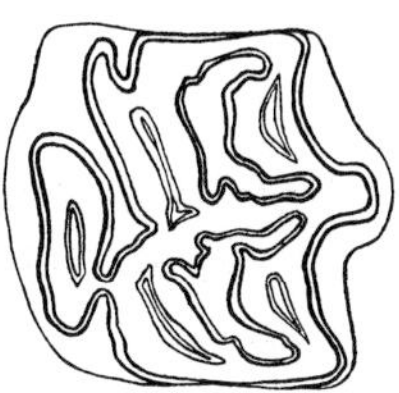

FIGURE 14. Restored cheek tooth of the horse, *Equus occidentalis,* from Ventana Cave. This is a composite restoration, based upon several specimens. Crown view, natural size

Remarks—The Ventana Cave fauna is characterized by the overwhelming preponderance of horse remains. This would indicate an abundance of forage, which in turn would point to the fact that climatic conditions were more moist and perhaps less harsh in this portion of North America than is the case at the present time. From the evidence of the horse we are justified in assuming that in the Arizona of that time there were large expanses of grasslands, probably cut by persistent flowing streams.

ARTIODACTYLA

Tayassuidae

Pecari sp.—Peccary

Materials—A right lower canine tooth (Pl. 18, *c*).

Horizon—Volcanic debris.

Description—A rather small canine, but very characteristically tayassuid because of its strong triangular cross-section.

Remarks—Even though the evidence for peccary at Ventana Cave must rest upon this single specimen, it is, none the less, quite valid, for there can be no mistaking of this peccary tooth. It might be said, however, that the generic identification is not so certain as that for the family, and it is realized that this tooth may well represent the genus *Platygonus,* rather than *Pecari.* Be that as it may, the presence of peccaries in this section of Arizona during the period which is under our consideration is not unexpected, in view of the presence of these animals in this region in Recent times. This may be an indication either of conditions parallel to those of modern times or to a moister climate conducive to a grassland rather than a desert ecology.

Cervidae

Large cervid—Deer

Materials—Portion of frontal with the pedicle of a right antler.

Horizon—Volcanic debris.

Description—Nothing very definite can be said about this fossil, in view of its fragmentary nature. From its size and the backward slant of the pedicle it would seem possible that it represents one of the western deer of the genus *Odocoileus.*

Remarks—Deer of the genus *Odocoileus* now range through southern Arizona, so the presence of such a form in the Ventana Cave fauna does not indicate environmental conditions strikingly different from those holding at the present time. It must be remembered, however, that these animals are, at the present time, wide-ranging forms, being found, in their specific and subspecific manifestations, over much of the North American continent and in a variety of climates. Consequently *Odocoileus* would be expected at Ventana Cave even with conditions quite different than they are at the present time.

Antilocapridae

Tetrameryx (Stockoceros) cf. *conklingi.*

Stock—Four-Pronged Antelope

Materials—Upper and lower cheek teeth (Pl. 18, *b*). Also a phalanx.

Horizon—Conglomerate and volcanic debris.

Description—There exists a reasonable doubt as to whether these antilocaprid fossils found at Ventana Cave should be referred to *Tetrameryx* or to *Antilocapra.* It is unfortunate that no horn cores were found, for these are quite definitive in the two genera, whereas differences in the dentition are at best very subtle. After a close comparison with representatives of both genera these specimens now under consideration have been assigned to the extinct form.

Remarks—Tetrameryx is known from adjacent regions in Arizona, notably from the Papago Springs Cave, near Sonoita. Therefore, its presence in the Ventana Cave fauna was to be expected. Its presence affords no positive evidence as to the environment in which it lived. Of course, pronghorns are at the present time found in the desert and grassland regions of the West, and it is supposed that *Tetrameryx* lived in similar habitats, or even under conditions more moist than those now prevailing in the range of *Antilocapra*. At any rate, *Tetrameryx* is a plains element in the fauna.

Bovidae

Bison sp.—Bison

Materials—Portion of a right lower third molar (Pl. 18, *a*), and fragments of two other teeth.

Horizon—Conglomerate.

Description—Typical bison teeth. Hypsodont.

Remarks—The bison, like so many other members of the Ventana Cave fauna, is a plains or prairie element in the assemblage. It is interesting to note the paucity of bison teeth as compared with the abundance of horse teeth. Since both of these mammals occupy essentially the same type of environment, it might be expected that the presence of *Bison* would be on a scale more or less comparable to that of the horse. It must be concluded, therefore (accidents of preservation aside), that the bison did not frequent this portion of the state at the time Early Man first entered the region. Probably, as in our recent past, this was an animal of the northern prairies.

REPTILIA

Chelonia

Fragments of the shell of a large turtle were found in the Ventana Cave deposits, but these were so incomplete that no attempt at an identification could be made.

Analysis of the Ventana Cave Faunas

Perhaps it might be well to give a listing of the Ventana Cave mammals, in order that there may be shown at a glance the composition of the two faunas, that of the conglomerate and that of the volcanic debris, and their relationships to each other. Also, in such a listing, the persistent and extinct forms may be indicated. With this list (Table 8) as a basis, it may then be possible to proceed with the analysis and interpretation of the faunas, in an effort to see in what manner they may bear upon the problem of Early Man at the Ventana Cave locality.

An examination of the faunas from the two levels gives the impression that we are dealing here with what is essentially a single zoological assemblage that persisted through the time during which the two layers, the lower conglomerate and the overlying bed, were being deposited. For instance, of the extinct mammals, the tapir, the horse, and the four-pronged antelope are found in both layers. The extinct cat, *Felis atrox,* and the sloth are found only in the upper layer, but there is every reason to think that they were living in this region when the lower layer was being deposited, so their absence is very likely due to

TABLE 8

FOSSIL MAMMALS FOUND AT VENTANA CAVE

		Conglomerate	*Volcanic debris*	*Persisting*
Lepus californicus	jackrabbit		x	x
Cynomys ludovicianus	prairie dog		x	x
Callospermophilus lateralis	Say's ground squirrel	x		(1)
Canis dirus	extinct wolf	x		
Canis latrans	coyote	x		x
Vulpes macrotis	long-eared kit fox	x		x
Taxidea taxus	badger		x	x
Felis atrox	extinct jaguar		x	
Nothrotherium shastense	ground sloth		x	
Tapirus sp.	tapir	x	x	(2)
Equus occidentalis	horse	x	x	
Pecari	peccary		x	x
Cervid	deer		x	x
Tetrameryx (Stockoceros) cf. *conklingi*	four-pronged antelope	x	x	
Bison sp.	bison	x		x

(1) Not south of Gila River.
(2) Not north of Oaxaca, Mexico.

the accidents of collecting. In a like manner, the absence of the extinct wolf from the upper layer may be due to the accidents of collecting, although it must be recognized that in this case there is the possibility of true extinction to account for the lack of *Canis dirus* in the volcanic debris. The other forms, so far as determinable, are living today so that their presence or absence in the Ventana Cave deposits has no particular significance.

When the composition of the mammalian assemblages from the conglomerate and from the volcanic debris are compared, the differences between the two layers become readily apparent. The comparison may be expressed by figures in Table 9:

TABLE 9

COMPARISON OF MAMMALIAN FAUNAS

Individuals	*Carni-vores*	*Rodents Lago-morphs*	*Sloth*	*Tapir*	*Horse*	*Antilo-caprid*	*Bison*	*Other artio-dactyls*
Volcanic debris	6	7	3	8	23	9	1	2
Conglom-erate	6	5	0	13	163	6	6	0
Percentages								
Volcanic debris	10	12	5	14	39	15	1.50	3.50
Conglom-erate	3	2.50	0	6.50	82	3	3	0

The point of greatest difference in the two assemblages is, of course, that of the horses, which are proportionately twice as abundant in the conglomerate as they are in the volcanic debris. Otherwise the differences between the mammals in the two levels are not so striking, there being no differences that cannot be accounted for by accidents of collecting.

These comparisons of the mammals from the conglomerate and the volcanic debris are set forth graphically in Figures 15 and 16.

Whether the difference in the number of horses found in the volcanic debris and the conglomerate is significant is a question difficult to answer. It is an interesting fact that leaving the horses out of account in both cases, the number of identifiable individuals from each layer was the same, namely thirty-six.

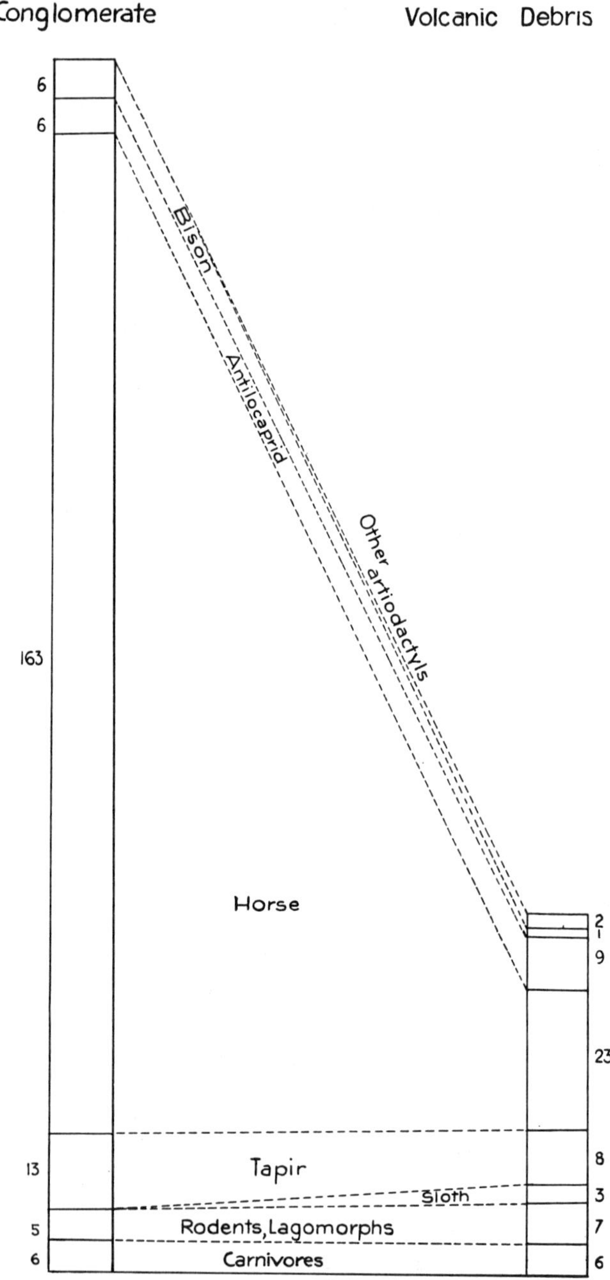

FIGURE 15. A comparison of the numbers of individuals comprising the mammalian assemblages found in the conglomerate and volcanic debris layers of Ventana Cave. The figures alongside the columns give the number of individuals of each category

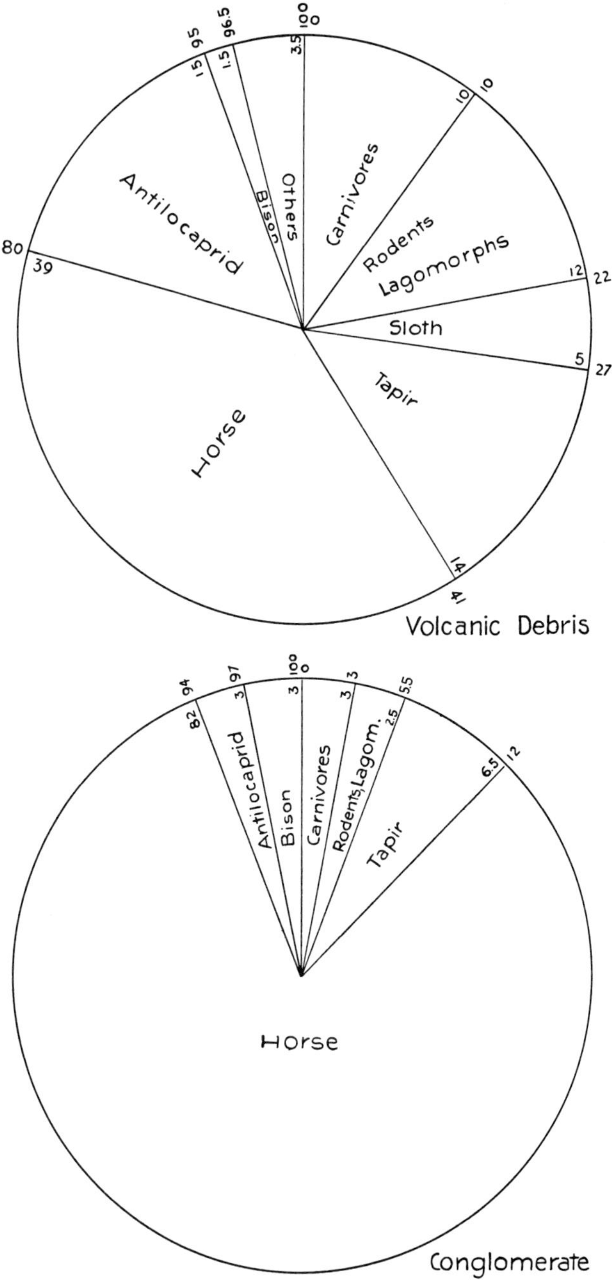

FIGURE 16. A comparison by percentages of the numbers of individuals comprising the mammalian assemblages found in the conglomerate and volcanic debris layers of Ventana Cave. The figures inside the circles give the percentages for each category, those outside the circles give the cumulative percentages

This being so, why were there so many more horses preserved in the conglomerate than in the volcanic debris? Is the presence of man at the time of volcanic debris deposition, as indicated by artifacts in the layer, connected in any way with the reduction in the number of horses?

Be that as it may, there is no doubt but that the mammals from both layers in Ventana Cave are predominantly "plains" forms, but with a rather curious intermixture of types from certain other ecological provinces. The "plains" elements are represented by such animals as the jackrabbit, prairie dog, wolf, fox, coyote, horse, peccary, antelope, and bison. The jaguar must be regarded as an animal which also might associate itself with a plains or desert fauna, as it does today in northern Mexico, although in the Neotropical region it is more characteristically a jungle animal. The ground sloth was probably quite capable of existing in a dry plains habitat. To this point the evidence does not preclude conditions similar to those of the present day, although some elements in the fauna, like the jaguar and the horse, would fit more conveniently into a picture of a moister climate environment than in a harsh desert.

Two elements of the fauna, however, fail to fit completely into the picture of a dry plains environment for the mammals of Ventana Cave. One of these is the ground squirrel, *Callospermophilus,* the other the tapir. At the present time *Callospermophilus* is not found south of the Gila River, which cuts across the center of the state, and within its modern limits it inhabits the rocky slopes and the open pine forests of the Canadian and Transition zones. It is possible that the habits of *Callospermophilus* were different in late Pleistocene and sub-Recent times from what they are today, but such a supposition seems, on the whole, a rather improbable manner of begging the question. Rather, it would seem that the presence of *Callospermophilus* indicates conditions similar to those in which it lives at the present time.

The tapir presents a far more difficult problem. It is easy enough to imagine the slight difference of conditions in southern Arizona between the late Pleistocene during the past ten or twenty thousand years that would account for the presence of *Callospermophilus* at Ventana Cave, but the differences that would have made conditions suitable for tapirs are something else again. We think of the tapirs as tropical animals, living along streams in the dense jungles, so that there is required a considerable stretch of imagination if these conditions are to be implied at the Ventana Cave site.

On the other hand, we are justified in thinking that the Pleistocene tapirs of North America were somewhat less tropical in habits than their present-day surviving relatives, since their remains are distributed into the middle latitudes of the United States. It is significant that except for the Ventana Cave locality, for a dubious record at El Paso, Texas, and for the Rancho la Brea site at Los Angeles, all of the discoveries of extinct tapirs in North America fall within the present-day twenty-inch mean annual precipitation limits. (It should be noted that the Rancho la Brea site is so close to the twenty-inch boundary that its location outside the heavier rainfall area is not particularly significant, considering the time element involved as well as the wandering proclivities and abilities of large mammals.) Therefore it seems evident that, although the North American tapirs of the Pleistocene might not have been tropical animals, they were, nevertheless, creatures of the moister areas, probably living in forests or savannahs.

Consequently, to account for the presence of tapirs at the Ventana Cave locality, one must imagine conditions somewhat different than they are at the present time. Certainly it was no region of jungles or even woodlands, but it very possibly might have been a savannah region, an open grassland crossed by permanent streams, rather than the desert with intermittent drainage that it is today. In such an environment there were numerous upland plains mammals such as the horse, bison, wolf, coyote, and the like, which today are spread through a variety of environments ranging from humid to desert conditions. In other words, the plains elements in the Ventana Cave fauna do not necessarily indicate a completely open plains condition, whereas the tapir there does indicate something of a reasonably moist, savannah type of habitat.

In this connection it might be well to compare the Ventana Cave fauna with the Pleistocene fauna of Florida, in which a similar mixture of tapir with horse, wolf, ground sloth, and other such mammals is found. Evidently in Florida the tapirs lived along the streams, while the horses and other grazing mammals roamed the more open grassy regions between drainage lines. So it may have been in Arizona in late Pleistocene and sub-Recent times. The tapirs probably kept to the moist borders of the rivers and streams, while the grazers such as the horses, bison, and antelope drifted across the open grasslands. Of course, mammals being what they are, the grazing forms often crossed the streams and thus associated with the tapirs, while the predators followed their prey wherever it might go.

In light of the above considerations, it is reasonable to think that the Ventana Cave site was not far distant from a constantly flowing watercourse. Naturally the advantages of such a site for human habitation are obvious.

One other question is raised by the occurrence of the Ventana Cave mammals. This is the ratio of extinct to persisting forms. On the basis of individuals alone, the extinct animals overwhelmingly outnumber those that live at the present time. Thus:

	Conglomerate	*Volcanic debris*
Extinct	184 or 92.50%	45 or 76%
Persistent	15 or 7.50%	14 or 24%

As concerns the species represented, the picture is somewhat different. Thus:

	Conglomerate	*Volcanic debris*
Extinct	4 or 50%	5 or 50%
Persistent	4 or 50%	5 or 50%

Yet, even on the basis of species rather than of individuals, the percentage of extinction is high, especially when one considers the relatively short period of geologic time involved. Here we are brought face to face with that perennial and perplexing question of the association of Man with extinct mammals in the Western Hemisphere. Man was present at Ventana Cave, *after* which time half of the species with which he was associated (as recorded) became extinct. Is there any significance in this fact?

Conclusions

Whether the study of the vertebrates found at Ventana Cave aids in the solution of the large problems of Early Man in America depends on the degree of correlation that can be achieved between the results presented here and those obtained by other students working along other lines of evidence obtained from the site. This much can be said:

(1) The vertebrate assemblages found at Ventana Cave include a high proportion of animals now extinct, either completely, or to a lesser degree, in this region of North America.

(2) The extinction of these animals came *after* Man had become established in Arizona. In other words, there is an indisputable association of Man with extinct forms at the Ventana Cave site.

(3) This association of Man with extinct animals may or may not imply a considerable degree of age for the association. The mammals now extinct, with which the Ventana Cave man was associated are "typical" Pleistocene forms. The fact must be recognized, however, that these "Pleistocene" mammals may have persisted until a comparatively recent date, measured by a few thousands of years. Unfortunately, the evidence of the mammals at Ventana Cave does not give any real clue as to the age of its human occupation; that is a problem in the province of the stratigrapher and the physiographer.

(4) However, the evidence of the mammals does indicate that climatic conditions in southern Arizona, at the time of Man's first occupation of the Ventana Cave site, were somewhat

different than they are at the present time. In those days, the climate was seemingly moister than it is now, so that the environment for the fauna was one of a savannah or plains, with persistent, shaded streams, rather than the desert, with intermittent drainage, which characterizes the region at the present time.

PART IV

Modern Fauna and Flora of the Cave Remains

From top to bottom the successive layers of Ventana Cave were very rich in animal bones, principally the vestige of animal food, which, from early to late, was highly important in the diets of the people. Plant remains, other than charcoal, were limited by the moist nature of the deeper layers to the upper dry zone of the midden. Both animal and plant evidences are significant for at least two reasons:

(1) As most of this material was brought into the cave by man himself and survives as a by-product of his quest for food or for other economically useful products, this dependence on various types of food, animal and plant, natural or cultivated, in the latter category, can be partially reconstructed.

(2) The length of time over which evidence of this sort accumulated in the cave provides a rare opportunity to gauge changes in the natural life of the area. While such information may be of greater interest to the zoologist and botanist than to the archaeologist and geologist, it nevertheless works the other way too, as both plant and animal life are indicative of climate, and climatic fluctuation, in turn, is one of the controls used in dating Early Man.

FAUNA

The identifications of mammal and reptile remains, other than those from the conglomerate and volcanic debris layers, were made by the late Dr. Glover M. Allen and by his successor, Dr. Barbara Lawrence, of the Museum of Comparative Zoology, Harvard University. Dr. Allen examined the lot resulting from the first season's excavations and Dr. Lawrence kindly undertook the study of the material accruing from the final season in the cave. Their respective lists have been combined.

Dr. Hildegarde Howard, curator of avian paleontology, Los Angeles County Museum, graciously undertook the study of approximately 120 elements of birds, and her identifications are also appended.[1]

Considerably over three hundred pounds of selected mammal bones were studied, running into thousands of elements. Bone was noticeably less abundant in the pottery layers of the midden than in the pre-pottery zone. This is the logical consequence of the introduction of the all-important plant food, corn, which came in roughly simultaneously with pottery, estimated to have been near the time of Christ.

While the list below, including the species from the red sand layer and midden, represents the important food animals of the region, it also includes others which to us would be quite unpalatable. Whether or not they were eaten or were brought into the cave for the skins, or simply died in the cave when it was not occupied by man, is a matter of conjecture; but in lean times one cannot be too choosy about what is eaten, and there is no reason to believe that the Ventana residents were ever free from want. Their economy, best characterized as one of scarcity, would have forced them to utilize every form of food possible.

★

1. The segregation of the bird bones from the mammal bones was done by Mr. L. L. Hargrave.

Mammals[2]

Jackrabbit *(Lepus californicus eremicus)*
Antelope Jackrabbit *(Lepus alleni)*
Desert Mule Deer *(Odocoileus hemionus ? canus)*
Coyote *(Canis latrans,* subsp. ?)
Berlandier's Badger *(Taxidea taxus berlandieri)*
Audubon Cottontail *(Sylvilagus auduboni arizonae)*
Pronghorn Antelope *(Antilocapra americana)*
Bighorn Sheep *(Ovis canadensis,* subsp. ?)
Rock Squirrel *(Citellus variegatus grammurus)*
Wildcat *(Lynx rufus baileyi)*
Gray Fox *(Urocyon cinereo-argenteus scotti)*
Yellow-haired Porcupine *(Erethizon epixanthum couesi)*
Kit Fox *(Vulpes macrotis arsipus)*
Sonora Deer *(Odocoileus couesi)*
Prairie Dog *(Cynomys ludovicianus arizonensis)*
Wood Rat *(Neotoma,* sp.?)
Mountain Lion *(Felis concolor azteca)*
Wolf *(Canis lupus,* subsp. ?)
Skunk *(Mephiles,* sp. ?)
Spotted Skunk *(Spilogale arizonae)*
Black Bear *(Ursus americanus amblyceps)*
Cacomistle, also "Ringtail" *(Bassariscus astutus flavus)*
Chipmunk *(Entamias,* sp.?)
Pocket Gopher *(Thomomys,* sp. ?)
Pocket Mouse *(Perognathus,* sp. ?)
Kangaroo Rat *(Dipodomys,* sp. ?)

Domesticated Mammals

Dog *(Canis familiaris)*
Horse *(Equus caballus)*
Sheep or Goat *(Ovis aries,* or *Capra hircus)*
Cow *(Bos taurus)*

★

2. No quantitative analysis was made because of obvious difficulties and the enormous amount of time involved. But the listing is roughly in order of frequency, from high to low, as based on the number of repetitions in the many test lots of bone.

REPTILES[3]

Berlandier's Tortoise *(Gopherus berlandieri)*
Gila Monster *(Heloderma maculatum)*
Horned Toad *(Phrynosoma,* sp.)
Snakes and Lizards (unidentified)

BIRDS

Red-tailed Hawk *(Buteo borealis)*
Horned Owl *(Bubo virginianus)*
Barn Owl *(Tyto alba)*
Turkey Vulture *(Cathartes aura)*
Raven *(Corvus corax)*
Roadrunner *(Geococcyx californianus)*
Marsh Hawk *(Circus hudsonius)*
Prairie Falcon *(Falco mexicanus)*
Gambel (?) Quail *(Lophortyx (gambeli ?)*
Scaled (?) Quail *(Callipepla (squamata ?)*
Mourning Dove *(Zenaidura macroura)*
White-winged Dove *(Melopelia asiatica)*
Brown Pelican *(Pelecanus occidentalis)*

The quantitative occurrence of the above species in the upper cave has been compiled in Tables[4] 10 and 11, accounting for mammals, both native and domestic; reptiles, and birds. The tabulation is based on the presence of species in each of the numerous lots of bone from the test sections, and a value of only *one* was assigned even though a given animal was represented by scores of elements. Questionable identifications have not been included.

As a further aid to understanding some of the faunal changes, a diagram is presented in Figure 17. This will be found useful in connection with the following comments.

The archaic character of the volcanic debris and conglomerate layer fauna is evident and needs no further comment, as

★

3. Partial identification.

4. It will be noted that a few species given in the list do not appear in the Tables, as they were represented only in the lower cave which has been omitted from the stratigraphic analysis.

Table 10

DISTRIBUTION OF MODERN MAMMALS, UPPER CAVE, GIVING FREQUENCIES BY LEVEL

Table 10
DISTRIBUTION OF MODERN MAMMALS, UPPER CAVE, GIVING FREQUENCIES BY LEVEL

	Stratigraphic Layer	Levels	MAMMA												
			Jackrabbit	*Mule Deer*	*Coyote*	*Badger*	*Audubon Cottontail*	*Pronghorn Antelope*	*Bighorn Sheep*	*Rock Squirrel*	*Wildcat*	*Gray Fox*	*Porcupine*	*Kit Fox*	*Sonora Deer*
Upper Cave	*Midden*	1	37 **20.2**	38 **22.2**	34 **20.2**	22 **17.2**	9 **10.8**	17 **23.6**	15 **28.3**	4 **15.4**	3 **14.3**	4 **20.0**	13 **68.4**	1 **5.6**	1 **8.4**
		2	35 **19.1**	29 **17.0**	29 **17.3**	12 **9.4**	9 **10.8**	13 **18.0**	15 **28.3**	8 **30.8**	4 **19.0**	3 **15.0**	3 **15.8**	6 **33.3**	3 **25.0**
		3	20 **10.9**	20 **11.7**	19 **11.3**	16 **12.5**	9 **10.8**	4 **5.6**	10 **18.9**	3 **11.5**	2 **9.5**		1 **5.3**	1 **5.6**	
		4	19 **10.4**	17 **9.9**	14 **8.3**	14 **10.9**	7 **8.4**	9 **12.5**	6 **11.3**	4 **15.4**	2 **9.5**	3 **15.0**		1 **5.6**	3 **25.0**
		5	21 **11.5**	18 **10.5**	22 **13.1**	20 **15.6**	11 **13.3**	9 **12.5**	3 **5.7**	3 **11.5**	5 **23.8**	1 **5.0**	1 **5.3**	2 **11.1**	2 **16.6**
		6	22 **12.0**	21 **12.3**	22 **13.1**	17 **13.3**	13 **15.7**	10 **13.9**	3 **5.7**		4 **19.0**	7 **35.0**	1 **5.3**	4 **22.2**	2 **16.6**
		7	16 **8.8**	14 **8.2**	17 **10.1**	17 **13.3**	14 **16.9**	5 **6.9**	1 **1.8**	2 **7.7**	1 **4.9**			1 **5.6**	
		8	8 **4.4**	8 **4.7**	6 **3.6**	6 **4.7**	8 **9.7**	2 **2.8**		2 **7.7**				2 **11.1**	
	Red Sand		5 **2.7**	6 **3.5**	5 **3.0**	4 **3.1**	3 **3.6**	3 **4.2**				2 **10.0**			1 **8.4**
		Totals	183	171	168	128	83	72	53	26	21	20	19	18	12
		Percent	**18.2**	**17.0**	**16.7**	**12.7**	**8.2**	**7.1**	**5.3**	**2.6**	**2.1**	**2.0**	**1.9**	**1.8**	**1.2**

											DOMESTIC ANIMALS					
	Mountain Lion	*Wolf*	*Spotted Skunk*	*Black Bear*	*Cacomistle*	*Chipmunk*	*Pocket Gopher*	*Kangaroo Rat*	*Totals*	*Percent*	*Dog*	*Horse*	*Sheep or Goat*	*Cow*	*Totals*	*Percent*
.5	3 **60.0**	2 **66.7**		1 **50.0**	1 **33.3**	1 **100.0**		1 **100.0**	212	21.0	1 **10.0**	5 71.4	4 **100.0**		10	**43.5**
.5	2 **40.0**		1 **50.0**		1 **33.3**				176	17.5	2 **20.0**	2 **28.6**		2 **100.0**	6	**26.1**
			1 **50.0**				1 **100.0**		107	10.6	2 **20.0**				2	**8.6**
3					1 **33.3**				102	10.1	2 **20.0**				2	**8.6**
									119	11.8	1 **10.0**				1	**4.4**
3									128	12.7						
		1 **33.3**							89	8.8	1 **10.0**				1	**4.4**
3				1 **50.0**					45	4.5	1 **10.0**				1	**4.4**
									30	3.0						
	5	3	2	2	3	1	1	1	1008		10	7	4	2	23	
7	.5	.3	.2	.2	.3	.1	.1	.1			43.5	30.4	17.4	8.7		

Table 11

DISTRIBUTION OF REPTILE AND BIRD REMAINS, UPPER CAVE, GIVING FREQUENCIES BY LEVEL

			REPTILES					*BIRDS*										
	Stratigraphic Layer	*Levels*	*Berlandier's Tortoise*	*Horned Toad*	*Snakes and Lizards*	*Totals*	*Percent*	*Red-tailed Hawk*	*Raven*	*Horned Owl*	*Barn Owl*	*Turkey Vulture*	*Roadrunner*	*Brown Pelican*	*Marsh Hawk*	*White-winged Dove*	*Totals*	*Percent*
Upper Cave	*Midden*	1	6 **21.4**		1 **100.0**	7	**23.3**	5 **20.8**	1 **14.3**	1 **16.6**	1 **20.0**	2 **40.0**	2 **66.6**	2 **100.0**		1 **100.0**	15	**27.7**
		2	6 **21.4**	1 **100.0**		7	**23.3**	3 **12.5**	2 **28.6**		2 **40.0**				1 **100.0**		8	**14.8**
		3	7 **25.0**			7	**23.3**	2 **8.3**	2 **28.6**	1 **16.6**		1 **20.0**					6	**11.1**
		4	4 **14.3**			4	**13.3**	3 **12.5**		1 **16.6**							4	**7.4**
		5						4 **16.6**		1 **16.6**	1 **20.0**	1 **20.0**					7	**13.0**
		6						6 **25.0**	2 **28.6**	1 **16.6**	1 **20.0**		1 **33.3**				11	**20.4**
		7	2 **7.1**			2	**6.7**	1 **5.0**				1 **20.0**					2	**3.7**
		8	3 **10.7**			3	**10.0**			1 **16.6**							1	**1.8**
	Red Sand																	
		Totals	28	1	1	30		24	7	6	5	5	3	2	1	1	54	
		Percent	**93.3**	**3.3**	**3.3**			**44.4**	**13.0**	**11.1**	**9.3**	**9.3**	**5.6**	**3.7**	**1.8**	**1.8**		

Dr. Colbert has covered this well (p. 126*ff*). It is also clear that the red sand fauna agrees in character with the midden fauna and not with that of the volcanic debris, thus assisting in confirming the idea suggested by the disconformity that considerable time elapsed between the formation of the two layers.

As for the mammal remains of the modern fauna, the common and antelope jackrabbit and the mule deer were staples in the meat diet throughout the period of midden accumulation. The dependence on jackrabbits of the late prehistoric people of the area is brought out time and again by the Papago legend of the Jackrabbit Eaters, who were allegedly dispossessed by them. It is worth noting that our excavations at the Jackrabbit Ruin and also at Ash Hill (Sells Phase) showed that jackrabbit bones were not only abundant but were in the overwhelming majority over those of other animals. Jackrabbits also supplied most of the fur that went into the robes.

The wealth of coyote bones is especially interesting in view

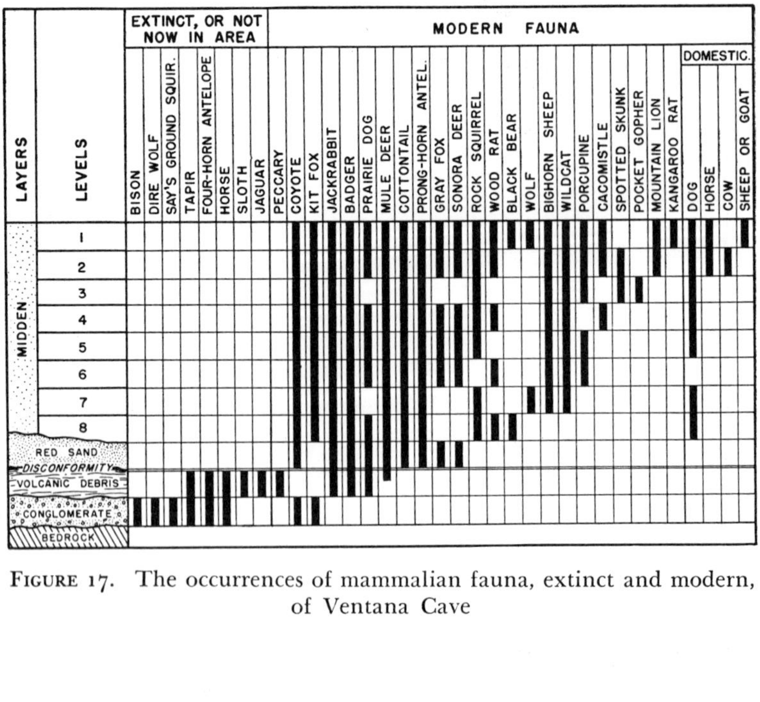

FIGURE 17. The occurrences of mammalian fauna, extinct and modern, of Ventana Cave

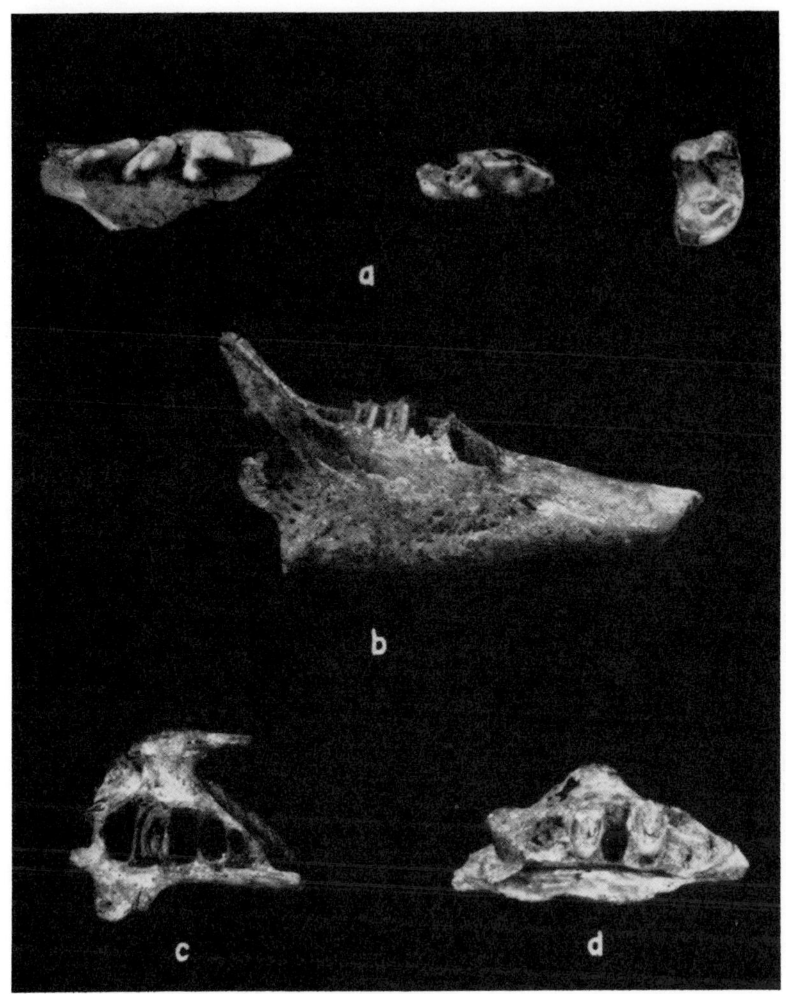

PLATE 17

Fossils from Ventana Cave, Arizona: *Vulpes macrotis,* left maxilla with last three premolars, lower left carnassial, upper right first molar, *a,* Conglomerate; *Lepus californicus,* right mandibular ramus with first two molars, *b,* Volcanic debris; *Lepus californicus,* left maxilla with last premolar, *c,* Volcanic debris; *Cynomys ludovicianus,* right maxilla with last premolar and second molar, *d,* Volcanic debris. Length of *b,* 42 mm.

PLATE 18

Fossils from Ventana Cave, Arizona: *Bison,* sp., portion of a right third lower molar, *a,* Conglomerate; *Tetrameryx (Stockoceros)* cf. *conklingi,* upper molars, *b,* Volcanic debris; *Pecari,* sp., canine, *c,* Volcanic debris; *Tapirus,* sp., fragments of three cheek teeth, *d,* Conglomerate and Volcanic debris; *Equus occidentalis,* upper and lower cheek teeth, *e,* Conglomerate and Volcanic debris; *Nothrotherium shastense,* cheek tooth and median phalanx, *f,* Volcanic debris; *Felis atrox,* blade of right upper carnassial tooth, *g,* Volcanic debris; *Canis latrens,* right upper first molar, *h,* Conglomerate; *Canis dirus,* left upper second and first molars, *i,* Conglomerate; *Taxidea taxus,* right maxilla with last premolar and first molar, *j,* Volcanic debris. Length of *a,* 60 mm.

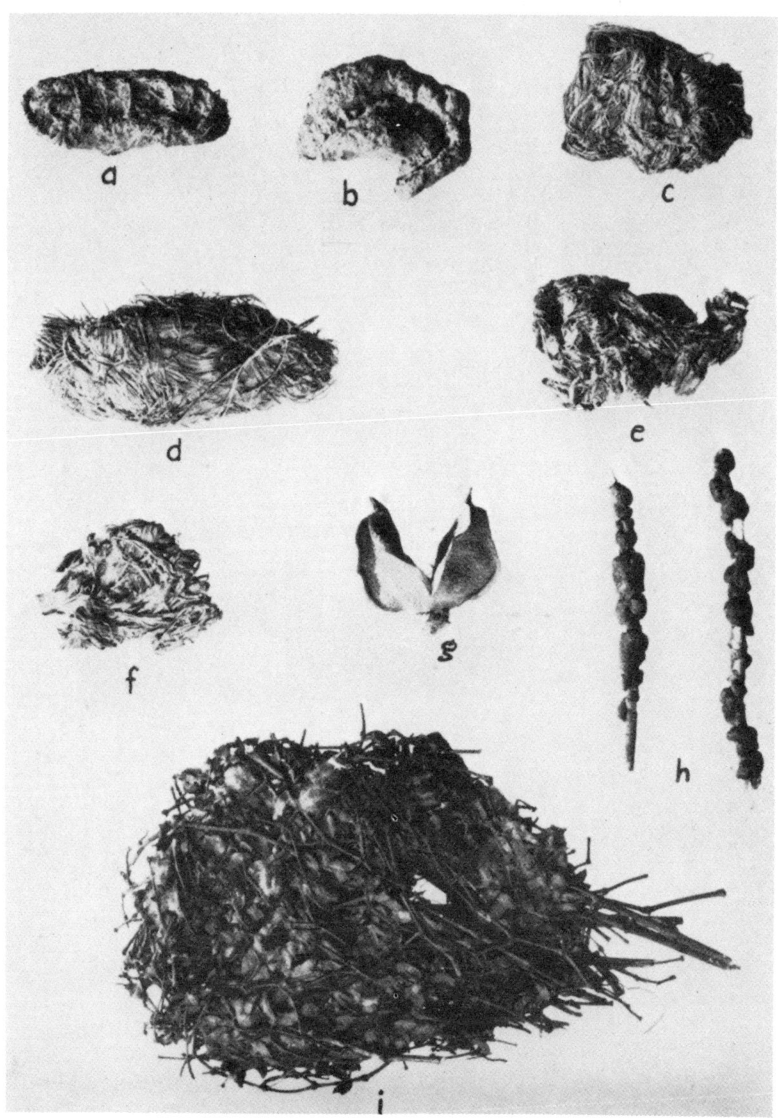

PLATE 19

Quids: fine fiber, *a, b;* coarse fiber, *c, d;* with mesquite seeds, *e;* corn husk, *f;* cotton boll, *g;* lac on creosote twigs *(Larrea divaricata), h;* and creosote pad, from burial 9, *i.* Length of *d,* 72 mm.

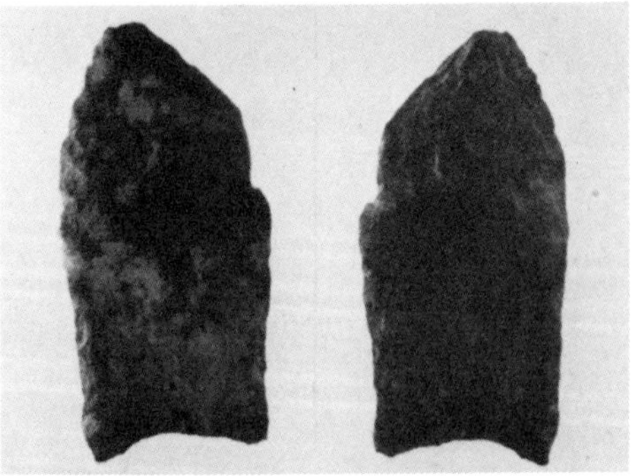

Plate 20

a (Upper). Crude side scraper firmly imbedded in the volcanic debris matrix.

b (Lower). Basalt projectile point from the volcanic debris. Length, 44 mm.

of the present Papago attitude toward this animal. The bones represent puppies as well as adults and Dr. Allen noted that they were always much broken and often charred. This can only mean that the coyote was used as food. The Papago repudiate any idea of eating the coyote nowadays as he is strongly linked with their mythology and is often regarded as an omen of dire events, especially death.[5] The badger and cottontail rabbit were important, too, as they could be easily taken at all times. Of even greater food value were antelope and mountain sheep, the largest animals hunted, next to the mule deer.

Concerning the bighorn, or mountain sheep, Table 10 reveals a situation which may bear on the history of the animal in the area. There were no sheep bones in the red sand or level 8, and only a few each up to level 3, whence they were plentiful. It is difficult to believe that the early hunters would have avoided taking this tasty animal if present at that time.

Authorities[6] state that bones of the bighorn *(O. Canadensis)* have been found in Pleistocene but not in Tertiary beds, suggesting lateness for the species, geologically speaking, and further, that the bighorn was a late immigrant to the New World from Asia. The evidence in Ventana Cave may yield a suggestion as to when this animal arrived, or at what approximate time it reached the mountainous and arid parts of the Southwest and Mexico, especially since Ventana Cave lies near the southern limits of the bighorn habitat. I am, of course, not competent to form a sound judgment in this matter, but the idea is offered for what it may be worth. The red sand and lower midden levels certainly formed after the last Pluvial, or during Early Recent times. These deposits contain the tools of hunters, along with bones of animals they hunted, but sheep bones are not among them. According to the best reckoning we are able to make now, it would appear that the bighorn was not present in the area until after B. C. 8000.

Among the other species present, highlights on a few need

★

5. E. F. Castetter and R. M. Underhill, 1935, p. 41, indicate that it was "sometimes shot" by the Papago.

6. W. B. Scott, 1929, p. 419; W. H. Flower and R. Lydekker, 1891, p. 357.

mention. The yellow-haired porcupine, most abundant in level 1 but occurring sporadically earlier, is out of its present timber habitat.[7] Dr. C. T. Vorhies informs me that in spite of its sluggish movements and its preference for a wooded environment, it sometimes wanders well beyond its element.[8] Curiously, no quills were recovered.

The cave also lies far from the present habitat of the prairie dog, the nearest recent colony being in Dragoon Pass, some 140 miles to the east.[9] The highly spotty and infrequent occurrence of the bones may mean that an occasional carcass was returned to the cave by some hunter who had gone far afield, or that if the animal occurred naturally near the cave it was rarely killed.

Such animals as the mountain lion and black bear were seldom molested and the small gophers, rats, and mice did not form any appreciable part of the diet.

The absence of javalina *(Pecari angulatus)* bones from all levels except the volcanic debris is difficult to account for, as this is one of the mammals which abounds in the area, can easily be taken, and is good eating.[10] Perhaps some food taboo must be held accountable.

Among the domesticated mammals, only one, the dog, was aboriginal. The others, horse, sheep or goat, and cow, were recent (since the latter part of the 17th century) introductions. An outline of the history of the horse, from late Pleistocene or Early Recent to modern times, is written in the cave's deposits. After the disappearance of the native but untamed horse *(Equus occidentalis)* of the volcanic debris layer from the local scene, is implied its survival and domestication in the Old World and its subsequent return to the New World, as man's servant, by the early Spanish Conquistadores. Table 10 indicates that elements of both the domestic horse and cow were found in level

★

7. W. P. Taylor, 1935, Figure 1, shows the range to lie considerably north of the Gila River, and east near the Arizona-New Mexico line.

8. A porcupine was observed within the city limits of Tucson in October, 1947.

9. Information from Dr. C. T. Vorhies.

10. Several were killed by our Papago workmen during the excavations and they were considered as welcome additions to the pot.

2, or somewhat deeper than would be expected for historic materials. This may be taken as evidence of the extent of the churning of the midden in recent times, attested also by some mixture of late prehistoric materials.

It is believed that Ventana Cave gives us some singularly new evidence on the antiquity of the dog in America. Heretofore probably the oldest North American dogs have been those associated with Basketmaker II remains,[11] dating from the early centuries of the Christian Era. In later horizons, dog remains, representing several breeds, are not at all uncommon.

Dog bones in Ventana were not abundant, according to the lists submitted by the late Dr. Glover M. Allen and his successor, Dr. Barbara Lawrence. But it should be born in mind that certain dog and coyote bones are frequently not specifically identifiable, and the lists repeatedly say "dog or coyote," or "probably dog." While, morphologically, these animals are much alike, they differ tremendously in what they meant to man, the one a wild creature and the other domesticated and man's companion. It is therefore necessary here to limit ourselves *only* to those elements which have been identified as dog beyond peradventure of doubt, and, on this score, both Drs. Allen and Lawrence, fully aware of the problem, have exercised the greatest care.

Undoubted dog remains occurred in eleven separate tests of both cave units (ten in upper cave), as against a listing of fifty-one instances of "dog or coyote" and "probably dog." This material ranged from such bone elements as maxillae to an entire mummy in the lower cave (Pl. 56, *a*). What is of greater interest is the vertical range through the midden, or the evidence reflecting the length of time the dog was known. As shown in the tabulation (Table 10), ten incidences of the dog in the upper cave were present in all levels except 6. This immediately focuses attention on the occurrences in levels 7 and 8 as the oldest evidence of the dog in the cave and doubtless in America. Concerning the one in level 7 (Test M-5) Dr. Law-

★ 11. S. J. Guernsey and A. V. Kidder, 1921, pp. 44-45.

rence states[12] "Of interest is the fragment of the anterior part of the lower jaw of a dog. . . . This animal was small, the symphysis of the jaw is narrow and the sockets for the incisor teeth are crowded out of line in a way not uncommon in such Indian dogs I have examined." The element in level 8 (Test D-1) was a maxilla, identified by Dr. Allen but not commented on further.

The cultural association of these dog remains was Chiricahua-Amargosa II Complex, and in terms of the Christian calendar, the age may be placed some millennia before the time of Christ. If we follow Antevs' dating[13] of the Cochise Culture this would have been between B. C. 8000 and 3000,[14] or after B. C. 2500 if we follow Bryan.

In the higher levels, notably 2, 3, and 4, dog bones were somewhat more frequent. These cover the time span from just before and through the first millennium of the Christian Era. Cultural affiliation ranges from the San Pedro Stage into the Hohokam Culture.

Dr. Allen's comments on the dog remains recovered during the first season's work are appended herewith:

Parts of three dogs *(Canis familiaris)* and an entire dried mummy of a fourth were almost the only remains that are undoubtedly Indian dogs. Two of these, including a skull and cervicals of one and cranium and limb bones of a second, are of nearly the same size, the second, however, younger and slightly smaller than the first. The entire mummy is a much younger animal, though it had acquired its permanent dentition. The small heavy-boned skull, shorter and more outwardly bowed tooth rows, especially of the lower jaw, are distinctive from those of the coyote which has . . . . more compressed teeth and the tooth rows are straighter, while in addition the lower premolars are more widely spaced.

The larger of the two adult skulls shows the following measurements:

★

12. Letter of June 7, 1943.
13. E. B. Sayles and E. Antevs, 1941, p. 55.
14. R. F. Heizer reports (letter February 9, 1948) the recovery of a partial dog skeleton in the Early Central Californian Horizon believed to date circa B. C. 2000.

Greatest length, including incisor	172.00 mm.
Basal length	152.00 mm.
Palatal length	86.00 mm.
Zygomatic width	92.00 mm.
Mastoid width	60.50 mm.
Width across condyles	35.50 mm.
Width outside first upper molars	58.30 mm.
Width across canines	33.30 mm.
Width of brain case	51.50 mm.
Width across postorbital processes	46.50 mm.
Alveolar length of upper tooth row	90.50 mm.
Outer length of fourth premolar	18.00 mm.
Outer length of first upper molar	12.50 mm.
Greatest length of first lower molar	21.00 mm.
Alveolar length of lower tooth row	91.30 mm.

The length of the adult humerus is 135.00 mm; of the middle two metatarsals, 52.00 mm.

These dogs were about the size of a large spaniel.

The mummified dog mentioned above probably lived less than a thousand years ago and was doubtless kept by members of the Hohokam Culture.

As to the origin of the dog known to the Basketmakers, Dr. Allen has stated, "These . . . . are true dogs, in no way derived from coyotes or other native dog-like animals of America. Their forebears probably reached America with their human masters, but their Old World ancestors still remain to be determined."[15] The oldest Ventana dogs may certainly be counted as among the "forebears" of the Basketmaker dogs, bringing the record that much nearer to their time of appearance on this continent. Dr. Allen found nothing in the Ventana evidence to alter his early opinion.[16]

In the reptile category (Table 11) [17] the only important food creature was the desert turtle. This attains a size of about twelve inches in length and was capable of producing enough meat to compensate for the task of extracting it from the shell. Turtle appears to have been utilized mainly by the Hohokam occu-

★

15. In S. J. Guernsey and A. V. Kidder, 1921, p. 45.
16. See also G. M. Allen, 1920.
17. This tabulation is based on the first season's excavations only.

pants of the cave. Even lizards and snakes may have been eaten in times of scarcity, as evidenced by occasional bones.[18]

In connection with the species of birds, Dr. Howard states: "All are about what one would expect for the region today, except for the brown pelican." The white pelican is not an uncommon sight along the shores of inland lakes, but apparently the brown variety does not stray far from its marine haunts. With the Gulf only ninety miles to the southwest of Ventana Cave, the opportunities for this bird to find its way there, naturally or by man's help, do not seem remote. The elements representing this species were vertebrae and a tibiotarsus.

Bones of the red-tailed hawk were particularly abundant and quite uniformly scattered through the debris.[19] Many of these represented immature individuals and it is likely that this hawk was captured young and kept until mature for its feathers. The Papago are known to keep the red-tail hawk, as well as other birds, for this purpose.[20]

Strangely, the game birds, as quail and doves, are poorly represented and bones of the turkey were not found. The latter probably did not range very near the cave, although turkey bones have been reported from Snaketown[21] in a semi-arid environment.

Insects

Utilization of insect products is limited to cocoons of a large moth (probably *Saturniidae*) for rattles, and lac, the secretion of tiny insects (*Tachardiella larrea*) which, in southern Arizona, live primarily on the creosote bush (*Larrea divaricata*) as the host plant.[22] This resinous substance, appearing on the infested branches, was collected by breaking off the superfluous

★

18. H. H. Bancroft, 1883, Vol. 1, p. 539, states that the Papago ate "snakes, lizards and toads" when they were in want.

19. Table 5 does not show this as only certain identifications, based on mature bones, have been included. Dr. Howard's study shows thirteen additional occurrences of *Buteo,* probably *borealis,* but the bones are of young hawks.

20. E. F. Castetter and W. H. Bell, 1942, pp. 70-71.

21. H. S. Gladwin, *et al,* 1937, p. 156.

22. H. S. Colton, 1943a, pp. 46-48; 1943b, pp. 21-32.

plant parts and stored for future use. A number of such pieces were found (Pl. 19, *h*). The chief local use was for mending pots, and making awl handles, and there is a lac hemisphere in the collection, but so far as our evidence goes it was not used as a plastic base for composite ornaments as reported by McGregor for the Flagstaff area.[23] It is probable that lac was the substance used by the River Hohokam in making their elaborate mosaic pieces.

FLORA

The plant remains are divisible on the basis of those which formed the vegetal part of the subsistence pattern and those which were used in other ways for string, basket and sandal making, etc., in short, accounting for a larger percentage of the material culture of a perishable nature. This record, unfortunately, applies only to the Hohokam and Papago, as the plant refuse of the older people has not survived.

Food

Cultivated

There are only two cultivated food plants represented, maize and pumpkin. It is difficult to explain why no samples of beans were found, as these were one of the staple crops aboriginally in the Southwest, and the Papago are credited by early white visitors with growing them.[24]

Maize—Corn cobs were found with regularity through the dry midden zone. The entire collection was submitted to Dr. Edgar Anderson, of the Missouri Botanical Garden, St. Louis, for study, and his report is appended herewith:

The material from Ventana Cave consists almost entirely of cobs. There is a single grain from level 1 (P-5) of the upper cave. It is apparently flour corn and is certainly not dented. A good many of the cobs look as though they had been harvested before they were fully mature, though I have no precise data

★

23. J. C. McGregor, 1943, Pl. II.

24. See E. F. Castetter and W. H. Bell, 1942, pp. 89-100, for an excellent review of the Papago use of beans.

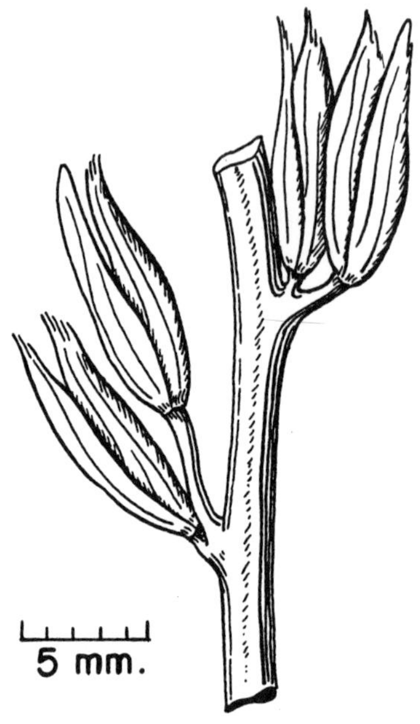

FIGURE 18. Portion of tassel branch showing four spikelets and two successive nodes. Note that, at the upper node, both of the spikelets are sub-sessile

on the subject since I have not yet made a collection of immature cobs for comparison. In four of the collections the kernels had been cut from the cob when it was green with a fairly sharp instrument. From one of the collections (upper S-3, level 1) there is a portion of a tassel (Fig. 18). It has a glume length of 10 mm. Some of its upper spikelets are sessile, or nearly so. There is no sterile zone at the base of the branches. The rhacis is thick, and about one-fourth of the internodes are markedly condensed. In all of these characters it is within the range of variation of modern Pima-Papago corn.

The bulk of the material has from eight to twelve rows per cob, both the mode and the median falling at ten. In both sections of the cave there are a few cobs of higher row numbers. All of this would be expected if the corn was essentially like modern Pima-Papago corn. Qualitatively, the cobs look essentially like those of Pima-Papago. There is very little pairing of the rows as in modern Pueblo corn. Only one cob in the entire collection (lower C-2) is so characterized.

There are two qualitative characters which are of some significance in the precise study of these collections. One is the midcob width. The other is a measure for the size of the grain. I am calling it kernel area if it is obtained from specimens with the grain attached, and cob-kernel area if computed from the cob. It is obtained by determining the average row width with a pair of dividers and the average thickness of the kernel in the other direction by measuring five or ten successive kernels, or places where kernels had been, and making the average. These two figures are multiplied by each other to give kernel area.

For the Ventana material, instead of plotting the position of each cob, I have plotted the position of the average of each collection in which there were more than three cobs (Fig. 19). For comparison I have first of all mature cobs grown in Missouri from material collected in the Southwest by George Carter and Hugh Cutler. You will note that the Ventana Cave material falls almost exactly in that of the Pima-Papago collections and is not at all like that of the Pueblo collections. If we allow for the immaturity of some of the cobs, the resemblance would be more striking. It is also in the area of the prehistoric material which I measured at Washington from Spruce Tree House and from Paragonah. The only other material in my collections which has cobs and kernels of the dimensions of this material are what Cutler and I have been calling Mexican pyramidal. This race characterizes the region around Mexico City. It has smaller kernel area on the average and is more variable in cob width. The row numbers of Mexican pyramidal, moreover, are higher on the average.

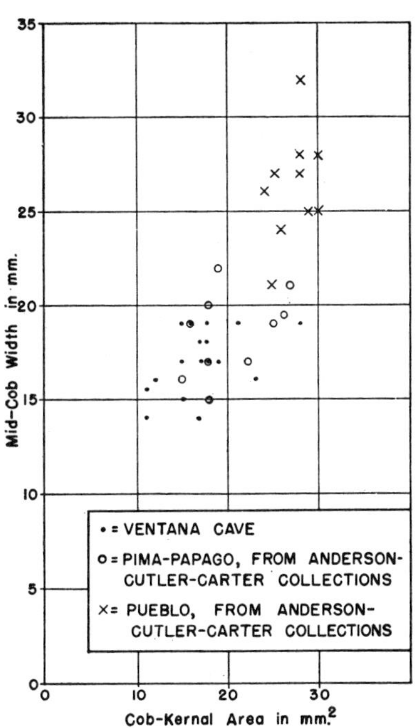

FIGURE 19. Comparison of mid-cob width and cob-kernel area of Ventana corn with Pima-Papago and Pueblo. Prepared by Dr. Edgar Anderson

To summarize, while we cannot be certain that the cobs from Ventana Cave came from maize essentially like that now being grown by the Pima and Papago Indians, there is nothing in the data to contradict such an hypothesis. It is very possible that some of the corn may have been more like Mexican pyramidal corn than is modern Pima-Papago, but it is quite certain that none of it was very much like the maize now being grown by the Pueblos.

Dr. Anderson's findings bring to the fore several important problems connected not only with corn but also with cultural continuity. First, however, it is necessary to dispose of a more elementary question: Could not all the Ventana Cave corn have been grown by the Papago in view of the favorable comparison which Anderson makes? Such an idea may be rejected because the cobs were well distributed through the dry midden zone whereas the Papago culture, with few exceptions, was superficial. This may be taken to mean that since Hohokam times the variety of corn grown in the area has been stable and unaffected by other strains. Supporting evidence for the antiquity of this type of corn is found in the fact that Basketmaker corn, the oldest now known in the Southwest, is similar to Pima-Papago corn.[25] It would thus appear that the early wave of corn brought similar though not identical kinds to the Hohokam and Basketmakers and that from then on the history of development differed. Anderson and Cutler show that subsequent to Basketmaker times the corn of the plateau received admixtures and culminated in what they term the Pueblo race.[26] But the Pima-Papago type was not so affected and has retained its early character.

After reviewing several corn lots on the Papago Reservation Dr. Anderson[27] commented that the type of corn now grown there has been cultivated for many centuries as indicated by pure botanical evidence. Obviously this has a bearing on one of our main problems, establishing the continuity between Hohokam and Pima-Papago. If a break is assumed, sometime between 1400 and 1700 for which we now have no archaeological evidence, Dr. Anderson believes that the immigrant Papago, beyond doubt, would have brought in with them other factors in their corn unless they came from within the area of distribution of this particular type of corn. The absence of these is a strong indication that modern corn of Papagueria, and Pimeria Alta too, survives today unchanged since its introduction cen-

★

25. E. Anderson and H. C. Cutler, 1942, p. 84.
26. *Ibid.*, pp. 84-85.
27. In company with the writer, May, 1943.

turies ago[28] and that throughout this time it has been tended by the same group of people.

Another question concerns the time of the arrival of corn. The Basketmakers had corn by the early centuries of the Christian Era and, as its origin is manifestly southern, the Hohokam therefore had it as early or earlier, assuming that corn passed through their territory or was transmitted by them. In Ventana, the evidence suggests that corn and pottery arrived about simultaneously. The oldest pottery types may be dated to about the time of Christ (p. 355), a date which may also then be adopted for the appearance of corn. Below the pottery line the evidence for corn is negative, although this was in the moist layer where cobs would not have survived. But there were no charred cobs and the metate type (basin) from the pre-corn levels was not customarily employed by corn-growing people. A change in the metate type in Ventana with the advent of corn is discussed under metates (p. 319).

Pumpkin—Only two pumpkin stems were recovered and Dr. Thomas W. Whitaker reports one of these to be *Cucurbita moschata* Duch. This species was grown aboriginally in the Plateau area where it has been reported from Anasazi ruins, but the Ventana specimen appears to be the first record from a probable archaeological horizon in the Hohokam area.

The second stem is believed by Dr. Whitaker to be *C. maxima* Duch. According to him, " . . . . *C. maxima* is known to be indigenous only to the southern parts of tropical South America (Brazil, Chili, Peru, Bolivia), and apparently was widely distributed after the coming of the Spaniards." He further notes that *C. maxima* occurs in a collection of fresh Papago material and the species is "thought to be of recent introduction." Unfortunately, the stratigraphic evidence of the two Ventana stems is not decisive, as they came from level 1 and could therefore be either of recent Papago or pre-Spanish origin.

★

28. See also George F. Carter, 1945, pp. 39-42.

Native

The proportionate evidence of native food plants as against cultivated plants lies heavily on the side of the former. While agriculture of sorts was practiced, this in no way supplanted the more ancient food gathering economy; and this pattern survives among the Papago, who, prior to white contacts, are said to have cultivated only about one-fifth of their food supply, the overwhelming balance of their diet having been derived from native plant and animal foods.[29]

The ethnobotany of Ventana Cave reads like that of the Papago, although it is much less complete because of the more limited nature of the evidence.[30] The following plant remains were found and it may be assumed that they were utilized as a food source by both Papago and pre-Spanish occupants:

Greens—

Cholla *(Opuntia,* sp. ?), buds.

Prickly pear cactus *(Opuntia Engelmannii),* leaves (evidence of slicing).

Sahuaro *(Cereus giganteus)* buds.[31]

Probably others, part of *Mamillaria robustispina* and *Mamillaria microcarpa* were found.

Fruits—

Sahuaro *(Cereus giganteus),* many hulls; probably including other varieties, too, as organpipe cactus *(Lemaireocereus thurberi)*,[32] and prickly pear.

Seeds—Numerous small seed caches yielded the following:

Sahuaro *(Cereus giganteus)*

Prickly pear *(Opuntia,* sp. ?)

Mesquite *(Prosopsis velutina),* pods and seeds.

★

29. E. F. Castetter and W. H. Bell, 1942, p. 57.

30. Good accounts will be found in E. F. Castetter and R. M. Underhill, 1935; E. F. Castetter and W. H. Bell, 1937 and 1942.

31. Not included by E. F. Castetter and R. M. Underhill, 1935, as now used by the Papago.

32. Ventana Cave lies just east of the main distribution of the organpipe cactus, but one large plant, probably man introduced, is now growing below the cave.

Blue palo verde *(Cercidium floridum)*, pods and seeds.
Bear grass *(Nolina microcarpa)*
Ironwood *(Olneya tesota)*
Coffee berry *(Simmondsia chinensis)*

Quids—One of the by-products of eating were the quids of fibrous material, ejected after chewing and getting the "good" out of plant parts. These are widely found throughout the Southwest, in caves, and in most cases are apparently the residue of eating agave, a plant which the Papago formerly relied on, too. But some of the quids are composed of other fibers and plant parts, as yucca, probably the leaf base near the stem, mesquite bean hulls, evidently chewed while the pods were young and tender, and even corn husks. Nichol observes[33] that young leaves of the agave were chewed as a tonic. Representative quids will be seen in Plate 19, *a – f*.

Plants Used, Other Than for Food

It is doubtful if any plants were cultivated near Ventana which were not immediately usable as food. One possible exception is the gourd *(Lagenaria*, sp. ?), which was easily converted into dippers, bottles, and cups. Fragments of gourd containers were found in the cave but no seeds were recovered. This might be interpreted as meaning that the gourds were imported.

Cotton fabrics were abundant but evidence that cotton was grown locally is scant indeed. Only half of a cotton boll (Pl. 19, *g*) was recovered, there being no other plant parts, seeds, or even free fibers in the cave litter. This cotton boll, submitted to Dr. T. H. Kearney, principal physiologist of the United States Department of Agriculture, brought forth the following reply:[34]

> I regret to say that Mr. Peebles and I are unable to identify the cotton boll you sent in. It resembles the bolls of Hopi cotton in shape but is about twice as large. Emory, in his "Military Reconnaissance" reported that the Pima Indians were growing

★

33. A. A. Nichol, 1937, p. 219.
34. Letter dated August 3, 1943.

cotton when he passed through their villages in 1846 and the culture may well have been an ancient one, but we have no record of just what type of cotton they grew. Very likely it was related to Upland cotton, to which, indeed, the cotton of the Hopi is distantly related. It may be conjectured that all of the cotton grown by Indians in the southwestern United States came originally from southern Mexico or Central America.

Early historic records make no mention of cotton grown by the Papago[35] and little or none is cultivated now. We can, nevertheless, be reasonably sure that the Papago did grow it in earlier times wherever conditions were favorable. But, as already stated, the absence of plant parts, lint, etc., would make it appear that most of the cotton in Ventana came from some distance, probably the Gila Valley, and possibly already made up as cloth.

Ventana adds nothing to our knowledge of tobacco cultivation. Castetter and Bell hold that neither the Pima nor the Papago grew tobacco aboriginally, but did make use of several native species.[36] It was probably these which were smoked in the pipes and cane cigarettes found in the cave.

A few pods of the unicorn plant *(Martynia louisiana)*, used in basketry, are small and likely came from wild, rather than cultivated, plants.[37]

As for the non-cultivated plants, the following list makes clear the extent to which the natural resources were exploited to supply all manner of materials for every day needs.[38]

Palmilla *(Yucca elata)*, fiber from leaves for cordage, whole leaves and stele fibers for sandals, leaves for basketry.

Century plant *(Agave deserti)*, retting of leaves produced good fibers for cordage and sandals.

Carrizo *(Phragmites communis)*, for arrows and cigarettes.

★

35. E. F. Castetter and W. H. Bell, 1942, p. 103.
36. *Ibid.*, pp. 108-113.
37. The cultivation of *Martynia* is believed to be recent, *Op. cit.*, p. 113.
38. The identification of all available material is not complete because of excessive alteration by man or because the diagnostic parts of plants are not present. See also list of fibers used for cordage, p. 391.

Desert willow *(Chilopsis linearis),* inner bark for breech clouts, rarely cordage, new shoots for basket splints.

Barrel cactus *(Echinocactus wislizeni,* or *E. covillei),* spines for sewing needles.

Creosote *(Larrea divaricata),* pads (Pl. 19, *i*), covering Burial 9; source of lac (Pl. 19, *h*).

Flat-top buckwheat *(Eriogonum,* sp.?), bundles, use unknown.

Cane Muhly *(Muhlenbergia dumosa),* possibly for arrow shafts.

Mesquite *(Prosopis velutina),* firewood, arrow bunts.

Palo verde *(Cercidium microphyllum),* main source of wood for various objects.

Ironwood *(Olneya tesota),* firewood, wooden tools.

Sahuaro *(Cereus giganteus),* cactus picks, dice (from ribs), callus vessels.

Dalea (sp.?), and numerous other grasses for padding and possibly bedding.

Arrowweed *(Pluchea sericea),* fire-making apparatus and possibly arrows.

Gourds *(Cucurbita foetidissima),* receptacles.

PART V

Material Culture

The stratigraphic and technological study of the specimens from Ventana Cave is greatly aided by the richness of the deposits. The duplication of the evidence in many instances and the opportunity to express values quantitatively gives the typologist a more secure footing than when the materials are more limited. Furthermore, these specimens reflect the life in the cave during an exceptionally long period of time, and indicate, with only a few apparent interruptions, several marked shifts in the economic dependence of the people. The interest in the collection as a whole is thereby enhanced.

The abundance of the remains hinged first upon the intensity of the occupation and second on the presence or absence of moisture in the cave. Thus the specimens from the layer of volcanic debris, for the most part a nature-laid deposit, were scarce per unit of volume because man entered the cave only occasionally; whereas those from the midden above, a deposit consisting chiefly of man's own trash, were present in quantity, because of more or less continual habitation. Finally, in the top layer, never reached by moisture, perishable goods greatly added to the cultural picture.

All told, more than 11,400 classifiable implements of stone

were recovered, not counting innumerable fragments too damaged for identification or so poorly worked that they could not be included in the system of classification. Artifacts of bone, shell, and the perishable materials aggregate another 1,900 items.

ANALYTICAL PROCEDURE

In a collection of such great size, it is natural that many problems should arise in connection with the analysis. Purely arbitrary judgments have had to be made to reduce this mass of tools to some semblance of order. No two people working independently on the collection would arrive at precisely the same results, although in generalities there should be agreement. The procedure employed here is briefly outlined below.

In the midden of both the upper and lower caves, the stone tools occurred in such great profusion that they presented a real problem in handling during the excavation. All small items of easily transportable nature were brought to the laboratory. The bulkier tools, as hammer stones, choppers, manos, and metates, sometimes reaching a total of more than a hundred items in a single test section, were piled separately and analyzed on the spot. Type examples were consistently kept for detailed laboratory study. It must be admitted that the field analysis was not as complete as it might have been because some of the finer distinctions brought out by the laboratory study had not been detected at the time. The numerical relationship among these larger tools as expressed here may not, therefore, reflect accurately the true conditions, but it is doubtful if the loss has been great.

A decision also had to be reached as to how the culture from the upper and lower caves was to be treated, whether separately or combined. In the description of the conditions in the lower cave it was pointed out that no deposits comparable to the conglomerate, the volcanic debris, or the red sand occurred. The partition effectively prevented these from extending into that area. If man was using the lower cave during the formation of these layers in the upper cave there was no evidence of it. In the lower cave the midden attained a maximum thickness of 2.20 m. and rested directly on bedrock. It reflected the same conditions as noted for the midden of the upper cave, *i. e.,* a bottom zone which, at some time in the past, had been moist, although dry today, and an upper zone never affected by moisture since its formation.

A preliminary inspection of the artifacts from these two layers of the lower cave revealed that the range of types was essentially the same as for those from the midden of the upper cave. On this evidence it was assumed that the upper and lower cave midden deposits were formed synchronously. For that reason the tools were combined in working out the preliminary step of establishing types, but in the frequency analysis they were again restored to their proper locale.

In the accompanying tables, use of the term "layer" refers to the stratigraphic units, as volcanic debris, red sand, and midden. The midden, because of its depth and homogeneous character, was divided into levels numbered serially top to bottom, each representing a depth of 0.50 m. It should be pointed out that level 8 (3.5-4.0 m.) was present only in a very limited area (test section D, upper) and that relatively few implements occurred in it, accounting for the fact that many traits are not present in this level. The miscellaneous category includes implements from areas not strictly placed within the stratigraphic sequence, as in the tunnel area of the partition.

Percentage values are figured to show: (1) the proportion of subtype to type, (2) the proportion of all subtypes to level, and (3) the proportion of all subtypes to the total implements comprising the type in any given level. Frequencies for the volcanic debris and red sand layers are not included in the tables because these layers represent well defined stratigraphic units from which the material culture has been examined separately.

The general procedure was, first, to arrange all specimens roughly into large type categories. This preview of the collection provided the necessary understanding for the final typing. Then followed, in order, the objective study of each type, the recognition of subtypes, the vertical distributional analysis of all samples of each type to determine the nodes of greatest frequency, and, finally, the correlation and interpretation. The first few steps are obviously abstractions, but here considered a necessity, nevertheless, in the effort to unravel the complex picture presented by stone tools.

The establishment of types was by no means the simplest of these steps. The makers of these tools were adhering to no rigid rules of form, although they must have had in mind the work which any given tool was to perform. The quality of the material, the shape and size of the original flake, oftentimes governed the final outcome. As Amsden has so aptly pointed out,[1] "many an implement started as 'something' and ended as 'something else.'" Furthermore, a number of tools were designed to do two kinds of work, as scraping and graving, involving a doubling up of criteria. All of these factors resulted in a merging and grading of types, one to the other, of knives to scrapers, of choppers to planes, etc., and the best that could be done was to try to recognize the nodes or the forms which recurred with the greatest frequency. Each type of implement, to be valid, must have a range, but not too great a range to lose its value as a possible diagnostic.

From the maker's standpoint, whether a stone was to be flaked on one side or on both sides seems to have been a primary decision. This difference of technique, uni-facial versus bi-facial chipping, is employed here to establish the basic division of chipped implements, particularly in the vast lot of tools from the midden. Other criteria then applied were shape, size, thickness or thinness, a flat or steep retouch, and the extent of the retouch, *i. e.,* whether part way or all the way around the perimeter of the tool.

Another question which arose was the stratigraphic placement. The conglomerate, volcanic debris, and red sand layers posed no problem in this connection as they were clear stratigraphic units. But the midden, lacking such distinctions, needed

★

1. In E. W. C. and W. H. Campbell, 1937, p. 56.

to be further subdivided vertically to pick up any possible changes within its depth. This had to be done on a purely arbitrary basis, by levels, the depth interval being 0.50 m. It is recognized that this system has its pitfalls. For example, the possibility of former slopes in the rising cave floor which did not conform to the contour of the surface when excavation started, and that any one of the levels, therefore, might cut across debris of both younger and older relative age. Testing this system

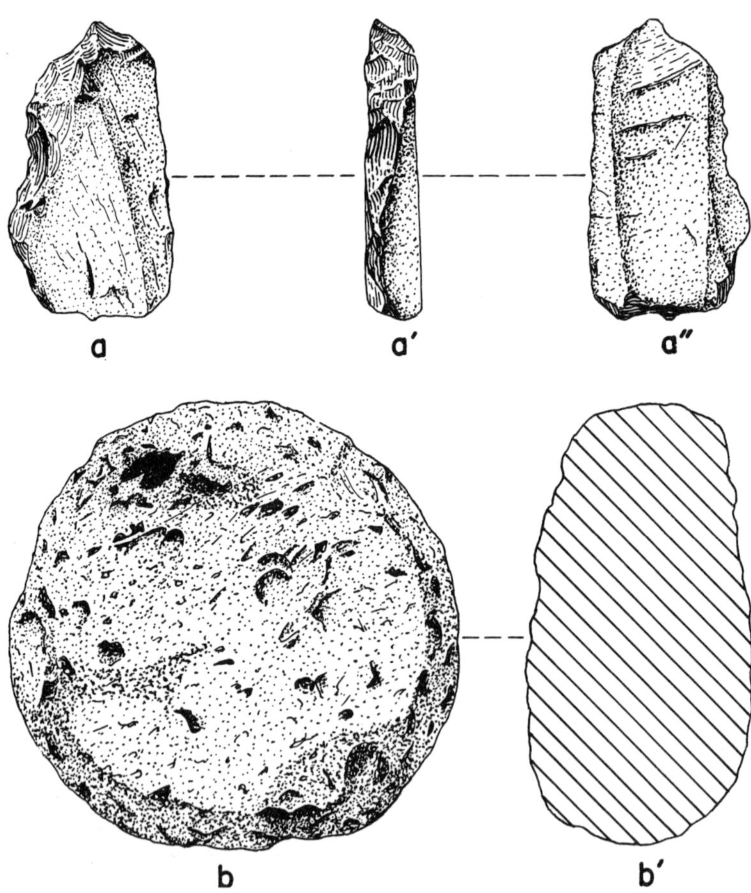

FIGURE 20. Doubtful implements from the conglomerate layer. Scraper (?), *a;* hammer stone (?), *b*. Both basalt. Diameter of *b,* 88 mm.

against the datum as a point of measurement showed no significant differences and the breakdown as employed may be assumed to be the best available under the circumstances.

In the tables, composite figures (totals of corresponding levels from all test blocks) are given to conserve space. Frequencies from each test block were examined, as a matter of course, for possible horizontal differences.

ARCHITECTURE

Throughout the entire excavation of Ventana Cave not the slightest evidence of architectural features was encountered. We know from other digging in the area that brush houses were built in open villages as early as about A.D. 800 and probably even long before. What the situation was among the gathering-hunting folk before the advent of pottery, we have no means of knowing. The fact is, that, within the natural rock shelter in this warm climate, no additional protection was necessary. In this respect, Ventana Cave, and most, if not all, of the caves in the desert area, differ from those of the plateau and mountain areas which, with few exceptions, have houses erected in the rock recesses.

It should be obvious to the archaeologist that absence of houses greatly simplified the digging procedure, although the stratigraphic picture might well have been helped by them.

IMPERISHABLE CULTURE

The Older Deposits

Those layers indicative of a climate wetter than today, the conglomerate, talus sand and rock, and the volcanic debris, are lumped together under the general heading of older deposits. The layers resting disconformably on these, the red sand and the midden, reflecting near modern or modern conditions, are called the younger deposits, as a convenient and significant temporal separation.

The Conglomerate Layer

Mention has already been made of the fact that the conglomerate contained some charcoal and two doubtful implements. One of these could pass for a discoidal basaltic hammer stone (Fig. 20, *b*) which lay in a horizontal position imbedded about halfway in the conglomerate with the upper half covered by volcanic debris. It is Hayden's opinion that the conglomerate had become hardened before erosion of it had set in and that the implement was partly exposed by this process, indicating a true association with the conglomerate layer. The second specimen (Fig. 20, *a*) is a basalt chip, suggesting a scraping tool, somewhat rolled, with fairly fresh chips removed along one edge from one face. It occurred well down in the conglomerate material.

While this evidence implies that man was present during the formation of the conglomerate, it is of such a scanty nature in the light of the more positive data we have from the volcanic debris layer that it may be regarded as inconclusive. There is no reason, of course, why man should not have been present in the area during the time the conglomerate was forming. As has been suggested, the conglomerate and the volcanic debris layers may be considered as two phases of essentially one climatic horizon, the markedly differing character of the two beds being due to local changes in the outlet channel. Thus the time element between the formation of these two zones need not have been very great and the human traces may well have come from the same people who later left more of their tools in the volcanic debris, when the floor of the cave had become drier and more habitable.

The talus sand and rock layer, contemporaneously laid down with the conglomerate, produced no artifacts and consequently can be ignored here.

The Volcanic Debris Layer

This bed rested on the conglomerate and produced the oldest clear-cut evidence of man in Ventana Cave. Before starting the analysis of the specimens it should be reiterated that the deposit reflects wetter conditions than today, that the layer was well cemented and that the associated fauna includes a number of animals which no longer exist.

The consolidation of the volcanic debris through the cementing action of lime and silica made the removal of the implements a difficult task (Pl. 20*a*). A few were unavoidably damaged. After trying several methods of excavation, the most expedient system proved to be one where the matrix was loosened with picks in sizeable chunks, and these were pulverized with wooden clubs preparatory to screening. The foreman on the "dig," by close supervision during this operation, was able to maintain accurate control over the work. Any other system would have been prohibitively expensive and it is doubtful if any further information would have been gained. The artifacts themselves were heavily encrusted with matrix. This could not be entirely removed even by prolonged acid treatment. Thorough cleaning was accomplished best by chipping and scraping off the silica crust, where this could be done without injury to the specimen.

The horizontal distribution of the tools through the layer was found to be quite even. This would indicate that the entire floor area of the cave was accessible to man and that there was little or no standing water such as existed during the formation of the underlying conglomerate. The flooding, the natural agency responsible for the bulk of the material forming the layer, was clearly intermittent and between times the cave floor was dry and tenable. The occurrence of tools vertically through the layer was also relatively uniform, suggesting man's presence throughout the period during which this layer accumulated. A few implements were found on the zone of contact which visibly marked the separation between the conglomeratic and volcanic debris layers.

Also scattered through the matrix were bits of charcoal ranging from tiny fragments to pieces as large as a walnut. The utility of this material as a climatic indicator, regretably, was not feasible. The primitive hunters obviously tarried in the cave long enough to build fires, and the charcoal from these became scattered and incorporated in the accumulation. There were no true hearths or concentrations of charcoal.

Although bones of animals were fairly abundant and well preserved, no implements of bone were found. An unexpected foreign material was marine shell. This was present in sufficient amount to indicate that shells were of some importance to the people.

Stone

The stone artifacts, totalling ninety, are, for the most part, very crude. This is chiefly due to the inferior quality of the material used and not to the inability of the people to work stone, as indicated by a few specimens expertly made from finer quality material. Most of the tools were made of basalt, which is very abundant locally but difficult to work into finished products. The following materials, some of which must have been brought in from a distance, are also represented by a few specimens: chert, quartzite, jasper, obsidian, clear quartz, and rhyolite, a smaller range of materials than is represented in the artifacts from the midden.

The implement classification is given below:

A. Projectile points (leaf-shaped) 2
   1. Rounded base, shallow notches, 1
   2. Concave base, 1

B. Knives 11
   1. Flakes, amorphous, 9
   2. Flakes, curved, 2

C. Scrapers 63
   1. Discoidal, 7
   2. Small core, 3
   3. Side, 37
      a. Irregular, 23
      b. Oval, 5
      c. Long, 6
      d. Hollow, 3

4. End, 5
5. Rough-flake, 11

D. Gravers	3
E. Choppers	3
1. Flake, 2	
2. Core, 1	
F. Planes	6
G. Hammer stones	1
H. Grinding stones	1
	90

A. Projectile points—The first of the two points in the collection is a leaf-shaped blade of clear quartz, 31 mm. long and 6.50 mm. thick (Fig. 21, *a*). A short segment at the point end has been broken off. Final shaping was accomplished by the pressure technique and, although quite irregular, the flake scars extend to, and in a few cases slightly beyond, the mid point on the faces. Attention should be called to the two shallow notches at the base which are too much alike in position and depth to be regarded as accidental.

The second point, leaf-shaped with concave base, is illustrated in Plate 20, *b,* and in Figure 21, *b*. In its fragmentary condition it is 44 mm. long, probably not more than 5 mm. having been lost through breakage. The greatest thickness is 4.80 mm. It was made from a thin flake of basalt by pressure flaking. The quality of workmanship was governed by the poor material and the small amount of chipping was further limited, by the original thinness of the flake, to the very edges, excepting toward the point, where the flake scars extend well over on the faces. From the basal tips toward the point for a distance of about 20 mm. the edges have been dulled by grinding, evidently to reduce the danger of cutting the sinew lashings when hafted.[2]

What immediately attracts attention is the resemblance of this specimen to the Folsom point. By measurement it is close to the average dimensions of the Folsom point given by Renaud[3] as based on a thousand specimens. The comparison:

★

2. E. B. Renaud, 1934, p. 3.
3. *Ibid.*, pp. 9-10

	Length	*Width*	*Thickness*
Average for Folsom	45.41 mm.	21.94 mm.	5.38 mm.
The Ventana Point	49.10*	21.50	4.80

* Reconstructed.

Apart from this similarity in dimensions, the outline may also be duplicated by numerous points illustrated in reports dealing with Folsom remains. What is missing is the channel flaking, the most distinctive of all Folsom point characters. But here the nature of the material would not permit the removal of such flakes. It would appear that the maker of the point was well aware of this, because a thin flake was selected which could be fashioned to the desired form with the original scars on the flake simulating the fluting normally achieved. While the Ventana point is therefore not of the true Folsom type as it has been defined, it is, nevertheless, too close to regard the similarity as strictly accidental. Consequently, taken with the evidence provided by a few other elements in the lithic complex, by the fauna, and by the geological placement, this single specimen may be assigned some weight in an endeavor to equate the culture.

B. *Knives*—Of the two classes, the first or amorphous group represents flakes which, for the most part, were picked up and used with little further alteration. Thus they lack uniformity both as to shape and to size. Most of the fine flaking along the sharp edges (Fig. 21, *c*) evidently was the result of use. Figure 21, *d,* is the butt end of what appears to have been a long flake with some intentional sharpening of the edges.

Two basalt knives, possibly representing a type, were made of curved flakes retouched on the concave side over approximately one-half the length of one edge (Fig. 21, *e*). Lengths: 72 and 73 mm.

C. *Scrapers*—These greatly outnumber all other classes of implements and may be divided into several types and sub-types. On the whole the workmanship is rough.

The discoidal scrapers share, as a lot, the characteristics of a flat face showing no chipping and a convex face with more or

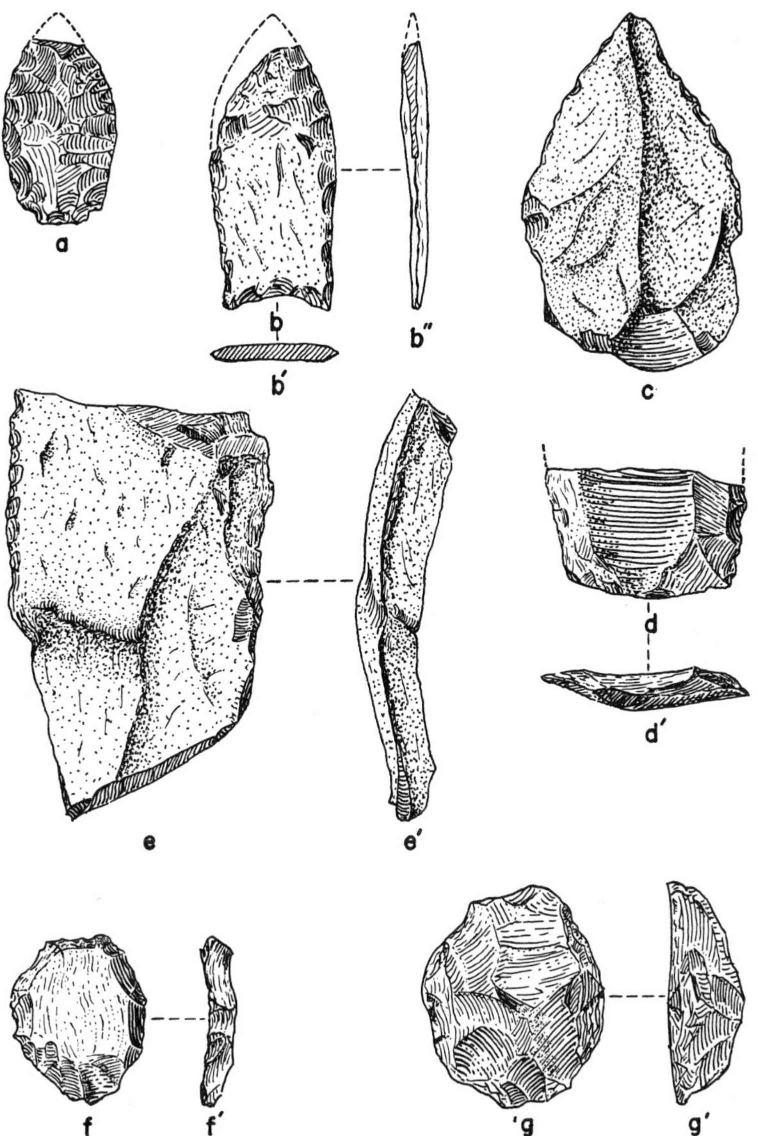

FIGURE 21. Implements from the volcanic debris layer. Projectile points, *a, b;* flake knives, *c, d;* curved knife, *e;* discoidal scrapers, *f, g: a,* quartz; *b-e, g,* basalt; *f,* obsidian. Length of *c,* 72 mm.

less all-over chipping (Fig. 21, *f, g*). These range in diameter from 23 to 66 mm., the thickness varying from one-third to one-fourth the diameter.

The core scrapers are small (maximum diameter 38 mm.), irregular, thick, and less perfectly chipped than the discoidal type (Fig. 22, a). The working edge extends over a relatively short distance along one of the sharper margins.[4]

Most numerous of the side scrapers are those of irregular form. These were made of any convenient flake, one margin of which could be dressed down (Fig. 22, *b-e*). The edges may be quite straight but more often are convex and the chipping is steep. Lengths: 28 to 63 mm.

The oval type differs from the above in that the chipping extends around the entire circumference and, like the discoidal scraper, they have a flat unworked and a convex chipped face (Fig. 22, *f, g*). Lengths: 32 to 63 mm.

Perhaps the most precisely made tools are the long side scrapers (Fig. 23, *a, b*). These were fashioned from selected long flakes by percussion flaking, restricting the process to the convex face of the blade. The long edges were given most attention but in a few examples the chipping was carried around the ends as well, which were either rounded or moderately sharpened. Lengths: 46 to 80+ mm.

The hollow scrapers are thick flake tools with steep chipping (Fig. 23, *c, d*). None of the Ventana specimens shows the deep and narrow concavity illustrated for scrapers from Lindenmeier[5] and Sandia.[6] Lengths: 50 to 67 mm.

End scrapers (Fig. 24, *a, b*), while not abundant, are clear enough as a type. The basalt of which they are made permitted no fine retouch and, as a consequence, they lack the perfection seen in the "snub-nosed" scrapers from Folsom sites and those of better materials from higher levels within the cave. Lengths: 41 to 103 mm.

★

4. These resemble the domed discoidal scraper from the midden, but are less exactly made.

5. F. H. H. Roberts, Jr., 1936, Fig. 3, *b*.

6. F. C. Hibben and K. Bryan, 1941, Pl. 8, *d*.

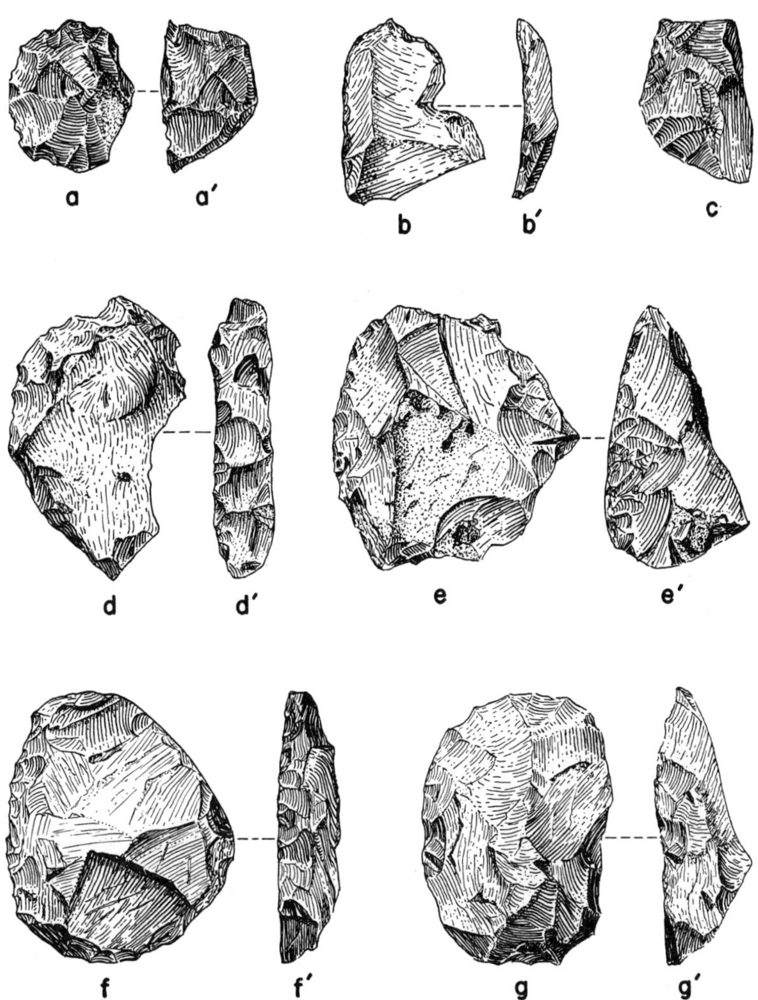

FIGURE 22. Scrapers from the volcanic debris layer. Small core, *a;* irregular side scrapers, *b-e;* oval, *f, g: a, d, e, g,* chert; *b, c, f,* basalt. Diameter of *f,* 63 mm.

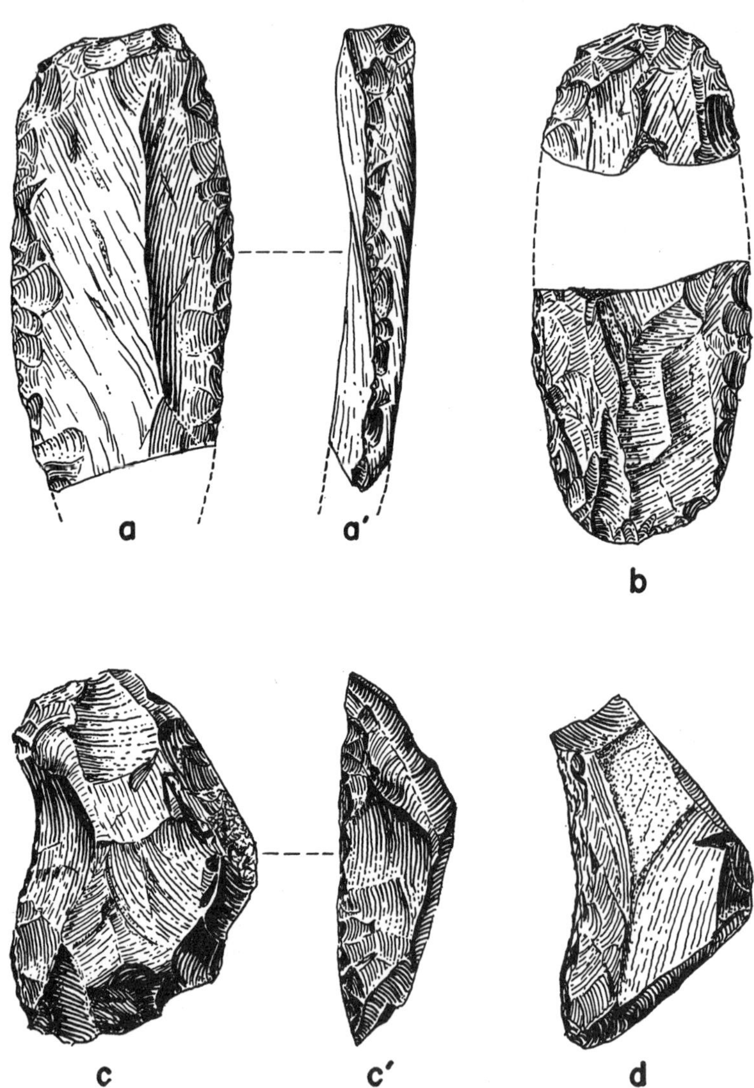

FIGURE 23. Scrapers from the volcanic debris layer. Long side, *a, b;* hollow, *c, d: a,* quartzite; *b-d,* basalt. Length of *a,* 80 mm.

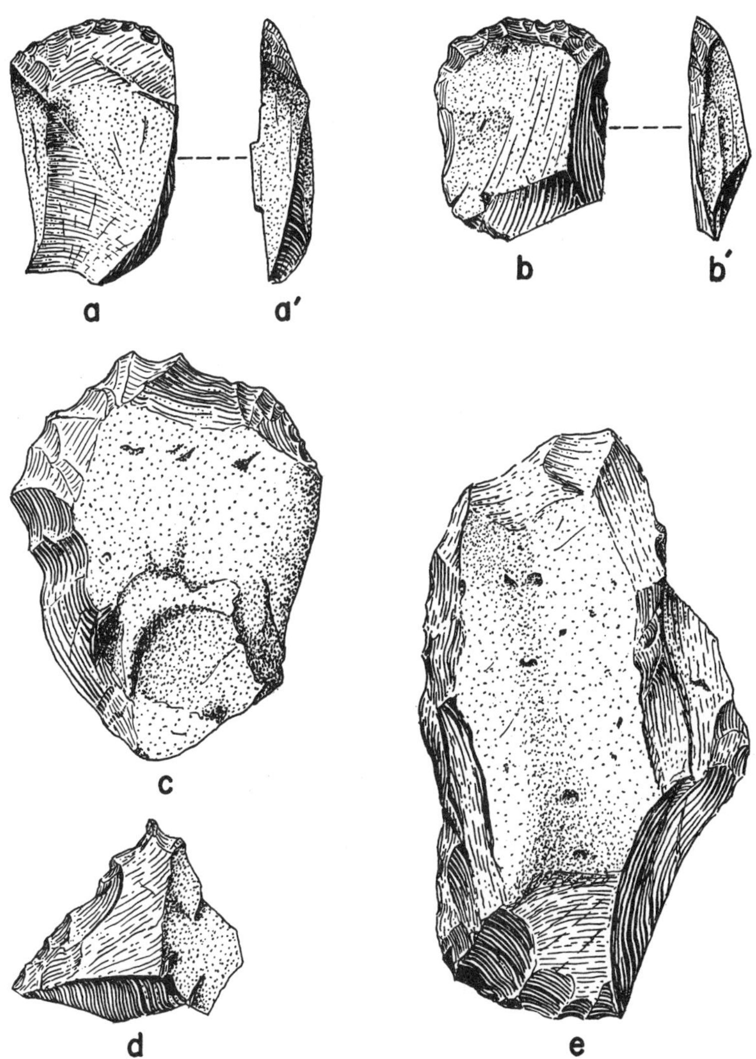

FIGURE 24. Implements from the volcanic debris layer. End scrapers, *a, b;* rough-flake scrapers, *c, e;* graver, *d: a, b, d, e,* basalt; *c,* chert. Length of *e,* 110 mm.

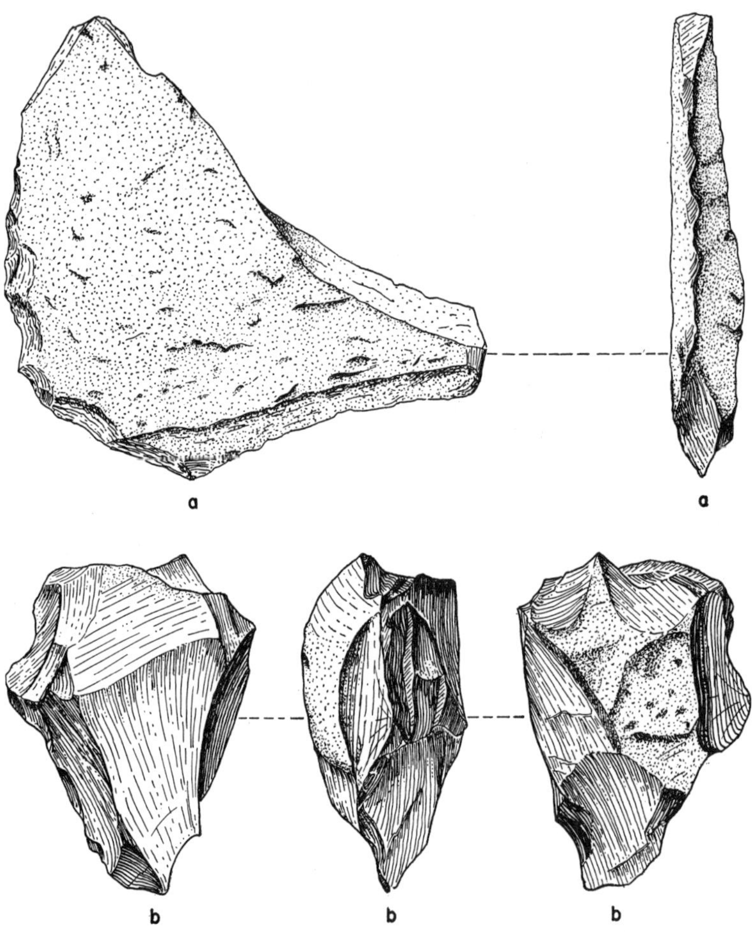

FIGURE 25. Choppers from the volcanic debris layer. Flake, *a;* core, *b:* both basalt. Length of *a,* 168 mm.

Implements with generalized scraper characteristics but too lacking in specific details to permit placing them in the above categories have been labelled as rough-flake scrapers. These were made of convenient large and thick flakes by jaggedly trimming down an edge (Fig. 24, *c, e*) so that all chips removed were from the convex side. Lengths: 60 to 115 mm.

D. *Gravers*—These tools were made of random flakes by working down one edge so as to leave a short point. One surface was bevelled by chipping while the other is flat and not modified (Fig. 24, *d*). Gravers of similar type but more varied in character occur also in the higher levels of Ventana Cave. Although designed for scratching hard surfaces, as bone, no such items were found in the volcanic debris layer. Lengths: 32 to 78 mm.

E. *Choppers*—Implements classed as choppers differ in thickness and in the extent of the chipping. The thin bi-face type was made of large flakes, one edge of which was sharpened by breaking flakes away from both faces (Fig. 25, *a*), whereas the thick type, of which there is but one example, is a core implement with all-over chipping (Fig. 25, *b*). This tool was clearly used as a chopper, the sharper and more jagged of the two edges having been used to do the work. Lengths: 96 to 168 mm.

F. *Planes*—These are cumbersome implements, made of angular rock which could be grasped in one hand. All have one flat face from which the chipping was directed along one edge as a means of sharpening (Fig. 26, *a*). None were modified around the entire margin producing the cone-shaped tools seen in later deposits. Rogers believes that tools of this sort were used as fleshing planes in dressing hides.[7] Evidently they have not been reported from Folsom sites. Diameters: 90 to 138 mm.

G. *Hammer stone*—The single specimen is a fragment of a stream pebble of hard crystalline rock, considerably battered.

H. *Grinding stone*—Evidence of grinding stones in this layer is limited to one mano. It is made of rhyolite, circular in outline

★

7. M. J. Rogers, 1939, p. 29.

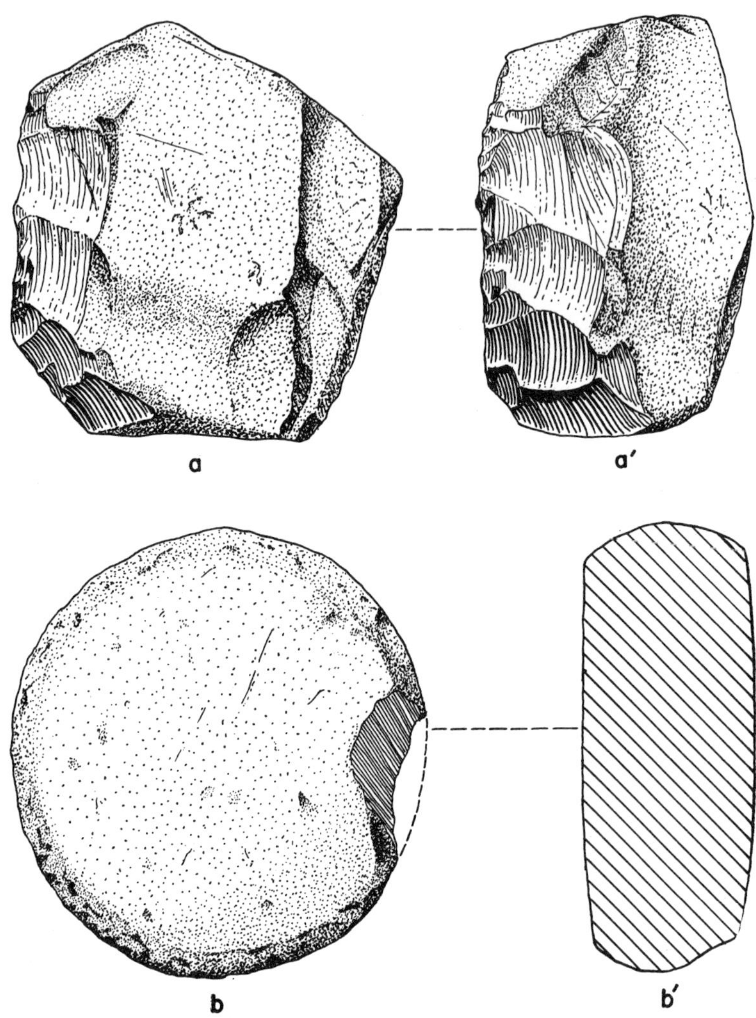

FIGURE 26. Implements from the volcanic debris layer. Plane, *a;* grinding stone, *b: a,* basalt; *b,* rhyolite. Diameter of *b,* 108 mm.

(diameter: 108 mm.) and has two work faces which give it an almost uniform thickness of 43 mm. (Fig. 26, *b*). The outer edge has been brought to shape by pecking, and the faces have been roughened by the same process. The flatness of the grinding surfaces would indicate that the implement was used on a perfectly flat nether stone or metate, but none were found.

The presence of this implement raises some interesting questions. It would appear first of all that that since there was only one, and since so many (about 1,350) were found in the midden above, this particular example might have drifted downward from later horizons. But this view must be dismissed because it was securely cemented in the volcanic debris matrix and because no others like it were found in higher levels. This specimen may be regarded, therefore, as a real associate of the other tools from the layer.

In view of the fact that the oldest grinding stones of the Cochise Culture from the Sulphur Springs Stage[8] are not of this type nor do they show the attention to shaping that this one does, it becomes all the more anomolous. Roberts[9] shows a granite rubbing stone of nearly circular form from Lindenmeier, but this appears to be single-faced and thin-edged.

While tools of this sort evidently did not enter prominently into the life of the early cave inhabitants as expressed in the remains, the people responsible for it were, nevertheless, well acquainted with the process of grinding. It may be regarded as a forecast of later times when, by preference or by force of changing environment, the people were more dependent upon a food-gathering economy.

Shell

It was somewhat of a surprise to find marine shells in the volcanic debris layer. At first it was thought that the few fragments recovered might not represent a true association; but, as time went on, repeated occurrences, well scattered through the layer and solidly cemented in it, erased all doubt.

★

8. E. B. Sayles and E. Antevs, 1941, p. 13.
9. F. H. H. Roberts, Jr., 1935, Pl. 16, g.

Of the forty-seven pieces recovered all represent fragments of a single species, *Cardium elatum* Sowerby, a familiar type in the late ruins of southern Arizona. These fragments obviously represent a smaller number of individuals than the total suggests, as some are doubtless from the same shell. It is an interesting fact that nearly all fragments are from large shells, measuring from about 100 to 160 mm. in diameter, while only three are from small individuals, probably in the neighborhood of 60 mm. in diameter. The fact that none of the fragments had been worked in any way, in contrast to the worked shell from higher levels, is also significant. These two details, the obvious selection of large shells and the lack of workmanship, give us some clue as to the possible use to which they were put. It may be suggested that they served as containers for liquids. Dating from a period long before knowledge of pottery in America and from a time for which there is no evidence of other types of containers, this assumption for a straight utilitarian use of shell is not unreasonable. The appreciation of shell as a medium for personal ornamentation did not come until about the time of the arrival of pottery and corn agriculture, insofar as the evidence from Ventana Cave is concerned.

The natural habitat of *Cardium elatum* includes the coast of California and also the whole of the Gulf of California. As Ventana Cave is only ninety air miles from Bahia de San Jorge, on the Gulf, it may be inferred that the shells came from there. This would mean that the early Ventana residents were acquainted with the coastal area personally or were in contact with other people who were already established there. In either event, the presence of shell in Ventana at this time suggests that research along the west coast of Mexico might well produce evidence of man as early as here.[10]

★

10. Mr. Julian Hayden, who has made several visits to the Tastiota-Libertad area, reports the presence of numerous shell middens, some with pottery and some without, the latter sometimes occurring at places now some distance from the sea, suggesting changing coastal conditions. One such midden produced stone implements which resemble those from the lower midden layers of Ventana Cave.

Discussion

What trend the interpretation of the implements from the volcanic debris layer takes depends first of all upon one's acceptance or rejection of the geologic implications of the layer. In consideration of the discussion already presented along this line by Bryan and Colbert, and in recognition of the early relative age of this material as dictated by the mass of overlying cultural material, there is no need for extended arguments establishing the validity of the implement-fauna association as might have been necessary a few years ago, when the studies of Early Man in the New World were meeting with blunt skepticism.

My position, therefore, is to accept the evidence as it stands, namely: (1) that the implements from the volcanic debris layer represent the oldest occupation level of the cave; (2) that their association with the bones of extinct animals is real, meaning that the people had the opportunity to, and probably did, hunt the larger game animals now extinct; (3) that moister climatic conditions prevailed which, according to Bryan, was between about 25,000 and 10,000 years ago.

We may now turn to the task of determining the cultural status. The accelerated research of recent years on America's first men has resulted in the identification of several culture types which existed in late glacial and early post-glacial times. The Sandia, Folsom, Cochise, and San Dieguito are but a few of the complexes. The equation of the oldest Ventana material with any of these must be based on a detailed comparison of both general and specific features, but we may, even then, have no absolute assurance that we are right in view of the double interpretation possible for some of the evidence.

Looking at the collection as a whole, and using the pre-pottery midden material as a standard of comparison, it would look as though these artifacts represent the products of a nearly true hunting culture. They were designed, almost without exception, to pierce, cut and scrape, to meet the needs of a hunting people. Implements designed for similar use were, of course, found in great profusion in the midden but these occurred with grinding tools in a ratio of about 2:1, indicating that the people of that level were heavily dependent on natural foods which needed preparation by grinding in addition to animal foods derived from their hunting pursuits. But in the volcanic debris layer only one grinding stone came to light, giving us a ratio of grinding to chipped tools of 1:89. No doubt these people relied on vegetal foods but evidently they had not yet reached the stage when many of the plants were converted into a more palatable form with implements we can recognize as designed for such work. At best, the economy may be described as hunting, food-gathering having been of lesser importance.

The implements represent a flake industry. Only a few, such as the bi-facial chopper shown in Figure 25, *b,* are core tools. Furthermore, 95 per cent of the specimens were flaked on one face only. As for percussion and pressure flaking, both processes were known.

This leaves the San Dieguito-Playa Complex of the Lower Colorado River Basin and the Folsom Culture of the Plains to be considered as possible correlatives of the Ventana remains with which we are now concerned. Before looking at the former it will be necessary to digress at this point to clarify the Southern Californian sequence as originally published by Rogers.[11] After visiting Ventana Cave and reviewing the collections from its successive layers of cultural debris, Rogers was convinced that changes were necessary because some of his complexes were represented at Ventana in different relationships, both temporally and culturally, than first constructed by his horizontal stratigraphical technique. A re-examination of his own material further persuaded him to make the revision which he has permitted me to include herewith (Table 12). This will be followed in the correlations of the culture complexes found in the younger deposits (midden), as well as the present material. Full particulars concerning this readjustment in the chronology will be awaited in a future report by Rogers.

★

11. M. J. Rogers, 1939.

TABLE 12

Revised correlation chart of Lower Colorado River Basin Cultures, according to M. J. Rogers

Old Sequence	*Revised Sequence*
Amargosa II	Basket Maker III (Lino Gray Intrusive)
Amargosa I	Amargosa III
Pinto-Gypsum	Amargosa II Amargosa I
Playa II	San Dieguito III
Playa I	San Dieguito II
Malpais	San Dieguito I

Looking now to the San Dieguito material and specifically Phase I:[12] This pattern is characterized by blades, planes, choppers, various plano-convex scrapers, and amulets. Rogers recognized a number of parallels between this assemblage and tools from the volcanic debris of Ventana Cave. He felt that the typological conformity was especially close in planes, choppers, knives, and, to a lesser extent, in some of the smaller tools, as the discoidal scrapers. The pattern conformity rests in the larger and bulkier percussion flaked tools, leaving a residue of traits which do not fit the western pattern. While this is not a very imposing list on which to base this correlation, the assignment seems to be the best possible at the present writing. One may adopt the stand, of course, that these were components common to a large part of the Southwest on an early time level and not necessarily indicative of the exact connections implied. Correlating the Ventana Complex with San Dieguito I chronologically presents the most serious problem. This will be dealt with elsewhere (p. 530). The associated fauna of San Dieguito I is not known.

★

12. M. J. Rogers, 1939, pp. 28-31.

The projectile points, where closer control over the material needed to be exercised, were pressure flaked, while, with a few possible exceptions, all other tools were shaped by percussion, making it the commoner of the two methods.

Before identification of the oldest Ventana remains is attempted, the culture groups of adjoining areas with which a possible relationship might be established should be reviewed. The Gypsum, Pinto, and Mohave Complexes may be eliminated by the lack of close parallels in the typology and more particularly because the analogies with these cultures occur in the specimens from the midden on a later time level. The Sulphur Springs Stage of the Cochise Culture may also be ignored, as the tools from that horizon were predominantly for grinding, and flaked implements were relatively scarce.[13] The Little Colorado River terrace material of north-central Arizona is, as yet, too imperfectly known to allow any direct comparison. Most of the tools illustrated by Bartlett would appear to be cores with bifacial chipping.[14] The recently discovered Sandia Culture may be accepted as both older and different from the material with which we are here concerned.[15]

For comparative information from the Folsom Culture we may now turn to the Lindenmeier site, of northern Colorado, which offers the best picture. Roberts has summarized the percentage occurrences of the implements as to type, based on a sample of 750 specimens.[16] These are arranged with the percentages of the Ventana specimens below, as based on a sample of ninety tools.

Implement Types	*Lindenmeier*	*Ventana*
Projectile points	11.3%	2.2%
Scrapers	32.8	70.0
Gravers	5.6	3.3
Chisel gravers	1.0	

★

13. E. B. Sayles and E. Antevs, 1941, p. 27. From Sayles' table it is clear that twelve grinding tools were found for every chipped implement.

14. K. Bartlett, 1942, pp. 37-41.

15. F. C. Hibben and K. Bryan, 1941.

16. F. H. H. Roberts, Jr., 1936, p. 34. These figures will doubtless be changed somewhat when the results of his later work has been added.

Knives	3.0	12.2
Large blades	6.3	
Choppers	0.5	3.3
Hammer stones	0.8	1.1
Planes		6.6
Rubbing stones	4.0	1.1
Flakes	19.0	(no figures)
Channel flakes	13.6	
Rubbed hematite	1.6	
Worked bone	.5	

As the scrapers in both collections outnumber all other types, these may be compared in greater detail, as follows:

Scraper Type	*Lindenmeier*	*Ventana*
Side	56.0%	58.7% (all sub-types)
Snub-nosed	26.6	
End	2.4	7.9
Discoidal		11.1
Core (small)		4.7
Broken	13.4	
Rough flake		17.4

The first list shows some discrepancies in the case of points, scrapers, and knives, as to absolute percentages but the pattern seems to run much the same. Several absences in the Ventana Complex should be noted: chisel gravers, large blades, hematite, and worked bone, while the planes are missing in the Lindenmeier series. None of these differences would appear to be serious handicaps in drawing a favorable comparison as some are naturally to be expected in sites about seven hundred miles apart and occurring in wholly different environments.

In the scraper class, the side-scraper type occurs with almost identical frequency. Long double-edged examples, as pictured in Figure 23, *a*, are about the same as tools illustrated from Lindenmeier.[17] These, it should be pointed out, have no exact parallels in higher levels of Ventana Cave nor among the San

★

17. *Ibid.*, Pl. 7, *d;* H. M. Wormington, 1939, Pl. opposite p. 18, left center.

Dieguito tools. Snub-nosed forms, a refined end scraper, are much more prevalent in Lindenmeier than at Ventana and discoidal scrapers are evidently not represented at all in Lindenmeier Folsom. The "broken" category of Roberts and the Ventana "rough flake" type may overlap to some extent and it is probably here that the difference is largely a matter of classification. Gravers are present in both sites, although those of the Folsom Culture are both more numerous and better made.

Roberts further indicates[18] that slightly less than 1.5 per cent of the Lindenmeier artifacts were core tools as measured against about 10.0 per cent for Ventana. This difference is largely due to the presence of planes, classified as core tools, which were lacking at Lindenmeier.

Another difference was the use of marine shells at Ventana and the lack of it at Lindenmeier. Accessibility to the supply for the occupants of Ventana is obviously the answer.

However this comparison may be regarded, there is no denying that, in general, the essential components of Lindenmeier Folsom are also represented at Ventana. One exception to this is the absence of the true Folsom point. But as already explained, the poor quality of rock of which most of the Ventana artifacts were made reduced the possibility of manufacturing fluted points. In place of it we have the one already described (Fig. 21, *b*) which, apart from the lack of fluting, must certainly be regarded as closely akin to the Folsom point.

It is not enough to use only the cultural material in this attempted correlation. Supporting lines of evidence must also be employed. Fortunately such evidence is available and its character is wholly in keeping with the cultural indications.

Bryan recognizes the layer of volcanic debris as reflecting moist conditions and has related its origin to late glacial times, or before ten thousand years ago, thereby assigning an age to the Ventana Complex on geological grounds which brings it within the period of time the Folsom Culture is believed to have existed.

★

18. *Ibid.*, p. 34.

The fauna of the volcanic debris layer has certain striking parallels and some dissimilarities with the faunal assemblages of other Folsom sites. A comparison is made below (Table 13), giving only the extinct forms.

Comparisons of this sort are not critical, of course, in evaluating exact contemporaneity of cultures. What does come out of it, however, is a certain common denominator which indicates that a similar pattern of animal forms was known to all groups. Four of the extinct Ventana genera are represented in other sites

TABLE 13

EXTINCT FAUNA ASSOCIATED WITH THE FOLSOM CULTURE IN FIVE SITES (Colorado and New Mexico) AS COMPARED WITH THE FAUNA ASSOCIATED WITH THE VENTANA COMPLEX

Species	*Lindenmeier (Colorado)*[1]	*Folsom (New Mexico)*[1]	*Sandia (New Mexico)*[2]	*Clovis (New Mexico)*[1]	*Burnet Cave (New Mexico)*[1]	*Ventana (Arizona)*[3]
Bison sp.				x		x
Bison oliverhayi		x?				
Bison antiquus taylori					x	
Bison taylori	x	x	x*			
Camelops sp.			x	x	x	
Parelephas cf. *columbi*				x		
Elephas sp.			x			
Equus tau					x	
Equus occidentalis			x*			x
Equus cf. *excelsus*				x	x	
Nothrotherium shastense						x
Nothrotherium sp.			x			
Tetrameryx onusrosagris					x	x
Preptoceras sinclairi neomexicana					x	
Canis dirus						x
Arctodus sp.					x	
Rangifer ? fricki					x	
Euceratherium collinum morrisi					x	
Tapirus sp.						x

1. E. H. Sellards, 1940.
2. F. C. Hibben and K. Bryan, 1941, p. 33.
3. E. H. Colbert, p. 126 herein.
* Near but not identical.

and two, tapir and dire wolf, so far, are unreported from Folsom sites. On the whole, therefore, the faunal association of the Ventana Complex supports the typological evidence of that relationship.

Summing up the foregoing discussion, the following conclusions may be reached:

(1) The artifacts from the volcanic debris layer of Ventana Cave, while not duplicating either the Folsom or the San Dieguito pattern, show parallels with both as to implement types and generally as to complexes, and are nearer these cultures than to any others now known.

(2) The implement-bearing layer dates from a wet cycle, which Bryan places at before ten thousand years ago, and is, therefore, within the time range when Folsom is judged to have existed. The assumed age of San Dieguito, about 1,000 to 2,000 B.C.,[19] is in sharp conflict with the Ventana date.

(3) The implements occur with a faunal assemblage of late Pleistocene or Early Recent character, and excepting the tapir and dire wolf, these were the animals also known to Folsom Man, together with some others not represented in Ventana.

Two other questions need to be answered before leaving this subject: (1) How much duplication is there in the implements from the layers later in Ventana and those from the volcanic debris layer? (2) What does the evidence suggest as to the intensity of occupation during the time the volcanic debris layer was forming?

In answer to the first question, those tools which are not exactly duplicated are: both projectile points,[20] curved flake knives, long, double-edged side scrapers, and the discoidal, bifacial grinding stone. All other forms are duplicated to a greater or lesser extent, although certain minor differences, as a smaller kind of concave scraper in later levels, may be noted. In consideration of the large sample of artifacts from above the vol-

★

19. M. J. Rogers, 1939, p. 74.

20. Similar points, of course, were found (Figs. 53, *a* and 55, *i*), but all lack the specific characters of these.

canic debris layer, it is surprising that the duplication was not complete. Further, what this does not show is the high frequency of traits in the upper levels which are totally absent in the bottom layer. Some idea of this will be had from a review of the next section of this report. Hence, one is inclined to regard the Ventana Complex material as an entity even from the standpoint of an intra-cave comparison.

Turning to the second question, several conditions may be interpreted as showing that the use of the cave during the time of volcanic debris formation was rather spasmodic. In the first place, the deposit was built up by a periodic flooding of the cave floor, a situation which would not allow permanent occupation. Secondly, the traces of culture were not abundant, compared, at least, to the wealth of material in the midden above. It would appear, then, that man entered the cave only occasionally, between wettings, using it as a stopping place, possibly, on hunting excursions. During such times he built fires, cooked his food, made implements, and left some behind. The single grinding stone is not the type of implement which would be regularly carried around, so some extended periods of use may be indicated.

THE YOUNGER DEPOSITS

Before proceeding with the analysis of the material culture from the higher and later deposits of Ventana Cave, namely, the red sand, talus, and midden, attention should be called once again to the fact that a considerable lapse of time is indicated between the ending of the formation of the volcanic debris layer and the beginning of the accumulation of the overlying materials. Obviously, this has a direct bearing on the cultural problem. During this interim, the climate changed from relatively moist toward modern conditions, an indeterminate amount of the hardened volcanic debris layer was worn away, certain animals became extinct or they migrated from the area, and the culture type changed.

The Red Sand

Like the volcanic debris layer, the products of this deposit should be presented as a unit because it represents a clear cut stratigraphic entity. The red sand is significant culturally because from it were recovered projectile points of a distinctive form, unmixed with other types as was the case higher in the cave fill. The implement complex may thus be regarded as being relatively pure, thereby providing a cultural stage of some diagnostic value.

This sand was limited to the area at the foot of the shoulder, covering a space of about 7 x 8 m. As previously shown, it may have had a water-borne origin, the source having been from the talus outside the cave, to the south. Much of the sand appears to have been removed by erosion subsequent to its formation. Only about three cubic meters remained. The time element involved in both the deposition and cutting need not have been long. The associated fauna was modern in character.

Remains attributable to man are of three kinds: stone tools, marine shell, and bone.

Stone

The stone tools, numerous (54) for the amount of sand, were crusted with lime, but not so heavily as those from the volcanic debris. The classification is as follows:

A. Projectile points and knives 21

- 1. Not stemmed (leaf-shaped), 4
  - a. Flake, little chipping, 1
  - b. Secondary chipping, both faces, 3
- 2. Stemmed, 17
  - a. Leaf-shaped, 1
  - b. Parallel-sided stem, 11
    - (1) Not serrated, 5
    - (2) Serrated, 6
  - c. Expanding stem, 5
    - (1) Narrower than blade, 4
    - (2) Wider than blade, 1

B. Knives[1] 7
    1. Flake, little chipping, 6
    2. Bi-facial blade (fragment), 1

C. Scrapers 22
    1. Discoidal (uni-face) (Fig. 39, *a*), 3
    2. Side, 13
        a. Irregular (Fig. 30, *g*), 4
        b. Keeled (Fig. 32, *h*), 4
        c. Elongate (Fig. 33, *c*), 5
    3. End (Fig. 36, *b*), 2
    4. Rough flake (Fig. 32, *a*), 4

D. Planes 4
    1. Oval, worked entirely around margin (Fig. 28, *c*), 1
    2. Elongate, one edge worked (Fig. 28, *e*), 3

Total 54

Shell

The five shell fragments, all unworked, are from large individuals of *Cardium elatum*. This duplicates the evidence already given for the volcanic debris layer. Whether these represent odd pieces picked up from the weathered surface of the volcanic debris or whether they actually indicate use of shell as utility articles during the time the red sand formed cannot be said.

Bone

Only one bone tool was found in this layer, a sawed metapodial awl of medium length (Fig. 86, *j*).

Discussion

It is doubtful whether the implements from the red sand represent all of the types which go with the complex. No grinding stones were present. In fact, it is noteworthy that few large

★

1. Since the collection of red sand implements is small and contains only types duplicating those found in larger numbers in the midden, no descriptive analysis will accompany this tabulation. The figure references are to examples from other layers, but which duplicate the specimens from the red sand.

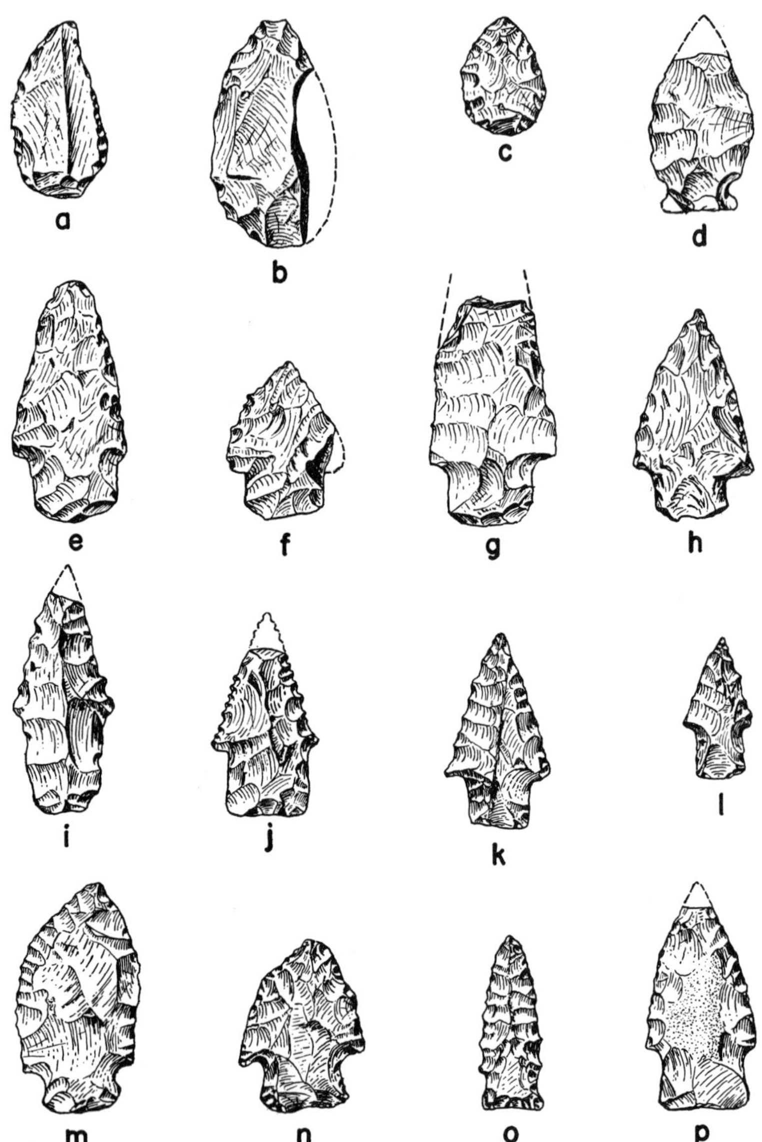

FIGURE 27. Blades and projectile points from the red sand layer. Leaf-shaped, not stemmed, *a-c;* leaf-shaped, stemmed, *d;* stemmed parallel-sided, *e-l;* stem expanding, *m-p. a, b, d, e, g, i, j, l, p,* basalt; *c, f, n,* obsidian; *h,* quartz; *k, o,* chert; *m,* jasper. Length of *e,* 48 mm.

implements of any sort occurred, possibly due to the thinness of the deposit. Those protruding above the surface may have been thrown to the side by the occupants who had occasion to walk over the surface of the red sand before further material had accumulated. Whatever the explanation for this may be, it is of less importance than the light which the layer in question throws on the earliest projectile point type of the younger deposits.

These points, nearly all of which are illustrated in Figure 27, were markedly uniform as to type. Excluding the leaf-shaped type (*a-d*) the main characteristics are: a triangular-shaped blade with parallel-sided or slightly expanding stem, base straight or somewhat rounded, edges occasionally serrated (*e-p*). In general, the type may be equated with the Pinto points from California.[21] There is, however, one singular difference. This is the absence of basal notching, which seems to run fairly uniformly in the Californian series. Typical Pinto points occur in Ventana in the pre-pottery midden layer, and these, on stratigraphic evidence, may be taken to be somewhat later than those from the red sand. It would appear, therefore, that the red sand culture is an early stage of Rogers' revised Amargosa I development. It should be pointed out that leaf-shaped points are also a part of Amargosa I and that examples *m* and *p* of Figure 27, evidently less typical, are duplicated also in the California collections.[22]

Rogers has informed me that the association of the red sand type of point with the standard Pinto type in California led him to suspect two developmental phases, but because neither of these had been isolated or found without the other he did not consider his evidence as adequate proof of the fact. The occurrence of both phases in Ventana in stratigraphic succession, the earlier in the red sand and the later in the midden, bears out his suspicion. The red sand complex therefore is labelled as Amargosa I and stands as the only pure manifestation of it now

★

21. E. W. C. and W. H. Campbell, 1935, Pl. 13; M. J. Rogers, 1939, Pl. 13.

22. E. W. C. and W. H. Campbell, 1935, Pl. 14, *f*; M. J. Rogers, 1939, Pl. 13, *t*.

known. To facilitate reference, the red sand point will be called the Ventana-Amargosa type.[23]

Such points were also found in the lower zone of the midden deposit, but here they were mixed with a variety of other types. The former may have been derived from the intermingling of the occupational trash accumulating during and after the period of sand formation but in parts of the cave not affected by the sand; or the mixture may represent the survival of the type into later times, a situation suggested by the Californian occurrences.

The tools, other than points, manifest no worthy departure from those described from the lower portion of the midden and, for the most part, they also duplicate the Pinto Basin collection (grinding stones excepted)[24] which can be assigned to Amargosa I.

The Talus Wedge

After the erosion of the red sand, conditions were such as to cause the talus from outside the cave to grow rapidly and a tongue of it advanced nearly to the back wall (Fig. 12, 5). Although a part of the mass in the talus was large angular rocks, there is ample evidence that man was intensively using the cave during this period. Beyond the area affected by the talus, the cave floor was more or less clear of rocks, and it was here that the actual living took place. To get to the spring from the lower part of the upper cave, traffic had to go over the talus. Evidence of hearths in the boulder-strewn talus and a few scattered implements are indications of this. Away from the talus and simultaneously with its invasion, the cave floor was slowly rising by the accumulation of trash. Because of this, no separate analysis is

★

23. Since the above was written, Harrington (1948) has presented his final work on the Borax Lake Site. Prominent among the projectiles from this station is the Borax Lake type, which bears a striking similarity to the Ventana-Amargosa type. The Borax Lake Complex is dated at the end of the Great or Provo-Pluvial, some ten thousand years ago. This is earlier than the presumed age of the red sand in Ventana, which formed during or after the early part of the post-pluvial. If the dating for both sites is correct, and the evident similarity of the projectile points actually connotes a cultural relationship, then the Ventana-Amargosa point must indeed be regarded as of Californian derivation.

24. E. W. C. and W. H. Campbell, 1935.

deemed significant of the few implements from the talus and these have been combined with the general lot of midden material from the same levels.

The Midden Layer

The bulk of the cave deposits were the direct result of man's intense use of the shelter. Trash began to accumulate after the erosion of the red sand and simultaneously with the encroaching tongue of the talus. This continued through the centuries to recent times. The greatest depth of occupational debris was toward the northeastern end of the cave with a thickness of about three meters.

As already stated, physical zones are recognizable in the midden (Fig. 8): (a) the upper layer, consisting of dust-dry refuse; and (b) the lower layer, slightly moist, and in which no organic materials have survived. The moisture line, as such, has no cultural significance, although in the analysis it would appear to have because of the richer complement of remains above it.

Profiles of the midden deposit illustrated in Figures 9 and 10 show a number of minor changes, as ash and rock concentrations, and trodden surfaces over small areas. Beyond illustrating the direction of slope of the cave floor during its growth, no stratigraphy helpful in the segregation of cultural levels was apparent. There were no uniform layers dating from any given occupation period and no evidence of an hiatus as might be indicated by a sharp change in material or by a sterile layer. Use of the cave appears to have been more or less continuous. Lacking physical guides in the composition of the trash, it becomes necessary to analyze the artifacts from the midden on a straight quantitative, typological, and depth basis. In the following pages, implements have been grouped according to type, accompanied by the best possible interpretation of their persistence through time as indicated by depth and as to those which occur with other types forming complexes. The earliest appearances of traits, as in the case of pottery, naturally is of vital importance, and such facts will be especially brought out. Disturbances in the trash were apparent in some areas. This was due to the work of rodents and to the activity of man himself. The upper dry zone suffered particularly in this respect in the digging of graves for the thirty-nine burials, doubtless causing much of the mixture of pottery types reported elsewhere. It is recognized that some of this mixture could well be the result of the arbitrary system of excavation by section, any one of which might include both younger and older debris. But where visible lines of separation are lacking there is no other alternative.

In spite of these shortcomings in the clarity of the midden stratification and in method of removal, the quantity of specimens available for analysis and therefore the repetition of the evidence probably eliminates fictitious situations to a large degree.

Stone Implements

The collection of stone comprises 11,288 items. Fully 75 per cent of these were made of basalt, the material available locally in unlimited quantity. Quartzite, chert, chalcedony, jasper, rhyolite, and obsidian are also represented but most of these are foreign to the immediate area.

For ready comparison and to outline the analysis which follows, the classification and enumeration of the main categories of stone objects is given herewith. The percentage figures are useful only in assessing the relative abundance of a tool type with respect to others as aggregates from all levels.

Flaked Stone Implements			7,329	65.0%
Flaked on one face only		3,184	43.4%	
Planes	230	7.2%	3.1	
Scrapers	2,706	85.0	36.9	
Flake knives	156	4.9	2.1	
Gravers	92	2.9	1.3	
Flaked on two or more faces		4,145	56.6%	
Flake knives	80	1.9	1.1	
Blanks	89	2.1	1.2	
Ovoids	110	2.6	1.5	
Discoidals	90	2.1	1.2	
Choppers	762	18.4	10.4	
Hammer stones	885	21.4	12.1	
Hoes	11	.3	.2	
Projectile points and knives	2,062	49.8	28.1	
Drills	54	1.3	.8	
Four-pointed objects	2	.1	.0	

Ground and Pecked Stone Implements (by use or by intentional shaping)		3,885	34.4%
Metates (whole and fragmentary)	2,287	58.8%	
Manos	1,355	34.8	
Mortars	2	.1	
Pestles	114	2.9	
Rubbing stones	18	.4	
Vessels	2	.1	
Rasps	14	.4	
Knives	2	.1	
Ground edge scrapers	35	.9	
Axes	2	.1	
Palettes	12	.3	
Discs	24	.6	
Pipes	4	.1	
Pendants	1	.0	
Nose plugs	2	.1	
Rings	2	.1	
Ball	1	.0	
Bead	1	.0	
Other worked stone	7	.2	
Miscellaneous		74	.6%
Lap stones	22	29.7	
Worked stones	45	60.8	
Painted stones	7	9.5	
Minerals			

Implements Flaked on One Face Only

Taken as a whole the chipped stone implements from the midden represent 7,329 specimens. Of these, 43.4 per cent show chipping on one face only. This is in sharp contrast to the implements from the volcanic debris where this category amounted to 95 per cent of all tools found. This difference is caused chiefly by the exceptionally large number of projectiles from the midden and the rarity of the same in the volcanic debris.

It is the general rule in Ventana material that when tools were chipped on one face they were made mostly of flakes. Considerable variability is seen in the thickness of the flakes, however, and some approach core status. Large primary flakes and the smaller ones resulting from finer work were adapted to a limited number of main types of tools and one of these, scrapers, has an uncommonly large number of subtypes.

Planes—A numerically small group of implements (3.1 per cent of all flaked tools), but showing considerable range in size and form, have been termed planes. The chief characteristics are thickness, a flat nether face which served as a striking platform, steep flaking from this face producing an upper conical or strongly convex face, and an outline varying from round to elongate. Tools of this sort were evidently intended to be used as push or pull planes, the flat face held more or less parallel to the material being worked. The smaller examples, rarely over 70 mm. in diameter, described by Rogers from the Phase I of the San Dieguito Playa Complex (now Amargosa I) of the Lower Colorado River and neighboring desert areas, have been specifically designated by him as scraper-planes, while the larger ones, especially those from the Pinto-Gypsum (Amargosa II) Complex, he labelled as pulping planes.[25] Functionally, they appear to be much the same, probably used in removing excess tissue and fat from hides and likely in the preparation of certain plant foods. Where a distinction is necessary in the Ventana collection, is in the smaller examples, 40 mm. or less in diameter. The downward grading in size drops appreciably from about 50 to 30 mm. with few representatives and the number then increases to make a small group between 18 and 30 mm. in diameter. Although identical in form these small replicas were grasped differently than the larger ones, *i. e.,* between thumb and forefinger instead of a full hand grasp; and they were quite consistently made of different materials which further strengthens the feeling that they should be treated separately. (See under Scrapers: domed discoidal, oval, and irregular.)

The Ventana planes were made either of thick flakes or cores which had a large bulbar scar. Using this face as a striking platform the edge was dressed down in a steep-flake technique[26] by percussion. Trimming sometimes extended entirely around the perimeter and more often only part way around, the striking platform becoming the base of the tool. Flaking ranges from the removal of rough large flakes to secondary dressing. Forms are round to elongate and the upper surface typically is conical or strongly domed. In some instances, the upper surface is quite

★

25. M. J. Rogers, 1939, pp. 29, 50.
26. See J. A. Barbieri, 1937, pp. 101-102, for further details on manufacture.

flat, representing the unmodified surface of the original flake. The thickness is usually about the equivalent of two-thirds of the diameter, ranging, however, from one-half to nearly equal the diameter.

Materials are almost exclusively basalt and other dense volcanic rocks.

The size range for planes including all subtypes is from 50 mm. to 122 mm., with an average diameter of about 80 mm. There appears to be no consistent difference in size between subtypes.

Based on form, the extent and placement of edge trimming, the 230 planes from Ventana are classifiable as follows:

Round[1]		88	38.3%
1. Viewed from top.			
Trimmed entirely around edge (Fig 28, *a*)	29	33.0%	12.6
Trimmed part way around edge (Fig. 28, *b*)	59	67.0	25.7
Oval		35	15.2%
Trimmed entirely around edge (Fig. 28, *c*)	28	80.0	12.2
Trimmed part way around edge (Fig. 28, *d*)	7	20.0	3.0
Elongate		103	44.8%
Trimmed on one edge only (Fig. 28, *e*)	74	71.8	32.2
Trimmed on one end (Fig. 28, *f*)	17	16.5	7.4
Trimmed on two sides and one end (Fig. 28, *g*)	12	11.7	5.2
Pebble planes (Fig. 28, *h*)		4	1.7%

Table 14 expresses quantitatively the distribution of planes through the successive levels of the midden from both cave units. It also shows the relative abundance of subtypes. For comparative purposes, frequencies within the red sand and volcanic debris layers are indicated but not included in the analysis. For the upper cave the following facts become evident: (1) The plane was a component in the cultural complex of each successive midden level.[27] (2) That they occurred in greatest numbers in levels 3 to 6 or in the mid-zone of the pre-pottery trash deposit. (3) The trend in the lower cave duplicates that of the upper cave, giving some measure of support to the above conclusion that planes are strongly diagnostic of the gathering-hunting people of pre-pottery times.

★

27. Excepting level 8, present only in a very small section of the cave.

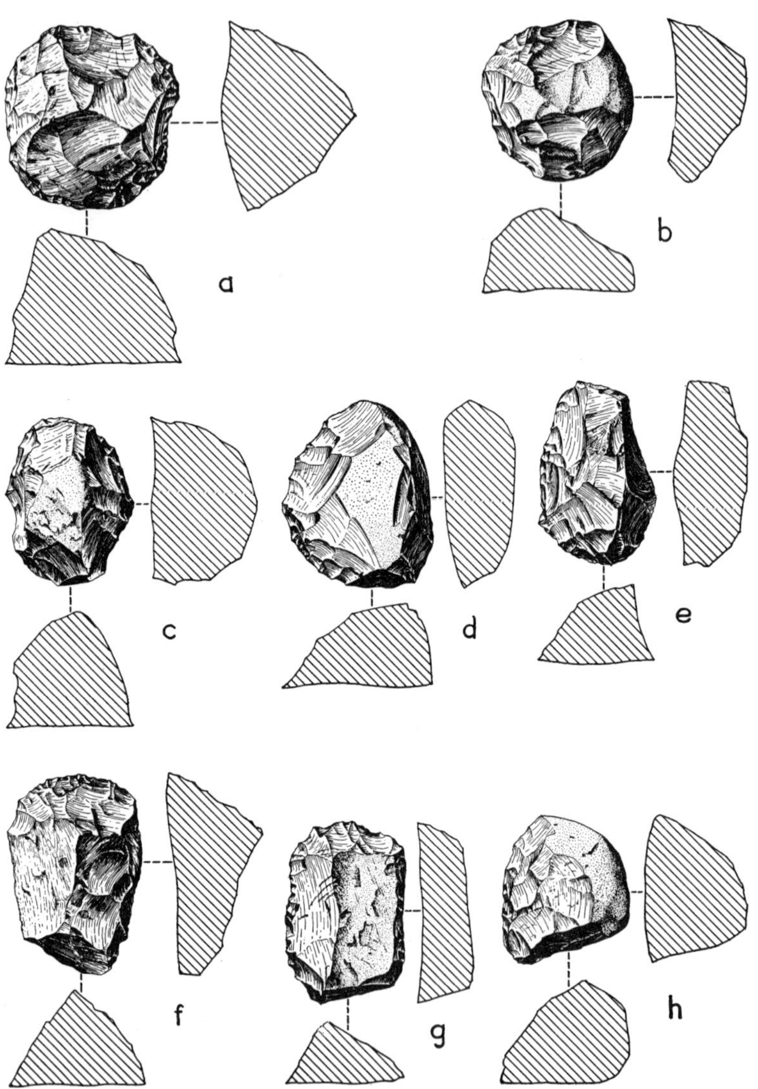

FIGURE 28. Planes from the midden. Round: trimmed entirely around edge, *a;* trimmed part way around edge, *b*. Oval: trimmed entirely around edge, *c;* trimmed part way around edge, *d*. Elongate: trimmed one edge, *e;* trimmed one end, *f;* trimmed two sides, one end, *g;* pebble, *h; h,* quartzite, all others basalt. Diameter of *a,* 94 mm.

Table 14

DISTRIBUTION OF PLANES IN MIDDEN LEVELS OF UPPER AND LOWER CAVES

Cave	Stratigraphic Layer	Levels	Round: Trimmed all around	Round: Trimmed partly	Oval: Trimmed all around	Oval: Trimmed partly	Elongate: One edge trimmed	Elongate: One end trimmed	Elongate: One end and two sides trimmed	Pebble planes	Totals	Percent of all types to level
Upper Cave	*Midden*	1	2 8.3	3 7.5	2 10.5		7 12.1	2 16.7	1 10.0	1 25.0	18	10.5
		2		2 5.0	1 5.3		6 10.3				9	5.2
		3	2 8.3	5 12.5	5 26.3	1 20.0	8 14.0	3 25.0	1 10.0		25	14.5
		4	9 37.5	9 22.5	5 26.3	3 60.0	12 20.6		3 30.0	1 25.0	42	24.4
		5	4 16.7	11 27.5	3 15.8		10 17.3	2 16.7	4 40.0		34	19.8
		6	4 16.7	6 15.0	1 5.3	1 20.0	12 20.6	3 25.0	1 10.0		28	16.2
		7	1 4.2	1 2.5			1 1.7	2 16.7			5	2.9
		8										
		Miscel.	2 8.3	3 7.5	2 10.5		2 3.4			2 50.0	11	6.3
		Totals	24	40	19	5	58	12	10	4	172	
		Pct.	13.9	23.3	11.0	2.9	33.8	7.0	5.8	2.3		
	Red Sand				1		3				4	
	Volcanic Debris			1			5				6	
Lower Cave	*Midden*	1		3 15.8		1 50.0	3 18.8				7	12.1
		2	2 40.0	2 10.5	3 33.3		2 12.5				9	15.6
		3	2 40.0	6 31.6	5 55.5		7 43.8	2 40.0	1 50.0		23	39.7
		4		3 15.8			1 6.3	1 20.0	1 50.0		6	10.3
		5		1 5.3				1 20.0			2	3.4
		Miscel.	1 20.0	4 21.0	1 11.1	1 50.0	3 18.8	1 20.0			11	18.9
		Totals	5	19	9	2	16	5	2		58	
		Pct.	8.6	32.8	15.6	3.4	27.6	8.6	3.4			

Scrapers—Most numerous of all chipped stone implements in either of the two main flake tool categories were scrapers. They account for 85 per cent of the single face class and 36.9 per cent of the total chipped stone collection. This predominance highlights an important domestic pursuit, the dressing of hides. But scrapers may be put to a multitude of uses and do not, in my opinion, necessarily reflect specialization in the working of skin. Although many scrapers were certainly used in preparing hides, they would also be useful in fashioning wood, and some types in the collection would appear to have been designed for that medium. Wood was an important raw material among the Papago and specimens of wood were fairly abundant in the dry zone of the midden. While none have survived from the moist zone, it was there that the scrapers were most abundant and it may be guessed on this evidence that the pre-pottery people also found wood a handy material.

Tools classified as scrapers have the following characteristics: (1) one flat or nearly flat face, not modified by chipping; (2) one convex face, low or high, modified by retouching to produce the working edge. General form, size, placement of the retouching, and steepness or flatness of same, are the criteria for breaking down the lot into types. Specific uses evidently lead to the development of specialized types as, for example, the hollow and serrated forms. But in the main the gradation from one type to the other is so complete that classification called for many arbitrary decisions. The collection has been reduced to types:

Scrapers					2,706
I. Side scrapers				2,077	76.8%
A. Thin flake			475	23.0%	17.6
B. Thick flake			529	25.4	19.5
1. Small		465	88.0%	22.4	17.2
2. Large		64	12.0	3.0	2.4
C. Rough flake			182	8.7	6.7
D. Oval			157	7.6	5.8
1. Thin flake		87	55.4%	4.2	3.2
2. Keeled		70	44.6	3.4	2.6
E. Elongate			558	27.0	20.6
1. Thin flake		201	36.0%	9.8	7.4
2. Keeled		357	64.0	17.2	13.2
a. Edge partly chipped	195	55.0%		9.4	7.2

b. Edge entirely chipped	162	45.0	7.8	6.0
F. Pointed		75	3.6	2.8
1. Thin flake	45	60.0%	2.2	1.7
2. Keeled	30	40.0	1.4	1.1
G. Rectangular		80	3.8	3.0
1. Thin flake	43	54.0%	2.0	1.6
2. Keeled	37	46.0	1.8	1.4
H. Serrated		14	.6	.5
I. "Steep-edged"		7	.3	.3
II. End Scrapers			216	8.0%
A. Rough flake		113	52.3%	4.2
B. Keeled		44	20.4	1.6
C. Round nosed		26	12.0	1.0
D. Square nosed		33	15.3	1.2
III. Hollow scrapers			138	5.0%
A. Thin flake		44	32.0%	1.6
B. Thick flake		43	31.0	1.6
C. Keeled		33	24.0	1.2
1. Edge partly chipped	22	67.0%	16.0	.8
2. Edge entirely chipped	11	33.0	8.0	.4
D. Pointed		6	4.3	.2
E. End		12	8.7	.4
IV. Discoidal			187	6.9%
A. Thin flake, small		88	47.0%	3.3
B. Domed		67	36.0	2.5
C. Large		32	17.0	1.1
V. "Thumbnail"			88	3.3%

I. Side scrapers: (A. Thin flake)—Implements of this and the thick flake type represent the least specialized of the scrapers. They were evidently hurriedly made whenever there was need for one and as quickly discarded. Shape was largely determined by the form of the original flake. The working edge, straight or convex, nearly always pressure flaked, extends only a part way around the perimeter of the flake. Standard features are the thinness of the flake, seldom exceeding 15 mm., and flatness of the retouch, forming an acute angle (30 degrees or less) to the flat nether surface. Maximum lengths range from 14 mm. to 88 mm., the average being about 35 mm. The material is predominantly basalt but there is a recognizable higher proportion of chert, chalcedony, obsidian, and jasper than among most other types. Figure 29 illustrates the full range of thin flake side scrapers, and the distribution to level is given in Table 15.

This scraper type is too unspecialized to be of real diagnos-

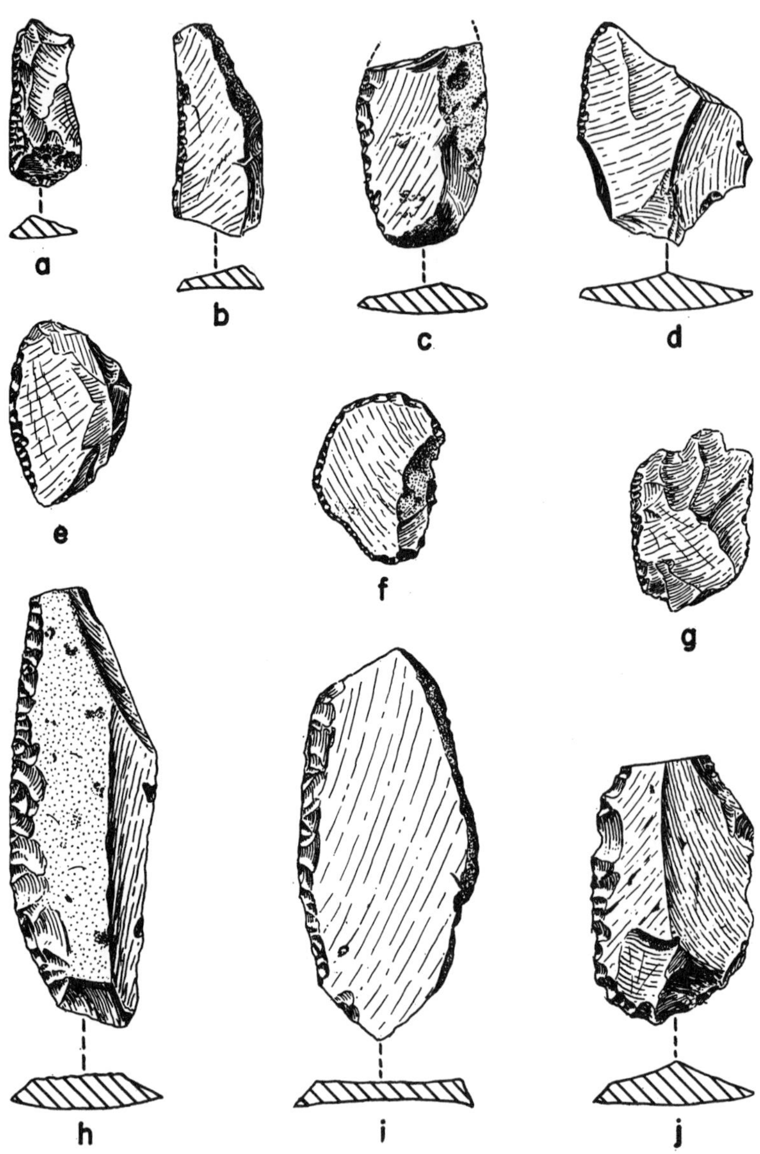

FIGURE 29. Implements from the midden. Thin flake side scrapers: *a-c, f,* chert; *d,* jasper; *e, h, j, i,* basalt; *g,* obsidian. Length of *h,* 88 mm.

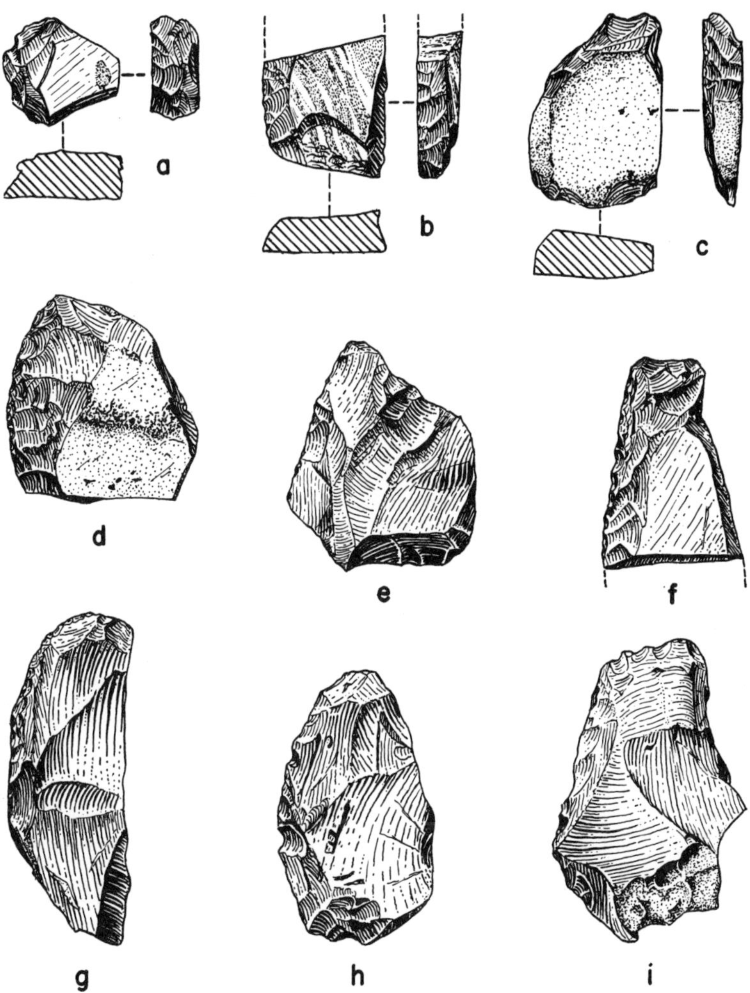

FIGURE 30. Implements from the midden. Small, thick flake side scrapers: *a, f-h,* (basalt); *b,* (quartzite); *c-e, i,* (chert). Length of *g,* 73 mm.

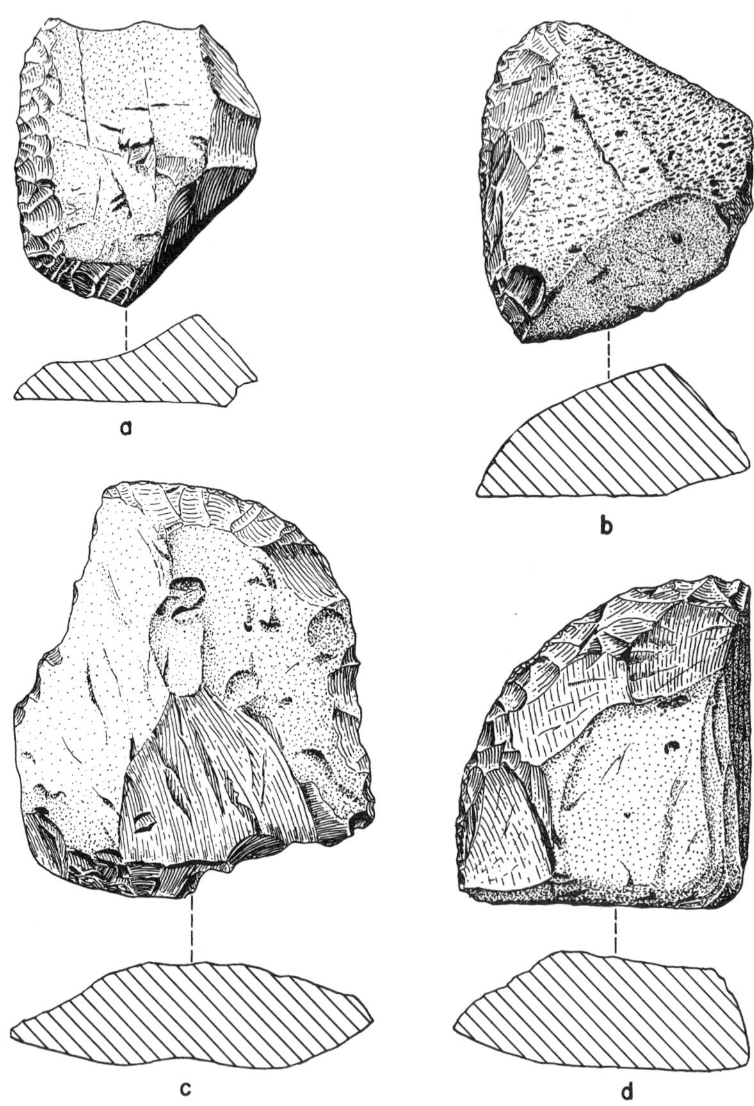

FIGURE 31. Implements from the midden. Large, thick flake side scrapers: *a,* (jasper); *b-d,* (basalt). Length of *c,* 105 mm.

Table 15

DISTRIBUTION OF SCRAPERS AS TO TYPE AND LEVEL

Table 15

DISTRIBUTION OF SCRAPERS AS TO TYPE AND LEVEL

	Stratigraphic Layer	*Levels*	*Side Scrapers*												
				Thick flake			*Oval*		*Elongate*			*Pointed*		*Rectangular*	
										Keeled					
			Thin flake	*Small*	*Large*	*Rough flake*	*Thin flake*	*Keeled*	*Thin flake*	*Edge partly chipped*	*Edge entirely chipped*	*Thin flake*	*Keeled*	*Thin flake*	*Keeled*
Upper Cave	*Midden*	1	96 23.6	79 21.2	4 11.1	29 20.6	11 15.5	6 10.0	35 20.8	27 17.3	11 9.2	13 31.0	5 23.8	3 8.6	1 2.9
		2	54 13.3	30 8.0	1 2.8	20 14.2	3 4.2	5 8.3	24 14.3	14 9.0	12 10.2	4 9.5	2 9.5	3 8.6	3 8.8
		3	50 12.3	38 10.2	6 16.7	18 12.8	9 12.7	7 11.7	15 8.9	16 10.3	10 8.5	3 7.1	1 4.8	7 20.0	3 8.8
		4	75 18.4	79 21.2	9 25.0	41 29.1	9 12.7	16 26.7	37 22.0	30 19.2	24 20.3	9 21.4	1 4.8	8 22.9	5 14.7
		5	54 13.3	73 19.5	4 11.1	14 9.9	14 19.7	12 20.0	18 10.7	27 17.3	34 28.8	6 14.3	5 23.8	8 22.9	7 20.6
		6	37 9.1	39 10.5	7 19.4	8 5.7	16 22.5	7 11.7	22 13.1	20 12.8	16 13.6	4 9.5	1 4.8	5 14.3	9 26.5
		7	26 6.4	19 5.1		3 2.1	6 8.5	2 3.3	8 4.8	13 8.3	6 5.1	1 2.4	3 14.3		4 11.8
		8	5 1.2	2 .5		1 .7			2 1.2	1 .6		2 4.8			
		Miscel.	10 2.5	14 3.8	5 13.9	7 4.9	3 4.2	5 8.3	7 4.2	8 5.1	5 4.2		3 14.3	1 2.9	2 5.9
		Totals	407	373	36	141	71	60	168	156	118	42	21	35	34
		Percent	18.5	16.9	1.6	6.4	3.2	2.7	7.6	7.1	5.4	1.9	.9	1.6	1.5
	Red Sand			4		4			4	5					
	Volcanic Debris			23		11	5				6				
Lower Cave	*Midden*	1	10 14.7	11 12.0	2 7.1	6 14.6	3 18.8		7 21.2	6 15.4	7 15.9		1 11.1	2 25.0	
		2	10 14.7	16 17.4	7 25.0	5 12.2	2 12.5	1 10.0	4 12.1	9 23.1	10 22.7	1 33.3	3 33.3	2 25.0	
		3	29 42.6	38 41.3	11 39.3	16 39.0	7 43.8	4 40.0	10 30.3	15 38.5	15 34.1	1 33.3	4 44.4	3 37.5	
		4	15 22.1	14 15.2	2 7.1	5 12.2	3 18.8	3 30.0	10 30.3	6 15.4	8 18.2		1 11.1		2 66.
		5	2 2.9	7 7.6		4 9.8		1 10.0	1 3.0	1 2.6	3 6.8	1 33.3			1 33.
		Miscel.	2 2.9	6 6.5	6 21.4	5 12.2	1 6.3	1 10.0	1 3.0	2 5.1	1 2.3			1 12.5	
		Totals	68	92	28	41	16	10	33	39	44	3	9	8	3
		Percent	13.2	17.9	5.4	8.0	3.1	1.9	6.4	7.6	8.6	.6	1.7	1.5	.

	End Scrapers				Hollow Scrapers						Discoidal					
							Keeled									
"Steep-edged"	Rough flake	Keeled	Round nosed	Square nosed	Thin flake	Thick flake	Edge partly chipped	Edge entirely chipped	Pointed	End	Thin flake	Domed	Large	"Thumbnail"	Totals	Percent
1 16.7	19 20.0	7 17.9	12 54.5	2 10.0	10 27.0	1 3.1	4 22.2	2 22.2		2 20.0	12 16.0	6 9.7	2 7.1	26 35.6	426	19.3
1 16.7	15 15.8	2 5.1	1 4.5	1 5.0	4 10.8	4 12.5	3 16.7				4 5.3	4 6.5		8 11.0	223	10.1
2 33.3	8 8.4	3 7.7	2 9.1	3 15.0	7 18.9	5 15.6		1 11.1	1 20.0	2 20.0	11 14.7	7 11.3	6 21.4	8 11.0	253	11.5
	23 24.2	13 33.3	1 4.5	2 10.0	6 16.2	4 12.5	3 16.7	1 11.1		3 30.0	13 17.3	15 24.2	12 42.9	11 15.1	453	20.6
2 33.3	9 9.5	4 10.3	1 4.5	5 25.0	6 16.2	4 12.5	5 27.8		3 60.0		14 18.7	16 25.8	4 14.3	11 15.1	360	16.3
	14 14.7	6 15.4	2 9.1	4 20.0	3 8.1	7 21.9	2 11.1	3 33.3		1 10.0	16 21.3	9 14.5	3 10.7	4 5.5	265	12.0
	3 3.2	2 5.1	2 9.1	1 5.0		5 15.6	1 5.6		1 20.0		3 4.0	1 1.6	1 3.6	3 4.1	114	5.2
	3 3.2			1 5.0	1 2.7					1 10.0				1 1.4	20	.9
	1 1.1	2 5.1	1 4.5	1 5.0		2 6.3		2 22.2		1 10.0	2 2.7	4 6.5		1 1.4	88	4.0
6	95	39	22	20	37	32	18	9	5	10	75	62	28	73	2202	
.3	4.3	1.8	1.0	.9	1.7	1.4	.8	.4	.2	.5	3.4	2.8	1.3	3.3		
	2											3			22	
	5					3					7	3			63	
					2 28.6						2 15.4			3 20.0	64	12.4
	1 5.6			2 15.4	2 28.6	3 27.3					2 15.4	2 13.3	1 20.0	2 13.3	86	16.7
1 100.0	7 38.9	3 60.0	1 25.0	5 38.5	3 42.9	4 36.4	3 75.0			2 100.0	3 23.1	8 53.3	2 40.0	6 40.0	203	39.4
	4 22.2	1 20.0	2 50.0	4 30.8		3 27.3	1 25.0	2 100.0	1 100.0		6 46.2	3 20.0		3 20.0	99	19.2
						1 9.1						1 6.7			23	4.5
	6 33.3	1 20.0	1 25.0	2 15.4								1 6.7	2 40.0	1 6.7	40	7.8
1	18	5	4	13	7	11	4	2	1	2	13	15	5	15	515	
.2	3.5	.9	.8	2.5	1.4	2.1	.8	.4	.2	.4	2.5	2.9	.9	2.9		

tic value. Table 15 does indicate that none were found in the volcanic debris and red sand layers and that the type was only weakly represented in the lower layers of the midden of the upper cave. Greatest frequency was reached toward the surface. In the lower cave, this situation is reversed, highest percentages occurring in levels 3 and 4. I doubt if this contradiction has any real significance. The main truth to be derived is that thin flake side scrapers were used throughout the period of midden formation, carrying up into pottery times.

(B. Thick flake [small]) —These differ from the foregoing in having been made from originally thicker flakes which determined that the retouch, either by percussion or pressure, be steep. The angle formed by the chipped and flat faces varies from about 30 to 90 degrees. Workmanship was limited to one-half or less of the margin and the quality of the chipping ranges from coarse and irregular to fine and regular. Thickness varies from about 10 to 25 mm. and extreme lengths range from 22 to 72 mm. (Fig. 30). Table 15 shows that these are most heavily concentrated in midden accumulation and that they closely follow the vertical distribution of the thin flake type.

(Thick flake [large]) —The distinction between these and the preceding is strictly a matter of size. As large specimens in the thin flake group were lacking, it was felt that some significance might be detected by making this breakdown. Thicknesses vary from 20 to 45 mm. and greatest diameters run from 70 to 120 mm. The material is almost exclusively basalt. For the most part, flaking is by percussion, steep and rough, and the edges are either straight or convex, as illustrated by the examples in Figure 31.

According to Table 15, the type is not represented in the deepest midden levels, becoming prevalent in the mid-zones of the midden in both the upper and lower caves, and surviving into the upper or pottery levels.

(C. Rough flake) —This is manifestly a "catch-all" category intended to take care of a large number of bulky scrapers with very rough chipping. Some may represent unfinished tools. The original flakes, mostly of basaltic material, were thick and large, ranging from 40 to 98 mm. in length and highly irregular as to outline. The working edges, usually limited to a relatively small segment of the perimeter, were jaggedly percussion flaked and there was little striving for the development of a keel. Typical examples are illustrated in Figure 32, *a-c*.

The distribution table shows that scrapers of this type reach maximum frequency in about the mid-portion of the midden in the upper and lower caves, or just before the appearance of pottery. They are strongly represented, however, in the pottery-bearing trash and as they also occurred in the volcanic debris and red sand layers, the type appears to have no particular diagnostic value.

(D. Oval)—As the name implies, the outline of these is oval and the workmanship has normally been extended entirely around the perimeter to achieve the desired shape. The thin flake variety, 80 per cent of which are basalt and the rest chert, ranges from 28 to 95 mm. in length, the thickness rarely exceeding one-third the maximum length. The chipping is rough to fine and may or may not extend over the entire upper surface (Fig. 32, *d-f*).

The size range and materials of the keeled ovals are approximately the same as in the foregoing. The difference lies in the thickness of the body, produced by the steep chipping which left a keel running more or less along the axis (Fig. 32, *g-i*). The thickness is always greater than one-third the length and in some cases is almost as great as the length. These are distinctly related by type to the keeled discoidal scrapers which in turn appear to be but miniatures of the plane.

Although present in all layers except the red sand (Table 15), oval side scrapers of both types occurred most heavily just below the mid portions of the midden in the upper and lower caves.

(E. Elongate)—These constitute a large group numerically and several sub-forms occur, depending again on thinness or thickness and extent of chipping. A distinctive characteristic

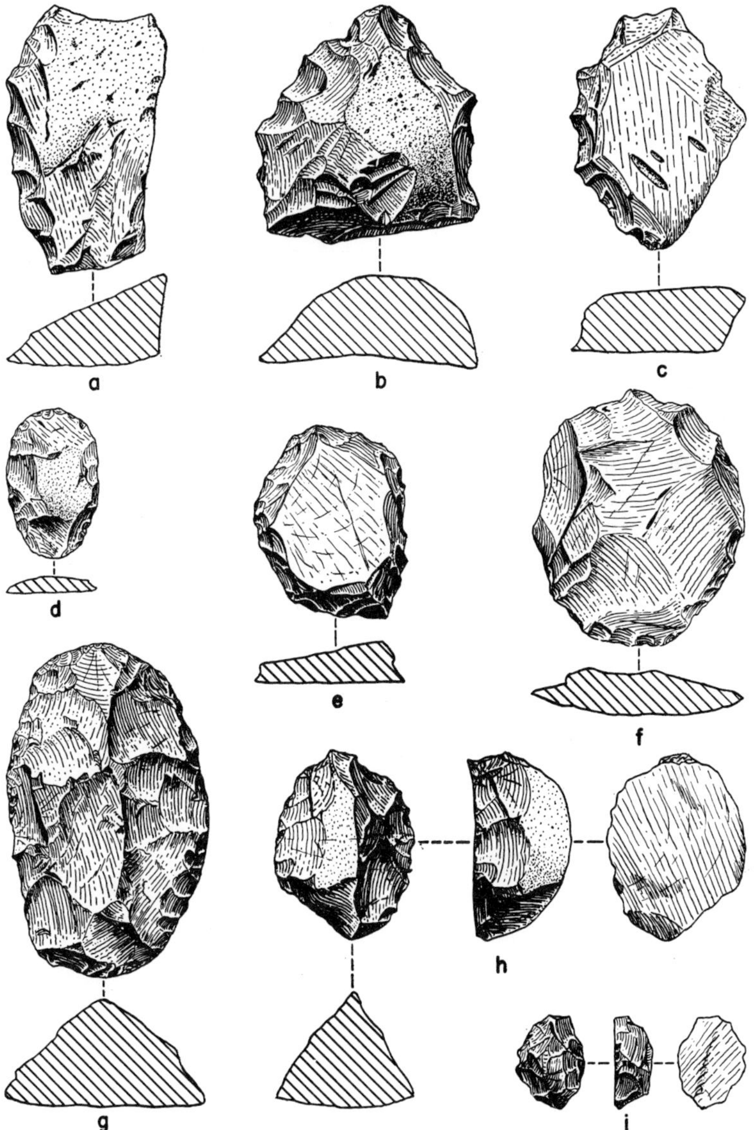

FIGURE 32. Side scrapers from the midden. Rough flake, *a-c;* oval, thin, *d-f;* oval, keeled, *g-i;* all basalt. Length of *g,* 87 mm.

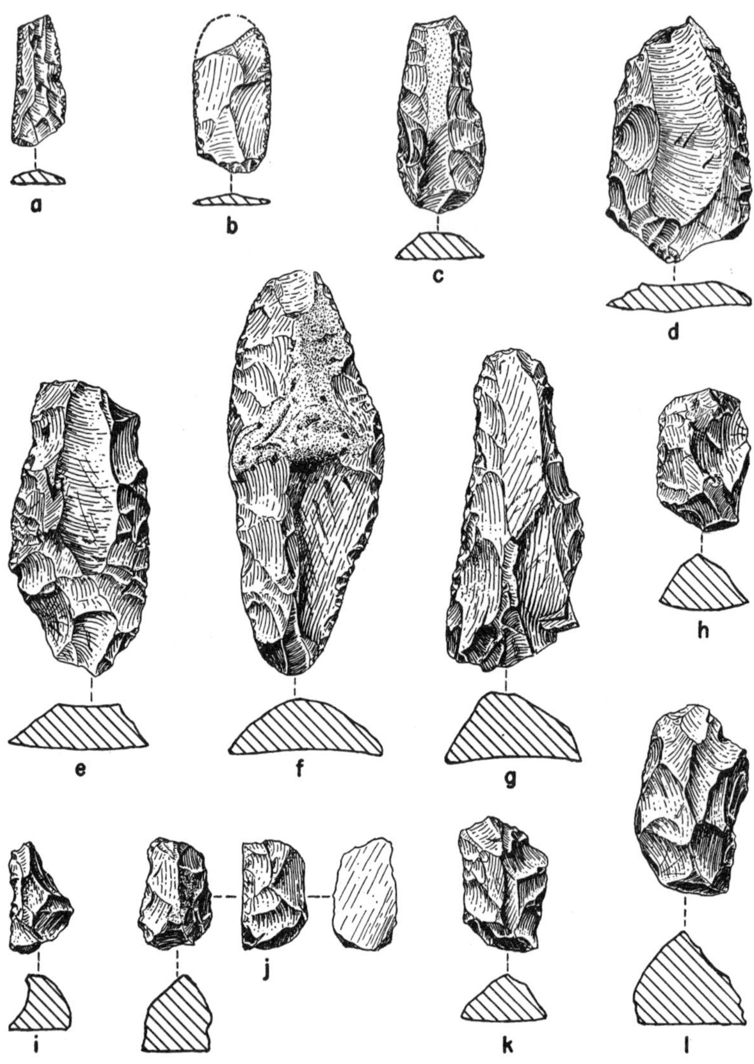

FIGURE 33. Elongate side scrapers from the midden. Thin flake, *a-g;* keeled, chipped part way around, *h;* keeled, chipped all the way around, *i-l: a, b, h, j,* chert; *c,* moss agate; *d, i, k,* jasper; all others basalt. Length of *f,* 108 mm.

of all is the elongation, but the outlines as such are highly variable.

The thin flake type ranges from 20 to 108 mm. in length (Fig. 33, *a-g*). The material is mostly basalt, although the smallest, which, incidentally, show the finest chipping, are chert and jasper. In a few examples highest perfection was reached by working down most or all of the edge, but this is the exception rather than the rule. Examples *d* and *e,* (Fig. 33), illustrate the average, and *f* is one of the best examples with chipping applied all the way around the edge.

The elongated keeled side scrapers with partial and complete edge chipping (Fig. 33, *h-l*) range from 23 to 85 mm. in length, being smaller on the average (about 40 mm.) than the preceding group. They also differ markedly in material, as the choice was chert, jasper, rarely obsidian, instead of the customary basalt. Those dressed only part way around, mainly on one long side (Fig. 33, *h*), differ from the thick flake side scrapers in the possession of a keel and, of course, in elongation. The perfected form with complete edge workmanship consistently shows steep chipping governed by the high keel. They were evidently put to use as small planes and as such must be regarded as a variation in form of that tool.

Once again the vertical distribution (Table 15) shows all varieties of elongate scrapers to have been well distributed through the midden, although weakest in the very bottom and reaching a minor concentration in the middle sections, a situation holding true for the upper and lower caves alike.

(F. Pointed)—Pointed scrapers are distinguished from all others in that they have two worked edges which converge, forming a point. While there are scrapers with points among some of the other categories as, for example, in the elongate class, in these the point is accidental as opposed to the intentional forming of the same in this group. Pointed scrapers are also recognized in the hollow edged type which were purposefully so made, but the concave scraping edge is given precedence over the pointing in that classification. Thin flake (Fig. 34, *a-d*) and

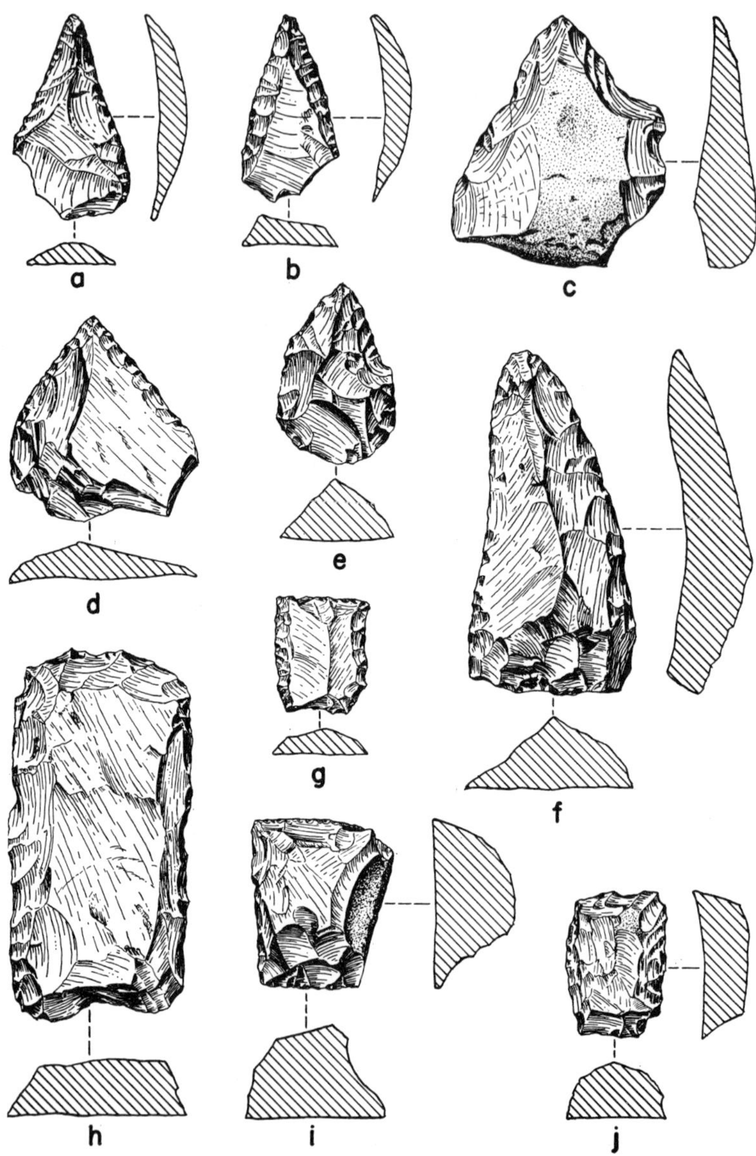

FIGURE 34. Scrapers from the midden. Pointed: thin flake, *a-d;* keeled, *e, f*. Rectangular: thin flake, *g, h;* keeled, *i, j*. *a, b, f,* chert; *c, d, h, i,* basalt; *e, g, j,* jasper. Length of *h,* 81 mm.

keeled (Fig. 34, *e, f*) subtypes are recognized, the former being somewhat more abundant. In size, the range is from 26 to 82 mm., there being no appreciable difference for the two subtypes. There are, however, some differences in material, as the thin flake form is chiefly basalt (70 per cent) whereas the keeled variety was made primarily of chert (60 per cent), an understandable difference, as basalt could not be so precisely worked as chert.

From the frequency analysis (Table 15), it appears that pointed scrapers have two nodes of occurrence, being heavy in the upper layer and again toward the middle section of the midden of the upper cave. Regrouping the thin flake subtype from layer 1 as opposed to layer 4, brings out some interesting details. The thirteen examples from the top layer comprise nearly all of the chert examples, which then places the basalt specimens to the deeper levels. The latter are, on the whole, much cruder, the chipping being more rugged and the edges more convex than in the late chert examples.

Comparable differences in the keeled subtype are not apparent. Culturally, the authorship of the late examples may be assigned to the pottery-making people, the Desert Hohokam, and the earlier ones to the pre-pottery food gatherers of the Chiricahua-Amargosa and San Pedro horizons. Pointed scrapers did not occur in the volcanic debris and red sand layers.

(G. Rectangular)—These were normally chipped along four edges with sharp to slightly rounded corners, producing a rectangular outline. Scrapers conforming to this shape, but worked on three edges only, have also been admitted to the type.

The thin flake subtype, varying from 22 to 90 mm. in length, was made chiefly of basalt, a few of other materials being present (Fig. 34, *g, h*). Among the keeled examples, chert and jasper predominate, a situation which appears to be fairly universal among all keeled scrapers. These have a size range from 21 to 62 mm. with an average of about 35 mm. (Fig. 34, *i, j*).

Reference to Table 15 shows that the thin form reached maximum abundance in layers 3, 4, and 5, whereas the keeled form was heaviest in layers 4, 5, and 6, with some scattering in other layers of the upper cave. The sample from the lower cave is small but the trend is about the same, the thin subtype appearing to be somewhat later. It would look as though the rectangular scraper was essentially a component of the pre-pottery people.

(H. Serrated)—A small lot of scrapers, generally of elongate form, show working edges which have been given special attention by serrating. This ranges from coarse to fine (Fig. 35, *a-c*) and was accomplished by pressure flaking. The material in about half is basalt, the rest being chert and jasper. The finest serrating is to be seen on the latter. The length range is 38 to 71 mm.

The associations of these (Table 15) are distinctly with pottery in the higher midden levels of both the upper and lower caves. The complete absence of the type in all deeper layers strengthens the belief that the authorship is assignable to the Desert Hohokam.

(I. "Steep-edged")—A curious and numerically small scraper type has been termed "steep-edged" for want of a better label. The distinguishing feature is the steep retouch away from a very narrow nether surface in contrast to other forms where this surface is as wide as the tool itself. This gives the specimens an extraordinarily high and sharpened back. The cross-section is shaped like an obtuse-angled triangle (Fig. 35, *d, e*). All examples are either chert or jasper, and lengths range from 30 to 57 mm.

Their occurrence in the cave was principally in the upper midden layers (Table 15), and like the serrated scrapers they may be regarded as a late form. Because of their rarity, no particular diagnostic importance need be assigned to them.

II. End Scrapers—End scrapers are distinguishable from other types in that the emphasis of the dressing was at one end of a flake with a long axis rather than along the edge. In common with other forms, the lower side is flattish, representing the cleavage of the original flake. In the more finished examples, the chipping was brought around the sides as well as on the end, which, in effect, made the tools combination side-end scrapers. Placement of chipping and thickness or thinness have been used in establishing subtypes.

(A. Rough flakes)—These show no appreciable difference from the few examples already cited from the volcanic debris and red sand. They are rough, irregularly outlined flakes, somewhat longer than wide, percussion-flaked at one end in varying degrees of convexity (Fig. 36, *a, b*). They reveal no refinement whatever and were doubtless hastily made when needed and

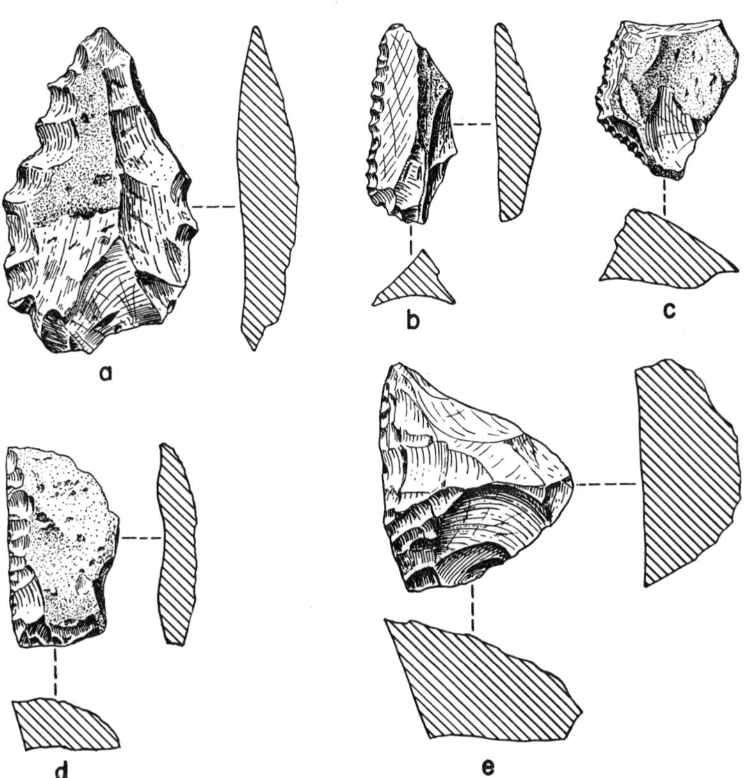

FIGURE 35. Scrapers from the midden. Serrated, *a-c;* "steep-edged," *d, e: a,* rhyolite; *b,* basalt; *c-e,* chert. Length of *a,* 73 mm.

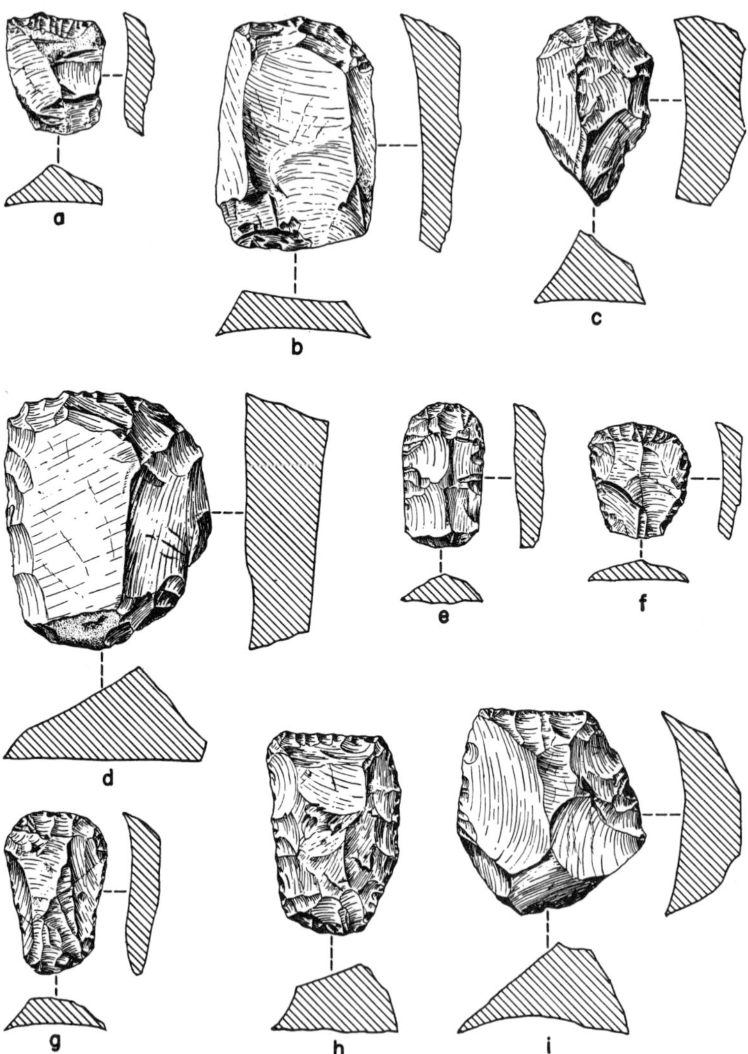

FIGURE 36. End scrapers from the midden. Rough flake, *a, b;* keeled, *c, d;* round nosed, *e, f;* square nosed, *h, i: a, e, f, h,* chert; *b, d,* basalt; *c, g, i,* jasper. Length of *b,* 64 mm.

quickly discarded. Basalt and chert are about equally represented, a few being of jasper and obsidian. The length range is from 20 to 98 mm. The type was erratically distributed through the midden (Table 15).

(B. Keeled) —As the name implies, these are thick-bodied because of the keel on the upper surface. Chipping may extend from the end down one or both sides, although the quality of side flaking is inferior to the workmanship on the end (Fig. 36, *c, d*). The materials are about equally divided between basalt, chert, and jasper, and the size range is great, from 31 to 106 mm.

Keeled end scrapers were absent in the volcanic debris and red sand layers but otherwise their distribution seems to be about the same as the rough flake end scraper (Table 15). The highest number was found in about the middle section of the midden of the upper cave, some being represented in all other layers except No. 8. None were found in the upper two levels of the lower cave. I cannot find any specific reference to anything quite like these among the desert cultures to the west or in the Cochise complexes, but it would appear from the evidence in Ventana that the type was more commonly in use by pre-pottery people than among those who had pottery.

(C. Round nosed and D. Square nosed) —These two types may be considered together since they share all characteristics except in the shape of the end, which was either well rounded (Fig. 36, *e, g*) or square (Fig. 36, *h, i*). The finest workmanship is seen on the ends. Thickness varies considerably and lengths (21 to 65 mm.) do not show the extreme range of other types. Materials again are chiefly basalt and chert, the former being slightly predominant.

The round nosed subtype closely resembles the "snub-nose" form so familiar in the Plains and recognized now also as present in more westerly sites of both early and late date.[28] These tend to have the same forward hump but the tapering of the "tail" is not so extreme.

★

28. F. H. H. Roberts, Jr., 1935, pp. 22-23; 1936, p. 23; A. V. Kidder, 1932, pp. 35-39.

The level analysis indicates that the two forms did not have a comparable usage. The round nosed subtype reached maximum as to numbers in late prehistoric times although represented in all but the deepest levels of the upper cave midden. In the lower cave the sample was too small to be of much value. The square nosed variety was more prevalent in the pre-pottery levels (Table 15).

III. Hollow Scrapers—In all classes of scrapers mentioned so far, the edge has been either straight or convex. When concave, the specimens were placed in a hollow scraper category with the idea that dressing down the edge thus was a somewhat more specialized treatment and that the tool had a more limited use. Only about 5 per cent of all scrapers belong here, indicating that the type was not particularly strong.

(A. Thin flake)—These were made by pressure retouch along one edge, of most any convenient thin flake, preferably chert or jasper, although basalt is also represented. A few examples have two edges worked and there is one combination concavo-convex edged scraper. Lengths range from 23 to 70 mm. with thickness less than one-fourth the length (Fig. 37, *a-d*).

The analysis to level (Table 15) indicates the type increasing generally from bottom to top in the midden of the upper cave, the strongest showing being in the upper layer. Regrouping the specimens to level brings out no significant details either as to form or material, and it must be admitted that the type was in use for a long time and is therefore of no great diagnostic value. In the lower cave the trend does not follow that of the upper cave, but the sample is small.

(B. Thick flake)—These differ from the preceding principally in thickness of the flake, this being from one-third to one-half the length. The retouching is consequently of a steep nature and the edge is sometimes more sharply concave. Materials and size range remain about the same as in the preceding (Fig. 37, *e-g*).

Distribution through the midden was more or less constant (Table 15) with an apparent falling off in the upper level.

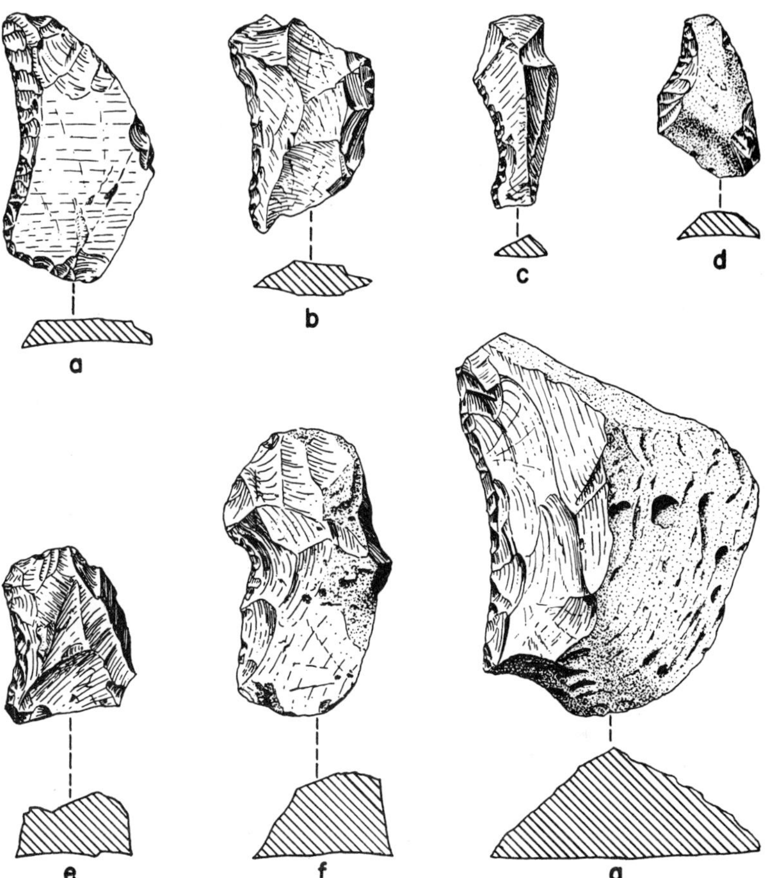

FIGURE 37. Hollow scrapers from the midden. Thin, *a-d;* thick, *e-g: a, d,* jasper; *b, g,* basalt; *c, e, f,* chert. Length of *g,* 90 mm.

(C. Keeled)—Scrapers of this subtype number only thirty-three and are differentiated from others in the high ridge running down the back. Chert and jasper were favored as materials and lengths vary from 23 to 60 mm. In the lot, a minor distinction has been made between those with chipping part way around the margin and those with completely worked edge (Fig. 38, *a-d*). There is no standardization of form among the latter.

The occurrence of both varieties was so spotty (Table 15) that little value is implied.

(D. Pointed)—There are only six scrapers which answer the following description but they are so much alike that they represent a true type. The materials are chert (3) and jasper (3), and the sizes vary only from 33 to 40 mm. Rather thick, triangular sectioned flakes were selected and two adjoining sides were steeply chipped to form concave edges coming together as a pronounced point (Fig. 38, *e-f*). Superficially they resemble gravers and it may well be that the points were so used, but here the chief attention has been paid to the edges and not the point.

Only one of the six was associated with pottery, the rest occurring deeper in the midden (Table 15). The indication therefore is that the type was fairly early and a component of the culture in Ventana with strong Californian desert relationships. Similar but not identical scrapers are illustrated from the Lake Mohave and Pinto Basin areas.[29] The type appears to be absent in both the Cochise and Folsom cultures.

(E. End)—The final subtype of hollow scrapers includes those of elongated form and hollowed at one end. They are thick-bodied, rather small (27 to 52 mm.), and of the 12, all are chert, jasper, or chalcedony, except three which are basalt. The specimens are not strictly keeled and the extent of the chipping varies from the concave end only to include the entire perimeter.

★

29. C. A. Amsden, 1937, Pl. XXXVI, *d;* C. A. Amsden in E. W. C. and W. H. Campbell, 1935, Pl. 10, *m*.

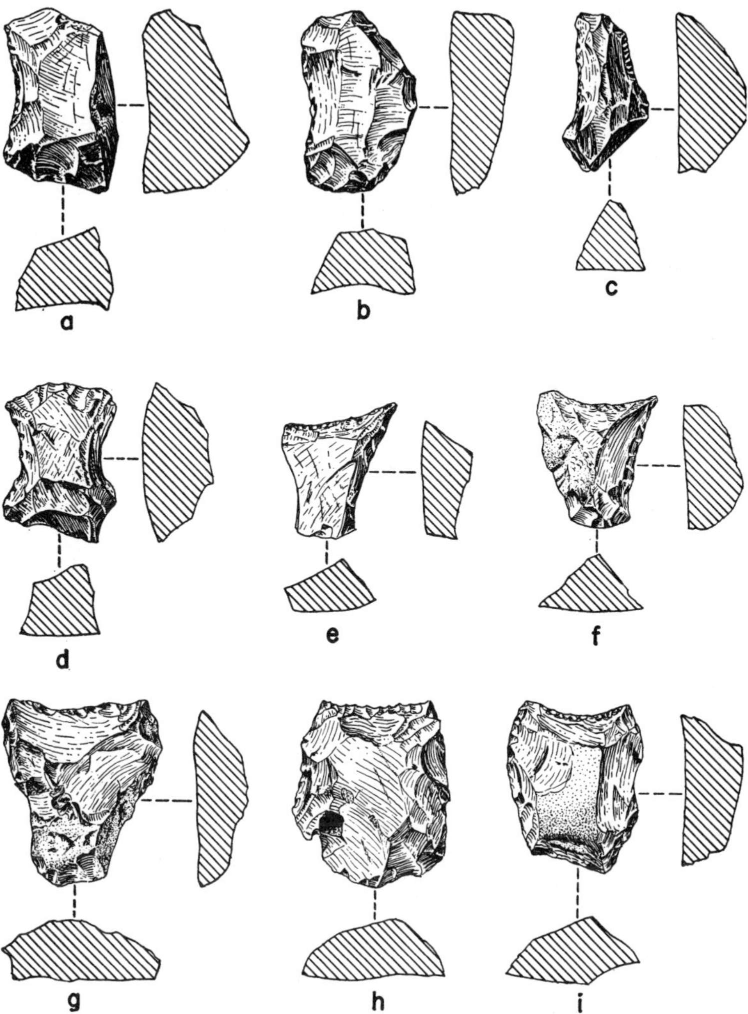

FIGURE 38. Hollow keeled scrapers from the midden. Trimmed part way around, *a;* trimmed all way round, *b-d;* pointed, *e, f;* end, *g-i: a, d, e, h,* jasper; *b , c, f, g,* chert; *i,* basalt. Length of *a,* 45 mm.

No satisfaction is found in the distribution (Table 15) as to the horizon or horizons which were characterized by the type.

IV. Discoidal Scrapers—Scrapers of discoidal form, chipped on one face only, make up about 7 per cent of the entire scraper collection from the midden. These reveal considerable differences in size and in thickness with attendant variations in the steepness of the pitch of chipping, factors which have been used in making the following distinctions.

(A. Thin flake) —The normal scraper in this subtype is plano-convex in cross-section although the bulbar surface may show either a slight concavity or even a slight outward curvature. The pitch of the chipping on the upper surface is flat and grades from an all-over treatment to edge trimming only, leaving a flattish top. A few examples have broad channel flakes removed from the upper surface. As a rule, chipping extends around the entire periphery but in a number of instances the cutting edge is irregular and jagged from the broadly spaced percussion flakes. Basalt was the common material with chert and obsidian also represented. Diameters run from 20 to about 50 mm. and thicknesses are equal to one-third the diameter or less (Fig. 39, *a-c*).

The stratigraphic analysis shows scrapers of this form to have been in use at all times (Table 15). It is noteworthy, however, that in the midden of both divisions of the cave the highest frequencies occurred in the lower layers before the advent of pottery and they would appear, therefore, to be most characteristic of the Chiricahua-Amargosa and San Pedro stages.

(B. Domed) —The difference between these and the preceding subtype is in the thickness of the body. An originally thicker flake was selected and the periphery was worked by percussion from the bulbar surface, leaving a cone- or dome-shaped top. These often give the appearance of being small cores, but the number (67) and the regularity of the flaking definitely places them in the implement category. Diameters vary from 16 to about 50 mm., the average being about 25 mm. (Fig. 39, *d-f*). Thicknesses exceed one-half the diameter and may even be as

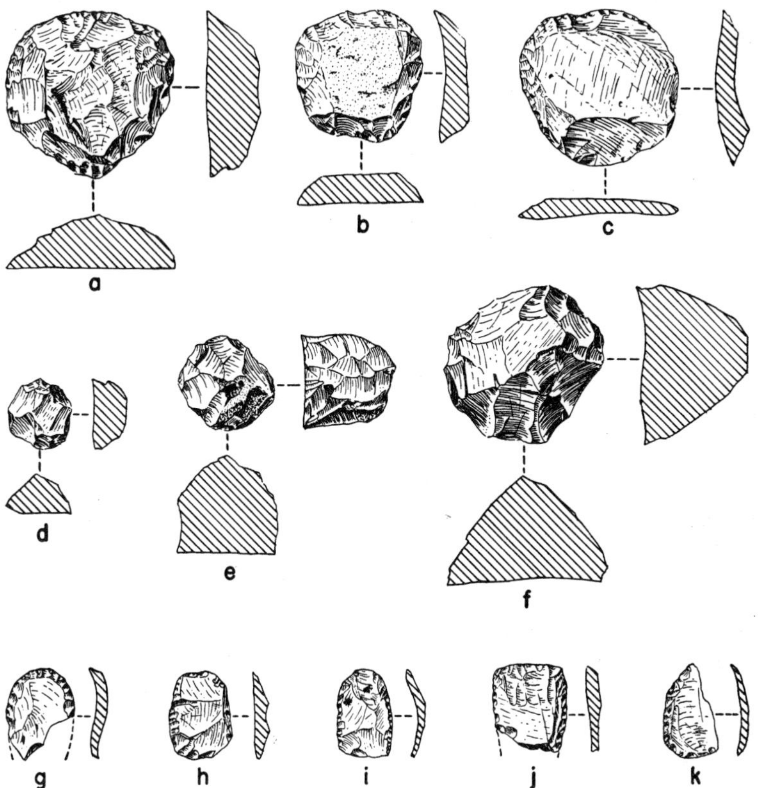

FIGURE 39. Discoidal and "thumbnail" scrapers from the midden. Thin flaked, *a-c;* domed, *d-f;* "thumbnail," *g-k: a-d,* basalt; *e, f, j, k,* chert; *g,* jasper; *h,* obsidian; *i,* moss agate. Diameter of *a,* 44 mm.

great as the diameter. Materials, in order of abundance, are: chert, basalt, jasper, and obsidian.

As has been pointed out before, these are but miniature copies of the plane and they are most nearly like the scraper-planes of Rogers of Phase II of the San Dieguito-Playa (now San Dieguito III) Complex.[30] In Ventana Cave, their occurrence (Table 15) indicates predominance in levels 4 and 5 of the upper cave and levels 3 and 4 of the lower cave. These are also the zones in which other strong desert culture traits appeared, which throws the relationship in that direction rather than toward Cochise, where the type appears to have been unknown. But their appearance in the midden of Ventana Cave is too late for a direct correlation with San Dieguito III. The volcanic debris and red sand layers produced none.

(C. Large)—Some of the discoidal scrapers in the collection attained a diameter much in excess of the thin flake type previously described as ranging from 20 to 50 mm. in diameter. Those with diameters over 60 mm. and up to 115 mm. have been grouped separately, purely as a typological expedient, with the idea that there might be some meaning, chronological or otherwise, in the large size category. Only a few of the thirty-two specimens show any extensive attention to the marginal chipping. Most of them were roughly battered out of an oval or circular flake (Fig. 40). Flake scars ordinarily cover the entire upper surface but the high dome or keel of the planes is lacking. Specimen *d* in Figure 40 is exceptional in that it has a large fluted scar on the upper surface.

Reference to Table 15 will bear out the statement that most of the specimens came from the non-pottery levels of the midden. None occurred in the pre-midden layers and the type was doubtless a complement of the food-gathering hunting folk inhabiting the cave well before the time of Christ.

V. "Thumbnail" Scrapers—This compartment has been established to take care of a number (88) of microlithic scrapers

★

30. M. J. Rogers, 1939, p. 29.

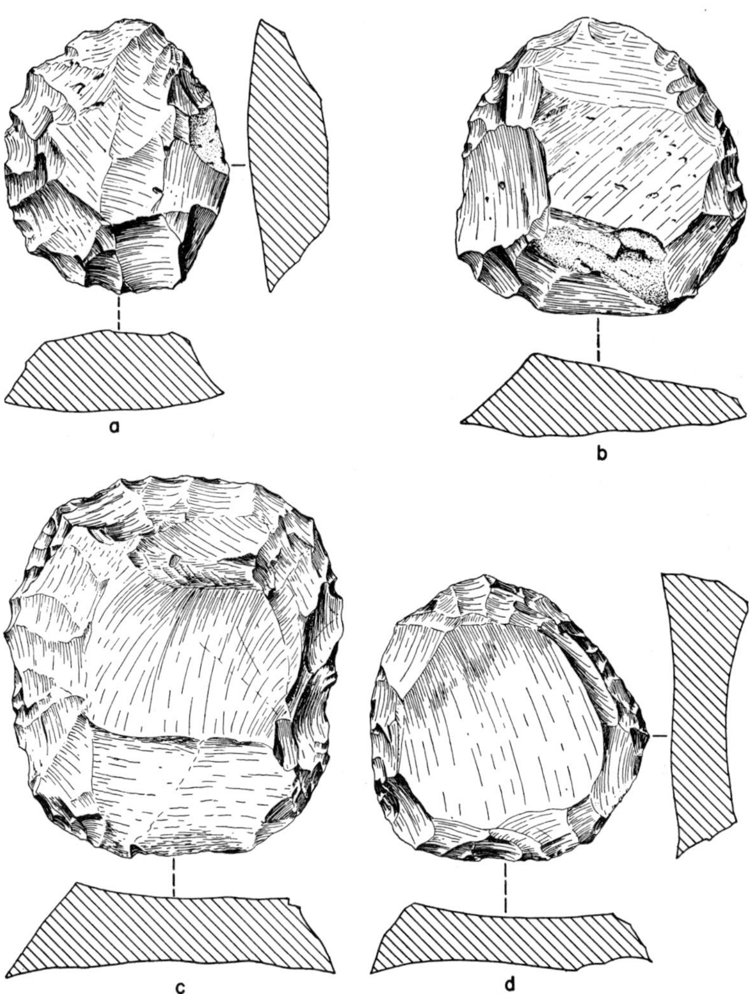

FIGURE 40. Large, discoidal scrapers from the midden. All basalt. Maximum diameter of *c*, 113 mm.

resembling those termed "Thumbnail" scrapers in the literature. Standardization in shape is lacking although the form is generally oval. A common characteristic is the thinness of the flake and extremely fine retouching, probably by shearing,[31] which may extend part way or entirely around the flake. A high proportion of the tools were made of good quality stone, as obsidian, chert, jasper, chalcedony, and there is one of moss agate. Basalt was also used but the fineness of flaking is lacking. Maximum diameters measure from 14 to 25 mm. and the thickness in most examples runs under 5 mm. A typical group is illustrated in Figure 39, *g-k*.

"Thumbnail" scrapers appear for the first time in Ventana in the lower levels of the midden and they reach maximum abundance in the top level of the upper cave, where over one-third of the sample was found. In the lower cave, this situation does not follow so clearly although the sample was much smaller (Table 15). The type may be considered essentially a component of the Desert Hohokam, with roots penetrating well into the pre-pottery horizon. Confirmation of this is found in a large Sells Phase site (Arizona Z:11:4) located several miles west of Ventana Cave, where these scrapers were particularly prevalent.

Flake Knives—The term flake knife, as here used, refers to any suitable flake having one or more sharp edges which was used as a cutting instrument with little alteration. Slight retouch is often present on one face, and less commonly on both faces, making a rather jagged cutting edge. Irregular chipping in a number of specimens was evidently the result of the work done by the tool. Flake knives differ from the thin scraper class in the irregularity of the chipping and in a much flatter retouch.

Where random flakes were put directly to use with so little modification it is obvious that there should be no uniformity as to size and shape. Lengths range from 22 to 108 mm. Seventy-five per cent of the 156 flake knives from the midden are basalt

★

31. J. A .Barbieri, 1937, p. 106.

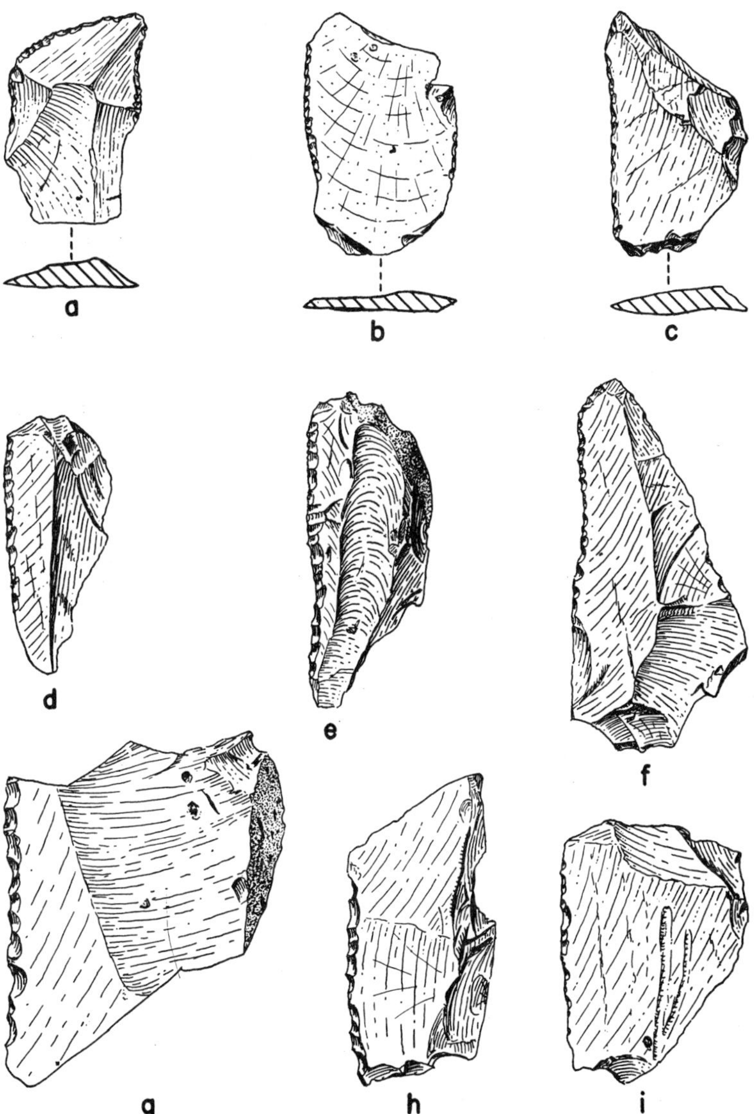

FIGURE 41. Implements from the midden. Flake knives chipped on one face only, all basalt. Length of *f*, 80 mm.

and the rest are of chert and jasper. They contribute only 2.1 per cent of the entire chipped tool category. Figure 41 illustrates typical examples.

Little cultural significance can be attached to such unspecialized tools as flake knives. They represent the simplest form of a cutting instrument. In Ventana, their presence is noted (see Table 16) in all levels with some increase indicated in the upper levels of the midden. The lower cave figures do not follow this trend and it is doubtful whether much weight may be attached to either. Included in the table are only the more obvious knives. It is certain that many times the number shown were discarded during the work, flakes which were not sufficiently altered by, or for, use to make their identification possible.

The curved flake knife (Fig. 21, *e*), represented by two specimens in the volcanic debris layer, did not recur in the higher levels.

TABLE 16

DISTRIBUTION OF FLAKE KNIVES BY LEVEL

	Level	*Upper Cave*	*Per Cent*	*Level*	*Lower Cave*	*Per Cent*
	1	30	24.3	1	6	17.6
	2	24	19.7	2	7	20.6
	3	23	18.8	3	15	44.0
	4	15	12.3	4	5	14.7
Midden	5	10	8.2	5	1	2.9
	6	12	9.9			
	7	6	4.9			
	8					
	Miscl.	2	1.6			
	Totals	122			34	
Red Sand		6				
Volcanic Debris		11				

Gravers—A number of terms, as gravers, chisel-gravers, borers, reamers, and drills, have been applied to assorted pointed implements from archaeological sites. As is evident in the Ventana collection, there are two general classes of pointed tools used as the terms indicate: (a) with chipping on one face only, tending to be short-pointed and bulky, and designed to scratch rather than to perforate; (b) with chipping on both faces, usually longer pointed and obviously intended as perforators al-

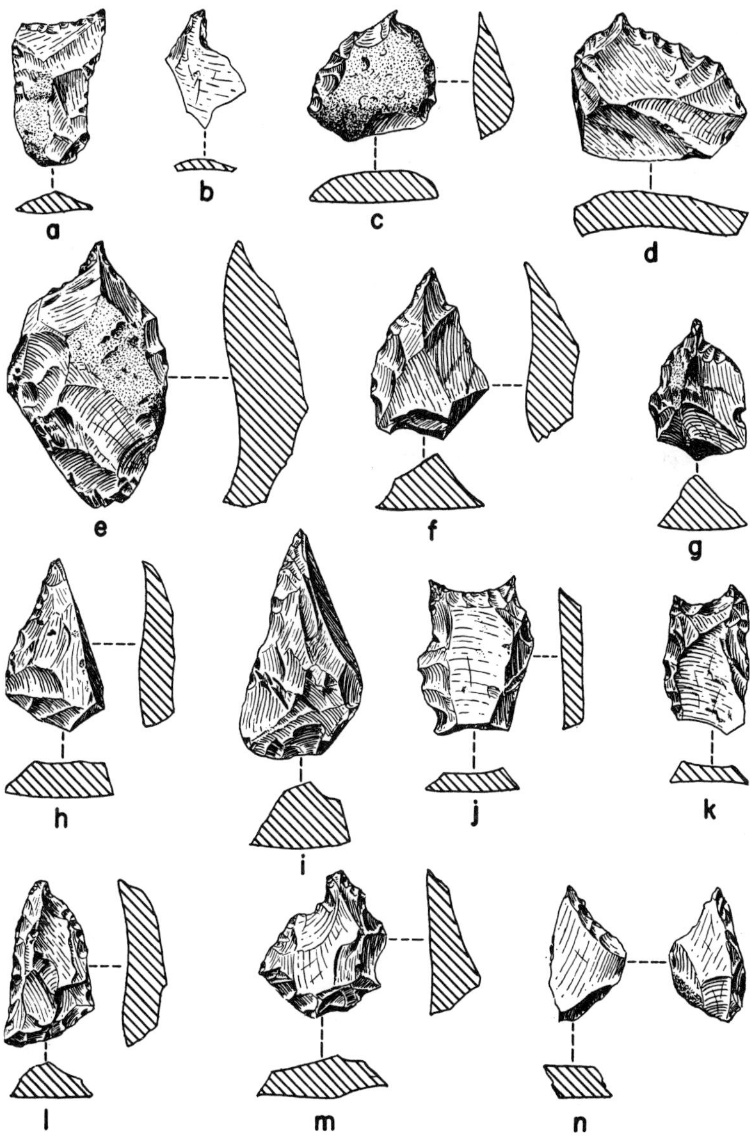

FIGURE 42. Gravers and chisel gravers from the midden. Thin flake, *a, b;* thick flake, *c-e;* prismatic flake, *f, g;* adapted from broken side scrapers, *h, i;* double pointed, *j, k;* chisel gravers, *l, m;* bevel edged, *n: a, b, d-i,* chert; *c,* obsidian; *j, k,* basalt; *l-n,* jasper. Length of *e,* 57 mm.

though scratching could also be done with them. To the first group the general term of graver is applied here, and the term drill to the second group, each having a number of subtypes (see p. 301 for the latter).

The separation of gravers from other tools with pointed projections resulting from irregular chipping was a difficult task. The selection was made finally on the following characteristics: (1) flaking directed with the obvious intent of making a point, and (2) a point scarred with long minute flakes, removed during the use of the implement by pressure applied at the tip. These are best seen under a magnifying glass. Gravers grade upward in size into the pointed scraper class. The points of the latter could also have been used graver-fashion but the care exercised in the trimming of the edges rather than the point is regarded as the distinguishing feature. Specimens with a somewhat broad and beveled point are labeled chisel-gravers, a term employed by Roberts.[32] Gravers account for only 1.3 per cent of the chipped stone collection.

Most of the gravers were made of chert, chalcedony, and jasper; a few of obsidian. In proportion to other types of implements, a very small number were of basalt for obvious reasons.

The graver classification follows:

Gravers		92
1. Thin flake (Fig. 42, *a, b*) Fine retouch on point, not suited for heavy duty. Lengths: 22 to 42 mm.	12	
2. Thick flake (Fig. 42, *c-e*) Extensive chipping on sides converging to form point; point strongly supported by keel; irregular outline. Lengths: 29 to 56 mm.	30	
3. Prismatic flakes (Fig. 42, *f, g*) Naturally pointed flakes with tips lightly flaked. Roughly triangular in outline and section. Lengths: 22 to 46 mm.	19	
4. Adapted from broken side scrapers (Fig. 42, *h, i*) Acute angle fragments; points used without much	7	

★

32. F. H. H. Roberts, Jr., 1935, p. 26.

modification. Curiously, all retouched edges on left (as illustrated) and fractured edges on right. Lengths: 29 to 50 mm.

5. Double pointed (Fig. 42, *j, k*) 7
Elongate flakes, one end chipped to concave to make two points; one or both points used. Lengths: 28 to 49 mm.
6. Chisel-gravers 17
   A. Thick flake (Fig. 42, *l, m*) 16
   Blunt, chisel-edged point, with keeled support. Lengths: 25 to 60 mm.
   B. Bevel-edged (Fig. 42, *n*) 1
   Thick flake with flat faces. Length: 28 mm.

The ninety-two gravers from the midden were distributed as indicated in Table 17. No gravers were recovered from the red sand layer, although they were present in the volcanic debris. It is interesting to note that they were not common in the lower midden levels but increased strongly toward the surface.

The thick flake graver, commonest throughout, was the only subtype from the volcanic debris, tending to make it the basic form. These are nearer the Folsom type than the others of the Ventana series. The late examples resemble the scraper-gravers of Amsden, keeled and flat forms[33] from the Mohave Lake area. Rogers found similar forms, his "borers," in Phase II of the Playa Complex[34] (now San Dieguito III), and Sayles does not indicate the trait as present in the Cochise Culture.[35]

Additional types listed are evidently modifications of the basic thick flake form, some being influenced by the selection of fortuitous flakes which could be adapted with little workmanship. The double pointed type is doubtless the most specialized. The divergence of the paired points on most of the specimens suggests that the points were used individually, not both at the same time. It seems to be unreported from other sites.

The Ventana chisel-gravers differ from the Folsom type in that the tips were not so long or so carefully shaped.

★

33. C. A. Amsden, 1937, pp. 72-73.
34. M. J. Rogers, 1939, p. 33.
35. E. B. Sayles and E. Antevs, 1941.

TABLE 17
DISTRIBUTION OF GRAVERS BY TYPE AND LEVEL

	Stratigraphic Layer	Levels	Gravers: Thin flake	Gravers: Thick flake	Gravers: Prismatic	Gravers: Adapted	Gravers: Double pointed	Chisel Gravers: Thick flake	Chisel Gravers: Bevel-edged	Totals	Percent
Upper Cave	Midden	1	3 37.5	4 16.7	3 21.4	2 28.6	2 33.3	3 21.4		17	23.0
		2	2 25.0	1 4.1	2 14.3	1 14.3	3 50.0	2 14.3		11	14.8
		3	1 12.5	1 4.1	1 7.2	1 14.3		2 14.3		6	8.1
		4		10 41.7	2 14.3	1 14.3	1 16.7	2 14.3	1 100.0	17	23.0
		5	1 12.5	5 20.4	2 14.3			1 7.2		9	12.2
		6		2 8.3	2 14.3			3 21.4		7	9.5
		7	1 12.5	1 4.2	1 7.2	1 14.3				4	5.4
		8									
		Miscel.			1 7.2	1 14.3		1 7.2			4.0
		Totals	8	24	14	7	6	14	1	74	
		Percent	10.8	32.4	18.9	9.5	8.1	18.9	1.4		
	Red Sand										
	Volcanic Debris			3						3	
Lower Cave	Midden	1									
		2		1 16.7	2 40.0					3	16.7
		3	2 50.0	4 66.5	2 40.0			2 100.0		10	55.5
		4	2 50.0	1 16.7	1 20.0	1 100.0				5	27.8
		5									
		Miscel.									
		Totals	4	6	5	1		2		18	
		Percent	22.2	33.3	27.8	5.6		11.1			

The occurrence of gravers in practically all levels in Ventana shows that they persisted over a long period of time. Their diagnostic value is thus somewhat reduced. The association of gravers with pottery in the upper levels of the upper cave is somewhat at odds with the evidence collected in open sites. Our work in the Jackrabbit and Valshni villages, estimated to range from about A. D. 800 to 1400, Hayden's tests in the Ash Hill Site near Santa Rosa, probably of 14th century date, and Gila Pueblo's work at Snaketown, produced no such tools. This may mean a mixing of late pre-pottery debris with the trash of pottery-making people and the implied persistence of the trait may, therefore, be fictitious. Some support for this is found in the lower cave, where the greatest frequency occurred in levels 3 and 4, which were pre-pottery in origin.

Implements Flaked on Two or More Faces

Implements fashioned on both major faces make up approximately 56 per cent of the chipped tools. This, of course, represents implements made over a long period of time and it may, therefore, be incorrect to make any comparisons of the lot as a whole against any other assemblages of more limited age. It is evident, nevertheless, that in the Mohave[36] and in the Cochise Culture[37] single face chipping was rather strongly predominant.

Flake Knives—The haphazard flaking on both faces of thinnish flakes distinguishes these from the flake knives of the single face chipped group. Generally elongated flakes were selected, of which one or both sides were quickly sharpened by pressure trimming. Flake scars seldom carry very far over the faces. With few exceptions the eighty knives (1.2 per cent of chipped tools) were of basalt; lengths run from 28 to 80 mm., and thicknesses from 3 to 15 mm. (Fig. 43, *a, b*).

These were most prevalent in the upper midden layers of both divisions of the cave (Table 18) and, although a simple and efficient tool, none were found in the pre-midden deposits.

★

36. C. A. Amsden, 1937, p. 76.
37. E. B. Sayles and E. Antevs, 1941, p. 27.

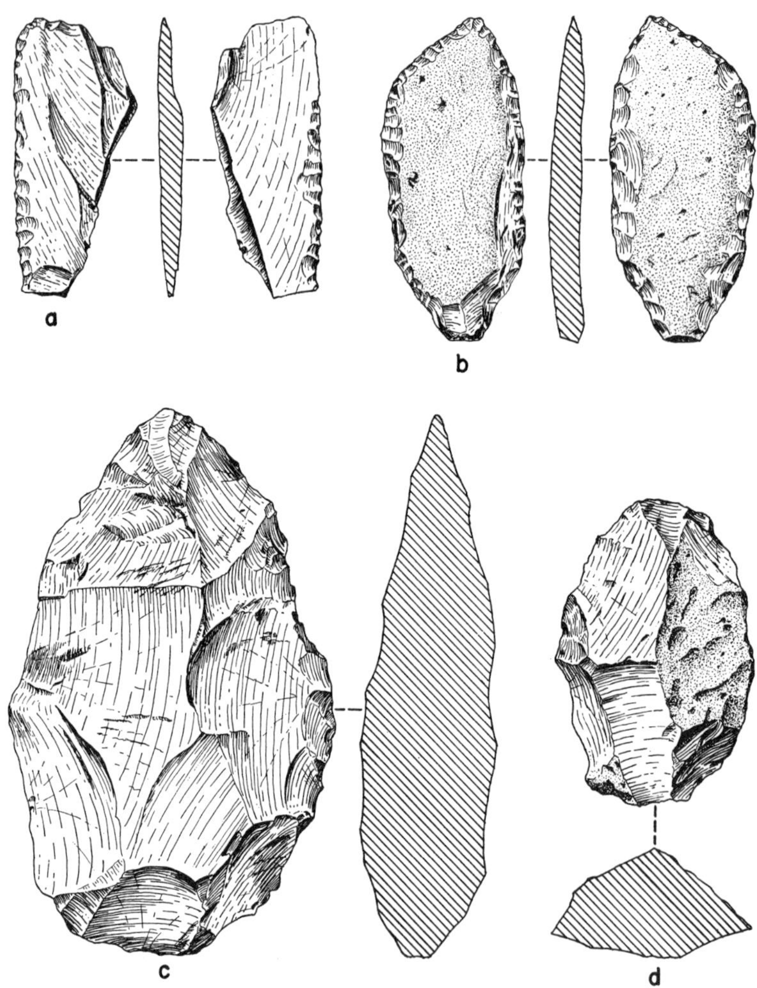

FIGURE 43. Implements from the midden. Flake knives, chipped both faces, *a, b;* blanks, *c, d: a-c,* basalt; *d,* rhyolite. Length of *c,* 134 mm.

Table 18

DISTRIBUTION OF MISCELLANEOUS BI-FACIALLY FLAKED TOOLS

	Stratigraphic Layer	*Levels*	*Flake Knives*	*Blanks*	*Ovoids*	*Discoidals*	*Hoes*
Upper Cave	*Midden*	1	17 24.6	16 20.8	25 28.8	15 20.0	3 37.5
		2	10 14.5	20 26.0	14 16.1	11 14.7	
		3	10 14.5	17 22.1	15 17.2	8 10.7	1 12.5
		4	16 23.2	9 11.7	14 16.1	18 24.0	4 50.0
		5	7 10.1	9 11.7	10 11.5	14 18.7	
		6	8 11.6	2 2.6	8 9.2	3 4.0	
		7	1 1.5	2 2.6		4 5.3	
		8					
		Miscel.		2 2.6	1 1.1	2 2.7	
		Totals	69	77	87	75	8
	Red Sand						
	Volcanic Debris						
Lower Cave	*Midden*	1	3 27.3	4 33.3	5 21.7	2 13.3	
		2	5 45.5	3 25.0	6 26.1	5 33.3	1 33.3
		3	1 9.1	2 16.7	5 21.7	6 40.0	2 66.6
		4	2 18.2	1 8.3	4 17.4	1 6.7	
		5		1 8.3	1 4.3		
		Miscel.		1 8.3	2 8.7	1 6.7	
		Totals	11	12	23	15	3

Blanks—A number of artifacts, hardly classifiable as implements, have been termed blanks. They are large (50 to 135 mm.) blades, roughly hewn out by percussion, of a variety of materials. None show any secondary edge dressing (Fig. 43, c, d). No doubt these represent implements in the process of manufacture, discarded because of imperfections in the material or such as were never completed.

Most of the eighty-nine examples were recovered from the late levels of the midden (Table 18).

Ovoids—This lot of roughly flaked, oval-outlined artifacts may be another form of blank but it is noteworthy that the chipping on the whole is somewhat finer and there is some secondary dressing of the edges (Fig. 44, *a, b*). Furthermore, the average

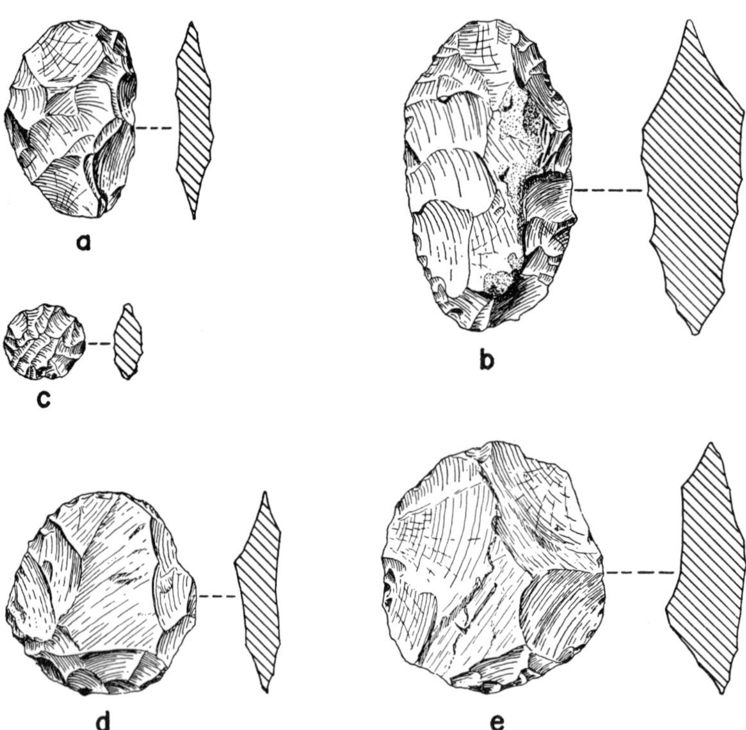

FIGURE 44. Implements from the midden, chipped on both sides. Ovoids, *a, b;* discoidals, *c-e: c,* obsidian, all others basalt. Length of *b,* 64 mm.

size is much smaller than in the preceding group, the extremes in length being 25 to 70 mm. The material is predominantly basalt. At least some of these would appear to be finished items, but what their use may have been is not clear.

Although represented in practically all levels of the midden the greatest numbers were found well toward the top (Table 18).

Discoidals—These differ from the ovoids principally in shape, being circular, and are unlike the discoidal scrapers in having bi-facial chipping. The quality of the flaking is rough and, in most cases, the scars extend over the entire face. Some secondary chipping is in evidence, giving the impression that these are finished tools (Fig. 44, *c-e*). This is also brought out by the small size of a few, especially five which are made of obsidian, (Fig. 44, *c*) from 15 to 30 mm. in diameter. Basalt and chert specimens reach a diameter of 65 mm. I assume that cutting must have been the chief practical use to which they were put.

The analysis (Table 18) indicates that the type was most common in the middle portion of the midden of both cave units, but survived strongly also toward the surface. It was absent in the volcanic debris and red sand layers of Ventana. A similar and perhaps somewhat more finely worked specimen is reported from the Pinto Basin Culture[38] and a more specific allocation is given by Sayles,[39] who reports five bi-face discs associated with the San Pedro Stage of the Cochise Culture. It is worth noting that in Ventana the type of projectile point associated with the greatest concentrations of discoidals was the San Pedro point, but it should be recognized that discoidals were also present well before the appearance of the type of point in question.

Choppers—The term chopper as here used refers to large implements which have bi-facial trimming by percussion flaking along the margin. They thus differ from the planes which were consistently dressed on one side only and away from the bulbar surface. The 762 choppers from Ventana can be further subdivided on minutiae which, in a few instances, would appear

★

38. C. A. Amsden, 1935, Pl. 14, *h*.
39. E. B. Sayles and E. Antevs, 1941, p. 27, Fig. 10.

to have some chronological value. The major criterion is the original character of the rock, *i. e.,* whether flake, core or pebble, secondarily, the shape and extent of the trim. The breakdown and enumeration follows:

Flake			67
Not sharpened		24	
Sharpened		43	
Core			667
Sharpened part way around		623	
Sharpened all way around		44	
Discoidal	25		
Oval	19		
Pebble			28
Spheroidal		9	
Long		8	
Flat		11	
Total			762

(Flake)—The first subtype to be presented, unsharpened flake choppers, does not conform to the primary requirement of flaking on both sides expressed above. But they so clearly belong with the choppers that for the sake of coherence their inclusion here seems advisable. What we have in these is the adaptation of natural basalt flakes, somewhat elongated, broken out along cleaveages which gave them sharp edges and roughly triangular sections. In the course of the work performed the edge became battered, but it is clear that there was no initial sharpening. Lengths run from 85 to 205 mm., although this would be of no great importance other than to select a stone with enough weight to stand up under the battering expected of it. A typical example is illustrated in Figure 45, *a.*

Choppers of this type were evidently never abundant, as they comprise only 3.1 per cent of the whole chopper collection; but it is worth noting that nearly all those found date from the upper levels, thus occurring with pottery (Table 19). Primitiveness in this instance distinctly does not mean earliness and we may consider the tool as a makeshift adopted by the late occu-

Table 19

DISTRIBUTION OF CHOPPERS BY TYPE AND LEVEL

	Stratigraphic Layer	*Levels*	*Flake Choppers*		*Core Choppers*			*Pebble Choppers*			*Totals*	*Percent*
						Sharpened Entirely Around						
			Not Sharpened	*Sharpened*	*Sharpened Part Way*	*Dis-coidal*	*Oval*	*Spheroidal*	*Long*	*Flat*		
Upper Cave	*Midden*	1	7 43.8	5 14.3	48 9.9	3 13.7	2 13.3	1 12.5	1 50.0	1 10.0	68	11.4
		2	3 18.7	4 11.4	46 9.5	2 9.1	3 20.0			1 10.0	59	9.9
		3	3 18.7	7 20.0	65 13.4	2 9.1	3 20.0			1 10.0	81	13.6
		4	2 12.5	4 11.4	76 15.6	7 32.0	4 26.7	4 50.0		1 10.0	98	16.5
		5		6 17.1	116 24.0	3 13.6		2 25.0		4 40.0	131	22.1
		6		5 14.3	107 22.0		1 6.7		1 50.0	2 20.0	116	19.5
		7		3 8.6	11 2.3	2 9.1	1 6.7				17	2.9
		8					1 6.7				1	.2
		Miscel.	1 6.3	1 2.9	17 3.5	3 13.7		1 12.5			23	3.9
		Totals	16	35	486	22	15	8	2	10	594	
		Pct.	2.7	5.9	81.8	3.7	2.5	1.4	.3	1.7		
	Red Sand											
	Volcanic Debris			2			1					
Lower Cave	*Midden*	1	1 12.5	1 12.5	40 29.0				1 16.7	1 100.0	44	26.0
		2		3 37.5	18 13.0	1 33.3	2 50.0		3 50.0		27	16.0
		3	4 50.0	2 25.0	63 46.0	2 66.6	2 50.0	1 100.0	2 33.3		76	45.0
		4	3 37.5	2 25.0	15 10.9						20	11.8
		5			2 1.4						2	1.2
		Miscel.										
		Totals	8	8	138	3	4	1	6	1	169	
		Pct.	4.7	4.7	81.7	1.8	2.4	.6	3.5	.6		

pants of Ventana as against the more standard and better made choppers from earlier levels.

The sharpened flake variety was an improvement over the foregoing, as there was some preparation of the edges to achieve greater efficiency. Most of the specimens of this lot are oval to round in form and quite thin sectionally, a primary flake having been selected as the nucleus. Trimming usually is limited to the thinner edge or away from the bulb of percussion if present (Fig. 45, *b, c*). Diameters range from 90 to 125 mm., and the materials are predominantly basalt, occasionally rhyolite and chert. They make up 5.6 per cent of the chopper collection and

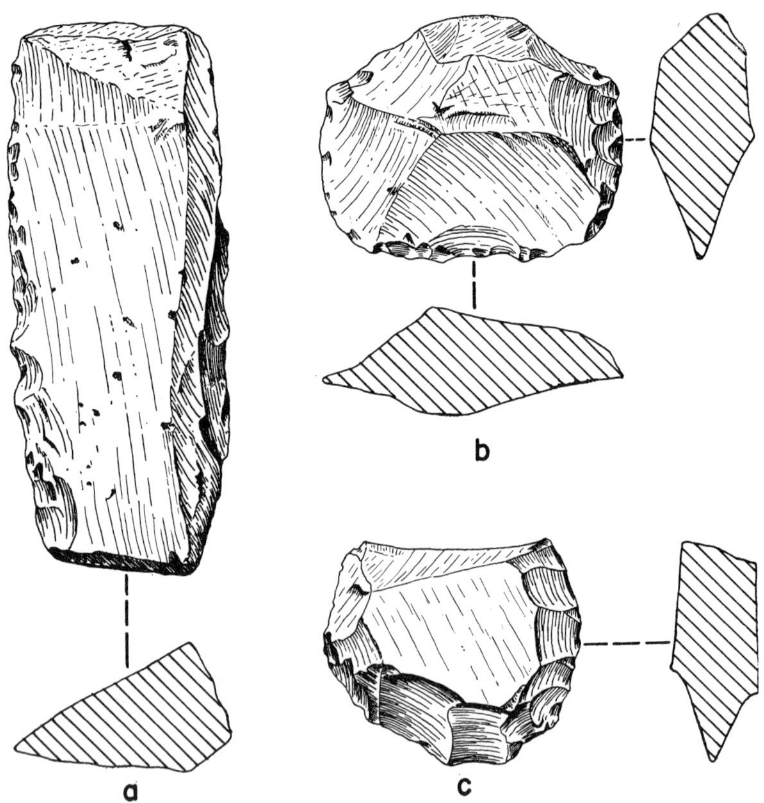

FIGURE 45. Choppers from the midden. Unsharpened flake, *a*; sharpened flake, *b, c*. All basalt. Length of *a*, 115 mm.

the vertical distribution through the midden was quite uniform (Table 19), indicating no particular peaks of use. The expedient of picking up a thin flake and sharpening it appears to have been a matter of common practice over a long period of time. The type occurs first in the volcanic debris.

(Core) –Core choppers greatly outnumber all other forms. Those trimmed only partly around the edge constitute 82 per cent of the whole chopper collection and would thus appear to represent the standard form of this tool. These are thick, crude affairs, displaying no consistent shape but always having large percussion flakes removed on both faces along a part of the mar-

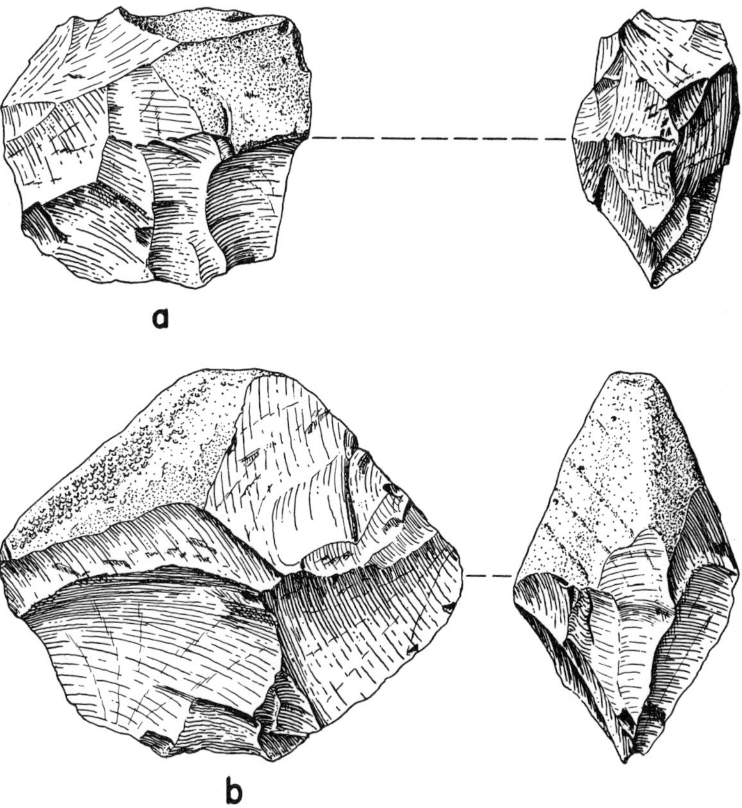

FIGURE 46. Core choppers from the midden, trimmed part way around perimeter. Both basalt. Length of *b*, 158 mm.

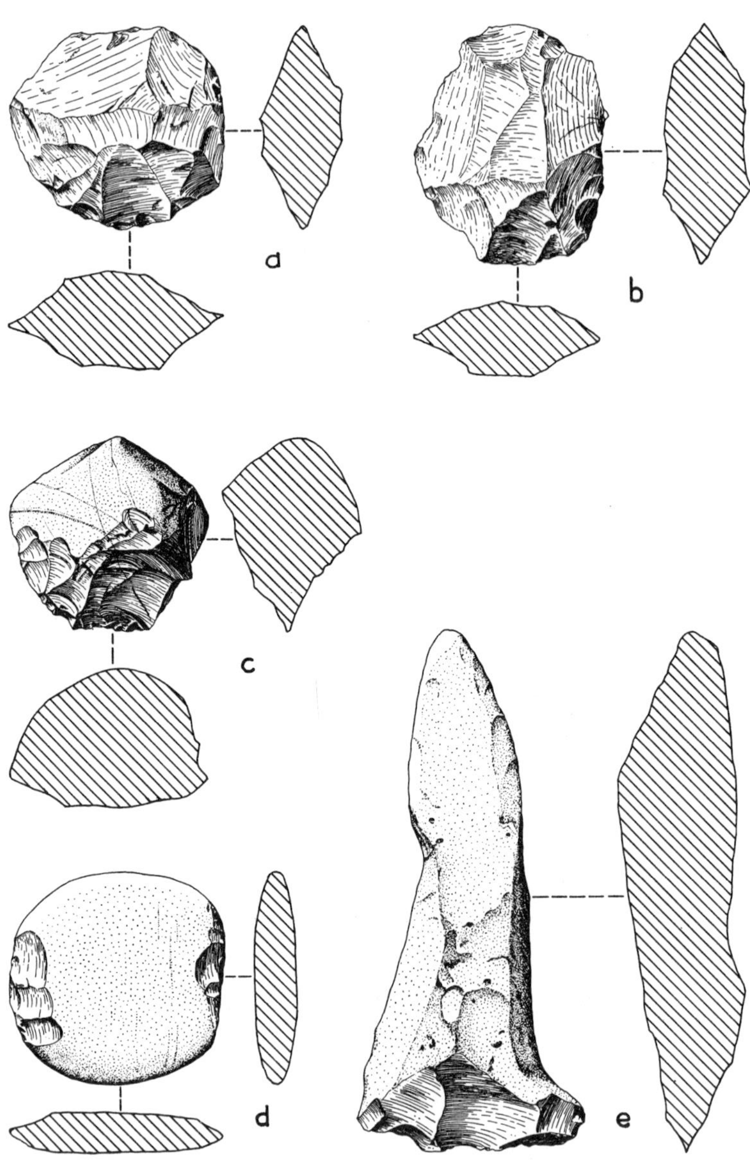

FIGURE 47. Choppers from the midden. Sharpened entirely around margin: discoidal, *a;* oval, *b*. Pebble: spheroidal, *c;* flat, *d;* long, *e*. *a, b, e,* basalt; *c,* fine-grained porphyry; *d,* quartzite. Length of *e,* 196 mm.

gin, to provide a sharp and sinuous cutting edge (Fig. 46). Many show the effects of extensive battering against some resistant material. Basalt was favored and chert and quartzite were used sparingly. Sizes range from 60 to 155 mm. in greatest diameter, and thicknesses almost invariably exceed one-half the diameter.

The abundance of this type gives us the best opportunity to appraise the occurrence of choppers to level (Table 19). The highest percentages occurred in levels 5 and 6 of the upper cave, after which there was a gradual decline. This peak comes synchronously with the implements characterizing the Californian desert cultures, an entirely harmonious situation, as choppers are reported as abundant in that area.[40]

The remaining core choppers with peripheries entirely sharpened are either discoidal (Fig. 47, *a*) or oval (Fig. 47, *b*) as to form. The diameter range is smaller (from 60 to 100 mm.), materials remain the same, and edges show the same crudeness of chipping. There would appear to be no special meaning in their distribution (Table 19) other than that they were produced on occasion over a considerable period of time.

(Pebble)—A small number of choppers (3.7 per cent) were turned out by selecting pebbles of basalt, limestone, and other hard crystalline rocks, and trimming a part of the margin on one or both ends to produce a usable tool. The spheroidal, long, and flat subtypes are illustrated in Figure 47, *c-e*. They show a rather erratic distribution through the midden (Table 19), although the spheroidal form would seem to have been somewhat earlier than the long subtype.

In every sense of the word, choppers are one of the simplest of tools and, therefore, probably also one of the most basic. It is apparent from the situation in Ventana that the type was not limited to any one horizon or to any one culture pattern. A few occurred in the volcanic debris layer, they were absent in the red sand, and in the midden they were one of the most common of tools. Highest frequency was reached in the pre-pottery part

★

40. C. A. Amsden, 1935, pp. 34-35; 1937, pp. 56-58; M. J. Rogers, 1939, pp. 49-50.

of the midden but they persisted strongly into the pottery-bearing levels. The evidence for choppers from other sites would tend to bear this out, including Lindenmeier,[41] the Californian desert groups,[42] Cochise,[43] and Snaketown.[44] I know of no actual record of their use by the Papago.

In Ventana, the height of chopper use came at a stage comparable culturally to Amargosa II (Pinto-Gypsum), of the California desert.

Hammer Stones—A great variety of shapes and sizes is recognizable in stones used as hammers. But a nearly consistent feature is the initial flaking of the core, doubtless as a measure of providing the tool with good biting edges. The abrasion of these edges varies, of course, with the extent of the use between sharpenings, from little modification of the edges to a near elimination of all flake scars and the reduction of the core to a sphere. Some were originally planes and ended up as hammer stones. The 885 specimens enumerated probably do not include all which were excavated, but the sample is large enough to demonstrate the pattern. The following subtypes have been recognized:

Irregular	858
Discoidal	16
Pebble	5
Pitted	6
Total	885

(Irregular)—These show a high range of materials and size. Basalt and quartzite are in greatest evidence. The largest and most unwieldy example measures 145 mm. in diameter and from this size they range downward to 40 mm. diameters, hammer stones of the lightest kind. Two average examples, little and much used, are shown in Figure 48, *a, b*. The level analysis (Table 20) of hammer stones yields no data which could be interpreted as indicating any change in the use of this type of ham-

★

41. F. H. H. Roberts, Jr., 1935, p. 29.
42. C. A. Amsden, 1937, pp. 56-58; M. J. Rogers, 1939, pp. 49-50.
43. E. B. Sayles, and E. Antevs, 1941, listed as axes.
44. H. S. Gladwin, *et al.*, 1937, Pl. XCVI, a.

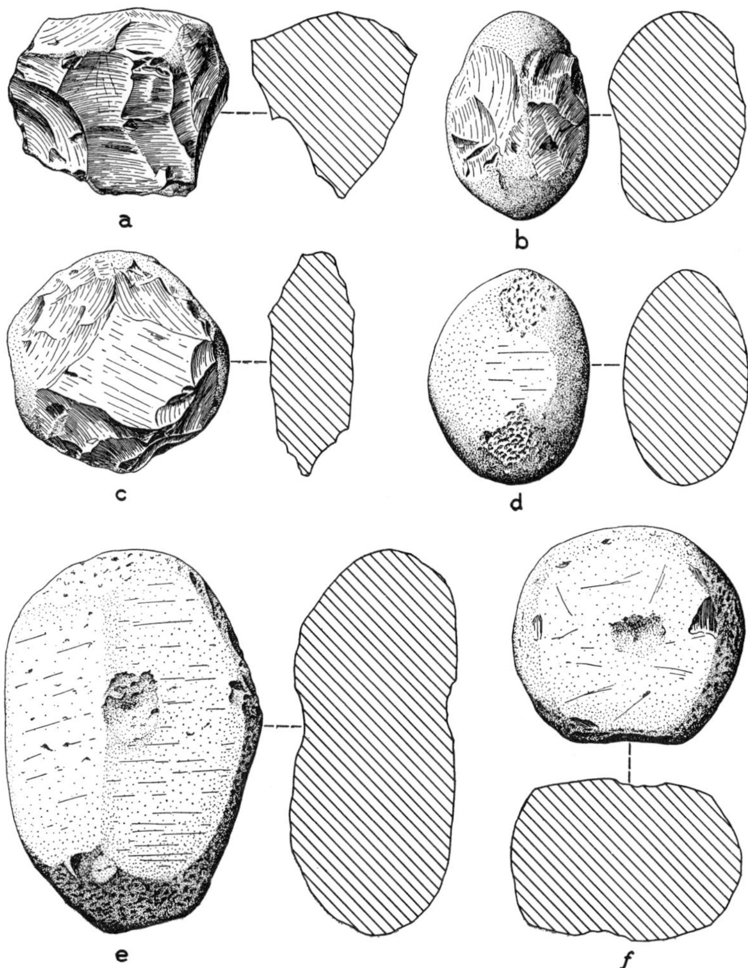

FIGURE 48. Hammer stones from the midden. Irregular: with initial flaking, *a* (little used) and *b* (extensively battered); discoidal, *c;* pebble, *d;* pitted, *e, f. a, c, e,* basalt; *b, d,* quartzite; *f,* porphyry. Length of *e,* 140 mm.

mer. But it is probably significant that none of them were found in levels 4 and 5, where chipped implements also were most numerous.

(Discoidal)—Hammer stones of this form also started as roughly hewn discs, and the abrasive work done with them was limited to the margin (Fig. 48, *c*). Diameters run from 60 to 110 mm. and the material is almost exclusively basalt.

With two exceptions, the sixteen discoidal hammer stones from the midden came from levels 1 to 4, suggesting that the type is a late one. Weighed against this evidence is the fact that one of the two doubtful implements from the conglomerate layer was a discoidal hammer stone (Fig. 20, *b*), making it one of the earliest implements from the cave, if genuine. It may be pointed out, however, that the form of this old specimen is different than the later examples in being larger and thicker and not trimmed by flaking.

(Pebble)—These are nothing more than quartzite stream pebbles, never prepared in any way for the work intended of them. They carry the abrasions and conchoidal fracture marks of work done with them (Fig 48, *d*). Sizes vary from 55 to 80 mm. in greatest diameters and no two came from the same level (Table 20). This, plus the small number, suggests only occasional use of the type; but it must be recognized that the rocks in question, being of stream origin, had to be brought into the cave deliberately from some distance.

(Pitted)—Every one of the six pitted hammer stones was converted from a bi-faced mano by centrally pitting the two flat faces. They occurred both in the pre-pottery and pottery levels of the midden (Table 20). One of the former, found directly above the volcanic debris layer, is illustrated in Figure 48, *e*, and a discoidal specimen (Fig. 48, *f*) came from level 1 or near the surface.

I find no mention of pitted hammer stones in the literature of the Californian desert complexes and in southern Arizona the oldest record seems to be that listed by Sayles from the Chirica-

Table 20

DISTRIBUTION OF HAMMER STONES BY TYPE AND LEVEL

	Stratigraphic Layer	Levels	Irregular	Discoidal	Pebble	Pitted	Totals	Percent
Upper Cave	Midden	1	56	2	1	1	60	
			10.3	22.2	25.0	16.7		10.7
		2	64	3			67	
			11.8	33.3				11.9
		3	83	1	1		85	
			15.3	11.1	25.0			15.2
		4	121	1		2	124	
			22.3	11.1		33.2		22.1
		5	119	2	1	1	123	
			22.0	22.2	25.0	16.7		21.9
		6	86		1		87	
			15.9		25.0			15.5
		7	5			1	6	
			.9			16.7		1.1
		8						
		Miscel.	8			1	9	
			1.5			16.7		1.6
		Totals	542	9	4	6	561	
		Percent	96.6	1.6	.7	1.1		
	Red Sand							
	Volcanic Debris				1		1	
Lower Cave	Midden	1	53	1			54	
			16.8	14.3				16.7
		2	73	3			76	
			23.1	43.0				23.5
		3	127	2	1		130	
			40.2	28.6	100.0			40.0
		4	62	1			63	
			19.1	14.3				19.5
		5	1				1	
			.3					.3
		Miscel.						
		Totals	316	7	1		324	
		Percent	97.5	2.2	.3			

hua Stage of the Cochise Culture,[45] with which the oldest Ventana specimens could be roughly equated. They are also shown as present in the San Pedro Stage.[46] This would suggest that the pitted hammer stone is a significant component of the Cochise Culture, with which those of Ventana are to be related. Their survival into pottery horizons is, of course, well documented. For the Papago area, Withers reports one from the Valshni Village, near Burro Pond.[47]

Hoes—The eleven stone hoes in the collection are all made of large wedge-shaped natural spalls of basalt. Little energy was expended in producing them, as the only workmanship was limited to the thin edge in the form of hasty flaking on both faces. Shapes, on the whole, are more or less oval (Fig. 49, *b*) and the sharpened edges are convex. One exception is the sharpened spall illustrated in Figure 49, *a*. On the five whole examples, the maximum lengths have the very small range of 135 mm. to 141 mm.

The hoe has long been recognized as a common tool in the ruins of southern Arizona, particularly those of the Salt and Gila River valleys.[48] It was originally thought to be strictly a product of the Hohokam, but considerable doubt has been thrown on this view by the excavations at Snaketown, where a single specimen only was found,[49] dating from the Sacaton Phase. Compared with Snaketown, hoes were abundant at Ventana, but weighed against the total number of stone artifacts, one must conclude that they could not have been considered as a particularly necessary implement among the Ventana residents. There was, in fact, little opportunity to use the hoe as a digging tool anywhere in the vicinity of Ventana, excepting in the trash of the cave itself. It would have been a useful implement for scooping out the shallow graves found in the upper levels. In this connection it should be noted that hoes were late

★

45. E. B. Sayles and E. Antevs, 1941, Pl. IX, i-j.

46. *Ibid.*, Pl. XV, f.

47. A. Withers, 1941, p. 60.

48. O. A. Turney, 1924; J. W. Fewkes, 1912, pp. 131-132; E. W. Haury, 1945, pp. 134-137.

49. H. S. Gladwin, *et al.*, 1937, p. 104.

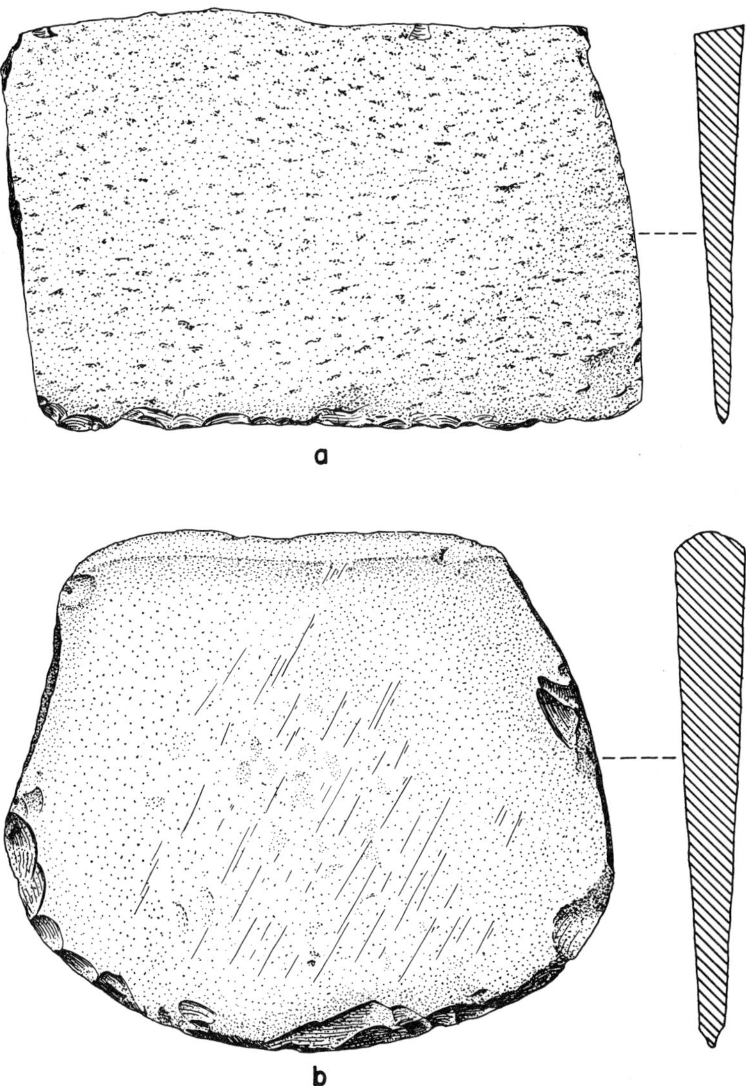

FIGURE 49. Hoes from the midden. These are characteristically wedge-shaped basalt spalls, sharpened along the thin edge. Length of *a*, 137 mm.

in the history of the cave, occurring with pottery and never below level 4 (Table 18).

Projectile Points and Knives—Anyone who has dealt extensively with chipped implements soon learns that a classification using functional terms eventually leads to difficulties. A case in point is provided here in a very large group of implements (2062) which may be broadly labelled as projectile points. But there are many in the lot which were certainly used as knives, possibly hafted in short handles. Size is somewhat of a criterion, but it is impossible to establish a maximum size for projectiles and a minimum size for knives because the Indian never thought of his tools in such precise categories. Consequently, following Kidder's example,[50] projectile points and knives are thrown together. It should be obvious to the reader that use of the term, knife, in this instance, refers to an all-over chipped tool, with premeditated shape, as distinct from the previous flake knives only partially chipped and of accidental form.

In spite of the above uncertainty as to the exact identification, I believe it may be stated that the majority of the specimens were used as projectile tips. The basis for this is the assumption that any hunter would have many more projectile points in his kit than knives, and the mortality of the former would be much higher, calling for the production of more. The damage to points is clearly reflected in the extraordinarily high proportion (55 per cent) of broken specimens. A single shot landing an arrow on stony ground, other than a lucky one, would shatter the point. One out of four points in the collection was so broken, in fact, that they could not be accurately classified and the damage to the rest was mainly loss of the tip or of one tang. It would appear that hunters, after retrieving their arrows or spears, supplied fresh points and discarded whatever was left of the original in the debris of the cave.

Most (about 80 per cent) of the Ventana projectile points and knives are made of basalt, with obsidian, chert, chalcedony, jasper, and quartzite also represented. The extensive use of

★

50. A. V. Kidder, 1932, p. 14.

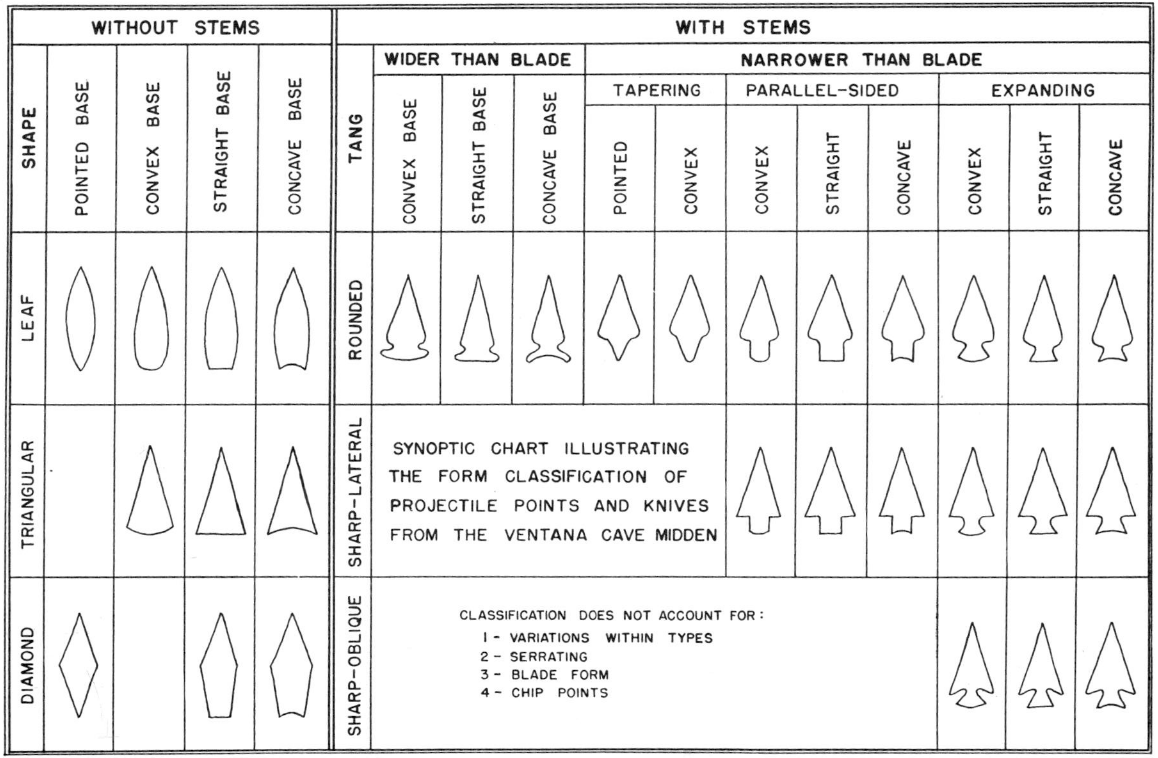

WITHOUT STEMS

SHAPE

POINTED BASE

CONVEX BASE

STRAIGHT BASE

CONCAVE BASE

LEAF

TRIANGULAR

DIAMOND

WITH STEMS

TANG

WIDER THAN BLADE

CONVEX BASE

STRAIGHT BASE

CONCAVE BASE

NARROWER THAN BLADE

TAPERING

POINTED

CONVEX

PARALLEL-SIDED

CONVEX

STRAIGHT

CONCAVE

EXPANDING

CONVEX

STRAIGHT

CONCAVE

ROUNDED

SHARP-LATERAL

SHARP-OBLIQUE

SYNOPTIC CHART ILLUSTRATING
THE FORM CLASSIFICATION OF
PROJECTILE POINTS AND KNIVES
FROM THE VENTANA CAVE MIDDEN

CLASSIFICATION DOES NOT ACCOUNT FOR:
1 - VARIATIONS WITHIN TYPES
2 - SERRATING
3 - BLADE FORM
4 - CHIP POINTS

FIGURE 50. Shape classification of projectile points and knife types

basalt, a low grade material and difficult to fashion, is responsible for the poor impression one gets of the Ventana occupants as chippers of stone. During all periods, points were made chiefly of this material and nearly all types in the collection show a predominance of it.

In classifying these tools I have avoided the use of formulae to express the shapes. Convenient as these are in the laboratory, they are little less than maddening in a published report, since the unraveling of the same sometimes amounts to so much work as to discourage one from doing it. Not that the word label system used here is perfect, but it will be somewhat more readily understood. Figure 50 illustrates synoptically the forms covering the range of Ventana points and knives. The major separation is made on the presence or absence of a stem. If absent, shape and base treatment provide further characters for classification; if present, the width and shape of the stem, as well as the tang form, become criteria. The nomenclature of the parts of projectile points and knives is given in Figure 51,[51] and the classification and census (exclusive of those from the volcanic debris and red sand) follows:

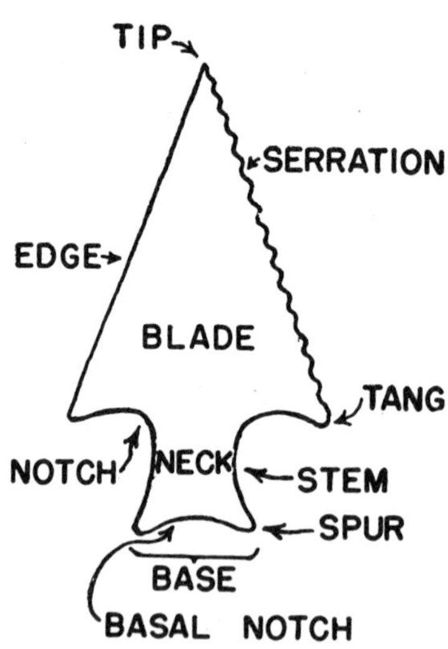

FIGURE 51. Nomenclature of projectile point and knife parts

I. Without stems — About 60 per cent of the classifiable points and knives lacked stems. A definite trend in the occurrence of the class as a whole is noticeable. In the deeper midden layers, they were found only now and again, but from levels 4 to 1, or from some time prior to the introduction of pottery to the end of the intensive use of the cave, the unstemmed point was common.

★

51. Adapted from *Stone Artifact Terminology* (Anonymous), Society for American Archaeology *Notebook,* Vol. 2, No. 4, pp. 67-69, April, 1942.

Projectile Points and Knives 2062

I. Without stems					967	62.7%[1]
A. Chips				7	.7%	.5%
B. Leaf shaped				726	75.0%	47.0%
1. Pointed at both ends			55	7.6%	5.7	3.6
2. Convex base			455	62.7	47.0	29.5
3. Straight base			106	14.6	11.0	6.9
4. Concave base			110	15.1	11.3	7.0
C. Triangular				148	15.3%	9.6%
1. Convex base			41	27.9%	4.2	2.7
2. Straight base			70	47.1%	7.2	4.5
3. Concave base			37	25.0	3.9	2.4
D. Diamond				86	8.9%	5.6%
1. Pointed at both ends			24	28.0%	2.5	1.6
2. Straight or convex base			36	42.0	3.7	2.3
3. Concave base			26	30.0	2.7	1.7
II. With stems					575	37.3%
A. Stem wider than blade				71	12.3%	4.6
1. Convex base			2	2.8%	.3	.1
2. Straight base			14	19.7	2.4	.9
3. Concave base			55	77.5	9.6	3.6
B. Stem narrower than blade				504	87.7%	32.7%
1. Tapering stem			76	15.1%	13.2%	4.9%
a. Sharp base		46	60.5%	9.1	8.0	3.0
b. Convex base		30	39.5	6.0	5.2	1.9
2. Parallel-sided stem			94	18.7%	16.4%	6.2%
a. Rounded tang		35	37.2%	7.0%	6.1%	2.4%
1. Convex base	7	20.0%	7.4	1.4	1.3	.6
2. Str. base	18	51.5	19.1	3.6	3.1	1.2
3. Concave base	10	28.5	10.7	2.0	1.7	.6
b. Sharp lateral tang		59	62.8%	11.7%	10.3%	3.8%
1. Convex base	19	32.2%	20.2	3.8	3.3	1.2
2. Str. base	19	32.2	20.2	3.8	3.3	1.2
3. Concave base	21	35.6	22.4	4.1	3.7	1.4
3. Expanding stem			334	66.3%	58.0%	21.6%
a. Rounded tang		122	36.6%	24.2	21.2%	7.9%
1. Convex base	37	30.3%	11.1	7.3	6.4	2.4
2. Str. base	19	15.6	5.7	3.8	3.3	1.2
3. Concave base	66	54.1	19.8	13.1	11.5	4.3
b. Sharp lateral tang		189	56.5%	37.5%	32.8%	12.2%
1. Convex base	102	54.0%	30.5	20.2	17.7	6.6
2. Str. base	62	32.8	18.5	12.3	10.8	4.0
3. Concave base	25	13.2	7.5	5.0	4.3	1.6
c. Sharp oblique tang		23	6.9%	4.6%	4.0%	1.5%
1. Convex base	6	26.1%	1.8	1.2	1.0	.4
2. Str. base	7	30.4	2.1	1.4	1.2	.5
3. Concave base	10	43.5	3.0	2.0	1.8	.6
III. Too fragmentary to classify						520

1. In figuring percentages the figure 1542 was used, derived by subtracting group III "Too Fragmentary to Classify" from the total.

(A. Chips) —Were it not for a quiver of arrows found with burial 9 it would be impossible to demonstrate certainly that fortuitous triangular flakes, showing little or no alteration, were used to tip arrows. Two of these, still with sinew binding, are illustrated in Figure 52, *a, b*. The points are of obsidian and are exceedingly small (14 mm.). If we had found these free in the trash it is doubtful if they would have been picked up. One suspects that many were discarded during the excavations and that the few specimens at hand do not accurately reflect how commonly these simple affairs were used. A somewhat larger specimen with just enough edge chipping to show what it is will be seen in Figure 52, *c*. It came from the dry or late part of the midden, as do the others in the collection, and is referable to the Desert Hohokam.

Chip points are also represented in a good many of the following categories, but they were shaped sufficiently to allow classification.

(B. Leaf shaped) —Most numerous of all were leaf shaped points and knives. These not only show an extreme range in size but also in thickness and workmanship. It is quite possible that many are unfinished or rejects.

Subtype 1, *Pointed at both ends* (Fig. 52, *d-i*): Lengths, 26 to 123 mm., average about 45 mm.[52] There are several distinctions within the lot which need to be pointed out. The larger specimens (5 over 65 mm., Fig. 52, *f, g*) may confidently be classed as knives, specimen *f* showing the best workmanship of all. Among the small specimens, about one-third are conspicuous in having thick bodies (Fig. 52, *h, i*) as compared with the rest, which are thin in section.

The analysis (Table 21) indicates the deepest occurrence of the type to be in level 6 of the upper cave, whence they increased in abundance in the higher levels. Both the thick- and thin-bodied forms were most prevalent in level 2, where they were associated with pottery. All larger specimens which may pass as knives came from levels 1 to 3.

★

52. All measurements are based on whole specimens only.

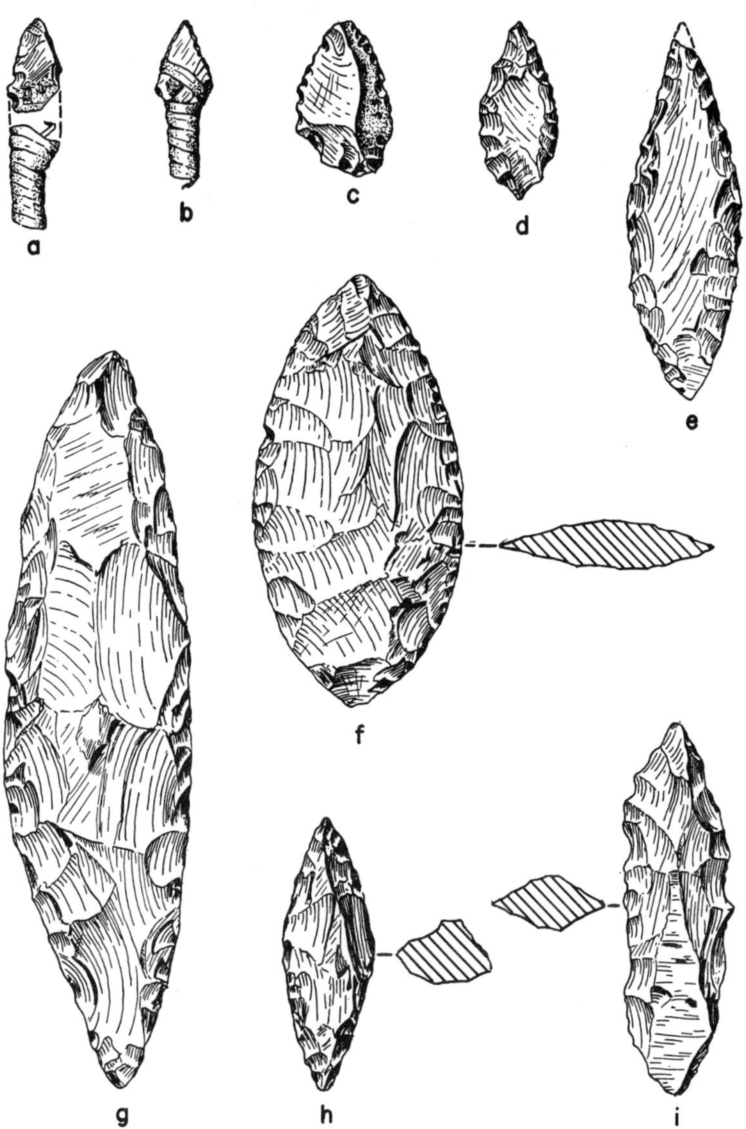

FIGURE 52. Projectile points and knives from the midden. Chip points with sinew lashing, *a, b;* without lashing, *c;* points and knives, pointed both ends, *d-i: a-c,* obsidian; *d, e, g, i,* basalt; *f,* chert; *h,* quartzite. Length of *g,* 124 mm.

Rogers[53] indicates double-pointed leaf blades as present in the Playa Industry, Phase I (now San Dieguito II), and Amsden[54] also records them for the Pinto and Mohave areas, although they seem to have been relatively uncommon. The earliest Ventana examples are associated with tools representative of the above industries and the evidence is, therefore, in harmony with that found in California. But it is clear that as a diagnostic, pointed leaf blades are somewhat more valuable critically in later times. Strangely enough, Sayles does not list them for any of the stages of the Cochise Culture and there are none in a large collection of artifacts from a surface site of the San Pedro Stage (Arizona FF:5:3) in the Arizona State Museum Survey. This suggests further that the affiliations at an early time, at any rate, are with the western cultures.

Subtype 2, *Convex base* (Fig. 53): Lengths, 19 to 98 mm., average about 50 mm. More implements of this form were found than of any single subtype and it is not surprising that considerable range should be manifested within the group. Simplest are chips which have been accorded just enough work to bring them to shape (*a*), followed by a large group somewhat below the average in length, pressure flaked, and with maximum widths at about the mid-point of the blade (*b, c*); a third variety, thin, and with flake scars, longer than average and with greatest width near the base (*d, e*); thick and crude percussion flaked examples, usually narrower in proportion to length than the foregoing (*f, g*); and finally, the larger specimens, dressed with some care and doubtless qualifying as knives (*h*).

Analyzed as a group (Table 21) it is apparent that most of them occurred in the upper four layers of the midden, the values diminishing rapidly through levels 5 to 8. The quartz blade from the volcanic debris (Fig. 21, *a*) is near these in shape but differs in having the shallow notches. In the table, no attempt has been made to pick up separately any possible distribution differences of the varieties mentioned above. A casual inspection shows

★

53. M. J. Rogers, 1939, p. 34, labelled small knives.
54. C. A. Amsden, 1935, Pl. 12, e; 1937, Pl. XL, b.

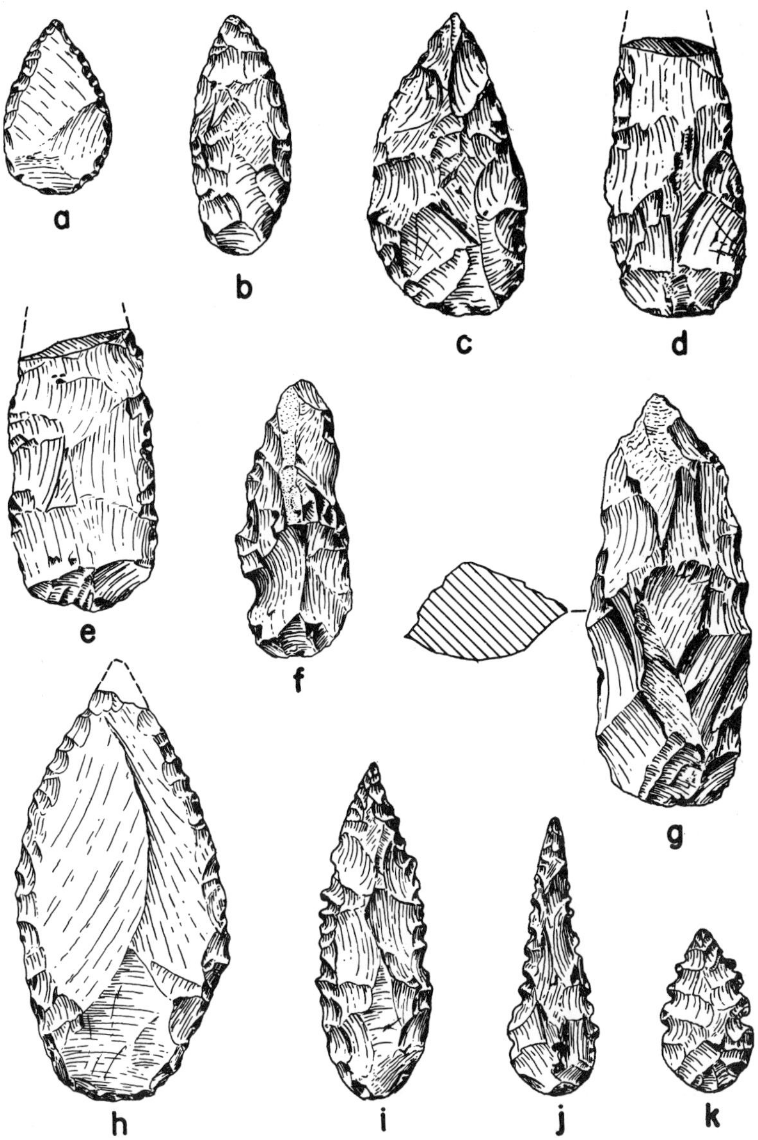

FIGURE 53. Projectile points and knives from the midden. Leaf shaped convex base. Retouched chip, *a;* greatest width near mid-section, *b, c,* long, greatest width near base, *d, e;* crude, thick bodied, *f, g;* large, *h,* serrated, *i-k*. All basalt except *k* which is chert. Length of *h,* 75 mm.

that, with few exceptions, the thick percussion flaked examples (Fig. 53, *f, g*) came from levels 1 to 3, and that the blades with greatest width near base (Fig. 53, *d, e*) came chiefly from levels 2 and 3. These, incidentally, are all broken, suggesting rather violent usage. Since nothing quite like them has been found in the pottery sites of the Papago Reservation or at Snaketown, and the form is somewhat specialized, I suspect that they may be companions of the San Pedro type of point, which they resemble in the quality of chipping and with which many were directly associated. This is plausible as they occurred just below and within the pottery zone and because the type form is also represented in our collection from Arizona FF:5:3, a San Pedro Stage site in the Sulphur Spring Valley. Sayles does not mention them and it may be reasonable to suppose that the above site in question was later in the sequence than any visited by Sayles, coming just before the introduction of pottery. The situation in Ventana would seem to bear this out.

Nothing significant is evident in the distribution of the other forms. Not mentioned as yet is the serration of the edges which occurs on ten specimens in the lot (Fig. 53, *i-k*). Apparently there is no time value to this characteristic, as they were well distributed vertically. Example *i* was found in level 7 and may be assumed to be the oldest.

The leaf shaped round base blade is evidently well represented in the Californian desert cultures.

Subtype 3, *Straight base* (Fig. 54): Lengths, 20 to 83 mm., average about 45 mm. About the same range is recognizable in these as in the foregoing subtype, although the number in the collection is much smaller. On all, the edges are convex, which distinguishes them from the straight edged triangular points. There are a few chips with a minimum amount of flaking, a majority of rather well-formed blades exhibiting both poor and refined chipping (*a-d*), the butts of large and thin blades (*e, f*), and a few of the thick clumsy type (*g*). Some show weakly developed serrations.

Stratigraphically, these straight based blades follow the trend of the round based form, with a moderately stronger showing in levels 2 and 3 than elsewhere (Table 21). The type does not occur in the cave before level 7 of the upper midden and then only as a very uncommon trait. Conspicuous again are the butt ends of the thin large blades (*e, f*), long in relation to width. These were heaviest in levels 2 and 3 and in chipping and size are like those of round base form previously suggested as being a San Pedro Stage component.

Subtype 4, *Concave base* (Fig. 55): Lengths, 20 to 63 mm., average close to 50 mm. The synoptic series illustrated for this interesting group includes chips (*a*), stubby and long varieties with great differences in chipping quality and thickness (*b-e*),

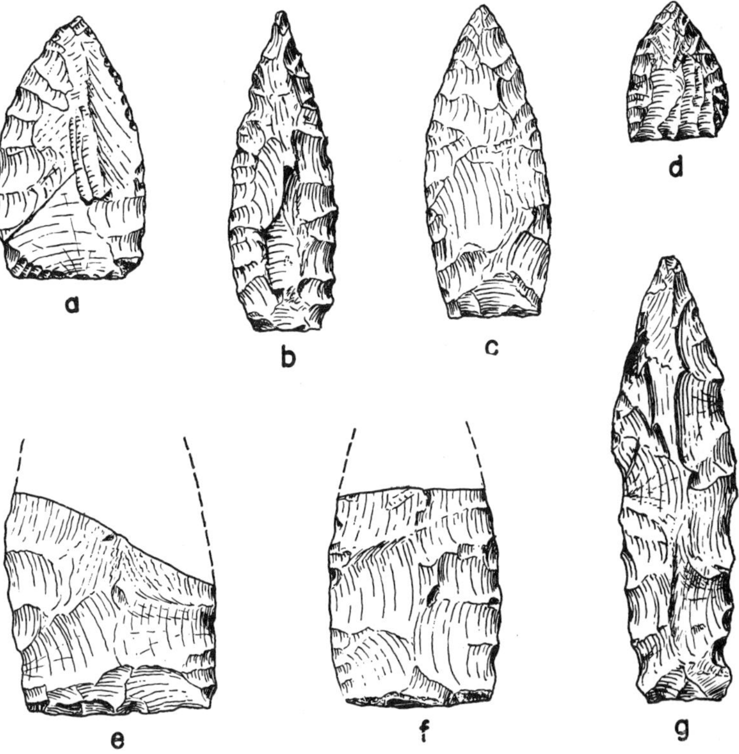

FIGURE 54. Projectile points from the midden. Leaf shaped, straight base; *d*, obsidian; all others basalt. Length of *g*, 66 mm.

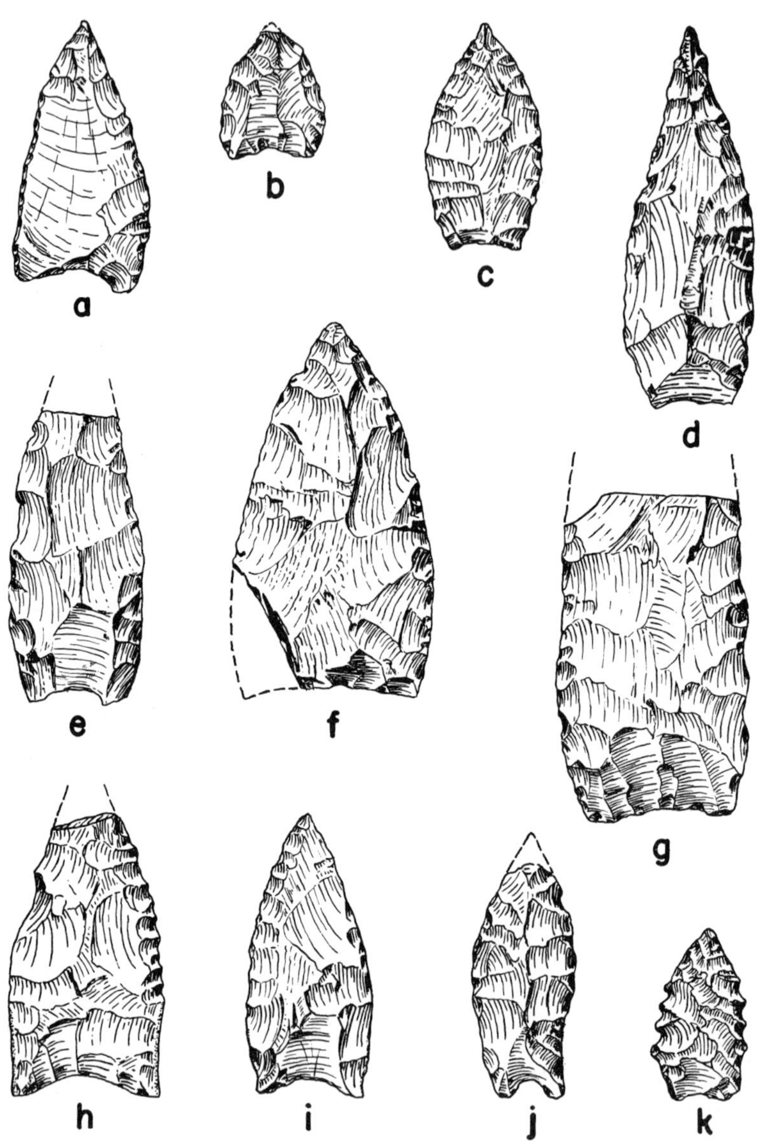

FIGURE 55. Projectile points and knives from the midden. Leaf shaped with concave base. Retouched, *a;* short, *b, c;* long, thick bodied, *d, e;* broad bladed form, *f, g;* with basal constriction, *h-j;* serrated, *k. a, d, e, g, i, j,* basalt; *b, c, f,* chert; *h,* rhyolite-porphyry; *k,* obsidian. Length of *d,* 64 mm.

broad bladed forms (*f, g*), and a few with edges slightly constricted toward the base (*h-k*).

Table 21 indicates that the majority were found in the top four levels of the upper cave with a scattering down to the very bottom of the midden. None were found in the red sand and one (Fig. 21, *b*) was associated with extinct fauna in the volcanic debris and is suggestive of the Folsom type. It shows the drawing in of the edges to a moderate degree. It is doubtless significant that all those from the midden with this feature were found in the deepest layers. All lack channel flaking and a few have their edges dulled by grinding near the base, which is not present in any of the examples from the higher levels. Obviously these are not Folsom points, to which they bear a vague resemblance in form, but it may be inferred that they represent the modified survival of the type into later times. Example *h* (Fig. 55) may be singled out as of special interest. It was found within a few centimeters of the bottom of the midden in section A, or just above the volcanic debris layer. Its material is a light gray rhyolite unlike that of any other point in the collection and it has been reshaped and evidently shortened considerably in length from the original. The chipping of the reworking process is quite fresh and irregular, in comparison with the somewhat eroded and regular original flaking. One cannot go so far as to claim that this point dates from the volcanic debris layer and was salvaged by later occupants of the cave, but its stratigraphic position and the re-use may be taken as indicators that it belongs early in the cave's history.

Only one point in this group has serrated edges (Fig. 55, *k*).

(C. Triangular): Subtype 1, *Convex base* (Fig. 56): Lengths, 27 to 60 mm., average about 50 mm. Three varieties of this subtype are distinguishable: (a) a small point with chipping well executed, (*a, b*), (b) a long, narrow form, all broken, most of which about reached the maximum length of this group (*c*), and (c) a bulky, broad bladed form (*d*).

The stratigraphy of this subtype as a whole is clearer than for most others (Table 21). None at all were found in the vol-

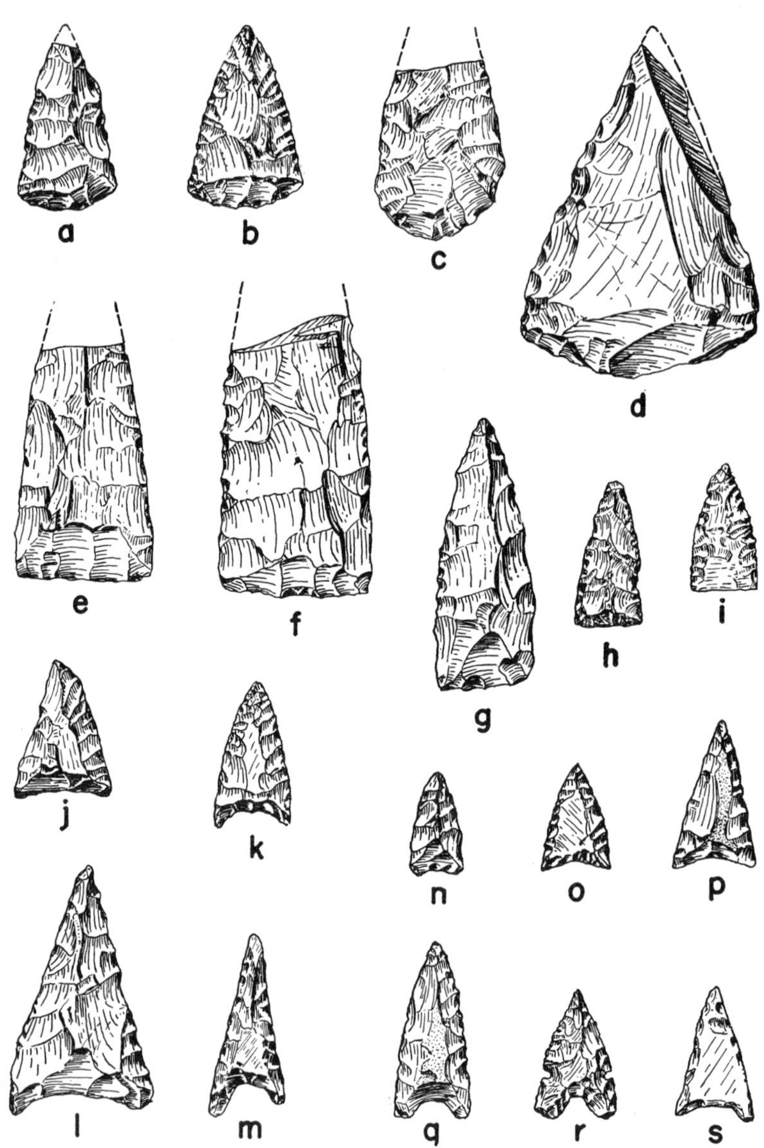

FIGURE 56. Projectile points and knives from the midden. Triangular: convex base, *a-d;* straight base, *e-i;* concave base, *j-m*. Points *n-s* are of latter type but of historic Papago origin from Batki. *a, d, e-g, l, n, p, q,* basalt; *b, i, o, r,* jasper; *c, j, m,* chert; *h, k,* obsidian; *s,* glass (probably of European origin). Length of *d,* 61 mm.

canic debris and red sand layers and only three occurred below level 3 of the upper cave midden. This places the high frequencies in the top zones. All three deep level specimens are of the small type (Fig. 56, *a*, from level 7), although this form persisted to the surface. The long, narrow form prevailed in levels 2 and 3, and by technology and size are but variations of the previous blades allocated to what I believe to be a San Pedro Complex. The broad bladed variety, of which there are only four, was well distributed in the upper three levels.

It seems safe to rule out these triangular points as of any consequence in the list of components of the early culture patterns of Ventana. The type burst into prominence shortly before the arrival of pottery and then persisted. It is quite likely that the few small specimens found in the top level are variations of the standard form of early historic Papago point.

Subtype 2, *Straight base* (Fig. 56): Lengths, 23 to 59 mm., average close to 50 mm. Again three varieties may be pointed out: (a) small (23 to 31 mm. range for 6 specimens) and thin, mostly of materials other than basalt (*h, i*), (b) a thick, roughly flaked medium length form (*g*), and (c) a thin but long, skillfully flaked form (*e, f*).

The distribution analysis (Table 21) shows a somewhat greater scattering for this subtype as a whole than in the previous one, but the highest percentages are reached in the upper levels of the midden. The small, finely chipped variety are all from near the surface and like their convex and concave based mates, may very well be of Papago origin. The style of the other outstanding variety, the large, thin bladed form, has by now become familiar and by prediction one would place them prevailingly in levels 2 and 3, which our analysis shows to be correct. Once again they may be related to the San Pedro Stage Complex.

Subtype 3, *Concave base* (Fig. 56): Lengths, 20 to 50 mm., average about 35 mm. These subdivide themselves into two categories, each with a fairly sharp time value: (a) a small form (*j, k, m*), pressure flaked, ranging less than 33 mm. in length, and (b) a large, crudely pressure flaked, thick bodied variety *(l)*. Highest frequencies for the former are noted in the upper two levels (Table 21), and of the dozen specimens from level 1, ten are of the small variety. The bulkier form occurred mainly in levels 3 and 4.

At this time, it will be well to identify the authorship and the age of the small variety of concave based triangular point. This can be done on sound evidence. In the Museum's survey of Papagueria this type of projectile point was found on several abandoned historic Papago village sites. Most notable of these is Batki (Ariz. Z:16:6), situated at the eastern foot of South Mountain and visited by Father Kino in 1697. This village was raided by the Apaches about the middle of the 19th century, when many of its occupants were killed and the houses burned. All but one of the twenty-two points picked up here are of triangular form, twenty of the lot show the concave base, and four in this group also have shallow lateral notches. Samples of these are illustrated in Figure 56, *n-s,* including one made of glass, which appears to be of European origin. The objection may be raised that these could have been made by the Apache and were shot on arrows during their raid. This idea, however, may be ruled out in the light of the following: seven of the Batki points were found in a cluster on the floor of one of the demolished houses, suggesting that arrows stored in the house were burned at the time of the raid. The type also occurs in a village where, as far as we know, the impact of the raiding was never felt. Proof for the recent Papago identity comes from a late 19th century or early 20th century grave near Coyote Village. This grave was liberally furnished with offerings of both native and American culture. On and about it, thirty-eight points of the type in question were picked up. Another association is recorded from the Santa Rosa area where the same style of point was found in a jar associated with other items of Papago origin. Although it cannot be said when the Papago first made use of the type, there can be no doubt that it has survived to very recent times, and that those which occurred in the upper level of Ventana Cave may be cited as further evidence of Papago occupancy.

Viewing the triangular point (or knife) broadly, the Ventana evidence would indicate that the form has no particular value until just before the arrival of pottery. Basically, it was a late development, doubtless as a refinement of the leaf shaped blade. The absence of triangular blades in the Californian desert cultures and the first two stages of the Cochise Culture tends to support this view.

(D. Diamond)—Diamond shaped blades, with variations listed below, made up only about 9 per cent of the unstemmed class and approximately 4 per cent of the collection as a whole, thus being one of the most weakly represented forms. Typologically these lean toward the tapering stemmed blades but the stem as such is not developed and it may therefore be regarded as an integral part of the blade.

Subtype 1, *Pointed at both ends* (Fig. 57): Lengths, 27 to 43 mm., average about 36 mm. Some range in shape is manifested by these, including nearly symmetrical forms (*a, b*), a few with shortened base (*c*), and three with convex edges (*d, e*). There appears to be no stratigraphic value in these differences. As a whole, the type occurred in all levels of the midden except the deepest and they were absent in the red sand and volcanic debris layers (Table 21). Highest frequencies occurred in levels 1 and 4. We may single out specimen *d* as being most nearly like the Lake Mohave type[55] of any in the collection. But it was found in level 1 of the lower cave, a stratigraphic position much too high for the Lake Mohave Complex.

Subtype 2, *Straight or convex base* (Fig. 57): Lengths, 19 to 72 mm. There are two varieties evidencing sharp stratigraphic values: (a) a long form (average 45 mm.), narrow in relation to length (*f-h*), and (b) a broad, short form (average 28 mm.) (*i, j*). The first of these is distinctly a late form, occurring almost without exception in levels 1 and 3, and the second form was predominantly in levels 5 and 6, accounting for the high percentages in those levels (Table 21). These are pretty certainly within the range of the Amargosa II (Pinto) type of point and

★

55. *Ibid.*, 1937, Pl. XLI.

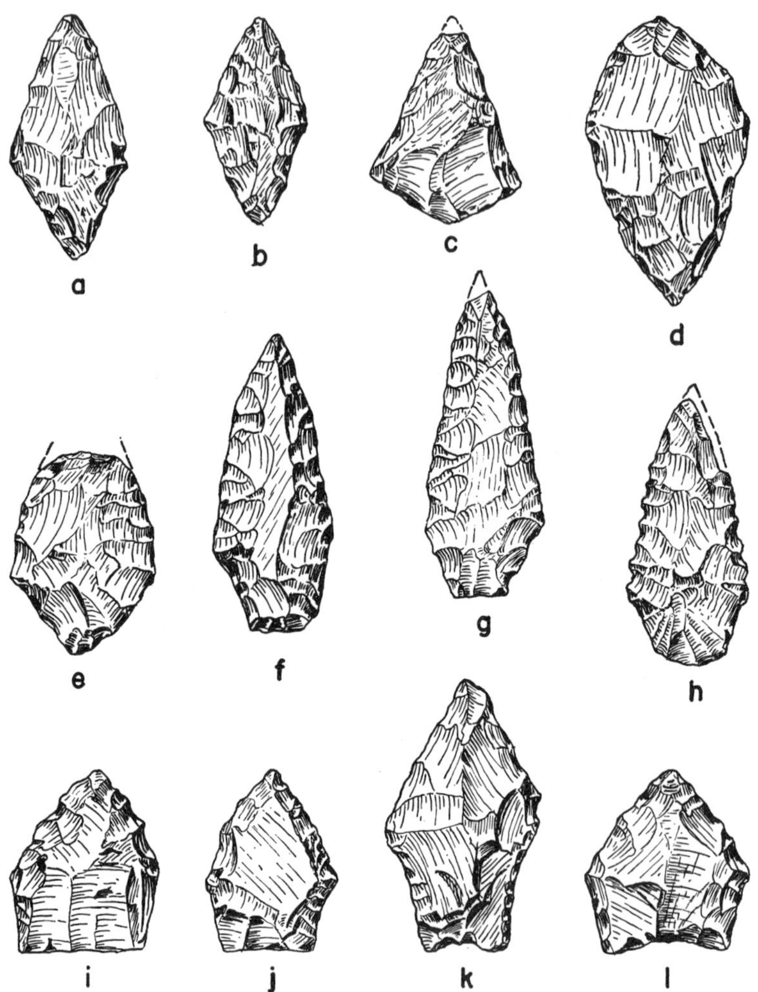

FIGURE 57. Projectile points and knives from the midden. Diamond shaped: pointed both ends, *a-e;* straight or convex base, *f-j;* concave base, *k, l.* *g, h,* chert; all others basalt. Length of *g,* 45 mm.

they are directly associated with the more orthodox examples of that type. Serration is present but infrequent in both varieties.

Subtype 3, *Concave base* (Fig. 57): Lengths, 17 to 46 mm. The same difference as between long (*k*) and short (*l*) forms noted above is in evidence here although the distribution is not so clear cut (Table 21). There was a stronger survival into higher levels of the short-bladed variety. A higher proportion (30 per cent) of the stubby variety of both straight and concave base subtypes was made of obsidian than evident in any other division of the classification. Serration again is rare.

II. With Stems—Although stemmed points make up only 37 per cent of the classifiable 1,542 specimens in the projectile point-knife category, the number of subtypes and varieties is much larger than in the unstemmed class. A true stemmed blade makes its earliest appearance in Ventana in the red sand layer.

(A. Stems Wider Than Blades)—Subtype 1, *Convex base* (Fig. 58, *a*): Lengths, 23 and 42 mm. This is a rare form, being represented by only two specimens. From their position in the midden (Table 21), it may be inferred that they were of late origin, although Rogers illustrates one bearing marked similarity to ours from the Amargosa II (Pinto) Complex.[56]

Subtype 2, *Straight base* (Fig. 58, *b-d*): Lengths, 21 to 55 mm. Numerically also a small lot, these, nevertheless, show a variation which appears to have some value. A large form nearly consistent, 45 mm. in length (*b, c*) runs to the deeper levels. A small variety is only represented by two examples but one of these (*d*), with sinew binding, is from the quiver found with burial 9 and therefore datable to after A. D. 1000. This small point, made of obsidian, is a familiar Hohokam type of the Sacaton Phase[57] whereas the large variety was not represented at Snaketown. One suspects the latter to be a variation of the Amargosa II (Pinto) point. Serration occurs on nearly all individuals of this subtype.

Subtype 3, *Concave base* (Fig. 58): Lengths, 12 to 50 mm.,

★

56. M. J. Rogers, 1939, Pl. 13, s.
57. H. S. Gladwin, *et al.*, 1937, Pl. LXXXV, e-h.

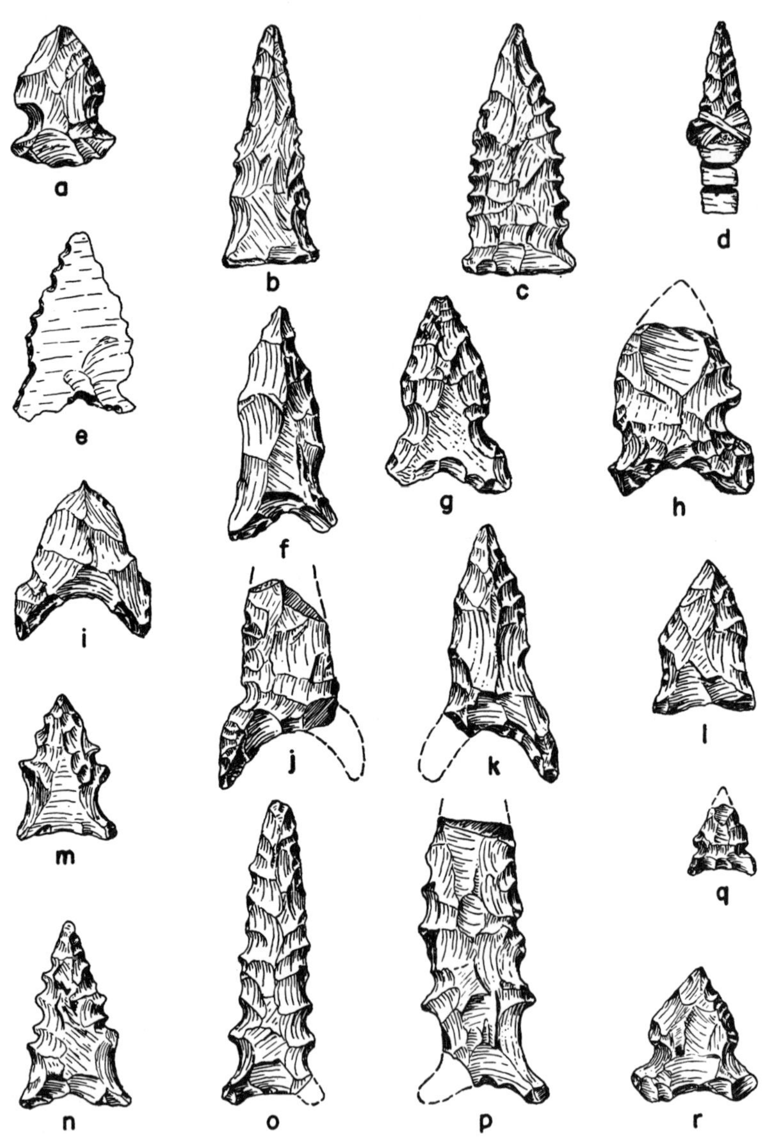

FIGURE 58. Projectile points and knives from the midden. Stem wider than blade: convex base, *a;* straight base, *b-d* (*d* with pitch and sinew binding); concave base, *e-r. a,* quartz; *b, c, f-i, l-n,* basalt; *d, e, q,* obsidian; *j, k, r,* jasper; *o, p,* chert. Length of *o,* 50 mm.

average about 35 mm. High variability is noted within this subtype. Simplest in the lot is an obsidian point (*e*) made from a paper-thin flake by merely breaking away the superfluous parts to bring it to form. It comes from level 6 (upper) and consequently carries the trait of thin chip points toward the lower levels of the midden. Most abundant in the group are points with shallow and narrow notches, relatively long flakes and no tang development (*f-h*), reaching in a few specimens a great exaggeration of the spur (*i-k*). Nearly as common is a variety with a broad notch and flaring, but relatively short, spurs (*l-p*). These are either long- or short-bladed and, in nearly all instances, pronouncedly serrated. Finally, there is a short, broad variety (*q, r*) with shallow notches.

The distribution (Table 21) of the subtype as a whole ranges through the midden, with most coming from the deeper levels. Examples *q* and *r*, however, occurred near the top and would appear, therefore, to be a late form. The rest, I believe, may again be recognized as within the range of the Amargosa II (Pinto) Complex, with the possible exception of specimens *o* and *p*. These are reminiscent of the traditional Sacaton Phase point[58] of the Hohokam but a direct comparison shows a minor difference in the more pronounced stem development by chipping out a broad notch. Point *p* emanated from level 7 of the upper cave midden, which would tend to fix it as an early point in spite of its "late" appearance.

(B. Stems Narrower Than Blade)—1. Tapering stem:—Specimens with narrow stems are strongly in the majority in the stemmed class (87 per cent) and among these there are relatively few (15 per cent) which have tapering stems. While not abundant, they, nevertheless, are of interest because of the marked similarity of some to the Gypsum type point. They resemble the diamond shaped, unstemmed type already described but are identified with this category because of a more pronounced development of tangs and a sharper delimitation therefore between the blade and the stem portions. Two subtypes are recognized:

★ 58. *Ibid.*, Pl. LXXXV.

Subtype a. *Sharp base* (Fig. 59, *a-i*) : Lengths, 20 to 83 mm., average 35 mm. The most frequently recurring form is illustrated by *a-f* with *b* showing serrated margins. Extra long tangs are seen in *c* and *d,* and *e* and *f* are assymetrical in outline. Nine small points, between 20 and 30 mm. in length, have very short rudimentary stems (*g, h*). With the exception of one, all were found in the upper level of the midden. They follow the pattern already set by other types in the retention, in miniature, of a shape present in earlier layers. The type in question at Snaketown dated from the Santa Cruz Phase and earlier[59] and I do not believe there need be any hesitation in assigning these to a Hohokam origin.

Most of the others in the lot came from the deeper midden levels (Table 21), where their chief companions were points of the Amargosa II Complex. These resemble and possibly have some relationship to the Gypsum Cave point.

There remains in Figure 59, specimen *i,* to which no specific reference has been made. This is a large blade, 83 mm. long, coming from level 3 in the midden of the lower cave. It is strikingly similar to a hafted knife found in Gypsum Cave[60] and a blade illustrated by Rogers,[61] from California. The evaluation of this specimen and the smaller copies, with respect to their relationship with the Gypsum Complex, will be postponed until a later section (p. 295).

Subtype b. *Convex base* (Fig. 59, *j-o*) : Lengths, 26 to 52 mm. These would appear to be related to the preceding subtype and although there are some minor variations within the lot there is no evident stratigraphic value in the differences. Specimens were well distributed through all but the deepest of the midden levels (Table 21) and there is only one with serration (*o*), coming from the top level.

2. Parallel sided stem:—a. Rounded tang. Subtype 1, *Convex base* (Fig. 60, *a, b*) : Lengths, 30 to 43 mm., average about 38

★

59. *Ibid.*, Pl. XCI.
60. M. R. Harrington, 1933, p. 46, Fig. 24.
61. M. J .Rogers, 1939, Pl. 14, e.

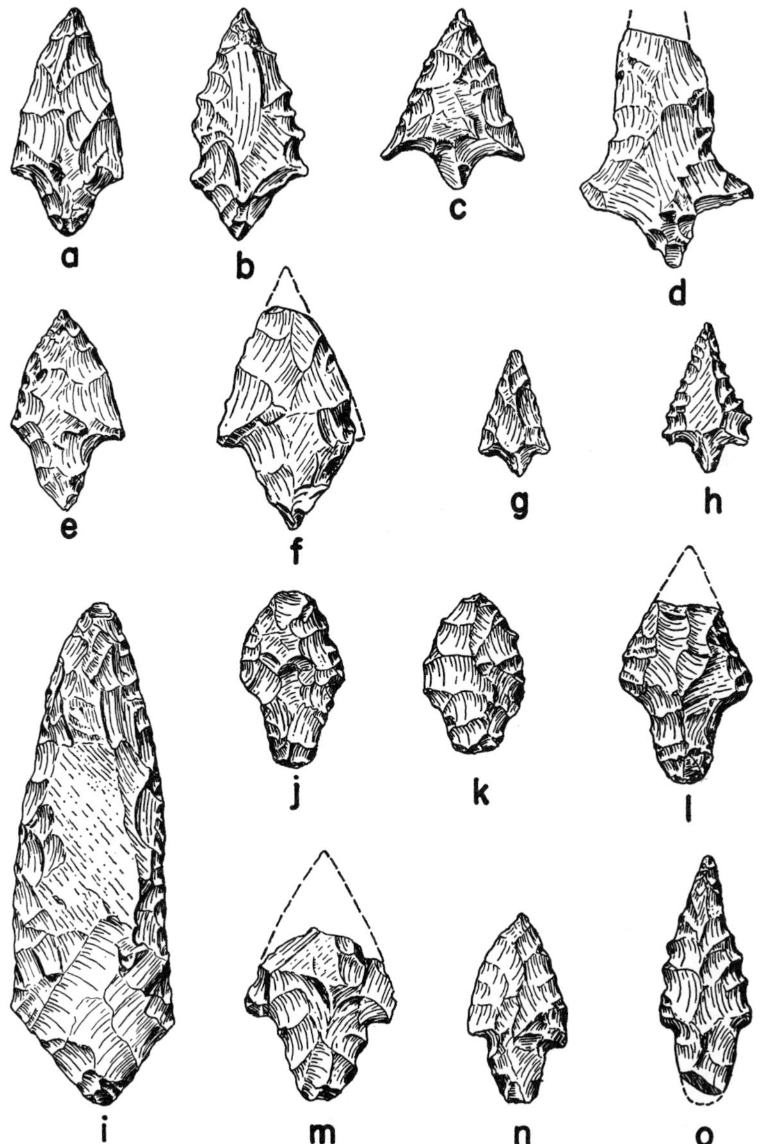

FIGURE 59. Projectile points and knives from the midden. Stems narrower than blade, tapering: sharp base, *a-i;* convex base, *j-o.* *h, m,* chert; *j, k,* obsidian; all others basalt. Length of *i,* 83 mm.

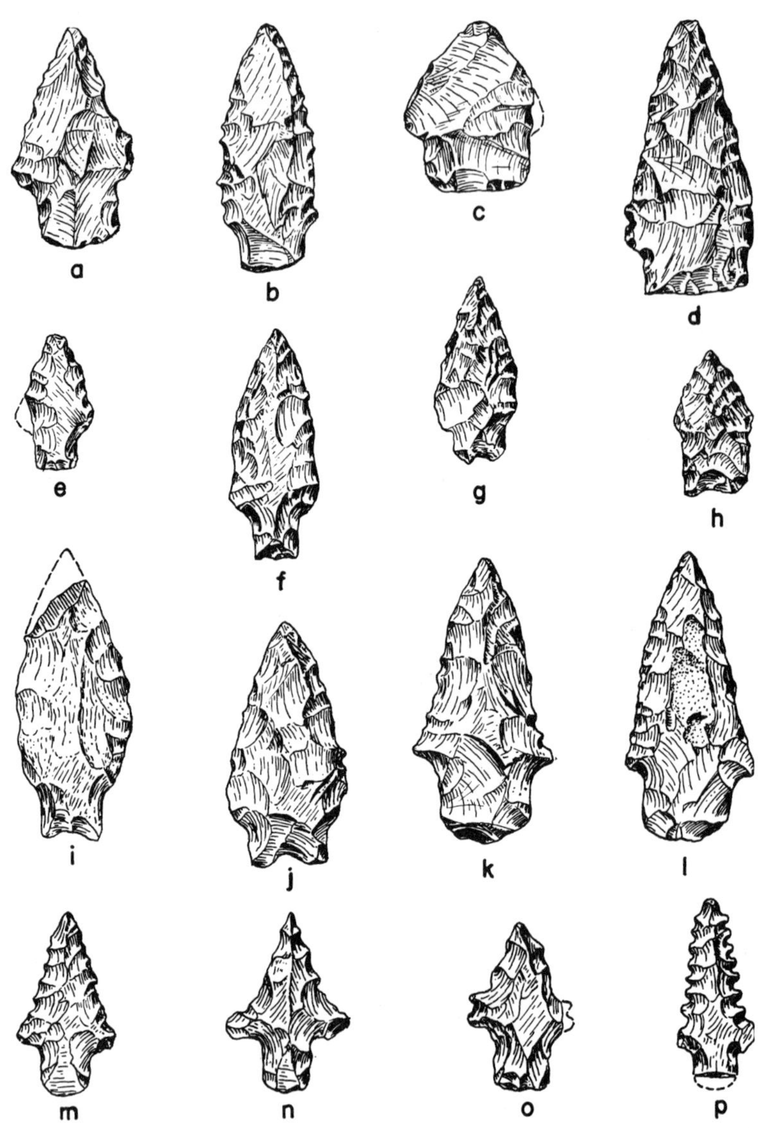

FIGURE 60. Projectile points and knives from the midden. Parallel sided stem, rounded tang: convex base, *a, b;* straight base, *c-f;* concave base, *g-j.* Sharp tang: convex base, *k-p. a, n,* jasper; *b, d-g, j-l, o,* basalt; *c,* obsidian; *h, m, p,* chert; *i,* quartzite. Length of *d,* 46 mm.

mm. A rare form, the seven examples in this lot nevertheless were well distributed through the midden (Table 21). They are crude, for the most part, the two illustrated coming from level 6, and suggest the form so well represented in the red sand layer (Fig. 27).

Subtype 2, *Straight base* (Fig. 60, *c-f*): Lengths, 22 to 50 mm. average about 38 mm. The eighteen points which qualify here show enough variability to be detected. There is a stubby broad-bladed form (*c*), limited chiefly to the deep levels; a larger variety, with a blade longer in relation to width than in the foregoing (*d*); and a small form (*e, f*). These three varieties are present in nearly equal proportions and the latter two, in contrast to the first one, with one exception, emanated from levels 2 and 3. Frequencies of the subtype as a whole are given in Table 21. Systematic serration is not present on any examples in the group.

Subtype 3, *Concave base* (Fig. 60, *g-j*): Lengths, 25 to 43 mm., average 37 mm. Although occurring in nearly all midden levels, most commonly in level 1 (Table 21), there is nothing in this type which strikes one as having any particular stratigraphic value. None are serrated.

b. Sharp lateral tang. Subtype 1, *Convex base* (Fig. 60, *k-p*): Lengths, 20 to 42 mm. There is a clear cut typological and stratigraphic separation to be made in the nineteen specimens of this subtype. The first variety (*k, l*) is large with broad stem (average length 40 mm.), coming from levels 5 to 7; and the second variety (*m-p*), restricted chiefly to level 1, is smaller (average length 30 mm.) with stem relatively longer and narrower in relation to blade than in the preceding variety. The tang is apt to be exaggerated. The older specimens may certainly be recognized as the Ventana-Amargosa type of the red sand layer, either derived from the red sand to become associated with the trash accumulation, or persisting as a component of the people who were responsible for the lower zones of the midden. The late variety looks suspiciously like Hohokam although nothing like them was found at Snaketown, the nearest being a type which was an element of the Santa Cruz Phase.[62]

Serration occurs consistently on the eleven examples of the late form, ranging from slipshod to precise arrangement of the teeth, and a rather fine serration is evident on two of the early examples.

Subtype 2, *Straight base* (Fig. 61, *a-d*): Lengths, 20 to 47 mm., average 35 mm. Although the distribution of this subtype through the midden (Table 21) suggests the possibility of the detection of an early and a late variety, the grouping of the points to level does not bring this out sharply. Generally speaking, the large, broad bladed form (*b, c*) is early and the stubbier form seems to run late (*a, d*); but there are so many exceptions that this trend may not be true. Serration occurs in about half of the nineteen points and is represented in all levels.

Subtype 3, *Concave base* (Fig. 61, *e-l*): Lengths, 19 to 50 mm., average 38 mm. This style of points is not divisible into varieties as in the foregoing categories. All run pretty much to a set pattern, although some slight deviations in tang development and serration are seen. Practically all specimens in this lot can be duplicated in collections of Amargosa II (Pinto) projectile points and the typological correlation with this complex can be made without question.[63]

The stratigraphic position of most of these points also lends support to the Amargosa connection, most of them coming from levels 4 to 6 (Table 21) of the upper cave midden, where they were associated with other points and implements so well known to the western desert. The presence of the type in the top two levels with pottery must be accounted for either by considering them to have been intruded upward from older parts of the trash or as contemporary products. The lack of this type of point in late pottery sites of the area, as Snaketown, Valshni, and Jackrabbit villages, throws the weight on the first alternative as being the most likely.

★

62. H. S. Gladwin, *et al.*, 1937, Pl. XCI, a.

63. For direct analogies see C. A. Amsden, 1935, Pl. 13, *k, n;* and M. J. Rogers, 1939, Pl. 13, *m.*

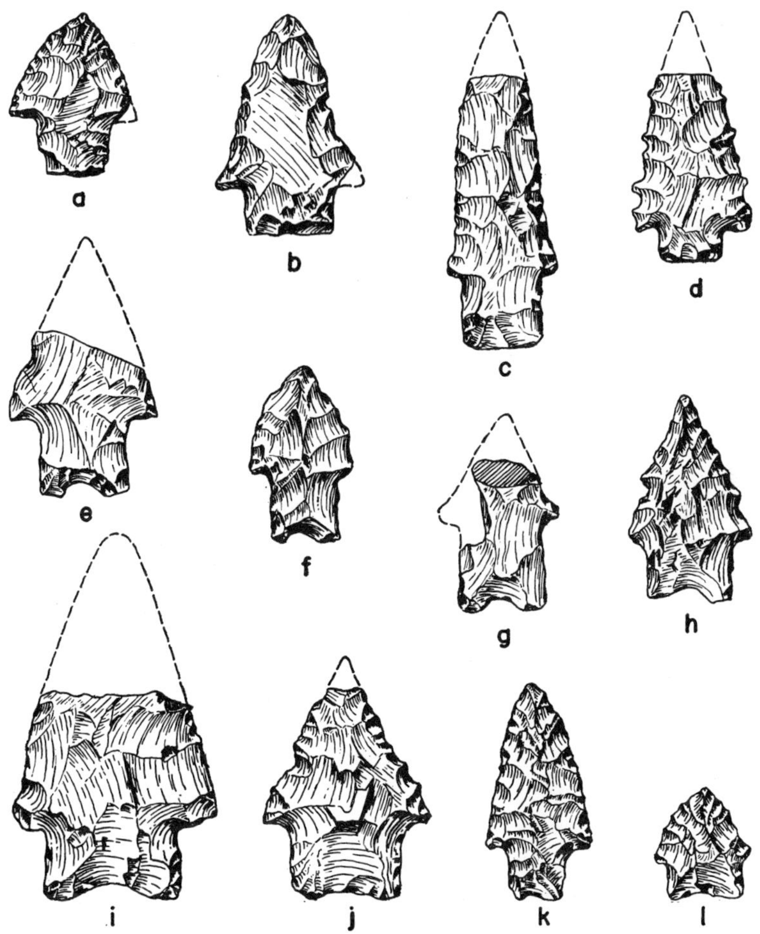

FIGURE 61. Projectile points and knives from the midden. Parallel sided stem, sharp lateral tang: straight base, *a-d;* concave base, *e-l.* *a, k, l,* obsidian; *b, c, f-h, j,* basalt; *d, e, i,* chert. Length of *c,* 46 mm.

3. Expanding stem:—a. Rounded tang. Subtype 1, *Convex base* (Fig. 62, *a-d*): Lengths, 23 to 65 mm., average about 45 mm. As in the preceding group, there are no definable varieties among these which appear to have any chronological value. According to the distribution chart (Table 21) the majority occurred in levels 1 to 3 of the upper cave, although the type made its appearance in the very bottom layer of the midden. Serration of a systematic kind was not represented at all although the edges of several specimens are rather sinuous, resulting from an extremely poor quality of workmanship. The material, with few exceptions, is basalt.

Subtype 2, *Straight base* (Fig. 62, *e-h*): Lengths, 22 to 43 mm., average about 35 mm. These manifest little difference in treatment over the preceding group except for the straight base. Relatively more occurred in the deeper midden layers but the sample, on the whole, is small and it is doubtful if any real diagnostic value may be assigned to this subtype. In general, many of these would appear to be variants of the more stylized Amargosa II (Pinto) point.

Subtype 3, *Concave base* (Fig. 62, *i-t*): Lengths, 20 to 68 mm., average about 40 mm. Two variations of this subtype are in evidence. First, points poorly chipped, cumbersome, and lacking serrations (*i-l*), and second, points given more care in fashioning and which, with few exceptions, show serrated margins (*m-t*). The former lot was recovered from levels 1 to 3 in the midden and the second group, more numerous than the first, occurred in the deeper portions of the midden (Table 21). These are assignable to the Amargosa Complex although some from Ventana show a more exaggerated form of serration than has been illustrated in the literature. The serration, in some cases, is limited to two or three pronounced projections just about the stem while in others this edge treatment continues forward to the tip. A rather interesting feature is a lengthened stem (*p*) which is also seen specifically on points from the Pinto Basin.[64]

Once again the predominant material is basalt but there is

★

64. E. W. C. and W. H. Campbell, 1935, Pl. 13, b.

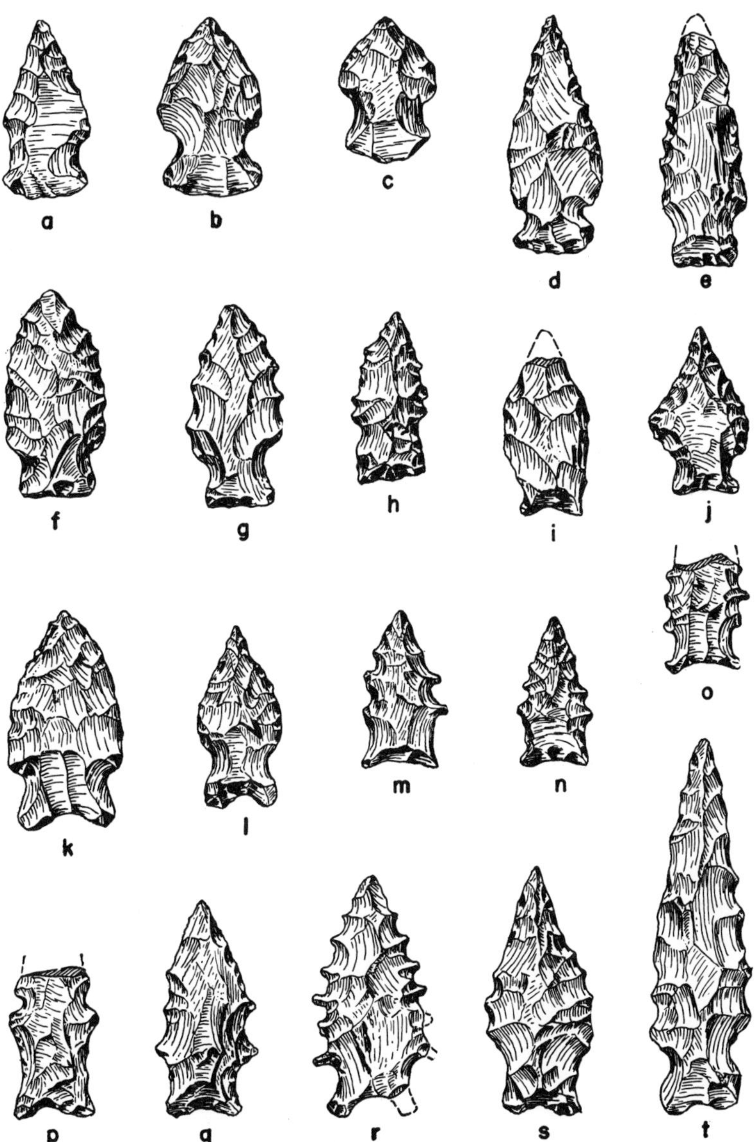

FIGURE 62. Projectile points and knives from the midden. Expanding stem, round tang. Convex base, *a-d;* straight base, *e-h;* concave base, *i-t.* *f, n,* obsidian; *h,* jasper; *j,* chalcedony; all others basalt. Length of *t,* 70 mm.

a noticeably higher per cent of obsidian (nine out of sixty-six specimens) and there is one example of clear quartz and a few of chert.

b. Sharp lateral tang. Subtype 1, *Convex base* (Fig. 63): Lengths, 28 to 75 mm., average about 50 mm. The sharp lateral tang on the points in this group are the results, chiefly, of a fairly deep notch. Three variations within this subtype, all adhering to the requirements of the classification, are recognizable. The first of these (*a-c*) shows a blade of moderate length in relation to width and the stem exhibits only slight flaring. These are quite clearly related by form to the type identified as coming from the red sand layer. The twelve specimens of this variety in the collection were found in levels 6 to 8 which would make them early as regards the age of the midden. The second variety is much smaller (*d-f*) and is represented by eight specimens. These occurred consistently in levels 1 and 2. This variety has, in fact, a rather marked resemblance to the Hohokam points of the Santa Cruz Phase[65] and may be assigned on the strength of this to the Desert Hohokam. The third variety, by far the most numerous (Fig. 63, *g-o*), is a large point. They were made by pressure flaking and manifest somewhat better craftsmanship than is evidenced in the other varieties of the subtype. On the whole, the lateral notches tend to be rather shallow and range from narrow to wide, often creating a stem with a long neck (Fig. 63, *j*). A somewhat oblique placement of the notch is also characteristic. There is no discernable difference in the emphasis of serrated edges in these three varieties. Approximately 50 per cent of the points in each show this treatment. Differences in material are likewise not in evidence, basalt being the usual stone used in each case.

Stratigraphically and typologically the third, or large variety of point in this subtype, meets the requirements of the San Pedro Stage type of point of the Cochise Culture.[66] In Ventana Cave, the San Pedro point occurs heavily in the upper part of the mid-

★

65. H. S. Gladwin, et al., 1937, Pl. XCI.
66. E. B. Sayles and E. Antevs, 1941, Pl. XVI, c, d.

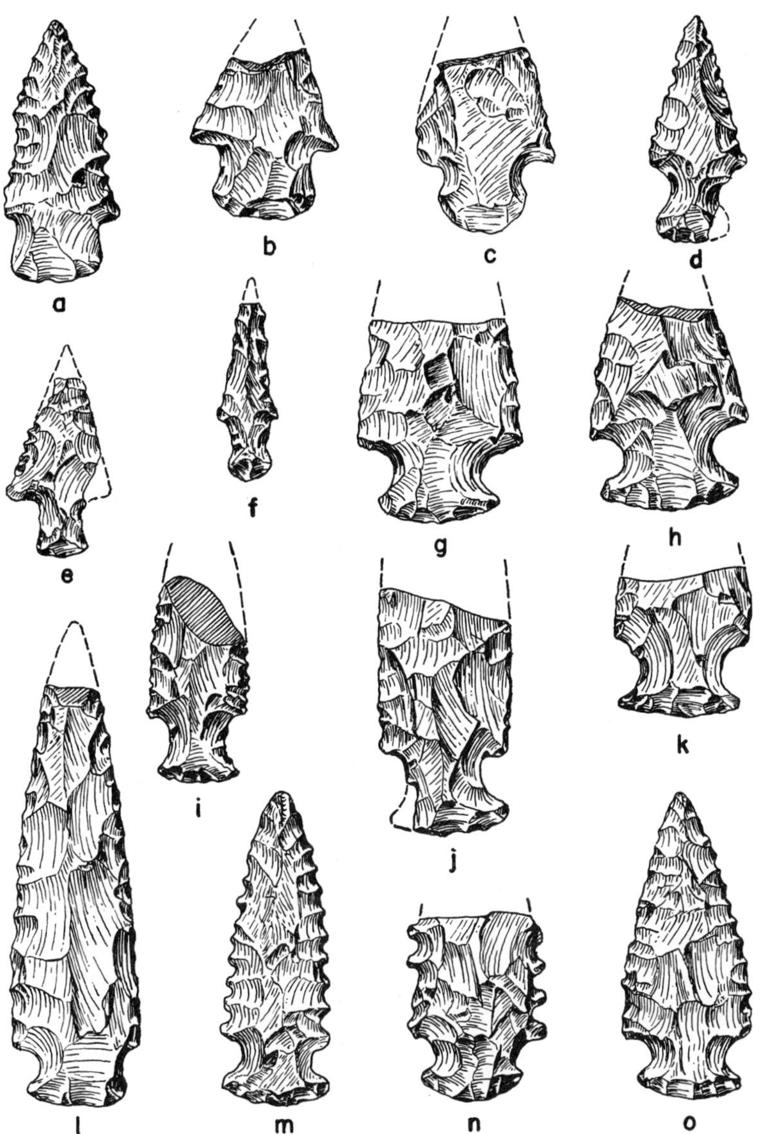

FIGURE 63. Projectile points and knives, from the midden. Expanding stem, sharp tangs, convex base: *e, o,* jasper; *g,* rhyolite; *n,* chert; all others basalt. Length of *a,* 43 mm.

den without pottery and in the lower zones of pottery-bearing trash. The inference here is that the type actually was in vogue before pottery arrived and then either persisted into early pottery times or individual points became mixed with later trash through the churning of the debris. This latter situation would appear to be the most likely in view of the fact that the San Pedro point has not been found as the normal type in ruins of southern Arizona which produce pottery.

Subtype 2, *Straight base* (Fig. 64, *a-g*): Lengths, 28 to 66 mm., average about 50 mm. Since the majority of these resemble the preceding groups in every respect, save the basal shape, they may be regarded as a variation of the San Pedro point. This appraisal is borne out also by stratigraphy (Table 21), since more were found in the upper four levels than elsewhere. The exceptions (*a, b*), it may be noted, are probably variants of the earlier Amargosa II (Pinto) types and cannot be confused with the much larger San Pedro point.

Plate 21 illustrates two San Pedro points, 58 and 61 mm. in length, lashed to a piece of yucca cord which occurred with the offerings of burial 9. Tied to this cord was also a marine shell *(Oliva angulata),* and a wooden nose plug, suggesting an appliance with possible magic qualities. There are reasons to believe that this burial was not made before A. D. 1000 (see p. 467). The presence of what appears to be an early type of point with a late burial, needs, therefore, to be explained, particularly as the previous surmise was that the presence of San Pedro points in pottery-bearing trash was chiefly a matter of accidental association. I suspect that in this instance we have a situation somewhat similar to the practices of modern Indians, who attach value to projectile points which they find on old ruins and carry them as amulets or which are used by medicine men in curing the sick.[67] The disharmony in this present association is also suggested by the fact that projectile points with burial 11, believed to be the same age as burial 9, were totally different (Fig. 58, *d*) than the ones in question.

★

67. C. Lumholtz, 1912, p. 180; Plate opposite p. 142, *b, e, f*.

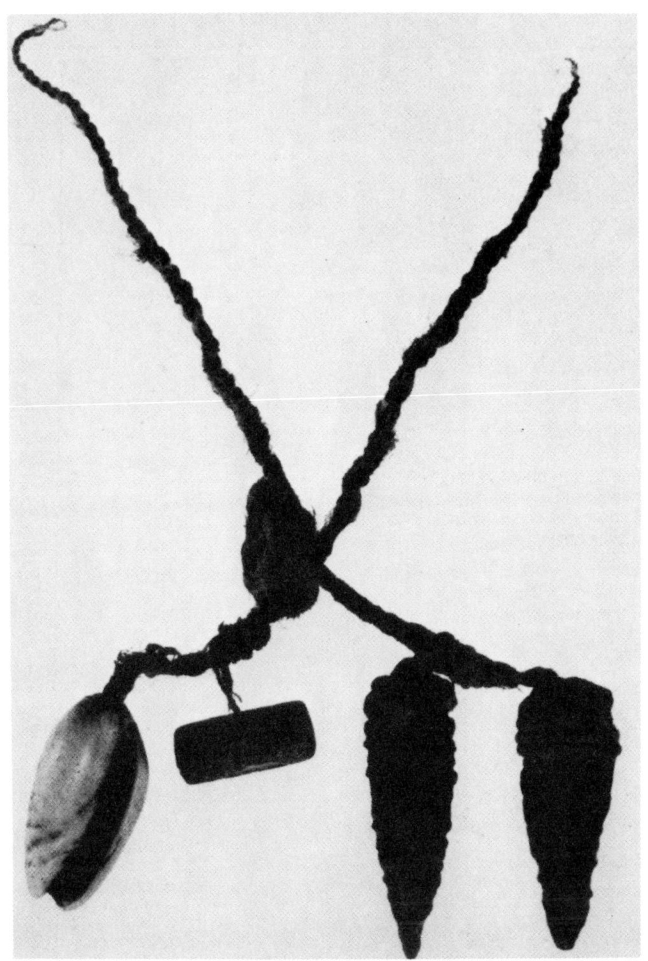

PLATE 21

Two projectile points of San Pedro type, tied to an amulet string, associated with burial 9, dating from after A.D. 1000. Other objects are a marine shell and a wooden nose plug.

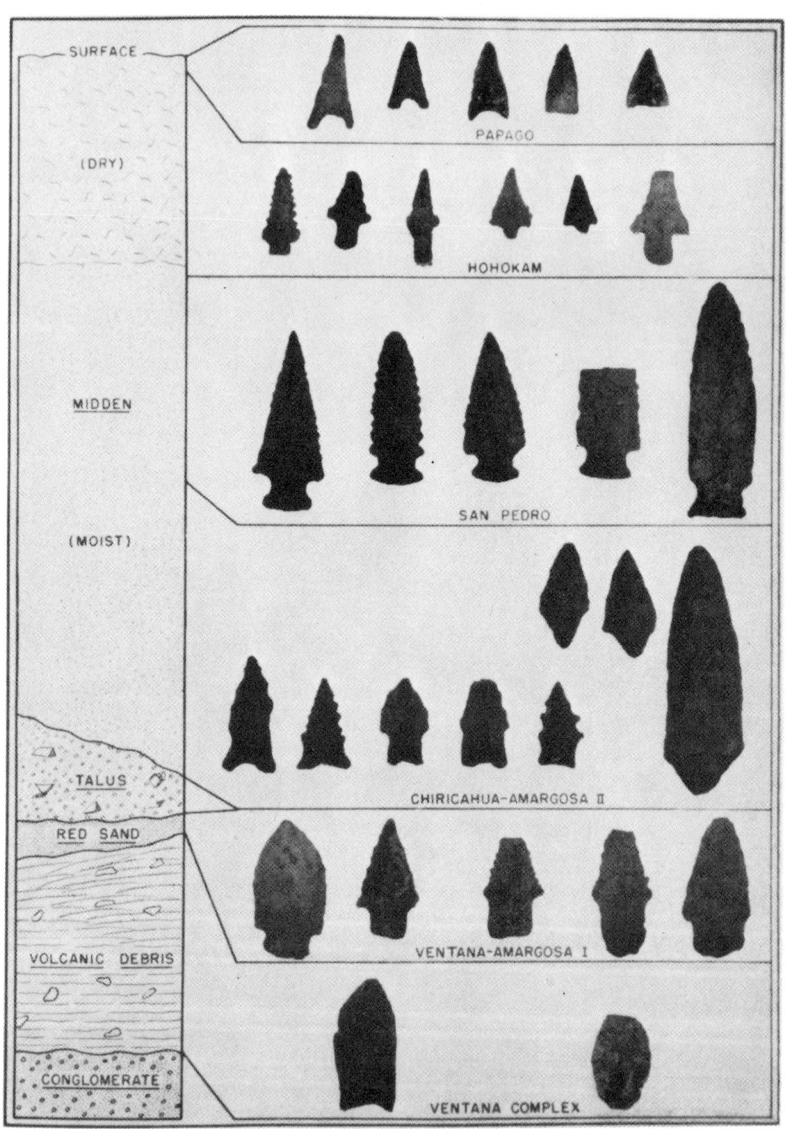

PLATE 22

Profile of Ventana Cave, and synopsis of projectile point types referable to the various levels.

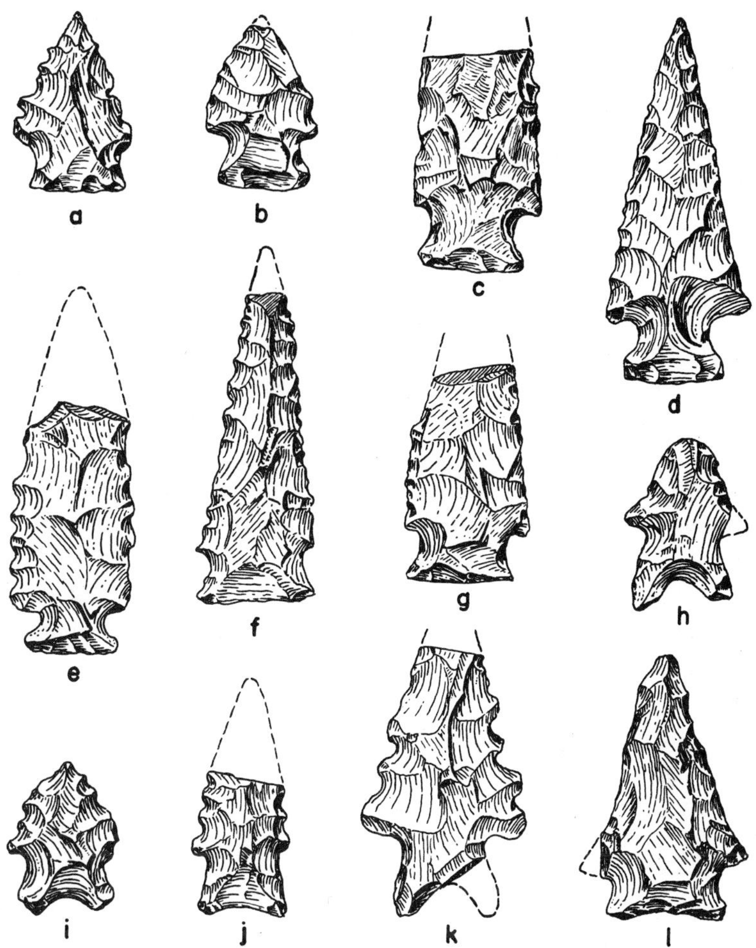

FIGURE 64. Projectile points and knives from the midden. Expanding stems, sharp tangs: straight base, *a-g;* concave base, *h-l. a, b, d, g, h, j-l,* basalt; *c,* rhyolite; *e,* chert; *f,* quartzite; *i,* jasper. Length of *d,* 51 mm.

Subtype 3, *Concave base* (Fig. 64, *h-l*): Lengths, 18 to 50 mm., average about 30 mm. Numerically, this subtype is represented by relatively few specimens. By inspection of the shape it will be quickly seen that practically all specimens within the lot represented nothing more than a variation of the Amargosa II (Pinto) style of point. This idea is borne out by the fact that the majority of these specimens came from the deeper levels of the midden and thus occurred in the same horizons with the more characteristic Amargosa points already described. Some survival of this evident early type of projectile into more recent parts of the midden (*i. e.,* level 2) is best explained by some disturbances within the deposit.

c. Sharp oblique tang: It will be seen from the few specimens which have been classified as having tangs directed back toward the base of the point that this was far from the usual treatment of the vast number of Ventana projectiles. The three subtypes were determined once again on the basis of the basal shape as illustrated in Figure 65. Table 21 does not exhibit any particular significance as to their distribution by level. Broadly speaking, the characteristic in question appears to be relatively late. Oblique tangs were fashioned occasionally on the various main types heretofore described but they were never consistently used on any one type.

We have now passed in review a great array of projectile point and knife types from a single site and representative of a number of cultural horizons. An effort must be made at this point to simmer down what appears to be a very complex situation into a few general and understandable facts. In so doing it should be borne in mind that no single type occurred exclusively in one or two levels. Excepting the lone Ventana point from the volcanic debris, once a type appeared it persisted into later levels, either because of a long life of the trait or because of the mixing of debris of different ages. It may be confidently pointed out, however, that certain standardized shapes did occur more frequently in certain zones than in others and that specific value with respect to relative age may therefore be accepted. It has

TABLE 21

DISTRIBUTION OF PROJECTILE POINTS AND KNIVES BY TYPE AND LEVEL

Table 21

DISTRIBUTION OF PROJECTILE POINTS AND KNIVES BY TYPE AND LEVEL

	Stratigraphic Layer	Levels	*WITHOUT STEMS*													
			Leaf Shaped					*Triangular*			*Diamond*			*Stem Wider Than Blade*		
			Pointed Both Ends													
			Thick Section	*Thin Section*	*Convex Base*	*Straight Base*	*Concave Base*	*Convex Base*	*Straight Base*	*Concave Base*	*Pointed Both Ends*	*Straight or Convex Base*	*Concave Base*	*Convex Base*	*Straight Base*	*Concave*
Upper Cave	*Midden*	1	2 11.1	5 19.2	75 20.2	16 16.7	16 16.1	11 27.5	18 30.5	12 36.4	5 23.8	5 15.6	1 4.7	1 100.0	2 20.0	[illegible]
		2	7 38.8	7 27.0	73 19.7	21 21.9	14 14.1	14 35.0	16 27.1	7 21.2	3 14.3	6 18.7	4 19.0			[illegible]
		3	3 16.7	5 19.2	68 18.4	22 22.9	20 20.2	12 30.0	10 16.9	4 12.1	3 14.3	5 15.6	3 14.3		2 20.0	[illegible]
		4	4 22.2	2 7.7	69 18.7	14 14.6	17 17.2	1 2.5	3 5.1	5 15.2	6 28.6	2 6.3	6 28.6		2 20.0	[illegible]
		5	2 11.1	5 19.2	31 8.4	13 13.5	10 10.1	1 2.5	5 8.5	2 6.1	2 9.5	7 21.8	2 9.5		1 10.0	[illegible]
		6		2 7.7	27 7.3	5 5.2	10 10.1		1 1.7	1 3.0	1 4.8	5 15.6	4 19.0		1 10.0	[illegible]
		7			11 2.9	2 2.1	6 6.1	1 2.5	2 3.4	1 3.0	1 4.8	2 6.3	1 4.7		1 10.0	[illegible]
		8			3 .8		3 3.0									[illegible]
		Miscel.			13 3.5	3 3.1	3 3.0		4 6.8	1 3.0					1 10.0	
		Totals	18	26	370	96	99	40	59	33	21	32	21	1	10	[illegible]
		Percent	1.4	2.0	28.1	7.3	7.6	3.0	4.5	2.5	1.6	2.4	1.6	.1	.8	[illegible]
	Red Sand				4										1	
	Volcanic Debris				1		1									
Lower Cave	*Midden*	1		2 20.0	16 18.8	3 30.0	1 9.1	1 100.0	2 18.2	3 75.0	1 33.3	1 25.0	1 20.0		1 25.0	[illegible]
		2	1 100.0	3 30.0	32 37.6	2 20.0	3 27.3		4 36.3	1 25.0	1 33.3		1 20.0	1 100.0	2 50.0	[illegible]
		3		4 40.0	28 33.0	2 20.0	5 45.5		4 36.3		1 33.3	2 50.0	3 60.0		1 25.0	[illegible]
		4		1 10.0	5 5.9	2 20.0	2 18.2		1 9.1			1 25.0				[illegible]
		5			3 3.5											
		Miscel.			1 1.2	1 10.0										[illegible]
		Totals	1	10	85	10	11	1	11	4	3	4	5	1	4	
		Percent	.4	4.6	38.6	4.6	5.0	.4	5.0	1.8	1.4	1.8	2.3	.4	1.8	

WITH STEMS																		
ering Stem		Stem Narrower Than Blade															Totals	Percent
		Parallel-sided Stem						Expanding Stem										
		Rounded Tang			Sharp Lat. Tang			Rounded Tang			Sharp Lat. Tang			Sharp Obl. Tang				
Base	Convex Base	Convex Base	Straight Base	Concave Base	Convex Base	Straight Base	Concave Base	Convex Base	Straight Base	Concave Base	Convex Base	Straight Base	Concave Base	Convex Base	Straight Base	Concave Base		
0	5 18.5	1 16.7		3 30.0	9 50.0	4 23.6	2 11.1	9 29.0	3 16.7	6 10.7	29 31.5	13 22.8	1 5.3		2 40.0	5 55.5	273	20.8
.8	4 14.8		5 35.8	1 10.0	2 11.1	1 5.9	2 11.1	3 9.7	3 16.7	5 8.9	28 30.4	19 33.4	4 21.0	3 50.0	1 20.0	1 11.1	266	20.2
3	4 14.8	1 16.7	2 14.3	2 20.0	2 11.1	1 5.9	2 11.1	6 19.4		5 8.9	11 12.0	11 19.3	1 5.3	1 16.7	1 20.0	1 11.1	220	16.7
0	6 22.2	1 16.7	1 7.1	2 20.0		5 29.4	5 27.8	3 9.7	4 22.2	12 21.4	8 8.7	7 12.3	5 26.3	2 33.3			213	16.2
.7	5 18.5	1 16.7	1 7.1	1 10.0	1 5.6	2 11.8	2 11.1	3 9.7	2 11.1	8 14.3	3 3.3	2 3.5	3 15.8			1 11.1	122	9.3
0	1 3.7	2 33.2	3 21.5	1 10.0	2 11.1	3 17.6	5 27.8	5 16.1	4 22.2	12 21.4	10 10.9	2 3.5	4 21.0		1 20.0		129	9.8
					2 11.1			2 6.5	1 5.6	4 7.2	1 1.1	1 1.7	1 5.3			1 11.1	42	3.2
			1 7.1			1 5.9				1 1.8	1 1.1						11	.8
3	2 7.3		1 7.1						1 5.6	3 5.4	1 1.1	2 3.5					39	2.9
	27	6	14	10	18	17	18	31	18	56	92	57	19	6	5	9	1315	
0	2.5	.5	1.1	.8	1.4	1.3	1.4	2.4	1.4	4.3	7.0	4.3	1.4	.5	.4	.7		
					3	8			1		1	3					21	
																	2	
0			1 25.0		1 100.0			1 16.7		1 10.0	3 30.0	3 60.0	1 16.7				47	21.4
6			1 25.0				1 33.3	2 33.3		4 40.0	2 20.0	2 40.0	2 33.3				68	30.9
2	1 33.3						2 66.7	3 50.0	1 100.0	2 20.0	2 20.0		1 16.7		2 100.0	1 100.0	67	30.4
2	1 33.3		2 50.0			2 100.0				2 20.0	1 10.0		2 33.3				27	12.3
											1 10.0						4	1.8
	1 33.3	1 100.0								1 10.0	1 10.0						7	3.2
	3	1	4		1	2	3	6	1	10	10	5	6		2	1	220	
2	1.4	.4	1.8		.4	1.0	1.4	2.7	.4	4.6	4.6	2.3	2.7		1.0	.4		

also become evident from the foregoing classification that the objective establishment of types somewhat clouds the stratigraphic picture. Specimens which fill the requirements of any given type often show variations which prove to have stratigraphic value when tested for provenience. This is seen, for example, in the sharp tanged points with parallel-sided stems and convex bases, wherein the larger specimens, normally of basalt, are distinctly earlier by stratigraphy than the smaller examples of chert. Bearing the above two factors in mind, we should then re-examine the lot, particularly with respect to the types already established elsewhere. The conclusions may be assembled in the form of a chart designed to show dominances. With the stratigraphic relationship thus presented, we will have a tool for appraising the validity of postulated sequences based on the work in other sites.

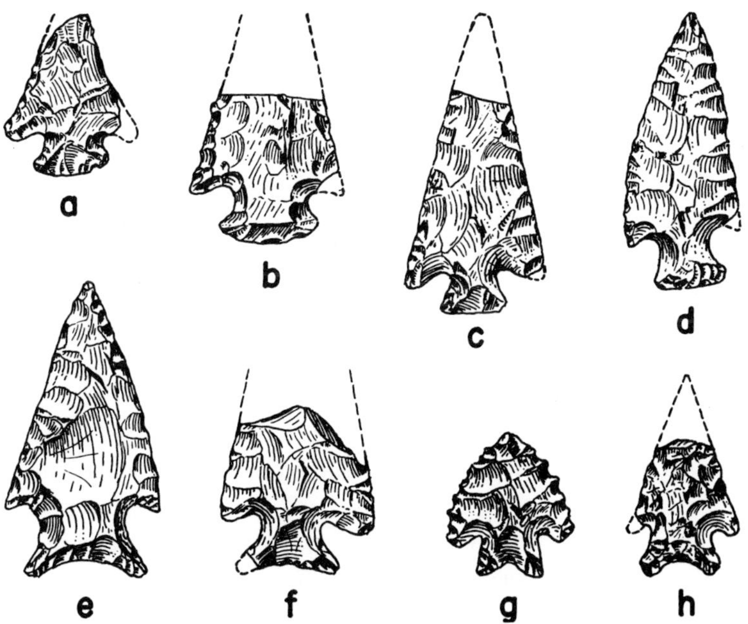

FIGURE 65. Projectile points and knives from the midden. Stem expanding and narrower than blade, sharp oblique tangs. Convex base, *a, b;* straight base, *c, d;* concave base, *e-h. a, b, d, f,* chert; *c, h,* chalcedony; *e,* basalt; *g,* obsidian. Length of *e,* 49 mm.

Plate 22 gives this broad picture of projectile point sequence within the cave. Such a presentation, an obvious attempt to simplify, does not recognize the full range of types present or the variations which occurred within a given standard form. But at the same time, it must be emphasized that there has not been undue selection since the pattern of succession is borne out by the level analysis. Beginning with the oldest, a few further comments are in order.

(Ventana Point)—The various aspects of the Ventana point from the volcanic debris layer have already been covered. But it should be reiterated here that it came from the deepest, and therefore the oldest, culture-bearing layer; that it resembles, but is not identical with, the true Folsom point; that some of the complementary tools are of a Folsom character; and that it was associated with an extinct faunal assemblage in a deposit interpreted as having been formed during wetter climatic conditions dating from late glacial times. These arguments are the basis for considering this point as a near relative of the Folsom type, and that Folsom Man, or a near relative, inaugurated the use of Ventana Cave by humans.

(Ventana-Amargosa I Points)—Second on the list is the Ventana-Amargosa I type, coming from the red sand layer and associated with modern fauna. The disconformity between the red sand and volcanic debris layers, together with the faunal change, is indicative of a considerable lapse of time between the genesis of these two respective layers.

Although this projectile point type, or one closely resembling it, is reported to occur in association with the Amargosa II (Pinto-Gypsum) Complex of California, it has never been found in purity to the extent indicated in Ventana Cave. Specific chronologic value may thus be assigned to it. Because it lies below the orthodox Amargosa II (Pinto) points, this value may be assumed to be in the early part of the complex.

The survival of the type into the lower layers of the midden has already been noted where companion points were principally of the Amargosa II (Pinto) type, thus paralleling the situation already mentioned for California. The origin of this type and its distribution are matters which must be left to further research, but I think it may safely be concluded that authorship is assignable to people with strong affiliations to the west.

(Amargosa II Points) —Next in time are two styles of points coming from the lower layers of the midden, which, from all appearances, were used contemporaneously. Points in the first group, Amargosa II (Pinto) points, are quite variable but nearly all share such features as serrations, expanding stems, and concave bases. They are almost exact copies of the California Pinto points in shape, materials, and chipping technique and the affinities with that area and culture are not to be doubted.[68]

The second lot, less numerous than the first, bears a general resemblance to the Gypsum point, first recorded by Harrington[69] from Gypsum Cave, Nevada. The co-existence of these two forms in Ventana is entirely consonant with the evidence produced by Rogers,[70] from California, where the Gypsum point is placed in Amargosa II (middle Pinto) times.

While on the subject of Gypsum points, attention should be called to the Pecos River focus of the Big Bend area of Texas,[71] in which the dominant projectile point resembles the Gypsum type. It occurred there, evidently, without the Pinto type, having appeared during the moist period marked by the Calamity Formation and persisted well into the first millenium, A. D.[72] No specific correlation between the Big Bend of Texas and Ventana Cave cultures is possible at this time, but the above analogy bears inspection as further work is done.

Another comparison worth noting is the similarity of the Amargosa II projectiles to those of the San Jose Complex near Grants, New Mexico.[73] This industry represents a hunting, food-gathering people who lacked pottery. No great age is claimed for

★

68. E. W. C. and W. H. Campbell, 1935, Pl. 13; M. J. Rogers, 1939, Pl. 13.
69. M. R. Harrington, 1933, pp. 105-109; see also M. J. Rogers, 1939, Pl. 14, a-e.
70. M. J. Rogers, 1939, pp. 55-57.
71. J. C. Kelley, T. N. Campbell, and D. J. Lehmer, 1940, pp. 24-27, Fig. 1.
72. *Op. cit.*, p. 162.
73. K. Bryan and J. H. Toulouse, Jr., 1943.

the material but, on the strength of an incomplete geological sequence, the possibility of time equivalent with the Chiricahua Stage is suggested.[74] Typologically, the San Jose material, particularly the projectile points, agrees with those from the lower zone of the Ventana midden, which, in turn, is thought to be equivalent to Chiricahua. Hence, there is some support for this correlation.

It will be seen in the distribution table (21) that some variations which have been put in the Amargosa II category occurred with the San Pedro points and even in the lower part of the pottery zone of the midden. I am confident that this association cannot be accepted at face value and must be attributed to the fact that cave deposits are subject to more extensive churning and consequent mixture of cultural remains than one would normally expect to find in a stratified site out in the open. The chief reasons for claiming that the points in question did not persist into the equivalent of San Pedro Stage times are: (a) that the Chiricahua Stage projectile points from southwestern Arizona, as reported by Sayles,[75] are stratigraphically antecedent to the San Pedro Stage, and may be regarded as a variation of the Amargosa II (Pinto) point; and (b) that collections from the San Pedro Stage sites, including both excavated and surface specimens, do not show this co-existence of Amargosa II and San Pedro types. On logical grounds, therefore, we may conclude that Amargosa II forms from Ventana which occurred above those levels where frequencies for the types were highest, principally 6, 7, and 8, reached those levels by upward intrusion.

(San Pedro Points)—Then follows an abundantly represented and stratigraphically well-placed projectile, the San Pedro point. This was consistently the largest form in the cave, even though relatively late, and offers a sharp contrast with all preceding styles. The lateral notched projectile point has significant mates in the unnotched blades of triangular and leaf forms.

The San Pedro point, segregated and dated by Sayles and

★

74. K. Bryan and F. T. McCann, 1943, p. 290.
75. E. B. Sayles and E. Antevs, 1941, Pl. XI, *c, d, g*.

Antevs,[76] is a diagnostic of the latest of three stages (San Pedro) in the Cochise Culture of southeastern Arizona. Antevs[77] places the inclusive dates at from about B. C. 3000 to 500, on geological evidence. This was one step prior to the introduction of pottery, which came in, presumably, about the time of Christ. In Ventana, the highest incidences of the San Pedro points occurred in the trash immediately below the ceramic line and it appears likely that the type persisted into the early part of the Christian Era.

(Desert Hohokam Points)—After the San Pedro point fell into disuse or was replaced, there was a marked style change in the projectile point sequence. This is evident in form and above all in size. The reason was quite clearly a basic shift in the economy, for the users of the San Pedro points were hunters and food-gatherers, while the makers of the small points, listed as Desert Hohokam, had made the important gain of agriculture with a consequent reduction of hunting.

The Hohokam points illustrated in Plate 22 are diagnostic principally of the Colonial and Sedentary periods, roughly between A. D. 800 to 1100. This leaves an interval in the early part of the Christian Era for which there is no good evidence as to the standard projectile form. It would appear that some little time elapsed between the adoption of agriculture and the development of the points shown.

(Papago Points)—Ending the sequence is the triangular concave based point of historic Papago make. It shows the Hohokam feature of small size but otherwise is distinctive.

Although this sequence is perhaps more complete than that of most sites found so far, there are, nevertheless, gaps in it. For example, we do not have a type or types to fill the supposed long interim of time represented by the disconformity in the beds, or, between the Ventana and the Ventana-Amargosa I forms. No specimen, even remotely resembling the Yuma type, was found

★

76. *Ibid.*, pp. 24 *et seq.*
77. *Ibid.*, p. 55.

These are generally concluded to overlap with the upper Folsom levels although, in the main, they are later.[78]

From the Ventana-Amargosa I type to the San Pedro point the succession appears to be fairly complete, but forms may eventually be added between the San Pedro and Colonial-Sedentary Hohokam, and between the latter and historic Papago.

Brief mention should be made of a few other well-known western types which were absent or only sparsely represented in the cave. As affinities were intimate with the California desert area, it is surprising that the Mohave and Silver Lake[79] forms did not show up more strongly. There was only a single undeniable Mohave point from the lower midden, where it was associated with the Amargosa II (Pinto) Complex, and no certain Silver Lake examples. This may be taken to mean that these were localized in California, or that the particular horizons represented by them left no impression among Ventana Cave occupants.

The Sandia point,[80] so far isolated only in New Mexico, by stratigraphy is older than Folsom and may be presumed to antedate even the oldest human evidence from Ventana.

In the Chiricahua Stage of the Cochise Culture, Sayles[81] notes several pressure flaked point types, the most common being one of short-bladed form with expanding stem and concave base. He considers these to have been an intruded element in that horizon and not native to it. In Ventana, several individual examples of this type were found, best illustrated by Figures 64, *i*, and 65, *h*, but they could not be assigned to any one culture level. Sayles[82] further holds that pressure flaking was not practiced by Chiricahua Stage people. Although the grinding tool pattern in Ventana is in the Cochise tradition, and pressure flaking was a common method of working stone at a time believed to be equivalent to the Chiricahua Stage in Ventana, it would thus appear that little contact existed between Ventana and southeastern Arizona, and least of all, that the alleged im-

★

78. F. H. H. Roberts, Jr., 1940, pp. 61-66; E. B. Howard, 1943, p. 234.
79. C. A. Amsden, 1937, pp. 80-84.
80. F. C. Hibben and K. Bryan, 1941, pp. 24-25.
81. E. B. Sayles and E. Antevs, 1941, Pl. XI.
82. *Ibid.*, p. 21.

ported points in the Chiricahua Stage of that area could have come from the west. This is particularly surprising since the Chiricahua Stage point, in size and concaving of base, suggests possible derivation from the Amargosa Complex.

As for the general Ventana projectile point sequence, if the main types had been arranged chronologically on the basis of evidence known prior to the excavation of Ventana Cave, the order would have been as illustrated in Plate 22, excluding the Ventana-Amargosa II type from the red sand, which is new. The Ventana stratigraphy thus validates the information so far obtained by other means and the two lines of inquiry combined present a most satisfactory picture.

Where non-pottery cultures are being dealt with, projectile points appear to be the best index for detecting local variations in sequence and even in determining affiliated groups. The marginal location of Ventana Cave to several centers of culture and the absence, for the most part, of local evolution, is sharply brought out by the influence pattern reflected by the projectile points, summarized as follows:

(1) Ventana: fundamentally from the high plains to the northeast, evidently the habitat preferred by the Folsom hunters.

(2) Ventana-Amargosa I: probably from the California desert area to the west.

(3) Amargosa II (Pinto-Gypsum) : from the northwest and west, or the California desert.

(4) San Pedro: a westward extension of the late stage of the Cochise Culture, best known at the moment in southeastern Arizona.

(5) Desert Hohokam: from the River Hohokam to the north, whose culture seems to have emerged in the permanently watered valleys of the Gila and Salt rivers.

(6) Papago: a problematical local evolution from Hohokam.

The serration of blade edges is an attribute of projectile points which has not been adequately studied. It is a fairly widespread treatment and has been used for a long time. In Ventana, there are some recognizable trends in serrating which suggest possible diagnostic value. The earliest occurrence is in the Ventana-Amargosa I points from the red sand, where the teeth are weakly developed. Amargosa II points, on the other hand, show this feature to a much greater degree, not only more consistently, but also to a much more exaggerated degree. Frequently there were only two or three widely separated projecting teeth. The makers of the San Pedro type evidently did not regard serrating with favor as only a few points show it, and so far as the local story is concerned, this attribute went into decline. The Hohokam, however, picked it up again and developed the idea so exuberantly that some of the points appear to be ornamental rather than basically useful.[83] Historically, the Papago have again lost, or did not make use of, the idea.

While this section has been concerned only with stone projectile points, it should be remembered that wooden points may also have been used. In the dry midden zone such were found, particularly bunt points. These are discussed in another section (p. 419). What the situation was in pre-pottery days we can only guess.

FIGURE 66. Sinew hafting on base of Amargosa II (Pinto) type of point from lower cave

Unfortunately, too, there is little information on hafting methods, and no new light on the recurring question as to when the bow replaced the atlatl. The quiver of arrows with burial 9 provides some indication as to the type of haft in late times, or between A.D. 1000 and 1400. Several examples of this have already been illustrated. These show the use of pitch to help fasten the point to the foreshaft, cross-crossing of the sinew lashing over stem and tangs, and the wrapping of the sinew well down on the foreshaft (Figs. 52, *a, b;* 58 *d*). By some miracle, the butt end of an Amargosa II (Pinto) point with lashing was

★ 83. H. S. Gladwin, *et al.,* 1937, Pls. LXXXIX and XC.

preserved to give the only suggestion of the early hafting method. This specimen (Fig. 66) shows no use of pitch, no criss-crossing of the sinew, and the lashing is carried from below the tangs to just below the stem spurs. Whether these were standard differences cannot be claimed on this slight evidence.

The atlatl-bow problem is equally unsolvable. Foreshaft diameters on the above example, measured from the lashings, are 4 to 5 mm. for the late arrow heads, and 10 mm. for the early head, indicating a considerable difference, which may have some significance. The sharp reduction in average projectile point size after the San Pedro type, or with the Hohokam points, may be indicative of a change in weapon type, too, but this is no more than a guess.

Drills—Drills, or perforators, are distinguished from other artifacts in normally having long, more or less parallel-sided shafts and thick sections. At no time in Ventana do they appear to have been used in any number, as they represent only 1.3 per cent of the tools flaked on both faces and .8 per cent of all flaked tools. Most of the drills were made of basalt, accounting for their crudity. A few were chert. Using shape and particularly basal treatment, the following classification has been set up with examples illustrated in Figure 67.

1. Sharpened flakes			6
a. Symmetrical (*a*)		5	
b. "Oblique" (*b*)		1	
2. Plain shafted (*c, d*)			5
3. Flanged			36
a. Small		16	
(1) Straight base (*e*)	6		
(2) Convex base (*f*)	4		
(3) Concave base (*g, h*)	4		
(4) Asymmetrical (*i*)	2		
b. Large (*j, k*)		19	
c. Extension above base (*l*)		1	
4. Unfinished (?)			4
5. Fragments not classifiable			3
Total			54

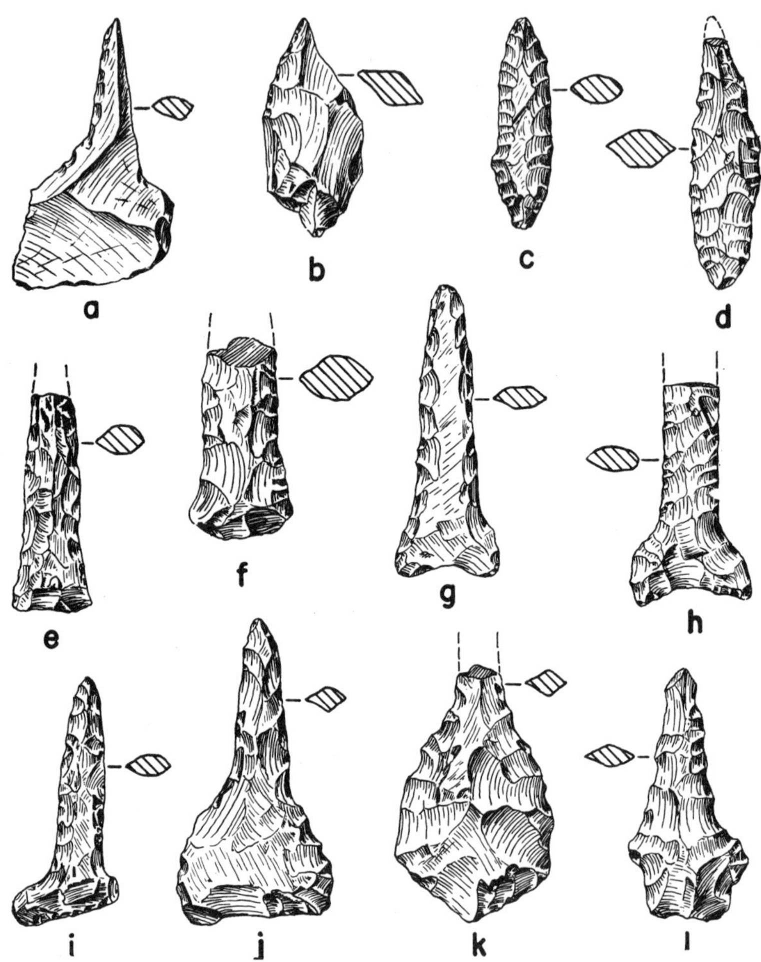

FIGURE 67. Drills from the midden. Sharpened flake: symmetrical, *a;* "oblique," *b;* plain shafted, *c, d;* small flange: straight base, *e;* convex base, *f;* concave base, *g, h;* asymmetrical, *i;* large flange, *j, k;* extension above base, *l.* *a, e-g, i, j, l,* basalt; *b, c, d, h, k,* chert. Length of *g,* 54 mm.

Table 22

DISTRIBUTION OF DRILLS BY TYPE AND LEVEL

Stratigraphic Layer	Levels	*Sharpened Flakes*		*Plain Shafted*	*Flanged*						*Unfinished*	*Fragments not Classified*	*Totals*	*Percent*
					Small									
		Symmetrical	*"Oblique"*		*Straight Base*	*Convex Base*	*Concave Base*	*Asym-metrical*	*Large*	*Extension Above Base*				
	1									1 100.0			1	2.7
	2				1 20.0				1 8.3				2	5.4
	3	1 50.0			1 20.0		1 33.3	1 100.0	1 8.3		1 33.3		6	16.2
	4			1 25.0			1 33.3		3 25.0		1 33.3	2 66.7	8	21.6
	5			1 25.0	2 40.0	2 100.0			4 33.3			1 33.3	10	27.0
Midden	6	1 50.0	1 100.0		1 20.0		1 33.3		3 25.0				7	18.9
	7													
	8			1 25.0									1	2.7
	Miscel.			1 25.0							1 33.3		2	5.4
	Totals	2	1	4	5	2	3	1	12	1	3	3	37	
	Percent	5.4	2.7	10.8	13.5	5.4	8.1	2.7	32.4	2.7	8.1	8.1		
Red Sand														
Volcanic Debris														
	1								2 28.6		1 100.0		3	17.7
	2	2 66.7							3 42.8				5	29.4
	3			1 100.0	1 100.0	2 100.0			2 28.6				6	35.3
	4	1 33.3											1	5.9
Midden	5						1 100.0						1	5.9
	Miscel.							1 100.0					1	5.9
	Totals	3		1	1	2	1	1	7		1		17	
	Percent	17.7		5.9	5.9	11.7	5.9	5.9	41.1		5.9			

The vertical distribution (Table 22) shows that the earliest occurrence of drills, a plain shafted example, was in level 8 of the upper cave, or in association with the Amargosa II (Pinto-Gypsum) Complex. Neither the red sand nor the volcanic debris layers produced any, although it may well be that the gravers in the latter were prototypes. Above level 8, excepting 7, the variety and number of drills increase to a maximum in level 5 and then taper off again in the recent or upper levels. Since the trend in the lower cave is roughly in keeping, it would appear that drills were most commonly used by the pre-pottery people. The rarity of this tool among the Hohokam is further indicated by the evidence from Snaketown.[84] Curiously, Sayles[85] reports no drills in the San Pedro Stage, but in Ventana they occur in the equivalent of that horizon. For California, both Rogers[86] and Amsden[87] illustrate drills from the Playa, Pinto-Gypsum Complexes and Lake Mohave area respectively. The latter are mostly of the large flanged type and the oldest of Roger's specimens are plain shafted. Taken with the Ventana evidence there is some indication that the plain shafted drill is an old form.

Four-Pointed Objects—Two specimens, not classifiable in any other category, have been labelled four-pointed objects, for want of a better term. They are 40 and 34 mm. in maximum length, respectively, and are rather thin sectioned (Fig. 68). The outline is asymmetrical to the extent that two points project laterally farther than the remaining two and the edges between are pronouncedly concave. Both were made of thin, basalt flakes by pressure flaking. Example *a* shows extensive wear on the flake scarred faces, as though from much handling, but the chipped edges remain quite sharp. They were found in levels 5 and 3 of the upper cave.

Similar items, generally somewhat larger in relation to width, have been reported from California.[88] They have been variously

★

84. *Ibid.*, Pl. XCIV.
85. E. B. Sayles and E. Antevs, 1941, pp. 21-26.
86. M. J. Rogers, 1939, pp. 33-34; p. 52.
87. C. A. Amsden, 1937, p. 73.
88. *Ibid.*, p. 76; M. J. Rogers, 1939, p. 36.

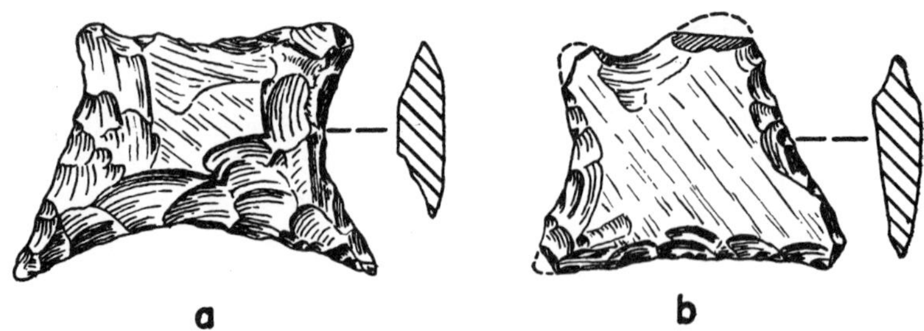

FIGURE 68. Four-pointed objects from the midden. Both basalt. Actual size

considered to be scrapers, scarifiers, and amulets. Whatever their use was, it is worth noting that both Ventana examples come from pre-pottery levels, the better of the two having been associated with the Amargosa II (Pinto-Gypsum) points. Sayles[89] describes a ground implement from the San Pedro Stage of southeastern Arizona called an abrading tool. It is analogous to these in shape only.

These recall the four-pointed stones, expertly made of very hard materials, from late sites of southern Arizona and northern Mexico,[90] which do appear to have had an amulet use. But there is no way of proving any developmental connection between these and the earlier forms at the present time. The Ventana stones may be cited as an additional trait held in common with the Californian area to make that relationship even more intimate.

Ground and Pecked Stone

Implements with pecked or smoothed surfaces constitute about 34 per cent of all stone tools from the midden. This includes, of course, those which have such surfaces resulting from work done with them, as for example, metates and manos. Some of these were modified intentionally by this process; but the bulk of them must be discounted in an appraisal of the relative use of chipping vs. grinding, or the polishing of

★

89. E. B. Sayles and E. Antevs, 1941, Pl. XV, *b*.
90. W. S. Fulton and C. Tuthill, 1940, p. 34; G .F. Ekholm, 1942, pp. 106-107.

stone. Those objects which could be made only by grinding, as pipes, nose plugs, etc., aggregate but the smallest fraction of the whole lithic complex. This can be narrowed down still more from the temporal standpoint. Ground and polished objects occurred high in the midden as invariable associates of pottery, indicating that this technique was late and that except for the very end of the time man used the cave he did not intentionally set out to create a ground and polished artifact.

Metates—Milling stones, the metate and inseparable mano, were present in amazing numbers. Nevertheless, the chronological picture is relatively simple. Of the 2,287 whole and fragmentary metates found, only one out of four was whole, so that the number may be sharply reduced, say by about 50 per cent, to get a truer notion of the frequency of the trait. When intact, metates were often found in an inverted position, evidently a measure to protect the grinding surface during times when the cave occupants went away.

Study of the metates, both in the field and in the laboratory, has brought out one significant character, namely, that throughout the cave's history a basin metate was used. But at all times they were so nondescript and so lacking in definitive details that classification is next to pointless. Whatever else may be said of the Ventana occupants, they took no pride in making this most useful implement. For the most part, any convenient flat-surfaced rock was selected, and except for breaking away bothersome corners, most mills received no further attention. With the hope that something might come from even so elementary a breakdown, metates have been grouped into two main classes: A, *Block,* those in which the raw material was a chunky, angular rock, and B, *Slab,* those consisting of a thin, tabular slab of stone. A further distinction is made among the latter on the presence or absence of shaping. A minority (about 30 per cent) of the slab metates show marginal dressing, but even these are far from the perfected tools one normally finds in late ruins. One bedrock milling basin in the upper cave should also be noted. It occurred on a large lava block lying near the shoulder. Many metates showed red paint stains from pulverizing pigment, evidently for rock painting, and metates were never set in bins as was customary among the Anasazi.

(A. Block) —Block metates, with few exceptions, were made of thick, angular pieces of basalt fallen from the cliff forming the roof of the cave itself or brought in from the talus. There was thus a never-ending supply of raw material, which probably accounts for the readiness with which the mills were abandoned and also for the fact that this type outnumbers all others. A few were made of scoriaceous lava, available nearby, and on rare occasions did anyone bother to bring in a stream boulder from the outside. The block metate seems to have been preferred at all times over the slab type, judging from the numbers recovered.

Many showed only a slight worn surface and those used over a longer period of time developed elliptical grinding depressions. What should be noted is the freedom of the grinding axis. This could be either straight down through the center or by curving strokes to the right or left. A true rotary motion was not used. Grinding surfaces on the reverse sides are practically absent. It is futile to give all dimensions but the average length would be about .4 m. An average well-worn specimen is illustrated in Figure 69, *a*. Any of the one-handed manos described in the following section could be used in this form of mill, but it is clear from the straight grinding surface along the longitudinal axis of the manos that most of them rode in much shallower metates than the one illustrated. Metates of this type occurred in all levels (Table 23), reaching greatest numbers in levels 4 and 5.

(B. Slab) (1) (Unshaped) —These were adapted from thin (seldom more than 50 mm. thick), irregular sheets of rock. Since the lava forming the cliff did not break out in tabular fashion the material had to be imported. A micaceous schist was preferred and the nearest outcrop is some nine miles to the east, near Santa Rosa. A few are hard sandstone, which may have been brought in from an even greater distance.

Generally speaking, slab metates are smaller (average length

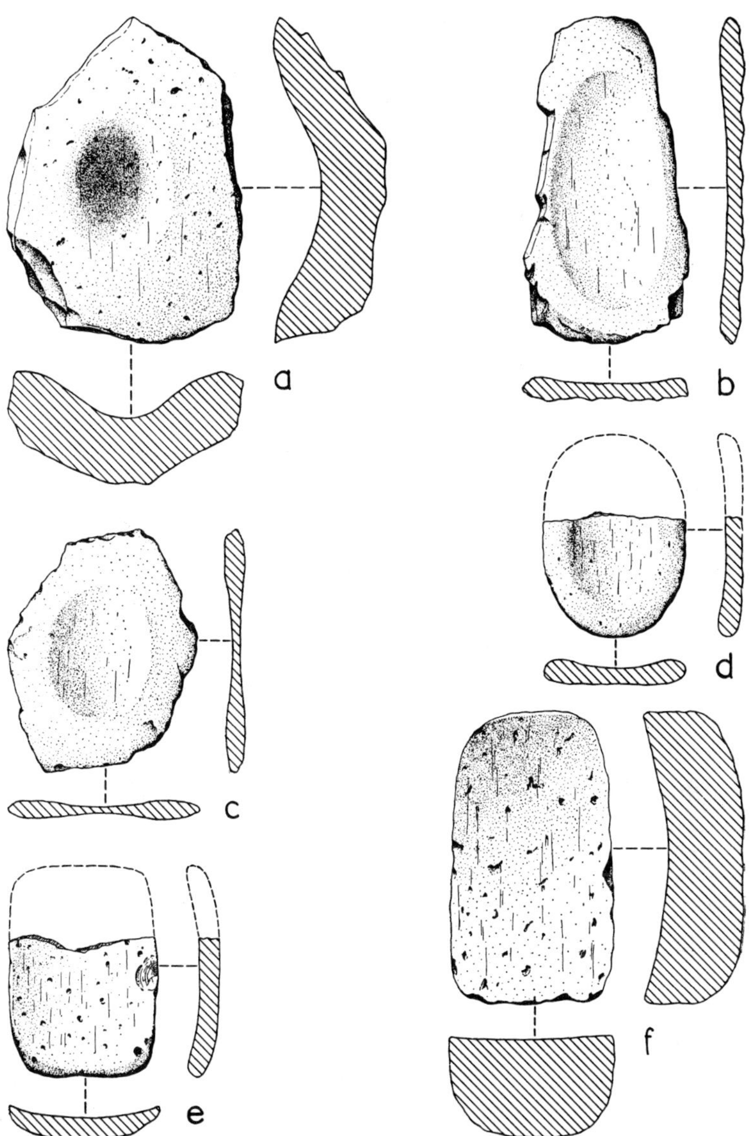

FIGURE 69. Metate types from the midden. Block, *a;* unshaped slabs: used one side, *b;* used both sides, *c;* shaped slabs, *d, e;* shaped block metate, *f* (from Ariz. DD:5:8, Topawa Phase). *b, c,* schist, all others basalt. Length of *a,* .45 m.

about .3 m.) than the block type. Thinness of the slabs prevented deep basins, so the entire flat surface shows abrasion with a slight central depression (Fig. 69, *b, c*). Both sides of the slab were often used and surfaces were sharpened by pecking.

Like the block metate, these appeared in all levels (Table 23), being most frequent in levels 4 and 5. Their similarity to Cochise Culture mills, particularly of the Chiricahua Stage, is to be noted.

(2) (Shaped)—Nearly 10 per cent of the metate samples tabulated (Table 23) showed marginal shaping by a crumbling process. These are seldom more than .3 m. long and the best ones were made of scoriaceous lava. In outline they are oval (Fig. 69, *d*) or approaching the rectangular (Fig. 69, *e*). One side only was normally used.

It is impossible to say that shaping was characteristic of any one horizon since the distribution pattern vertically follows that of the other types.

Manos—As was to be expected, the moment metates appeared in Ventana, so did manos, because the one is of no use without the other. The impressive feature is that there were so many, 1,355 all told, sometimes occurring in bunches from twenty to thirty in number, lying close to the cliff wall. The only other stations known to the writer which approach this cave in abundance of grinding tools are the sites of the Cochise Culture in southeastern Arizona.

In classifying manos, special attention has been given to form, number, and nature of grinding surfaces, and material. Out of the great number of specimens, a fairly simple picture emerges. As previously stated, a rough analysis was made in the field but not all characteristics were observed at that time. What is believed to be a typical laboratory sample of 236 specimens was made representing about 17 per cent of the total collection and the following data is based primarily on this lot. In the accompanying table (24), manos from the upper cave only have been included. The system of grouping is as follows:

Table 23

DISTRIBUTION OF METATES BY TYPE AND LEVEL

	Stratigraphic Layer	Levels	Block	Slab		Totals	Percent
				Unshaped	Shaped		
Upper Cave	*Midden*	1	22 **4.1**	14 **4.4**	3 **3.0**	39	**4.0**
		2	54 **10.0**	32 **10.0**	9 **8.9**	95	**9.9**
		3	97 **18.0**	48 **15.0**	13 **12.9**	158	**16.5**
		4	150 **28.0**	90 **28.0**	31 **30.6**	271	**28.3**
		5	138 **25.7**	70 **22.0**	39 **38.6**	247	**25.8**
		6	69 **12.8**	58 **18.1**	5 **4.9**	132	**13.8**
		7	8 **1.5**	8 **2.5**	1 **1.0**	17	**1.7**
		8					
		Miscel.					
		Totals	538	320	101	959	
		Percent	**56.0**	**33.4**	**10.6**		
	Red Sand						
	Volcanic Debris						
Lower Cave	*Midden*	1					
		2					
		3					
		4					
		5					
		Miscel.					
		Totals					
		Percent					

TABLE 24

DISTRIBUTION OF MANOS BY TYPE AND LEVEL

	Stratigraphic Layer	Levels	Uni-face: Irregular	Uni-face: Spheroidal	Uni-face: Rectangular	Uni-face: Petaloid	Bi-face: Oval	Bi-face: Sub-rectangular	Bi-face: Rectangular	Multi-face	Totals	Percents
Upper Cave	*Midden*	1	7 **41.2**	7 **38.8**	10 **71.4**	4 **100.0**	3 **4.9**	19 **29.2**	5 **83.2**		55	**28.1**
		2	1 **5.9**	2 **11.1**	2 **14.3**		4 **6.5**	6 **9.2**	1 **16.8**	1 **9.1**	17	**8.7**
		3	2 **11.8**	6 **33.3**	2 **14.3**		12 **19.7**	6 **9.2**		6 **54.5**	34	**17.3**
		4	2 **11.8**	1 **5.6**			9 **14.7**	12 **18.5**		2 **18.1**	26	**13.3**
		5	4 **23.4**	1 **5.6**			24 **39.4**	17 **26.2**		1 **9.1**	47	**24.0**
		6		1 **5.6**			5 **8.2**	3 **4.6**		1 **9.1**	10	**5.1**
		7	1 **5.9**				4 **6.6**	2 **3.1**			7	**3.5**
		8										
		Miscel.										
		Totals	17	18	14	4	61	65	6	11	196	
	Red Sand	Pct.	**8.7**	**9.2**	**7.1**	**2.0**	**31.1**	**33.2**	**3.1**	**5.6**		
	Volcanic Debris											
Lower Cave	*Midden*											
		1										
		2										
		3										
		4										
		5										
		Miscel.										
		Totals										
		Pct.										

1. Uni-face
   a. Irregular
   b. Spheroidal
   c. Rectangular
   d. Petaloid
2. Bi-face
   a. Oval
   b. Sub-rectangular
   c. Rectangular
3. Multi-face

An outstanding characteristic of Ventana manos is the fact that, with few exceptions, they are of the one-hand type, *i. e.*, designed to be operated in one hand rather than two, as was customary among the Anasazi. The exceptions were all in the uppermost layer and therefore were late.

The number of grinding faces, used above as a primary distinction, shows some significant differences, top to bottom, through the midden. The ratio of single to double face in three levels sampled runs as follows: level 1, 1:1; level 4, 1:5; level 6, 1:7. Thus, bi-face manos are characteristic for the early levels, whereas in the late ceramic levels the uni- and bi-face types occur in about equal proportions. Multi-faced manos are not seen at all among the specimens from the pottery horizon and they appear only occasionally among the earlier ones.

(1. Uni-face)—a. Irregular. b. Spheroidal. Taking up the uni-face category first, both irregular and spheroidal forms represent convenient hand-size rocks without shaping. In the former group (Fig. 70, *a*), basalt was the common material; in the latter, quartzite and rhyolite pebbles predominate (Fig. 70, *b*). Diameters range from 80 to 155 mm. No particular significance is to be attached to their distribution in the midden, although these makeshift tools appear to have been commonest in late times.

c. Rectangular. These represent a clear cut lot from the standpoint of type and stratigraphy. They are made of vesicular basalt, almost without exception, and considerable care was expended in shaping them by pecking. The grinding face is only slightly convex in both axes (Fig. 70, *c*) and does not extend over on the ends, indicating that this type of mano was not used in a troughed metate but on a slab of the type illustrated in Fig. 69, *e*. Furthermore, there is no asymmetry of the grinding surface, best seen in the oval bi-face type and the product of a rocker motion as described later. The upper surfaces or backs are strongly convex and the ends are usually vertical. Finger grooves in the sides are absent. Dimensions are quite uniform: length range, 154 to 178 mm., average, 168 mm.; width range, 86 to 104 mm., average, 93 mm. Thickness depends on the amount of wear, range 38 to 68 mm. Size, and the symmetry of the work surface, leave no doubt that these were designed for two-handed use, which distinguishes them further from all others except the petaloid and the rectangular bi-face forms.

Stratigraphically these are late (Table 24). All came from the high midden deposit and mostly from the upper half meter.

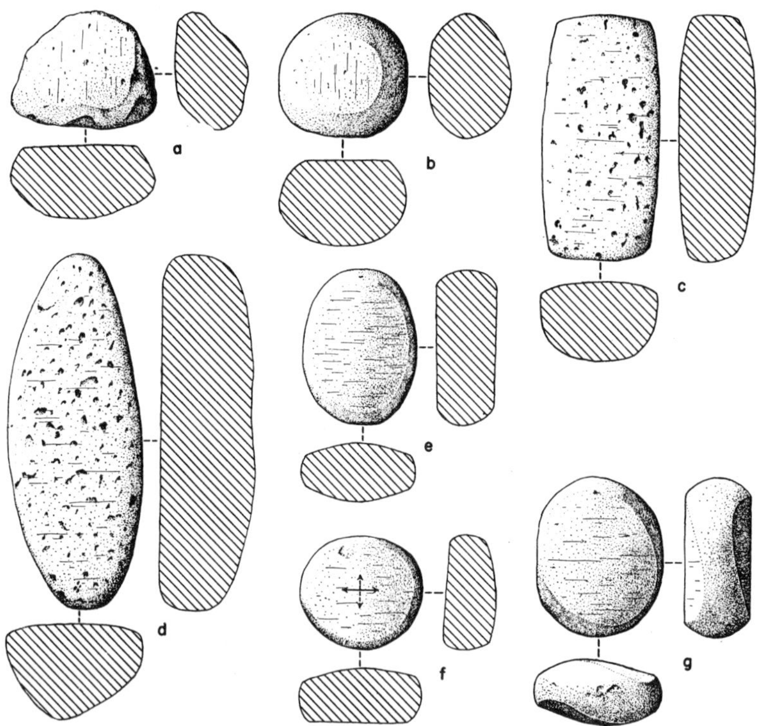

FIGURE 70. Mano types from the midden. Uni-face: irregular, *a;* spheroidal, *b;* rectangular, *c;* petaloid, *d.* Bi-face: oval, *e, g;* mano with grinding axes at right angles to each other on opposite faces, *f. a, c, d,* basalt; others quartzite. Length of *d,* 25 cm.

d. Petaloid. There are too few in this group to ascribe much significance to them. All characteristics of the rectangular manos are shared except shape (Fig. 70, *d*) and they may be regarded as a variety of that type. All appeared in level 1 (Table 24).

(2. Bi-face)—a. Oval. We now come to the most numerous of all types, the oval, double-faced mano. Flattened hand-size stream pebbles were selected. Approximately three out of four show some shaping about the edges by pecking to produce a uniformly oval outline (Fig. 70, *e*). The type of material preferred was quartzite and indurated sandstone, and occasionally granite. Only three manos are basalt, and, as these all came from high in the midden, we can say that in early times basalt was not used at all. This is a sharp contrast to the materials of late manos which were predominantly basalt. An interesting feature which develops here is the fact that the stream channels of the Ventana district, a volcanic area, do not have supplies of quartzite and hard sandstone pebbles. These were obviously imported and probably from a considerable distance. It is worth noting that the materials of the early Ventana manos and those of the Cochise Culture are essentially the same.

The grinding faces are flat or nearly flat on the long axes and convex on the transverse axes. Greatest convexity, however, is reached on a line drawn at about 45° from the longitudinal axis (Fig. 70, *g*). This is correlated with the right handed use of the tools. In pushing the mano over the metate surface greatest pressure was first applied on the left part of the leading edge and as the stroke continued the mano was rocked slowly back and the weight was then transferred to the right half of the trailing edge at the end of the stroke (Fig. 71). This is a highly characteristic feature of Cochise Culture hand stones and comes from use in flat surfaced or shallow basin metates. The normal position of the hand stone was so that its long axis rode at right angles to the long axes of the metate.

Seven examples show this feature on one face, but to use the opposite face the stone needed to be turned 90°, throwing the axes of the two grinding facets at right angles to each other

(Fig. 70, *f*). This is also occasionally seen on Cochise Culture manos.

Manos with wedge shaped sections are not common and sharpening the work surfaces by pecking was practiced. Many were used as hammer stones in addition to their primary function, and a few have shallow central pits for finger grips.

Although there is considerable range in maximum diameters, from 77 to 150 mm., most examples have a diameter of about 100 mm.

Table 24 reveals that this type was present in all levels except 8, but predominated in 3 to 5. The significant fact is that in all details these manos fit the Chiricahua Stage type described by Sayles[91] which may be taken to mean that there was both a cultural connection and general equivalence in time, a fact suggested by other evidence also.

b. Sub-rectangular. In shape these differ from the preceding lot only in having a slightly more angular outline, approaching a rectangle, but corners are well rounded. Shape alone does not permit this type to be broken down into subtypes but other characters do. Table 24 shows two peaks in the vertical distribution, in levels 1 and 5, and an inspection of the manos from these two levels reveals the following significant differences:

	Level 1 (late) Fig. 72, a	*Level 5 (early) Fig. 72,* b
Material	Predominantly vesicular basalt	Mainly quartzite and indurated sandstone
Shaping	Extensive on sides and ends	Usually all around but most extensive on ends, probably from incidental use of mano as hammer stone
Grinding faces	Flat to slightly convex on both axes; usually lie in parallel planes	Straight on long axis, strongly convex in oblique axis as in oval bi-face type
Size		
Length	Range, 105 to 143 mm., average, 115 mm.	Range 87 to 123 mm., average, 100 mm.
Width	Range, 72 to 90 mm., average, 80 mm.	Range, 61 to 88 mm., average, 80 mm.
Thickness	Range, 24 to 51 mm., average, 35 mm.	Range, 33 to 54 mm., average, 40 mm.

★

91. E. B. Sayles and E. Antevs, 1941, pp. 18-19.

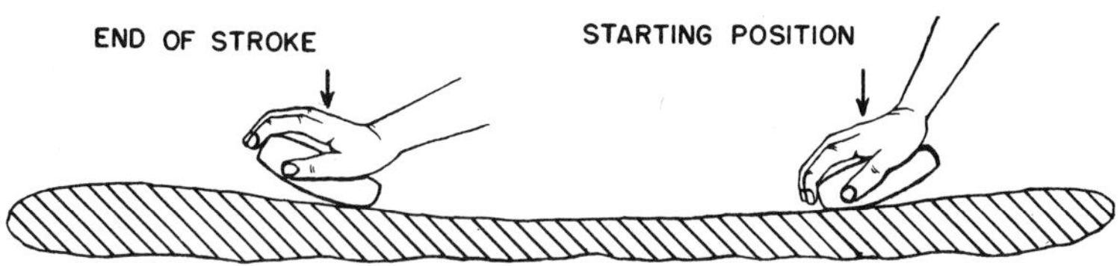

FIGURE 71. Sketch illustrating shift of weight on Cochise type mano, from left leading to right trailing edges, accounting for assymetrical wear

The dissimilarity in grinding faces is largely the result of a rather basic difference in the way the manos were pushed across the metate surface. The late, flat-faced form was not rocked as was the older type, so that the whole face was always in contact with the milling slab. Just why this was, is not easy to establish, but it may have been influenced, in part at least, by the substances being pulverized. The flat-faced manos do not occur in the pre-agricultural deposits of the cave and it may well be that corn could be milled more easily with this type, while the harder and

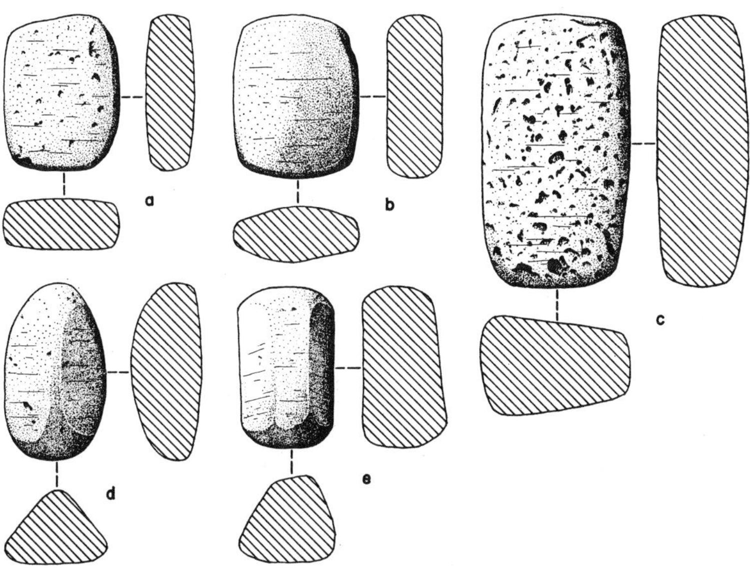

FIGURE 72. Mano types from the midden. Sub-rectangular, *a* (late), *b* (early); rectangular, *c;* multi-face, *d, e.* *a, c,* basalt; *b, d,* quartzite; *e,* porphyry. Length of *c,* 187 mm.

presumably smaller native seeds could be reduced more effectively by a slight rocking motion of the mano.

The early subtype is clearly a close relative of the oval mano and its occurrence, too, in Chiricahua Stage sites, is to be noted. The later form appears to be a one-handed version of the two-handed, rectangular mano and has been found in Hohokam sites[92] in the Gila Basin and the type is fairly common in pre-Spanish sites on the Papago Reservation.[93]

c. Rectangular. By type and stratigraphy these belong with the rectangular uni-face group. They show about the same range in size and material and differ only in having two worn faces (Fig. 72, *c*). This is distinctly a late type (Table 24) and was intended for two-handed use on a nearly flat-surfaced metate.

(3. Multi-face)—These are chunky, thick-sectioned stones with three (Fig. 72, *d*) to four (Fig. 72, *e*) grinding facets and battered ends from evident use as pestles. The material is hard sandstone and porphyry. None are of basalt. The vague resemblance between the three-surfaced examples and the late Pueblo type[94] must be regarded as a coincidence rather than as any cultural connection. Most of the specimens came from level 3 or deeper (Table 24) and are therefore pre-pottery in age.

Several general problems relative to milling stones remain to be discussed. The first of these concerns time of appearance in the cave. As previously noted, a single discoidal hand stone was found in the volcanic debris layer but there was no accompanying metate. Curiously this specimen was unlike any of the hundreds found in later deposits. This merely shows that grinding was known, but evidently not commonly resorted to in that early culture level. The red sand produced no milling stones whatever, but this absence has been attributed to the smallness of the artifact sample. From the base of the midden upward, beginning in level 7,[95] both manos and metates were present in

★

92. H. S. Gladwin, *et al.*, 1937, Pl. XLVI, *b*.

93. F. H. Scantling, 1940, p. 48; A. M. Withers, 1941, p. 59.

94. A. V. Kidder, 1932, p. 71.

95. Level 8 occurred in but a small segment of the cave, hence level 7 may be considered as the base.

sufficient numbers to indicate that they were a standard complement of the material culture. From this point upward the numbers increased sharply to levels 4 and 5, thence dropped off again toward the surface. Plotted, the entire metate and mano sample from the upper cave appears in Figure 73.

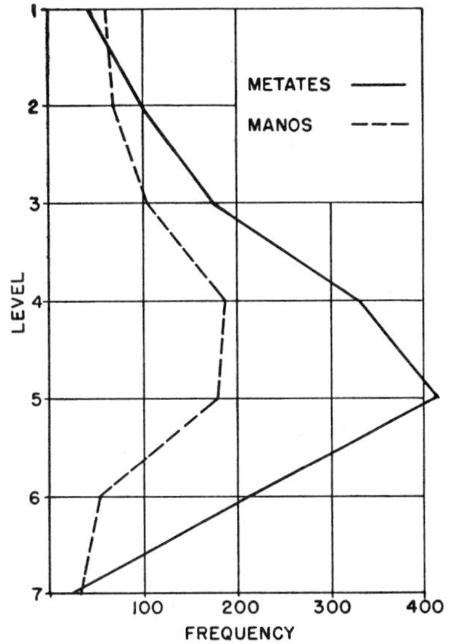

FIGURE 73. Plot of level distribution of all metates (1284) and manos (678) in the midden, upper cave

What this peak in frequency in levels 4 and 5 means may be interpreted in two ways. Either more people were using the cave at that time, with a consequent increase in numbers of mills, or the grinding of food played a much more prominent part then than in earlier and later times. I know of no way in which this problem can be settled. But it may be suggested that the sharp increase in grinding tools from levels 7 to 5 and the detailed similarity of these tools to those of the Chiricahua Stage of the Cochise Culture might indicate an increasing use of the cave by that group.

The San Pedro Stage sites of southeastern Arizona have fewer grinding tools than the earlier stages[96] and the Ventana evidence agrees, since, in level 3, the equivalent of the San Pedro Stage by culture and stratigraphy, there had been a sharp reduction in milling tools. This trend continued, even after the introduction of corn.

But what happened with the arrival of this important plant was the adoption of a new form of mano, the two-handed rectangular type, made of lava, and presumably a new type of metate, too. For some unaccountable reason none of these was

★

96. E. B .Sayles and E. Antevs, 1941, p. 24.

found in the cave, although they are known from other sites in the area. To illustrate the type one has been selected from a Topawa Phase site (Ariz. DD:5:8) near Burro Pond (Fig. 69, *f*). This is a thick block of lava, well shaped, roughly rectangular in outline, with a grinding surface covering the whole upper face, concave in the long axis but not basin shaped. We can be sure that such metates existed in Ventana because the late two-handed manos will not fit any of the metates recovered but will fit this type perfectly. This metate form, incidentally, is much like that used by the modern Papagos.

The full trough metate of the Gila Basin Hohokam appears to have been used in Papagueria very sparingly and then only

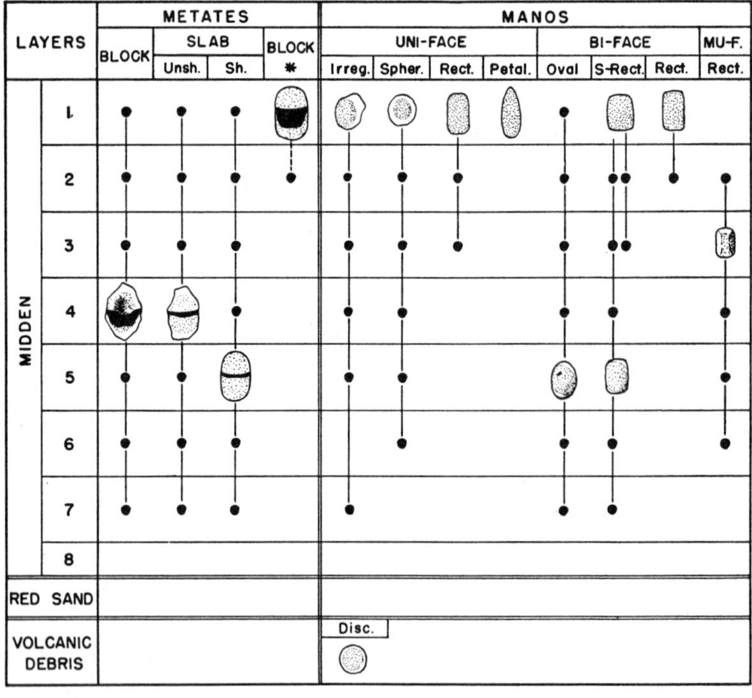

FIGURE 74. Stratigraphic summary of metates and manos (not drawn to same scale) from the upper cave. Types are drawn in level of greatest frequency and dots indicate presence. Solid areas in metates represent cross sections. Block metate with asterisk represents type not found in cave but present in area during formation of midden levels 1 and 2

in the Sells Phase.[97] This highlights another difference between the River and Desert branches of the Hohokam Culture.

The story of Ventana milling stones is summarized visually in Figure 74. Its simplicity belies the importance of this implement complex, basic to subsistence itself. The significant fact is the change in type coincident with the arrival of corn. For the nether stone, this meant a substitution of a large longitudinally concave surface for the earlier basin-shaped grinding depression, and in manos the differences are:

Early	*Late*
One-hand type	One- and two-hand type
Oval to sub-rectangular	Sub-rectangular to rectangular
Bi-face	Uni- and bi-face
Metamorphic rock types	Lava
Transversely convex grinding face	Nearly flat faces, both axes

Since corn arrived late, relatively speaking, what was ground in the early metates? Unfortunately no dry caves have been dug in the Southwest with food products of pre-agricultural people, so one can only guess. The choice is more or less limited to the native seeds of the area. Even now, these are still abundantly used.[98] As the evidence in the Cochise Culture has shown, confirmed by the data from Ventana Cave, the presence of metates no longer implies agriculture.

That the milling stones of Ventana are indicative of a close Cochise Culture connection should be obvious by now. Whereas in southeastern Arizona there was a fairly distinctive mano and metate form for each of the three stages determined,[99] this situation does not hold for Ventana. Sulphur Springs Stage implements are lacking because that horizon is not represented in the cave. For the Chiricahua Stage there was parallelism, but the large round mano and deep basin metate of the San Pedro Stage is not present in the equivalent horizon of Ventana. Instead, the Chiricahua Stage type persisted although the associated chipped

★

97. F. H. Scantling, 1940, p. 45.
98. E. F. Castetter and W. H. Bell, 1942, pp. 59-64.
99. E. B. Sayles and E. Antevs, 1941.

tools were of orthodox San Pedro vintage. The difference may be ascribed to unequal regional developments.

Mortars—Mortars are of two types, boulder and bedrock. Only two of the former were found, both from the dry midden zone (level 2). The better of the two is illustrated in Figure 75. This is a basalt chunk, used as a metate on both sides and finally as a mortar. Judging from the number of pestles in the cave, particularly from the deeper levels of the midden, and the absence of mortars from those same levels, one suspects that wooden mortars may have been used (see also below).

Bedrock mortars, fourteen in number, occurred on the high, flat part of the shoulder (Pl. 7, *b*; Fig. 5). All but one of these were visible before excavation started and the exception was covered by trash. In cross-section these were cone shaped with rounded bottom and somewhat flared at the upper margin. Depths varied from 180 to 480 mm., and top diameters ranged from 180 to 300 mm.

Pestles—Of the 114 pestles, only about half were complete enough to classify. The primary criterion used was the nature

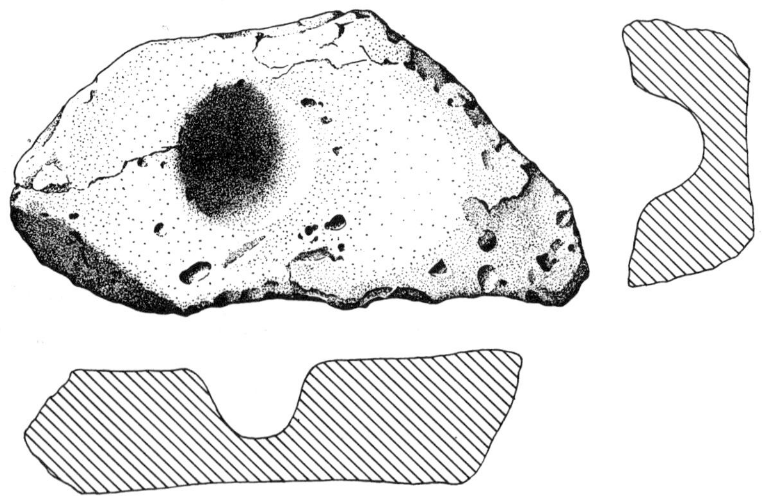

FIGURE 75. Boulder mortar of basalt. Length, .54 m.

of the working end, whether round or flat. This is believed to provide some clue as to use. Shaping, or lack of it, was also considered. The classification follows:

A. Flat ended			36
1. Shaped		30	
a. Conical	17		
b. Cylindrical	13		
2. Not shaped		6	
B. Round ended		16	
1. Shaped		11	
2. Not shaped		5	
C. Fragments, unclassified			62
Total			114

(A. Flat ended)—1. Shaped. The conical and cylindrical pestles represent the most refined types from the cave. They were shaped by pecking, in most cases of scoria; a few are of schist, granite, and rhyolite. The length range is great, from 120 to 392 mm. Typical examples are shown in Figure 76, *a, b*. The grinding ends are quite flat centrally but the edges are rounded and sometimes battered. These could have been, and probably were, used in the bedrock mortars in the rock shoulder in the cave. The distribution in the midden was compactly centered in levels 4 and 5 of the upper cave midden (Table 25). They thus date from pre-pottery times and are associated partly with the Chiricahua-Amargosa II level but more particularly with San Pedro. Sayles reports[100] similar examples from San Pedro sites of southeastern Arizona.

2. Not shaped. These are rough, elongated stones, put to work without any attempt at forming. The size and material range follows the pattern set by the preceding types, and the vertical distribution was spotty (Table 25).

(B. Round ended)—1. Shaped. These differ from the flat ended pestles in being generally longer in relation to diameter, oval as opposed to round in section, and particularly in the na-

★

100. *Ibid.*, Pl. XV, *h*.

Table 25

DISTRIBUTION OF PESTLES BY TYPE AND LEVEL

	Stratigraphic Layer	Levels	Flat ended: Shaped: Conical	Flat ended: Shaped: Cylindrical	Flat ended: Not shaped	Round ended: Shaped	Round ended: Not shaped	Totals	Percent
Upper Cave	Midden	1			2 50.0		1 25.0	3	7.5
		2				1 12.5		1	2.5
		3	3 21.2			1 12.5	1 25.0	5	12.5
		4	5 35.8	5 50.0	2 50.0	3 37.5	2 50.0	17	42.5
		5	5 35.8	4 40.0		3 37.5		12	30.0
		6	1 7.2					1	2.5
		7							
		8							
		Miscel.		1 10.0				1	2.5
	Red sand	Totals	14	10	4	8	4	40	
	Volcanic Debris	Percent	35.0	25.0	10.0	20.0	10.0		
Lower Cave									
	Midden	1		2 66.7		1 33.3		3	25.0
		2	3 100.0	1 33.3		2 66.7	1 100.0	7	58.3
		3			2 100.0			2	16.7
		4							
		5							
		Miscel.							
		Totals	3	3	2	3	1	12	
		Percent	25.0	25.0	16.7	25.0	8.3		

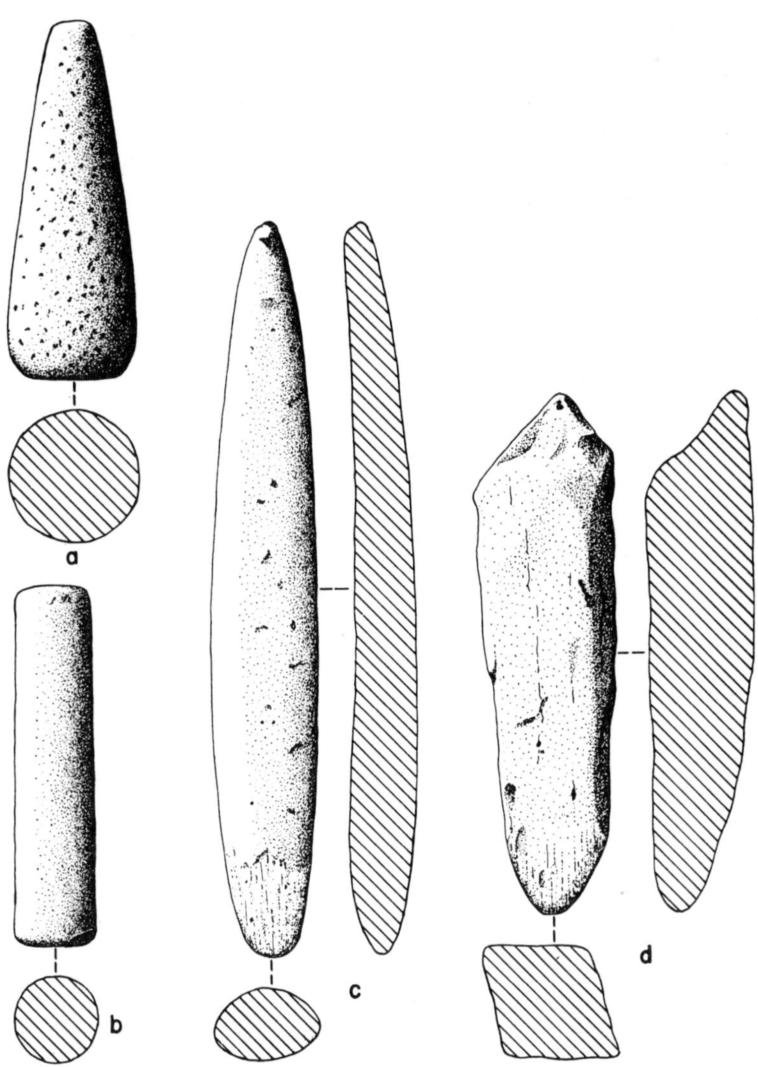

FIGURE 76. Pestles from the midden. Flat ended: conical, *a;* cylindrical, *b*. Round ended: shaped, *c;* not shaped, *d*. *b,* rhyolite; others basalt. Length of *c,* 45.5 cm.

ture of the working ends, which are rounded or slightly wedge shaped (Fig. 76, *c*). The ends evidently did not come into contact with a flat resistant surface to wear them down and it would appear that this might result from use in a wooden mortar. Furthermore, the abrasion may extend upward on the body of the pestle for as much as 80 mm. The scouring caused faint irregular grooves and the more resistant particles of the rock protrude.

The shortest example is 250 mm. long and the longest is 455 mm. The material is predominantly basalt.

The time range appears to be about the same as for the conical and cylindrical forms (Table 25).

2. Unshaped. Same as above, except not shaped (Fig. 76, *d*).

Mortars and pestles appear in the Southwest at an early date. In the original work done by Dr. Byron Cummings on the Double Adobe site north of Douglas, the type location for the Sulphur Springs Stage[101] of the Cochise Culture, a pestle was found suggesting that the trait was known to the earliest food-gatherers. They also occur in succeeding pre-pottery stages and were, of course, employed widely by later people, especially those heavily dependent on natural vegetal food. During the Sells Phase a short, bulky pestle was used in a boulder mortar[102] and historically the Papago have made use of this grinding combination. In Ventana Cave, pestles were primarily associated with the trash of pre-agricultural people.

Rubbing Stones—The collection contains eighteen small rubbing or polishing stones, ranging from 25 to 60 mm. in diameter. They are rounded stream pebbles, showing small abraded surfaces, probably from polishing pottery. It is significant that most of them came from the pottery-bearing zone, and one was with burial 9.

Stone Vessels—Two hollowed stones have been placed in this category. One, a fragment of tufaceous rock, has an oval depression about 180 mm. in diameter and 35 mm. deep, and is

★

101. *Ibid.*, p. 12.
102. F. H. Scantling, 1940, p. 49.

not dressed exteriorly. It came from the deepest level of the lower cave and is of a type found in some Cochise Culture sites. The other, an oval basalt tray (Fig. 77), was evidently made from a small, shaped metate. It is late, coming from level 1 of the upper cave. Neither of these two specimens shows any wear in the basin, so use as a metate may be discounted.

Rasps—Implements classified as rasps, or files, number fourteen and are made of an abrasive schist. Most of them are elongated with elliptical sections and showing well-worn curved facets (Fig. 78, *a, b*). Tools of this type have been reported from the Colonial and Sedentary Periods of Snaketown where they are

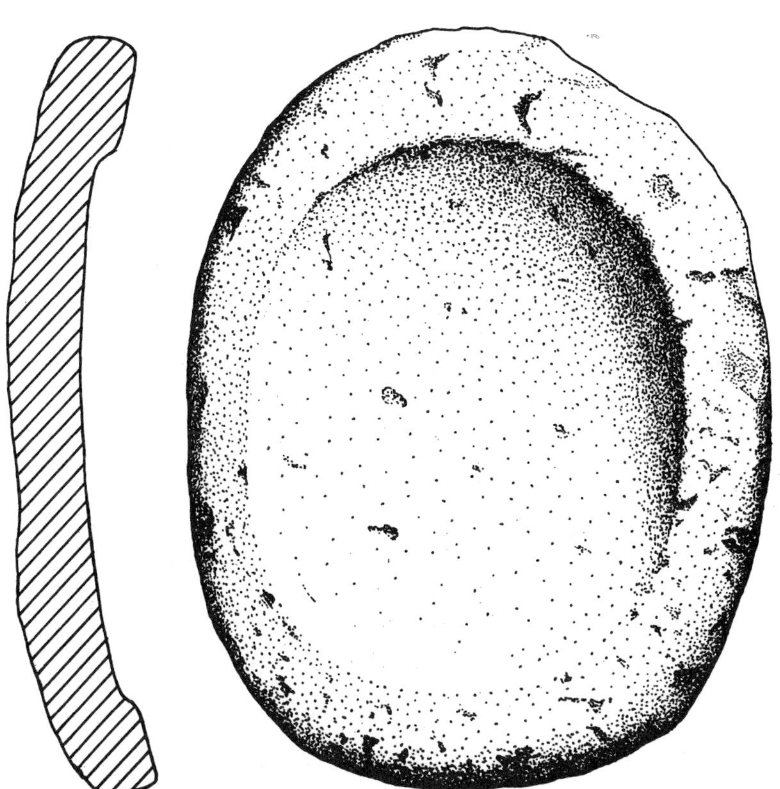

FIGURE 77. Basalt tray. Length, 27.3 cm.

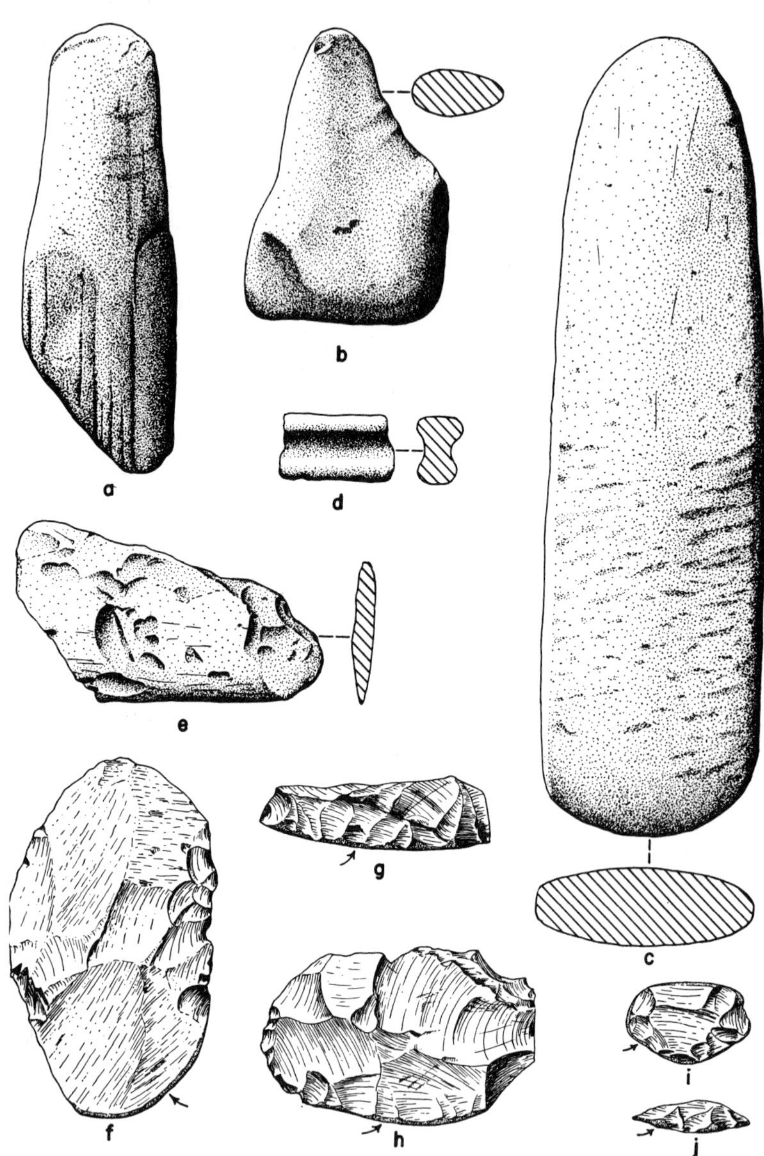

FIGURE 78. Implements from the midden. Rasps, *a-d;* ground edge knife, *e;* ground edge scrapers (indicated by arrows), *f-j*. *a-c,* schist; *d,* pumice stone; *e,* mud rock; *f-j,* basalt. Length of *c,* 22.3 cm.

believed to have been used in working shell[103] and several were found in the Ash Hill site (Ariz. Z:12:6), near Santa Rosa, a Sells Phase ruin. In Ventana, it is significant that all examples occurred in the upper two levels, coincident with the presence of worked shell. Figure 78, *c*, a long, blade-like tool and somewhat different than the foregoing, may have served as a rasp also, judging from the scars on both faces. But this identification is not certain. A final specimen is a segment of a double-grooved rod of pumice (Fig. 78, *d*). Such a file would work well in smoothing wooden or bone shafts.

Knives—There are two thin knives, both from level 2 of the upper cave. These started as thin flakes of a fine grained, laminated rock and one edge was ground sharp (Fig. 78, *e*). Fine striations along the cutting margin run parallel to the edge.

Ground Edge Scrapers—This lot of tools evidently had a rather specialized function, probably scraping adherent materials from the surface of metates. Ground edge scrapers were first roughly flaked from basalt and, subsequently, one edge, either at one side or one end, was repeatedly drawn over an abrasive surface, wearing it smooth. While no standard shape is evident, the collection can be reduced to two lots on the basis of size and stratigraphy. The larger examples (Fig. 78, *f-h*), with diameters from 63 to 112 mm., occurred in levels 3 to 6, while the small chip scrapers (Fig. 78, *i, j*), from 33 to 52 mm. in greatest dimensions, were from levels 1 and 2 (Table 26). Whether or not both forms served the same purpose is uncertain.

Particular significance may be attached to the large early type. These are reported[104] as having been characteristic in Chiricahua Stage sites of southeastern Arizona and their appearance in Ventana in a culture level, believed to have been the equivalent of that stage, may be regarded as more than a coincidence. It adds one further trait to the list of Chiricahua

★

103. H. S. Gladwin, *et al.*, 1937, p. 138, Pl. XXXVIII.
104. E. B. Sayles and E. Antevs, 1941, p. 18, Fig. 10.

TABLE 26

DISTRIBUTION OF MISCELLANEOUS STONE OBJECTS BY TYPE AND LEVEL

	Stratigraphic Layer	Levels	Scrapers Ground Edge	Perforated Stone Discs	Lap Stones	Worked Stones
Upper Cave	Midden	1	4 13.3	2 11.1	1 8.3	
		2	3 10.0		1 8.3	3 15.0
		3	3 10.0	4 22.2	2 16.7	9 45.0
		4	9 30.0	8 44.5	1 8.3	1 5.0
		5	5 16.7	1 5.5	1 8.3	3 15.0
		6	5 16.7		4 33.3	4 20.0
		7				
		8				
		Miscel.	1 3.3	3 16.7	2 16.7	
		Totals	30	18	12	20
	Red Sand					
	Volcanic Debris					
Lower Cave	Midden	1	1 20.0		2 20.0	5 20.0
		2		3 75.0	2 20.0	9 36.0
		3	4 80.0	1 25.0	4 40.0	11 44.0
		4			2 20.0	
		5				
		Miscel.				
		Totals	5	4	10	25
		Percent				

Stage parallels. The small type may be a late derivative but it has not been reported from other sites in southern Arizona.

Axes—Ventana Cave yielded two axes, both fragmentary. Only one (Fig. 79, *a*) includes the groove which is of the full type. Both examples are late, *i. e.*, associated with pottery. The normal axe for both River and Desert branches of the Hohokam was the three-quarter groove type, but for some unaccountable reason the tool was poorly represented.

Palettes—One of the outstanding features of the River Hohokam is the schist palette with decorated border. Such items are very rare in Papagueria. In Ventana, the equivalent was a thin schist slab, usually of sub-rectangular shape and wholly lacking in decoration, but carrying red or black paint stains and worn surfaces from pulverizing paint materials. A wedge-shaped example with heavily scarred and pigmented surface is illustrated (Fig. 79, *b*). All specimens are from the pottery levels.

Discs—Of the twenty-four stone discs, twenty-two are centrally perforated. They were all made of schist, from 36 to 74 mm. in diameter and averaging 8 mm. in thickness. The customary way of producing them was by breaking and then smoothing the rough corners by abrasion (Fig. 79, *c*). Only one is well made (Fig. 79, *d*, from level 1). Drill holes are bi-conical and not always centrally placed. Two were painted red.

Next to nothing is known about these discs. Figure 79, *d* was doubtless a spindle whorl, but the rest would appear not to have been well suited for this function. The majority came from the pre-pottery levels (Table 26).

Pipes—Considerable interest is attached to three fragmentary and one whole pipe. The fragments, two of fine-grained stone and one of volcanic scoria, are from tubular pipes, probably not over 70 mm. in length. The bit end of one example (Fig. 79, *e*) is quite tapered. The levels represented are 1, 3, and 5, which, if taken at face value, suggests pipe smoking as early as the Chiricahua-Amargosa II cultural stage.

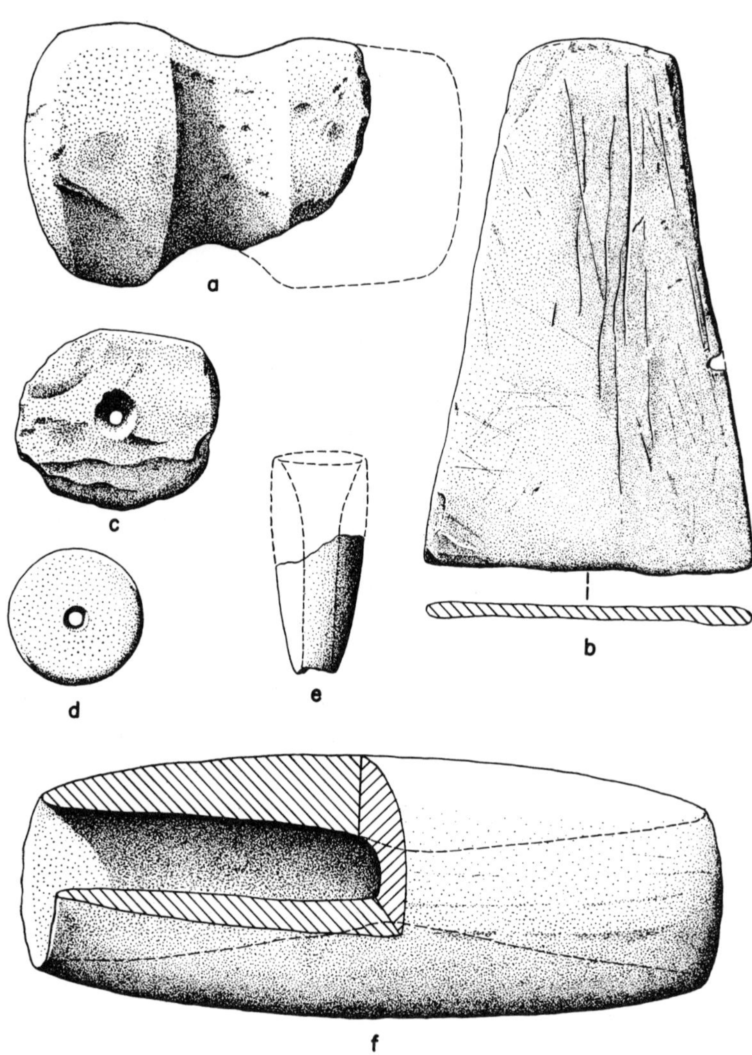

FIGURE 79. Stone objects from the midden. Grooved axe, *a;* paint palette, *b;* perforated discs, *c, d;* pipes, *e, f,* the latter double bowled. *a,* andesite porphyry; *b,* schist; *c,* mica schist; *d,* granite porphyry; *e,* fine grained volcanic; *f,* arkosic sandstone. Length of *f,* 184 mm.

The fourth specimen, also tubular (Fig. 79, *f*), is exceptional because of its great size (length 184 mm., mid-diameter 70 mm.) and in having a bowl at each end. At first this would appear to argue against its use as a pipe, but heavy tobacco cake in both bowls leaves no other alternative interpretation. This also means that stems were not inserted to make smoking easier. Since bowl diameters are 47 mm., it represented a considerable stretch of the lips to smoke the pipe. That this was done is indicated by the stained outer bowl rims. The specimen was made of a pinkish arkosic sandstone and was bored from both ends with a mid-bore diameter of 17 mm. It is possible that a perforated plug was originally lodged in the bore to keep the tobacco from going through such a large opening, although no evidence of this remains. This pipe was found near the surface in the lower cave and it may, therefore, be of historic or late prehistoric origin.

Several attempts were made to have the cake in the bowls analyzed as a further means of absolutely establishing the pipe's use. But those who were approached on this step felt that little was to be gained by it. Mr. R. E. Heineman, aware that tobacco extract fluoresces under ultra-violet light, suggested this test, and under a lamp with long-wave length (3600 to 3800 Å) ultra-violet light the stained bowl rims of the stone pipe reacted in the same way as the stained bit of a modern briar pipe. A bluish fluorescence was noted in each case. Further, aqueous solutions, made by boiling the cake from the stone pipe and also from a modern pipe as a control, gave the characteristic pale blue fluorescence.

This test, of course, is not definitive; but as far as it goes, the evidence for the use of tobacco in the pipe is confirmatory.

While examining the pipe under ultra-violet light, another feature showed up which had not only gone unnoticed but which without this treatment could not have been detected at all. This is a simple design running lengthwise on the pipe, as seen in Plate 23, *a*. Evidently this pattern was painted on with some organic dye and was absorbed by the porous base. A sufficient quantity of it is still present to mask the fluorescence of the stone, although through time, handling, and bleaching it is no longer visible in normal light. The pattern offers no clue as to the further dating of the specimen.

This chance discovery of an unseen character on the pipe led to the examination of nearly all of the Ventana collection under ultra-violet light but without producing any significant results.

Smoking, as such, was known among the Hohokam, but, to date, no pipes have been reported from orthodox Hohokam sites. In places, cane tubes packed with tobacco are the only tangible evidence.[105] The Ventana pipes are, therefore, among the first found in southern Arizona. Nothing has been learned from the Papago which might help explain the large double bowled specimen.

Pendant—Jewelry items of stone were next to absent. A lone schist pendant (Fig. 80, *a*), 46 mm. long, came from level 1 of the upper cave.

Nose Plugs—That wooden nose plugs were worn by some of the late prehistoric people of Ventana Cave is well documented (p. 422). Whether they used stone for the same purpose is a matter of conjecture, although stone nose plugs are well known elsewhere.[106] Two pieces of shaped calcite from Ventana probably belong in this category. The one whole example is cylindrical except for a flat and slightly concave longitudinal undersurface (Fig. 80, *b*). It is 31 mm. long and 16 mm. in greatest diameter. The fragmentary plug is somewhat more triangular in section. These were found in levels 1 and 2, which places them in the same general chronological position as the mummy with the wooden nose plug (Pl. 59).

Rings—A familiar stone artifact from Hohokam sites is the stone ring, often referred to as a "doughnut." The two from Ventana were both in level 1 and may be related to that culture. The material is scoriaceous lava, diameters are 89 and 66 mm. (Fig.

★

105. E. W. Haury, 1945, pp. 194-196; see also p. 426 herein.
106. J. C. McGregor, 1941, pp. 204-209; 1943, p. 280.

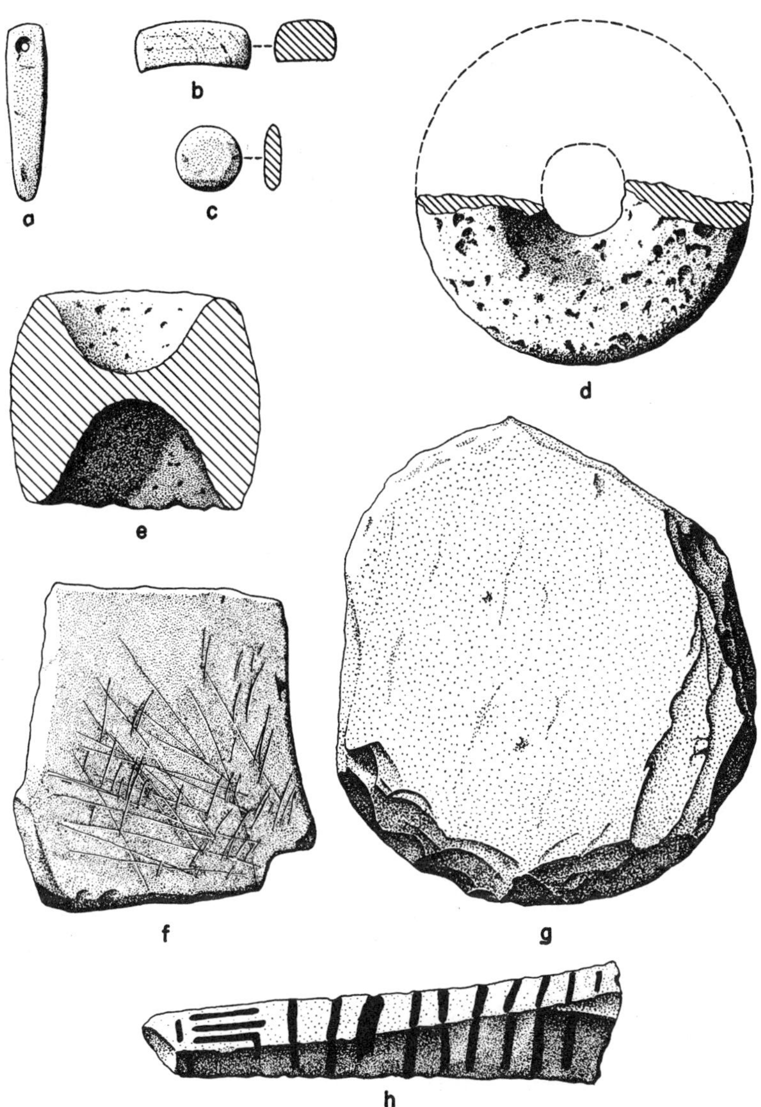

FIGURE 80. Stone artifacts from the midden. Pendant, *a;* nose plug, *b;* disc, *c;* rings, *d, e* (latter partly finished); lap stone, *f;* worked stone, *g;* painted (red) stone, *h. a, g,* schist; *b,* gypsum; *c,* argillite; *d, e,* scoriaceous lava; *f, h,* basalt. Length of *h,* 133 mm.

80, *d, e*). The smaller of the two was broken in manufacture before the bi-conical perforation had been completed, and is thicker than the usual ring.

Ball—The collection contains a single ball (level 4, upper cave) laboriously pecked out of rhyolite. Its diameter is 127 mm., which is more than twice as large as the stone kick balls found in some Papaguerian and Gila Basin sites[107] and which survive among the living Indians of the area.[108]

Bead—A fragmentary cylindrical stone bead, of mottled red and greenish argillite, appeared in level 1 of the upper cave. It is bulky, with a diameter of about 25 mm., and was perhaps twice as long.

Other Worked Stone—Included are two polished discs (Fig. 80, *c*), a piece of worked soapstone, and four shaped stones not classifiable. All are from level 1 of the upper cave.

Miscellaneous

This category includes a residue of items not fitted in elsewhere.

Lap Stones—There was constant need for a stone anvil in performing certain types of operations. These were probably held in the lap or balanced on the leg. The primary requirement appears to have been a flat surface, but beyond this there is no uniformity. Sizes run from 80 mm. to 230 mm. in length. A characteristic common to all is a scored surface (Fig. 80, *f*), mostly short slashes as might result from cutting skin with a flake knife.

No accurate count was kept of all lap stones found, but the twenty-two returned to the laboratory range almost throughout the entire depth of the midden (Table 26).

Worked Stones—A considerable number of thin schist slabs, more or less worked around the edges by breaking, came to light in nearly all levels (Table 26) during the excavation. They

★

107. J. W. Fewkes, 1912, p. 131; Ariz. Z:11:4, Arizona State Museum Survey.
108. F. Russell, 1908, pp. 172-173.

vary in diameter from about 100 to 150 mm. and are mostly circular to oval in form (Fig. 80, *g*). The Papago workmen identified these as rocks used formerly by them in cooking rabbits. Dressed rabbits are said to have been laid on hot coals and ricked over with such rocks which had been pre-heated. Some of these do show the effects of fire but many do not.

Painted Stones—A few rock chips show daubs of red paint trimming about the edges and in the most elaborate case a striped pattern on all four faces of a square, rod-like stone (Fig. 80, *h*). Almost all are late, having come from the upper two levels of the midden. There is no reason to believe that these are connected in any way with the painted pebbles from the lower Pecos and Big Bend regions of Texas.[109]

Minerals—The collection contains 286 mineral specimens, most of which were picked up by the early cave occupants because of their color or form. A few were found with burials, but, for the most part, they appeared at random in the debris.

Table 27 shows the vertical distribution of those found in the upper cave. Most common were chalcedonic concretions (70 per cent of the collection) called "desert roses" because of their exotic and often flower-like form (Pl. 23, *b-e*). These could be gathered in the immediate vicinity of the cave where they weather out of certain volcanic formations. This was the only mineral which appears to have been collected by the oldest residents in the cave for strictly non-utilitarian purposes, and, as time went on, succeeding people evidently took more and more to gathering these curiosities. This pattern, in fact, is generally true for other minerals, too, as most of them occur in the late debris.

Crystal forms, notably calcite, and color-producing minerals appear to have attracted most attention. Among the latter, specularite for red paint was more prevalent than other types but

★

109. J. W. Davenport and C. Chelf (no date); Bulletin V, Witte Memorial Museum, San Antonio.

TABLE 27

DISTRIBUTION OF MINERALS, UPPER CAVE ONLY

	Stratigraphic Layer	Levels	Chalcedony Concretions	Calcite	Obsidian Nodules	Quartz Crystals	Muscovite	Gypsum	Psilomelane	Malachite	Pyrolusite	Rhyolite Spherulites	Red Hematite	Black Hematite	Specularite	Prepared Paint	Totals	Percent
Upper Cave	Midden	1	23 / 32.0	10 / 50.0	2 / 33.3	2 / 40.0	1 / 25.0						1 / 16.7		3 / 27.3	3 / 100.0	45	32.1
		2	11 / 15.3	3 / 15.0	2 / 33.3		1 / 25.0	1 / 100.0		2 / 40.0			1 / 16.7		3 / 27.3		24	17.1
		3	12 / 16.7	2 / 10.0			1 / 25.0			3 / 60.0	1 / 100.0	1 / 50.0	3 / 50.0		3 / 27.3		26	18.6
		4	10 / 13.9	3 / 15.0	1 / 16.7	1 / 20.0			1 / 33.3					1 / 100.0	1 / 9.1		18	12.9
		5	7 / 9.7	2 / 10.0	1 / 16.7		1 / 25.0		1 / 33.3			1 / 50.0	1 / 16.7		1 / 9.1		15	10.7
		6	6 / 8.3			2 / 40.0			1 / 33.3								9	6.4
		7	3 / 4.2														3	2.1
		8																
		Miscel.																
		Totals	72	20	6	5	4	1	3	5	1	2	6	1	11	3	140	
		Percent	51.5	14.3	4.3	3.6	2.9	.7	2.1	3.6	.7	1.4	4.3	.7	7.9	2.1		

scarce in view of the high number of metates showing red stains from grinding the material. Prepared pigments such as mixtures of clay and colorants are limited to a few small cakes of red paint, all of which were found in level 1 of the upper cave. There are two rhyolite sphirulites (Pl. 23, *f*), and one chunk of galena from the lower cave was rubbed to a cubic form (Pl. 23, *g*).

General Discussion of Stone Artifacts

We have now reviewed over eleven thousand items made of stone, and a few general observations are in order. The sheer bulk of the collection and the repetition of the evidence for a relative temporal placement of many stone traits does much to inspire confidence in the validity of that evidence. But such large problems as the correlation of the Ventana lithic assemblages with other cultural patterns still display baffling aspects.

First, the technology of stone presents a relatively simple picture. Flaking by percussion and pressure were known from the earliest to the latest times represented by the human debris in the cave. Pressure flaking may have been secondary to percussion in the Ventana Complex, just as percussion was behind pressure flaking in levels 1 and 2 of the upper cave midden, although this relationship is little more than an impression. The reduction of stone by pecking was known in the Ventana Complex as evidenced by the simple discoidal mano. Subsequently, in the lower two-thirds of the midden, pecking was common. It is worth noting that this treatment was restricted to utilitarian objects. Polished stone in the pre-ceramic layers resulted from work done with the tools. On the other hand, true polishing, done to bring a stone to desired form and finish, was limited to the upper zone of the midden. This was the only basically new stone technique added during the cave's long history and it may be regarded as significant that this appeared with or after the arrival of pottery and agriculture.

This situation does not coincide with Sayles' reconstruction for the Cochise Culture,[110] where ground (by use, not for use) and percussion flaked tools characterized the Sulphur Springs Stage; pressure flaked tools, believed to be intrusive, were added in the Chiricahua Stage, and chipping in general, by both techniques, was preponderant in the San Pedro Stage. The disparity may be explained in terms of differing economies of early western people who eventually came together at Ventana Cave. The changes in emphasis in lithic techniques appear to have little more than regional value.

Any attempt to relate the people of Ventana Cave to those of other areas prior to the introduction of pottery must be done primarily on the basis of their stone work, because this is the only common denominator which has survived in quantity. And such an appraisal must lie in the strength of tool assemblages or patterns rather than on individual traits. Several segregable but not entirely distinctive patterns in stone work emerge. In other words, while a few tool types appeared to have been definitive of one period or another there were, nevertheless, a number of types which persisted through several periods.

The names for the various assemblages used here demand a word of explanation. The oldest pattern, A, is called the Ventana Complex, being distinctive in that it manifests characters of both Folsom and San Dieguito I but is not quite like either of these. In the Ventana-Amargosa I horizon, B, the assemblage appears as a relatively pure complex, whereas in the Californian manifestations the elements are mixed with implement types characteristic of Complex C, the Chiricahua-Amargosa II. This label recognizes both the Cochise and the Californian elements in the total assemblage of the horizon. Complex D is San Pedro, essentially indistinguishable from, and doubtless the temporal equivalent of, the San Pedro Stage of the Cochise Culture of southeastern Arizona. Then follows E, the Hohokam, and F, Papago, which are self-evident.

★

110. E. B. Sayles and E. Antevs, 1941, p. 8.

A. *Ventana Complex*

Stratigraphic Position: Volcanic Debris Layer

Tool Assemblage:

- Projectile Points:
  - Leaf-shaped, round and concave bases (the latter Folsom-like, one recovered)
- Knives:
  - Curved flakes
- Scrapers:
  - Discoidal, small core, side (of varying shapes), end, and rough flake
- Gravers
- Choppers
- Planes
- Grinding Stone (1)

B. *Ventana-Amargosa I Complex*

Stratigraphic Position: Red Sand Layer

Tool Assemblage:

- Projectile Points:
  - Stemmed: stem parallel-sided or expanding
- Knives:
  - Amorphous flakes
- Scrapers:
  - Discoidal, side, end, and rough flake
- Planes:
  - Oval and elongate
- Grinding stones and choppers absent

C. *Chiricahua-Amargosa II Complex*

Stratigraphic Position: Base of midden, levels 5 to 8

Tool Assemblage:

- Projectile Points:
  - Leaf-shaped, convex, straight, and concave bases; triangular, straight base; diamond
  - Stem wider than blade: concave base
  - Stem narrower than blade: tapering
- Scrapers:
  - Large, thick flake; oval, thin flaked and keeled; elongate, thin flaked and keeled; pointed, thin flaked and keeled; rectangular, thin flaked and keeled; end, keeled, round and square nosed; hollow, thin and

thick flaked and keeled; pointed; discoidal, thin flaked and domed; "thumbnail"

Flake knives:
Gravers: Thick flakes, prismatic, chisel
Choppers: Sharpened flakes, core, and flat pebble
Metates: Block and slab forms
Manos: Small single hand type
Pestle: Flat and round ended
Ground edge scrapers

D. *San Pedro Complex* (Stage) :

Stratigraphic Position: Midden, levels 3 to 5

Projectile Points:
Stemmed, short lateral tang, long. Some carryover of previous forms

Blades:
Triangular or leaf-shaped

Choppers:
Chiefly core types; pebble type abundant

Planes and Scrapers:
Nearly all previous types

Gravers:
Thick flake, some others

Drills:
Large and small flanged forms

Metates:
Both block and slab types

Manos:
Small single hand type

E. *Hohokam*

Stratigraphic Position: Midden, levels 1 and 2

Projectile Points:
Small, expanding stems, sharp lateral tang

Choppers:
Flake and core types

Scrapers:
All types in ranging frequencies. Distinctive are serrated, pointed, and "thumbnail" forms. Rare are oval and rectangular keeled types

Gravers: Doubtful
Drills: Rare

Metates:
  Shaped block with full grinding surface
Manos:
  Two-handed, rectangular
Mortars:
  Boulder type
Rasps
Axes:
  Three-quarter groove
Palette:

F. Papago
  Simple, undecorated
  Stratigraphic Position: Mostly surface, locally deeper
  Probably considerable use of rough tools duplicating older forms, but assemblage not certainly definable
  Projectile Points:
    Small, triangular, concave base

Further discussion of these assemblages will be deferred to the concluding section of the report.

Pottery

The presence of pottery in Ventana Cave and where it appeared in the trash are important to this study; but what pottery reveals by way of local ceramic development is relatively unimportant. The reasons for this will become apparent presently.

Most of the pottery was found in the dry layer of the midden and just within the upper few centimeters of the moist layer, rarely occurring deeper than 2.00 m. below the surface. Roughly, the moisture line in the trash marked the lower limits of pottery. But this appears to be purely a coincidence and is not believed to represent a true cultural boundary. Exceptional disturbances into early trash by pottery-using people did let pottery down below the 2.00 m. line in a few places. The absolute maximum depth for pottery was 3.50 m. in section D of the upper cave, where the situation was rather special. This is at the point where the cave wall is sharply undercut and evidently the cave floor, since the arrival of pottery, sloped from front to back into this undercut section making that area accessible for the deposition of trash. The dip in the weakly developed stratification lines in this area bears out this contention.

Horizontally, pottery was distributed over the full length of the shelter, with a noticeable concentration in the upper part, especially in sections A to D, where maximum sunshine, coupled with best protection, was afforded. Practically no pottery was to be found on the talus outside the cave, indicating that such pottery as was taken inside the shelter ultimately found its resting place in the trash accumulating over the occupied area.

Although the depth of the pottery-bearing layer was great enough to anticipate stratigraphy within it, the analysis of the sherds showed that this was not the case. Pottery known to be of different ages, as established, for example, in the stratigraphic studies at Snaketown, often occurred together. The obvious explanation of this situation is that through constant churning of the debris, as would result from making burials (36 burials were found in the pottery layer), the pottery of various ages became extensively mixed. Thus it is impossible to draw any fine chronologic distinctions within the pottery zone. Generally speaking, however, most of the oldest pottery lay deep, and most of the younger material was high in the fill. Early historic and modern Papago pottery, as well as glass, rarely went below the surface. This would indicate little disturbance of the trash by the Papago.

The screening of almost all of the trash in both the upper and lower parts of the shelter makes us feel reasonably sure that a high percentage of the pottery ever used there was recovered, providing an almost complete sample for study. Considering the amount of the pottery-bearing trash screened, the actual bulk of the pottery is small. The total sherd sample amounts to 31,400 pieces, and only one whole vessel was found. Matched against equal amounts of rubbish from caves in the San Juan area this return in pottery is very small. Since open sites in Papagueria and those farther north along the Gila show a great abundance of pottery, and as the people who frequented the shelter were of the same basic stock, the argument that pottery was relatively unimportant to them cannot be advanced. This situation calls for speculation as to the kind of occupation the shelter had since pottery was introduced into the area.

We know that today the Papago use the cave seasonally, limited chiefly to a few weeks late in June and in early July, during the sahuaro fruit harvest. The cave has also been visited occasionally because of the permanent water supply it affords. The camp residue of such visits is negligible. This intermittent usage probably extends well into prehistory, thereby accounting for such a relatively small amount of pottery. Further, painted types of all classes and indicative of a long span of time were rare (about 2 per cent of all pottery), whereas in permanently occupied village sites these types run to respectably high percentages of the total pottery produced. Conversely, the plain utility pottery is excessively represented (94 per cent). This can be interpreted in terms of simple economy. Seasonal dependence on the cave coinciding with the ripening of cactus fruit called for the use of pottery which would be most efficient in reducing the fruit to consumable form, and that was the plainware jar. Other types naturally found their way in, too, but a true notion of the ceramics at any one time must be determined from permanently inhabited open sites. Ventana Cave offers nothing on the problem of local ceramic evolution.

In view of this situation there is no need of presenting the Ventana pottery in detail. Some types have already been well described and others, relatively unknown, should be so treated only when good collections are made from sites where their chronological position and companion types can be more accurately determined. However, a listing of the types present in the cave and pertinent facts must be included.

Plain Wares

The overwhelming fraction (94 per cent) of the sherd collection is classifiable as plain ware. This is far from satisfactory analytical material because culinary wares were relatively stable over long periods of time and they incorporate so few definitive characteristics. A primary difference is observable in the presence or absence of mica in the paste. A thick, non-micaceous plain ware is normal for Papagueria in all horizons thus far determined. This is known as Sells Plain.[111] It appears to have undergone no appreciable changes structurally or in form in about six hundred years. There was, however, a notable decrease in amount from early to late, coincident with the increase of red ware and painted pottery.[112] Recent Papago plain ware shows features of Sells Plain, so much so that in sherd form most of it is inseparable from the older type. One clear cut diagnostic feature, however, is seen in the rims of both bowls and jars. This is the addition of a coil at the rim, creating a band about the orifice (Fig. 81, *a, b*). It occurs on painted pottery and red ware

★

111. F. H. Scantling, 1940, pp. 33-35.

112. Vamori Phase, 96 per cent; Topawa Phase, 77 per cent; Sells Phase, 43 per cent. (A. M. Withers, 1941, p. 48.)

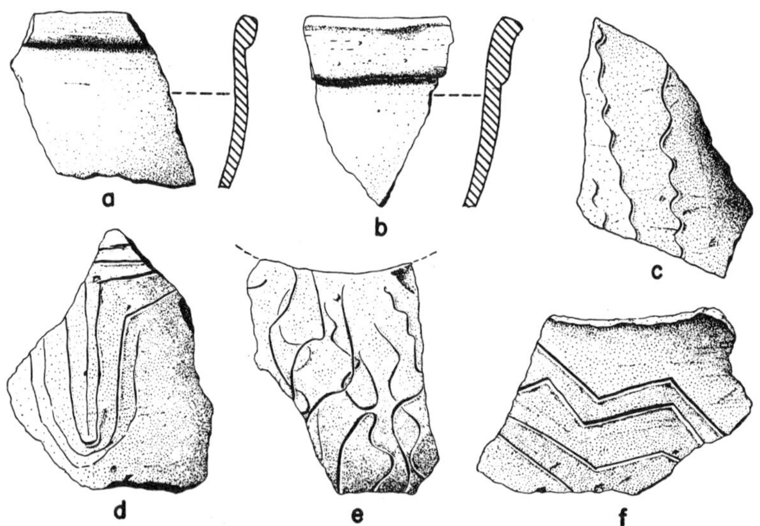

FIGURE 81. Sherds from the midden. Nineteenth century Papago rim-coil plain ware, *a, b;* incised sherds, possibly of Yuman affinity, *c-f*. Length of *f*, 68 mm.

as well, and has been found to be a most useful hallmark of 19th century Papago pottery.

In Ventana, mica-free plain ware accounts for about 65 per cent of the pottery in this category, including modern, as well as the full range of prehistoric products.

In the lot there are eight incised sherds which merit special mention, as this treatment is rare in Papagueria. These all represent neck or upper body portions of jars (Fig. 81, *c-f*) of an unpolished hard brown ware. Incising was done while the clay was still plastic. A few do not appear to be local and it may be that these are fragments of jars made to the far west in the Yuma area.[113]

In the non-micaceous class of pottery, about 1.5 per cent of the sherd sample is a thin, hard, and well smoothed ware of chocolate brown color. This, too, is unlike anything previously found by us on the reservation. Vessels were evidently exclusively jars. Wall thickness, the striking feature, ranges from 2.50 to 4 mm., as against a range of 5 to 22 mm. for Sells Plain. It was made by the coil paddle-and-anvil technique. M. J. Rogers, of the San Diego Museum of Man, has inspected some of this pottery and noted one sherd as specifically identifiable to Yuma II from the Lower Colorado River and dating before 1500. The rest was not typical but the resemblance to Yuman pottery is present. This reflects some measure of late prehistoric contact between the Papaguerian and the Yuma area to the west.

Coming to the micaceous class of plain ware, amounting to 33.5 per cent of the total, we are dealing with another pottery type which does not appear to be native. Its identity is easily established as Gila Plain[114] and a few samples will qualify as Vahki Plain,[115] both types being associated with the River Hohokam. That Gila Plain should have been so strong as an intrusive type is surprising, but if we remember that Ventana Cave lies just

★

113. M. J. Rogers informs me that incised pottery is found in Yuma archaeology and that the style of patterns on the Ventana sherds, particularly on the one illustrated in Figure 81, *d*, is suggestive of that culture.

114. H. S. Gladwin, *et al.*, 1937, pp. 205-211.

115. *Ibid.*, pp. 211-212.

south of its home in the Gila Valley, a long importation is not implied. Furthermore, its abundance emphasizes the intimacy of the contact between the Desert and River branches of the Hohokam.

Red Wares

Red ware, in greater or lesser amounts, has been made in practically all horizons of southern Arizona archaeology. The task of separating early from late types is rendered difficult because of the similarity of red pottery over long expanses of time. The best one can do is to show what was present in Ventana and then to pin types down where possible.

Numerically, red ware of all kinds amounts to about 4 per cent of the total sherd collection. Within the red ware the bulk of it (65 per cent) is specifically identifiable as Sells Red.[116] It has a brick-red color and was produced mostly as bowls with thickened and somewhat everted rims. Polishing marks, horizontal at the rim and vertical on the body, are characteristic. In typical Sells Phase sites, as Jackrabbit and Ash Hill, this type was made in about the same proportions or even a little heavier than plain ware and is one of the important diagnostics of the phase. Its companion painted type is Tanque Verde Red-on-brown. As the latter is the prevalent painted ware in the cave, it is logical to assume that Sells Red should also have been well represented.

The next most abundant red ware is of Papago origin. These are sherds from small vessels, sometimes displaying the rim coils. Some of this pottery has a dense black core derived from the vegetal temper in the paste, a certain historic trait. Also, another form of red pottery is easily picked out. This has a light red color and the paste shows an abundance of white temper in a brown matrix. Papago settlements abandoned comparatively recently have yielded such wares. The similarity of some of the red Papago pottery to Sells Red is so striking that direct relationship may be suspected.

★

116. F. H. Scantling, 1940, pp. 30-33.

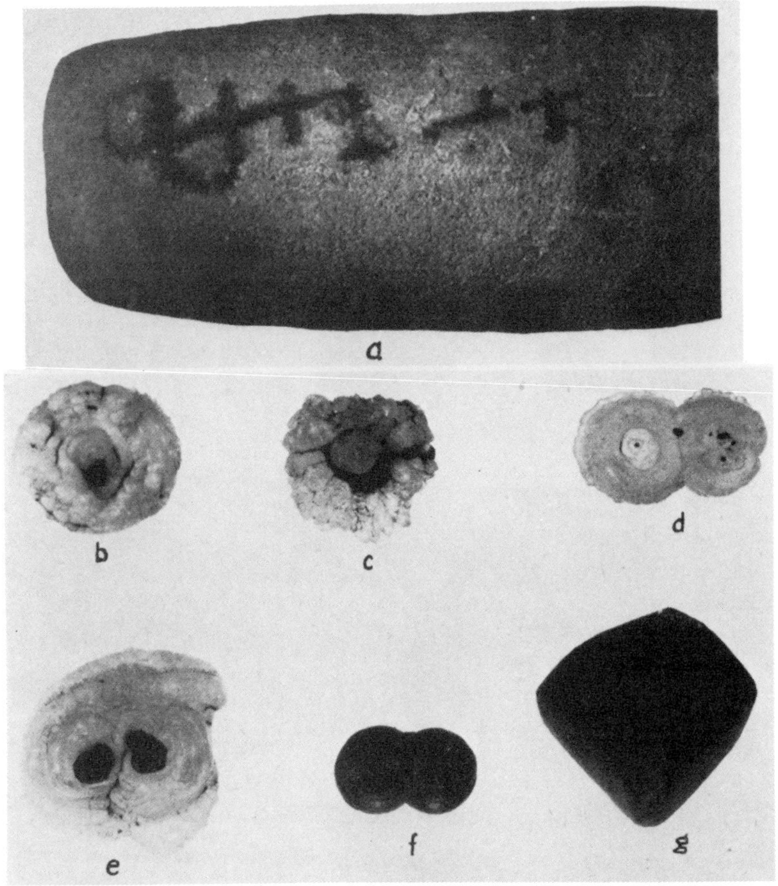

PLATE 23

Luminogram of double-bowled tubular stone pipe, *a,* bringing out the normally invisible painted pattern. (On X-F Panchromatic film, G filter, 10 minute exposure at F.32; light source, hot type mercury vapor filtered ultraviolet lamp, 3600-3800 Angstrom units).

Concretions and minerals from the midden: *b-e,* chalcedonic concretions; *f,* rhyolite sphirulite; *g,* galena. Length of *d,* 30 mm.

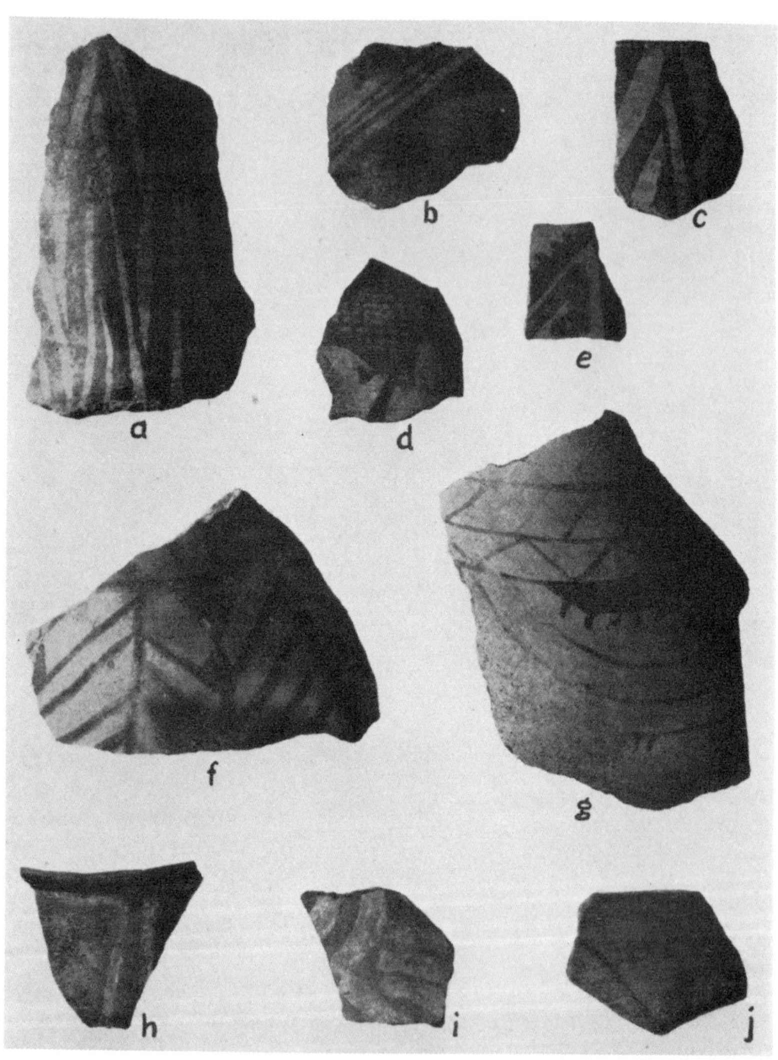

PLATE 24

Native painted pottery from the midden. Prehistoric: Tanque Verde Red-on-brown, *a-e*. Papago: 19th century broadline red-on-buff, *f;* late 19th and early 20th century narrowline red-on-buff, *g;* white-on-buff, *h, i;* black-on-red, *j*. Length of *a,* 140 mm.

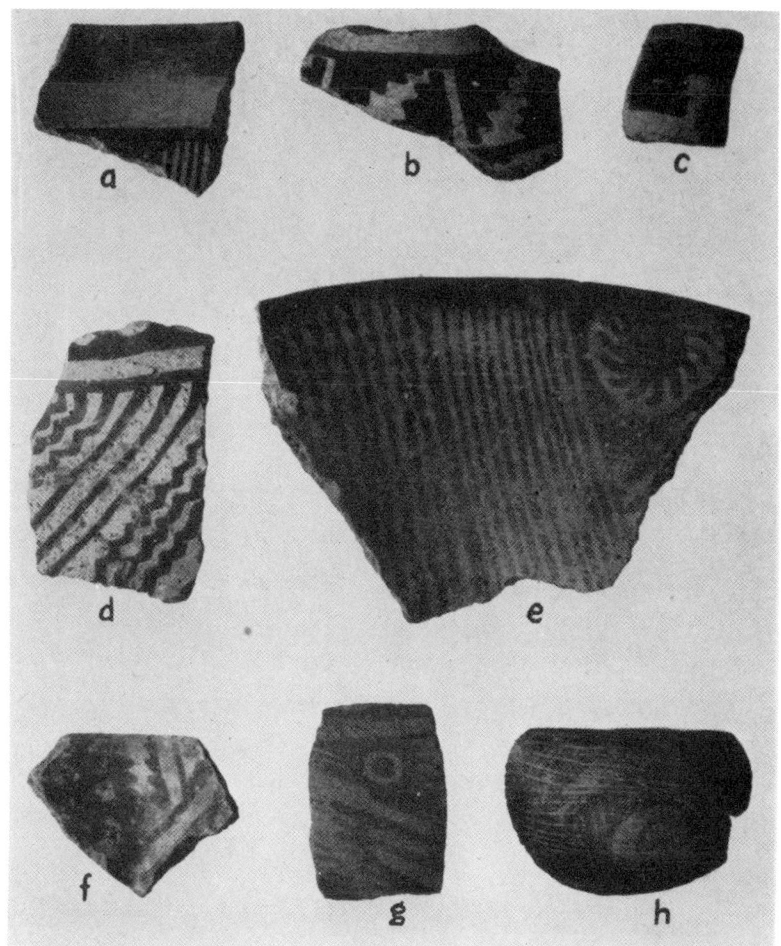

PLATE 25

Intrusive painted pottery from the midden. Gila Polychrome, *a, b;* Tonto Polychrome, *c;* Sacaton Red-on-buff, *d;* Santa Cruz Red-on-buff, *e;* Gila Butte Red-on-buff, *f, g;* Snaketown Red-on-buff, *h.* Length of *e,* 160 mm.

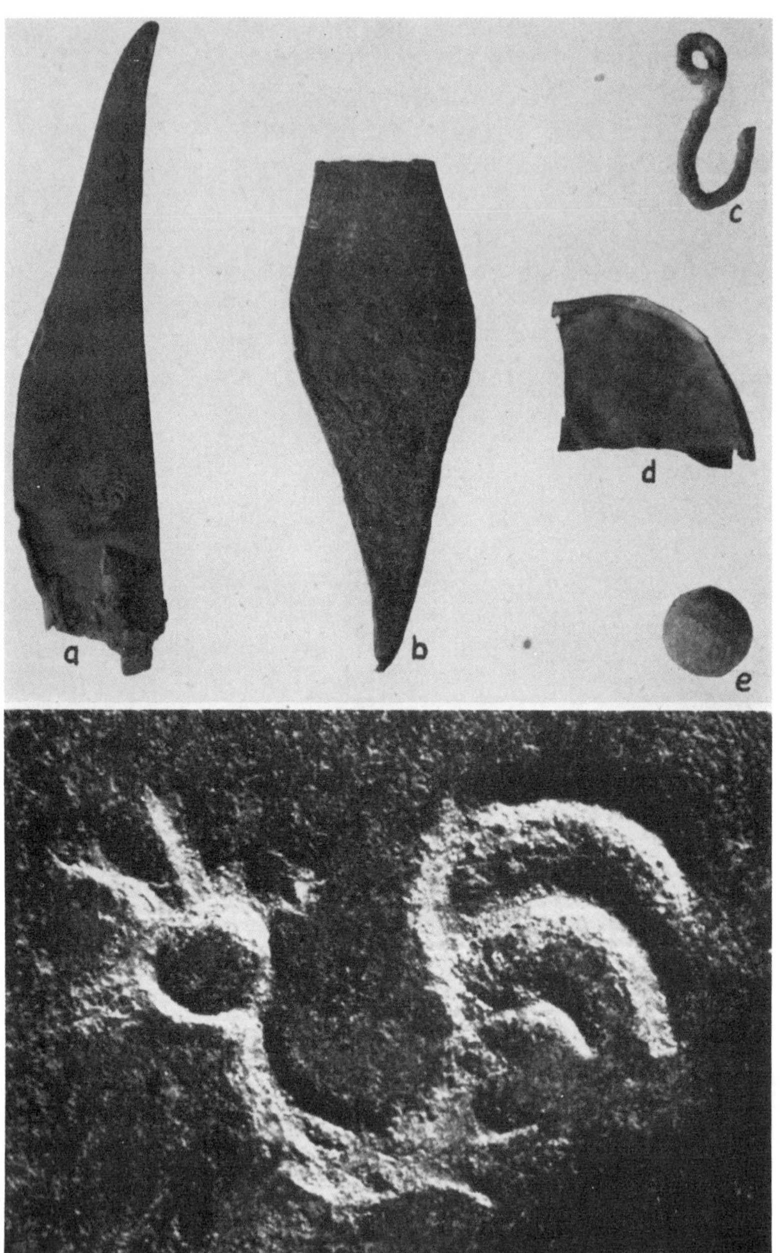

Alfred A. Cohn Photo

PLATE 26

Metal objects from the surface layer of the midden. Iron knives, *a, b;* wire hook, *c;* scrap of zinc can, *d;* lead musket ball, *e*. Length of *a,* 130 mm.

f (Lower). The hallmark visible on the face of the iron blade *(a)* above. Greatly magnified.

Intrusive red wares include a few sherds of the thin, micaceous Vahki Red,[117] a Pioneer Period type of the River Hohokam, and a handful of Gila Red sherds also from the Gila Basin of Classic Period times. The smudged black interiors of Gila Red calls for a general observation to the effect that smudging of interiors of red vessels was not practiced in Papagueria. This is a northern and eastern trait.[118] It begins to look as though the origin of the red ware, which eventually gave rise to Sells Red was independent of the northern red ware development. A southern link is therefore suggested, possibly with Guasave Red ware of Sinaloa.[119]

Painted Wares

In the total pottery sample of 31,400 sherds, only 2 per cent is painted, representing both native and foreign types. What this low percentage means has already been discussed. Regardless of the amount, the types present do yield significant chronological and cultural information.

Indigenous

The story of the indigenous painted pottery on the reservation has so far been only vaguely sketched,[120] and it is of such a nature that segregation of the three chronologically sequent types, Vamori Red-on-brown, Topawa Red-on-brown, and Tanque Verde Red-on-brown, is not easily accomplished when they are all thrown together as they were in the midden. This is due to the fact that technically poor examples of the late form, Tanque Verde Red-on-brown, may resemble the earlier parent type, Topawa Red-on-brown, and so on. But as we already have the knowledge that the cave was in use during nearly all phases of the River Hohokam development, it stands to reason that all locally made painted types should be represented, too.

These have therefore been lumped together, accounting for

★

117. H. S. Gladwin, *et al.*, 1937, pp. 204-205.
118. E. W. Haury, 1940, pp. 87-90.
119. G. F. Ekholm, 1942, pp. 78-82, 125.
120. A. M. Withers, 1941, pp. 48-53.

70 per cent of the painted pottery recovered. By far the majority of these sherds are easily recognized as Tanque Verde Red-on-brown, and this may be taken as indicative of the latest pre-Spanish horizon, when the cave was used intensively. A few comments on the type are in order.

Tanque Verde Red-on-brown, occuring widely through south-central Arizona, unfortunately has not been described in available sources.[121] It takes its name from the Tanque Verde Village[122] some twenty-five miles east of Tucson. A hard, semi-polished brown paste pottery, it occurs in both bowls and jars. Bowl interiors are often blackened by smudging, which may or may not have been intentional. Designs appear on both inner and outer bowl surfaces, the latter being most extensive. Jars often have tall vertical necks, somewhat vertically compressed bodies, and may have a curious angular indention near the

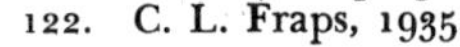

121. I. Kelly, in preparation; F. H. Scantling, 1940, pp. 27-30.
122. C. L. Fraps, 1935.

FIGURE 82. Design on Tanque Verde Red-on-brown bowl, found with burial 22. Interior, *a;* exterior, *b*. Diameter, 280 mm.

base. A typical selection of sherds is shown in Plate 24, *a-e*.

In Ventana, the only nearly whole clay vessel recovered during our entire work, an offering with burial 22, was of this type. Its design, inside and out, is shown in Figure 82.

The inclusive dates for Tanque Verde Red-on-brown in the Tucson area may be put from about A.D. 1200 to 1300. These dates are based on its repeated association with Gila Polychrome of the Salado Culture, which, in turn, has been dated by tree-rings. It degenerated some time during the 14th century to a heretofore undescribed type, Pantano Red-on-brown.[123] But in Papagueria, while it is obviously as old as in the Tucson area, the ware did not degenerate but persisted as Tanque Verde Red-on-brown into the Sells Phase (ca. 1250-1400), for which it is the chief ceramic component. On the strength of this type, the last intensive habitation of the cave may be accredited to the 14th century. Tanque Verde Red-on-brown was most heavily represented in level 1 of the midden.

Recent and Modern Papago Pottery—No systematic analysis of Papago pottery has ever been made. Although this was one of the aims of our Papaguerian studies, now is not the time to treat it in detail and only enough will be said to cover the data as pertaining to the cave.

On the whole, Papago painted wares are not difficult to segregate from the pre-Spanish types in spite of the fact that, in some, the color combinations are about the same. Workmanship, form, and particularly design, are the main identifying criteria. Criticism of the stratigraphy within the pottery-bearing zone of the midden has been voiced. Nevertheless, it must be noted that Papago pottery consistently occurred near the surface, and where digging was done on a .25 m. vertical basis, it was found predominantly in the top zone rather than in the second .25 m. level.

Quantitatively, Papago painted pottery accounts for only about 8 per cent of all painted pottery recovered. The following painted types may be listed:

★

123. Determined through recent excavations in the University Indian Ruin.

Red-on-buff	39
White-on-buff	14
Black-on-red	8
Total	61

(Red-on-buff)—Recent and modern red-on-buff of the Papago is mainly in the form of spheroidal-bodied jars, with rather high necks and relatively small mouths. A few bowls also occur. Painting is usually restricted to the upper half or less on jars, both inside and outside on bowls; the pattern layout is simple and open, and line work is markedly crude. Vessel surfaces may carry a thin wash and are sometimes lightly polished. Two styles have been noted: one with rather heavy line work (Pl. 24, *f*), dated from the 19th century,[124] and the second with narrow line work (Pl. 24, *g*) of late 19th and early 20th century age. Both of these are present in Ventana, the former being predominant. The sherds are small, so, in illustrating, the type examples have been selected from other sites.

(White-on-buff)—Occasionally the Papago substituted a thick white paint for red in executing patterns on both bowls and jars (Pl. 24, *h, i*). This appears to have been applied after firing, as it is extremely fugitive. The paint was applied as a thick, creamy liquid, accounting for its caked and smeary appearance. Only a broad-line technique is represented, and the evidence, so far, from the reservation suggests this to be essentially a 19th century type.

(Black-on-red)—Highly burnished red pottery decorated with a watery carbon paint, derived from mesquite gum and bark, has been made in recent times by the Maricopa,[125] Pima,[126] Kwahadk,[127] and Papago. As yet no one has attempted to unravel the story of this pottery as to who made it first and when. Because it is much alike among the above tribes it may be

★

124. Undoubtedly earlier, too, but we have no evidence as yet to prove it.
125. L. Spier, 1933, pp. 108-110.
126. F. Russell, 1908, p. 127.
127. *Ibid.*, p. 129.

erroneous to assign the few Ventana sherds (Pl. 24, *j*), to the Papago. It could easily have come in as trade material. There is, however, a detail which may help in the placement. One bowl fragment shows the diagnostic rim coil so common on Papago pottery of the 19th century. Whether the other tribes used it too, I do not know. In Papagueria, the rim coil appears to have faded by about 1875, suggesting that black-on-red painting may have been adopted by that time. Batki, abandoned in 1850, has not produced pottery of this type. Nowadays it is purely a sale product.

Ceramically there are no grounds for claiming that the Papago used Ventana Cave much before 1850, but it must be remembered that the early limits of the 19th century type have not been ascertained. Native Papago glazed pottery, a post-Spanish innovation of the early 19th and possibly of the late 18th century, was not found.

Intrusive

Anasazi—Salado. One of the best dating guides we have in southern Arizona is the polychrome pottery of the Salado division of the Anasazi. This is so because the particular types involved, Gila and Tonto Polychromes,[128] have been dated accurately by tree-rings to the 14th century. Assuming, as we may rightfully, that this pottery reached Ventana reasonably soon after it was made, it helps in dating the latest intense horizon of occupation of the local people, the makers of Tanque Verde Red-on-brown of late Sells Phase times.[129] The Salado people spread into Southern Arizona soon after 1300, but did not establish a strong foothold in Papagueria. The sample of their wares from Ventana (35 sherds) represents more sherds than have been found collectively from all ruins on the reservation by us.

★

128. W. and H. S. Gladwin, 1930, pp. 6-9; E. W. Haury, 1945, pp. 63-80.

129. Further justification for this is hardly necessary, but for those unfamiliar with southern Arizona archaeology, the Gila Polychrome-Tanque Verde Red-on-brown association has also been noted in the Jackrabbit Ruin (F. H. Scantling, 1940), University Indian Ruin, Martinez Hill Ruin, and in the Gila Valley. In many ruins (as Casa Grande) it is a companion of Casa Grande Red-on-buff, a collateral type of Tanque Verde Red-on-brown.

It is well to note that the cave lies near the southwestern limit of Salado distribution which gave good opportunities for contact. Also, skeletal remains include several persons resembling the Pueblo racial type (p. 495), suggesting more than mere diffusion of cultures. The general problem of Salado influence on the Desert Hohokam is dealt with elsewhere (see p. 17). The Salado sherds, a few of which are illustrated in Plate 25, *a-c,* are typical in every respect. This pottery is so much alike over a wide area that it is impossible to pin it down to a precise source. Stratigraphically nearly all Salado sherds came from level 1 and a few were in level 2. It may be concluded, therefore, that only a half meter or so of rubbish was added to the enormous fill of the cave after about A. D. 1300.

Trincheras Culture—The area south of the International Boundary was inhabited by people who have come to be known as the Trincheras Culture. They take their name from the extensive terracing of hillsides for defensive home sites. One of the characteristic types of pottery produced by them was Trincheras Purple-on-red,[130] a highly polished ware, chiefly in the form of jars with deeply scored inner surfaces. By trade, this pottery, with a few variant forms, found its way into southern Arizona at a time prior to about 1100. Its association at Snaketown was with three phases of the Pioneer Period.[131] In the light of what has been learned since Snaketown was dug, I am sure that these associations were not real and that the horizon must be put considerably later. Trincheras intrusives were present at Gleeson, a site roughly contemporary with the late Colonial and early Sedentary horizons of the Gila Basin.[132] Also at Valshni Village, near the Mexican border, it occurred heaviest in Vamori Phase contexts and in association with Santa Cruz and Sacaton Red-on-buffs of the Gila Basin.[133] Furthermore, Arizona Hohokam

★

130. C. Sauer and D. Brand, 1931, pp. 107-109; D. Brand, 1935, pp. 298-299. This and several variant forms more recently described by A. M. Withers, 1941, pp. 36-43.

131. H. S. Gladwin, *et al.*, 1937, Fig. 105, called Sonora Red-on-brown.

132. W. S. Fulton and C. Tuthill, 1940, pp. 47-48.

133. A. M. Withers, 1941, pp. 39-40. Arizona DD:5:8, a site tested by the Arizona State Museum in 1941, shows the same situation.

intrusives, in one of the largest sites of the Trincheras Culture in Sonora, located on the Boquillas River at La Playa,[134] are of Colonial-Sedentary age. Thus the general period of the Trincheras development, in its best form, at least, appears to be bracketed. Trincheras wares have not been found during extensive diggings in sites of Classic Period age, specifically in the Tanque Verde or Tucson Phases of the middle Santa Cruz area or in the Sells Phase of Papagueria. Either the culture died out by the 14th century or newly developed characteristics identifying it have not been recognized. In all probability the former alternative was the case.

In any event the fifteen Trincheras Purple-on-red sherds from Ventana are evidence of contact with this southern group, certainly on a pre-Sells Phase level. Nine were in the first .50 m. of trash and six occurred from .50 to 1.50 m. (levels 2 and 3).

Hohokam: River Branch—Thanks to several easily recognizable and highly definitive features, the red-on-buff of the Gila Basin is easily determined, both as to provenience and to horizon. The numbers of painted sherds from Ventana for the respective phases as ascertained at Snaketown stand as follows:

Period	*Phase*	*Type*[1]	*Number*
Sedentary	Sacaton	Sacaton Red-on-buff	32 (Pl. 25, *d*)
Colonial	Santa Cruz	Santa Cruz Red-on-buff	19 (Pl. 25, *e*)
	Gila Butte	Gila Butte Red-on-buff	8 (Pl. 25, *f, g*)
Pioneer	Snaketown	Snaketown Red-on-buff	7 (Pl. 25, *h*)
	Sweetwater	Sweetwater Red-on-gray	6
	Estrella	Estrella Red-on-gray	4
Total			76

1. For a description of these types see H. S. Gladwin, *et al.*, 1937, pp. 171-202.

This placement is made solely on typology, as the stratigraphic situation in the cave is entirely unsatisfactory within the vertical limits of the occurrence of these sherds.

It has been determined through our excavations on the reser-

★

134. C. Sauer and D. Brand, 1931, pp. 93-94; Arizona State Museum Survey, Sonora F:10:3.

vation that the painting of pottery here lagged far behind that of the River Hohokam in time, quantity, and quality. The oldest local decorated ware was probably no older than Santa Cruz Phase times and little of it was produced until the Sells Phase, or after about 1250. Undoubtedly, the stimulus for painting came from the River Hohokam through rather extensive introductions of Santa Cruz and Sacaton Red-on-buffs.[135] The recovery of Pioneer Period sherds from Ventana shows that this flow of pottery from north to south extended back to even earlier times. If the Desert Hohokam were inspired by it to take up ceramic decoration, no evidence of it has been found. It does not appear that the numerical increase of River Hohokam sherds, from early to late, in the pottery-laden trash may be interpreted as an intensifying of contacts. This trend pretty closely follows the curve of painted pottery production in relation to the total pottery output in the Gila Valley.

Why some Classic Period pottery (Casa Grande Red-on-buff) did not find its way into the cave is not easy to explain. The most likely answer is that, by Sells Phase times, local pottery painting had reached its peak and was stabilized, whereas, in the Gila Valley, disintegration already appears to have set in. It is generally true that Casa Grande Red-on-buff seldom occurs as trade material in sites of comparable age outside of its native area.

The importance of Hohokam pottery in Ventana lies in the fact that it shows a persistent use of the cave by Hohokam peoples through practically the full range of their history as we now know it.

Miscellaneous Notes on Pottery

A lump of prepared potter's clay, impressed with the coils of the basket in which it was originally stored, may be taken as an indication that some pottery was produced in the cave. The clay is of the mica-free type used in Sells Plain.

★

135. Particularly true of the Valshni Village, where River Hohokam Red-on-buff accounted for about 75 per cent of all decorated pottery (A. M. Withers, 1941, p. 43, *et seq.*).

There is one sherd with coiled basket impression on the inside, a rare feature on pottery of southern Arizona. Cracks in vessels were mended either by drilling holes on each side of the crack and lashing with vegetal fiber, or more commonly by liberally applying a smear of *lac* (see p. 443) on each surface of the vessel over the crack. Holes up to 15 mm. in diameter through vessel walls were also plugged with *lac,* the excess material being flattened on both surfaces.

Discussion

If any doubt exists as to the recency of pottery in southern Arizona, relative to the length of time man has been there, such misgivings should be dispelled by the findings in Ventana Cave. But this recency cannot be measured in terms of a few centuries. As is explained below, the oldest pottery may be dated near the time of Christ. The addition of pottery to the long list of culture elements coming from a succession of stratified deposits is in a perspective we have not had heretofore from a single station.

The question of age of the Ventana pottery bears on the much wider problem of the antiquity of pottery in the Southwest. While opinions on this are still at variance with each other, proof is mounting in favor of the idea that pottery was made earlier among the Hohokam and Mogollon groups than among the Anasazi. The most recent clue comes from the Forestdale Valley, where a Mogollon site with tree-ring dates in the early A. D. 300's had an accompanying local brown ware, intrusive Hohokam pottery, but *none* of Anasazi authorship.[136] Nevertheless, we have no precise data, so far, to show exactly when pottery did appear in southern Arizona. Early estimates for the beginning of pottery in the Hohokam Culture put the initial date at about B. C. 300.[137] Subsequently this was revised to A. D. 600.[138] My personal belief is that a date somewhere between these two extremes will be more nearly correct, say

★

136. A. E. Douglass, 1942, pp. 2-7; E. W. Haury, 1942, pp. 7-8; E. W. Haury and E. B. Sayles, 1947.

137. H. S. Gladwin, *et al.,* 1937, p. 247, *et seq.*

138. H. S. Gladwin, 1942, p. 4.

about the time of Christ. There is still a strong element of guesswork in arriving at such a date, but the above estimate accommodates the facts better than the other proposed dates. I cannot caution the reader too strongly that a date of A. D. 1 for the appearance of pottery in southern Arizona is provisional.

The vertical distribution of pottery in the Ventana midden suggests an intensification in its use from early to late, *i. e.*, after its introduction it gradually gained in momentum until it finally became a truly important factor in the culture. It is recognized, however, that conditions peculiar to caves, as intermittent use and the bringing into the cave of only such pottery as would be used there in specialized economic pursuits, may go far to nullify the above statement. The following figures demonstrating the trend are put down for what they may be worth. These apply to the upper cave only.

Level	*Per Cent of Pottery Recovered*
1	85.0%
2	11.5
3	3.0
4	.5

Below level 4 there were only rare sherds, obviously downward intrusions, and as level 4 was practically a pure San Pedro Stage horizon, it may be suspected that the .5 per cent (168 sherds) of pottery in this level were similarly not in their true context.

Figure 83 has been prepared to show approximately where the various pottery types fit into the last two thousand years of time. Two significant features become evident. First, that the oldest types are not native to the area, but emanated from the River Hohokam to the north. The composite results of both excavation and reconnaissance on the reservation have indicated no locally made pottery identifiably older than about A. D. 800. This may be taken to mean that the Desert Branch of the Hohokam emerged after the River Hohokam developed. As a postulate, one might hold that the River people drifted into the desert area and, after establishing themselves, their culture slowly degenerated or its development was held in check because of the environmental restrictions.

Second, pottery is one of the best clues for telling us who used the cave since the time of Christ. In review, these include, first of all, the River Hohokam, followed (about 800 to 1400) by the newly emerged Desert Branch of the same people. Transient contact was made with the Trincheras Culture of northern Sonora in the neighborhood of A. D. 1000, and with the Salado and Yuma in the 14th century. Historically, the occupation terminates with the Papago. A conspicuous gap, ceramically, occurs from about 1400 to 1700 (Fig. 83). Either the cave was not inhabited during this time or the pottery of the period has escaped identification.

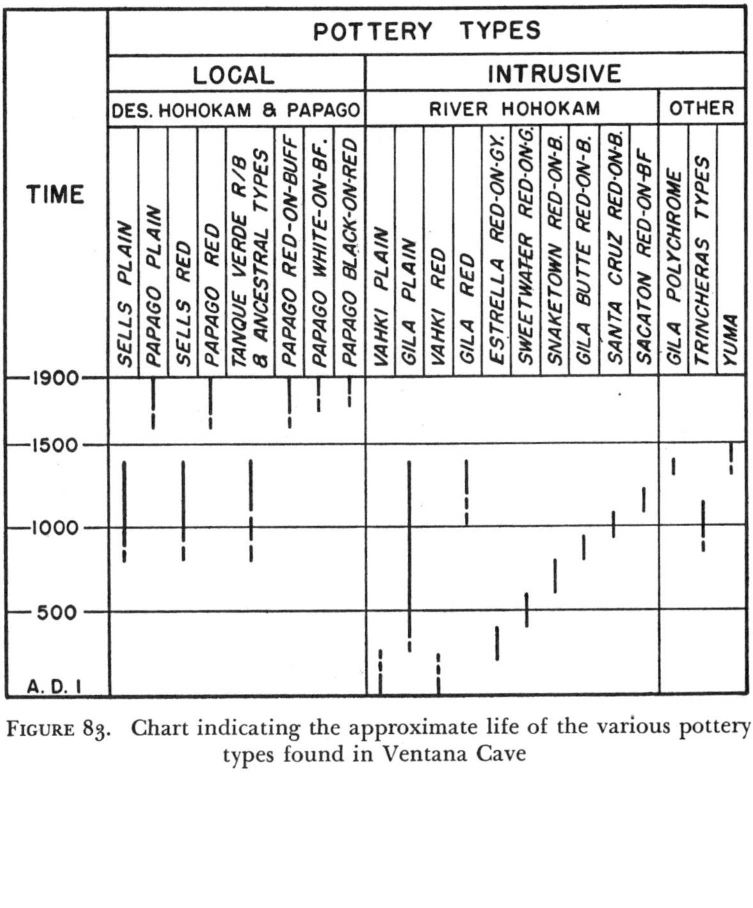

Figure 83. Chart indicating the approximate life of the various pottery types found in Ventana Cave

Because the oldest pottery in the cave came from the River Hohokam, the present evidence offers nothing new on the problem of the ultimate origin of pottery. This points back to the center of Hohokam culture in the Gila Basin as the place where more work is needed.

Another important question is what, if anything, came in with pottery. I believe we can be sure it was not an accident that the earliest evidence of corn coincides roughly with the appearance of pottery. There is nothing decisive in the cave's stratigraphy to indicate that corn was grown before the arrival of pottery as was true among the Anasazi (Basketmaker II and III). Coincident with the arrival of corn was the change in metate form from basin to trough. Inferentially, the change in projectile point styles, from the large San Pedro to the small Hohokam types, would indicate the introduction of the bow and arrow at about this time, too, and extensive working of shell is seen only in pottery times. As for perishable goods, there is no basis for judging these, as none were preserved in pre-ceramic levels.

I look upon these additions as the result of diffusion, chiefly from the south. There appears to be no basis for holding that a new people arrived, who introduced agriculture and pottery to the natives of Papagueria. Nothing in the physical composition of the trash itself indicates a cultural upheaval, and the survival of many lithic elements from pre-ceramic to ceramic levels would argue that pottery came to, and was accepted by, the local people, who, at that time, near the beginning of the Christian era, were still in the San Pedro Stage of development. This idea, the acceptance of pottery by late Cochise people, has been hinted at in the Mogollon area also.[139]

Miscellaneous Clay Objects

Clay objects other than vessels numbered only eighty-nine, and most of these were made from potsherds. A few were unfired. The breakdown follows:

★

139. E. W. Haury, 1943, p. 262; E. W. Haury and E. B. Sayles, 1947, pp. 87-88.

Fired objects				83
Secondary manufacture (worked sherds)			71	
Jar tops		4		
Discs		53		
Not perforated	47			
Perforated	6			
Irregular		14		
Primary manufacture			12	
Spindle whorls		2		
Figurines		9		
Pipe		1		
Unfired				6
Figurines			4	
Clay ball			1	
Pendant (?)			1	

Secondary Manufacture

Worked Sherds—Jar tops were made of large sherds, roughly trimmed to circular form. These were laid over jar mouths, concave surface up, and sealed with *lac* or pitch about the edge. The few in the collection are apparently prehistoric but the Papago retained this custom until recently.

Pottery discs, omnipresent in Southwestern ruins, range from 16 to 89 mm. in diameter and run the whole scale from the crudest shaping to precisely ground edges. Such discs are used by the Pima (also probably the Papago) in a guessing game,[140] and a more strictly ritual use has been noted in Winchester Cave,[141] where they occurred wrapped in pairs with other shrine material. None of the Ventana examples were so found. All appear to be made of pre-Papago pottery types. Perforation was rare.

The irregular worked sherds offer no clue as to possible use. There is no uniformity of shape but all have abraded edges.

Primary Manufacture

These include objects moulded of clay and then fired. First are two fragmentary spindle whorls with diameters of 30 and 34 mm. respectively and sections as illustrated in Figure 84, *a, b.*

★

140. F. Russell, 1908, pp. 177-178.
141. W. S. Fulton, 1941.

One is plain brown and unpolished, and the second is slipped red and polished.

Papagueria has produced more spindle whorls than any other section of Arizona and many of these show clearly their Mexican derivation. What makes them significant is the fact that they are one of the best horizon markers of the Sells Phase. While there is some evidence that clay whorls appeared in southern Arizona by late Sedentary times, they did not take hold generally until later. A northward spread took them into the Gila Basin but not much beyond.[142]

The fired figurines are represented chiefly by peg-like limb

142. E. W. Haury, 1945, pp. 115-121.

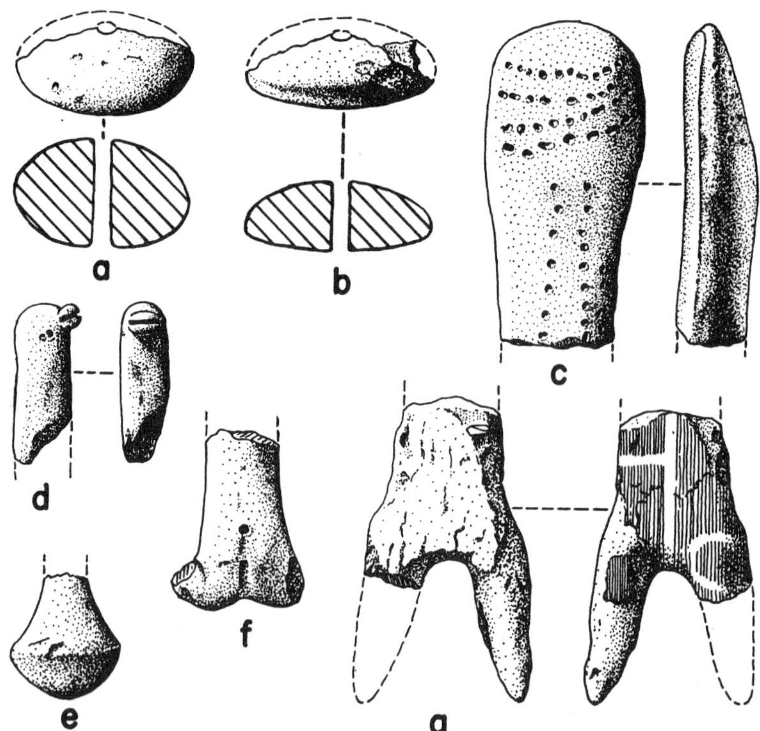

FIGURE 84. Clay objects from the midden. Fired: spindle whorls, *a, b;* figurine fragment (?), *c*. Unfired: figurines, *d, f, g* (latter with black and white body paint); pendant (?), *e*. Length of *c*, 54 mm.

fragments made of a fine, brown paste and unpolished. One questionable figurine fragment with punctate pattern (Fig. 84, *c*) is reminiscent of the Basketmaker technique of decorating figurines. There is no clue as to its horizon.

A piece of tubular pipe from the bowl end is the only evidence of pipes in this material. The bowl diameter was about 30 mm., and its exterior surface is highly smoothed. The paste, hard, black, and fine, is unlike that of any other local clay product, and the specimen was probably a trade item.

Among the unfired clay pieces, the modelled figurines are of special interest. Included are: a questionable bird head with incised pellet for the beak (incision painted black, Fig. 84, *d*); a torso (Fig. 84, *f*); and a trunk with lower limbs (Fig. 84, *g*). The latter is rather badly checked but on the back is preserved a section of black and white body paint. Another notable feature is a small (4 mm.), well formed quartz crystal pressed into the clay on the front side at about the heart position.

These figurines fall well within the Hohokam pattern as determined at Snaketown.[143] Specific resemblances are limb and torso type, painting, and appliqued "coffee bean" pellets. Since face style is the best criterion of phase, it is too bad that none were recovered in Ventana to assist in allocating them. They are probably of Sedentary Period age or earlier.

The remaining unfired objects are a ball (diameter 40 mm.) and a small, pendant-like piece (Fig. 84, *e*) with broken end.

Shell

Considering the amount of occupational debris removed from Ventana Cave, the quantity of shell, both finished items and wastage, was large, although many are represented by one or two individuals only. The clear cut vertical distribution of shell in the cave's levels makes possible several significant statements and inferences. Identifications were kindly furnished by Dr. Howard R. Hill, zoologist, of the Los Angeles County Museum. The following list gives the species in order of

★

143. H. S. Gladwin, *et al.*, 1937, pp. 233 *et seq.*

abundance, including fragments but excluding shells from the volcanic debris layer reported on in an earlier section.

Marine Shells

Cardium elatum Sowerby: about 150
Glycimeris maculatus Broderip: about 50
Cardium procerum Sowerby: 10
Oliva angulata Lamarck: 7
Columbella strombiformis Lamarck: 3
Pecten circularis Sowerby: 3
Pecten excavatus Turton: 2
Turritella tigrina Kiener: 2
Scurria mesoleuca Menke: 2
Ostrea chilensis Philippi: 1
Dosinia ponderosa Gray: 1
Conus mahogani Reeve: 1
Spondylus limbatus Sowerby: 1
Haliotis fulgens Philippi: 1
Agaronia testacea Lamarck: 1

Fresh Water

Anodonta cynea beriniana (Middendorf) : 2

Land Shells

Sonorella siticus Pilsbry and Ferriss: 3

The distribution of marine shells leads to a significant conclusion concerning the nature of contact with the west. All species save one, *Haliotis fulgens,* occur in the waters of the Gulf of California, the exception being limited to the coast of California. A few species, as *Cardium elatum* and *Pecten circularis,* are found in both waters. As the Gulf of California is within easy range of the inhabitants of Ventana Cave, it may be assumed that the source of the shell was there. The single specimen of *Haliotis fulgens* is slim evidence on which to base a belief of extensive contact between Ventana occupants and the coastal tribes of California *at any time.* Pre-ceramically, Lower California Desert Culture elements were strongly represented, but this westerly tie did not reach far enough to allow the importation of Pacific coast shells. In Hohokam times, this connection was equally restricted, being rather with the Gulf region to the southeast. Real Southwestern-California ties as reflected by shell distribution must be sought in the remains of the Anasazi.[144]

The fresh water clam (*Anodonta*) was evidently brought in from some little distance, as there are no living streams nearer to the cave than the Gila River, about fifty miles to the northwest. Land snails still occur in favored spots in the area.

The shell remains are classifiable as follows:

- I. Unworked shell
- II. Worked shell
  - A. Utilitarian
    - 1. Containers
    - 2. Scrapers
      - a. Bivalve
      - b. Univalve
  - B. Ornaments
    - 1. Beads
      - a. Whole shell
    - 2. Pendants
      - a. Whole shell
      - b. Ground shell
      - c. Cut shell
    - 3. Bracelets
    - 4. Perforated shells
    - 5. Ear plugs (?)

I. Unworked Shell

There are only two unworked whole shells in the collection, both *Glycimeris maculatus*. One of these and a few fragments of others have been altered through much handling. The majority of the fragments of *Cardium elatum* show no workmanship, but the fact that the fragments were so numerous suggests that these shells had some functional and rough use.

II. Worked Shell

The processes used by the occupants of Ventana for reducing shells to the desired objects were grinding, chipping, drilling, and cutting, abrasion by grinding being the most common. These add nothing new to the methods described for other sites, as Snaketown,[145] but it should be noted that several methods known to the River Hohokam, as carving and etching, are not

★

144. E. W. Gifford, 1947, p. 62.
145. H. S. Gladwin, *et al.*, 1937, p. 138.

represented in the cave at all. This is in keeping with the evident minor use of shell among the Desert Hohokam, as touched upon in the discussion.

A. Utilitarian

1. *Containers*—We have no whole examples to bear out the claim that shells were used as receptacles by the people whose trash formed the midden. Fragments of large individuals of *Cardium elatum,* believed to have been used as such and reported from the volcanic debris and red sand levels, continued to appear in the midden. These ranged from bottom to top with no appreciable differences in concentration. Although a few of the finished objects, notably cut shell pendants, were made of the thinner wall sections of *Cardium,* there are far too many fragments to account for them all as wastage from this source. *Cardium* shells, more so than any others present, were suited by size and depth as small containers and dippers. These would have been particularly useful in fetching water from the cave's spring and might even have been favored by a pottery-making people where the supply was as accessible as it was to the people of Ventana. It may be mentioned that ladles and dippers in pottery are not represented in the cave.

2. *Scrapers*—Some use of shell as scrapers appears to have been made. This is seen in the worn edges of eight examples. The bivalve most commonly selected was *Cardium,* the crenulated margin being entirely worn away in a few cases. Broken pieces were also put to use in this manner. Such scrapers were well distributed through the midden and the practice doubtless extended over a considerable period of time.

To my knowledge, the type of univalve scraper described below has not been previously reported. There are three examples, made of two species of shell which superficially resemble each other, *Conus mahogani* and *Oliva angulata.* The scheme was to chip off the spire down to about the point where the shell reached its maximum diameter. This provided an open spiral cutting edge which was evidently efficient on certain types of material. The three shells (Fig. 85, *a-c*) conveniently show three stages: (1) a freshly chipped margin, (2) the fractured edge partly smoothed by use, and (3) excessive rounding by use. These resemble somewhat the *Conus* tinklers commonplace in the Southwest, but the lack of perforations for suspension and the rugged broken and worn edges are the features which distinguish them.

All three examples were found in the upper or first level of the midden and they may, therefore, be assigned to a late occupation.

B. Ornaments

1. *Beads*—a. Whole shell. Only five whole shell beads were recovered, all coming from the highest four levels of the upper cave. They were, therefore, associated with pottery and may be considered relatively late in point of age. The species represented are *Columbella strombiformis,* commonly known as Dove Shell (3 specimens, Fig. 85, *d*); *Agaronia testacea* or Olive Shell (1 specimen, Fig. 85, *e*); and a land shell, *Sonorella siticus* (1 specimen, Fig. 85, *f*). In all but the latter, the spires were removed and, in the case of the *Columbella,* perforations were also made through the side wall near the mouth. The *Sonorella* was pierced about 10 mm. from the mouth in the outer wall.

It should be mentioned here that not a single disc shell bead was recovered. Although very abundant at Snaketown[146] and in most other Southwestern ruins, they were evidently never strongly favored in Papagueria by the Desert Hohokam. Scantling found none[147] at Jackrabbit Ruin, and Withers reports only three from his extensive digging at Valshni.[148]

2. *Pendants*—a. Whole shell. Whole shells pierced for suspension as pendants number seven. These include one small *Glycimeris maculatus,* one limpet (*Scurria mesoleuca,* Fig. 85, *g*), two *Turritella tigrina,* and two large individuals of *Oliva angulata.*

★

146. *Ibid.,* pp. 139-140.
147. F. H. Scantling, 1940, p. 58.
148. A. M. Withers, 1941, p. 70.

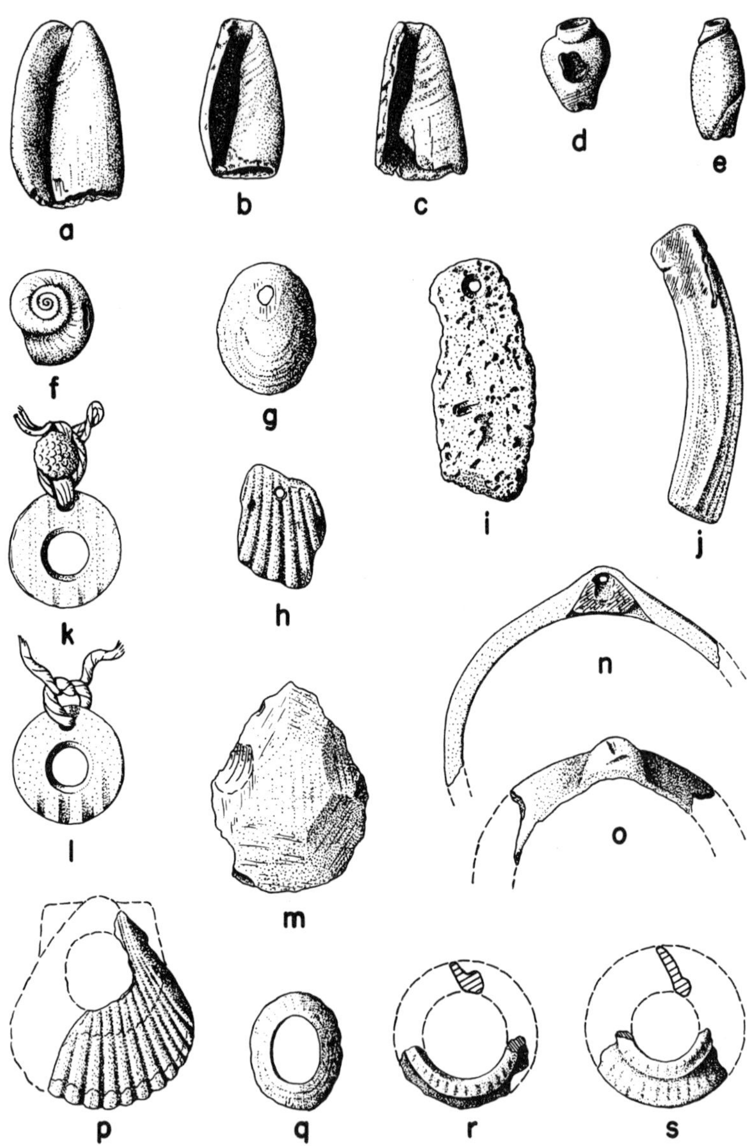

FIGURE 85. Shell objects from the midden. Univalve scrapers, *a-c;* whole shell beads, *d-f;* whole shell pendant, *g;* ground pendants, *h-j;* cut shell pendants, *k, l;* waste piece from bracelet manufacture, *m;* bracelets, *n, o;* perforated shells, *p, q;* ear plugs (?), *r, s.* Length of *a,* 40 mm.

They differ in no way, as to perforation, from the *Agaronia* identified as a bead, but some indications as to use are seen in Plate 21, where one of the specimens is fastened pendant-wise to a string, together with a wooden nose plug and two projectile points, found with burial 9. The second example came with the same burial but was unattached.

Four of the foregoing were found in the first level of trash in the upper cave, and the fifth specimen occurred in level 2.

b. Ground shell. There are three pendants of shell whose original form has been considerably altered by grinding. Two, of irregular form and pierced near one end, were made of scallop (*Pecten circularis,* Fig. 85, *h*) and thorny oyster (*Spondylus limbatus,* Fig. 85, *i*) respectively. The third example, a long, blunt-ended crescentic pendant, was fashioned from the green abalone (*Haliotis fulgens,* Fig. 85, *j*). It lacks a perforation but, instead, has shallow notches near one end, evidently for the attachment of a string. There is also a light incrustation of pitch at this end, which was probably applied to prevent the string from slipping off.

All three examples come from within the top meter of the midden and they may, therefore, be considered as of late date.

c. Cut shell. Hohokam sites have produced an abundance of pendants of geometric and effigy shapes, cut from thin-walled bivalves. Ventana Cave yielded only two. These are of identical form (Fig. 85, *k, l*) and originally were attached to the ears of a male mummy (burial 9), illustrated in Plate 59. These pendants were discoidal, having a large central perforation and smaller holes near the rim through which cotton yarn was passed for attachment to the ears. On one of the pendants a small bundle of single-strand cotton yarn has been securely fastened in the tie between two overhand knots so as to fall between the ear and the shell.

The time of burial of the man concerned cannot be accurately fixed but it is estimated to have been some time between

A. D. 1000 and 1400. Identical pendants were found at Snaketown, dating chiefly from the Sacaton Phase.[149]

3. *Bracelets*—Ventana Cave yielded no complete bracelets and even fragmentary examples were rare considering their abundance in the ruins of southern Arizona. Of the thirty fragments in the collection, eight represent finished bracelets and twenty-two are fragments of bracelets broken in manufacture. This, together with five blanks (Fig. 85, *m*) removed from the centers of the shells[150] by processes of rasping, cutting, and breaking, would suggest that, to a limited extent, shell ornaments were actually finished from the rough shells in the cave.

As near as can be told, a single species of shell is represented by the bracelet fragments, *Glycimeris maculatus,* the shell customarily used for this purpose throughout the Southwest. Nearly all came from the upper cave and the fragments distributed to midden levels are as follows:

Level	*No. Fragments*	*Level*	*No. Fragments*
1	16	5	1
2	8	6	0
3	3	7	0
4	2	8	0

This has particular interest, inasmuch as with the long occupation indicated in the cave we gain a fairly precise notion as to when shell bracelets, as a trait, made their appearance in southern Arizona, assuming that our evidence is flawless.

The deepest occurrence of pottery was in level 5, and then only in the form of rare sherds. This was also the maximum depth at which a lone fragment of a bracelet was found. It may be inferred that bracelets were an attribute of the pottery-making people. Bracelets are unreported for all stages of the

★

149. H. S. Gladwin, *et al.,* 1937, Pl. CXVI.
150. A. Woodward, 1936, pp. 117-125.

Cochise Culture[151] and also in the Californian Desert Complexes with which the material in the lower midden deposit was related, thus substantiating the Ventana findings. Bracelet fragments became progressively more numerous in the younger levels of the trash, where they were associated directly with the greatest density of ceramic material.

At Snaketown it was found that the earliest bracelet type was thin and fragile[152] and that later on, particularly in the Sedentary Period, bracelets became much heavier and broader. It is probably significant, as bearing out this evidence, that the deepest and probably earliest Ventana fragment from level 5 was of the thin type (Fig. 85, *n*), while most all others from higher levels, of the finished group, were of the heavy type (Fig. 85, *o*).

Carving of the umbo or the band is not seen in any of the specimens.

Mr. M. J. Rogers has indicated to me that he sees good evidence for believing most of the shell used throughout the Southwest, excepting those types exhibiting iridescent nacres, was not fresh but old material, *i. e.*, dead shells were picked up on modern beaches, on raised Pleistocene beaches, or were even gathered from old shell heaps. Almost never does one see any pigmentation in such species as *Glycimeris* from the Hohokam ruins, and the unworked shells often manifest considerable abrasion as though rolled by water. Additional evidence for this claim is found in a bracelet fragment from Ventana (Fig. 85, *n*) which, on the inside of the umbo, retains an extremely hard siliceous matrix, worn smooth as the bracelet was made and later partly chipped away as the umbo was perforated. This cemented accretion could hardly have come about in any other way except by long burial of the shell.

4. *Perforated shells*—Occasionally bivalve shells are found with large perforations centrally placed in the valve or near the umbo. Nothing appears to be known as to how they were used, whether

★

151. E. B. Sayles and E. Antevs, 1941.
152. H. S. Gladwin, *et al.*, 1937, p. 142.

as pendants or for some other special purpose. The Ventana collection has four such shells, three of *Pecten excavatus* and *P. circularis* (Fig. 85, *p*) and the fourth is a fragile limpet (*Scurria mesoleuca,* Fig. 85, *q*) shell. The latter came from level 4 of the upper cave and the remainder from levels 1 and 2.

5. *Ear plugs* (?)—There are two similar ornament fragments whose use is not clear. These are discoidal pieces about 35 mm. in diameter with large central holes. Bordering this opening there is a flange which rises above the main band or body portion of the object (Fig. 85, *r, s*). There is a marked similarity between these and some of the ear plugs of Mexico. This suggestion is not too far fetched since we have evidence of a positive nature that plugs were worn in the nose (Pl. 59),[153] and circumstantial evidence that labrets were also used.[154] This tendency to decorate the face by inserting foreign bodies into perforations would doubtless also have been extended to include the ear. Snaketown figurines show such articles in use and two of the Sacaton Phase stone specimens, identified as ear plugs, were also found there.[155] Both Ventana specimens were from level 2 of the upper cave, in which occurred the majority of the Hohokam pottery of Colonial and Sedentary Period age. The ear plugs evidently fall somewhere within this time range.

Discussion

The long and more or less continuous occupation of Ventana Cave and the clear-cut evidence bearing on the distribution of shell throughout the cave deposits provide us with an admirable opportunity to inspect shell from three standpoints: (a) the vertical distribution of species and traits, (b) the occurrence of worked shell in relation to unworked, and (c) the significance of shell culturally. The discussion will be limited to the upper cave because all species save one (*Agaronia testacea*) occurred there, as did the bulk of the shell material.

★

153. J. C. McGregor, 1941, pp. 204-209.
154. H. S. Gladwin, *et al.*, 1937, pp. 128-129; J. C. McGregor, 1941, p. 209.
155. *Ibid.,* Pl. CCII, *g*; Pl. CVIII, *d*.

TABLE 28

FREQUENCIES OF SHELL SPECIES BY LEVEL

Worked shells have been included where the species was identifiable. All from upper cave except (*), *Agaronia testacea,* which came from the lower cave. The Miscellaneous category includes shells associated with burials

	Level	*Cardium elatum*	*Glycimeris maculatus*	*Cardium procerum*	*Oliva angulata*	*Columbella strombiformis*	*Pecten circularis*	*Pecten excavatus*	*Turritella tigrina*	*Scurria mesoleuca*	*Ostrea chilensis*	*Dosinia ponderosa*	*Conus mahogani*	*Spondylus limbatus*	*Haliotis fulgens*	*Agaronia testacea* *	*Anadonta cynea beriniana*	*Sonorella siticus*	*Totals*
Midden	1	21	32		4		5	1	1	1			1	1		1		1	69
	2	15	8	1		2		1	1						1		1		30
	3	13	2			1					1								17
	4	15	3	3						1								2	24
	5	11	1									1							13
	6	6	1														1		8
	7	7	1	1															9
	8	3																	3
	Miscel.	2	1		2														5
Red Sand		5																	5
Volcanic Debris		47																	47
Totals		145	49	5	6	3	5	2	2	2	1	1	1	1	1	1	2	3	230

The compilation of the incidences of species (fragments included) to level is given in Table 28. Percentages are not shown because of the high number of species represented by only one or two individuals. The striking feature here is the fact that only one species, *Cardium elatum,* occurred in all levels and that approximately one-third of the total fragments were present in the volcanic debris level. This is, beyond doubt, the oldest evidence for the spread of marine material in the Southwest, which, according to Bryan's determination, may have taken place more than ten thousand years ago. As previously suggested, the role of this particular shell appears to have been utilitarian rather than decorative.

Adopting level 4 as the average greatest depth to which pottery was found, we have only *Cardium procerum, Glycimeris maculatus, Dosinia ponderosa,* and the fresh water *Anadonta cynea beriniana,* in addition to *Cardium elatum* of the volcanic debris layer, occurring before pottery and after the formation of the red sand. These appeared in such small quantities as to be negligible. Above level 4 and after shell work became established, the number of species sharply increased, a trend which has been noted for Snaketown.[156]

The actual working of shell coincides more or less with the arrival of pottery or chiefly above level 5. This is brought out in Table 29, where the traits are tabulated to level. The only forms occurring earlier than pottery are the problematical whole shell containers and one instance of a bivalve scraper which was the product of work done with it rather than the result of intentional modification. Most worked shell is limited to the upper two levels. What this means is that the ornamental use of shell was restricted, insofar as Ventana was concerned, to the agricultural pottery-using inhabitants, in round numbers since the time of Christ, thus becoming one of the better diagnostics in the differentiation of the latter from the less advanced, food-gathering, hunting people. I believe this trend will also hold generally in the Southwest, as indicated by the lack of reference to marine

★

156. *Ibid.,* p. 152.

Table 29

FREQUENCIES OF SHELL ARTIFACTS BY LEVEL FROM THE UPPER CAVE

Cardium containers (?) listed as present only (x) since all are fragmentary. The Miscellaneous category is for specimens associated with burials

		Unworked		*Worked*											
				Utility		*Ornament*									
				Scrapers		*Beads*	*Pendants*			*Bracelets*					
Level		*Glycimeris*	*Cardium Containers* (?)	*Bivalve*	*Univalve*	*Whole Shell*	*Whole Shell*	*Ground Shell*	*Cut Shell*	*Thin*	*Heavy*	*Blanks*	*Perforated Shells*	*Ear Plugs* (?)	*Totals*
Midden	1	8	x	3	3	1	4	2		2	14	4	2		43
	2		x	3		2	1	1		1	7	1	1	2	19
	3		x			1				2	1				4
	4		x	1		1				2			1		5
	5		x							1					1
	6		x												
	7		x	1											1
	8		x												
	Miscel.						2		2						4
Red Sand			x												
Volcanic Debris			x												
Totals		8		8	3	5	7	3	2	8	22	5	4	2	77

shells in the reports of pre-pottery Southwestern groups, specifically Cochise,[157] Folsom, Mohave, and Pinto.

The task of assigning authorship to the shell ornaments rests on the general problem of who made use of the cave since the time of Christ. The conclusion was reached that the Ventana residents before A. D. 1400 were the Desert Hohokam. The rigors of the desert habitat and the more precarious existence they followed, because of a less stable and less abundant food supply, deprived them of many of the "luxuries" seen among the River Hohokam. The shell industry of Ventana reflects these restrictions. Certain techniques known to the River Hohokam are absent in Ventana. These include mosaic work, etching, painting, and carving. Generally speaking, there was also a much smaller and simpler array of productions. Nevertheless, the complexion of the Ventana shellwork is Hohokam.

The sparseness and simple character of the shell industry in Papagueria as a whole is also seen in the Jackrabbit[158] and Vashni[159] villages, ranging in time from about A. D. 800 to 1400.

Bone and Horn

All layers of the cave were rich in bone, mostly the elements of animals used as food. But combing approximately three hundred pounds of food bones for artifacts produced a disappointingly small number (198 in all), including those modified by use as well as those fashioned for use. The ratio of bone to stone tools was 1:56, disregarding the time factor.

Many bones bore the marks of human activity accidentally produced when the animals were dismembered. This has been well noted by Kidder for Pecos.[160] Methods of working bone, too, have been fully recorded by the same author[161] and it will suffice here to say that, in Ventana, sawing was the chief system

★

157. One exception must be noted here as Sayles (and E. Antevs, 1941, p. 55) reports a single *Olivella pedroana* in a Sulphur Springs Stage context.

158. F. H. Scantling, 1940, pp. 58-60.

159. A. M. Withers, 1941, pp. 70-73.

160. A. V. Kidder, 1932, pp. 196-199.

161. *Ibid.*, pp. 190-200.

for deriving desirable pieces from shafts, which were then further reduced by grinding.

The collection of bone and horn objects has been classified as follows:

- I. Bone 151
  - A. Awls 111
    - 1. Not sawed 26
      - a. Whole bone 8
      - b. Splinter 18
    - 2. Sawed 34
      - a. From proximal end .. 24
      - b. From distal end 10
    - 3. Unclassified tips, shafts 51
  - B. Flakers 17
  - C. Fleshing tool 1
  - D. Scrapers 3
    - 1. Rib 2
    - 2. Others 1
  - E. Spoons 2
  - F. Tubes 9
    - 1. Mammal bone 4
    - 2. Bird bone 5
  - G. Dice 1
  - H. Painted bone 1
  - I. Wrapped rodent jaws 4
  - J. Perforated pieces 2
- II. Horn 47
  - A. Awl handles (?) 4
  - B. Hammers 5
  - C. Flakers 31
  - D. Spoons 6
  - E. Spatula 1

I. Bone

A. *Awls*— (1) Not sawed. The first class, whole bone awls, were made of the distal ends of deer and mountain sheep metapodials (Fig. 86, *a-c*) and the proximal ends of ulnae (Fig. 86, *d*). Unfortunately the tips are not preserved on any specimens, but enough of the altered portion remains to show that, by grinding, unwanted parts were eliminated. Sawing appears to have been

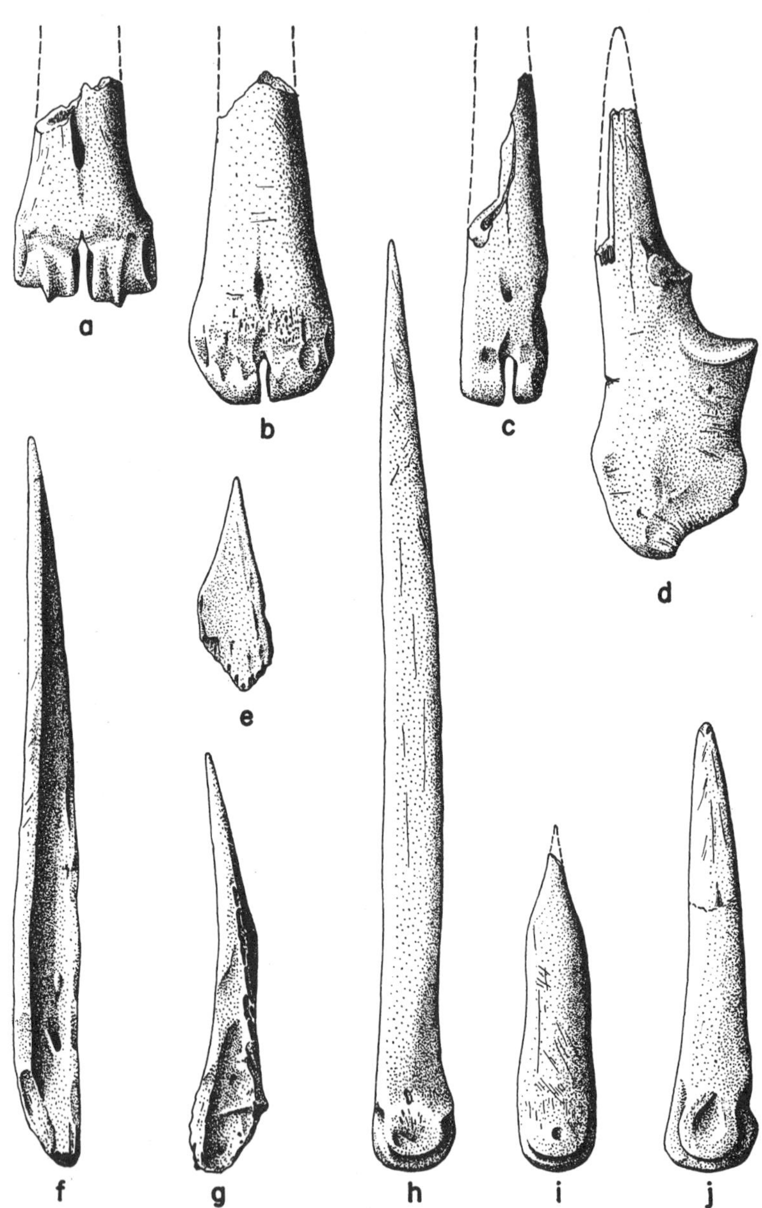

FIGURE 86. Bone awls from the midden and red sand layers. Not sawed: whole bone, *a-d;* splinter, *e-g;* sawed (distal end type), *h-j* (*j* from red sand). Length of *h,* 200 mm.

TABLE 30

DISTRIBUTION OF BONE OBJECTS BY TYPE AND LEVEL

Table 30
DISTRIBUTION OF BONE OBJECTS BY TYPE AND LEVEL

	Stratigraphic Layer	Levels	AWLS					Flakers	Fleshers
			Not Sawed		Sawed		Unclassified		
			Whole Bone	Splinter	Proximal	Distal			
Upper Cave	Midden	1	2 33.3	5 31.2	6 30.0	2 22.2	5 10.4	3 20.0	
		2		1 6.2	2 10.0		3 6.2	2 13.3	
		3		2 12.5		1 11.1	3 6.2	1 6.6	10
		4	1 16.6	4 25.0	7 35.0	2 22.2	24 50.0	3 20.0	
		5	2 33.3	3 18.7	1 5.0	1 11.1	4 8.3	3 20.0	
		6			1 5.0		6 12.5	2 13.3	
		7	1 16.6						
		8							
		Miscel.		1 6.2	3 15.0	3 33.3	3 6.2	1 6.6	
		Totals	6	16	20	9	48	15	
		Percent	4.5	12.1	15.1	6.8	36.4	11.4	
	Red Sand					1			
	Volcanic Debris								
Lower Cave	Midden	1	1 50.0		4 100.0		1 33.3	1 50.0	
		2		1 50.0			2 66.6		
		3		1 50.0				1 50.0	
		4	1 50.0						
		5							
		Miscel.							
		Totals	2	2	4		3	2	
		Percent	11.1	11.1	22.2		16.7	11.1	

SCRAPERS			*TUBES*							
Rib	*Other*	*Spoons*	*Mammal*	*Bird*	*Dice*	*Painted Bone*	*Wrapped Rodent Jaw*	*Perforated Pieces*	*Totals*	*Percent*
1 **100.0**			1 **33.3**		1 **100.0**		3 **75.0**		29	**21.9**
			1 **33.3**	1 **25.0**					10	**7.6**
	1 **100.0**	1 **100.0**	1 **33.3**	1 **25.0**				1 **50.0**	13	**9.9**
									41	**31.0**
									14	**10.6**
				1 **25.0**				1 **50.0**	11	**8.3**
									1	**.8**
				1 **25.0**			1 **25.0**		13	**9.9**
1	1	1	3	4	1		4	2	132	
.8	**.8**	**.8**	**2.2**	**3.0**	**.8**		**3.0**	**1.5**		
									1	
1 **100.0**						1 **100.0**			9	**50.0**
		1 **100.0**							4	**22.2**
									2	**11.1**
			1 **100.0**	1 **100.0**					3	**16.6**
1		1	1	1		1			**18**	
5.5		**5.5**	**5.5**	**5.5**		**5.5**				

restricted to lengthwise cutting of bone shafts. Over-all lengths must be calculated in all cases as in excess of 100 mm.

No particular value appears to be attached to this type chronologically, except that it occurred sporadically enough in various levels of both caves (Table 30) to indicate that metapodial and ulna awls, with little alteration except sharpening, were known over a long period of time.

The second class of awls not sawed were improvised from bone splinters with only enough shaping by grinding to bring the tips to the desired sharpness. All appear to be from mammal long bones, but exact identification is nigh impossible. Articulations are never preserved. The length range is from 45 to 158 mm. (Fig. 86, *e-g*), and the distribution in the upper cave was limited to levels 1 to 5 inclusive.

(2) Sawed. Sawed awls, the only remaining category of this type of implement, were fashioned from deer or mountain sheep metapodials by halving the shaft lengthwise. Each half was then capable of being further reduced, the articulations serving as the butts. In most cases, the joints were rubbed down to eliminate bothersome projections. A division in the classification has been made on the basis of whether the awl came from the proximal or distal end of the bone to test the temporal distribution. Although the proximal end type (Fig. 87, *a*) [162] is more numerous, the distribution pattern is about the same for both kinds (Table 30). The length range for both is great and of about the same proportions, 68 to 201 mm.

In two cases the grip ends have been improved by adding, respectively, a ball of pitch[163] or *lac* and a wrapping of bark (Fig. 87, *b, c*). This appears to be a late feature, as the pitched example was with burial 14 and the other in level 1 of the midden (upper cave).

These awls of the distal end type are shown in Figure 86, *h-j*, the latter having been found in the red sand layer, to make it

★

162. The finely tapered point of this awl suggests use in basket weaving.

163. F. Russell, 1908, p. 106, notes this practice among the Pima of providing iron awls with handles.

the oldest bone implement in the cave. The only observable difference between early and late specimens in this class is that the latter tend to be longer, but these did not replace the short type in late horizons.

If the awls made of proximal segments are grouped according to two general zones, those occurring with pottery and those associated with non-pottery debris, a minor difference becomes apparent. The early ones tend to be broad based (Fig. 87, *d*) while the late examples, with one exception, are slender, including the butt (Fig. 86, *a*). One awl in the early lot has a notched end (Fig. 87, *e*).

(3) Unclassified tips and shafts. While unclassifiable fragments have no particular typological meaning, they do show

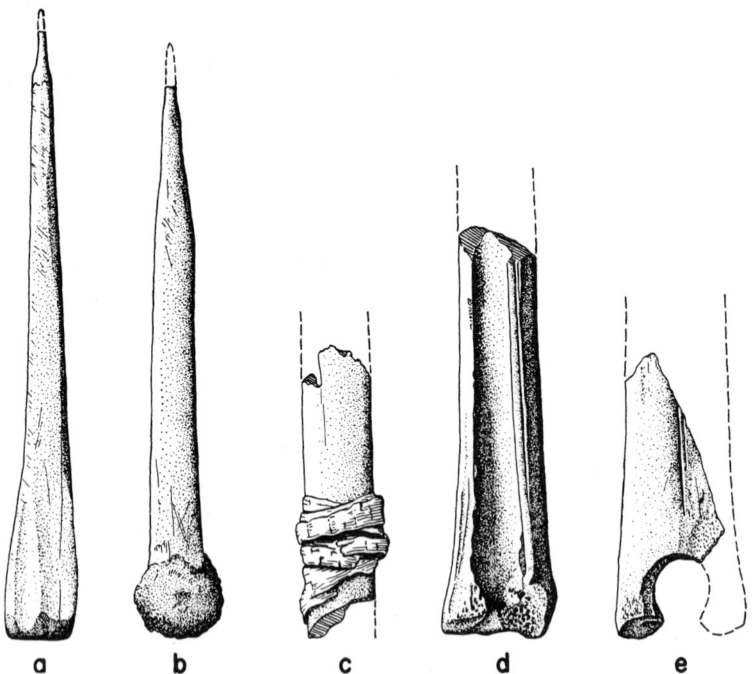

FIGURE 87. Bone implements from the midden, made from proximal ends of deer or mountain sheep metapodials by sawing and grinding. Length of *a*, 136 mm.

when bone awls were employed (Table 30). Fragments were distributed from levels 1 to 6 of the upper cave midden with a peak in level 4. This evidence, taken with splinter and sawed awl distributions, reveals two nodes of awl use, the early one during the Chiricahua-Amargosa II to San Pedro cultural transition and the late one in Hohokam times.

B. *Flakers*—Flakers have awl characteristics but the ends are blunt, often irregularly chewed and chipped as would develop from flaking stone (Fig. 88, *a-d*). Both ulnae and long bone shafts are represented, the latter usually made of splinters. The range through the midden was quite uniform (Table 30).

C. *Fleshing tool*—This specimen, from level 3 (upper cave), is a mammal leg bone shaft fragment, ground down to a chisel-like edge at one end (Fig. 88, *f*). It resembles tools previously reported from Anasazi sites[164] and is duplicated more or less exactly, both as to type and approximate age (Santa Cruz Phase), by a specimen from Snaketown.[165]

D. *Scrapers*—It is quite likely that many rib scrapers (probably deer) were not caught in the sorting of the bone, accounting for the small showing (two) of the type. Rib sections, without further attention, were put to use (Fig. 88, *g*) and unless they show the effects of hard service they are not easily detected. Both are from late debris (Table 30). There is also a well worn, leg bone scraper (Fig. 88, *e*).

E. *Spoons*—Were it not for the fact that the collection has several curious horn items, almost certainly spoons, the suggestion that the two bone artifacts following were so used could not be made. One is the distal end of a deer metapodial, sliced laterally and hollowed out (Fig. 88, *i*). The pores of the cancellous tissue are filled with what appears to be food. The other example is the proximal end of an ulna, with the outer bony table on the flat side broken out along with the underlying can-

★

164. F. W. Hodge, 1920, Pl. XXIII, *k;* A. V. Kidder, 1932, pp. 233-237.
165. H. S. Gladwin, *et al.*, 1937, Pl. CXXV, *o*.

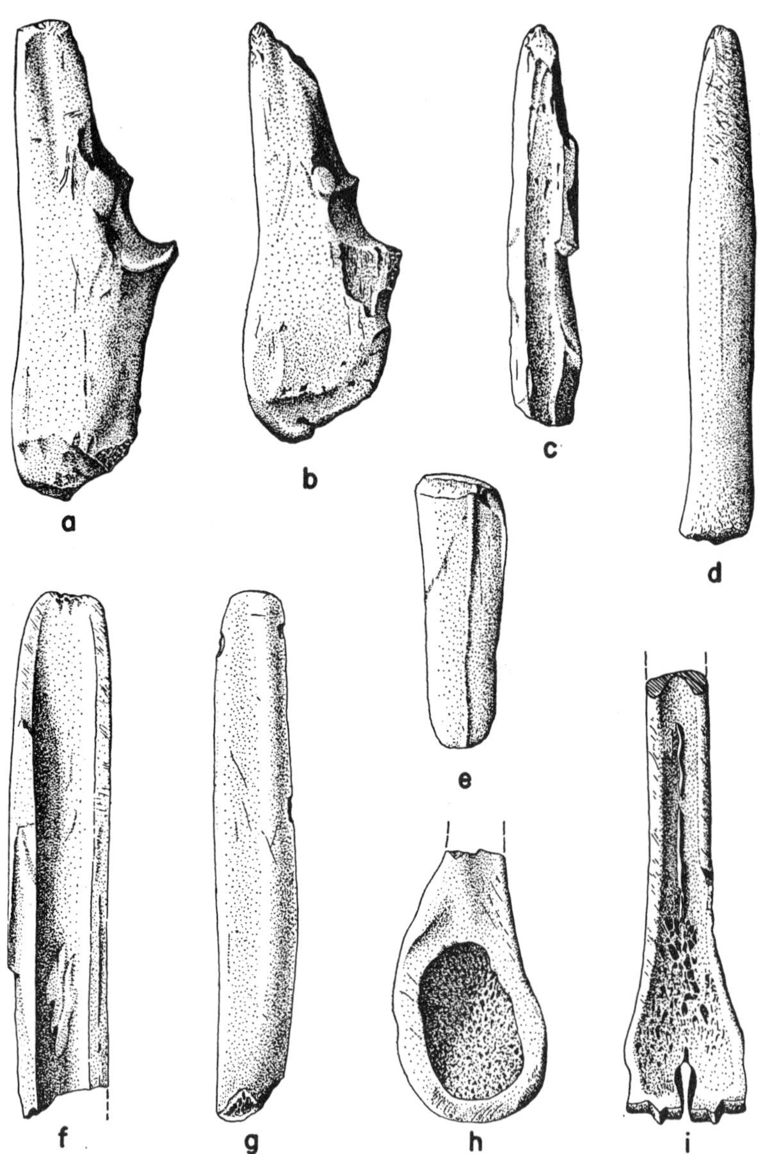

FIGURE 88. Bone implements from the midden. Flakers, *a-d;* scrapers, *e-g* (latter rib type); spoons (?), *h, i.* Length of *a,* 104 mm.

cellous bone, thus forming a convenient basin for holding food (Fig. 88, *h*).

Both are late (Table 30) but would appear to be somewhat earlier than the horn spoons.

F. *Tubes*—There are two general types: those of mammal leg bones and those of bird bones. The former represent both long (71 to 90 mm.) and short (27 to 37 mm.) varieties. One short example has a heavily scored surface (Fig 89, *a*), and one fragmentary long tube carries an incised pattern (Fig. 89, c). Ornamental tubes of this sort have become familiar accompaniments of the Hohokam Culture[166] and the Ventana examples were associated with Hohokam remains. The two plain tubes are from levels 3 and 4 and may be regarded as earlier (Table 30). At Snaketown it was found, however, that plain tubes were generally associated with Sedentary Period trash.[167] Admitting that the evidence is meager, it looks as though plain bone tubes were known in the pre-ceramic period, that they persisted or were taken over by the Hohokam, who customarily incised them during the Pioneer Period, and that decoration was then lost by the Sedentary Period.

Bird bone tubes are short (23 to 35 mm.), small in diameter, and apparently served as beads (Fig. 89, *b*). The earliest occurrences are in levels 6 (upper cave) and 4 (lower cave), as recorded in Table 30. If their identification as beads is correct, then these objects, along with a perforated bone disc described below, are the oldest ornaments from the cave.

G. *Dice*—Figure 89, *d,* is a fragment of rib bone, bearing a zigzag incised pattern on the flatter of the two faces of the bone. This is clearly one in a set of dice of the kind that the Papago use, although nowadays they are normally made of wood. It came from the first 25 cm. in DII of the upper cave. The small gaming bones associated with the Anasazi have not been reported from southern Arizona.

★

166. *Ibid.,* Pl. CXXVII.
167. *Ibid.,* p. 155.

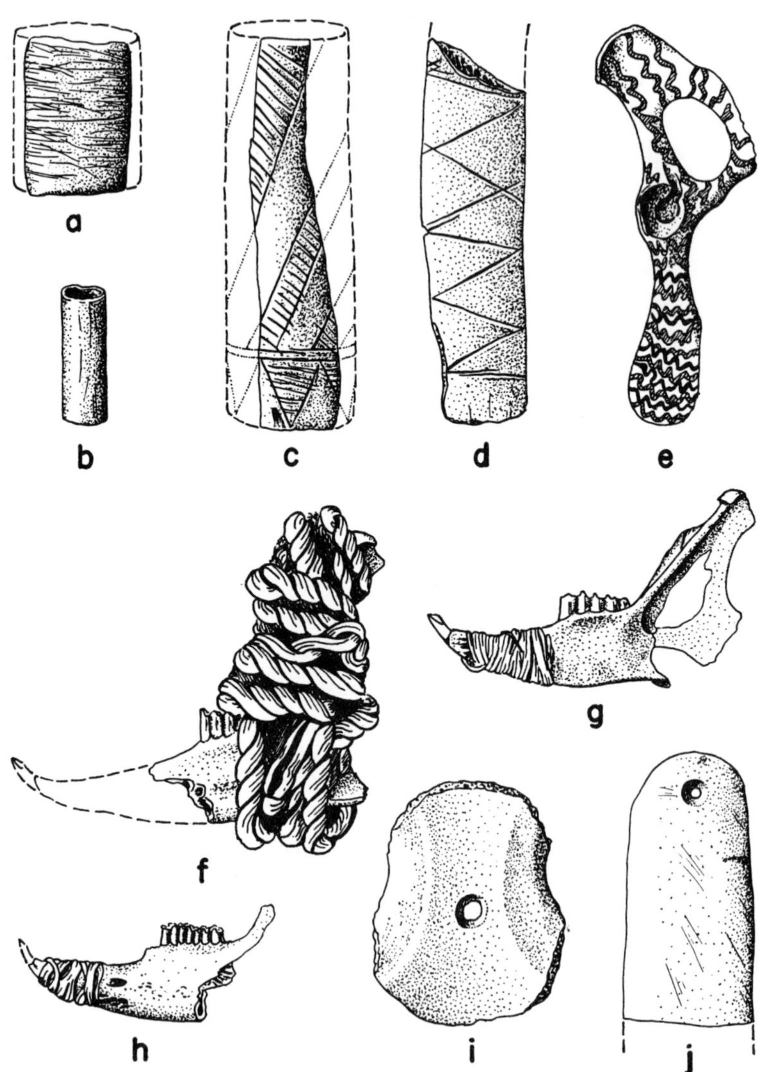

FIGURE 89. Bone artifacts from the midden. Tubes, *a-c;* rib dice, *d;* painted pelvis (in black and red), *e;* wrapped rodent jaw engravers, *f-h;* perforated bones, *i, j*. Length of *c*, 71 mm.

H. *Painted bone*—Only one painted bone was recovered. This is the left half of a cottontail pelvis, entirely covered with alternating black and red zig-zag lines (Fig. 89, *e*). Its location was level 1 of the lower cave. Hodge[168] reports that among the Zuñi it was customary to paint one bone element of a hunter's first kill with red or black paint, or both. As the Ventana bone was unworked and pelvic bones, as such, were not known to have been used ornamentally, a similar idea may be involved here. Painted deer antlers were found at Snaketown.[169]

I. *Wrapped Rodent Jaws*—Four jaws, three cottontail and one jackrabbit, were specially wrapped, either with two-ply cord (Fig. 89, *f*), or with vegetal fiber and sinew between the incisor and molar teeth (Fig. 89, *g*, *h*). The fact that, in three specimens, the long, sharp incisor teeth have been broken out of their sockets suggests they were subjected to rough treatment. The remaining incisor shows a blunted and slightly chipped edge, increasing the suspicion that these jaws were used as natural chipping or engraving tools. Vaillant[170] notes that sixteen gopher jaws were found with a burial at Ticoman, in the Valley of Mexico, and in a later work[171] he expresses the belief that these jaws were used for cutting and scraping. Pond[172] shows a similar tool used by Mr. H. L. Skavlem in chipping arrow heads. The wrapping of the jaws comes at exactly the point where the strain would have been greatest, and the cord wrapping on the larger jackrabbit jaw made a better grip.

All are late, three having come from level 1 of the upper cave (Table 30) and one with burial 31, an adult female.

J. *Perforated Pieces*—Two perforated bones represent a disc, made from an animal sternum (Fig. 89, *i*), and a fragmentary flat piece cut from a long bone (Fig. 89, *j*). The disc is of interest because of its earliness (level 6) and, other than the small

★

168. F. W. Hodge, 1920, p. 141.
169. H. S. Gladwin, *et al.*, 1937, Pl. CXXX.
170. G. C. Vaillant, 1931, p. 313, Pl. XCI.
171. *Ibid.*, 1941, Pl. 16.
172. A. W. Pond, 1930, Pl. 3, No. 5.

bone tubes, is the only item identifiable as an ornament from the Chiricahua-Amargosa II culture level.

II. Horn

Implements of horn or antler were only one-third as common as those of bone, and there are only four well defined classes of products. All horn specimens were made of deer antlers, both white- and black-tail. It is strange that the horn of the mountain sheep, an animal extensively killed, was not put to good use.

A. *Awl Handles* (?) —There are four stubby antler tools, believed to have been handles for awls (Fig. 90, *d, e*). None contained awls when found, or even awl butts, but handles of this general style, although now generally of wood, are used for the iron basket awls among the Papago. These handles are 43 to 54 mm. long with diameters averaging 33 mm. The sockets, let into the spongy core of the horn, are from 20 to 27 mm. deep and 9 to 17 mm. in diameter. These accommodate the splinter type of bone awls and the small-butted variety of sawed awls. One of the so-called handles is nicely tapered toward the socket (Fig. 90, *e*). It came from level 1 (upper cave) and is reminiscent of Papago awl handles. The rest are cylindrical. The distribution (Table 31) suggests that this device was in use for some little time but probably not before the advent of pottery. Antler handles reported from both Hawikuh[173] and Pecos[174] are generally much longer and slenderer than these.

B. *Hammers*—Sections of black-tail deer antlers, taken at the base of the horn, appear to have been used as hammers (Fig. 90, *f, g*) and in one case as a rubbing tool as well. Lengths range from 65 to 88 mm. Actual experiment shows these to be serviceable in percussion flaking of stone, but there is no sure way of telling that these specimens were so used.

This type of tool, so far, has been found mainly in late Pueblo sites.[175] In Ventana, three examples occurred in the

★

173. F. W. Hodge, 1920, pp. 136-137.
174. A. V. Kidder, 1932, pp. 276-278.
175. F. W. Hodge, 1920, Pl. XXVI, *c, d;* J. A. Jeancon, 1923, Pl. 26, *c, d, e;* A. V. Kidder, 1932, Fig. 231.

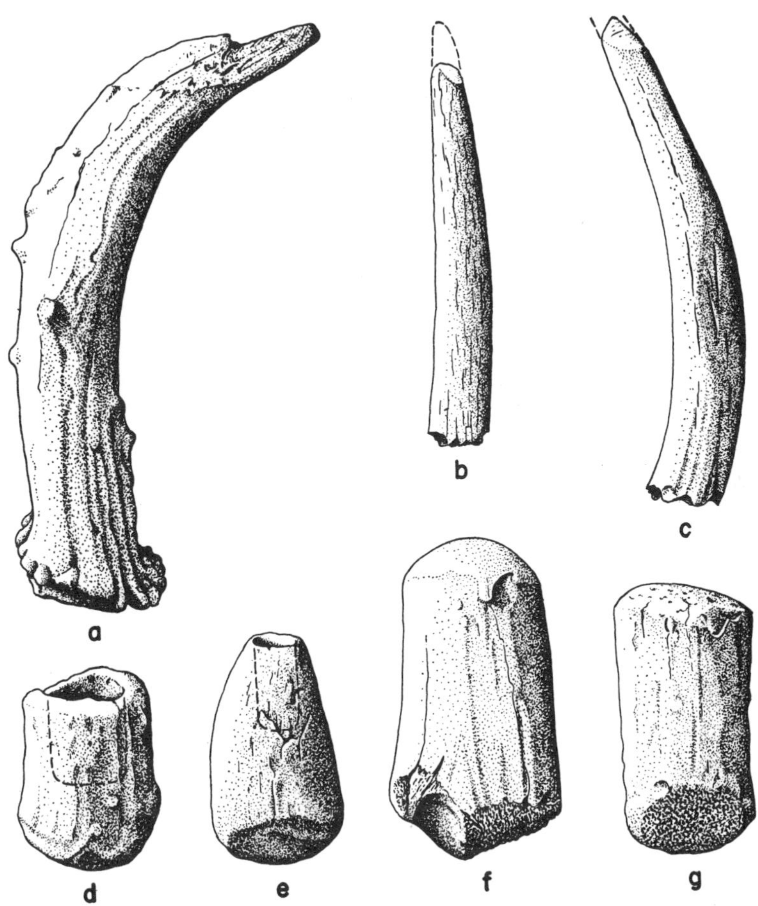

FIGURE 90. Horn implements from the midden. Flakers, *a-c;* awl handles (?), *d, e;* hammers, *f, g*. Length of *a*, 150 mm.

Table 31

DISTRIBUTION OF HORN TOOLS BY TYPE AND LEVEL

	Stratigraphic Layer	*Levels*	*Awl Handles (?)*	*Hammers*	*Flakers*	*Spoons*	*Spatula (?)*	*Totals*	*Percent*
Upper Cave	*Midden*	1	1 **50.0**		5 **22.7**	1 **33.3**		7	**21.9**
		2			4 **18.2**	2 **66.7**		6	**18.8**
		3			1 **4.5**		1 **100.0**	2	**6.3**
		4	1 **50.0**	1 **25.0**	8 **36.4**			10	**31.3**
		5		1 **25.0**	1 **4.5**			2	**6.2**
		6		1 **25.0**	2 **9.0**			3	**9.3**
		7							
		8							
		Miscel.		1	1			2	
		Totals	2	4	22	3	1	32	
		Percent	**6.2**	**12.5**	**68.7**	**9.3**	**3.1**		
	Red Sand								
	Volcanic Debris								
Lower Cave	*Midden*	1	1 **50.0**	1 **100.0**	2 **22.2**	3 **100.0**		7	**46.6**
		2			5 **55.5**			5	**33.3**
		3	1 **50.0**		2 **22.2**			3	**20.0**
		4							
		5							
		Miscel.							
		Totals	2	1	9	3		15	
		Percent	**13.3**	**6.6**	**60.0**	**20.0**			

deeper midden levels of the upper cave (Table 31), while the remaining two appear to be late.

C. *Flakers*—Flakers, thirty-one in number, uniformly represent antler tines. These were ready-made and highly serviceable in the flaking of stone by the pressure technique. They received no intentional shaping but the tips are irregularly worn and scored from the work performed with them (Fig. 90, *a-c*). Nearly all levels of both cave middens produced them (Table 31) and there is no recognizable difference between those from pre-ceramic and ceramic deposits.

D. *Spoons*—Unique among the antler artifacts are six Y-shaped pieces, almost certainly identified as spoons. To make these, a branching section of a large antler was removed and sliced trans-

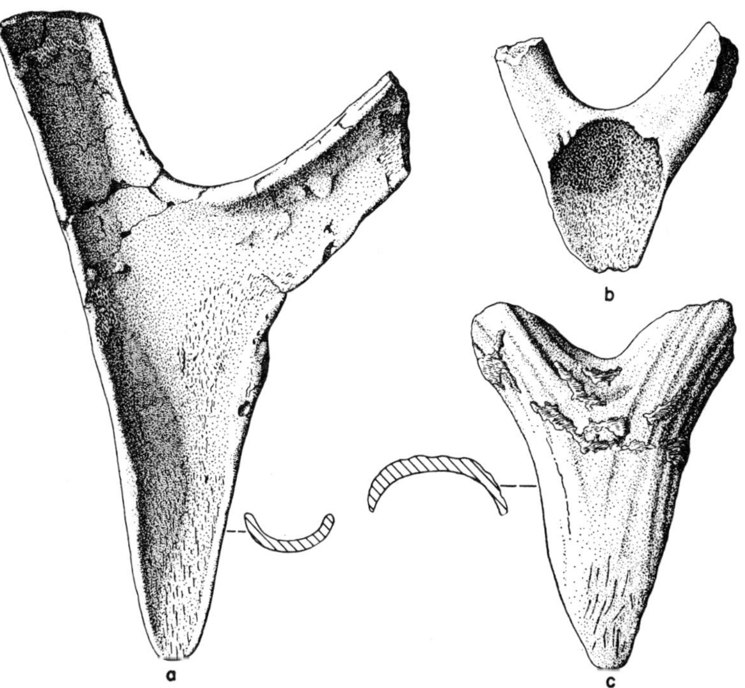

FIGURE 91. Horn spoons from the midden. Length of *a*, 209 mm.

versely. Porous tissue was then scraped out and the end representing the main stem of the antler was tapered to a rounded and well polished tip (Fig. 91, *a*). The smallest example (Fig. 91, *b*) was not so lavishly worked but the net effect was the same. Lengths range from 75 to 207 mm. All are heavily caked and smeared with what appears to be food, but the polished or eating end is licked clean (Fig. 91, *c*). The branching end made a convenient handle.

In age these may be allocated to late prehistoric times (Table 31) and they are probably the products of the Hohokam. Such items have not been found in Hohokam sites heretofore and there appears to be no reference to them elsewhere in the Southwest. The Papago deny any knowledge of them.

E. *Spatula* (?) —There remains to be noted a single flat spatulate piece of antler from level 3 of the upper cave.

Discussion

The chief interest in the Ventana bone and horn industry lies in the fact that so little emphasis was placed on the use of these materials over such a long period of time. As food bones were abundant in all levels, and because all bone was well preserved, the possibility that implements were lost through decay must be discounted. The ever replenished supply of raw material provided the opportunity for working in this medium, but, by choice, the cave inhabitants did not do so. Hard desert woods may have taken the place of bone (see p. 413). For Hohokam times, the situation in Ventana Cave is borne out in other sites where worked bone is never abundant.

Looking at the story of bone and horn within the cave, no tools of these materials were found in the volcanic debris layer. A sawed awl from the red sand layer is the oldest bone implement and this one, along with others from the lower midden levels, provides a trait heretofore unreported from the Chiricahua or Amargosa culture levels. The specialized tools, namely spoons, rib dice, and rabbit jaw flakers, are late.

Caucasian Culture

Eighteenth and nineteenth century contacts of the Papago with Whites is reflected in a small amount of material, mostly, if not all, of American manufacture. Stratigraphically these specimens were all late, in the first few centimeters of the cave fill. The list follows:

Glass			21
Bottle fragments		20	
Shoe button		1	
Porcelain			4
Metal			10
Iron		4	
Knives	2		
Hook	1		
Sheet	1		
Zinc		3	
Copper		1	
Lead		2	
Wood			1
Total			36

Glass

Glass is represented chiefly by bottle fragments dating after 1870. Some of these showed chipped edges but no finished glass artifacts were recovered. There is also one opaque white shoe button of late 19th or early 20th century age.

Porcelain

Included here are two fragments of a yellow porcelain dish, either of 19th century European or American manufacture and two pieces of a porcelain doll of very recent date.

Metal

Iron

There are two hand-wrought blades, probably of a 19th century Mexican origin. The first (Pl. 26, *a*) is thin (2 mm.) and the haft with which it was last equipped was of Indian origin, judging from the *lac*-encrusted tenon end. Near the base the blade is stamped with an unidentified hallmark (Pl. 26, *f*). In general appearance, the knife resembles those from late refuse at Pecos.[176] The second piece seems to be a short lance head (Pl. 26, *b*). Finally, there is a heavy wire hook (Pl. 26, *c*) and a strip of thin sheet iron, evidently cut from a tin can.

Zinc and Copper

Thin sheet metal of various kinds, from cans, was cut up, possibly for making ornaments, although none of these were found. Only the scraps remain in Ventana (Pl. 26, *d*). These are common, too, in early Papago villages.

Lead

Lead is represented by two smooth-bore musket balls (18 mm. diameter, Pl. 26, *e*), believed by Woodward to be of Mexican or Indian origin.

Wood

The only wooden object foreign to the native culture is a thread spool of recent vintage.

PERISHABLE CULTURE

It is unfortunate that, in the evaluation of the material remains of the early Ventana occupants, no perishable materials were available to round out the picture of their life. This must await the discovery of a cave where circumstances for preservation were more favorable. The dry upper midden zone did, however, yield much fine material assignable mainly to Hohokam and Papago origin. Even this is a decided asset, since southern Arizona has produced little dry material of any description and our knowledge of Hohokam perishable culture is practically a blank. The collection has been classified as follows:

Perishable Culture	1506
A. Cordage	653
B. Knotted Elements	141

★

176. A. V. Kidder, 1932, Fig. 250, *a*, *b*.

C. Twisted and Coiled Elements			16
D. Netting			16
E. Basketry			114
F. Wood and Plant Artifacts			268
G. Leather			24
H. Feather			5
I. Dress			265
1. Breech Clouts		12	
2. Fur Blankets		13	
3. Sandals		99	
4. Textiles		141	
a. Historic	72		
b. Prehistoric	69		
J. Personal Adornments			1
1. Wig		1	
K. Objects from Insect Products			3

A. Cordage

The importance of string in the everyday life of people is nowhere better shown than in Ventana Cave. Cordage remnants were thickly strewn through the dry zone of the midden and from these may be judged the quality, the materials, and the techniques of manufacture.

A complete analysis of the fiber in all samples has not been possible because the task of determining this is a tedious one and demanding of a wide range of control samples not now available. Cotton is, of course, readily identified, as are hair and sinew. But most cordage was made of other fibers, both coarse and fine. A selected sample of these was submitted to Dr. A. C. Whitford, of Newburgh, New York, who has kindly supplied the following identifications:

Agave utahensis, (Century Plant)
Agave lecheguilla, (Lecheguilla)
Cowania stansburiana, (Cliff Rose)
Asclepias mexicana, (Milk Weed)
Nolina microcarpa, (Bear Grass)
Yucca elata, (Soap Weed)
Yucca baccata, (Banana Yucca)

In checking the present distribution of these plants with Dr. Robert A. Darrow, of the Botany Department, University of Arizona, I find that all species occur locally in the Papaguerian desert, except *Agave utahensis,* which ranges on the plateau in northern Arizona, and *Agave lecheguilla,* which occurs principally in west Texas. The nearest local counterparts to these species are *Agave deserti* and *Agave schottii* respectively. Since it is not likely that the people of Ventana Cave roamed far afield for fibers, in view of a good native supply, it is quite probable that the above named species supplied the fibers in question. It will be noted that *Apocynum* does not occur in the list.

To arrive at some notion as to what materials were preferred or were most accessible, the string remnants were sorted on the basis of Dr. Whitford's identified samples and other easily recognized fibers into the following lots:

Yucca and agave	434
Milk weed	145
Bear grass	28
Cotton	15
Cliff rose	11
Bark (not identified)	8
Human hair	6
Grass	3
Sinew	3
Total	653

The data, with respect to type of yarn, direction of twist, and diameters, are summarized in Table 32, and cord types are illustrated in Plate 27. It appears that a 2-yarn strand, regardless of material, and left-twisted cordage were dominant. But the range, nevertheless, was great, occasioned by so much latitude in the degree of fiber maceration, selection of materials, direction and firmness of twist, and choice of strand numbers.

Hair was made up chiefly as rope, designed for heavy duty work because of its great tensile strength. For some unexplained reason this was prepared usually by right twisting.

The use of color was restricted to *Asclepias,* or milk weed, and cotton, both soft fibers which would readily hold the dye. But even then this treatment was not common. Red seems most frequently used, followed by brown and black. There is only one piece in which two colors, red and white, were combined (Pl. 27, *h*).

Two fragments of fine (diameter 2 mm.) 2-yarn strands deserve special mention. These show a flat vegetable fiber serving (Fig. 92), a rare technique from pre-Columbian sites.

Braiding, or sennit, involving the interlacing of three or more elements, was not plentiful among the cordage remnants

TABLE 32

ANALYSIS OF CORDAGE REMNANTS

Dominant forms in bold type. Terminology under TYPE from J. T. Burgess and J. Irving, 1941, pp. 8-9

MATERIALS	TYPE										TWIST		DIAM. in mm.		
						ROPE									
	YARN	2-YARN STRAND	3-YARN STRAND	4-YARN STRAND	9-YARN STRAND	2-2 YARN STRAND	3-2 YARN STRAND	6-2 YARN STRAND	9-2 YARN STRAND	3-4 YARN STRAND	LEFT	RIGHT	MINIMUM	MAXIMUM	AVERAGE
YUCCA, AGAVE, BEAR GRASS	X	**X**	X	X		X					**X**	X	1.5	12.0	4.0
MILK WEED	X	**X**		X	X	X				X	**X**	X	1.0	5.2	1.6
BARK, CLIFF ROSE		X									X		2.0	6.0	5.0
COTTON	X	X	X			X	X				**X**	X	.3	3.2	1.5
HUMAN HAIR		X				X	X	X	**X**		X	**X**	1.5	4.0	225

from the cave. But considerable variety is represented nonetheless. Below is a listing of the types, including materials:

1. Common sennit[177]
   - A. 3 element: long stems and leaves of an unidentified plant. Width, 20 mm. (Pl. 28, *a*).
   - B. 3 element: (one strand is 2-yarn); yucca. Width, 3 mm. (Pl. 28, *b*).
   - C. 4 element: milk weed. Width, 2 mm. (Pl. 28, *c*).
   - D. 5 element: milk weed. Width, 4 mm.; red paint applied after braiding. (Pl. 28, *d*).
   - E. 5 element: (6- to 10-yarn); cotton. Width, 10 mm. (Pl. 28, *e*).
2. Flat sennit
   - A. 6 element: (2-yarn); milk weed. Width, 5 mm. (Pl. 28, *g*).
3. Round sennit
   - A. 8 element: (around a 2-yarn yucca cord hearting); plant stem (unidentified). Diameter, 3.50 mm. (Pl. 28, *f*).

It has been impossible to detect any time differences in the cordage types. Once again it should be noted that none of this material can be dated earlier than the time of Christ and that most of it probably ranges from A.D. 800-1400 in point of time.

1. Cordage for Fur Blankets

Fur blankets (p. 430) required the manufacture of specialized cordage, which may be analyzed here. A sizeable number of cord remnants, plus several robes, provide a good opportunity to determine both ranges and the average for manufactures of this sort.

★

177. The Bluejackets Manual, U. S. Naval Institute, 1940, p. 396.

FIGURE 92. Fiber serving on a 2-yarn strand

The base was normally a 2-yarn agave cord with an average diameter of 4 mm. before wrapping with fur strips. Milk weed was also used, predominantly 2-yarn, with an average diameter of 1.50 mm. before applying the fur. Even with the addition of the latter, this produced uncommonly fine fur string. There are a number of pieces in which light base cords were wrapped with fur strips, then paired and twisted together. String was also produced without any vegetal fiber base merely by twisting fur strips on themselves. The type of fur string and incidences are as follows:

Yucca base: simple wrapping (Fig. 93, *a*)	
1-yarn	1
2-yarn	27
Milk weed base: simple wrapping (Fig. 93, *a*)	
1-yarn	1
2-yarn	11
Yucca or milk weed: 2-yarn base, each yarn wrapped before twisting (Fig. 93, *b*)	
1-yarn	1
2-yarn	8
2 2-yarn rope	1
No base: fur strips twisted (Fig. 93, *c, d*)	
1 strip	7
2 strip	2
3 strip	1
Fur tufts held by twisting (Fig. 93, *e*)	1

For the most part, the fur is rabbit, but skins of other small animals were undoubtedly used as well. There is only one small piece showing that feathers were employed on rare occasions (p. 428). This sparing use of feathers contrasts sharply with Anasazi practices, especially during Pueblo III, when feather-wrapped cordage was standard for robe manufacture.

A word must be said about the methods of attaching the fur. Commonest was the insertion of the strip ends between the cordage yarns. This was normal, too, among the Basketmaker.[178] On

★

178 A. V. Kidder and S. J. Guernsey, 1919, p. 174.

1-yarn, cord ends appear not to have been fastened. The robe on a child burial (No. 6) shows a special method in which tufts of hair stripped from the hide were twisted into the 2-yarn base cord (Fig. 93, *e,* and Pl. 61 *a*).[179]

B. Knotted Elements

Many (141 saved) knotted elements, mostly yucca leaves, strips of bark, sundry fibers, sinew and even gut, came to light. All of these appear to be remnants, as from sandal lashings and

★

179. This same method, but with feather tufts replacing the fur, was rarely used by the Basketmakers. (A. V. Kidder and S. J. Guernsey, 1919, p. 174, footnote.)

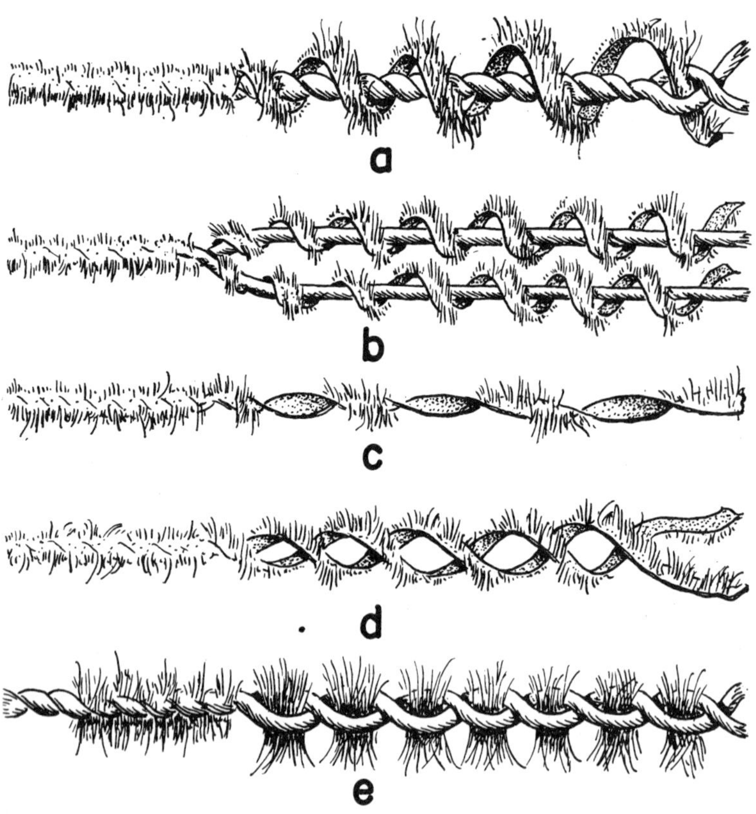

Figure 93. Types of fur cordage

from various things which were united by tying. A typical lot is shown in Plate 29. About the only utility such material has is in the study of knots.

1. Knots

This survey of knots is based not only on the above mentioned specimens but on all cordage and perishable goods, as well, wherever cords were joined by tying. To pay any attention to knots at all may seem a waste of time, but it was an operation which had to be performed nearly every day by every one. A piece of string became useful only as its owner learned the art

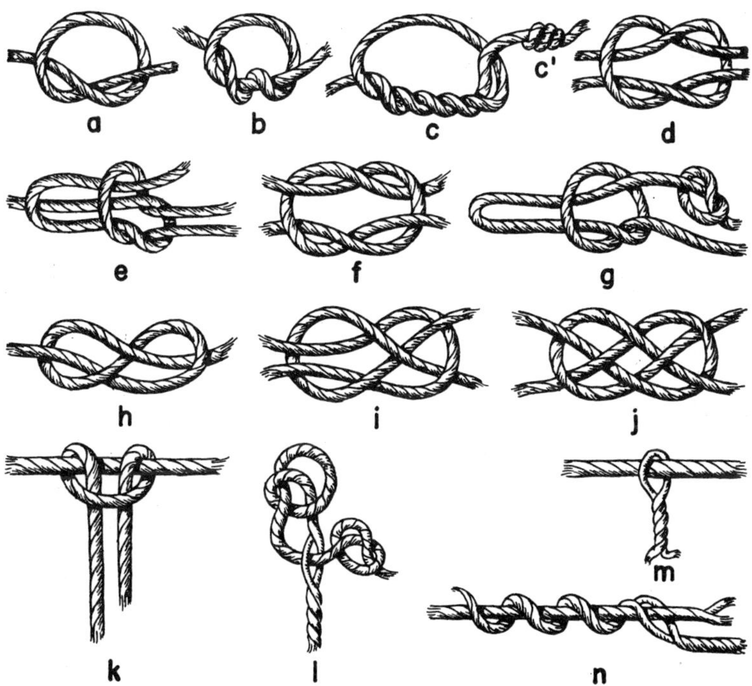

FIGURE 94. Types of knots. Overhand or thumb, *a;* double, *b;* treble, *c;* treble knot drawn taut, *c';* reef or square, *d;* draw knot or single bow, *e;* false or granny, *f;* running or slippery knot with overhand knot at end, *g;* figure-of-eight, *h;* common or sheet bend, *i;* carrick bend, *j;* lark's head (var.), *k;* overhand knot in standing part, stopped by tucking, overhand knot in end, *l,* joining by strand and twist, *m;* simple splice, *n*

of knot tying, and it is not too much to hope for that some day, as the body of data increases, cultural differences will be noted.

Attention has been paid only to those knots of standard form.[180] There are, of course, some clumsy efforts at knotting which the tier himself probably could not duplicate, and such have no value here.

The chief method of preventing cords from untwisting was the overhand knot (Fig. 94, *a*) but it was rarely used as a stop (Fig. 94, *g, l*). Double and treble knots (Fig. 94, *b, c*) were also employed at cord ends or in shortening cords, as in the case of one of the fur blankets where too much length had been allowed in laying out the work. The standard knot for uniting was the reef or square knot (Fig. 94, *d*), sometimes made as a draw knot for easy opening (Fig. 94, *e*). The granny knot (Fig. 94, *f*) is rare, as are the running and figure-of-eight knots (Fig. 94, *g, h*). In netting, the sheet bend (Fig. 94, *i*) was the norm, used also in joining cords. There is but one instance of a carrick bend (Fig. 94, *j*), on a sandal. Examples *k, l, m* in Figure 94 are individually represented, and there is one example of simple splicing (Fig. 94, n).

C. Twisted and Coiled Elements

In addition to the above, there are sixteen sundry specimens, twisted or coiled. Little can be said about the purpose of these, but they are included to complete the record. Illustrated in Plate 30 are: a twist of bark (*a*); bark handle (*b*); bark ring (*c*); and a spiral of the same material (*d*); grass coil, probably a head ring (*e*); and a large flat spiral of grass (*Dalea* sp., *f*).

D. Netting

The sixteen examples of netting are all small fragments and one can only guess as to what the original products were like. Technically, a subdivision may be made on a basis of whether the netting was knotless or knotted.

★

180. Terminology based on J. T. Burgess and J. Irving, 1941.

1. Knotless

This is generally referred to as coiled netting[181] and is represented by four pieces, three of 2-yarn agave fiber and one of 2-yarn milk weed cord. The technique is illustrated in Figure 95, *a,* and was often used in the Southwest in making small bags.

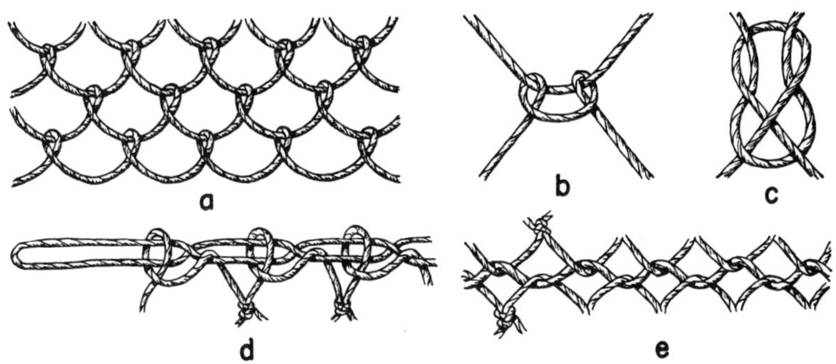

FIGURE 95. Loops and knots used in netting: coiled netting, *a;* knotted netting: lark's head, *b;* sheet bend, *c;* starting method of bag, *d* (Pl. 31, *a*); method of lacing netted bag, *e* (Pl. 31, *c*)

The finest Ventana example has two coils and three loops per cm., taken both ways of the fabric, and there is one piece put together very loosely with mesh about 2 cm. square.

Coiled netting was extensively used throughout most of the Southwest from Basketmaker times on. Recently the Papago burden basket (*kiaha*) was made by this method,[182] but there are now only a few women who still know how to produce them.

2. Knotted

In this form of netting, succeeding additions to the fabric are united by knotting. A double loop arrangement (lark's head) is illustrated in Figure 95, *b,* seen in a cylindrical bag (Pl. 31, *c*), but the prevalent knot is the sheet bend (Fig. 95, *c*).

Most of the Ventana knotted netting is large mesh (9 pieces), from 40 to 70 mm. square. While these could be bits of carry-

★

181. S. J. Guernsey and A. V. Kidder, 1921, p. 77.
182. M. L. Kissell, 1916, pp. 225-244.

ing bags, it is more likely that they are remnants of rabbit nets of the type described by Guernsey and Kidder for the Basketmaker.[183] But there is no need to assume that these are of Basketmaker age, as nets of this type have been used historically by some Western tribes. I find no record of the trait among the Pima or Papago.

One fragment, the bottom of a bag (Pl. 31, *a*), clearly shows the method of starting, as it retains the loop of the primary cord, which was initially attached to some anchor. A piece of twine, doubled, served as the frame, and loops of the weaving cord were formed around it, as shown in Figure 95, *d*. After the addition of eight such loops, the second row was added on a circular basis. This item is made, evidently, of cordage remnants, because in it are included four different gauges of yucca cord and one piece of milk weed fiber cord. Bags of this character are said to have been used by the Papago to carry venison.[184] Plate 31, *c* shows a section of a small mesh (10 mm. square) cylindrical bag, woven of a fine-fibered 2-ply thread. Both ends are missing, but what there is of it is 40 cm. long. It was presumably made of a rectangular piece of netting, two edges having been laced together with a stout cord as illustrated in Figure 95, *e*. This stretches to a diameter of about 90 mm. The netting knot is a sheet bend.

The foregoing specimens are probably pre-Spanish, but we have good information for only two rabbit net sections. These were with burial 9, one piece having been tied around the man's body, evidently the supporting belt for his breech clout, and the other was in the bundle of odds and ends placed under his head. From the things found with him we may judge that he was interred about A.D. 1200.

The two final fragments available for study are confidently of Papago manufacture. These are evidently from the netting stretched over the wooden framework of the *kiaha,* the conical carrying basket. The mesh is extraordinarily fine (5 mm. square,

★

183. S. J. Guernsey and A. V. Kidder, 1921, pp. 77-79.
184. R. Underhill, 1940, p. 16.

Pl. 31, *b*) and the 2-ply milk weed (?) fiber threads were joined with the sheet bend. While the knotting and material are unlike that of recent Papago netting, an important identifying character is the painted pattern on the netting in red and blue-black colors. This is exactly the color combination used by the Papago to accentuate the patterns worked out in the netted foundation.[185] These two pieces came from level 2, lower cave, which is a deeper occurrence than for the usual Papago goods. If there were some way of accurately establishing the antiquity we might have, in this material, a significant link between the new and old.

E. Basketry

As far as the Ventana Cave evidence goes, basketry was an important cultural asset to the local residents since about the beginning of the Christian Era. It is possible, of course, that some form of basketry was made earlier, but no traces have survived in the moist rubbish if this was the case. The ability to bring basketry down from archaeological horizons to the present day inhabitants of southern Arizona offers an excellent, and, perhaps, our first opportunity for a historical study of this trait. Knowledge of basketry here has lagged far behind what is known of basketry in the Plateau, primarily because adequate archaeological material has not been recovered. Several good analyses of modern Papago basketry are available and these will serve as a useful departure point in arriving at certain conclusions.

The cave yielded 114 basket fragments, only a few being nearly complete. These were uniformly distributed through the dry midden zone, vertically and horizontally, in both cave units, and ten were associated with burials. The basic techniques represented in the collection are:[186]

1. Plaited	5
2. Coiled	108
3. Twined	1
Total	114

★

185. M. L. Kissell, 1916, p. 233; M. Shreve, 1943.

186. In the description of basketry the general approach and terminology are patterned after that used by E. H. Morris and R. F. Burgh (1941) in their comprehensive and systematic analysis of San Juan Anasazi basketry.

1. Plaited

For some reason not readily explained, the simple technique of plaiting appears not to have been favored. There are only five fragments, all small, and none show the selvage. Doubt may be expressed, therefore, as to whether or not the pieces are actually from baskets; but this is a fairly safe assumption, as the weaving elements are narrower than in matting, particularly the matting produced until recently by the Papago.

In all cases the weave is a twill in a 2-2 rhythm with the elements laid in at right angles to each other. Weaving materials are of two kinds: (a) a sedge (*Scirpus,* sp. ?, Pl. 32, *a*) which grows wherever there is a sufficient water seepage to support it; and (b) yucca (probably *Y. elata,* Pl. 32, *b*). The latter material, seen in one fragment only, is quite fresh looking. As it was found just below the surface, the origin is probably recent Papago. Kissell[187] reports that sotol (*Dasylirion wheeleri*) was the customary material for this type of weaving, but a more recent analysis of Papago basketry shows that *yucca elata* was also used.[188]

The specimens twilled of sedge may be considered to be older. One piece was found with burial 13, a child, which labels it as pre-1400.

2. Coiled

All coiled basketry is of the close-coiled simple stitch type,[189] but there is an astonishing array of wall techniques considering the amount of basketry recovered.

Wall Techniques—Using wall structure, *i. e.,* foundation, as the basis for differentiation, and ignoring for the moment stitch details, a survey of the collection gives the following kinds of foundation, with frequencies.

I.	Bundle	32
II.	Bundle-with-rod-core	25

★

187. M. L. Kissell, 1916, p. 150.
188. M. Shreve, 1943, p. 7.
189. E. H. Morris and R. F. Burgh, 1941, p. 6, *et seq.*

Table 33

ANALYSIS OF BASKETRY TYPES AND OCCURRENCES IN HIGHER MIDDEN LEVELS OF BOTH CAVE UNITS

TABLE 33

ANALYSIS OF BASKETRY TYPES AND OCCURRENCES IN HIGHER MIDDEN LEVELS OF BOTH CAVE UNITS

Foundation	Material	Stitch					Stitches per cm.
		Not Interlocked	*Interlocked*	*Not Split*	*Split*	*Slant* *	
I **Bundle**	Shredded yucca leaf cattail (?) or finely split twig	 x	x	x x	x	\or/	2 4
II Bundle-with-rod-core	Bundle: shredded yucca leaf (?) Rod: not identified	 x	x	x x -	x	/	2
III One-rod	Not identified	x	x	x	x	\or/	2½-3½
IV One-rod-and-bundle, stacked	As in II		x		x	/	2
V One-rod-and-slat, stacked	Rod: not identified Slat: cattail (?)		x		x	/	3
VI Two-rod, stacked	Not identified	x		x		/	3
VII Two-rod-and-bundle, bunched	Rods: not identified Bundle: shredded yucca leaf (?)	 x	x	x x	x	/	2-6
VIII Two-rod-and-slat, bunched	Rods: Not identified Slat: cattail (?)		x	x	x	/	3-4
IX Three-rod, bunched	Not identified		x		x	/	3-5
Totals							

* denotes direction of work (E. H. Morris and R. F. Burgh, 1941, p. 61) where determinable. All baskets worked from concave surface.

Coils per cm.	*Rim*	*Center*	*Provenience*									*Burials*	*Grand Total*
			Upper Cave Levels					*Lower Cave Levels*					
			1	2	3	4	Total	1	2	3	**Total**		
1-2	Self	Spiral	11 3	4			15 3	5	5 2	1 1	11 3		26 6
1			 3	1 1	 1		1 5	1 6	5 6	1	7 12		8 17
2-2½	Self	Spiral	3	1			4	6	4		10	9	23
2		Spiral							1	1	2		2
2								1			1		1
1½			1				1						1
1½-3			1 2	2 6		 1	3 9	 2			 2		3 11
2									1	1	2		2
2-3			2	1			3	3		1	4	1	8
			26	16	1	1	44	24	24	6	54	10	108

III.	One-rod	23
IV.	One-rod-and-bundle, stacked	2
V.	One-rod-and-slat, stacked	1
VI.	Two-rod, stacked	1
VII.	Two-rod-and-bundle, bunched	14
VIII.	Two-rod-and-slat, bunched	2
IX.	Three-rod, bunched	8
Total		108

The general information and stratigraphic placement concerning each of these is contained in Table 33, but a few additional facts, as well as historical considerations, need to be brought out for each.

I. Bundle (Fig. 96, *a*; Pls. 32, *c, d;* 33, *a-c*). Particular interest is attached to bundle foundation baskets because this wall technique is standard in the Papago and Pima basketry of today. Some of the specimens, especially those from the surface litter of the midden, are of undoubted Papago origin. Those from deep within levels 1 and 2 are certainly assignable to the pre-Spanish Hohokam. Technically there is no appreciable difference between the new and the old; and the dominance of the type, past and present, in the area leaves one with the impression that the two are historically connected.

II. Bundle-with-rod-core (Fig. 96, *b;* Pl. 33, *d*). This was one of the main techniques, producing stiff baskets with a rather coarse weave. Stitching, whether interlocked or not, was normally far apart, exposing the foundation material. Both interlocked split and non-interlocked unsplit stitches may occur in the same piece.

The type is most strongly represented in levels 1 and 2 of both caves but occurs also in level 3, indicating fairly early and continued use. It may be assuredly dated to prehistoric times as nothing like it has survived historically in the area. Elsewhere in the Southwest this type of basketry seems to be limited. Two cases have been reported in Utah, where one is dated to Basketmaker II and the other one to the same horizon by analogy, and there is a questionable specimen from Burnet Cave, New Mex-

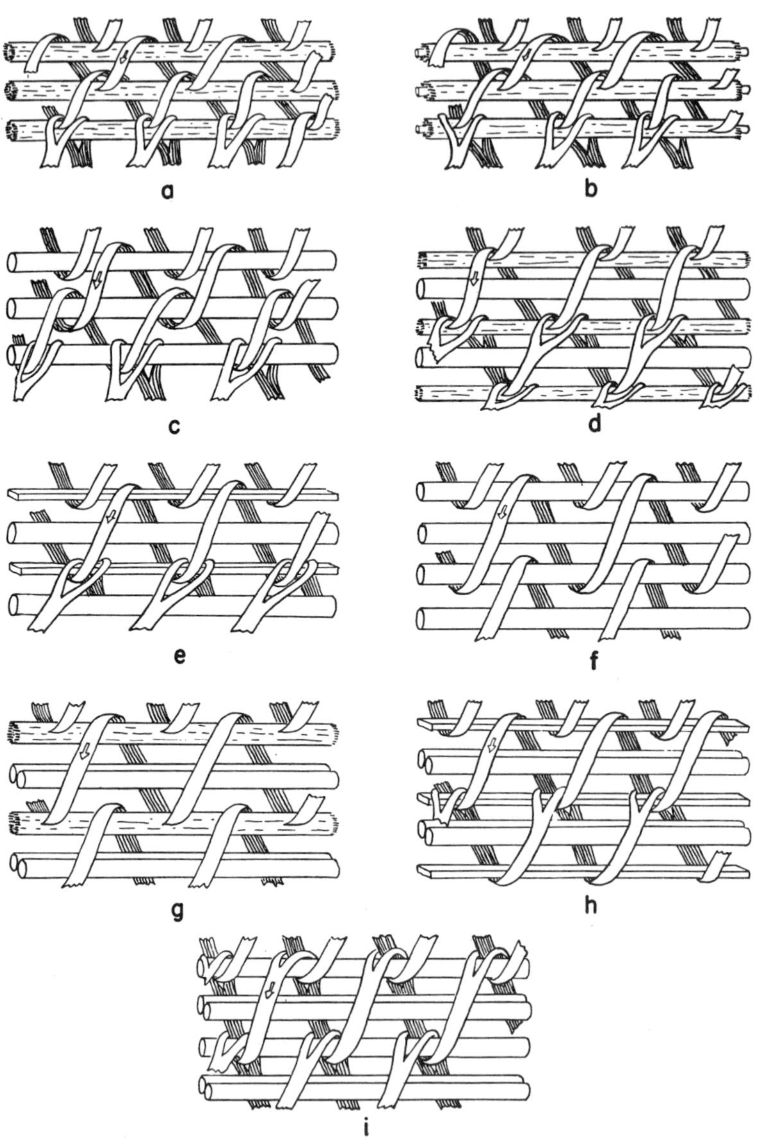

FIGURE 96. Wall technique of Ventana Cave close-coiled, simple stitch baskets. Direction of weave, bottom to top and right to left

ico,[190] of unknown age. The abundance of the bundle-with-rod-core foundation in Ventana indicates it to be in or near the focus of distribution. The basketry of northern Mexico, about which next to nothing is known at present, will doubtless shed more light on the problem. Provisionally the type may be considered one of the basic forms of Hohokam basketry.

III. One-rod (Fig. 96, *c;* Pls. 32, *e;* 33, *e*). Technically one-rod foundation baskets are among the best from the cave. They were woven both tightly and evenly, using either wooden or fibrous sewing elements. Split interlocked stitches, usually on the non-work face but sometimes on both faces, greatly outnumber the non-interlocked stitch technique. In one case, the splint was carried through the rod of the preceding coil, creating a minor and probably unimportant variety. Rods are normally peeled twigs, from 3 to 4 mm. in diameter.

In ten instances where baskets were associated with burials, nine are of this type. This is an excellent basis for dating, since, as is explained elsewhere (p. 467), the burials fall somewhere between A.D. 1000 and 1400. The same type is reported from the Sacaton Phase, at Snaketown,[191] which fits within this time bracket. Morris and Burgh[192] discuss this type of basket at length (*i. e.,* with interlocked stitch), since its indigenous character in the Anasazi area has been questioned.[193] They convincingly show that one-rod basketry is native to the area and that it is one of the three most frequently recurring processes, dated to Basketmaker III, and Pueblo I and III horizons. The nearest modern basketry of this type is among the northern Paiute.[194] This is mentioned here as further support for the aboriginal dating of the Ventana specimens and to show that one-rod baskets were well known to both the Anasazi and the Hohokam.

Two shallow bowl baskets of this type, found with burials, have diameters of 380 and 450 mm. respectively. They are

★

190. *Ibid.,* p. 11.
191. H. S. Gladwin, *et al.,* 1937, p. 159.
192. E. H. Morris and R. F. Burgh, 1941, pp. 7-9.
193. G. Weltfish, 1932, p. 43.
194. *Ibid.,* 1930, p. 469.

fragile, as most of the foundation rod has been destroyed by insects.

IV. One-rod-and-bundle, stacked (Fig. 96, *d*; Pl. 33, *f*). From their stratigraphic positions, the two examples of this wall type appear to be early. It is probably correct to assume the weave to be but a variation of the bundle-with-rod-core variety. The nearest approach to it in the Anasazi area is a half-rod-and-bundle (Pueblo III), which is rare and is considered to be a variant of local standard types.[195]

V. One-rod-and-slat, stacked (Fig. 96, *e*). This is obviously a further and rare variation of IV, wherein a flattish reed was substituted for a fiber mass.

VI. Two-rod, stacked (Fig. 96, *f*). This technique is seen in one fragment only. Its archaeological occurrence elsewhere is doubtful,[196] and as there is but this one instance, from level 1, in Ventana, its precise date even there is uncertain. The technique among living tribes in the Southwest appears to be limited to the Ute.[197]

VII. Two-rod-and-bundle, bunched (Fig. 96, *g*; Pl. 33, *g*, *h*). The finest textured baskets are of this type, unfortunately represented by small fragments only. In a few, the stitches run six per cm., completely hiding the foundation elements, but the weave may also be quite open and coarse (2 stitches per cm.), resembling the stitching in the bundle-with-rod-core baskets. While non-interlocking stitches predominate, interlocked and split stitches on the reverse surface also occur. In fact, both classes of stitches are recognizable on one piece.

Baskets of the two-rod-and-bundle wall type are standard in the Anasazi, dating from Basketmaker II to the present time. Some difference between those of Basketmaker III and Pueblo III have been detected,[198] and while essentially these same variations are observable on Ventana baskets, there is nothing in the

★

195. E. H. Morris and R. F. Burgh, 1941, p. 11.
196. *Ibid.*, p. 12.
197. G. Weltfish, 1930, p. 472.
198. E. H. Morris and R. F. Burgh, 1941, p. 12.

stratigraphy to indicate any inequality in age. It should be borne in mind, however, that the sample is quite inadequate.

Probably the oldest basket remnant from the cave (level 4, upper) was of this type, an indication of its early, widespread use all over the Southwest. But types I, II, and III, as listed here, were numerically superior. This technique is not employed by the Papago.

VIII. Two-rod-and-slat, bunched (Fig. 96, *h*). This is evidently an infrequent variant of the preceding type, accomplished by substituting a flattish and soft piece of rush for the customary fiber bundle.

IX. Three-rod, bunched (Fig. 96, *i*). The final type has three rods, all of about the same diameter and kind of material, held together by fine and snugly fitted stitches, interlocked and split on the reverse surface. Elsewhere in the Southwest the same foundation system, but with non-interlocking stitching, occurs archaeologically in Pueblo III and IV and rather extensively among historic people,[199] the Pima and Papago excepted. In Ventana, the technique may be accredited to a pre-Spanish level. Otherwise it would be most easily explained as an intrusion from the Western Apache with whom the Papago were constantly at war until after 1850. Neither stratigraphy nor technological details favor this view.

So far nothing has been said of several other significant basketry criteria, namely, rim and center type, splice, form and design. All of these can be covered very briefly, not because they appear unimportant, but because the excessively fragmentary nature of the Ventana collection provides a poor opportunity for observing such details.

Rims—The few rim segments all show what Morris and Burgh call the self-rim,[200] made in the same way as the basket wall. A single rim tip shows tapering but no false braid. The ornamental rim treatment (overstitching) of Papago basketry of today[201]

★

199. *Ibid.*, p. 14.
200. *Ibid.*, p. 22.
201. M. Shreve, 1913, pp. 121-124.

seems to be a fairly recent innovation, possibly correlated with the commercialization of basketry.

Center—All centers preserved are of one type: wrapping of the foundation material in a tight spiral and stitching (Pl. 32, *c-e*), with stitches sometimes extending over more than one coil. In only one example (Pl. 33, *d*) is there a small opening in the starting spiral. Within this sample of basketry the center treatment thus has no particular technical significance, but when compared with modern Papago basketry it does have meaning, for precisely made knots or plaiting are the normal methods of starting a new basket.[202]

Splice—Morris and Burgh have demonstrated that the method of splicing, *i. e.*, disposition of the fag and moving ends of splints at those points along the coils where sewing elements were renewed, has diagnostic value in Anasazi basketry.[203] Where splices have been determined in Ventana baskets, one basic procedure was followed. The fag end of the splint was laid in between the coil already in place and the one being added, pointed in the direction of work, where it was completely concealed by succeeding stitches of the newly added splint. The end of the new splint is a visible stub on the work face (Fig. 97, *a*). This type of splice has been recorded and appears to be normal in one-rod, one-rod-and-bundle stacked, and bundle foundation wall forms of the Ventana lot. The coarsely woven bundle-with-rod-core baskets are spliced as in Figure 97, *b*, differing from the above only in that the moving end was cut off on the reverse face

★

202. M. L. Kissell, 1916, pp. 206-208; M. Shreve, 1943.
203. E. H. Morris and R. F. Burgh, 1941, pp. 23-25.

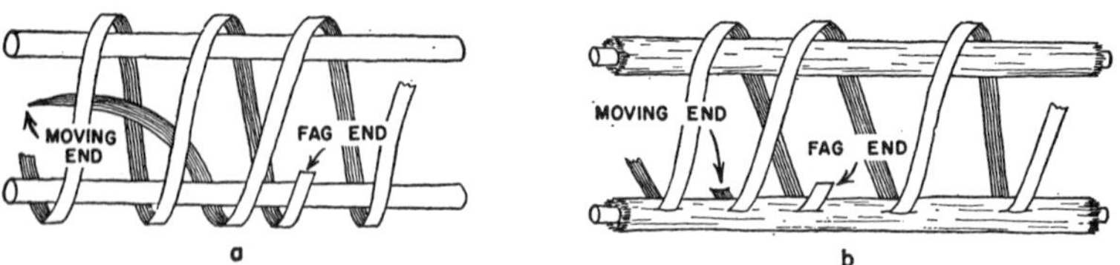

FIGURE 97. Splice types found in Ventana Cave basketry

and not laid in between the coils. Both of these systems are employed by the Papago basket makers today.[204]

On the whole, these mechanical processes are less complicated than those found in most Anasazi basketry. The first type described above is duplicated but twice in Pueblo III baskets studied by Morris and Burgh.[205]

Form—The appraisal of basket forms leaves much to be desired because of the highly fragmentary nature of the collection. All of these appear to be from shallow, bowl-shaped containers resembling the historic Papago basket bowl. There is no indication whatever of any closed or eccentric forms, suggesting a restrained tradition which differed considerably from the more varied forms of Anasazi and modern Papago basketry.[206]

Design—Here, again, there is nothing to go on. Cleaning of the more durable fragments has revealed no patterns at all except in the bottom of one, a bundle foundation, yucca splint basket, carrying a faded black design of Papago type. Its weave, design, and location near the surface identify it as a recent Papago product. The determination of the decorative characters of the early baskets, if they existed, must await further discoveries.

Mending—A final note on coiled baskets concerns mending. Given enough comparative data, even this process may prove to have either regional or time values, or both. Where weaknesses developed or the bottom became worn, a straight stitching technique was commonly used to prolong a basket's usefulness. This included one or more coils adjacent to the split. In two instances, bottoms were stitched in such a way as to enclose from five to six coils and these stitches were further tightened by a lacing at right angles to them as shown in Plate 32, *e*.

Pitching of Baskets—While there is no direct proof that baskets were coated with pitch or like material to render them water-

★

204. M. Shreve, 1943, p. 91.

205. E. H. Morris and R. F. Burgh, 1941, Fig. 9, *c*.

206. Modern basketry has, of course, been heavily stimulated by commercialism and, as a consequence, exotic forms wholly foreign to the native tradition have appeared. (M. Shreve, 1943, pp. 95-103.)

tight, a few of the basket fragments, when placed under ultra-violet light, fluoresced a yellow color similar to the fluorescence of *lac,* hinting that some baskets may have been coated with this substance.

3. Twined

The remains of an infant (burial 24), found at a depth of .80 m. in the upper cave, were deposited in a flexible bag and further encased in a grass "nest" (Pl. 56, *b*). Only a few small pieces of the bag have survived so its shape and size cannot be reconstructed. But the technique, a simple twine (Pl. 33, *i*), is significant because it and a second small fragment represent the only occurrence of this weave in the entire lot of fabrics. Warp (2 per cm.) and weft (3 or 4 per cm.) are of identical material, a bast fiber resembling shredded willow bark. The second fragment, evidently of the same fiber, was compactly twined with 2-yarn cords over warp of the same cord type. It came from level 2 of the upper cave. Excepting the bark breech clout (p. 429), no other products manufactured of this kind of fiber were found. Hence, both technique and material set these apart from all the rest of the woven pieces from the cave, arousing the suspicion that they may not have been native to the area. They may have come from the river area to the north, where willow grew in abundance. The archaeological horizon for the burial bag can be fixed only in round numbers, roughly between 1000 and 1400.

The Papago do not make twined baskets or bags, but use the twining principle in the manufacture of certain specialized appliances, as doors, strainers, cradles, etc.[207] Twined bags are one of the high lights in Basketmaker crafts, but technical and twine differences between these and the Ventana pieces preclude any probability of relationship.

Discussion

From the foregoing description of Ventana basketry certain generalizations can be drawn. Although some of the specimens

★

207. M. L. Kissell, 1916, pp. 140-149; M. Shreve, 1943, pp. 38-42.

may be as early as the first centuries of the Christian Era, it is my belief that most of them will date considerably later, or from around A.D. 800 to 1400. A few are of historic Papago origin. Throughout the time range, whether long or short, emphasis was on coiling. Plaiting appears to have been a marginal technique, and there is no good evidence to show that twining was native to the cave.

Taken as a whole, the coiled basketry shows nothing but straightforward sewing, of a rather coarse texture. There was no fancy stitching, no manipulation of the weaving elements to produce patterning, nor any evident attempt at color decoration, and no great variety of form. This becomes particularly obvious when the collection is matched against a comparable lot of Anasazi or modern Papago baskets. Except for foundation differences, southern Arizona basketry of pre-Spanish time was restrained and evidently stable.

In the San Juan area, the dominant and long-lived techniques were "non-interlocked stitches on two-rod-and-bundle foundation, bunched and interlocked stitches on one-rod foundation,"[208] whereas, in Ventana, bundle and bundle-with-rod-core foundation in both stitch forms were dominant. One-rod foundation with interlocked stitch is a strong third and, finally, there is the two-rod-bundle type. The situation was not parallel in the two regions and there was no mutual exclusion of main techniques. The difference between Anasazi and Hohokam basketry was one of emphasis.

Apart from giving us our first good glimpse of Hohokam basketry, another problem worthy of speculation concerns possible Papago basketry derivation from the cave prototypes. Today, and as far back as there are adequate records, the Papago have habitually used a bundle foundation and either willow, cottonwood, or yucca leaf sewing splints.

In the cave, bundle foundation baskets (shredded yucca leaf, split twigs, grass, etc.) with stitch and splice type paralleling Papago usages occurred more frequently than all other forms,

★

208. E. H. Morris and R. F. Burgh, 1941, p. 59.

principally in levels 1 and 2. Some of these are obviously of Papago make but the majority may be assigned to pre-Spanish times. While it cannot be absolutely proven, yet, logically, and by such support as is given by pottery and other traits, I believe the odds greatly favor modern Papago basketry as a surviving local type of the aboriginal Hohokam form. If this was the case, certain changes, of course, have been made through the years: (1) an almost complete substitution of yucca for willow as sewing material, a shift correlated chiefly with the development of sale baskets;[209] (2) the addition of rim braids or overstitching; (3) adoption of a characteristic center or starting knot; (4) many new shapes; and (5) development of design and design techniques. High standardization is evident in all of these individual features today, and this applies to basketry as a whole, too. It must be recognized, however, that the early Ventana techniques, even such common ones as bundle-with-rod-core foundation, do not occur in the area today.

One bit of negative evidence from the cave is most perplexing. This is the lack of the so-called "bird's nest" coiled storage baskets of the Pima and Papago, the Lower Colorado River Yumans, and some southern Californian groups. Archaeologically it has been found in the Sierra Ancha[210] during Pueblo IV and, possibly, in Salado Culture[211] sites of the same horizon, but there are no acceptable pre-Spanish records of it in the area where the trait was strongest during recent times. The same may be said of coarse coiling, by which process large and durable storage baskets were made.[212] The evidence does not warrant, as yet, the conclusion that these are old styles of basketry in the

★

209. M. Shreve, 1943, pp. 67-69.

210. E. W. Haury, 1934, pp. 73-74.

211. Clay platforms, obviously pediments for storage baskets, are fairly common and sometimes they carry ossier impressions of the bottom-most coil laid in the soft clay, as at Rye Creek Ruin, excavated by Gila Pueblo in 1930, and in the Tres Alamos ruin reported by Tuthill (1947, pp. 27-29).

212. Reported from the Sierra Ancha (E. W. Haury, 1934, pp. 74-75) of Pueblo IV date, and several fine examples, of uncertain age, were recovered from McEwen Cave, near Safford. (Arizona State Museum and Gila Pueblo collections).

Hohokam area, spread to the adjacent Anasazi. It may have worked the other way.

In this analysis of basketry I have not been able to convince myself that certain deviations in technique are culturally as significant as some students have suggested. Specifically the mechanical details I have in mind are: right or left direction of weaving, interlocking and non-interlocking of stitches, and splitting or not splitting of stitches. Direction of weave may be either way in the same basic type of basketry, although one form usually prevails. The Papago normally work from right to left, and whether the working surface is the concave or convex side is largely determined by the shape.[213] Likewise, I have recognized non-interlocking, interlocking but not split, and interlocking and split stitches all on the same basket. The craftsman may set out to achieve uniformity but carelessness, haste, and loss of interest may produce mechanical sloppiness. In all of these the individual factor is great.

Consequently, it appears to me that cultural affinities and related historical problems must be based on the aggregate of wall technique, splice, center and rim finish, shape, and design, in combination with the above details.

F. Wood and Plant Artifacts

The desert yields a number of woods, both hard and soft, which are capable of being made up into a variety of useful articles. Among the Pima and Papago, wood has long been one of the more important raw materials for the manufacture of a wide array of goods. Previous to the Ventana excavations, one could only guess that the Hohokam, too, recognized the value of this material and produced many articles from it.

Among the following items some are to be credited to the Hohokam with certitude, but it is not always possible to make a clear-cut distinction between them and Papago articles. A number of the latter, however, show steel knife cuts, which establishes their recency.

★

213. M. Shreve, 1943, pp. 91-93.

1. Wood

The enumeration of the 220 wooden objects follows:

Fire-making apparatus			3
Fire tongs			1
Digging stick			1
Axe handle			1
Scraper			1
Kiaha helping stick			1
Cactus picks			40
Awl			1
Spatula			1
Cut sticks			7
Hook			1
Paddles			5
Stoppers (?)			2
Burred pieces			8
Perforated sticks			2
Bow			1
Arrows			96
Reed		14	
Solid		26	
Foreshafts		12	
Bunt points		44	
Type A	40		
Type B	4		
Grooved clubs			6
Beads			3
Nose plugs			4
Pillow			1
Dice			6
Painted disc			1
Prayer sticks			9
Miscellaneous			18

Fire-making apparatus—We have no evidence as to how the early occupants of the cave made fire. But, in late times, the agricultural people employed the drill and hearth so prevalent in Southwestern cliff ruins. The one identifiable drill was made of arrow weed *(Pluchea sericea)*, having a diameter of 8 mm. (Pl. 34, *a*). The customary materials for hearths were split sahuaro ribs, flat on the socketed face and convex below. Anasazi hearths appear to have been in round sticks[214] as a rule. The drill sockets were flared well to the side and notched to allow the spark to kindle the tinder (Pl. 34, *b*). There is no evidence that the bow drill principle was known.

Fire tongs—This is a simple device made of two twigs (length 188 mm.) held together at one end with a fiber wrapping (Pl. 34, *c*). The spreading ends are charred from picking up hot coals, probably for transfer to parching trays.[215] Coming from level 1 (lower cave), there is no way of determining whether this tool was of Papago origin or whether it was the product of earlier people.

Digging stick—A single, rod-like digging stick, of desert hard wood (length, 640 mm., diameter, 12 mm.), is probably of pre-Papago origin (upper cave, level 2). The working end is slightly pointed and worn but there is no blading.

Axe handle—The method of hafting the three-quarter grooved axe is well understood from such discoveries as reported by Morris from the Verde salt mine.[216] The handle was a stout, J-shaped branch, thinned in the crook of the J to expedite bending around and fitting into the groove of the axe head. The free end was notched and securely lashed to the handle below the head. The Ventana specimen represents only the haft portion (Pl. 34, *d*), having a diameter of 28 mm. All shaping was done with a stone knife and it may be assigned to the Hohokam level. The idea is prevalent that three-quarter grooved axes were hafted with the ungrooved face up, or away from the handle.[217]

★

214. A. V. Kidder and S. J. Guernsey, 1919, pp. 120-121.

215. F. Russell, 1908, p. 68, notes that parching of cereal foods was general among the Pima, and verbal reports also account for the method among the Papago.

216. E. H. Morris, 1928, pp. 86-89.

217. This notion even exists among the Pima. Some years ago, a Pima presented the author with an aboriginal axe head, mounted by him on a modern handle with the head reversed.

Scraper—A split branch (length, 222 mm., diameter, 17 mm.) served as a scraping tool, judging from caked material collected along the margins (Pl. 34, *e*). This might come from cleaning baskets. The ends are also charred, suggesting use as a fire poker. Freshness of the crusted substance suggests Papago origin.

Kiaha helping stick—The netted conical burden basket (*kiaha*) of the Pima and Papago requires the use of a forked helping stick when being loaded on the ground. This stick forms a tripod with the two long front frame sticks. Russell accurately describes the use of the *kiaha,* and the helping stick illustrated by him[218] is duplicated by the one from Ventana (length, 1.04 m.). It was resting against the cave wall and has probably been used by the Papago within the last fifty years.

Cactus picks—As has been brought out earlier, the cave was used seasonally by the Papago during the sahuaro harvest. One of the tools used in handling the spiny fruit is a sharpened wooden stick and it is not surprising that a goodly number (40) were found. These were made either of suhuaro ribs (Pl. 34, *f*) or palo verde twigs (Pl. 34, *g*). One still has impaled on it a part of a cactus plant (Pl. 34, *h*). Lengths vary from 112 to 235 mm. and most in the lot were found in the surface debris. These show steel knife cuts, but a few from level 2 were formed by more primitive means, attesting the pre-Spanish use of such picks, as well as the Papago.

Awl—Only one hard wood awl, probably mesquite, was found. It was fashioned of a split twig 10 mm. in diameter and 140 mm. long. The base was cut off square and the long and slender point is of a type adapted for basket weaving (Pl. 34, *i*). Coming from the first 25.cm. of the upper cave refuse, it is probably assignable to the Papago.

Spatula—This is a thin section of mesquite branch, well worn at one end (Pl. 34, *j*), from level 1 of the lower cave.

★

218. F. Russell, 1908, pp. 140-142, Fig. 64.

Cut sticks—Seven sticks (lengths, 90 to 205 mm.) show pointed or rounded ends (Pl. 34, *k*). The bark is generally intact and both stone and steel knife cutting is represented. They come mostly from level 1. No guess is made as to their use.

Hook—Figure 98 illustrates a wooden hook made of a forked branch by hacking off one prong (length, 57 mm.). It came to light in level 3 (lower cave) and may be considered a Hohokam attribute.

FIGURE 98. Wooden hook. Length, 570 mm.

Paddles—Of the five paddles, four may be definitely connected with the art of pottery making. All have been severely damaged, two by fire and two by termites. The wood, in all cases, is mesquite or ironwood, laboriously worked down by cutting, gouging, and scraping with stone tools. The handle and blade ends of two are illustrated in Plate 35, *a, b*. These differ in shape from modern Papago pottery paddles in that they lack the angularity where blade and handle connect, evidently a feature developed after the adoption of steel tools. Overall lengths were in the neighborhood of 240 mm. These paddles are undoubtedly of Hohokam origin as two came to light in level 2 (upper cave) and the others were placed at the left shoulder of burial 17, an adult female.

The fifth paddle of ironwood is much smaller (139 mm. long) than the above (Pl. 35, *c*). It has a well-polished surface and a chisel-shaped distal end. What its specific use was is not known, as no modern parallels are reported.

Stoppers (?)—Two Papago, steel-cut objects may have been used as bottle stoppers (Pl. 35, *d*). The one not illustrated is chunky and tapered but lacks the long extension.

Burred pieces—The first specimen or two of short stubs with macerated and burred ends were considered at the time of discovery to have no particular significance, but the objects recurred so many times (eight) that they are considered worthy of recording, in spite of the fact that no suggestion can be made as to use or of what process they may be a by-product. Lengths vary from 40 to 120 mm. and diameters from 7 to 25 mm. All have one blunt, stone-cut end and the other frayed, with the fibers bent over and outward (Pl. 35, *e, f*). Several types of wood are represented. Most, if not all, of these are of pre-Spanish origin. Similar items are reported from Winchester Cave.[219]

Perforated sticks—There are two sahuaro rib sections, 145 and 410 mm. long respectively (Pl. 35, *g*), each with a single central perforation. While they are certainly of Papago origin, I have not been able to learn what use they may have made of such pieces.

Bow—Complete bows were not found but there is one wing tip which has been intentionally severed from the main body by steel knife cuts. As the string notches and the trimming were also done with white man's knife, this item may be classed as Papago. The wood is probably willow.

Arrows—For arrows there is better evidence; both recent and old examples, all fragmentary, exist. Two types are recognizable, those made of the reed *Phragmites communis* and those made of the solid stem of the arrow weed, *Pluchea sericea.*

The former lot of twelve includes nine arrows, badly deteriorated, found in a skin quiver with burial 9 (Pl. 39, *a*), which helps to assign them to the Desert Hohokam. The remaining reed arrows were found in pre-Papago trash and the type may be conceded as an early one. There is no information on lengths or feathering. Such arrows were originally fitted with hard wood foreshafts (see below).

The solid arrows of arrow bush were, without exception, found in level 1 of both caves and their Papago authorship is not to be doubted. Again, overall dimensions cannot be determined. The fore-end of the shaft was sharpened and the arrow

★

219. W. S. Fulton, 1941, Pl. XI, *c, d*.

was thus used without further attention. There is no indication, in this lot, of stone tipping, although the Papago are known to have employed a small, triangular, concave-base point. One yucca stalk arrow has a foreshaft let into the soft pithy center (Pl. 36, *a*).[220] On all examples where evidence remains two feathers were used, lashed with sinew at the ends and sometimes at intervals between (Pl. 36, *b, c*).[221] The feathered sections of a few arrows were painted a solid red.

Foreshafts of hard wood, for reed arrows, were notched for the stone tip (Pl. 36, *d*) or merely sharpened (P*l*. 36, *e*). In the former, the stone tips were securely seated with pitch or *lac* and sinew-tie (Fig. 58, *d*). The one complete foreshaft is 240 mm. long and the ends, fitted into the main shaft, are long-tapered on all specimens. None shows the shoulder found on some Anasazi arrows. Foreshaft painting is absent.

Bunt points, of which there are forty-four, are of two types: the solid wood bunt and a stick work type attached to the foreshaft. The former, mostly of mesquite, range in length from 45 to 150 mm., having long basal tapers and fore-ends of varying degrees of bluntness (Pl. 36, *f-i*). The tips of some are four-sided and one has a triangular section. Since all but two of the lot were found in the surface trash and were whittled with steel knives, Papago origin is assured. The two bunts from deeper levels are somewhat different (Pl. 36, *j, k*), evidently the early type. As these bunts are not suited for use in arrow bush arrows it must be assumed that they were seated in reed or yucca stalk arrows, probably the latter, as one such arrow with bunt in place was found in the Bat Cave (Sonora C:4:7) excavated by Scantling in 1938.

Stick-work bunts were made by lashing two or four short (22 to 32 mm.) sticks to the foreshaft, just back of the point, to prevent deep penetration (Pl. 35, *h, i*). These have a rather

★

220. F. Russell, 1908, p. 96, notes that the Papago sometimes supplied the Pima with yucca stem arrows.

221. Russell *(op. cit.)* further states that, among the Pima, two-feathered arrows were used in hunting and three-feathered arrows were reserved for war.

wide distribution in the western United States[222] and historically have been used by the western Apache. The four Ventana examples may be Papago or earlier. No use of them among the Papago, however, has been reported.

Before leaving this subject it should be mentioned that positive evidence of the bow and arrow was limited to levels 1 to 3 of both caves. It may have been employed earlier, but it would appear on these indications, plus the radical change from large to small stone points already noted between the San Pedro and Hohokam Culture levels, that this weapon arrived at about the same time as did pottery and agriculture.

Grooved clubs—It was somewhat a surprise to find six fragmentary grooved throwing clubs of a type well known from the Colorado Plateau,[223] southern New Mexico,[224] and West Texas.[225]

All of the Ventana clubs are fragmentary but they appear to differ in no way from those reported elsewhere (Pl. 37, *e, f*). The S-curve type seems not to be represented. Grooves number three, where these can be counted, and none are interrupted. One shows an incised zigzag pattern on both faces and traces of pitch at the end. There is no doubt that the fragmentary nature of these clubs is due to misuse by later people who found them in the trash. Four are partially burned and the rest are shattered. Evidently they were used as fuel or as pokers in tending fires.

Grooved clubs are usually recognized as a Basketmaker trait, or as associated with people on a Basketmaker level of culture. Stratigraphically the Ventana clubs ranged from levels 1 to 3, as is to be expected if they were salvaged by later people and used in ways other than their original intent. They are certainly not of Papago origin and it is impossible, on the present evidence, to say whether the Hohokam shared the use of the club

★

222. L. S. Cressman, 1942, p. 70.

223. S. J. Guernsey and A. V. Kidder, 1921, pp. 88-89.

224. C. B. Cosgrove, 1947, pp. 58-60.

225. F. H. H. Roberts, Jr., 1929, pp. 11-13; E. B. Sayles, 1935, Table 8; G. C. Martin, 1933, pp. 30-32.

with the Basketmakers or whether it was strictly an intruded feature. Sayles[226] notes one from Chihuahua, but to my knowledge none have been reported so far west as those from Ventana.

Beads—Among the scarce ornaments from the cave are three wooden cylindrical beads, 7 mm. long and 4 mm. in diameter (Pl. 37, *a*). The material, other than being a plant stalk with a pithy center, has not been identified. They came to light in level 1 (upper cave) and authorship is uncertain.

Nose plugs—Heretofore, wooden nose plugs from archaeological horizons in the Southwest have not been reported. The finding of one in the nasal septum of a male mummy (burial 9, Pl. 59) leaves no room for doubt about the identification. Three of the four plugs in the collection are wooden cylinders with square cut ends and slightly rounded margins. The one on burial 9 measures 29 mm. long by 12 mm. in diameter; a second, found with this mummy, attached to a piece of string, is 31 mm. by 13.50 mm. (Pl. 21); and the third is somewhat larger, 47 by 14 mm. (Pl. 37, *b*). The latter was carved with a steel knife, which arouses the suspicion that nose plug wearing has persisted from aboriginal times to the Papago. The probability of this will be examined further in a moment. The fourth plug differs in being sharpened at both ends and having one curved margin as illustrated in Plate 37, *c* (length, 42 mm., diameter, 7 mm.). Further, it is perforated lengthwise with a small hole, evidently for the attachment of additional elements.

The pre-Spanish use of nose plugs is well documented, since burial 9 may be dated somewhere between A. D. 1000 and 1400. Stone cylinders, roughly comparable to the wood plugs in size but often of slightly crescentic form, occur plentifully in the La Playa site of northern Mexico; they have been found on the Papago Reservation in Sells Phase sites,[227] at Snaketown,[228]

★

226. E. B. Sayles, 1936, p. 78, Pl. XXIX, *b*.
227. Jackrabbit Ruin and the Ash Hill Site.
228. H. S. Gladwin, *et al.*, 1937, Pl. CVIII, *g* (not recognized as such at the time the Snaketown report was written).

and perhaps most abundantly near Flagstaff,[229] where their use has been well established.

The wearing of nose ornaments historically is recorded for the Lower Colorado and Gila River people[230] and Russell records for the Pima that "a very brave man pierced the septum of his nose and wore therein a skewer of neatly polished bone, or else suspended from it a bit of turquoise or shell. Two men yet living in the Santan village have pierced noses, though they long ago abandoned the practice of wearing anything in them."[231]

I have been unable to find any such reference for the Papago, although on the following evidence it may be supposed that the custom was present among them, too. Their word for nose decoration is *dák-osh-a-táh*. It may be inferred that the type of ornament they have in mind involved the piercing of the septum. Jose Francisco, of Akchin and Comobabi, alleged to be 110 years old, remembers[232] as a boy seeing wooden nose plugs of the Ventana type worn by Papago men for no other reason than that they "looked pretty." Jose Francisco also related a folk tale which bears on this general problem. The gist of it runs as follows:

A wise man was in love with a pretty girl, but being reluctant to approach her himself he sent Coyote to her with a handful of jewelry as a present. As Coyote held out his hand, offering the jewels, the girl struck his hand from below, showering the jewels over a wide area. Ever since, the shrubbery in this region has grown luxuriously and the Papago formerly went there to get wood for their nose plugs.

★

229. J. C. McGregor, 1941, pp. 204-209; 1943, p. 280. McGregor's reference (1945, p. 306) to the uniqueness of nose plugs in the Flagstaff area therefore requires modification.

230. Font, in 1775-1776, saw Yumas wearing various articles in their noses and "some who were content to wear a little stick thrust through the cartilage" (H. E. Bolton, 1930, p. 301). C. D. Forde (1931, pp. 151-152) describes a nose-piercing ceremony for boys among the Yuma and, farther south, the Cocopa war chief formerly wore a shell bead and blue abalone shell pendant suspended from the nasal septum when going into battle (data from William H. Kelly). The Kiliwa wore bright objects in their noses (P. Meigs, 1939, p. 49). Among the Gila River Yumas, noses were pierced for pendants, which hung over the mouth (L. Spier, 1933, pp. 102-103).

231. F. Russell, 1908, p. 163.

232. Interrogated for the writer by Enos Francisco, March, 1943.

At best, it looks as though the custom among the Papago was waning a century ago and memory of it among the younger generations has already been lost. What is of interest is the fact that the type of plug worn aboriginally and by the Papago was the same, accepting Jose Francisco's account and the Papago-made plug from the cave at face value. This provides one more possible link between the dead and the living groups.

Pillow—Under the head of burial 6, a child of about five years, was a bundle made up of a mass of cotton cloth remnants. Peeling off layer upon layer of cloth revealed, inside, the shell of a wooden block about 210 mm. long, 80 mm. wide, and 40 mm. thick. This has been entirely consumed by wood-eating insects, leaving only the thin surface layer to preserve the form. A heavy bundle of brown-dyed cotton yarn was first wrapped about the block (Pl. 61, *c*) and, finally, such cloth fragments as were available to make a soft padding over the hard core.

I find no information to the effect that wooden pillows were used historically by the Papago, but the trait does occur prehistorically in the Plateau among the Anasazi.[233]

Dice—Each of the six stick dice was made from a split sahuaro rib segment and has a flat and a convex face. Lengths range from 82 to 151 mm. Only two show black-painted incised markings in the manner of recent Papago dice (Pl. 37, *g, h*). Two of the plain dice came from level 2 (both cave units) which may possibly carry the trait into prehistoric times although there is no further support for this notion (see also *bone dice*, p. 381).

Painted Disc—Plate 37, *d,* is an interesting wooden disc 67 mm. in diameter and 5 mm. thick with a painted radiating pattern in red and black on the face and solid red on the back. Through a central perforation protrudes a tuft of cotton string. The piece has been reduced to a mere shell by termites. It was found in the upper cave within 30 cm. of the surface and whittling scars suggest the use of a steel knife. There is not much doubt

★

233. Several Pueblo III burials with wooden pillows were found by the Arizona State Museum in Vandal Cave, northeastern Arizona, 1927.

that the Papago made it, and it looks suspiciously like the symbolic wood carvings used curatively by Papago medicine men.

Prayer sticks—Papago prayer sticks found about shrines and sacred spots are usually peg-like affairs with flat upper ends, frequently painted red. The nine from Ventana were indiscriminately strewn about the surface or in the surface debris. Lengths range from 120 to 320 mm. The one illustrated (Pl. 37, *i*) has a string tied about the upper end which originally may have held feathers in place.

Miscellaneous—The eighteen miscellaneous items of wood include a variety of remnants and artifact pieces too fragmentary to be of any value.

2. *Plant Artifacts*

In this category are considered those items made from plant parts with only such alteration, by cutting or bending, as was required to bring the object to shape. The list includes:

Sahuaro callus receptacles	5
Gourd vessels	6
Gourd rind and bark discs	2
Gourd rind gaming ring	1
Flute (?)	1
Wrapped stick	1
Cane cigarettes	29
Needles	2
Box weave	1
Total	48

Sahuaro callus receptacles—The sahuaro cactus (*Cereus giganteus*) repairs wounds by forming a hard, tough callus about the injury. Such wounds are often caused by woodpeckers in building nests in the cactus. When the plant dies and the trunk disintegrates, the tough callus is one of the few parts to remain. These were gathered by the people of Ventana and broken or cut in two to make containers. Three such items were found, from 145 to 315 mm. long, with burials (Pl. 38, *a*), and two fragments were loose in the debris. One was evidently from a scoop. There is no indication that the Papago made use of this natural material. Velarde, in 1716, noted that calabashes (gourds) of water[234] were buried with Pima men, and it may very well be that, aboriginally, callus vessels were a substitute for the gourd in this practice.

Gourd vessels—These are represented by fragments only. They were evidently made from the largest of the native gourds *(Cucurbita foetidissima)* by halving them lengthwise. A cultivated variety, *Lagenaria,* appears also to be represented. Gourd dippers are still used by the Papago but they were doubtless employed also in earlier times. The Ventana specimens all came from level 1.

Gourd rind and bark discs—These two discs, 29 and 21 mm. in diameter respectively, are centrally perforated (Pl. 38, *b*). The gourd rind example, from level 2 (lower cave), is probably old.

Gourd rind gaming ring—The pin-and-ring game among the Papago was played by catching rings of gourd or squash rind on the pin. Plate 38, *c* illustrates a fragment of one of these rings left in the cave by the Papago. Its diameter is 40 mm. and at opposite poles on the reverse (inner) side there is a black and a red dot.

Flute (?)—There is one small fragment of carrizo *(Phragmites communis)* with three burnt holes (diameter, 3 mm., and 19 mm. apart), probably all that is left of a flute.[235] It was found in the surface debris of the upper cave and is probably of Papago origin.

Wrapped stick—This is a tapered stick wrapped spirally with a strip of bark (Pl. 38, *d*). Slipped over the pointed end is the butt of a feather. The cultural identity is uncertain (from lower cave, level 1) but Russell illustrates a vaguely similar article used ritually by the Pima.[236]

★

234. R. K. Wyllys, 1931, p. 136.
235. Russell (1908, p. 166) describes Pima flutes as three-holed.
236. *Ibid.,* Figure 100 (left).

Cane cigarettes—From levels 1 and 2 of both cave units were recovered twenty-nine butts of cane cigarettes *(Phragmites communis)*. These were made by cutting out segments of the cane, including a node near an end (Pl. 38, *e, f*). The septum of the node was then pierced to permit the drawing of air through the opposite end. All but one of the Ventana cigarettes have been smoked. The original packing from one of these cigarettes, when burned, smelled like the aromatic scaly bark of the ocotillo. Tobacco has been found in reed cigarettes from the Salt River Valley.[237]

Cane cigarettes have survived from prehistoric times among the Pima[238] and probably among the Papago as well, particularly for ritual smoking. Those from Ventana may well represent both culture levels.

Needles—There are two varieties of needles, both ingeniously adapted from natural plant spines. One (Pl. 38, *g*) is the spike end of an agave or yucca leaf. The fibers of the leaf, after removal of outer covering and pulp, remain attached to the spike. These were twisted into a 2-yarn cord producing a handy needle-and-thread combination in one unit. The needle was cut off and thrown away when the cord was used up. Similar needles are recorded for the Anasazi in the Sierra Ancha.[239]

The second variety of needle is no different from ours of today except in material. The only one recovered from Ventana (Pl. 38, *h*) was stuck into the hair wig found under the head of burial 9. It is a long, straight spine of the barrel cactus *(Echinocactus wislizeni* or *E. covillei)*, measuring 69 mm. in length. Spines of these varieties of cactus are ideally suited for conversion to needles, with comparatively little alteration. The crossribs, giving the natural spine a rough surface, have been eliminated and the shaft was given a high polish. The eye end was neatly round-tapered and the eye itself (diameter, 1 mm.) was

★

237. E. W. Haury, 1945, p. 194.
238. F. Russell, 1908, p. 112.
239. E. W. Haury, 1934, Pl. LV, *b*.

drilled from two sides. A remnant of agave fiber cord, doubled and twisted upon itself, is still threaded in the eye.

Box weave—This object (Pl. 38, *i*) is of only passing interest as it adds one more to the variety of techniques seen among the objects from the cave. The material is composed of narrow (3.50 mm.) yucca leaf strips and the weaving begins by crossing two elements in the center, folding the four free ends over each other in rotation, and always inserting the fourth element through the loop made by the first. This is commonly known as a box weave and is used variously as ornamental trapping nowadays.

G. Leather

There is no doubt that skins were widely used throughout the entire Ventana occupation, but concrete evidence was found only in the dry midden. The use of skin strips in making robes is described elsewhere (p. 395) and what remains is an imposing list of articles. Included is a tubular quiver of buckskin (?) found with burial 9 (Pl. 39, *a*). This is now without a bottom piece. The two edges are held together with cotton string in a fagoting stitch. Nine reed arrows were snugly packed inside.

There is also one heavily worn buckskin sandal from the surface refuse of the upper cave. It had two thong perforations at the toe and paired holes along the sides near the heel for ties (Pl. 39, *b*). This is much like the rawhide sandals still occasionally seen on the reservation and probably is of Papago origin.

A disintegrated article, perhaps a bag, made of a small animal hide was found with burial 17.

The remaining twenty-one leather fragments are all remnants of thongs, trimmings, and the like. A few are rawhide although the majority are well-tanned pieces of buckskin.

H. Feathers

With the exception of their use on arrows, feathers appear to have been associated chiefly with ritual paraphernalia. The evidence of feathers in the ash daubs from the cave wall, and the attaching of feathers to prayer sticks, have already been noted.

There remain five pieces to be mentioned: (1) a feather butt tied with yucca string; (2) a slender stick wrapped with yucca string with downy feathers caught in the wrappings (Pl. 39, *c*); (3) a feather with butt doubled back on the shaft and tied (Pl. 39, *d*); (4) the badly deteriorated remnants of a feathered plume (Pl. 39, *e*), made by tying the ends of downy feathers together with yucca string and forty to fifty of such elements were then attached to a wooden shaft with a fiber wrap (found with burial 12, a middle aged male); and (5) a short piece of milk weed cord wrapped with a smaller, red-dyed cord of the same material which held in place the fine downy parts of feathers (Fig. 99). This is the only instance where feathers were substituted for fur in the production of cordage for robes.

FIGURE 99. Feather cord

I. DRESS

Before the influence of white man, the living groups in southern Arizona had as standard clothing some scanty form of breech cover, sandals, buckskin shirt, and a blanket, none being classifiable as fitted garments. The people of Ventana Cave followed this same pattern, at least back to about A. D. 1000. Our evidence does not take us beyond this. The deductions as to body clothing are based on the mummies which were interred, presumably with their full complement of dress. Thirteen were wrapped in fur robes and four in cotton blankets; breech clouts were on five, sandals on two, and a cotton, poncho-like garment was found with one. The art of weaving, well established by A. D. 1000, resulted in the manufacture of some pieces of considerably more aesthetic interest than has been recorded for the Pima and the Papago.

1. *Breech Clouts*

Although several of the mummies have no loin cover it is evident that, as a rule, clouts were worn. Three classes of material are represented: (1) cotton cloth (one example), (2) milk weed cordage (ten examples), and (3) bark (one example). The principle of wearing breech clouts, regardless of material, appears to have been the same. The cloth cover on a male burial (No. 9) consists of several strips of fabric about 100 mm. wide, tucked before and behind under a belt made of a section of rabbit netting. This cloth was cut to form, probably having been salvaged from a worn blanket.

Eight of the ten cordage loin covers were on burials and two were found in the trash. The burials, Nos. 2 and 6 (wearing one and two extras at side of body), No. 11 (one extra), Nos. 16 and 31, are all mummies of females varying in age from five or six years old to adults. There are consistently two units, the cover proper and the belt. The former, in all cases, is a mass of loosely twisted 4- to 6-yarn milk weed cordage, worn closely against the body and lodged under the belt, front and back (Pl. 40). The cordage ends were free and dropped over the belt for a short distance. Belts were masses of cotton or milk weed cordage, smaller in diameter than the clout cords. The one on burial 2 (Pl. 57, *a*) has over two hundred strings. How the belt ends were joined cannot be determined as this was evidently in back where the disintegration has been the greatest. In one case (burial 11) the loin cords were dyed red.

The final clout (Pl. 41), a fragment from the rubbish (level 1, upper cave), is made of shredded bark fiber. Probably willow strands of the fiber were joined by a 2-element twine as diagrammed in Figure 100. This is essentially the same technique as employed in the free-hanging bark skirt of the Maricopa.[240] It is too fragmentary to tell whether it was worn as a fringe or gathered between the legs and fastened behind. This piece very likely came from the Gila Valley, to the north, as willows are

★

240. L. Spier, 1933, p. 95.

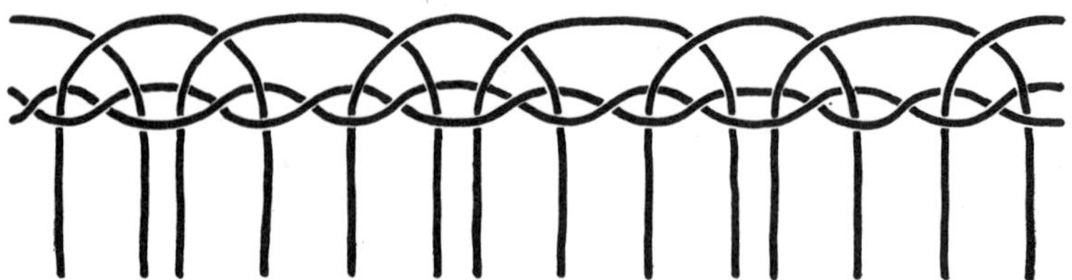

FIGURE 100. Diagram illustrating the method used in constructing willow bark (?) breech clout shown in Plate 41

extremely rare in Papagueria, particularly in the vicinity of the cave.

2. *Fur Blankets*

Robes or blankets were of two kinds, cotton and rabbit skin. The cotton blankets are discussed in the special section on textiles by Mrs. Tanner, so we may limit ourselves here to the fur variety.

Thirteen of these, in various states of preservation, were found with burials, and the trash produced a quantity of fur cordage remnants, indicating that capes of this material were abundant. As was the custom among the living Indians of the area until recently, these must have been the chief body protection in winter. How the fur cordage was made is presented elsewhere (p. 395). The actual method of putting the cordage together was rather simple. Whether this was done with the elements in a vertical or horizontal position is not known, but some sort of anchorage points were necessary.[241] These numbered four and the system, with variations noted in the Ventana material, may be set down as follows (see Fig. 101 for composite diagram): single or double loops of fur cord were fixed around anchors to form the framework (1, 2); fur string (body cord, 3) was tied to one frame end, then carried back and forth between frame cords and simultaneously lashed by simple looping (4) or by marling (marline hitch) (5); body cords were further held in place by lengthwise twining at intervals from 5 to 50 mm., being continuous (6) or separate units, the fag ends being

★

241. *Ibid.*, p. 96, notes that among the Maricopa one end of the foundation piece was fastened to the worker's toe, the other end to her belt.

tied after crossing the fabric (7). The twining interval was normally over-one, but one blanket is twined over-two (8). A piece of cordage tied in one corner (9) evidently was used in uniting two corners about the neck when the garment was worn. On all examples, the fur-covered body cords were laid in closely enough to make a fairly tight and consequently warm fabric. The three best preserved specimens are shown in Plates 42 and 43.

Fur robes were evidently worn by people of both sexes and of all ages, those for children being correspondingly smaller than the adult models. Even the latter were small and would have hung only to the waist when worn over the shoulders.

There is good documentation to the effect that both Yuman and Piman peoples used the rabbit skin robe historically.[242] Descriptions would indicate these to have been little different

★ 242. *Ibid.*, p. 96; F. Russell, 1908, pp. 157-158.

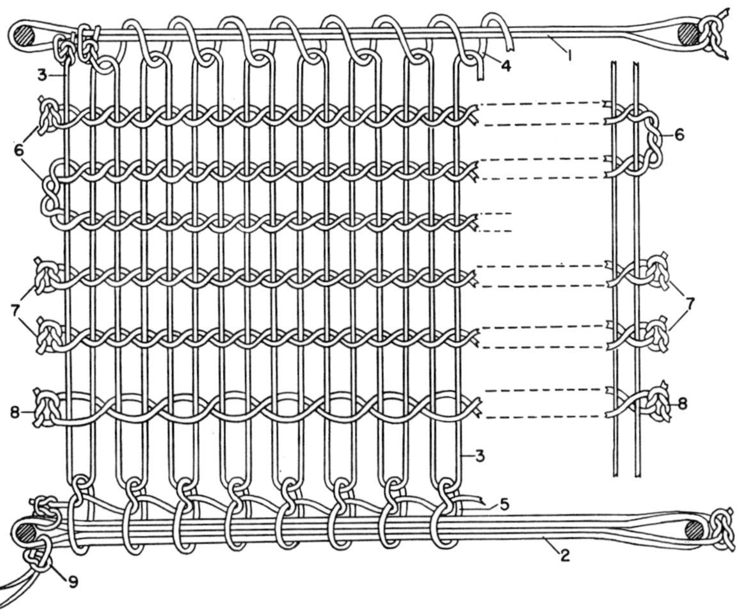

FIGURE 101. Composite diagram showing construction techniques for fur robes

from those recovered in Ventana. Although the information is not sufficiently complete to make detailed comparisons, there can be no doubt that the Ventana robes are the direct forerunners of those used in the area until recently.

From about A. D. 1000[243] to 1400, skin was the standard material for trimming the cords that made up the body of each robe. This establishes a significant contrast between the Hohokam fur robe and the feather robe of the late Anasazi. In the Plateau the Basketmaker II habitually used fur.[244] By Basketmaker III times, feather stripping was gradually taking the place of fur[245] and this eventually became dominant through the rest of Anasazi prehistory. The only reference to feather cloth for southern Arizona was made by Fewkes,[246] who reported it at Casa Grande, but as that was jointly occupied by Anasazi and Hohokam, the specimen in question might well have belonged to the former group. On the present evidence it would look as though the boundary line between feather and fur was culturally determined. Technically the robes were made similarly in both areas with some differences in details. Guernsey illustrates the marline hitch[247] in Basketmaker fur cloth for fastening the fur cords to the selvage, comparable to one of the Ventana forms for executing the same step.

3. *Sandals*

Excepting the single buckskin sandal (Pl. 39, *b*) and the sandal listed below with gut weft, all other examples of footgear were made of plant fiber. While the variety of sandals from Ventana is not great, the technological extremes between the simpler ones and those with most complicated weave are about as far apart as is possible.

The collection of ninety-nine whole and fragmentary sandals is classifiable as follows:

★

243. Fur robes were certainly in use before this date, but our evidence does not show it.

244. S. J. Guernsey, 1931, p. 115.

245. F. H. H. Roberts, Jr., 1937, p. 8.

246. J. W. Fewkes, 1912, p. 148.

247. S. J. Guernsey, 1931, Pl. 54, *a*.

A. Natural fiber 9

B. Wickerwork 77

- 1. Yucca warp 70
  - a. Whole yucca leaf weft 55
  - b. Macerated yucca leaf weft 10
  - c. Macerated wood weft 3
  - d. Bark strip 2
- 2. Cordage warp 7
  - a. Macerated yucca leaf weft 4
  - b. Macerated wood weft 1
  - c. Bark strip 1
  - d. Gut weft 1

C. Sewed 13

A. *Natural fiber*—Sandals not woven but made of a native material, requiring merely trimming to shape and attaching foot lashings number only nine. Their occurrence in levels 1 to 3 suggests probable pre-Spanish to recent use. The material is the matted and laminated fiber forming the outer covering of the stele of mature yucca *(Yucca elata)* plants. This was cut into pads of foot size (Pl. 44, *a*) and about 10 mm. thick. Although the individual fibers are tough they tend to pull apart and the pads are apt to separate into layers. This weakness was generally overcome by a yucca leaf stitching as shown by Plate 44, *b*. Ties were fastened, too, by stitching through the fiber. At best, these sandals could not have been very serviceable but they show, along with the materials employed in some of the following sandals, a willingness to improvise and to test any possible raw products. The same type has been reported from Etna Cave, southern Nevada.[248]

B. *Wickerwork*—The majority (seventy-seven) of the sandals fall within the wickerwork class and the general type represented by them may be considered to be the norm for the area during Hohokam times. Variations, as recognized here, are accounted for chiefly by materials. The basic technique of manufacture

248. S. M. Wheeler, 1942, p. 15.

remains the same throughout. In the all-yucca sandal a half-dozen or so yucca leaves *(Yucca elata)* were bent to form an oval, the ends being securely tied. This produced a fairly substantial 2-warp frame closed at the ends. Long narrow yucca leaves were then closely packed by weaving back and forth, over and under across the warp, the ends protruding on the underside to give a a cushion effect to the sandal. The knotted end of the frame always falls at the heel, and the general form of the finished product was oval (Pl. 44, *c*). Rights and lefts are not distinguishable. The technique as a whole is like that used by the late Anasazi in some of their sandals,[249] but there are minor differences: the Ventana sandals have a more oval shape, single instead of double knotted frame (2-piece), and longer leaves were employed for weftage.

In descending order of prevalence of weft materials there is first the whole yucca leaf, followed by macerated leaves of the same plant (Pl. 44, *d*), then shredded wood, and finally bark strips (Pl. 45, *a, b*). Reinforcements were sometimes effected by stitching the sandal lengthwise.

Cordage warp, sometimes substituted for the stiff yucca leaf warp, was stout 2-ply yucca cord, and in the sandals of burial 2, a young adult female, 3-ply human hair string was the foundation. Whole yucca leaves were not used as weftage on these but shredded leaves are present. Macerated wood, bark strips (Pl. 45, *d*), and gut weft (Pl. 45, *e*) are individually represented.

Many of these sandals are small, probably belonging to children, but one wonders whether or not some were worn by adults, too, as padding under the ball of the foot. In only one instance was there any added wrapping at the heel for a cushion to protect it against abrasion (Pl. 45, *c*).

Curiously, most of these sandals came from the lower cave, particularly from level 2, in a relatively small area toward the southwest end. The distribution to level in both caves runs as follows:

★

249. A. V. Kidder and S. J. Guernsey, 1919, p. 103.

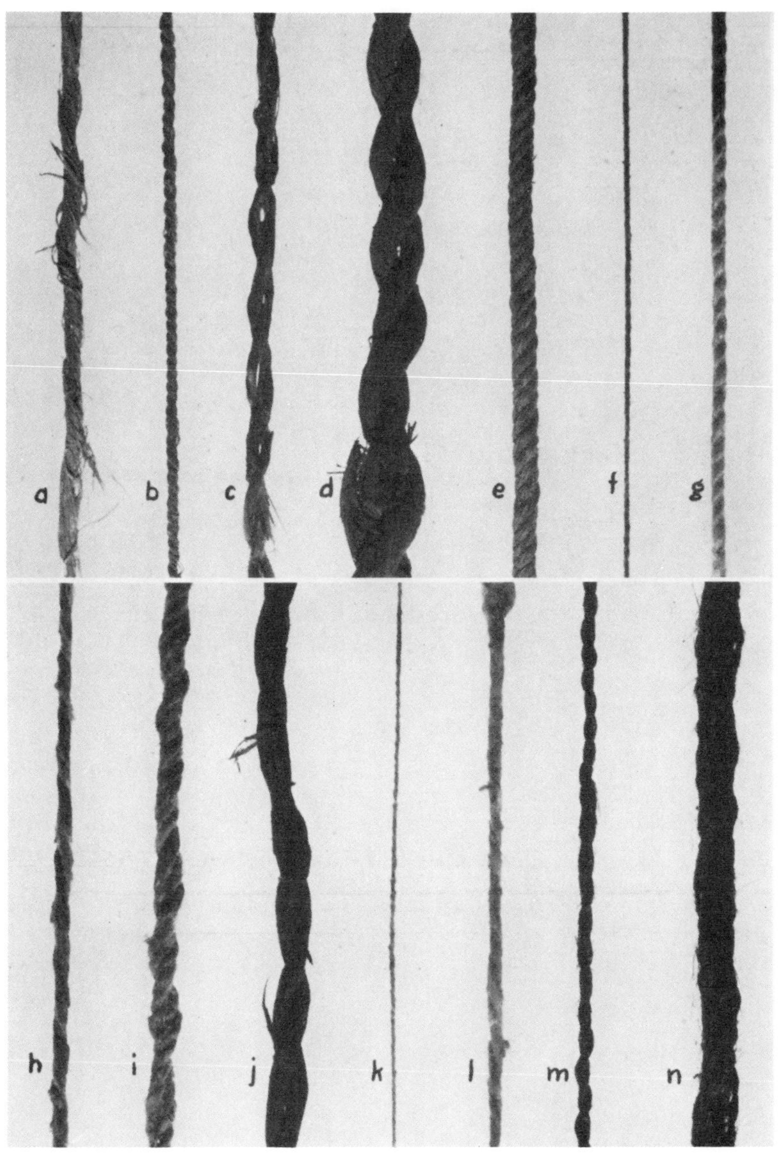

PLATE 27

Types of cordage. Yucca or agave fiber: yarn, *a;* 2-yarn, *b-d;* 4-yarn, *e;* milk weed: 2 yarn, *f, g;* 4-yarn in paired white and red, *h;* 2 2-yarn rope, *i;* bark: 2-yarn, *j;* cotton: 2-yarn, *k, l;* human hair: 2-yarn, *m;* 9 2-yarn rope, *n.* Diameter of *e,* 3.50 mm.

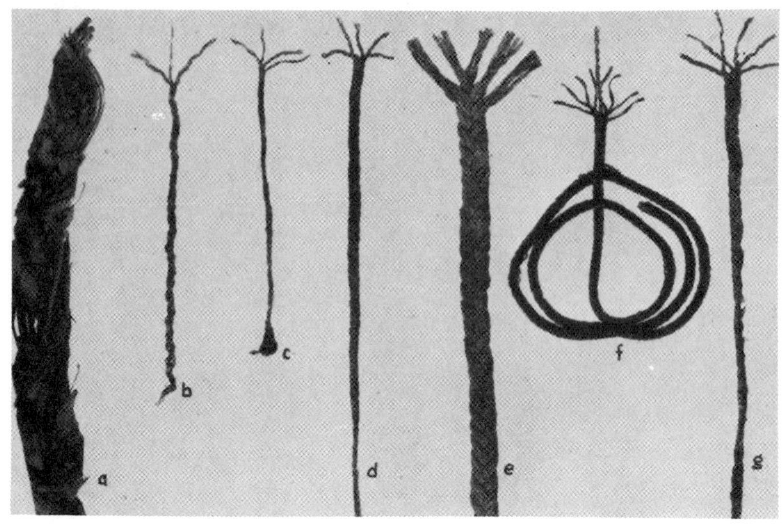

PLATE 28

Forms of sennit: common, *a-e*; round, *f*; flat, *g*. Width of *e*, 10 mm.

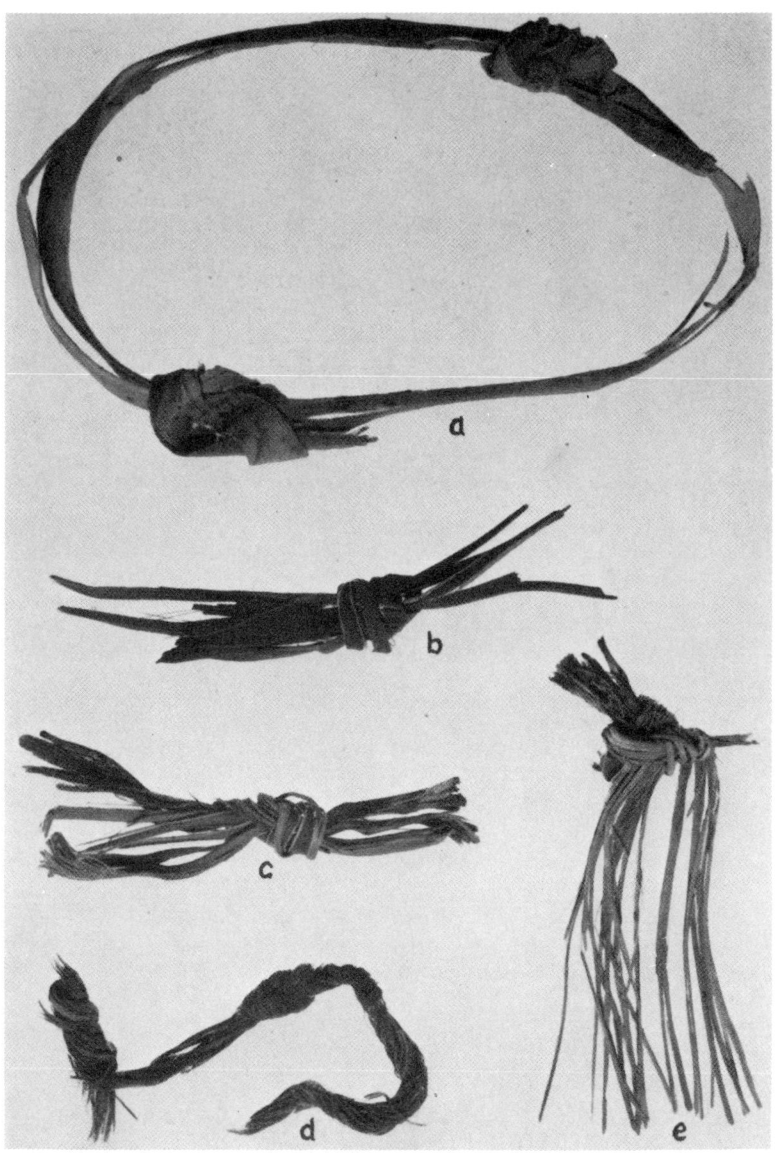

PLATE 29

Miscellaneous knotted elements. Bark strip hoop, *a;* yucca leaves, *b-e.* Length of *a,* 180 mm.

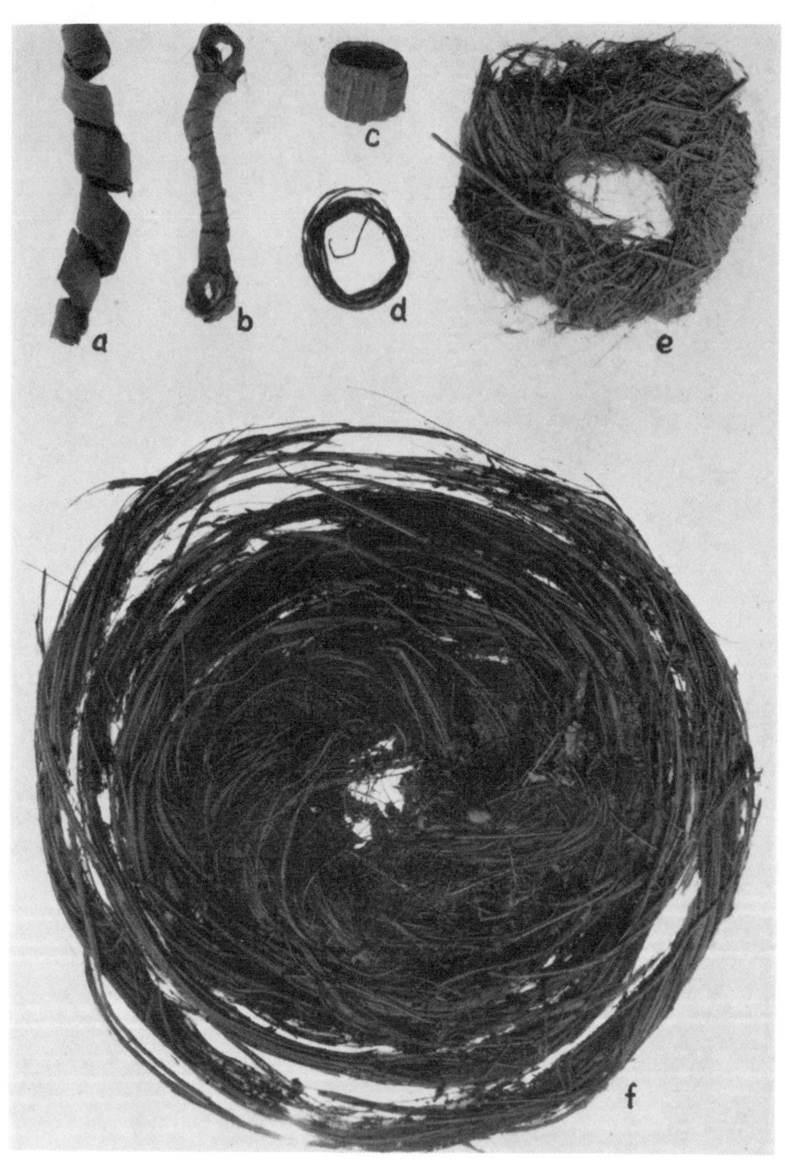

PLATE 30

Miscellaneous twisted and coiled elements. Diameter of *f*, 260 mm.

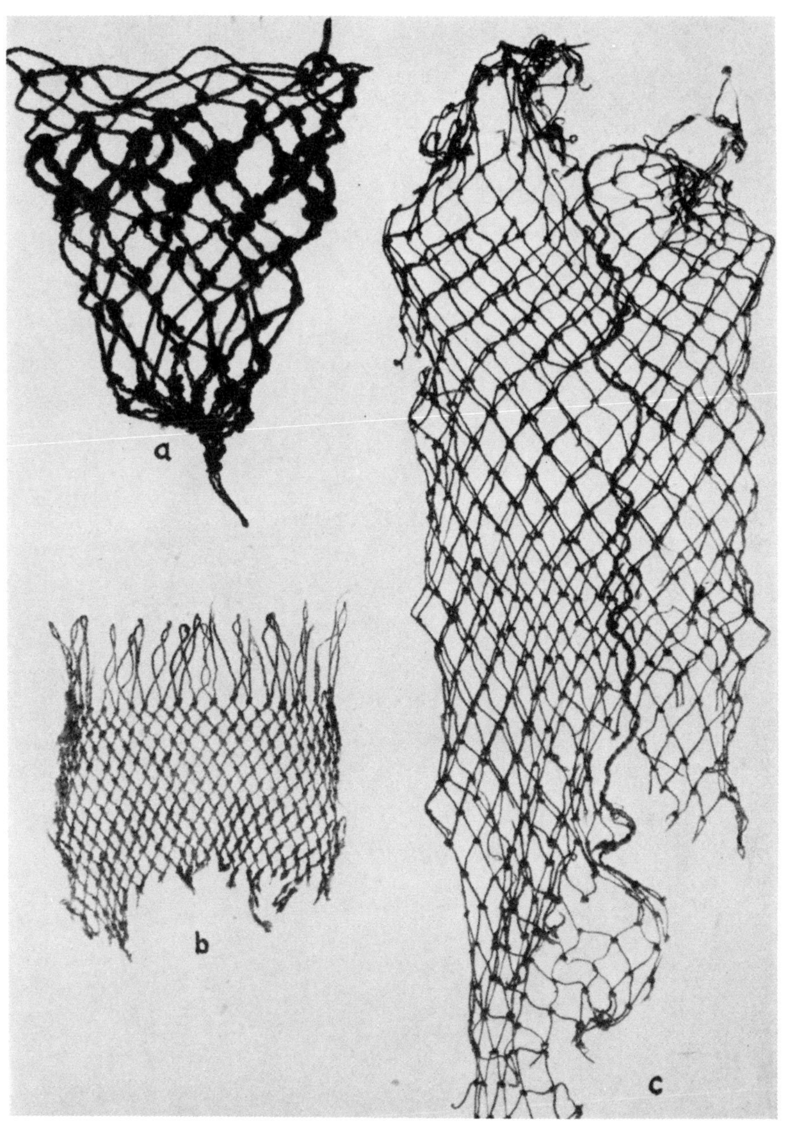

PLATE 31

Knotted netting. Bottom of bag, *a;* fine mesh netting, *b;* segment of cylindrical bag, *c.* Length of *a,* 145 mm.

PLATE 32

Basketry from the midden. Twill-plaited, *a* (*Scirpus* sp.?), *b* (yucca leaf); close coiled centers, *c-e: c,* bundle (split twigs) foundation, non-interlocked stitch (reverse surface shown); *d,* bundle (split twigs) foundation, interlocked split stitch (reverse surface shown); *e,* one-rod foundation, interlocked split stitch and showing mending stitches. Greatest diameter of *e,* 305 mm.

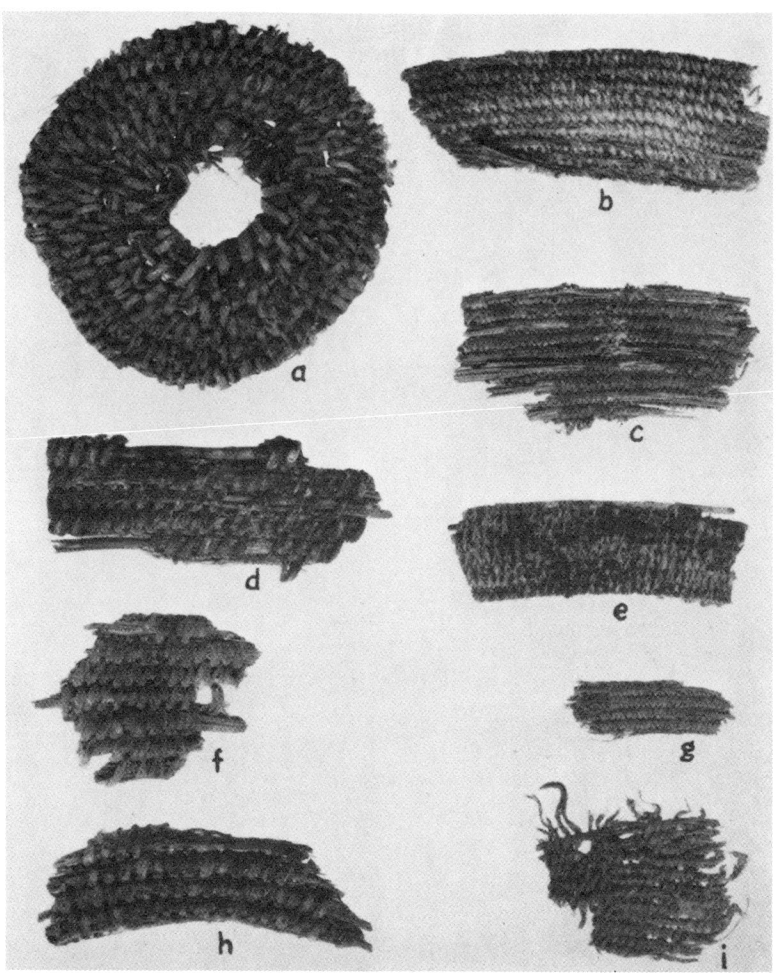

PLATE 33

Basketry from the midden: *a,* bundle foundation (shredded yucca), yucca leaf splint, interlocked split stitch (reverse surface shown); *b,* bundle foundation (shredded yucca), yucca leaf splint, interlocked stitch, split both faces (working face shown); *c,* bundle foundation (shredded cattail?), willow splint, interlocked split stitch (working face shown); *d,* bundle-with-rod-core foundation, willow splint, both non-interlocked and interlocked split stitches present (reverse face shown); *e,* one-rod foundation, willow splint, interlocked, wood splint, non-interlocked (reverse surface shown); *f,* one-rod-and-bundle foundation, stacked, wood splint, non-interlocked (reverse surface shown); *g,* two-rod-and-bundle foundation, bunched, willow splint, stitching variable (reverse face shown); *h,* as above, but coarse weave; *i,* fragment of twined woven bag. Diameter of *a,* 140 mm.

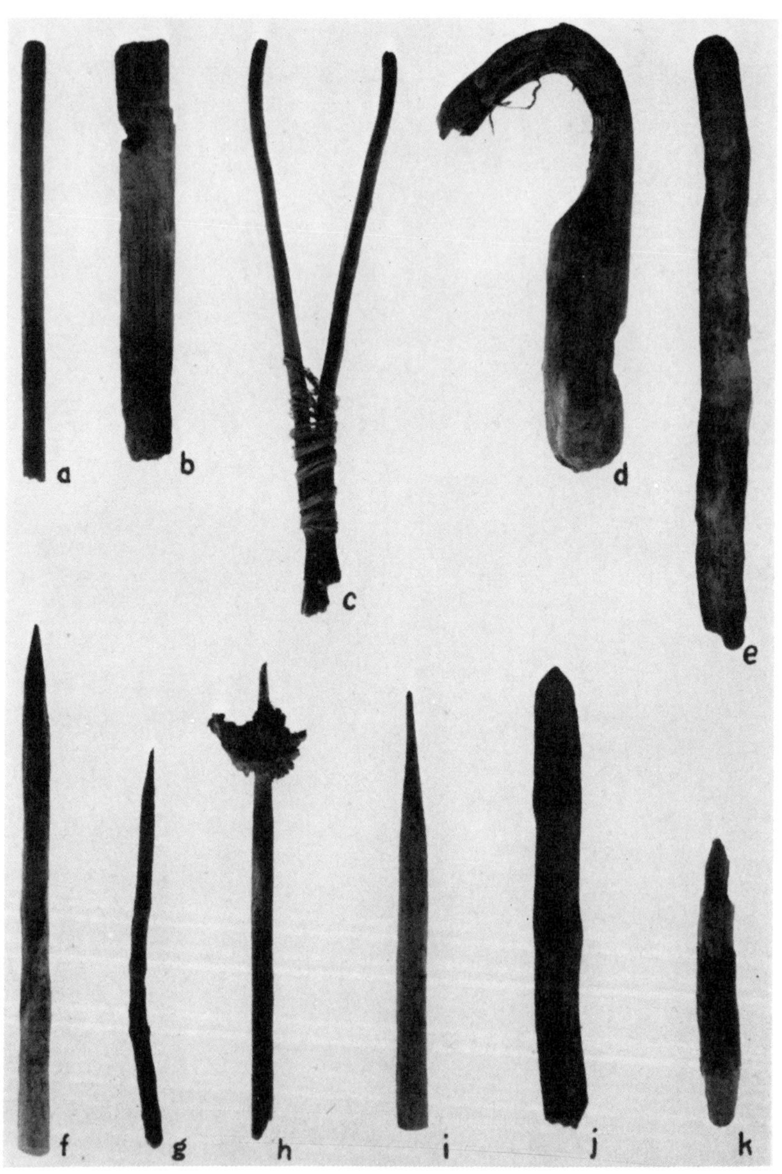

PLATE 34

Objects of wood from the upper layers of the midden. Fire-making apparatus, *a, b;* fire tongs, *c;* axe handle fragment, *d;* scraper, *e;* cactus picks, *f-h*; awl, *i*; spatula, *j;* cut stick, *k*. Length of *e,* 203 mm.

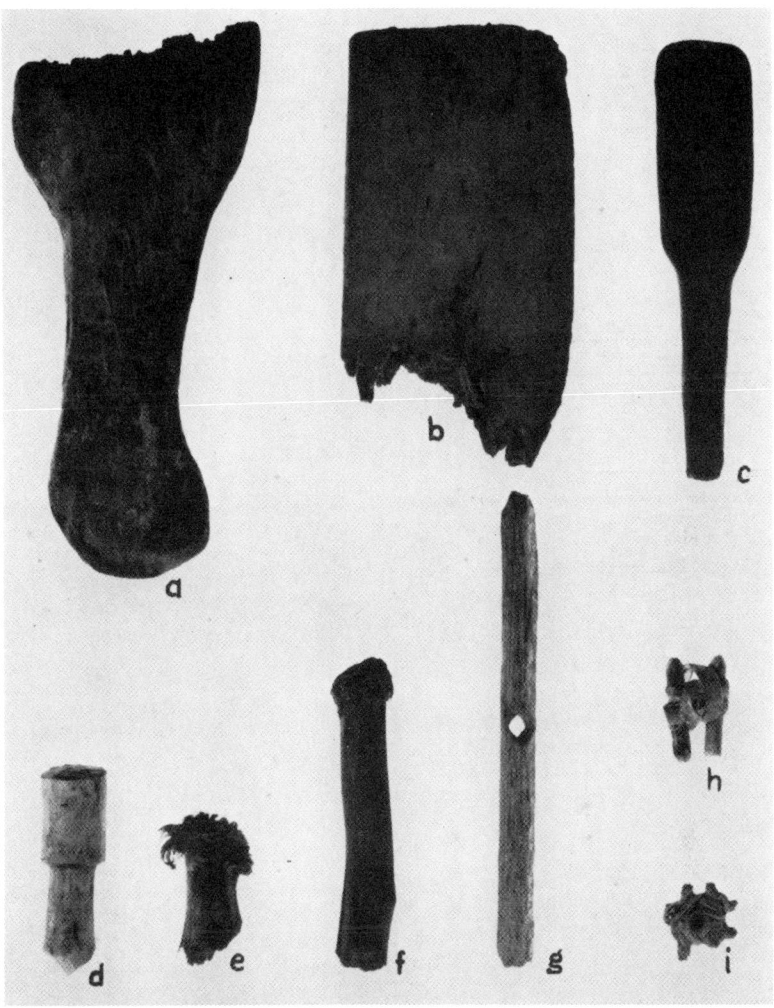

PLATE 35

Objects of wood from the upper layers of the midden. Paddles, *a-c;* stopper (?), *d;* burred pieces, *e, f;* perforated sahuaro rib, *g;* stick-work bunts for arrows, *h, i.* Length of *a,* 165 mm.

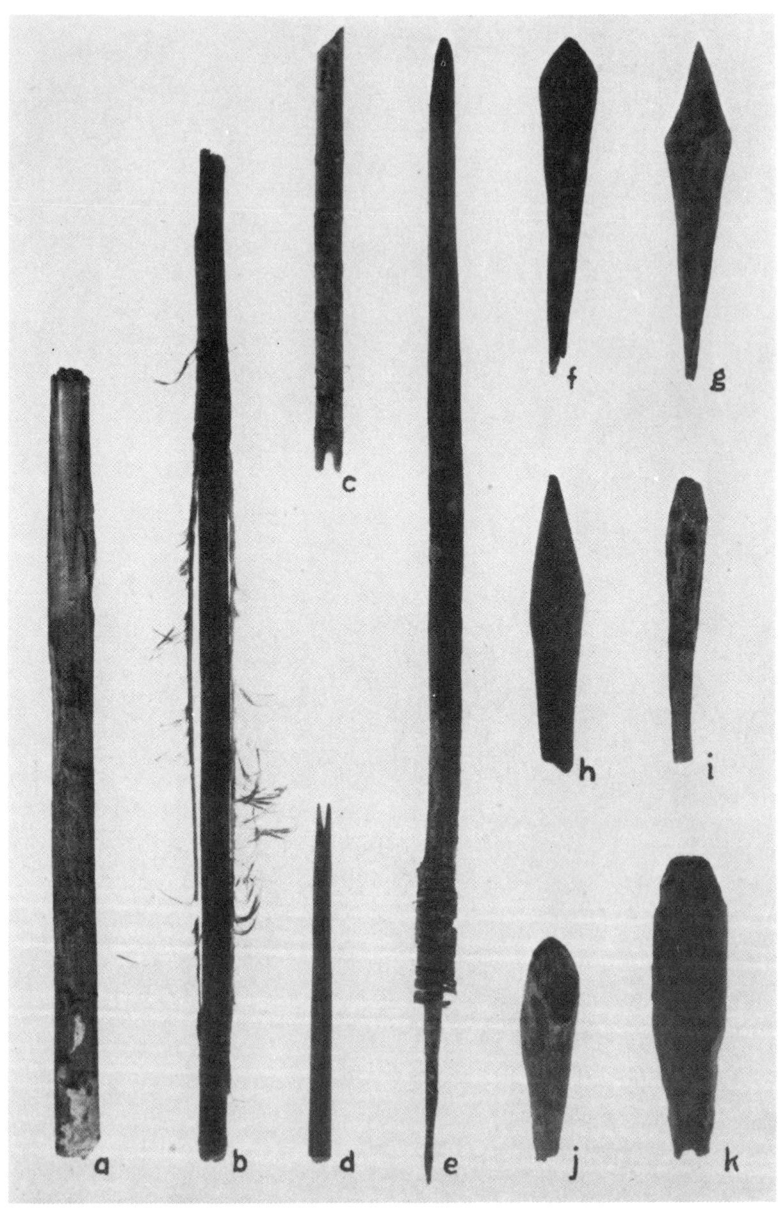

Plate 36

Arrow parts from the upper layers of the midden. Solid shaft, with base of foreshaft in place, *a;* feathered butts, *b, c;* fragment of notched foreshaft to receive stone tip, *d;* hardwood foreshaft without stone point, *e;* bunt point, *f-k.* Length of *e,* 240 mm.

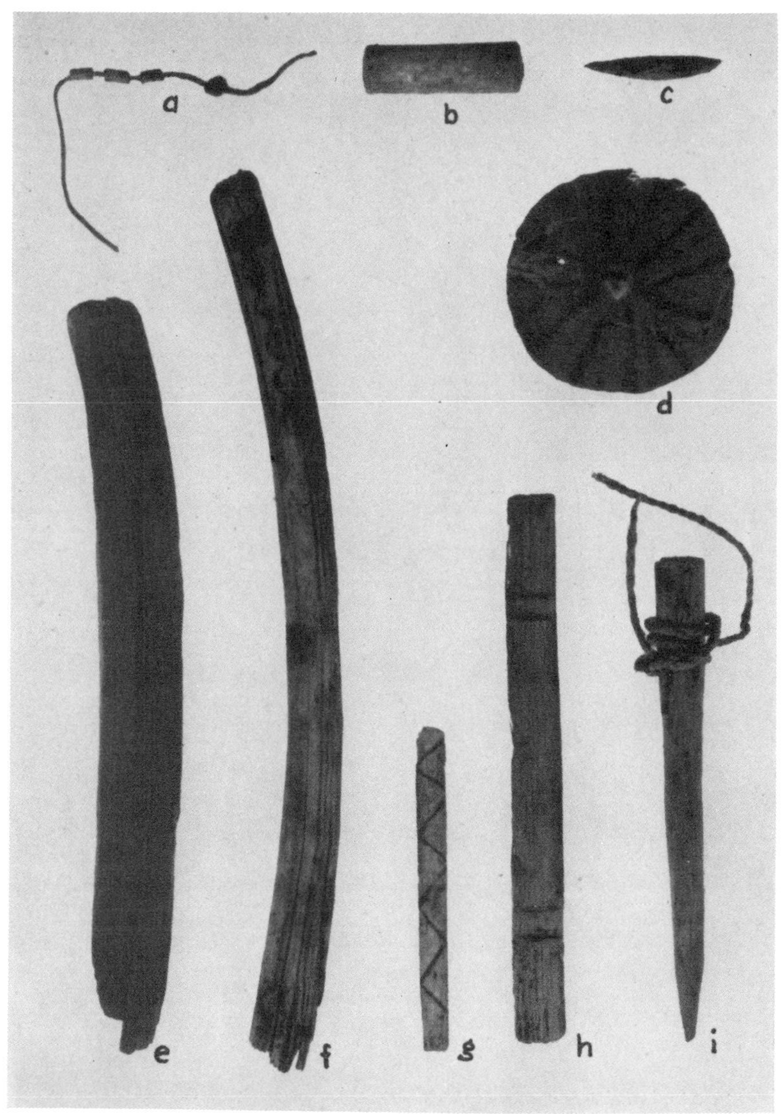

PLATE 37

Objects of wood from the upper layers of the midden. Beads, *a;* nose plugs, *b, c;* painted disc, *d;* grooved clubs, *e, f;* dice, *g, h;* prayer stick, *i.* Length of *f,* 245 mm.

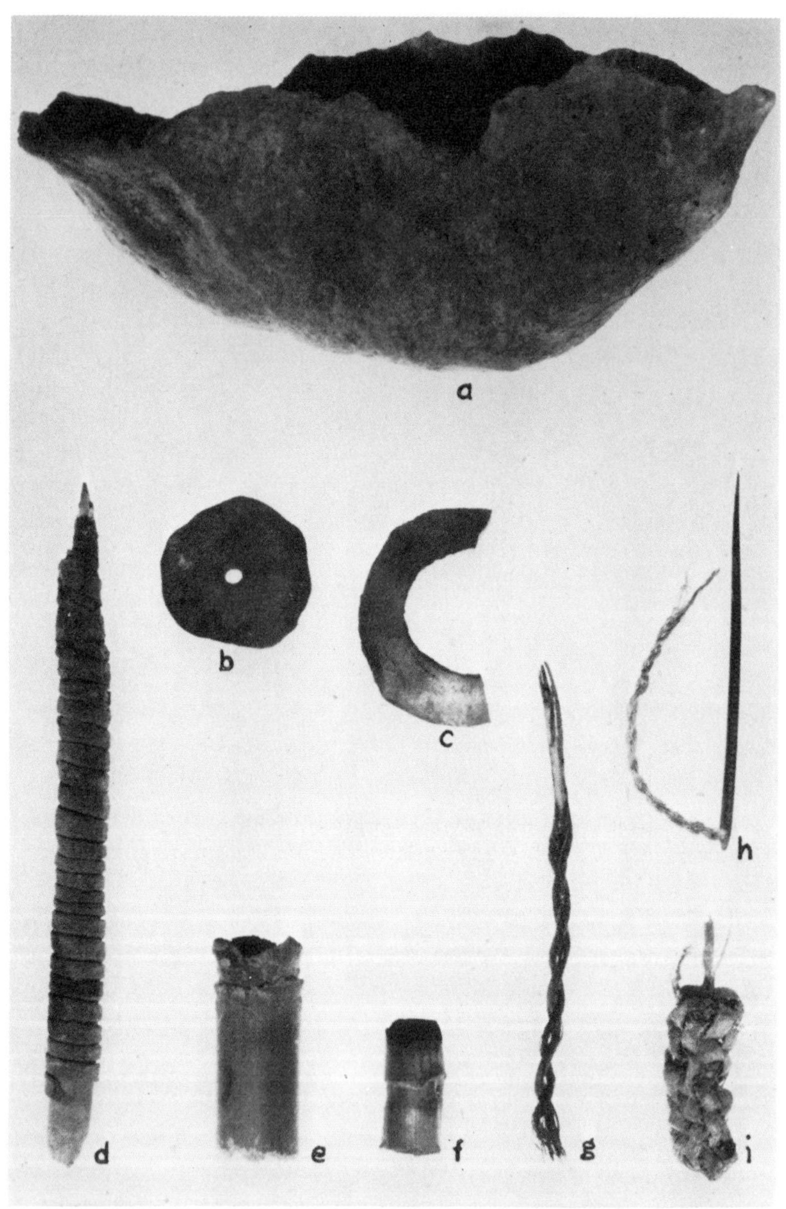

PLATE 38

Artifacts made of plant parts with little modification. Sahuaro callus receptacle, *a;* gourd rind disc, *b;* gourd rind gaming ring, *c;* wrapped stick, *d;* cane cigarette butts, *e, f;* agave or yucca leaf spine needle, *g;* cactus spine needle, *h;* example of box weave, *i.* Length of *a,* 146 mm.

	Levels	Number
Upper Cave	1	8
	2	2
	3	1
Lower Cave	1	7
	2	36
	3	11
	4	7
Miscellaneous		5
Total		77

While there are superficial resemblances between the Ventana wickerwork sandals and some of Cosgrove's[250] 2-warp types from the Huecos, the similarity becomes more apparent than real when a point-by-point comparison is made. The abbreviated scuffer-toe sandal is lacking in the western desert and the "fish-tail" effect is not seen either.

C. *Sewed*—Thirteen sandal fragments of a unique type present a most unsatisfactory source for technological determination. The fragmentary nature and the extensive damage done to them by termites prevent dissection over more than small areas, and excessive wear has eliminated some characters necessary for the successful reconstruction of the technique. A few characteristics, however, are determinable and the details of manufacture can be postulated.

In general outline, these sandals were shaped to fit the foot to the extent that the toe section was enlarged, but rights or lefts are not distinguishable. Both toe and heel ends were rounded. The upper surface presents what appears to be rows of braided agave fiber (Pl. 46, *b*), secured in such a way as to make a flat sole cover. On worn examples, the under-surface however, is quite different. Visible are the worn ends of fiber bundles, and between them, running indiscriminately, are many individual fibers (Pl. 46, *c*). The sole thickness, even in the present worn

★

250. C. B. Cosgrove, 1947, pp. 82-98.

state of the fragments, is from 7 to 10 mm., or much thicker than could be achieved by sewing "braids" together when these are only 4 to 5 mm. in diameter. It thus becomes obvious that the "braiding" is merely a deceptive overlay on some base, achieved by a sewing technique. Dissection of several fragments substantiates this idea. But since sewing presupposes the use of a base material, as cloth, a problem is posed as to the nature of that base. The indiscriminate fiber matting already mentioned, and further illustrated by a partially dissected specimen in Plate 46, *d,* is the only substance which qualifies at all as a possible foundation. We have a good clue as to the nature of this from the matted yucca fiber sandals described previously, indicating that its utility had been recognized. Further, some of these were occasionally strengthened by sewing (Pl. 44, *b*). Some alert person must have recognized the value of this fiber mat as the foundation for an all-sewed sandal and the type in question eventually was evolved.

Having selected a fiber pad, the procedure appears to have been as follows: A prepared 2-yarn yucca cord (diameter, about 3 mm.), doubled, was the sewing element. The needle may have been either the spike end of the leaf itself or the pointed ends of the cord may have been inserted through awl-made holes in the fiber. A chain stitch was then laid on. Judging from a nearly complete specimen (lacking heel) from Winchester Cave[251] and the heel portion of a Ventana sandal (Pl. 46, *a*), sewing was begun centrally in the toe end by applying a short, straight line of stitches. This was then enclosed in two concentric rows of stitching, forming the nucleus of the expanded toe end. One line of stitches of the next addition was carried down toward the heel end. Successively other concentrically stitched rows were added until the required width and length of the sandal were achieved. The technique is shown schematically in Figure 102.

What the pattern of stitching was on the under-surface is not known because this has been worn away on all specimens.

★

251. W. S. Fulton, 1941, Fig. 4.

Actual duplication of the technique in the laboratory produced a series of bumps where the fat yarn was turned back through the fiber. These would be the first to wear away when the sandals were put into service, leaving the yarns exposed as bundles.

The final step was the addition of a selvage, consisting of two units. This was accomplished by turning and hemstitching a part of the projecting ends of the fiber mat base to the outermost row of "braid," forming a slight rim about the whole sandal. The technique was then repeated directly below with the remaining free fiber (Fig. 102).

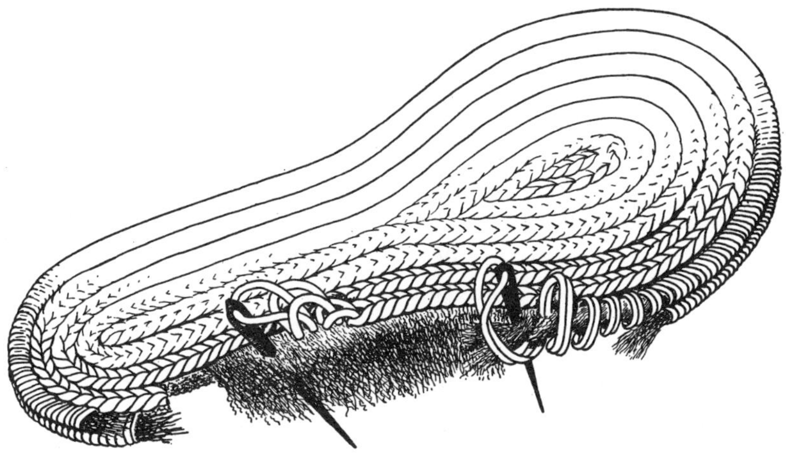

FIGURE 102. Drawing of sewed sandal. Needle on left illustrates stitching through matted fiber base to produce the "braid" effect by means of a chain stitch; needle on right shows selvage stitch

Two partially burned sandals from the feet of burial 11 show a red painted trimming in the crease formed between this double selvage. Alternating human hair and yucca were used as the sewing elements of the selvage in one instance.

As the cohesiveness of the basic fiber mat was not particularly great and the appliquéd rows of stitches were in no way interlocked to give strength, additional sewing seems to have been called for. Here and there may be seen thin, 2-yarn, yucca cords running at right angles to the direction of the "braid" stitch.

These were probably added as sewing progressed. Fulton has illustrated them as holding the braided elements together.[252]

It may appear as though altogether too much space is being devoted to this sandal type. There are good reasons, however, for considering it in detail. In the first place, it is a sewed sandal, a new departure in Southwestern footgear techniques. Secondly, it has a high potential value, both culturally and temporally.

Heretofore, fragments of similar or identical sandals have been found in Gila Basin Hohokam sites. All pieces recovered have been with cremations where, by some curious quirk, the fibers were both incrusted and replaced with what appears to be siliceous material. Diagnosis of the weave in such material is most difficult even in the best preserved pieces, because all flexibility has been lost. Efforts at reconstructing the weaves were attempted in the Snaketown report[253] and these were shown as double warp affairs. In the light of the Ventana evidence, some doubt is cast on the correctness of this interpretation, particularly as the surface of the sintered pieces looks like those reported on here. That there was some variation in the technique is evident from the upper surface of a fragmentary sandal taken from the left foot of burial 34 (old female) shown in Plate 46, *e*. Analysis of it is impossible owing to its termite-riddled condition. The Winchester Cave specimen, already referred to, is the most nearly complete one recovered so far. Examination of the same, kindly made possible by Mr. W. S. Fulton, shows it was made by the process outlined here and not as originally described.

The best evidence of horizon for sewed sandals comes from their association with mummies. A pair were on the feet of burial 9, unfortunately damaged by a Papago fire built on this mummy's feet. There was also a badly worn pair, as well as several odd fragments, in a bundle with other things under this man's head. While the period when he lived cannot be accurately determined, I venture to say it was sometime between

★

252. *Ibid.*
253. H. S. Gladwin, *et al.*, 1937, p. 161, Fig. 60.

A. D. 1000 and 1400. At Snaketown the age of the fragments from cremations was late Colonial or early Sedentary Period. The Winchester Cave sandal is evidently from the Sedentary horizon as the associated Hohokam pottery is Sacaton Red-on-buff.[254]

Until contradictory evidence is found, the sandal may be considered to have been a Sedentary Period trait, and if any sandal lends distinctiveness to the Hohokam it is this type. Curiously, a sandal of apparent identical type occurs in Peru.[255] But direct examination of a complete and several fragmentary sandals[256] indicates that the manufacturing method was entirely different.

Sandal ties

On only a few sandals are the ties complete enough to indicate how they were attached to the foot. Basically there was a toe loop for one or more toes, centrally placed, and a heel loop, the two being variously joined with lashings running over the foot and around the ankle. Three ties complete enough for analysis are shown in Figure 103. On the fiber mat sandal (*a*)

★

254. W. S. Fulton, 1941, Pl. VII, lower left.

255. Handbook of the South American Indian, Vol. II, Pl. 59 (bottom, center), from Surco, Peru.

256. Courtesy American Museum of Natural History, New York.

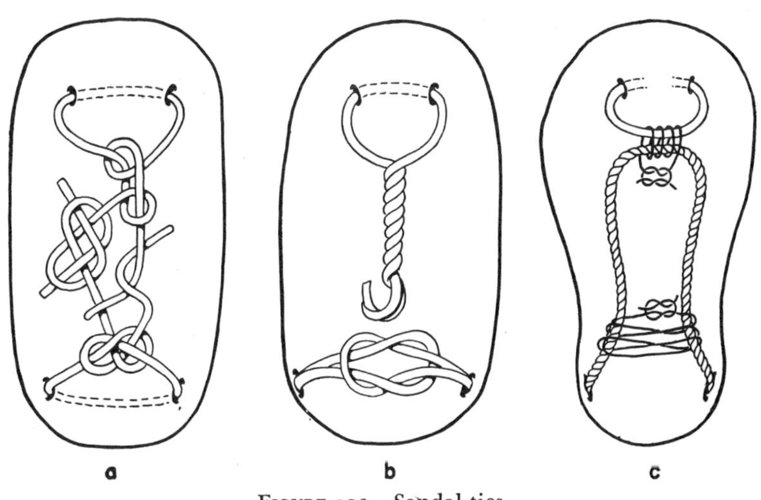

FIGURE 103. Sandal ties

two shredded leaves of yucca were stitched through the foundation and united above as shown. Tie (*b*), on a shredded leaf wickerwork sandal, has a toe loop with the two ends brought together and twisted. Evidently this was attached somehow to the heel loop composed of two doubled pieces, anchored to the warp frame. The only sewed sandal with a recognizable tie (*c*) has a toe loop, complete in itself, and a 4-ply cord fastened to the selvage near the heel, taken forward, lashed to the toe loop and returned to the heel on the opposite side. A criss-cross string around the main cord fell behind the heel when the sandal was worn. This method was well known in east-central Arizona.[257]

J. Personal Adornment

There is little information about how extensively personal ornaments were employed by the late prehistoric Ventana residents. The collection is pitiably lacking in the beads, pendants, and bracelets which normally accompany Hohokam sites in quantity. We do know that ears were pierced for pendants and that plugs were worn in noses. But out of thirty-nine burials, ornaments either on the body or included in the graves as offerings occurred in only one case. One is led to suspect that the Desert Hohokam were less addicted to personal decoration than were their River relatives.

Close inspection of the mummies has revealed no trace of face painting or tattooing, and the patchiness of the hair deprives us of all chances of reconstructing the mode of hairdress.

1. *Wig*

An outstanding piece is a human hair wig. It was found wrapped in a bundle, along with cloth, sandal remnants, sinew, bone awls, cactus spine needle, charm, etc. (Pl. 60) under the head of an old male (burial 9). This individual, with his nose plug, ear pendants, and sundry accessories, appears to have been a person of some note in his community. It should be made

★

257. E. W. Haury, 1934, pp. 66-68, Fig. 12.

clear from the start, therefore, that the wig, while it could have been worn as an adornment, more likely is to be linked with a deep-seated social practice. What this may have been will be judged later.

This wig is one of the most intricate and ingenious articles recovered from the cave. Original wear and tear, damage during interment, and the readily appreciated difficulty of unsnarling hair has hindered the technical analysis. A complete understanding of it was not developed even after extensive study.

Its overall length is .55 mm. (Pl. 47). The basic unit is a small (3 mm. wide on the average), 4-element, flat sennit, from which tufts of hair were dropped on one face as braiding progressed (Pl. 48, *a* and Fig. 104). The tufts (up to 120 mm. long)

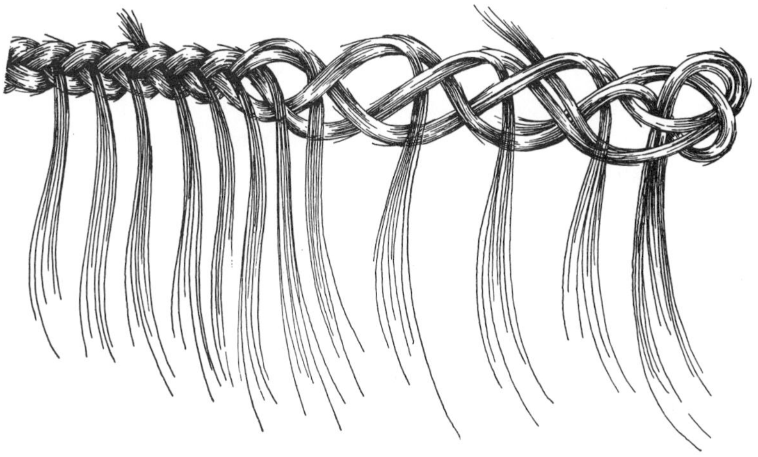

FIGURE 104. End of braid in human hair wig showing the method of tufting

from scores of braids form a bushy mat of hair which was exposed to view when the wig was worn and completely concealed the braids below. Braid ends were either tied or the two ends of a strand of hair were inserted in the braid a few centimeters above the end, worked into the sennit, and finally twisted together and tied with an overhand knot.

At the opposite ends, the braids were individually wrapped

with cotton cord and a dozen or so were brought together and joined to form a U-loop. Four such bunches make up the wig and a cotton cord is drawn through all of them, as is a length of 21-strand flat sennit. On one loop the pendant braids have been burned off and a second has almost entirely disintegrated.

To give the wig cohesiveness and to prevent the braids from parting, they were interlaced with cotton string. Two systems were used: (1) closely spaced twining with cotton string (Pl. 48, *b*) at the upper end, and (2) a rather loose and random gathering up of the braids with cotton string (Pl. 48, *c*). All details of this work are visible on the under-surface only.

It is most difficult to find any references in the literature dealing with modern Yuman and Piman people which might shed light on the possible meaning of this wig. Modern parallels do not appear to exist. Some practices among both groups may conceivably be related, but there is no way of determining this as a certainty. For example, the wig could be a ceremonial appliance, a forerunner of the hair robes worn by Kiliwa men in the "Talking with the Dead" ritual.[258] Spier mentions another possibility when he intimates that the Lower Colorado River tribes artificially lengthen their hair.[259] The Pimas did the same thing, using horsehair.[260] It is well established that many of the desert people cut off their hair, or singed it, as a sign of mourning when a member of the family died. Russell explicitly states that men "added the hair of their women, who trimmed their hair in mourning for lost relatives."[261] The Ventana wig has hair of variable shades, black to a deep reddish brown, suggesting that it did not all come from the same head; but if this is in any way connected with the wearing of hair in mourning, considerably more care was expended on it than was customary historically. The age of this wig may be set between A. D. 1000 and 1400.

★

258. P. Meigs, 1939, p. 52. "The sacred robes were composed of heavy tightly woven nets of mescal fiber, to which were attached closely spaced tufts of long, black, human hair. When worn only the hair must be visible. . . . No one knows how to make them. . . ."

259. L. Spier, 1933, p. 98.

260. F. Russell, 1908, p. 158.

261. *Ibid.*, pp. 158-159.

K. Objects from Insect Products

1. *Cocoon*

A favorite form of rattle among the Indians in southern Arizona and Sonora, Mexico, are strings of pebble-filled cocoons, generally wrapped around the calves and ankles of the legs. Russell states[262] that these "were obtained (by the Pima) from the Papagos or Yaqui of Sonora." The Ventana collection contains two cocoons found near the surface of the upper cave, which are from assemblies of the type still in use. The origin is certainly Papago. The cocoon is probably from the giant silkworm *(Saturniidae)*.[263]

2. *Lac*

The resinous secretion of the insect (*Tachardiella larrea*) which lives on the creosote bush was used practically in mending pottery. There is also a small hemisphere (diameter, 21 mm.) of this material. It is precisely made, pressed to form while plastic, but there is no indication as to its use.

Ventana Cave Textiles[264]

All textiles from Ventana Cave were found in the dry zone of the midden. Cloth of recent and historic times, both commercial and native, occurred in the thin layer of surface debris, and goods of prehistoric age were in the remainder of the dry level below, which has been dated from *ca.* A. D. 1 to 1400. It is doubtful if any of the prehistoric materials date before 800 or 900, and most of them likely fall between 1000 and 1400. Many of the textiles from the prehistoric stratum were found with or on burials, and some odd fragments came to light in the debris.

All textiles recovered are included in the following list. Historic materials are classified on the basis of plain or printed commercial fragments, or pieces of native weave. Prehistoric materials are classified on a basis of weave.

★

262. *Ibid.*, pp. 168-169.

263. Identification by Dr. L. P. Wehrle, Associate Entomologist, Agricultural Experiment Station, University of Arizona.

264. By Clara Lee Tanner, Assistant Professor of Anthropology, University of Arizona.

Historic Textiles		
Commercial		70
Plain	25	
Prints	45	
Native weave		2
Plain[265]	1	
Twill	1	
Total		72
Prehistoric Textiles		
Cloth		60
Plain weave	54	
Gauze weave	1	
Weft-wrap openwork	5	
Belts		9
Plain	3	
Braided	4	
Tapestry weaves	2	
Total		69

Historic Textiles

Associated with metal, glass, and pottery of historic age in the surface debris of Ventana Cave were found fragments of more than seventy different textiles. An analysis of these[266] reveals the following general commercial types: printed calico, which is in the majority, percale, men's shirting, shepherd's check, mull, and denim. Also a cotton piece of native manufacture, doubtless made during historic times, was found with these. Oddities include a piece of very poor quality and much-frayed binding.

The term calico has been applied to a material in common use before better woven, heavier, and better printed percales were manufactured. Most of these cotton prints may be anywhere from several to fifty or sixty years of age. A few pieces may be as old as seventy-five to eighty years. Minute floral pat-

★

265. Considered to be historic as it was found in an ash daub from the cliff wall, most of which are thought to be of recent origin.

266. Discussions were held on the historic materials with Miss Edith S. Ranney and Miss Mildred Jensen, both of the Home Economics Department, University of Arizona, and Mrs. Edna Boyd, Tucson.

terned prints of sixty years ago are represented (Pl. 49, *a*), as are the poorer dyes and odd colors of the same day. What is thought to be the oldest piece has an interesting fagoting pattern. Fragments of very recent date include a heavily "loaded" print (Pl. 49, *b*), and shepherd's check in blue and white (Pl. 49, *c*). On the prints, both hand and machine sewing are to be noted, certainly the work of Papago Indians as there are no records that the cave was ever used by anyone else. The numerous snippings suggest that sewing was done in the cave, doubtless during cactus fruit gathering expeditions. A hand sewed sleeve of "mutton leg" style, popular among the Papago Indians for a long period of time, is especially noteworthy.

The fragment of twill which is like balbriggan (Pl. 49, *d*) closely resembles a material which was in common use some thirty-five to forty years ago for men's underwear. However, in the West the cloth in question continued to be popular for the same purpose among cowboys until quite recently. The same survival is likely among the Papago cowboys. It is well known that many materials were sold to out-of-the-way Indian trading posts long after their popularity or use had dwindled elsewhere.[267] Burlap (Pl. 49, *e*) is, of course, one of our commonest fabrics and its presence in the cave is not surprising.

An interesting example of possible native weaving of historic times is the small fragment of brown and tan twill illustrated in Plate 49, *f*. It proves to be made, in part at least, of wool. The weaving is regular; the texture of the cloth is quite coarse. The two colors are woven in such manner as to emphasize the diagonal twill.

The historic textiles from Ventana Cave, far behind those of pre-Columbian times in importance, illustrate, nevertheless, a few of the types of manufactured cloth used by the Papago; they corroborate the general conclusion of occupation of the cave for the past fifty or sixty years; and they suggest the possible continuation of native weaving in this vicinity into relatively late historic years.

★

267. This same point must be kept in mind relative to the probable age of all other historic commercial textiles at Ventana Cave.

Prehistoric Textiles

The finest collection to date of prehistoric textiles from the Hohokam area was excavated at Ventana Cave. At the present writing the fabrics from southern Arizona have been too fragmentary and too few in number to give us a good picture of the Hohokam textile industry. These circumstances are due to the open nature of Hohokam sites plus the common custom among these people of cremating the dead. Both of these conditions are overcome in the protected and dry cave and in the presence of many inhumations.

Although actual examples of weaving are rare in Hohokam ruins, the excellent quality of the few pieces found, and indirectly, the textiles of the Anasazi adjoining the Hohokam, forecast the variety and abundance which might be expected in this area. Charred fragments and impressions at Snaketown;[268] cotton seed and textile impressions at a Colonial Period Hohokam site;[269] fragments of a belt decorated with zigzag patterns woven in and with the end embroidered, and a second "lace-like piece," described by Fewkes from Casa Grande;[270] chance recoveries of fabrics by the Hemenway Expedition in the Salt River Valley;[271] numerous spindle whorls at many Hohokam sites; and even historic reference to the cultivation and use of cotton,[272] all would seem to point to the prehistoric development of this craft among the Hohokam and its survival into recent times.

Technical equipment for weaving recovered in Ventana was limited to several clay spindle whorls (Fig. 84, *a, b*). As yet, no direct remains have been found in the Hohokam area indicative of the loom type used by them. There is, however, indirect evidence which, together with early historical references, may be

★

268. H. S. Gladwin, *et al.*, 1937, pp. 161-162.

269. V. Jones, 1936, p. 5.

270. J. W. Fewkes, 1912, pp. 147-148.

271. E. W. Haury, 1945, pp. 163, 172, 178, 201-202.

272. V. Jones, 1936, p. 3, summarizes the observations of Bartlett, Emory, and Whipple as reporting "that considerable cotton was grown and used by the Pima at about 1850."

significant. Reports written between 1848 and 1908[273] constantly refer to the horizontal loom among the Pima-Papago peoples. The probability that this was the aboriginal form also is seen in the dimensions of the loom products, especially blankets. Mrs. Kate Peck Kent, currently making a comprehensive study of native Southwestern cotton textiles, has pointed out that four of the five Ventana blankets are "markedly different from the overall dimensions of blankets woven by peoples farther north," *i. e.*, within the Anasazi region where the vertical loom was used.[274] The northern examples are nearly square and, not infrequently, the weft dimension is slightly the longer. The four blankets with burial 22 in Ventana contrast sharply in that the weft stretches are much smaller than the warp stretches. The long, narrow cloth may well be the result of horizontal-loom weaving.

The probable size of the loom is indicated by some of the blankets already mentioned. Several pieces, minus selvages, are more than 1.30 m., which is in excess of the loom width suggested by Haury on the basis of textiles from Canyon Creek Ruin.[275] Another example, a much mended robe from burial 22 (Pl. 50), measures 2.12 m. in length, selvage to selvage, but the width is not determinable because of its shredded condition. This is the greatest loom length recorded at Ventana. Smaller fabrics are also found, one, for example, showing a width of .21 m. and a length of .70 m., all selvages being present.

Both Beals[276] and Russell[277] intimate that, historically, belts were made on the horizontal loom by the Papago. Goddard,[278] however, states definitely that the belt loom was used for the making of both belts and head bands. Several examples of belts from Ventana would indicate that Goddard's statement could be applied to the probable ancestors of the Papago, the prehistoric inhabitants of Ventana, as well.

★

273. V. Jones, 1936, p. 9.
274. C. A. Amsden, 1934, pp. 24-25.
275. E. W. Haury, 1934, p. 89.
267. R. L. Beals, 1934, p. 27.
277. F. Russell, 1908, pp. 150-152.
278. P. E. Goddard, 1931, p. 136.

As to primary evidences relative to weaving, as actually done at or near Ventana, there are the following points to be considered: one cotton boll (Pl. 19, *g*), some cotton yarn, and the large number of textiles themselves. Cotton string is conspicuously rare; other and more durable fibers were generally used in the making of cordage. Actual cultivation of cotton in this region has not been known since the early years of this century. As mentioned above, some writers report extensive cultivation of cotton by the Pimas[279] in 1850, and Papagos today say that cotton was formerly grown.[280] These facts, coupled with the many evidences of aboriginal weaving, would, therefore, lead one to conclude that earlier cultivation on an appreciable scale in the Hohokam area was highly probable, especially along the Gila and Salt rivers.

Cotton is and has been important in ritual. Castetter and Bell indicate early usage in ceremonial ways: "Papago informants stated cotton was used ceremoniously on their sticks to symbolize clouds."[281] In the Wiikita today it is used to make piles of fluffy clouds.[282] As ritual materials tend to survive in unchanged form for a longer while than many another culture trait, it is suggested that cotton is by no means new to the Papago.

The fibers mainly employed in the weaving industry at Ventana were cotton and yucca. Each was used in separate pieces, and there seems to have been no combining of the two materials in one piece of cloth as reported by Haury at Canyon Creek Ruin[283] and by Fewkes at Casa Grande.[284] Yucca was used sparingly as only several pieces of cloth of this fiber were noted.

Quality of cord or yarn used in textiles at Ventana varies considerably. Some were tightly spun, presumably by a spindle; other threads are heavy and loosely twisted, either by spindle or by hand. Most yarns were evenly spun throughout, while

★

279. V. Jones, 1936, p. 3.
280. E. F. Castetter and W. H. Bell, 1942, p. 105.
281. E. F. Castetter and W. H. Bell, 1942, p. 198.
282. J. Chesky, 1942, p. 3.
283. E. W. Haury, 1934, p. 102.
284. J. W. Fewkes, 1912, says that the combination of cotton and agave fiber "was common."

a few were poorly prepared, being fat at one point and lean and weak at another. Although the weft is quite generally heavier than the warp, there are many cases where warp and weft are indistinguishable as to quality. Except for selvage and end cords, which are usually 4-yarn, 1-yarn warps and wefts predominate. One exception to this is the 2-yarn yucca belt on burial 2 (Pl. 54, *a*).

Thread counts are indicators of not only the quality of the weave but also of the quality of the thread employed by the weaver. Counts vary considerably, from 20 warps and 17 wefts per square 2.50 cm. (approximately 1 square inch) in the coarser fabrics to 38 warps and 32 wefts for the same area in the finer textiles. A piece-by-piece survey of the Ventana collection by Mrs. Kent[285] shows that, almost without exception, the warp number exceeds weft number over comparable dimensions by ratios ranging from 1:2 to 5:7. Although the series is small (24 specimens), here again there may be a suggestion that Hohokam textiles were woven in a different manner than Anasazi textiles, characterized by a more nearly square count of warp and weft elements. Mrs. Kent points out further that Peruvian belt-loom plain fabrics and contemporary Southwestern belt-loom products show the same dominance of warps over wefts seen in the Ventana fabrics.

Most of the yarn employed in these textiles appears to be natural in color. Some discoloration has taken place through the centuries, but, despite this condition, a dull white predominates. Yarns were sometimes dyed before weaving, as unwoven but dyed threads from the refuse would indicate. In a few solidly colored pieces, red or brown, irregularities in color suggest the use of a dye after the whole fabric was woven. In one example only is the warp lighter in color than the weft. Most of the brown cloth comes from burial 22, there being two distinct shades, a dark brown and a rusty brown.

One other color was used at Ventana, namely, a light red. This was employed for both cloth and cordage. The latter was

★

285. K. P. Kent, in preparation.

used chiefly for sewing, as in uniting two torn edges, and sometimes it was aimlessly sewed across a fragment of cloth.

All pieces of the red cloth are in plain weave, coarsely done, and they have extremely weak wefts. The most interesting example is a red robe or blanket found with burial 22 (Pl. 50, *a*). In places, the soft weft yarns have completely disintegrated and the owner had mended it either by sewing or by twining (Pl. 50, *b*), to prolong its life. It was finally rolled into a bundle and used as a pillow for a deceased child.

Weaves—Several different weaves are represented in the Ventana textiles. These include plain, gauze, weft-wrap openwork, and several belt-loom types. High technical ability is demonstrated in these styles. An important addition to aboriginal Southwestern textile studies is made here, for the Ventana specimens extend geographically some of the more elaborate techniques, as gauze and weft-wrap openwork. In his report on Canyon Creek Ruin, which well summarized the situation prior to Ventana excavation, Haury says, "The Southwestern occurrences of gauze weaving, so far, are pretty well confined to the east-central part of Arizona."[286]

1. Plain Weave. Plain weave cloth shows some variations in texture, attributable to thread sizes and compactness in the weave itself. Typical examples of coarse and fine weaves will be seen in Plate 51, *a, b*. Usually the warp threads tend to be a fraction smaller in diameter than the weft, due to a tighter twisting of the yarn in spinning. The finer warps result in a somewhat greater relative spacing than is seen in the weftage in spite of the fact that warp strands commonly outnumber wefts, as already indicated. Being fatter, the weftage gave the cloth body while warps imparted the strength. The loose spinning of wefts apparently accounts for their extensive disintegration, so characteristic in Ventana textiles. This is clearly visible in Plates 50, *b* and 51, *b*.

Several cloth fragments reveal the use of different colored

286. E. W. Haury, 1934, p. 97.

warps and wefts, for example, light colored warps and dark brown wefts, which impart a simple pattern.

A variation in plain weave is seen in several pieces from burial 22 in which two weft threads were carried over paired warps.

Since most blankets were done in plain weave, a word should be included here on their sizes. As previously stated, the length (warp dimension) exceeds the width (weft dimension). Three pieces with burial 22 will illustrate the point.

	Length	*Width*
(1)	2.04 m.	.74 m. (incomplete)
(2)	1.22 m.	.38 m.
(3)	1.15 m. (incomplete)	.38 m.

2. Gauze Weave. Simple gauze weave can be defined as follows: two warps are twisted in such fashion that when one or more weft threads pass betwen them they retain this twisted position. As there are usually three or more wefts done in plain weave between each gauze weft, the result is an openwork effect. The openwork lines run from selvage to selvage, following the weft lines in the textile, and resulting in a lace-like banding.

A most interesting example of gauze weave from Ventana is in the form of a poncho from burial 22, a long, slender piece too small for anyone but a child. A slit torn or cut slightly off center and from side to side (Pl. 52) suggests its use as a poncho. The piece measures .70 m. in length and about .22 m. in width. In general it resembles the simpler type of gauze weave from the Tonto Ruin[287] except that the width of plain bands between the single wefts which hold the warps in twisted position is more irregular in the Ventana example. A few heavy brown wefts are inserted toward one end of the poncho, seemingly for no purpose, for they in no way add to the design scheme.

Near the center of this small poncho there is also an openwork design done in the technique described below. The head slit was made just to the side of this pattern so that when worn it would fall over the child's chest.

★

287. *Ibid.*

3. Weft-wrap Openwork. A second decorative technique found at Ventana is weft-wrap openwork. There are a few examples of this weave, although the exact number cannot be determined because of the possibility that several fragments may belong to the same original cloth. This technique resembles eyelet embroidery except that it is done as the worker weaves. Let us say that the working weft is to utilize four each of the warp and preceding weft strands. As this weft is woven in, it deviates from the plain weave as follows: first it enwraps (all at once or over-1-under-1) the next four warp strands, then drops down and enwraps the last four weft strands. Each completed wrapping is pulled taut so that an opening is produced wherever this is done.[288] The weaver plans each of these openings so as to make distinct designs, as triangles, frets, diamonds, T-shaped patterns, and zigzags, or combinations of several of these. Weft-wrap designs are done all over the woven piece, or are confined to border patterns, or as centered motives.

The child's poncho (Pl. 52, *b*) is a good example of this technique. The weft-wrap pattern is produced during the actual weaving process, with no introduction of additional threads. The presence of selvages proves this, for the wefts can be traced back and forth in regular order as part of the whole weft pattern.

Unfortunately, other examples of weft-wrap are in such poor condition as to deny complete identification of pattern. One fragment, from burial 34, measures approximately .43 m. in each dimension, only one selvage being present (Pl. 53). An all-over pattern, exceptionally intricate, is made up of opposed rows of small joined triangles, interspersed with keys, which run in oblique lines across the textile (Fig. 105). A second piece, from burial 9, dark brown in color, shows two rows of joined and opposed oblique triangles, but more distinct than the textile above (Fig. 106). This specimen also illustrates a variation of the weft-wrap technique in achieving larger openings in the manner illustrated in Figure 107. An additional

★

288. For a more detailed and illustrated explanation see *Ibid.*, pp. 91-94; C. B. Cosgrove, 1947, pp. 76-79.

FIGURE 105. Reconstructed design on weft-wrap open-work textile shown in Plate 53. Hachured parts of design are restored. *Courtesy Mrs. Kate Peck Kent*

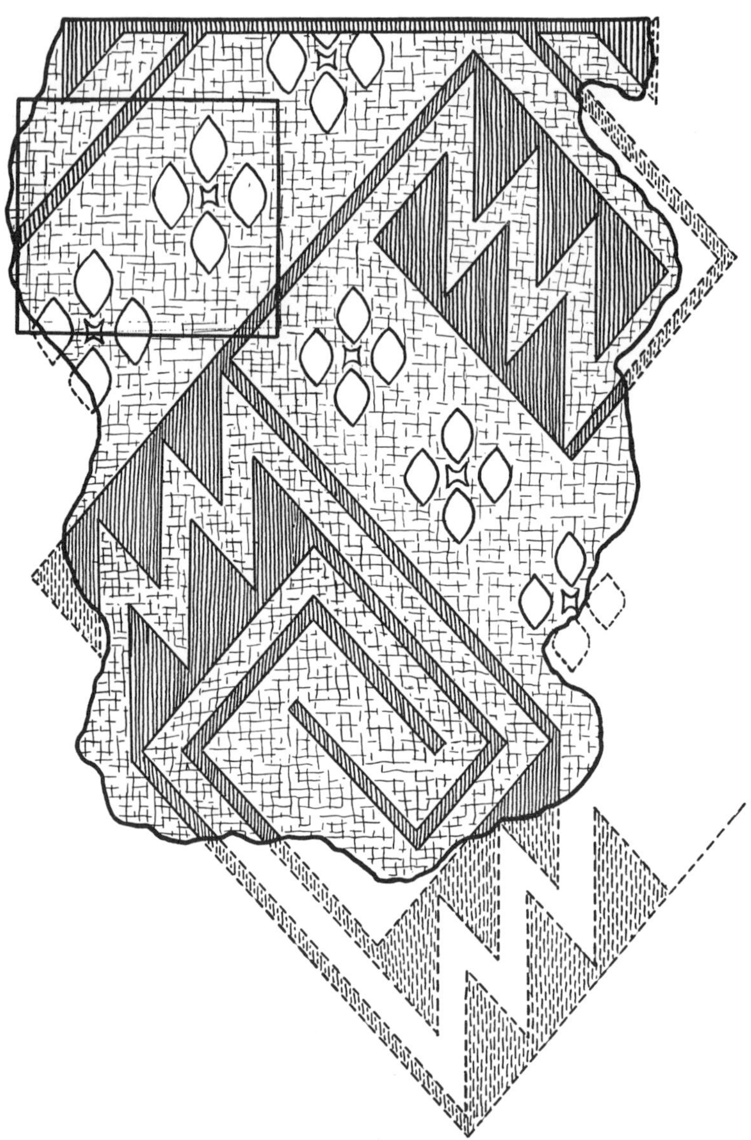

FIGURE 106. Fragment of cotton blanket with burial 9 showing design layout in weft-wrap technique. Boxed area (upper left) is enlarged in Figure 107 to illustrate how pattern was made. *Courtesy Mrs. Kate Peck Kent*

fragment shows a diamond pattern in connective arrangement. The presence of this weave at Ventana extends its distribution into a new locality, for the southernmost site previously reported was Casa Grande.[289] The Casa Grande and Snaketown examples and those from Ventana Cave are indicative of the fact that the Hohokam were either well acquainted with the technique or were in direct touch with the producers of it.

Still another design is produced by a technique related to weft-wrap. It uses a loose wrapping, more on the order of an overcasting of individual threads.[290] The result is a soft outline to the eyelet and not the heavy ridged outline noticeable in the weft-wrap. A border of this appears on one of the weft-wrap pieces.

★

289. W. Hough, 1914, pp. 76, 78-79.
290. H. S. Gladwin, *et al.*, 1937, p. 161.

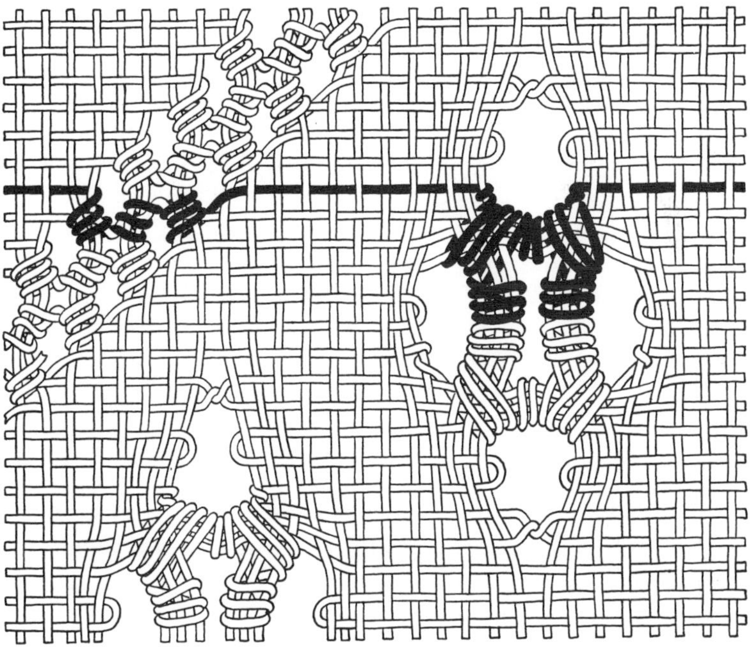

FIGURE 107. Weft-wrap openwork technique employed in blanket design shown in Figure 106. *Courtesy Mrs. Kate Peck Kent*

An interesting feature in connection with the fancy weave textiles is that they have a higher thread count as a whole, while the plain weaves present a wider range in thread count, with many low ones. In the gauze weave, there is an estimated 30 warps and 20 wefts per 2.50 cm. (approximately 1 inch). In the weft-wrap textiles there are thread counts of 29 to 34 warps and usually 26 wefts per 2.50 cm. Of course, this is to be expected, for, as a general rule, it is the better weaver who has the imagination and ability to wander from the well worn paths of traditional techniques.

Belts—1. Plain Weave. Certainly the belt-loom was used to produce the belts found at Ventana, and from all indications remained popular into historic times among the Papago. Two specimens show the warps, but the wefts are hidden. In one fine complete belt, apparently of yucca fiber, from burial 6 (Pl. 54, *a*), the thread count is 23 warps and 7 wefts per 2.50 cm. The length of this belt is 2.80 m., the width, 2.50 cm., the ends being finished in single and double braids respectively, the latter knotted at the end. The method of weaving this belt is shown in Figure 108, which employs both a plain weave and a gauze technique.

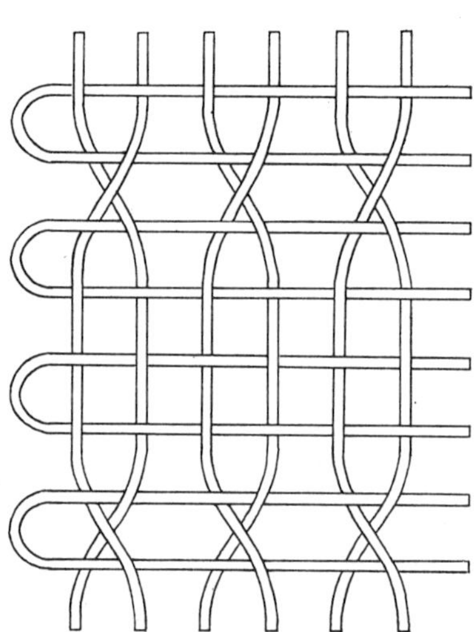

FIGURE 108. Technique used in weaving belt shown in Plate 54, *a*

The second belt, of soft fiber in plain weave, is somewhat narrower and has a thread count of 10 warps and 5 wefts per 2.50 cm. The threads are 2-yarn.

2. Braided. Braided sashes resembling the Ventana Cave examples are made by the Hopi today. The technique involves the use of a horizontal loom, a continuous warp, and a number of

small rods which serve as heddles. Rods are inserted as the braiding or manipulation of the thread progresses.[291]

Braided belts and bands (Pl. 54, *b*) are much more common than the above type. Many fragments of braiding were found in burial 9, some others in burial 6. These pieces vary in width from 1.30 cm. to 3.20 cm. Fragments of several belts are more than 45 cm. in length; total length cannot be computed for no complete example remains. Some are made of natural cotton, some of yucca fiber. The braided belts and bands are made up of from 21 to 43 threads, most of them of double twist yarn.

3. Tapestry. A small yucca fiber (?) belt or band (Pl. 55) might well be classed as a prehistoric "sampler," for it incorporates three styles of weaving. The warp web supports, in the central section, a closely packed decorative field, done in an interlocking tapestry weave (Fig. 109, *a*), using natural color and black-dyed wefts. Diagonally across the field are two lines which produce a ribbed effect (Fig. 109, *b*). This was achieved

★ 291. See K. P. Kent, 1940, pp. 46-50, for detailed description and illustrations.

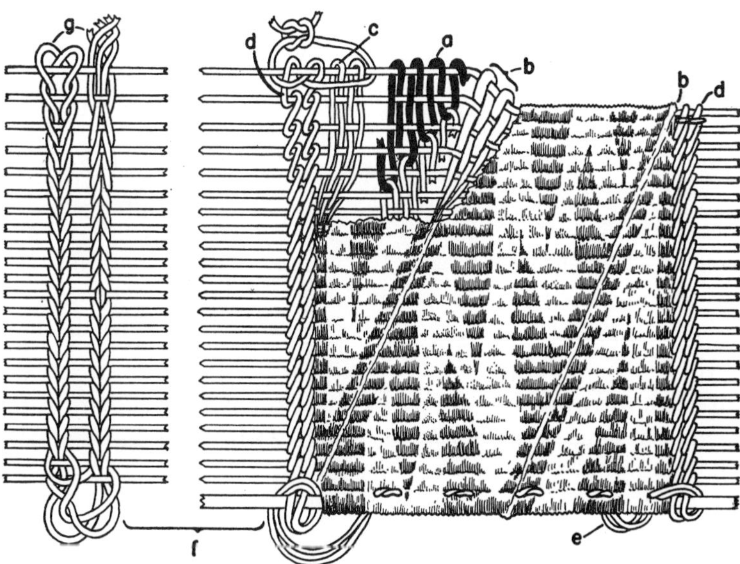

FIGURE 109. Weaving techniques in belt-like specimen shown in Plate 55

by inserting four wefts larger in diameter than the wefts in the body of the piece. Apart from the relief thus obtained, these zones are interesting in that the wefts do not run at right angles to the warps, as is the case with the wefts producing the design (Fig. 109, *c*). The tapestry section is bordered by paired rows of wrap-twining (Fig. 109, *d*), the two cords of one border having been sewed through the fabric before passing on to make the matching border (Fig. 109, *e*). Unwoven zones (Fig. 109, *f*) adjoin the tapestry and toward the end of the warp these elements are held in position by double rows of plain twined cords (Fig. 109, *g*).

To all appearances this specimen is incomplete and there are no indications as to its possible use. The piece is so out of keeping with the rest of the textiles from Ventana Cave and so strongly favors the early Anasazi (Basketmaker) technique of belt weaving that it may be identified with that culture.

Selvage Treatment—Selvages are varied in the cotton textiles. Some are very heavy and others are extremely light. Good stout cord is used. Some selvage cords are made of paired 2-ply strings twisted together, others of pairs of 4-yarn string. Ends are finished, as a rule, by the use of cords heavier than warp or weft, which are twisted together. Each of these is caught through the alternate loops of warp yarns.

Mending—Evidences of mending are found on a large number of cotton textiles. However, mending is not the explanation for a number of cases where heavy threads are aimlessly sewed back and forth through the cloth. A few examples of mending follow. In one fragment, from burial 34, a fairly heavy 2-yarn thread is sewed in half-running, half-back stitch, slightly gathering the cloth, obviously with the idea in mind of making more sturdy the worn parts. A mend in a small blanket fragment from burial 17 is made with a back stitch. Otherwise most of the mending shows a careless sewing together of torn edges or of areas weakened by wear, without benefit of stitch type.

The red robe from burial 22 (Pl. 50) shows the most amazing piece of mending. In places the weft threads have entirely

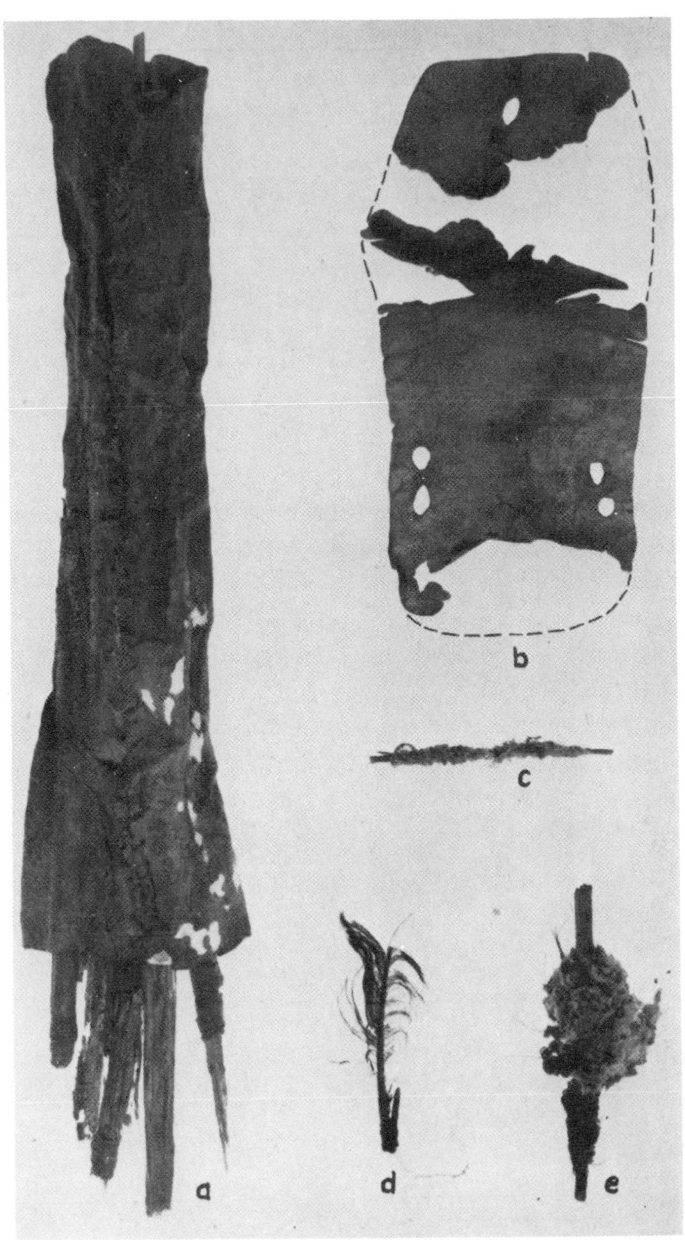

PLATE 39

Leather and feather objects from the upper layers of the midden. Quiver with reed arrows, *a;* sandal, *b;* feathered stick, *c;* feather with shaft doubled back and wrapped, *d,* feathered plume, *e.* Length of *a,* 305 mm.

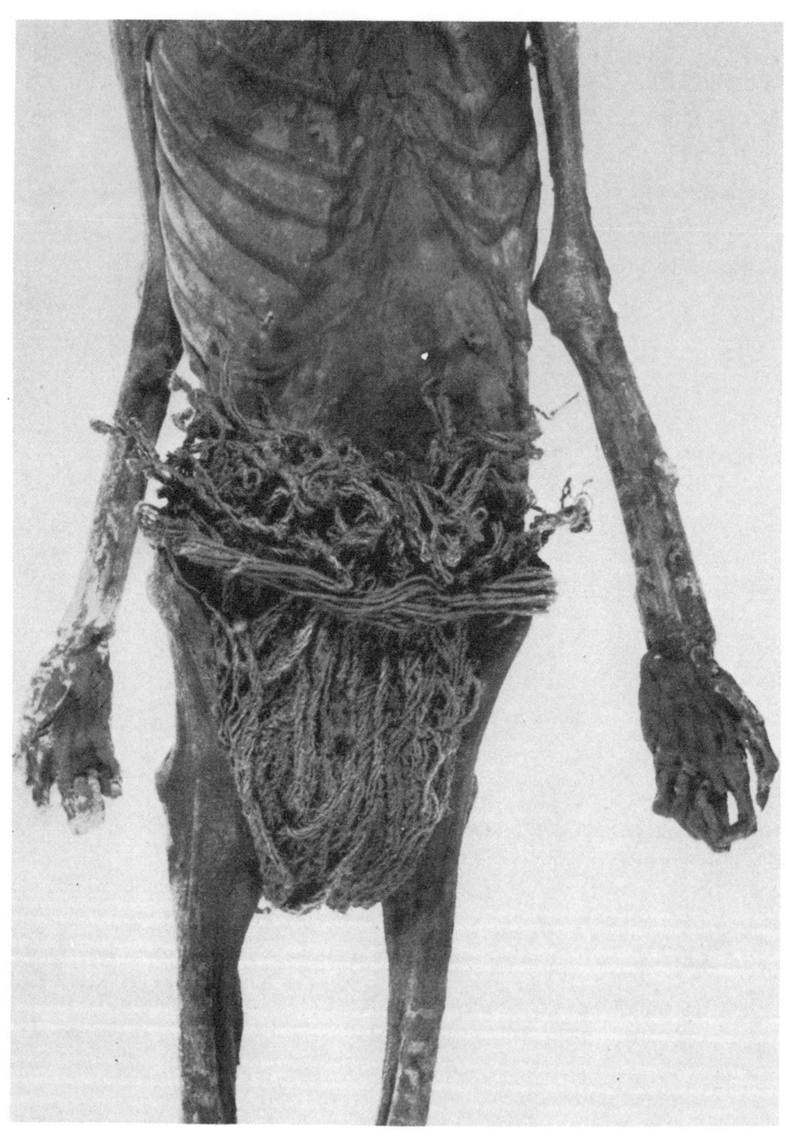

Plate 40

Typical breech cover worn by occupants of Ventana Cave of about A.D. 1000 to 1400 (burial 6, a girl of about five years).

Plate 41

Willow bark (?) breech clout. Length, 270 mm.

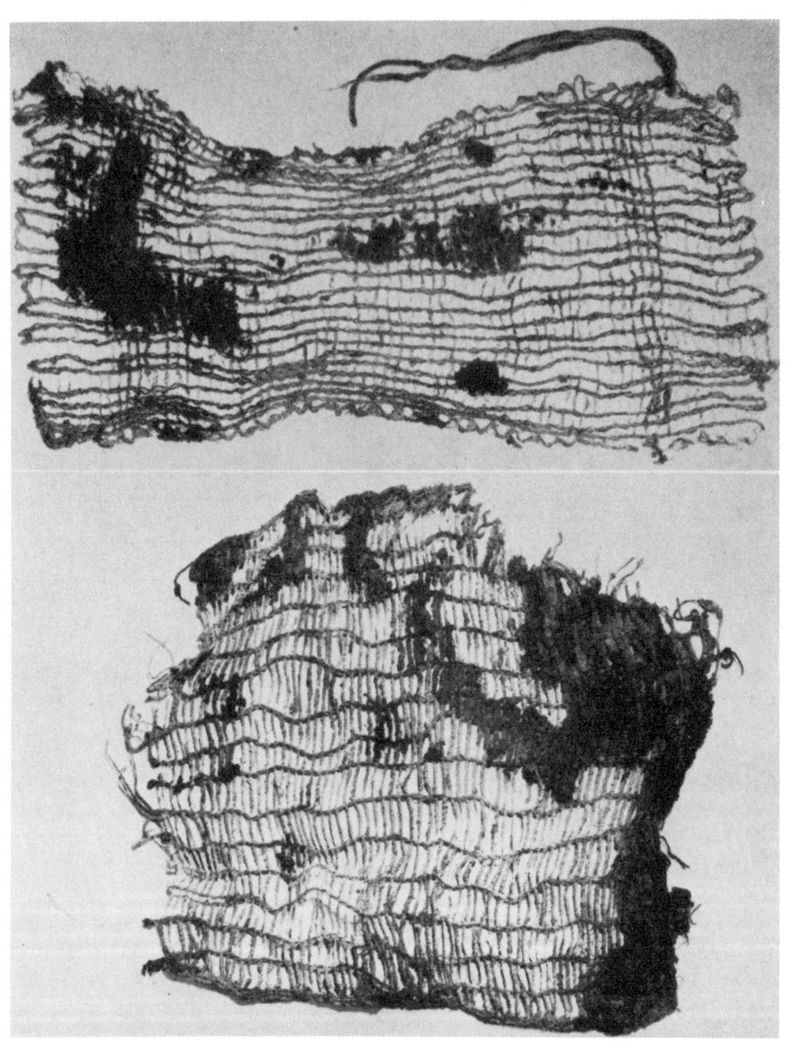

PLATE 42

Fur robes: *a* (Upper), with burial 6 (child); .35x.75 m., milk weed base, 2-yarn framing cords, body cords tufted, cotton cloth strip tie.

b (Lower), with burial 2 (young adult female); .81x.85 m., yucca fiber for all cords, frame and body cords 2-yarn wrapped with fur strips, 2-yarn twining cords.

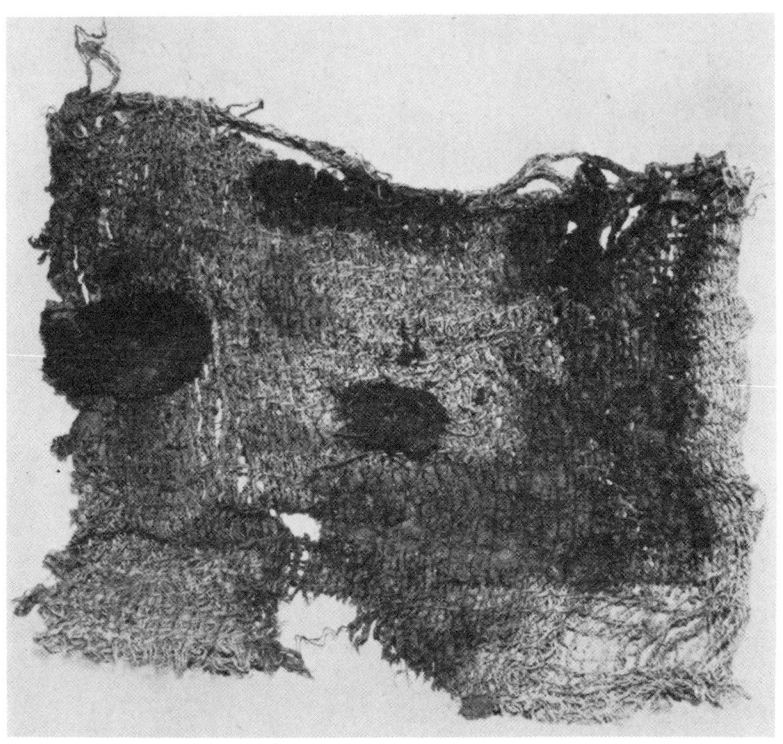

PLATE 43

Fur robe with burial 9 (adult male); .55x.85 m., yucca fiber for all cords; fur cords, 2 2-yarn skin wrapped before twisting; twining cords, 2-yarn paired.

PLATE 44

Sandals from the upper layers of the midden. Natural matted fiber, *a;* the same with stitched reinforcing, *b;* wickerwork, whole yucca leaf warp, whole leaf weft, *c;* shredded leaf weft, *d*. Length of *a,* 220 mm.

PLATE 45

Sandals from the upper layers of the midden: wickerwork (bark strips), *a, b;* heel pad on wickerwork sandal, *c;* wickerwork, cordage warp and bark strip weft, *d;* same with gut weft, *e.* Length of *a,* 120 mm.

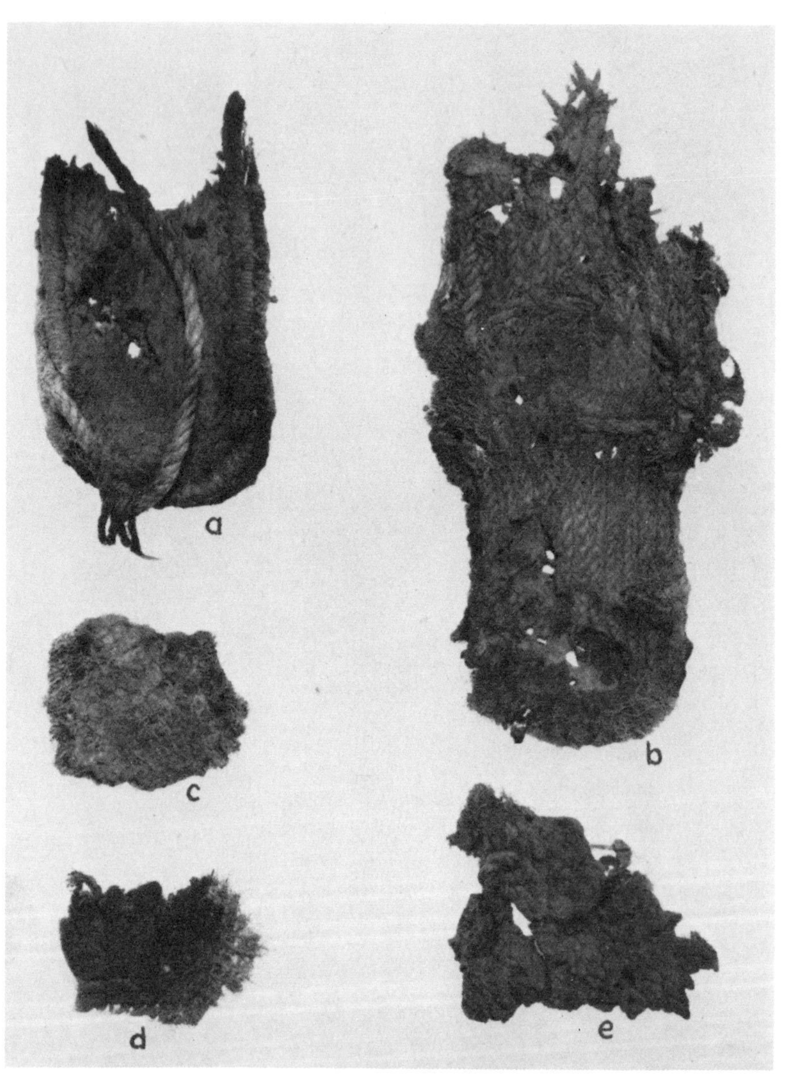

PLATE 46

Sewed sandals from the upper layers of the midden. Braided effect is seen on these sandals, *a, b;* under-surface, *c;* sole partially dissected showing matted fiber (right and lower edge), *d;* variation of weave, *e*. Length of *b*, 190 mm.

PLATE 47

Human hair wig found with burial 9. Length, .55 m.

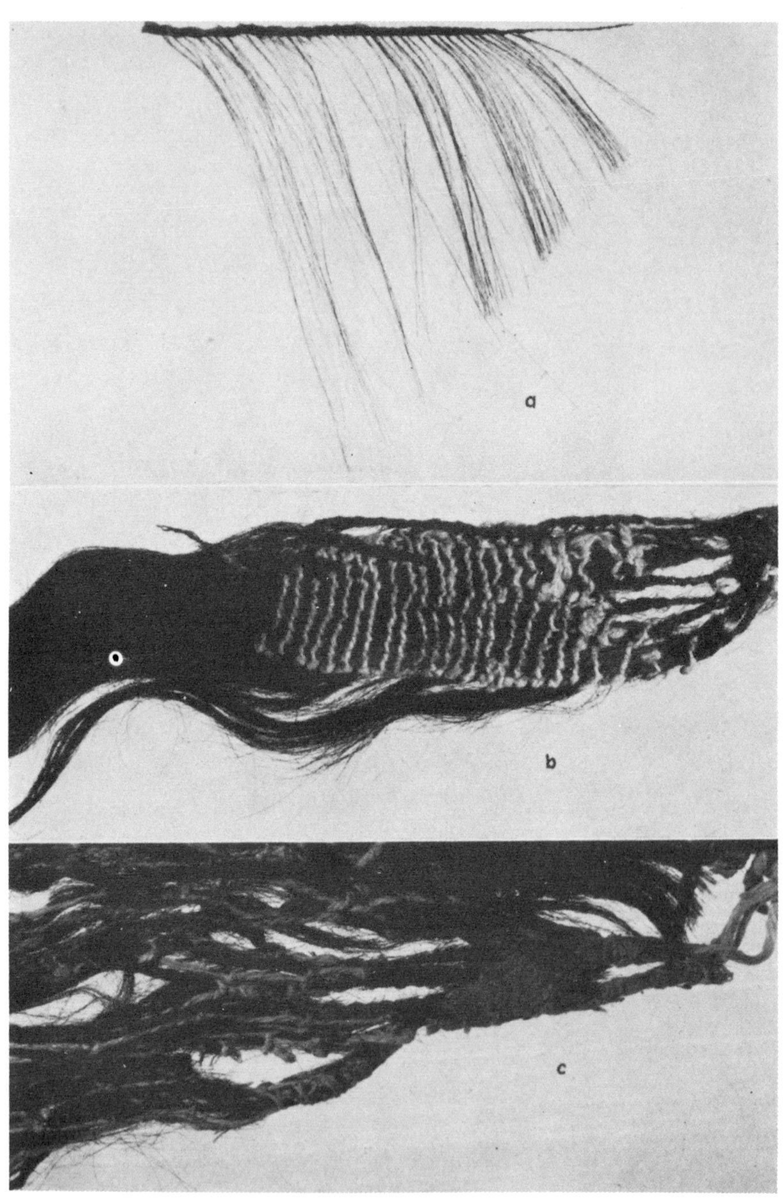

PLATE 48

Details of human hair wig. Tufted braids, *a;* cotton string twining uniting braids into larger units, *b;* alternate method of uniting braids, *c.* Length of *a,* 120 mm.

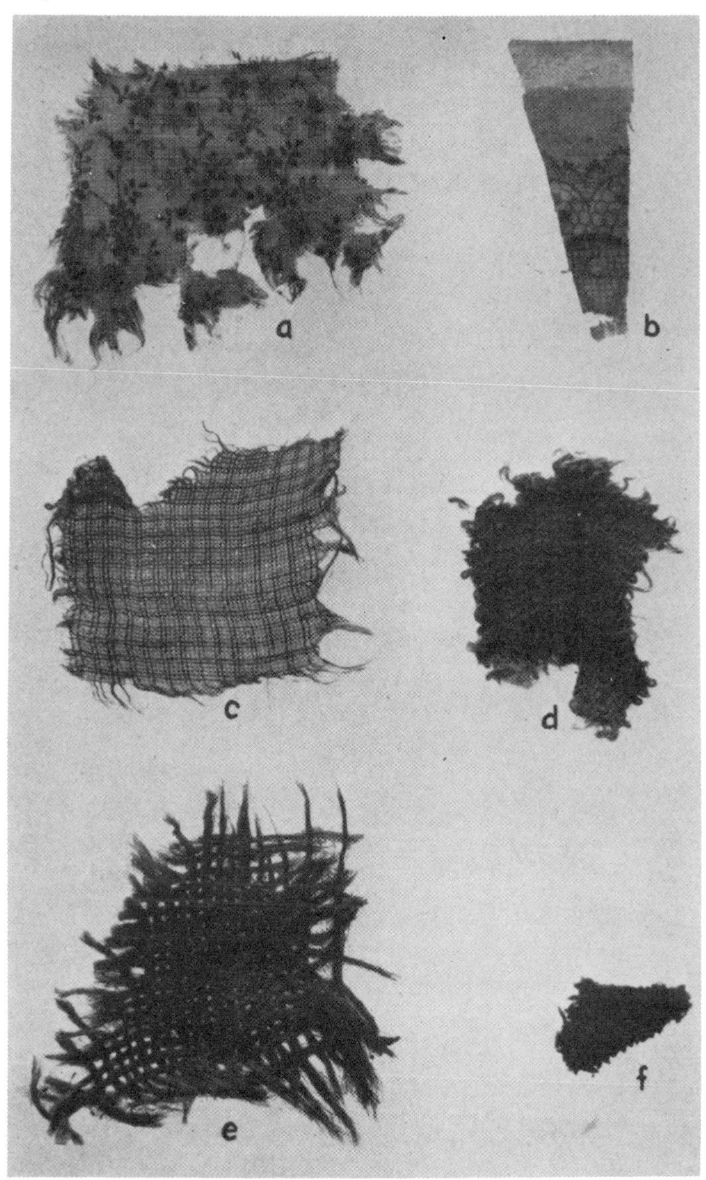

PLATE 49

Historic textiles: Calico, *ca.* 60 years old, *a;* a modern, heavily "loaded" print, probably no more than several years old, *b;* shepherd's check, *c;* a twill which resembles balbriggan, *d;* burlap, *e;* fragment of native woven cloth, probably of historic times, *f.* Length of *b,* 50 mm.

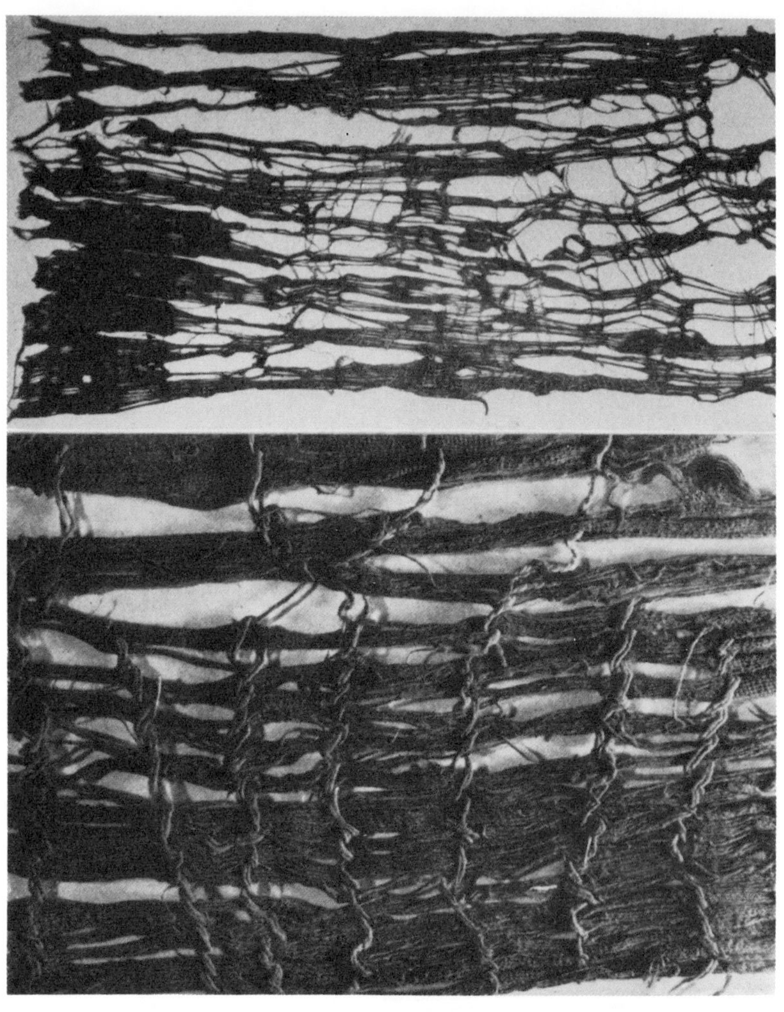

PLATE 50

Red robe or blanket from burial 22. General appearance (full length, selvage to selvage, 2.12 m.), *a* (Upper); detail, showing method of mending, *b* (Lower).

PLATE 51

Plain weave textiles: plain weave, coarse, *a;* plain weave, fine, *b*. Length of *b,* 145 mm.

PLATE 52

Child's poncho, from burial 22: full view, length, .70 m., *a* (Upper); detail of neck slit and weft-wrap openwork design, *b* (Lower).

Plate 53

Textile in weft-wrap technique with a key or meander pattern. From burial 34. Width, 430 mm.

PLATE 54

Belts: belt-loom product of yucca fiber (burial 2), *a;* braided belt fragment, cotton (burial 9), *b.* Length of *a,* 2.80 m.

disappeared and the mender twined the remaining warp threads together. Practically the entire robe is mended in this manner, save for a small unworn portion at each end. The mender carried her double twining threads on into the adjoining unworn section of the cloth, simulating the twining effect by an evident sewing with two needles. Pieces of dark brown cloth from the same burial are mended in identical fashion.

In summary of mending, the following stitches were known and used: even and uneven running stitches, half back stitch, twining in weftless sections and its counterpart as done with a needle in unworn textiles, overcasting, oblique running stitch, and, in one instance, a cross stitch.

A few general statements can be made in conclusion. First, the prehistoric textiles of Ventana date largely between A.D. 1000 and 1400, with the possible exception of the interlocking tapestry belt which, as mentioned above, seems by type to be of greater antiquity. These textiles indicate a high development of the craft among the Hohokam. They point to a knowledge of most of the techniques and skills of this art familiar to the Anasazi, for, with the exception of tie-dying and slit tapestry, a favorable comparison of the industry in the two areas can be made. This introduces an important problem. The most highly developed of the Anasazi textiles belong to the southern part of the Pueblo area, adjacent to the Hohokam region. Were the Hohokam, then, the leaders in the textile industry, and were they the teachers of the Anasazi? Obviously additional excavation and investigation will do much to solve this problem.

PART VI

Burials and Pictographs

BURIALS

It will be recalled that, during the first visit to Ventana Cave, scattered human bones were seen on the surface, forecasting the recovery of burials. Excavation had scarcely begun before a workman found one, and four others came to light during the first day. All told, thirty-nine burials were recovered, not counting a few which had been completely scattered. The bodies, in ten instances well mummified, together with their accompaniments, have added much to our knowledge of material possessions of the people and particularly of the racial characteristics. The latter are treated separately in a special study by Dr. Norman E. Gabel (p. 473).

All of the bodies were interred in pre-Spanish times, thirty-six being in the upper pottery-bearing zone, and three were found well down in the debris of the pre-ceramic people. A more precise appraisal of the age will be given shortly. There was no indication whatever that the Papago have used the cave as a burial place, a fortunate situation for us, as otherwise the excavations would certainly have come to an enforced stop.

In spite of the relatively high number of graves the cave was not a burial cave in the strict sense of the word. The dead were put down under the very feet of the people who occupied it, attested to by the extensive accumulation of everyday trash contemporaneous with the burials. Evidently the occupants held no fear of the dead. This is at odds with our evidence from such ruins as Jackrabbit and Valshni,[1] where, collectively, only four burials were recovered. It appears as though the custom was to inter them some distance from the village.

The burials were about evenly distributed through the northeastern half of the upper cave and all of the lower cave (Fig. 110). There seems to have been some conscious effort not to deposit them too near the spring.

Graves were shallow (Pl. 56, *a*), probably not much more than .50 m. Several bodies were all but exposed on the surface and mention has already been made of one case (burial 11) where a Papago fire was built directly on the feet of the mummy, burning the toes and sandals. The deepest of the late graves, *i. e.*, those dating from pottery times, was 1.40 m. below the surface, but in all considerable rubbish probably collected above it after burial.

Adult graves received no attention beyond scooping out the soft debris. For four infants, the graves were lined with grass and the bodies were covered with it before the graves were closed. One infant, burial 24, was enveloped in a twined bag surrounded by grass (Pl. 56, *b*).

In nearly every instance the bodies were oriented on a northeast-southwest line, paralleling the cave wall but not necessarily near it, with heads in either direction. In twenty burials from the pottery level, where the determination was certain, eight lay with heads northeast and twelve with heads southwest. Similarly, there was no uniformity as to the position of the body, ten being extended and ten flexed, heads oriented to either of the above directions. Extended bodies normally rested on the back and those flexed were on the back and right side chiefly, with a single one lying on the left side. This lack of standardization is evident from Table 34.

★

1. F. H. Scantling, 1940, pp. 25-26; A. M. Withers, 1941, pp. 26-28.

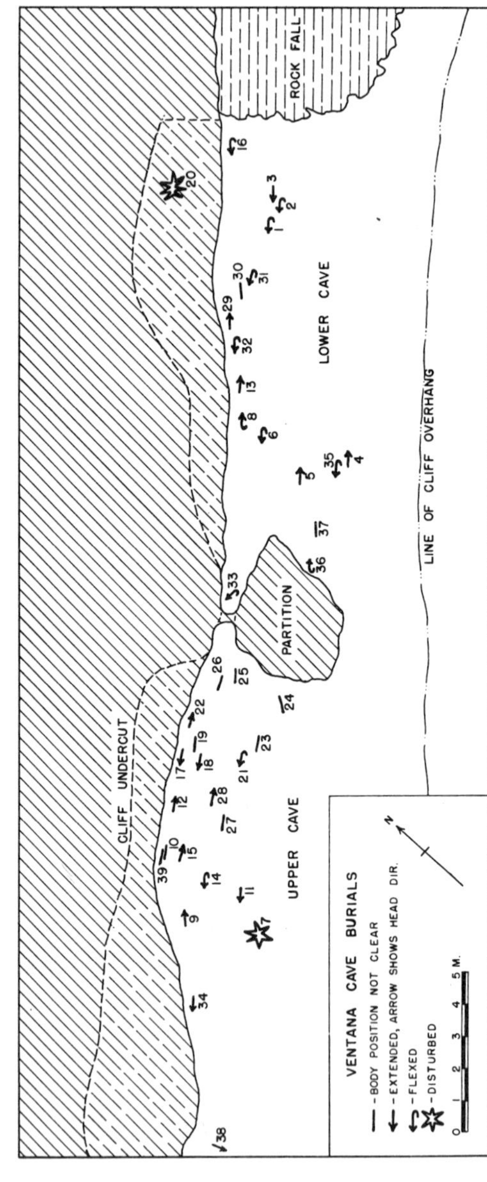

FIGURE 110. Plan of Ventana Cave, showing location and orientation of burials

Table 34
ORIENTATION AND POSITION OF 20 BURIALS FROM THE POTTERY LEVEL

Body Position	Flexed		Right Side	Left Side	Back	Extended		Right Side	Back
Head Orientation	NE	SW				NE	SW		
Infants		4	1		3	3			3
Males	1	2	2		1	2			2
Females	1	2	1	1	1	1	4	1	4

Gabel's analysis of race demonstrates that several morphological types were present in the Ventana population, including the deformed high vaulted Anasazi. The Salado, from which these are most likely extracted, customarily buried their dead extended. But of the three individuals of this racial make-up from Ventana, one (No. 8) was flexed, head northeast; the second (No. 12) was extended, head northeast; and the third (No. 21) was flexed, head southeast. Age, sex, and possible ethnic differences evidently were wholly irrelevant in influencing the body posture and orientation at time of burial, and it is safe to conclude that there was considerable individual choice in the matter. The only rigid feature seems to have been that the body be inhumed and not burned.

For the pre-pottery burials (Nos. 20, 35, and 36) there is no data on one (20) because of excessive disturbance. No. 35, a male, was flexed with head to the southwest and No. 36, a female was flexed with head northeast. There is thus nothing significant in actual disposal methods between the early and late burials. More early bodies might have shown that flexing was the rule.[2] The degree of flexure varies from doubling up the legs without drawing them up to the chest (Pl. 57, *a*) to tight flexing (Pl. 57, *b*), the latter being the more general. A binding about the legs is seen in the case of the former. In flexed bodies, arms were usually folded across the chest, while in extended bodies they

★

2. A pre-pottery burial, possibly of Chiricahua Stage (Cochise Culture) age, recovered by the Arizona State Museum in April, 1943, in the banks of Cienega Creek, Empire Valley, was flexed.

lie at the sides or the hands rest on the abdomen. Two extended mummies with burial wraps are shown in Plate 58.-

As the photographs show, some of the bodies were exceptionally well preserved. Here, as elsewhere in the dry Southwest, this was strictly the result of natural desiccation. There is no evidence whatever that evisceration or other artificial means of preserving were known.

There is no need in describing in detail each of these burials. Burial 9, however, merits special attention and the highlights of a few others will be brought out. This person (Pls. 58, *a;* 59), a middle aged male, was found in the upper cave (Section C) within 10 cm. of the surface. Apart from being a good example of an extended burial, and well preserved, he had with him and was wearing items of interest. First of all let us take up dress and body decoration. Cotton cloth stripping formed his breech clout, held in place by a belt made of a section of rabbit netting. The burial shroud, doubtless his blanket in life, was a fur robe (Pl. 43) covering found in the position shown in Plate 58, *a*. The robe was thickly encrusted with hand-sized pads of creosote branches, plucked when the bush was in full leaf and flower. A wooden nose plug, worn through the septum, and circular shell pendants, attached with cotton string to the ears through perforations in the lobes, constitute the body decorations. A section of yucca cord, caught between the chin and neck, may be all that is left of a charm or ornament worn about the neck.

Other accessories include a skin quiver (Pl. 39, *a*) with cane arrows lying at the right side of the body, and a bundle of oddments (Pl. 60) under the head. On opening the bundle, it was found to contain the following items:

A cord with attached shell, nose plug, and projectile points (Pl. 21)
Four bone awls
Human hair wig (Pl. 47)
Cactus spine needle (Pl. 38, *h*)
Several fragments of sewed sandals

Miscellaneous cotton cloth fragments including some with weft-wrap openwork technique

Human hair cord
Two small bundles of sinew
A small section of rabbit net
Braided belting (Pl. 54, *b*)
About 4 m. of cotton cloth strips rolled into a cord

Such a mixture of material obviously represents the earthly possessions of this individual, his work kit, weapons (excepting his bow), dress, and ornament. The careful garnering of cloth remnants suggests the premium put on this material and, if the cactus needle belonged to him, it may be inferred that the men of his day were not beyond doing a little sewing.

As to this man's position in his community, the reader's imagination is as good as mine. No other burials were equipped with so many tangible goods, no others were wearing nose plugs or jewelry. The wig and charms may mean that he was endowed with special powers. Perhaps he was no more than a respected old gentleman.

Considerable speculation developed in the laboratory as to how this individual looked in life. Visiting in Tucson at the time this work was in progress was Mr. Oscar F. Davisson, an accomplished and professional sculptor, who became much interested in the problem. Mr. Davisson kindly offered to try a plaster reconstruction, the results of which are illustrated in Plate 59, *b, c*. His first move was to exactly duplicate the head of the mummy and then to add flesh on half of the face based on flesh-thickness measurements given in Martin's *Lehrbuch der Anthropologie*. The restoration may be presumed to bear a general likeness to this person. The mode of wearing the hair is, of course, speculative, and the ear pendants have not been added.

Burial 9 belongs in Gabel's undeformed, mesocranial, low vaulted morphological type, which has much in common with the Papago type of today. I do not believe we would have to look very far among the Papago to find someone resembling Mr. Davisson's reconstruction.

Burial 11 (Pl. 58, *b*), the mummy of a female, was covered with a cotton robe and she wears the characteristic cordage breech clout. This was one of two mummies in the lot with sandals on the feet. Plate 61, *a* and *b*, illustrate additional examples of burials, the latter being an infant bundle, done up in a fur robe.

There was no consistency about the nature of offerings or where they were placed with the body. Beyond the burial wrap and articles of dress, many lacked accessories. Pottery was found with only one (burial 22, infant) which had a bowl of Tanque Verde Red-on-brown turned over the head. This lack of pottery is in decided contrast to Anasazi burials and even the cremations of the River Hohokam, where, frequently, a variety of offerings accompany the ashes of the dead.

It appears that placing objects over the head was a part of the burial ritual. The bowl already mentioned, two baskets, two Sahuaro callus receptacles, and a cotton blanket were so found.

In three instances, pillows occurred under the heads. Examples are the bundle of odds and ends with No. 9, a wooden block well wrapped with textiles with No. 6 (Pl. 61, *c*), and a wadded up cotton blanket (Pl. 50) with No. 22.

The recovery of the mummies in Ventana Cave aroused considerable interest among some of the personnel of the Indian Service as to the possibility of tracking down diseases. Dr. Joseph D. Aronson, then special investigator in tuberculosis for the Service, and engaged in research on valley fever *(coccidioidomycosis)*, arranged to have the mummies x-rayed. The incidence of valley fever among the Papago is very high and it was hoped that some evidence might be found to show whether or not the earlier residents in the area were afflicted, too. The findings were negative, at least to the extent that no trace of the disease was revealed if it was present, and nothing significant appeared from a pathological standpoint either.

One of the chief questions concerning the burials has to do with their age, or time of interment. As already said, three burials (Nos. 20, 35, and 36) were recovered in a pre-pottery trash con-

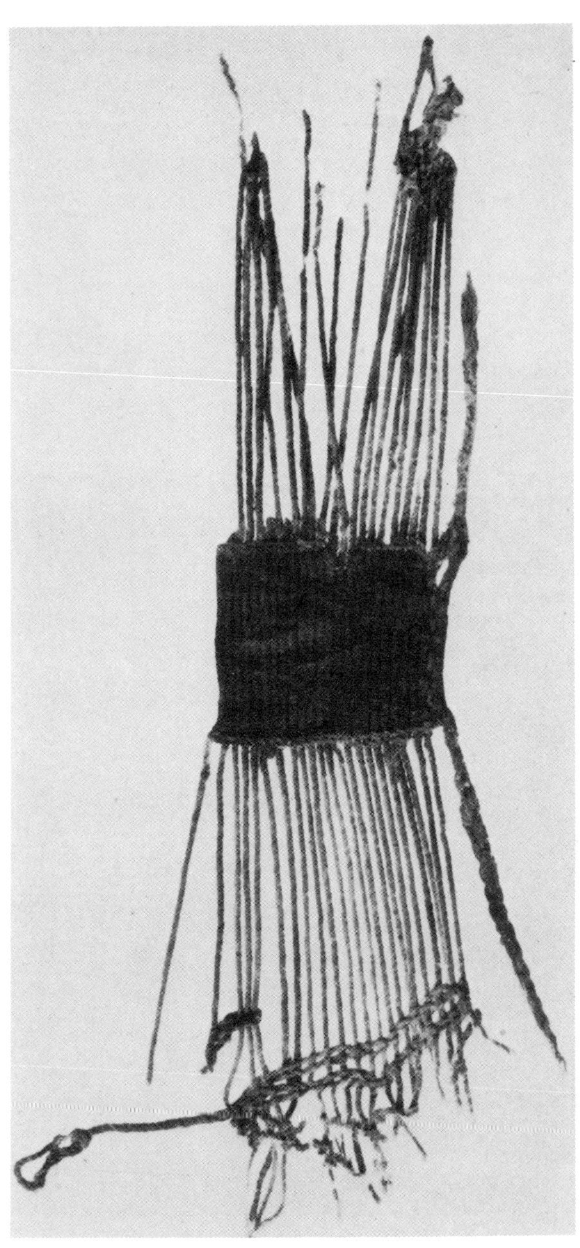

PLATE 55

Small belt-like specimen with mid-portion done in interlocking tapestry weave. Mid-portion, 45 mm.

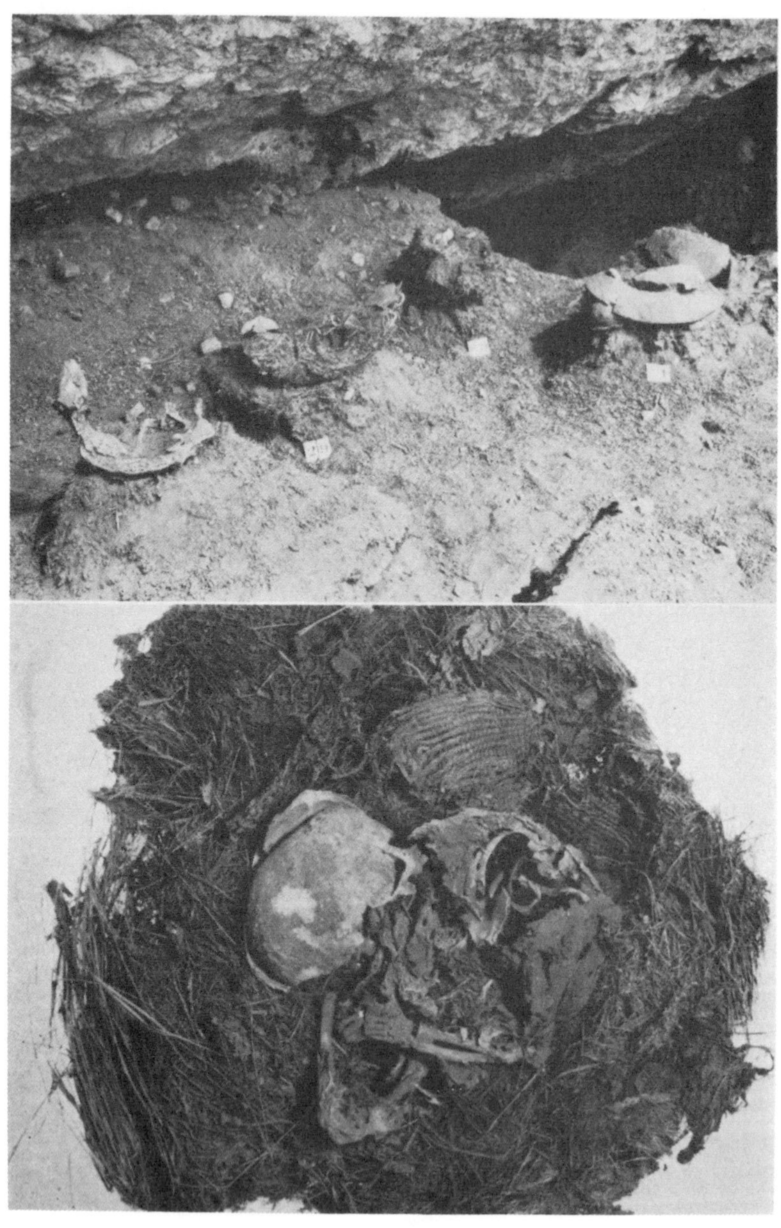

PLATE 56

Ventana Cave burials. *a* (Upper), in lower cave with surface debris stripped away. Nos. 29 and 30, infants in fur robes; No. 31, adult female with basket over head. Note dog burial, lower left.

b (Lower), infant in twined bag and grass nest (upper cave, burial 24).

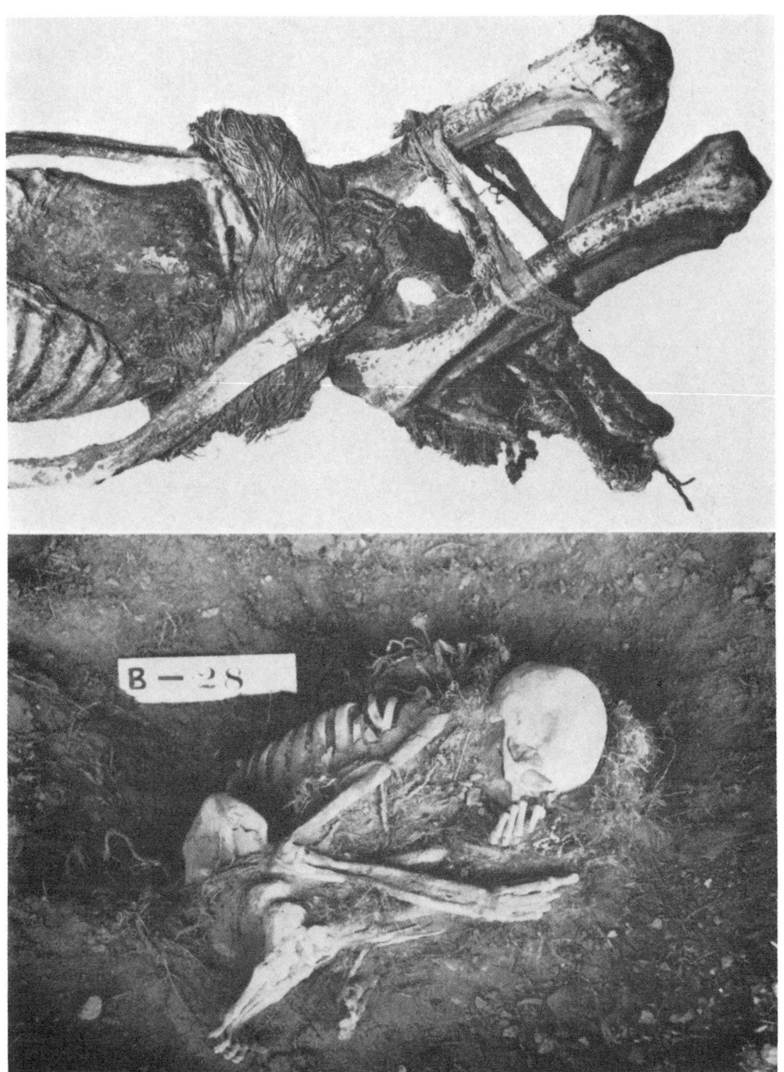

PLATE 57

Burials from the pottery level: *a* (Upper), lower extremity of burial 2 (young adult female).

b (Lower), burial 28 (middle aged female).

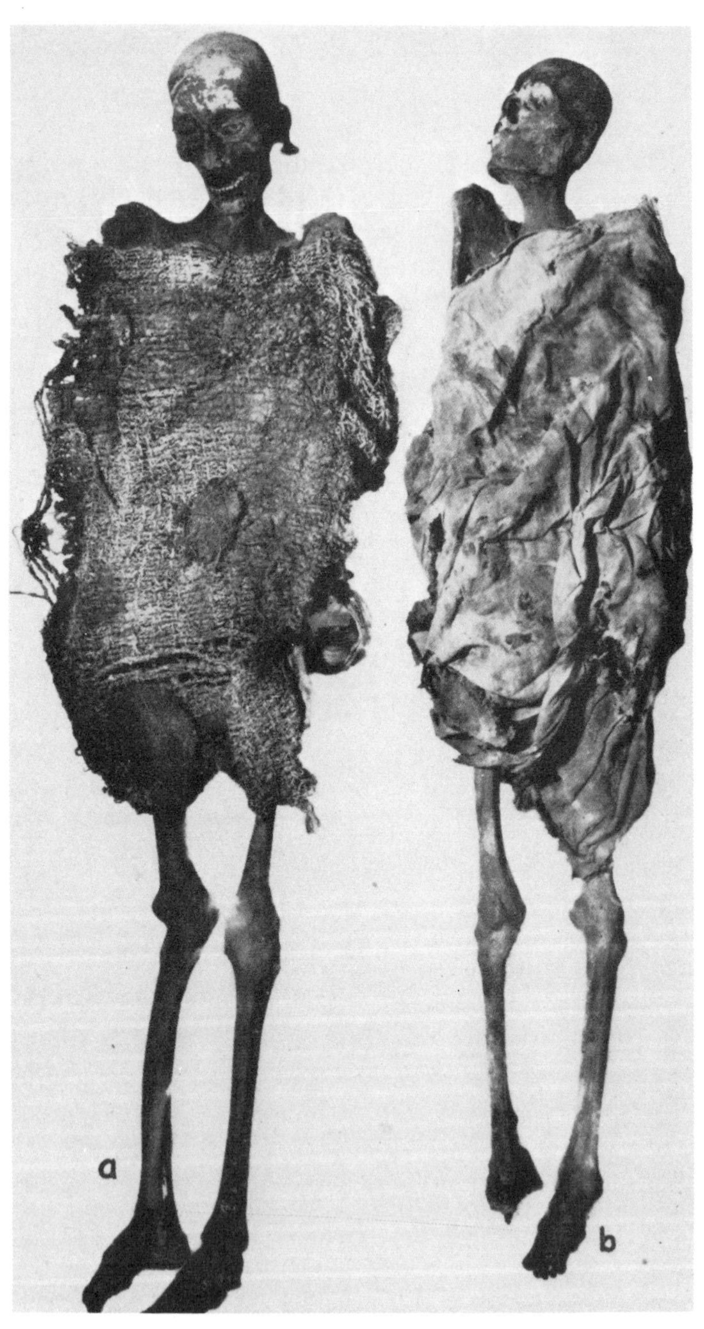

PLATE 58

Mummies from Ventana Cave: *a,* burial 9, male; *b,* burial 11, female.

text of the lower cave, the location of No. 20 being indicated in the profile given in Figure 7, *a*.

Gabel's determination that two of the three (the third skull being too fragmentary for observation) represent a different morphological type than that exhibited by the pottery level burials, and the alteration of the bone because of burial in a once moist deposit which is now dry, goes a long way to eliminate the possibility that late, or pottery level burials, were intruded downward in older trash. All of them were found near the rock floor, which means that interment was made after enough rubbish had collected to cover them. Or, they could have been put down in a fairly deep grave from a higher level of trash, but before the arrival of pottery and the accumulation of the lens of waste rock from the cliff face (Fig. 7.) This is especially true of burial 35, which lay well away from the cave wall (Fig. 110).

As the stratigraphy in the lower cave was much less satisfactory than in the upper cave, it is impossible to assign these burials to a specific culture level. The limits, however, may be defined. They cannot be older than Chiricahua-Amargosa II times, nor more recent than the San Pedro Stage. We may be certain that they do not represent the oldest inhabitants of Ventana Cave, who were contemporaneous with animals now extinct. Yet, these fragmentary skeletons are probably among the oldest discovered to date in southern Arizona.[3]

Pottery level burials are datable with somewhat greater accuracy because, in a number of instances, the accessories are assignable to phases of the Hohokam Culture of the Gila Basin, of which the approximate age is known. To come to cases in point, the sewed sandals (on the feet of burial 11) so far have been found in Santa Cruz and Sacaton Phase contexts; projectile points or arrows (with burial 9) are of a Sacaton Phase type; nose plugs (burial 9) appear to be essentially of the late Colonial and early Sedentary periods; and a Tanque Verde Red-on-brown

★

3. A Sulphur Springs Stage burial, morphologically similar to the Ventana remains, has been reported by E. B. Sayles and E. Antevs, 1941, p. 13; see also A. M. Brues, 1946, p. 16.

bowl (burial 22) is the key type for the Sells Phase, of Papagueria, and the Tanque Verde Phase, for the Tucson area, which was the chronological equivalent of the Civano Phase, of the Classic Period. In terms of years, this type falls between A. D. 1250 and 1400. The overall range for the late burials may be placed from about 1000 to 1400. It is conceivable that some might be earlier, but this cannot be proved.

Finally we come to the question of inhumation *vs.* cremation as methods for disposal of the dead. One of the most consistent features of the Hohokam was their practice of cremation. In all of the Gila Basin, inhumations have been found but rarely in pre-Salado times. After the arrival of the Salado people, who brought with them a tradition of inhumation, there is good evidence to the effect that both burial practices were followed by these two ethnic groups during the time they lived in the same villages.[4]

The near absence of cremations in Papagueria[5] has stood in the way of accepting the local archaeological remains after about A. D. 800 as of Hohokam origin. But, measuring the total culture against that of the Gila Basin, one notes too many parallels to regard it as otherwise. It must be admitted, therefore, that the Desert Hohokam departed from the River Hohokam custom of cremation in this important respect. A logical explanation of why this was so cannot be voiced, but it must be accepted as fact, unless future findings show the situation to have been otherwise. The pottery level burials from Ventana must be regarded as prime examples of the burial practice of the Desert Hohokam.

PICTOGRAPHS

The description of Ventana Cave would not be complete without giving due notice to the extensive rock paintings on the cliff wall and to the rock-cut figures outside the cave along the main trail leading to the cave.

★

4. E. W. Haury, 1945, pp. 43-48.

5. Only one has been found by us in Arizona DD:2:7, located at the north foot of the Quinlan Mountains, in the eastern part of the Reservation. It comes from a Santa Cruz Phase site.

The cave wall presented far from an ideal working surface, as it is very rough and badly cracked. This may have had something to do with the generally poor quality of execution of the figures, but the paintings on a few smooth surfaces are no better and one gains the impression that the level of artistry was definitely inferior. This, coupled with the spalling off of the cliff face since the paintings were made, has reduced many of the figures to a vagueness that makes identification of the subjects impossible.

The paintings were all situated above the surface of the cave fill at the time excavations were begun, and it is clear that they were made by persons standing on the surface of the debris after most or all of it had collected. Only in a few places were they high, requiring some sort of a support to reach them. One group of red lines in particular, some 8 or 10 m. above the floor, on the face of the cliff, may have been reached by scaling the rock face, although this is quite impossible now. It seems more probable that a brush was tied to a long pole and the lines thus applied.

Obviously the distribution of the paintings in both cave units where they could be conveniently reached from the present surface has a bearing on their age. It can be said with confidence that none of the pictures date from the pre-pottery level and that they are either of Hohokam or Papago origin, as will presently be brought out.

There are several bits of evidence to suggest, however, that the earlier occupants also made rock paintings. Paint stained metates were found down to the base of the midden, as were a few paint-daubed rocks, and here and there on the cave wall were spots of red paint, doubtless the vestiges of paintings. These were below the moisture line, which accounts for the fact that they have not survived. The colors of the surviving paintings include white and black and several shades of red, and it is impossible to detect any age difference on this basis.

Most of the figures are of a geometric nature and a few are distinctly life forms. The former could be of either Hohokam or

Papago authorship, and for some of the latter it is possible to make more specific assignments.

A complete canvass of the geometric figures was not made, but the elements recurring most frequently are a series of near-vertical lines, either in one color or alternated in two (Fig. 111, *a, b*). These, the Papago say, are tallies and mnemonic signs of the kind they formerly made for keeping record of the duration of sickness. Some further calendrical ideas may be involved, too, as the Papago did keep records on calendar sticks by an assortment of lines, dots, and other symbols. There is also a dotted rectangle in white (Fig. 111, *c*), a series of joined triangles in red (Fig. 112, *c*), and a curious figure in black (Fig. 111, *d*), possibly all of Papago authorship.

Life forms certainly of Papago artistry include a horse with rider in red (Fig. 111, *e*) and a group of figures in black (Fig. 111, *f*). Two large polychrome figures may, I believe, be iden-

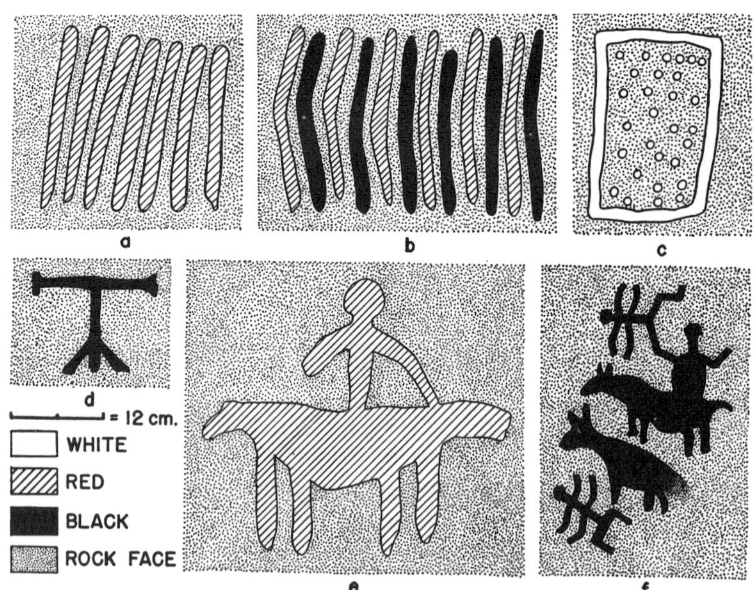

FIGURE 111. Wall paintings in Ventana Cave. Tally marks (?), *a, b;* geometric figures, *c, d;* horsemen (Papago), *e, f*

tified as of Hohokam origin. One of these is a square shouldered, stylized human representation (Fig. 112, *a*) over 3 m. high. The bottom part fades where it extended below the surface of the midden. The second (Fig. 112, *b*) and most complicated of all paintings is slightly more than 2 m. high, and also appears to be a highly formalized human figure with extensive embellishments at the side. The head ornament is strongly reminiscent of the human figures seen on some River Hohokam pottery of the Sacaton Phase.[6]

The Papago workmen referred to this last figure as the "devil," and did not believe it to be Papago work. They were at a loss to explain how they knew it was the devil. One of the men finally admitted that he did not see how they could say it was the devil when he "changes his ways and looks every generation."

★

6. H. S. Gladwin, *et al.*, 1937, Pl. CLII, n.

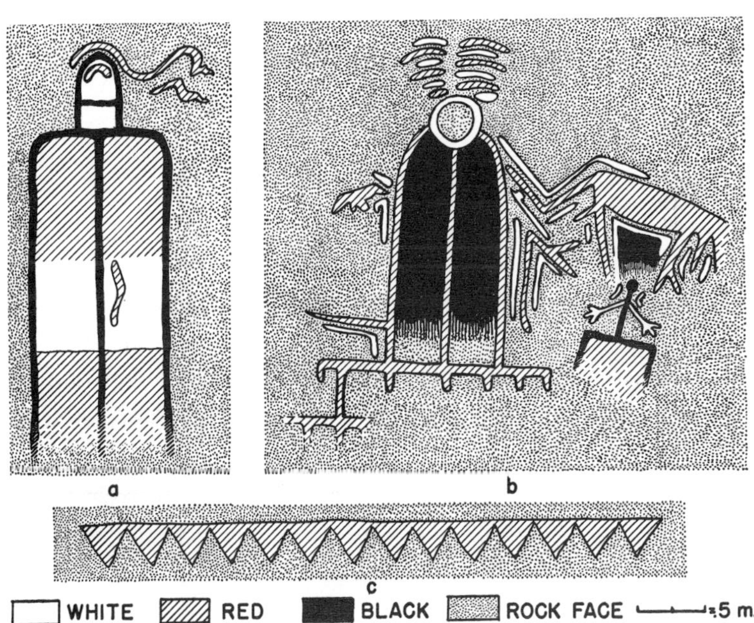

FIGURE 112. Wall paintings in Ventana Cave. Conventionalized human forms, possibly Hohokam, *a, b;* joined triangles, *c*

The rock-cut figures, a snake (Pl. 62), several mountain sheep, deer, and geometric figures, were pecked through the desert varnish on basalt boulders along the main trail into the cave from the northeast. There is no good clue as to their age but they are probably pre-Papago.

Pictographs are notoriously difficult to pin down as to authorship, although this can certainly be done for many with systematic study. Such an analysis for Papagueria and neighboring areas has not been made in spite of the fact that rock-cut pictures are to be found everywhere. For this reason nothing more can be done on the Ventana drawings beyond noting their presence. What they mean, or meant to the artist, is such a speculative problem that there is no point in devoting space to it here. Painted pictographs are far from common in southern Arizona and those in Ventana, indistinct as they are, are probably one of the best groups.

PART VII

The Skeletal Remains of Ventana Cave[1]

NUMBER AND PRESERVATION

Thirty-nine burials were recovered from Ventana Cave. Of these, all but one were excavated during the first season, of 1941, and only one was found subsequently in 1942 (see Fig. 110 for locations).

On the whole, the specimens are well preserved owing to the dryness and otherwise protective nature of the cave and the cave debris. A number of the remains are excellent examples of natural mummification (Pls. 58, 59). At the other extreme are several fragmentary remains, some of them too badly disintegrated for reconstruction and analysis. Other burials are variously intermediate. That is, some parts of the skeletal frame are partly articulated by dessicated remnants of skin, ligament, and cartilage.

A few of the burials were so extremely disturbed that it was impossible for us to recover all of the scattered elements and relate them to the respective interments. The disarrangement of these interments was due to human agency, arising chiefly from the excavation of new graves through the old.

★

1. By Norman E. Gabel, Associate Professor of Anthropology, Dept. of Social Sciences, University of California, Santa Barbara College, Santa Barbara, California.

CULTURAL ASSOCIATION

Thirty-six of the burials were located in the dry zone of the cave midden and in direct association with pottery and other evidences of the Hohokam Culture. The remaining three came from lower depths of the midden in a pre-pottery context. On the basis of this difference in position plus difference in the chemical nature of the bone tissue, which will be described later, it seems justifiable to ascribe these latter three specimens to the earlier pre-pottery horizon in which they were found. In other words, it is believed that this trio was not intruded downward from the later pottery culture into the trash of earlier people. For this reason the human remains of the ceramic and pre-ceramic strata will be separately described, analyzed, and compared.

THE BURIALS OF THE POTTERY HORIZON

A total of thirty-six burials comprises the sample associated with a ceramic culture identified in earlier pages as the Desert Hohokam. Particular interest attaches itself to this collection because it is the first and only known instance of Hohokam Culture reflecting inhumation practices instead of the usual cremation, which characterizes the funerary customs of the Hohokam people in the Gila Basin.

Sex Incidence

The sex ratio in this series shows a preponderance of females. There are twenty adults from the pottery level. Four of these could not be sexed. The remaining sixteen show a ten to six excess of females.

Age Incidence (Table 35)

Although the small size of the sample does not permit too positive an assertion, age incidence suggests a high frequency of infant and child mortality. Of the thirty-six individuals from the pottery level, ten are infants less than three years old, and five are children between four and six years, accounting for over 40 per cent of the total.

TABLE 35
AGE INCIDENCE

	No.	Pct.
Infant (0-3 yrs.)	10	27.8
Child (4-6 yrs.)	5	13.9
Child (7-12 yrs.)	1	2.8
Adolescent (13-17 yrs.)	0	0.0
Sub-adult (18-20 yrs.)	1	2.8
Young adult (21-34 yrs.)	1	2.8
Middle aged (35-55 yrs.)	10	27.8
Old adult (55-X yrs.)	3	8.3
Unknown age	5	13.9
Total	36	100.0

Beyond early childhood there is a striking dearth of burials until the beginning of the middle age category. Late childhood is represented by only one specimen and there are no adolescents at all. The sub-adult class contains but one individual, a male, and the same is true of the young adult group, this one being a female. The middle aged category, represented by four males and six females, marks the peak of adult mortality as far as this small series is concerned. Hooton, in his analysis of the prehistoric Pecos population, demonstrates a comparable excess of deaths in this age class.[2] Old adults are three in number, one male and two females. The indeterminate burials are all adults.

Deformation

Three of the four male crania show artificial deformation, presumably the result of cradling practices. Two of these have pronounced occipital flattening and the third exhibits a slight amount of lambdoidal distortion. For the females, a curious reverse condition occurs. Six of the seven female skulls used in the following analysis are undeformed and only one shows some lambdoidal flattening. A number of other cranial variations, metrical, indicial, and morphological, ally themselves with the deformed and undeformed specimens, so that there is good reason to believe, as will be demonstrated later, that the variations in cradling practices may coincide with ethnic differences in the Ventana population.

★

2 E. A. Hooton, 1930, p. 25.

The Vault (Tables 36 and 37)

Obvious and considerable contrasts obtain between the deformed and normal crania of this series. The lone undeformed male specimen (Pl. 63) markedly exceeds the deformed in absolute head length and is as strikingly deficient in cranial breadth and height, particularly the latter. The ratios associated with these diameters describe the normal skull as mesocranial and the deformed ones as hyperbrachycranial. Similarly, the undeformed individual is low vaulted in relation to both head length and breadth, while the distorted males (Pl. 64) are hypsicranial and metriocranial, excepting one, which is tapeinocranial. The undeformed male has a narrower forehead than the others but this is owing to lesser size of the whole skull. There is no significant difference in the ratio of least frontal to maximum cranial breadth; all are stenometopic.

The cranial capacities of the males range from very small to moderate. At the low end of the distribution is the undeformed example with a volume of only 1,120 cubic centimeters.

TABLE 36

MEASUREMENTS AND INDICES OF THE VAULT—MALE

	Undeformed		*Deformed*		
	B14[1]	*B8*	*B12*	*B21*	*Mean*
Head length (Glabello-opisthocranium)	177mm.	167mm.	148mm.	168mm.	161mm.
Head breadth	137	149	141	151	147
Cranial index	77.4	89.2	95.3	89.9	91.5
Basion-bregma	120	142	138	135	138.3
Height-length index	67.8	85.0	93.9	80.4	86.4
Height-breadth index	87.6	95.3	97.8	89.4	94.2
Auricular height	104	125	122	122	123
Auricular height index	63.5	74.9	82.3	72.6	76.6
Minimum frontal	87	92	89	94	91.7
Fronto-parietal index	63.5	61.7	63.1	62.2	62.3
Cranial capacity	1120cc.	1410	1245	1420	1358.3
Max. circumference	495mm.	498	470	503	490.3
Sagittal arc	335	360	350	363	357.3
Transverse arc	289	343	320	339	334
Cranial module	144.7	152.7	142.3	151.3	148.8
Foramen magnum diameter	31.5	31.5	29.0	30.5	30.3
Parietal thickness	6.3	6.0	4.8	6.7	5.8

1. In this and subsequent tables, the "B" followed by a numeral designates burial number.

TABLE 37

MEASUREMENTS AND INDICES OF THE VAULT—FEMALE

	Undeformed		Deformed
	Range[1]	Mean	B17
Head length (Glabello-opisthocranium)	159 - 179mm.	167.5mm.	148
Head breadth	127 - 137	132.0	143
Cranial index	70.9- 83.0	79.0	96.6
Basion-bregma	120 - 135	128.2	138
Height-length index	69.3- 83.0	76.7	93.2
Height-breadth index	91.6- 100.0	97.1	96.5
Auricular height	109 - 117	111.8	119
Auricular height index	60.9- 73.6	66.9	80.4
Minimum frontal	79 - 91	87.2	90
Fronto-parietal index	61.2- 70.9	66.1	62.9
Cranial capacity	1020 -1210cc.	1095cc.	1230cc.
Maximum circumference	459 - 494	478.5	468
Sagittal arc	337 - 362	347.2	329
Transverse arc	292 - 312	297.7	325
Cranial module	138.7- 146.3	142.6	143
Foramen magnum diameter	25.5- 31.0	28.7	31
Parietal thickness	4.7- 6.6	5.4	4.3

1. For six skulls.

The remaining males vary between 1,245 and 1,420 cc. Differences in maximum skull circumference between the deformed and undeformed individuals are not great, but the nasion-opisthion and the transverse arcs are both considerably less in the undeformed skull. When the respective absolute lengths, breadths, and heights of the skulls are combined, averaged, and compared with one another, the conspicuous contrasts shown by the individual diameters are largely eliminated. The cranial module of all the males ranges only about 10 mm., from 142.3 to 152.7 mm. The male excess over the females in mean diameter of the foramen magnum and in skull thickness is an expected sex difference.

The female series shows a reversed majority of undeformed crania. Five specimens are normal, one is slightly and one markedly deformed. As among the males, the deficiency in head length of the deformed type and the associated excess of head breadth result in hyperbrachycephaly. The undeformed females range from dolichocephaly to moderate brachycephaly, with an average tendency toward high mesocephaly. The mean basion-bregma height of the normal females is 128.2 mm., which is well below the head height of the undeformed female. The vaults of the normal crania are fairly high compared with maximum lengths; that of the deformed skull is excessively so. Height-breadth ratios are not so widely scattered and tend to fall in the middle class. All three of these cranial diameters describe the skulls as small in size regardless of usual sex differences.

The foreheads of the female series are quite narrow, both absolutely and relative to maximum head breadth; the undeformed group show a low metriometopic average while the deformed specimen has a lower fronto-parietal ratio.

Mean cranial capacity (1,095 cc.) for the undeformed females is very small; the deformed specimen is somewhat larger. Maximum horizontal circumference of the deformed skull is less than the average value of the six undeformed individuals, which is as one expects, and the same is true of the sagittal arc. The reverse condition holds for transverse arcs. Differences in cranial module are relatively small since all the values fall within a range of less than 8 mm.

The Total and Upper Face (Tables 38 and 39)

In keeping with the usual Indian tendency, the total facial breadth of the Ventana males is pronounced, while the maximum height of the face is also generous. The average bizygomatic diameter of the females is a good deal lower. Only one female yields a total facial height measurement and it is very low. Breadth-height ratios for the males are moderate for the most part; the deformed series runs to relatively longer faces. The one female which possesses a measurable lower jaw shows a euryprosopic ratio due mostly to deficiency in face height. Upper facial indices of the males are clearly mesene, and data for this feature are lacking for the undeformed skull. The female upper facial average is also in the middle class, though somewhat lower, and their range extends farther down into the euryene category. The ratio of bizygomatic breadth to total cranial width is considerably lower in the deformed skulls, where the head

TABLE 38

MEASUREMENTS AND INDICES OF THE TOTAL AND UPPER FACE—MALE

	Undeformed		*Deformed*		
	B14	*B8*	*B12*	*B21*	*Mean*
Bizygomatic breadth	137mm.	140mm.	131mm.	141mm.	137.3
Gnathion-nasion height	118	—	120	124	122
Total facial index	86.1	—	91.6	87.9	89.8
Nasion-prosthion height	—	75	71	70	72
Upper facial index	—	53.6	54.2	49.7	52.5
Cranio-facial index	100.0	94.0	92.9	93.4	93.4
Basion-nasion	100	100	93	97	96.3
Basion-prosthion	93	94	95	107	98.7
Gnathic index	93.0	94.0	102.2	110.3	102.2
Nasal height	52	55	48	49	51.7
Nasal breadth	22	24	23	26	24.3
Nasal index	42.3	43.6	47.9	53.1	48.3
Orbital height—R	36	34	34	35	34.3
Orbital breadth (dacryon)—R	38	41	40	40	40.3
Orbital index—R	94.7	82.9	85.0	87.5	85.1
Orbital height—L	36	34	33	34	33.7
Orbital breadth—L	40	40	39	39	39.3
Orbital index—L	90.0	85.0	84.6	87.2	85.6

TABLE 39

MEASUREMENTS AND INDICES OF THE TOTAL AND UPPER FACE—FEMALE

		Undeformed		*Deformed*
	No.	*Range*	*Mean*	*B17*
Bizygomatic breadth	5	117 -126	122.6	131
Gnathion-nasion height	1	—	100.0	—
Total facial index	1	—	79.4	—
Nasion-prosthion height	4	57 - 65	61.8	69
Upper face index	3	48.4- 52.9	51.0	52.7
Cranio-facial index	4	90.7- 96.2	94.4	91.6
Basion-nasion	5	93 - 98	95.4	97
Basion-prosthion	5	90 - 98	92.6	89
Gnathic index	5	93.8-101.1	97.1	91.8
Nasal height	6	42 - 49	45.3	49
Nasal breadth	6	23 - 25	24.0	22
Nasal index	6	50.0- 56.8	53.0	44.8
Orbital height—R	6	32 - 34	33.3	36
Orbital breadth (dacryon)—R	6	36 - 38	37.5	38
Orbital index—R	6	84.2- 94.4	88.9	94.7
Orbital height—L	6	31 - 34	32.7	37
Orbital breadth—L	6	36 - 38	37.3	38
Orbital index—L	6	81.6- 91.9	87.6	97.4

breadth has been artificially increased. Males tend to relatively narrower faces in relation to head width than do the females.

Prognathism, as expressed by the gnathic index, is moderate in the deformed males and lacking in the undeformed male and in all of the females.

Diameters of the nose are not large and the nasal proportions vary a good deal. The undeformed male is leptorrhine while the deformed males range from leptorrhini to platyrrhini. Most of the undeformed females are platyrrhine and the single deformed individual has a relatively narrow nose.

Orbital proportions vary between meso- and hypsiconch. The orbits of the undeformed male are relatively higher than those of the deformed series. An opposite contrast is exhibited by the females.

The Lower Face (Tables 40 and 41)

The proportions of the palate are brachyuranic for all the males, although the palates of the deformed examples are considerably less broad. A conspicuous sex difference is also in evidence: the female average is much lower than the male. The lower jaws of the deformed males are larger and relatively longer than the undeformed. Relative to facial breadth the mandible of the deformed male is narrower between the gonial angles. The males have relatively wider jaws than the females and the remainder of the mandibular measurements show usual sex differences.

Morphological Observations of the Vault

The four crania representing the male series of the pottery horizon show several contrasts in general morphology. The undeformed specimen is smaller and manifests less development of muscularity. For that reason in part, the sex criteria are not as clearly marked. All of the males have moderately heavy skulls. The vault shape of the undeformed skull is pentagonal (Pl. 63); the deformed vaults approximate a broad oval outline (Pl. 64). Two of the males are old adults and two are middle-aged.

TABLE 40

MEASUREMENTS AND INDICES OF THE LOWER FACE—MALE

	Undeformed	Deformed			
	B14	B8	B12	B21	Mean
Palatal length, (ext.)	46mm.	52mm.	54mm.	54	53.3
Palatal breadth, (ext.)	62	67	66	67	66.7
Palatal index	134.8	128.8	122.2	124.1	125.0
Mandibular length	101	—	115	109	112
Bicondylar breadth	118	—	116	123	119.5
Mandibular index	85.6	—	99.1	88.6	93.9
Bigonial breadth	86	—	94	107	100.5
Zygo-gonial index	62.8	—	71.7	75.8	73.8
Symphyseal height	35	—	41	38	39.5
Asc. ramus height	64	—	58	56	57
Asc. ramus breadth (min.)	22	—	31	37	34
Angle of mandible	113°	—	117°	120°	118.5°

TABLE 41

MEASUREMENTS AND INDICES OF THE LOWER FACE—FEMALE

		Undeformed		*Deformed*
	No.	*Range*	*Mean*	*B17*
Palatal length, (ext.)	3	48 - 52	50	48
Palatal breadth, (ext.)	3	52 - 58	54	61
Palatal index	3	100 -120.8	108.3	127.1
Mandibular length	4	94 -110	100.5	108
Bicondylar breadth	4	107 -118	112	112
Mandibular index	4	83.1- 98.3	89.9	86.4
Bigonial breadth	4	77 - 91	85.8	94
Zygo-gonial index	4	61.1- 74.4	69.8	71.8
Symphyseal height	3	27 - 32	30	33
Asc. ramus height	4	43 - 57	51.5	50
Asc. ramus breadth (min.)	4	27 - 31	29.3	29
Angle of mandible	4	119° -133°	124.5°	127°

The female sample, which is composed of six undeformed and one deformed crania, shows less variation. Muscularity is consistently submedium, as is skull weight. Four of the undeformed vaults are pentagonal from the *norma verticalis* while the remaining two, as well as the single deformed female, are ovoid. They range in age from young adults to very old.

The Frontal Region (Tables 42 and 43)

The foreheads of the Ventana males range equally between submedium and medium height, and the females show a stronger tendency in the submedium direction. Frontal slope is characteristically present among all the individuals of both sexes, varying from slight to pronounced. The males exhibit moderate development of the supraorbital ridges for the most part, while the females show the expected sex difference. Brow ridge type in males divides itself between the median and divided forms in a ratio of one to three; the median form is in the majority among females. The glabella is pronounced in two of the males; in the remaining two it is moderate and slight. All but one of the females has a submedium glabella.

Traces of metopism are discernible in half of the series. Postorbital constriction is moderate for all of the males and is more marked on the average among the females. Development of the frontal bosses follows the recognized sex pattern. All of the males have some elevation of the median sagittal plane of the frontal bone though it is never pronounced. The female series lacks a median crest in three specimens although among the remaining

TABLE 42

OBSERVATIONS, FRONTAL REGION

			Frontal Height[1]			
	O	ssm	sm	+	++	
Males (4)						
Females (8)	0	0	2	2	0	
			Frontal Slope			
	O	ssm	sm	+	++	
Males (4)	0		1	2	1	
Females (8)	0		3	3	2	
			Brow Ridge Type			
		Median			Divided	Continuous
Males (4)		1			3	0
Females (7)		5			2	0
			Brow Ridge Size			
	O	ssm	sm	+	++	
Males (4)		0	0	3	1	
Females (8)		3	5	0	0	
			Glabella			
	O	ssm	sm	+	++	
Males (4)			1	1	2	
Females (8)			7	1	0	

1. Symbols used in recording observed qualities indicate: O-absent; ssm—very small; sm—submedium; +—medium; ++—pronounced; +++—very pronounced.

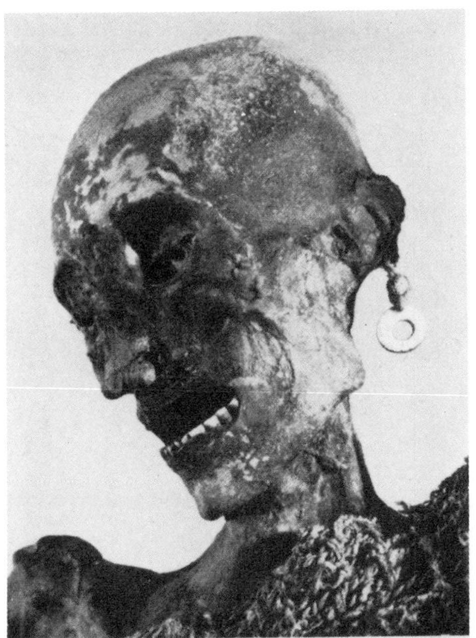

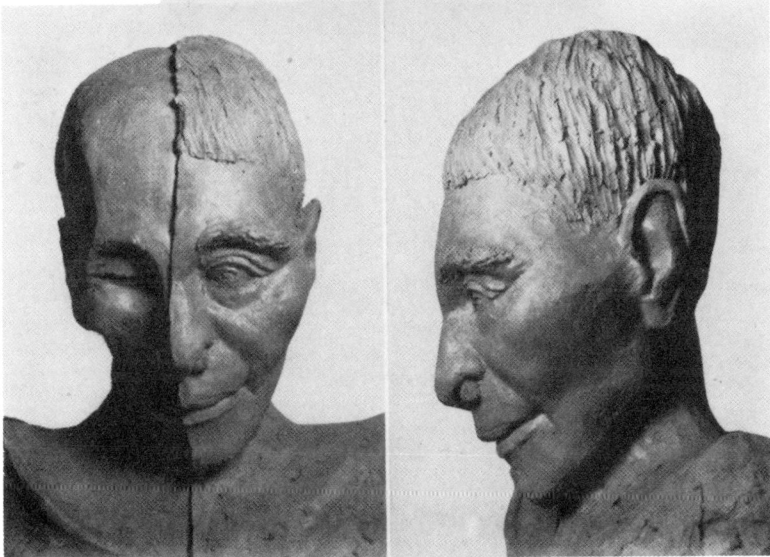

PLATE 59

Head of male mummy (burial 9): *a* (Upper), showing nose plug and shell ear ornaments; *b, c* (Lower), partial reconstruction of the facial features. Bust by Oscar F. Davisson.

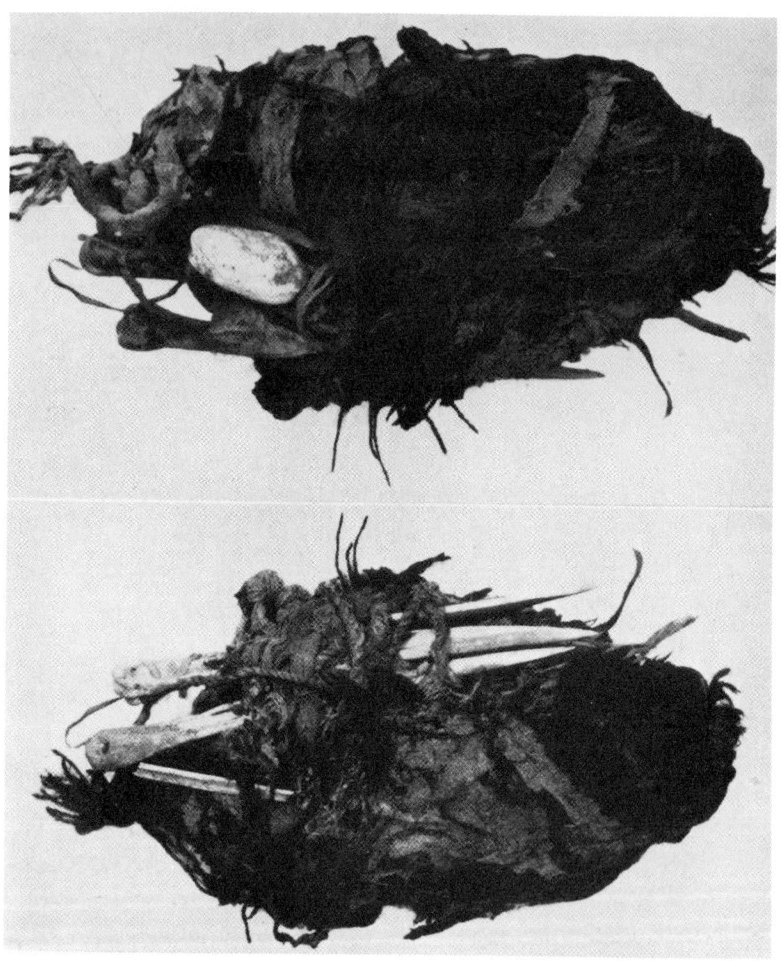

PLATE 60

Bundle of sundry articles found under the head of burial 9: *a* (Upper), hair cordage, the human hair wig, and a marine shell are in evidence; *b* (Lower), the other side of the bundle. This shows bone awls, sinew, and fabrics. Length, 265 mm.

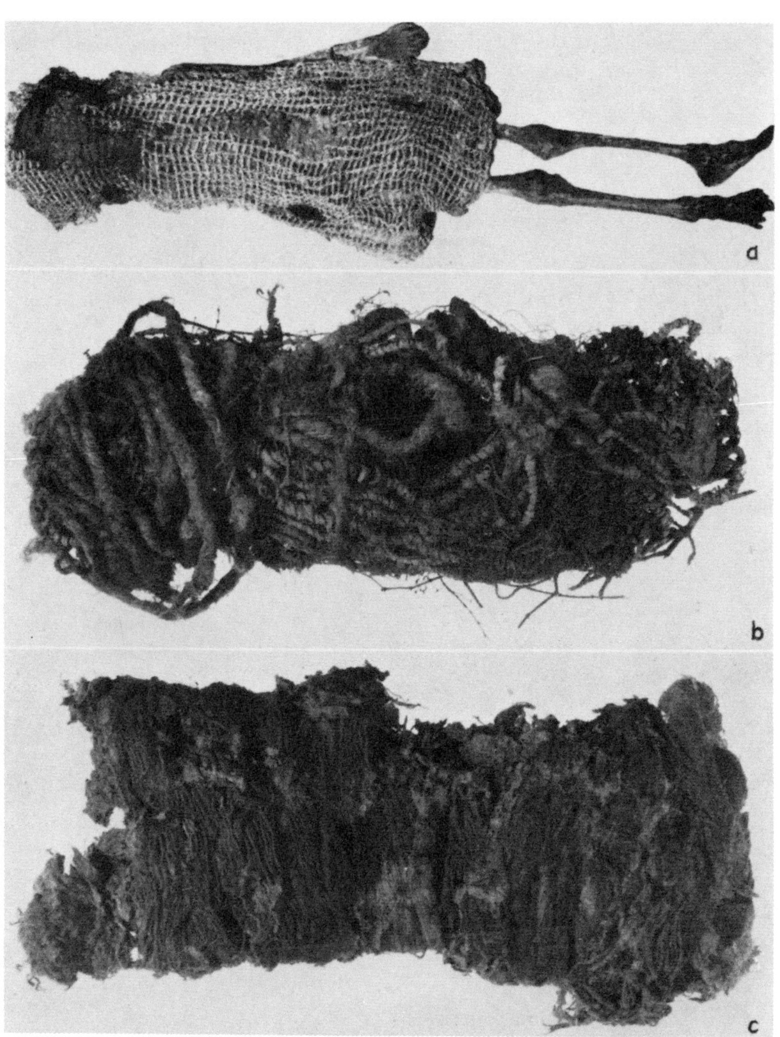

PLATE 61

Pottery level burials *(a, b)* and pillow *(c)*: *a* (Upper), burial 6, four to six year old girl; *b* (Middle) burial 29, infant in fur robe shroud. Length, .65 m. *c* (Lower), bundle of cloth remnants with a wooden block core, used as a pillow under head of burial 6. Wrapping includes a skein of brown cotton yarn. Length of *c*, 270 mm.

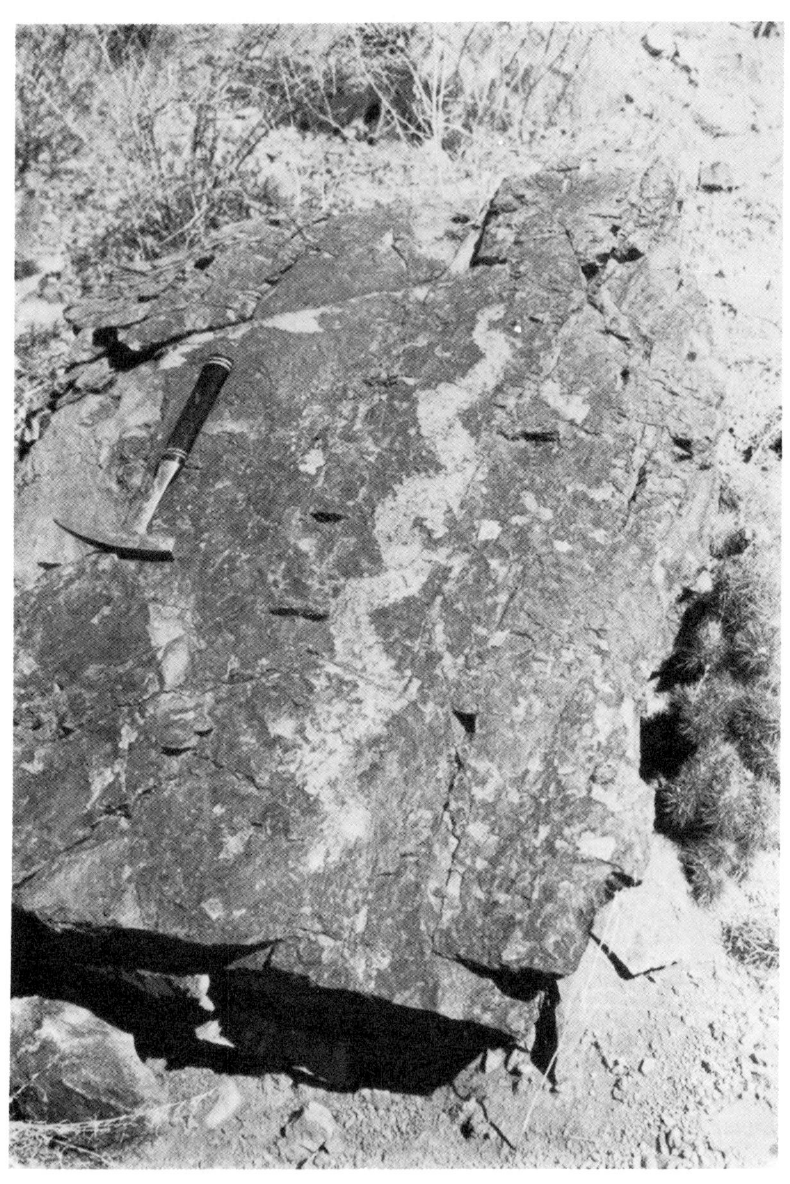

PLATE 62

Snake pictograph (rock-cut type) along trail leading to Ventana Cave.

TABLE 43

OBSERVATIONS, FRONTAL REGION

	Metopism		
	Trace	Complete	Absent
Males (4)	2	0	2
Females (8)	4	0	4

	Post Orbital Constriction			
	O	sm	+	+ +
Males (4)		0	4	0
Females (8)		0	5	3

	Frontal Bosses			
	O	sm	+	+ +
Males (4)		1	3	0
Females (8)		0	6	2

	Median Crest			
	O	sm	+	+ +
Males (4)	0	2	2	0
Females (8)	3	4	0	1

	Frontal Breadth			
	O	sm	+	+ +
Males (4)		2	2	0
Females (8)		4	4	0

individuals one has a pronounced elevation in this plane. Breadth of the frontal region leans toward the submedium, both sexes being equally divided between small and moderate frontal width.

Parietal Region (Table 44)

The median sagittal plane of the parietal area is characteristically elevated in all of the specimens except one. Particularly is this true of the males. None of the series shows postcoronal depression. The parietal bosses are well developed throughout, more so among the males in whom pronounced bosses are associated with occipital flattening. Parietal foramina are either small or lacking in all of the specimens.

Temporal Region (Table 45)

Fullness of the vault in the temporal region is moderate among the male crania that are deformed, and submedium in the undeformed individual. The females vary evenly in the same

TABLE 44

OBSERVATIONS, PARIETAL REGION

	O	sm	+	++
		Sagittal Elevation		
Males (4)	0	0	3	1
Females (8)	1	3	3	1
		Postcoronal Depression		
Males (4)	4	0	0	0
Females (8)	8	0	0	0
		Parietal Bosses		
Males (4)	0	0	1	3
Females (8)	0	0	6	2
		Foramina		
Males (4)	1	3	0	0
Females (8)	3	4	1	0

TABLE 45

OBSERVATIONS, TEMPORAL REGION

	O	sm	+	++
		Fullness		
Males (4)	0	1	3	0
Females (8)	0	4	4	0
		Crests		
Males (4)		2	2	0
Females (8)		8	0	0
		Supramastoid Crest		
Males (4)		0	1	3
Females (8)		4	3	1
		Sphenoid Depression		
Males (4)			4	0
Females (8)			4	4
		Mastoid Size		
Males (4)		0	2	2
Females (8)		4	3	0

two categories. Temporal crests are small or moderate in equal proportions among males and altogether slight among females. The males show average sphenoid depression while the females tend definitely toward the more pronounced condition. Supramastoid crests are strongly developed in the males and, though a good deal smaller, are present on all the female skulls. The male mastoids are medium and pronounced in size in equal ratio while the females follow the usual tendency to relative smallness.

Occipital Region (Table 46)

The degree of curvature of the occipital plane is, of course, directly correlated with the amount of posterior deformation, and this association precludes a true description, at least for the males that are predominantly deformed. Among the females, only one of which is distorted, the central tendency is moderate convexity. The size of the occipital torus is not unusual for either sex and the mound type of torus predominates over the ridge form.

Table 46

OBSERVATIONS, OCCIPITAL REGION

		Curve		
	O	sm	+	++
Males (4)	0	2	1	1
Females (8)	0	2	4	2
		Torus – size		
	O	sm	+	++
Males (4)	0	1	2	1
Females (8)	0	6	2	0
		Torus – type		
	Ridge		Mound	
Males (4)	1		3	
Females (8)	0		8	
		Transverse Suture		
	Absent		Present	
Males (4)	4		0	
Females (8)	8		0	

Suture Serration (Table 47)

Complexity of the suture patterns is rarely pronounced in this series. In no instance is the serration of the coronal or the sagittal suture more than moderately intricate; more often than not it is rather simple. On the whole, the lambdoidal suture is the more serrated. Sex differences are not clearly defined although the small samples involved may obviate the expected variation.

TABLE 47

OBSERVATIONS, SUTURE SERRATION AND OCCLUSION

	?	O	sm	+	++	+++	Complete
Suture Serration							
Coronal							
Males (4)	0		2	2	0	0	
Females (8)	2		3	3	0	0	
Sagittal							
Males (4)	1		2	1	0	0	
Females (8)	2		4	2	0	0	
Lambdoidal							
Males (4)	0		0	2	2	0	
Females (8)	1		0	5	2	0	
Suture Occlusion							
Coronal							
Males (4)		0	1	2	1		0
Females (8)		2	3	1	0		2
Sagittal							
Males (4)		0	0	1	2		1
Females (8)		1	2	2	1		2
Lambdoidal							
Males (4)		0	1	2	1		0
Females (8)		3	3	1	1		0

Wormian Bones (Table 48)

Island bones occur on nearly all of the crania but with one exception they are all located on the lambdoidal suture and for the most part they are neither numerous nor large.

TABLE 48
WORMIAN BONES

	Lambdoidal			
	O	1-3	4-6	7-X
Males (4)	0	4	0	0
Females (6)	1	4	0	1
		Others		
		Coronal	Sagittal	Squamous
Males (4)		0	0	0
Females (7)		0	0	1

Form of Pterion (Table 49)

The bulk of the crania exhibit the H-type pterion. The K-form is represented by one male and one female and the X-type by the right side of a single female.

TABLE 49
FORM OF PTERION

	Right			
	H	K	X	Retournné
Males (4)	3	1	0	0
Females (7)	5	1	1	0
	Left			
	H	K	X	Retournné
Males (4)	3	1	0	0
Females (7)	6	1	0	0

Basal Region (Tables 50, 51, 52)

The height of the occipital condyles is submedium and moderate; the males showing a greater proportion of slight elevation. Similarly, the basal region is never conspicuously elevated. Styloid size is usually moderate among the males and submedium in females. A pharyngeal tubercle is occasional in both sexes but the fossa condition is lacking. The lacerate foramina are typically moderate in size among males and smaller in females. Glenoid fossa depth follows a similar sex pattern. A small postglenoid process occurs on two of the male specimens. Thickness of the tympanic plate is largely divided between medium and thin. The majority of males possess ellipsoid external auditory meatuses; those of the females tend to be somewhat broader.

TABLE 50

OBSERVATIONS, BASAL REGION

	O	sm	+	++
Condyle Elevation				
Males (4)		3	1	0
Females (7)		3	3	1
Basion Elevation				
Males (4)		2	2	0
Females (7)		1	6	0
Styloids — Size				
Males (4)		1	3	0
Females (7)		6	1	0
Pharyngeal Tubercle				
Males (4)	2	0	2	0
Females (7)	5	2	0	0
Pharyngeal Fossa				
Males (4)	4	0	0	0
Females (7)	7	0	0	0

TABLE 51

OBSERVATIONS, BASAL REGION

	O	sm	+	++
Lacerate Foramen Size				
Males (4)		1	3	0
Females (7)		6	1	0
Glenoid Fossa Depth				
Males (4)		0	4	0
Females (7)		7	0	0
Postglenoid Process				
Males (4)	2	2	0	0
Females (7)	7	0	0	0
Tympanic Plate Thickness				
Males (4)		2	2	0
Females (7)		3	4	1
Auditory Meatus Shape	Round	Oval	Ellipse	Slit
Males (4)	0	1	3	0
Females (8)	0	7	1	0

TABLE 52

OBSERVATIONS, BASAL REGION

	Petrous Depression			
	O	sm	+	++
Males (4)	0	1	2	1
Females (7)	0	1	5	1
	Ext. Pterygoid Plate Size			
	O	sm	+	++
Males (4)		1	1	2
Females (6)		3	3	0
	Int. Pterygoid Plate Size			
	O	sm	+	++
Males (4)		0	4	0
Females (6)		4	2	0

Depression of the petrous portion of the basal region is more often than not moderate; the exceptions are in both directions in equal proportions. The pterygoid plates show a normal sex difference in size, the external lamina of the males being pronounced in two of the four skulls.

The Orbits (Table 53)

The shape of the orbits quite characteristically approaches a square and the horizontal inclination ranges between slight and moderate. An infraorbital suture is occasional. Suborbital fossae are consistently shallow in males, less so among the females. The articulation between the lacrimal and ethmoid bones is medium in length in the males and typically less extensive in the other sex.

The Malars (Table 54)

The usual sex differences in malar size is shown by this series; the males run to moderate development, the females to submedium. Strong lateral malar projection is characteristic of the males, the females less so, while pronounced anterior projection of the zygomata is also rather typical. Zygomatic thickness shows the usual sex variation.

The Nasal Region (Tables 55 and 56)

Depression of the nasion is divided between submedium and medium among the males while the females show lack of de-

TABLE 53

OBSERVATIONS, THE ORBITS

		Shape			
	Oblong	Rhomboid	Square	Ellipse	Round
Males (4)	0	0	4	0	0
	Oblong	Rhomboid	Square	Ellipse	Round
Females (8)	0	2	5	0	1
		Inclination			
	O	sm	+	++	
Males (4)	0	2	2	0	
Females (7)	0	5	2	0	
		Infraorbital Suture, Right			
		None	Face	Orbit	
Males (4)		4	0	0	
Females (8)		7	0	1	
		Infraorbital Suture, Left			
		None	Face	Orbit	
Males (4)		3	0	1	
Females (8)		7	0	1	
		Suborbital Fossa Depth			
	O	sm	+	++	
Males (4)	0	4	0	0	
Females (8)	1	4	2	1	
		Lacrimo-Ethmoid Articulation			
	O	sm	+	++	
Males (4)	0	1	3	0	
Females (8)	0	7	1	0	

TABLE 54

OBSERVATIONS, THE MALARS

		Size	
	sm	+	++
Males (4)	0	3	1
Females (8)	6	2	0
		Lateral Projection	
	sm	+	++
Males (4)	0	0	4
Females (8)	0	7	1
		Anterior Projection	
	sm	+	++
Males (4)	0	1	3
Females (8)	0	5	3
		Zygomatic Thickness	
	sm	+	++
Males (4)	0	2	2
Females (8)	5	3	0

Table 55

OBSERVATIONS, NASAL REGION

	O	sm	+	++	+++
Nasion Depression					
Males (4)	0	2	2	0	
Females (8)	3	5	0	0	
Root Height					
Males (4)		1	3	0	0
Females (8)		7	1	0	0
Root Breadth					
Males (4)		1	2	1	0
Females (8)		0	5	3	0
Bridge Height					
Males (4)		0	1	3	0
Females (6)		2	4	0	0
Bridge Breadth					
Males (4)		1	3	0	
Females (7)		1	5	1	

Table 56

OBSERVATIONS, NASAL REGION

Profile	Straight	Concave	Con-Con	Convex
Males (3)	0	0	1	2
Females (5)	0	0	3	2
Sills	Absent	Dull	Medium	Sharp
Males (4)	1	2	1	0
Females (8)	0	4	3	1
Spine	O	sm	+	++
Males (4)	0	2	2	0
Females (8)	0	8	0	0
Subnasal Grooves	O	sm	+	++
Males (4)	2	1	1	0
Females (8)	6	1	1	0

pression to a greater extent. Nasal root height is usually moderate among the males and lower for the females. Breadth of the root ranges from submedium to pronounced. The males show a clear tendency to a high nasal bridge, more so than the females. Bridge breadth is more often moderate in both sexes.

All of the specimens display a convex or concavo-convex nasal profile. The sills of the nasal aperture are not usually well defined and the nasal spine is never large. Subnasal grooves are shown by two of the four males and by two of the six females.

Prognathism (Table 57)

Two of the three male skulls display some total prognathism but it is not pronounced. The females, without exception, are orthognathous. Midfacial prognathism is only occasional and never striking. Alveolar projection, however, seems to be rather characteristic of the majority of skulls, particularly the males.

Table 57

PROGNATHISM

	Total Prognathism			
	O	sm	+	++
Males (3)	1	1	1	0
Females (6)	6	0	0	0
	Midfacial Prognathism			
	O	sm	+	++
Males (4)	2	1	1	0
Females (8)	6	1	1	0
	Alveolar Prognathism			
	O	sm	+	++
Males (4)	1	1	0	2
Females (8)	2	3	2	1

The Palate (Table 58)

The form of the palate is prevailingly parabolic, the one exception, a female, being small U-shaped. Most of the males have moderately high palates and the females more often have low ones. A palatine torus is fairly frequent in both sexes but it is never pronounced in size. The direction of the transverse palatine suture is usually at right angles to the intermaxillary

TABLE 58

OBSERVATIONS, THE PALATE

		Shape			
	Parabolic	Hyperbolic	Elliptic	Small U	Large U
Males (4)	4	0	0	0	0
Females (7)	6	0	0	1	0
		Height			
	O	sm	+	++	+++
Males (4)		0	3	1	0
Females (5)		3	2	0	0
		Torus Size			
	O	sm	+	++	+++
Males (4)	2	1	1	0	
Females (7)	4	0	3	0	
		Torus Form			
	Ridge	Mound	Lump	Normal	
Males (4)	1	1	0	2	
Females (7)	1	2	0	4	
		Transverse Suture			
	Transverse	Anterior	Posterior		
Males (4)	3	0	1		
Females (6)	4	0	2		
		Postnasal Spine			
	O	sm	+	++	+++
Males (4)	0	2	2	0	
Females (7)	0	4	3	0	

line; the exceptions are directed posteriorly. The postnasal spine ranges between small and moderate for both sexes.

The Mandible (Tables 59 and 60)

All of the male lower jaws are medium in size while the females show a predominance of small jaws. The chin form is bilateral in only one instance, a female. Projection of the chin is marked in two of the three males and is more moderate in the females. Alveolar prognathism is not characteristic of either sex.

The geneal tubercles vary in size between medium and small, the submedium type being more characteristic of females. Development of the mylo-hyoid ridge also follows a definite sex pattern: moderate in males, submedium in females. The same is true of the bony relief at the pterygoid attachments. Gonial eversion varies in degree from slight to pronounced in males and from none to moderate in females.

The Teeth (Table 61)

Data on dentition is rather unsatisfactory because of the high frequency of tooth loss, both ante- and post-mortem. Some of the

TABLE 59

OBSERVATIONS, THE MANDIBLE

			Size				
			O	sm	+	++	+++
Males (3)				0	3	0	0
Females (7)				6	1	0	0
			Chin Form				
			Median			Bilateral	
Males (3)			3			0	
Females (6)			5			1	
			Chin Projection				
	Neg.	Neut.	O	sm	+	++	+++
Males (3)	0	0		0	1	2	
Females (6)	0	0		0	5	1	
			Alveolar Prognathism				
			O	sm	+	++	+++
Males (3)			2	1	0	0	
Females (6)			6	0	0	0	

TABLE 60

OBSERVATIONS, THE MANDIBLE

		Geneal Tubercles			
	O	sm	+	++	+++
Males (3)	0	1	2	0	
Females (5)	0	4	1	0	
		Mylo-hyoid Ridge			
	O	sm	+	++	+++
Males (3)	0	0	3	0	
Females (6)	0	6	0	0	
		Pterygoid Attachment			
	O	sm	+	++	+++
Males (3)		0	2	1	0
Females (6)		5	1	0	0
		Gonial Eversion			
	O	sm	+	++	+++
Males (3)	0	1	1	1	
Females (6)	2	1	3	0	

skulls are edentulous and some lack the lower jaw altogether. Hence, the table on caries, for example, is not reliable. Tooth decay may have been much more prevalent than the figures indicate. Abscesses were fairly common. Most of the teeth show pronounced attrition, nor is this condition confined to the oldest individuals. On the whole, the teeth of this series are good. Observations on shovel-shaped incisors and the types of bite cannot be made because the front teeth are either missing or fragmentary. Likewise, the patterns of the molar cusps are obliterated by attrition.

Table 61

OBSERVATIONS, THE TEETH

Ante-Mortem Loss

	0	1-4	5-8	9-12	13-16	17-20	21-24	25-28	29-X
Males (3)	1	0	1	0	1	0	0	0	0
Females (6)	0	0	1	1	1	1	1	0	1

Caries

	0	1-4	5-8	9-16	17-X
Males (4)	3	0	1	0	0
Females (4)	3	0	1	0	0

Wear

	O	sm	+	++	+++
Males (3)	0	0	0	1	2
Females (6)	0	0	1	5	0

Abscesses

	0	1-3	3-X
Males (3)	0	1	2
Females (7)	4	3	0

Morphological Types

A review of the cranial features of the Ventana material suggests a lack of homogeniety in physical type. Some of the contrasts can be largely attributed to occipital deformation practices as reflected by several of the specimens. Thus the deformed skulls are broader and more oval than the undeformed skull when viewed from above; they are hyperbrachycranial and hypsicranial, while the undeformed specimen is mesocranial and low vaulted. On the other hand, it is imprudent to claim that these variations are entirely the result of cradling practices. When the contrasts in vault conformation are extreme and when they are accompanied by other structural differences that cannot be similarly explained, it raises the suspicion that artificial deformation has only accentuated certain differences which were a part of the inherent constitution of the Ventana population. This possibility is strengthened by the presence of other contrasting characteristics which are unaccountable on the basis of cranial deformation. Thus the deformed skulls show moderate cranial capacity while the long head is greatly inferior in this trait. The deformed series exhibits greater general size and more rugged relief. Nasal indices are higher in the deformed specimens and the orbits are considerably less hypsiconch. Similarly, the larger hyperbrachycephals are a good deal less brachyuranic and they exhibit much greater alveolar prognathism and chin projection. The mandibular indices describe the jaws of the deformed skulls as relatively narrower and longer.

The most serious obstacle to the suggestion that two different morphological types are represented in the Ventana series is the size of the sample. The three deformed male crania form a well defined type, it is true. This type is characterized by very broad heads, high vaults, moderate cranial capacity coupled with medium proportioned facial contours, moderate nasal ratios, rather high orbits and broad palates. The lower face is marked by rather pronounced alveolar prognathism and strong chin projection. In the main, such a type conforms with similar deformed brachycephals of the Anasazi Culture which existed farther north in the Southwestern archaeological province.

The other suggested morphological variant is a good deal less rugged in general appearance. The skull is undeformed, mesocranial, low vaulted, and it has a much smaller cranial capacity. The vault is more scaphoid, the forehead recedes more sharply, the temporal area is flatter and the occiput more curved. The facial skeleton is marked by a narrow nose and by orbits that are relatively higher than the deformed series. Jaw development is noticeably less in the undeformed specimen and the mandible is relatively broader.

The obvious objection to presenting this latter cranium as a second morphological type is not lack of contrasting features but the use of one skull only on which to base a separate physical type. Many of the variations enumerated could result from a single undersized individual who had escaped the cranial deformation practices shown by the other specimens. This objection taken alone is a valid one.

There are, however, certain considerations relative to the female series that bolster the indications of heterogeneity among the Ventana people. It is possible to distinguish among these some fairly close feminine counterparts of the male types described above. As far as vault conformation is concerned, most of the females resemble the undeformed male. They are mesocranial on the average, low vaulted, and they have strongly receding and constricted foreheads. Only one of the females has as low a vault as the undeformed male, an indication that the latter is not representative in that trait. Comparisons with the females suggest also that the undeformed male cranial capacity is unusually small. One of the female crania is hyperbrachycephalic and high vaulted like the deformed males; others conform closely to neither one or the other of the suggested male types, they are variously intermediate, resembling one type in some features and approaching the other type in other aspects.

Despite the inadequate size of the sample, it is believed that the combined evidence warrants the opinion that more than one morphological type constituted the Ventana population. The one is quite clear cut and represented by the three deformed males and one female. This is allied to the Anasazi or Pueblo population to the north. The other type is based on the undeformed individuals, male and female. It approaches the Basketmaker type of Hooton's[3] as closely as any other described in the Southwest.

★

3. *Ibid.*, p. 231.

Ventana-Papago Comparison

The material culture of the ceramic level at Ventana Cave is essentially Hohokam. But the usual Hohokam funerary practice of cremation is lacking, and in its place is a form of inhumation like that practiced among the Anasazi. Since Ventana Cave is located in the territory of the modern Papago, the question of physical relationship between the prehistoric and historic people of this area is immediately raised. What, in other words, can the Ventana skeletal material add to our present knowledge of Papago beginnings?

The origin of the Papago has been the subject of considerable discussion among Southwestern anthropologists. Attempts to bring them into their present habitat during later prehistoric times are met with grave obstacles. Physical differences alone preclude the probability of their being descendants of the Pueblo tribes of the north.[4] An eastern origin is no more tenable, since that area was occupied by their traditional Apache enemies, and archaeological support to such a theory is lacking. To the south, the general lack of evidence from that province makes any prehistoric immigration from Mexico purely hypothetical as yet. Westward lies the Yuman country, and the last word from that region is a denial of anything but occasional contact across the desert waste that separates the Colorado peoples from the Papago.[5]

A good deal of archaeological interest has centered about the prehistoric inhabitants of the modern Piman speaking area. The southwestern part of Arizona is rich in archaeological material and a prehistoric sequence of cultures has been delimited, at least for the northern part of the area centering in the Gila Valley. The work of Gila Pueblo at Snaketown has been largely responsible for extending the Hohokam horizons back to the early centuries of the Christian Era. A period of dual occupation in this same area around the 13th to the 14th centuries has been

★

4. N. E. Gabel, 1941.
5. M. J. Rogers, 1941.

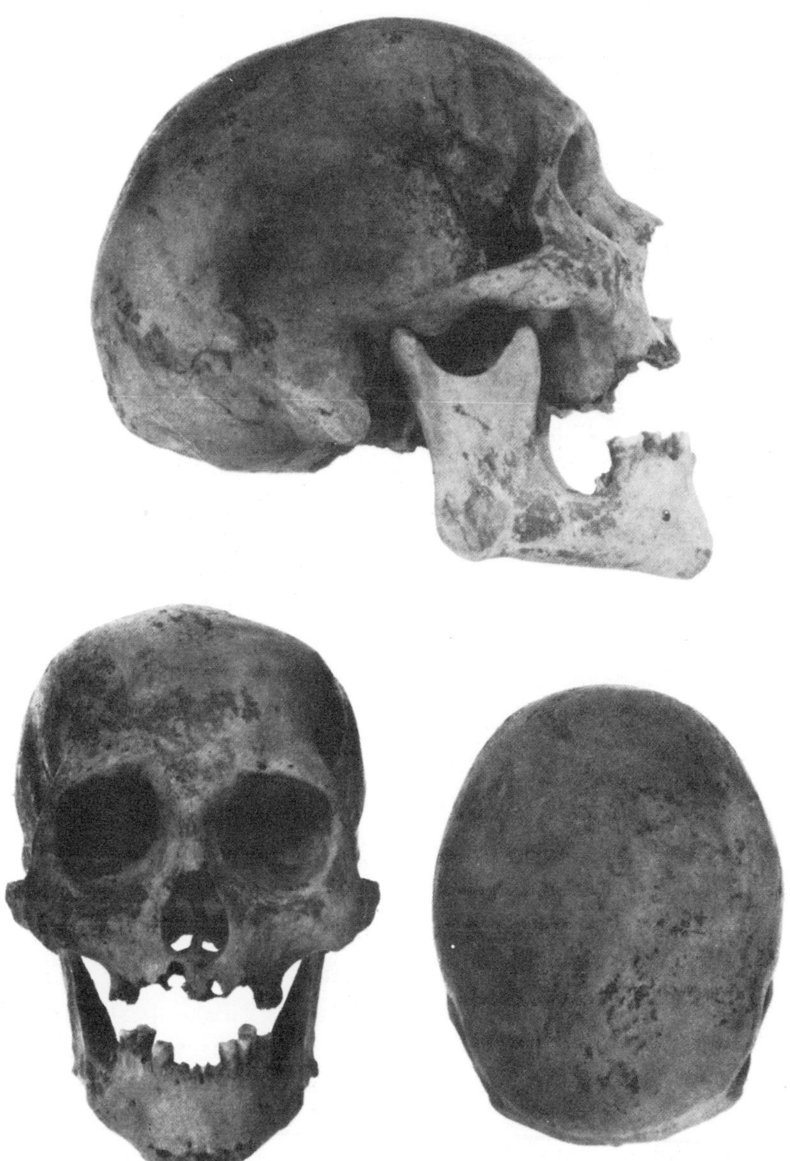

Plate 63

Burial 14. Hohokam, undeformed male.

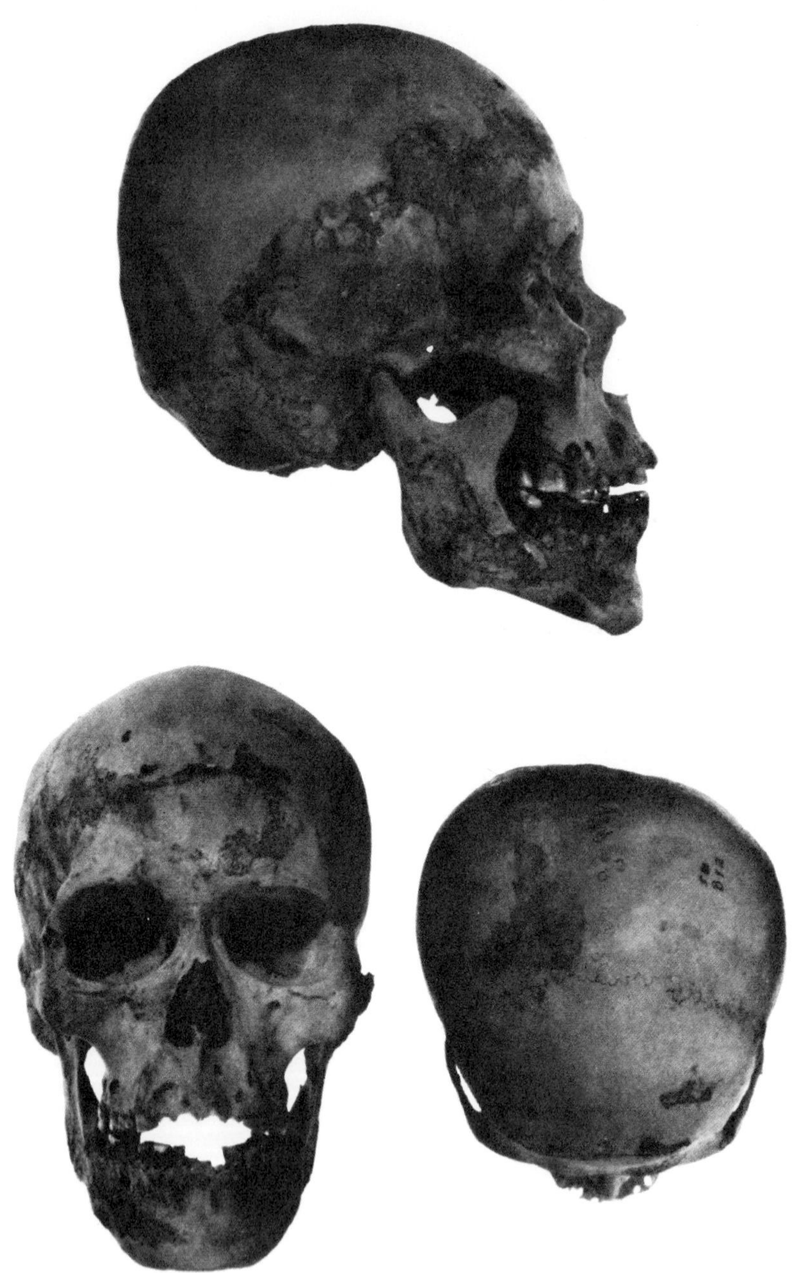

PLATE 64

Burial 12. "Pueblo" type, deformed male.

demonstrated.[6] This was the result of a transitory intrusion of the Salado people from the Pueblo country, and it brought in such northern traits as communal houses, pottery, and inhumation of the dead. Seemingly, the native Hohokam practices of paddle-and-anvil pottery finish, cremation, semi-subterranean family unit houses, and extensive irrigation systems were continued with little interruption during this Salado visitation. And after the withdrawal of this apparently peaceful invasion in the later 14th or early 15th century, the Hohokam story becomes obscure. In fact, the period between the abandonment of the large houses of the Salado people (in the neighborhood of 1400) and the earliest mention of the modern Papago at the close of the 17th century has been almost a complete blank. Several striking cultural resemblances occur between the Hohokam and the modern Indians of the same area and these have suggested to some investigators a direct ethnic relationship between the two. Similarities in pottery technique and design, the same use of irrigation canals, and several affinities in house type are the strongest links in this line of reasoning. Gladwin's analysis of the story is that the modern Papago are a remnant of the Hohokam who were forced by nomadic pressure into their present habitat.

"The arrival of the Athapascans is all the excuse needed to explain the disappearance of the Salado people from the Gila Basin. It is quite possible that the Eastern Salado sites were in no way connected with the more Western Salado sites in the Gila Basin and Tucson, that these western groups were killed off, and that the remnants of the Hohokam sought refuge in the desert country of the Papagueria."[7]

The greatest impediment to this theory of a Hohokam ancestry to the modern Piman-speaking people has been the necessity of accepting a change from cremation customs, as practiced by the Hohokam, to inhumation, which is the custom of the modern Papago.

★

6. H. S. Gladwin, 1928; E. W. Haury, 1945, pp. 205-213.
7. H. S. Gladwin, *et al.*, 1937, p. 102.

The skeletal remains from Ventana Cave give us our first opportunity to compare the physical appearance of individuals definitely associated with Hohokam Culture and modern Papago. For this purpose the writer has made use of all the available skeletal data (Tables 62 and 63). These are limited to a series of ten crania, five males and five females. Measurements and indices are available for all ten, but morphological observations could be obtained for only one male and one female, since the remainder of the collection is no longer in our possession and could not be obtained. From the Ventana collection only one male specimen is included in the comparison (Burial 14, Pl. 63). The other males are excluded for the present because they are so clearly unlike the Papago crania; they are artificially deformed, which the Papago are not, and they are generally Puebloid in appearance, which the Papago are not. The female Ventana series is composed of six crania, all of which are undeformed. Although handicapped by the small size of the respective samples, the comparisons are not without value.

The horizontal cranial indices describe the males of both series as mesocranial. The pronouncedly low vault of the Ventana male results in chamaecranial and tapeinocranial ratios, both considerably lower than the same indices of the Papago males. The Ventana vault also shows lesser frontal breadth; it is stenometopic while the Papago average is metriometopic. Both series have small cranial capacities, the Ventana specimen particularly. The horizontal vault circumference of each is practically identical while the sagittal and transverse arcs are greater for the Papago crania. Cranial modules are closely alike. Facial diameters agree fairly closely: the total and upper facial ratios of both series are mesoprosopic and mesene although the Ventana values indicate a slighter, broader face. Face breadth relative to vault width, as expressed by the cranio-facial index, is nearly the same for both groups. Close similarity is also shown by the orthognathic index values. The nasal proportions of the Ventana male are leptorrhine while those of the Papago are in the middle category. Orbital ratios for both series are clearly hypsi-

Table 62

VENTANA AND MODERN PAPAGO CRANIA—UNDEFORMED

	Male		Female	
	Ventana (1)	*Papago (5)*	*Ventana (6)*	*Papago (5)*
Head length	177mm.	178.3mm.	167.5mm.	166.5mm.
Head breadth	137	135.0	132.0	130.2
Cranial index	77.4	75.8	79.0	78.2
Basion-bregma	120	132.0	128.2	127.2
Height-length index	67.8	74.0	76.7	76.5
Height-breadth index	87.6	97.9	97.1	97.8
Auricular height	104	113.0	111.8	....
Auricular height index	58.8	62.3	66.9	....
Min. frontal breadth	87	91.2	87.2	88.0
Fronto-parietal index	63.5	67.6	66.1	67.6
Cranial capacity	1120	1265	1095	....
Max. vault circumf.	495	495.6	478.5	469.0
Sagittal arc	335	361.2	347.2	340.7
Transverse arc	289	301	297.7	283.5
Cranial module	144.7	148.5	142.6	141.1
Foramen magnum diam.	31.5	32.0	28.7	30.3
Left parietal thickness	6.3	4.5	5.4	....
Max. face breadth	137	134.2	122.6	122.6
Max. face height	118	120	100.0	....
Total facial index	86.1	89.5	79.4	....
Upper face height	69	72.4	61.8	65.0
Upper facial index	50.3	53.9	51.0	53.0
Cranio-facial index	100.0	99.7	94.4	94.2

Table 63

VENTANA AND MODERN PAPAGO CRANIA—UNDEFORMED

	Male		Female	
	Ventana (1)	*Papago (5)*	*Ventana (6)*	*Papago (5)*
Basion-nasion	100.0	99.0	95.4	93.5
Basion-prosthion	93.0	94.6	92.6	91.7
Gnathic index	93.0	94.3	97.1	97.9
Nasal height	52.0	52.2	45.3	46.2
Nasal breadth	22.0	25.6	24.0	25.5
Nasal index	42.3	49.1	53.0	55.5
Orbital height—R	36.0	35.8	33.3	34.5
Orbital breadth—R	38.0	39.8	37.5	38.5
Orbital index—R	94.7	90.1	88.9	89.6
Orbital height—L	36.0	36.4	32.7	34.5
Orbital breadth—L	40.0	40.0	37.3	39.0
Orbital index—L	90.0	91.1	87.6	88.5
Palate length ext.	46.0	50.8	50.0	48.5 (st)
Palate breadth ext.	62.0	65.6	54.0	57.7
Ext. palatal index	134.8	129.5	108.3	119.0 (st)
Mandibular length	101.0	107.0	100.5	....
Bicondylar breadth	118.0	122.0	112.0	....
Mandibular index	85.6	87.7	89.9	....
Bigonial breadth	86.0	92.0	85.8	....
Zygo-gonial index	62.8	68.7	69.8	....
Symphyseal height	35.0	34.0	30.0	..
Asc. ramus height	64.0	63.0	51.5	....
Asc. ramus br. (min.)	22.0	27.0	29.3	....
Angle of mandible	113°	114°	124.5°	....

conch and palate proportions are prevailingly broad. Although the Ventana mandible is smaller in absolute gross measurements the mandibular index lies close to that of the Papago average. The bigonial diameter of the Ventana specimen is less than that of the Papago, both absolutely and relative to bizygomatic breadth. The heights of the mandibular symphysis and of the ascending ramus are nearly the same for both groups, although the Papago mandibles excel in breadth of the perpendicular ramus. The mandibular angles for both series are nearly identical.

The female series, which is much more satisfactory from a standpoint of size, exhibits a very impressive array of physical likenesses. Both groups are mesocranial, both fall in the lower brackets of hypsicephaly, both are metriocranial and metriometopic. Close agreement also holds for cranial capacity, which is low notwithstanding the sex. Cranial module, vault circumference, sagittal and transverse arcs are nearly alike. The facial diameters are very similar and the upper facial indices are mesene in both series. Cranio-facial ratios are practically identical as are the gnathic indices. Both groups are platyrrhine and hypsiconch. The palatal proportions of the Ventana females are mesuranic, those of the Papago are brachyuranic. Mandibular comparisons are not possible because the Papago skulls all lack the lower jaws.

The strikingly close likeness demonstrated by the female series from Ventana Cave and the modern Papago is particularly significant in view of the fact that the male sample from Ventana consists of only one undeformed specimen. The combined evidence suggests that this lone male is an aberrant individual in several ways, hence, he may not be representative of the true undeformed Ventana male, and the above comparisons with modern male Papago may not be truly indicative.

Several considerations combine to support the probability that the undeformed Ventana male is an individual variant. The extreme lowness of the cranial vault is an instance in point; it is considerably less than the comparable average for the females of the same series. This condition has, of course, marked influence on the length-height and breadth-height ratios of the vault. Similarly, the pronounced deficiency in cranial capacity may be an exaggeration of the true size of a typical sample. Facial comparisons between the Ventana and Papago males agree much more closely; the only significant difference among those values is in nasal proportions: the Ventana specimen has a relatively narrow nose, while the Papago average is mesorrhine.

Comparison of Morphological Observations (Table 64)

The following tabulations present a comparison of morphological observations between the single undeformed Ventana male cranium (Pl. 63) and the one available Papago skull (Pl. 65).

To summarize the more significant observations, it is clear that the Ventana and Papago crania show close similarity in a number of morphological characters. These include moderate development of muscular relief, medium weight of the skull, and pentagonal outline of the vault viewed from above. Development of the supraorbital ridges and the glabella are the same. Both specimens have markedly sloping and rather low foreheads. Each has the same degree of median sagittal elevation on the frontal as well as in the sagittal region. Neither of the temporal areas is well filled, the Papago the lesser of the two. The Ventana skull has small temporal crests and large supramastoid ridges, while the Papago shows more moderate development of the same features. Sphenoid depression and mastoid size are medium in both crania. Close agreement is also the case in the moderately curved occipital regions and in the size of the occipital torus. Correspondence in the basal region occurs in the moderately sized glenoid fossae, small styloids, and medium height of basion relative to the general skull base. Average depression of the petrous parts of the temporal characterize each specimen and each possesses elliptical external auditory meatuses. Moderate suture serration typifies both examples as does the H-type pterion.

TABLE 64

OBSERVATIONS, VENTANA AND PAPAGO CRANIA

	Ventana	*Papago*
GENERAL		
Age	Old	Young adult
Musculiarity	+	+
Weight	+	+
Deformation	O	O
Skull form	pentagonal	pentagonal
FRONTAL REGION		
Brow ridges		
Type	median	median
Size	+	+
Glabella	+	+
Frontal height	sm	sm
Frontal slope	++	++
Metopism	trace	trace
Postorbital constriction	+	+
Bosses	+	sm
Median crest	sm	sm
Breadth	+	sm
PARIETAL REGION		
Sagittal elevation	++	+
Postcoronal depression	O	O
Bosses	+	sm
Foramina	sm	sm
TEMPORAL REGION		
Fullness	sm	sm
Crests	sm	+
Supramastoid crest	++	+
Sphenoid depression	+	+
Mastoids	+	+
OCCIPITAL REGION		
Curve	+	+
Inion	sm	+
Torus		
Size	+	+
Type	mound	crest
BASAL REGION		
Condyle height	sm	+
Basion height	+	+
Styloids	sm	sm
Lacerate foramen	+	sm
Glenoid fossa	+	+
Postglenoid process	O	O
Tympanic plate	sm	+
Auditory meatus	ellipse	ellipse
Petrous depression	+	+
SUTURES		
Serration		
Coronal	+	+

TABLE 64 (Continued)

	Ventana	*Papago*
Sagittal	?	+
Lambdoidal	+	+
Occlusion		
Coronal	sm	trace
Sagittal	+++	O
Lambdoidal	++	O
PTERION		
Right	H	H
Left	H	H
ORBITS		
Shape	square	square
Inclination	+	+
Lacrimo-ethmoid articulation	+	+
Suborbital fossa	sm	sm
MALARS		
Size	+	+
Lateral projection	++	++
Anterior projection	++	++
Zygomatic thickness	+	+
NASAL REGION		
Nasion depression	sm	sm
Root height	+	sm
Root breadth	+	+
Bridge height	++	+
Bridge breadth	+	+
Profile	concavo-convex	concavo-convex
Sills	dull	dull
Subnasal grooves	O	O
Aperture height	+	+
Aperture breadth	sm	+
PROGNATHISM		
Midfacial	O	O
Alveolar	sm	—
Total	O	O
ALVEOLAR BORDERS		
Absorption	++	sm
Preservation	poor	+
PALATE		
Shape	ellipse	ellipse
Height	+	+
Torus	O	O
Transverse suture	transv.	transv.
Postnasal spine	sm	?
MANDIBLE		
Size	sm	+
Chin form	median	median
Chin projection	+	—
Alveolar prognathism	O	O
Geneal tuber	sm	sm
Mylo-hyoid ridge	+	+

TABLE 64 (Continued)
OBSERVATIONS, VENTANA AND PAPAGO CRANIA

	Ventana	*Papago*
Gonial angles		
Pterygoid attachment	+	+
Eversion	+	sm
TEETH		
Eruption	complete	complete
Loss		
Ante-mortem	16	3
Post-mortem	8	27
Wear		
Quality		
Caries		
Abscesses: number, size		

Structural agreement is continued in the square shape of the orbits, their moderate inclination and the small size of the suborbital fossae. The malars are of the same general size although the Ventana zygomae are slightly more projecting. Nasal features common to both specimens include slight depression of the nasion, moderate root and bridge breadth, concavo-convex nasal profile and dull sills.

Both skulls are orthognathous as far as total or mid-facial protrusion is concerned but each shows some alveolar projection. The outlines of the palate in each case are ellipsoidal and the palatal heights are moderate. The mandible of the Ventana male is somewhat smaller than that of the Papago. Each jaw has a moderately projecting chin of the median type. The other mandibular features agree closely with each other.

SUMMARY

It is clear that the single undeformed male of the Ventana series resembles the modern Papago crania in several metrical and indicial characters, and in some other respects there is a lack of agreement. The most striking dissimilarities are the lowness, both absolute and relative, of the cranial vault and the lower nasal index of the Ventana specimen. Among the female series the metrical averages are strikingly alike in nearly every case. Because the vault of the Ventana male is considerably lower than the average female of the same series, it is suggested that this male is not representative in this particular trait. The same may be true of the nasal proportions: the male ratio is much lower than the expected sex difference warrants. If this were the case it would place the undeformed Ventana type metrically very close to the modern Papago. Such a suggestion would be extremely bold were it not for the very close agreement between the Ventana and Papago females.

Close similarity is also the rule when the non-measurable morphological traits of the males are considered. In general conformation and in the majority of cranial details, the Ventana and Papago have a great deal in common.

The insufficient quantity of data does not warrant any conclusive interpretation, but there are rather emphatic indications that no striking change in morphological type occurred between some of the Hohokam occupants of the area considered and the present day inhabitants. This suggestion, of course, applies only to the non-Puebloid element of the Ventana people.

THE BURIALS OF THE PRE-POTTERY HORIZON

The fragmentary remains of three burials (20, 35, and 36) were recovered from the pre-ceramic level of the lower cave (see Fig. 7, *a* for location of Burial 20). Two of these could be sufficiently reconstructed to allow a few measurements of the cranial vault as well as numerous non-metrical observations on the vault and on portions of the face. The third specimen was too shattered and incomplete to permit detailed analysis.

The sub-pottery position of these remains was not the only indication of an earlier time level. The nature of the bone tissue itself was unlike that of the pottery horizon. This difference was largely a matter of much lower content of organic substance in the deeper burials. In the case of one skull, deposits of potassium nitrate were adhering to some of the bone fragments. This in itself is not necessarily an indication of greater age, but, coupled with the long history of the cave, the case for pre-ceramic age is supported. These nitrates were leached out of the organic matter contained in the cave debris under conditions of greater moisture than prevailed during the pottery period, and this is particularly true of the lower cave which was not affected by the spring. Since potassium nitrate was deposited on some of the skull fragments they must have been in the midden during this wetter phase, although the deposit was dry when excavated. Had this burial been intruded downward from the ceramic level during the time the cave was dry, these water soluble salts could not have been formed.

The two other skull fragments that came from the previously moist stratum have no mineral substance adhering to them but the bone tissue is like the first burial just mentioned, strikingly more friable and porous than that of the upper dry level, indicating a greater loss of organic material.

Description of Burial 35

Burial 35, found at a depth of 1.70 m., near the southwestern end of the lower cave, consisted of a fragmentary skull (Pl. 66). The remains were represented by most of the skull cap although none of the vault bones are complete. The squamous portions of each temporal are lacking as is the adjoining part of each parietal. There is a gap below lambda and most of the skull base was not recovered. The facial skeleton is very fragmentary and incomplete. The upper parts of the nasal region, medial and lateral fragments of the upper maxillae, and portions of the right and left zygomatic bones are present. Parts of this specimen were encrusted with crystals of potassium nitrate as mentioned above.

These remains represent a young adult male. The sex criteria are quite clear although the broken condition of the vault was a handicap in determining the age. The weight of the skull is pronounced and the bones of the vault are very thick. The skull is undeformed and from the *norma verticalis* the outline of the vault is ellipsoid.

The marked thickness and weight of the vault bones is of particular interest. Since the left parietal along the squamous suture is missing, it is not possible to record the bone thickness at that region. However, various measurements were made at other parts of the vault. The parietals averaged 9 mm. in thickness at the bosses, nearly 11 mm. at the anterior superior angle, and about 6 mm. at the anterior lower corner. The posterior superior angle of the parietal averaged nearly 10 mm. and the lower posterior portions were between 6 and 7 mm. thick. The frontal bone at the temples showed a mean of 4 mm. and the right and left bosses were 11 and 12 mm. respectively. The occiput is 8 mm. at asterion and 20 mm. at inion. The thickest parts of the vault are clearly along or near the median sagittal plane.

There is good reason to believe that this thickened condition of the skull is not normal but is due to *osteoporosis symmetrica*, or, more precisely, to recovery from this affliction. Hooton[8] says in this connection:

> Recovery from the condition is marked by a deposition of a very thick compact layer of bone over the extended diploë and the latter becomes to a considerable depth compact. The healed surface of the bones is rough, to some extent pitted, and has the appearance of scarification.

This describes accurately the appearance of the skull under consideration.

The glabello-occipital diameter of 196 mm. defines the vault as long. Since fragments of the lower borders of the parietals are missing, the cranial breadth could not be measured exactly, but a careful approximation gives a value of 130 mm. as the total breadth. These diameters result in a hyperdolichocranial index of 66.3. Obviously this ratio is open to question as far as its being the exact value is concerned, but visual examination of the vault contours leaves an unmistakable impression of relative narrowness. The auricular height of 120 mm. in relation to cranial length defines the specimen as orthocranial (61.2).

★

8. E. A. Hooton, 1930, p. 318.

The frontal region is conspicuously constricted laterally. Least frontal diameter is 84 mm. and the frontoparietal index is stenometopic (64.6). The supraorbital ridges are pronounced in size and they form a continuous torus over the orbital and nasal parts of the face. Development of the glabella is also more than moderate. Although the cranial vault is not low as described by the auricular height, the forehead is receding. Postorbital constriction is marked. The frontal bosses are but slightly developed and there are traces of metopism over the nasion. A median crest is slightly in evidence.

In the parietal area the median sagittal elevation is more developed. The bosses are but slightly protrusive and parietal foramina are lacking. The temporal region is marked in two respects: the region of the temples is very flat and the crests, though moderate in development, are very high on the sides of the vault. Most of the occiput is lacking, but the remaining parts indicate that the region was more than moderately curved. A mound type of torus of medium development is present and the inion is pronounced.

Suture serration ranges in complexity from simple along the coronal line to moderate in the sagittal and lambdoidal parts. External occlusion seems not to have begun as far as the lambdoidal and sagittal sutures are concerned, although parts of the lambdoidal are lacking. No Wormian bones appear but this is not conclusive, because of the missing portions of the lambdoidal suture. Observations on the pterion region are not possible and the same is true of most of the skull base. Enough of the petrous parts of the temporals remain to discern that the glenoid fossae are moderate in size and that a postglenoid process borders the posterior edge of each fossa. The tympanic plates are thin and the shape of the external auditory meatuses is round.

On the face only some of the upper and lower parts of the nasal region remain. The nasion depression is moderate, the root of the nose is low and about average in width. At the lower aspect the nasal sills are very poorly developed and there is moderate development of subnasal grooves.

Description of Burial 36

The second pre-ceramic burial is represented by the fragmentary remains of most of the skull cap. The cranial base is entirely missing. The facial parts include nearly all of the right maxillary and a part of the left. A piece of the left zygomatic bone is also present. Part of the right mandible is preserved along with ten teeth, five of them in the jaw fragments and the other five loose.

The condition of these remains is more fragmentary, more fragile, and more friable than the preceding specimen. Probable causes for this contrast lie in the pathological nature of burial 35, described above, which thickened and reinforced the bone structure as well as the more advanced age of burial 36. The latter skull is that of an old adult.

Criteria of sex are not so unmistakable as are those of the preceding individual, but male characteristics predominate.

The general shape and proportions of this vault conform to those of burial 35. The horizontal outline is ellipsoidal and the occiput is well curved. Maximum cranial length is 191 mm. and the reconstructed total breadth is 126 mm. The resulting hyperdolichocranial index of 66.0 is almost identical to that of burial 35. The auricular height is recorded as 115 mm. although the reconstruction of this axis leaves the measurement open to some question. With this in mind, the approximate auricular height index defines the skull as orthocranial (60.2). Minimum frontal breadth is 88 mm. and the fronto-parietal index is 67.7.

The frontal region of the vault exhibits pronounced slope and less than average height. Development of the brow ridges is average and in type they are divided. The glabella is moderate. Postorbital constriction is quite marked, the frontal bosses are slight, and a small median crest is present. Traces of metopism occur between nasion and glabella. The general frontal breadth is submedium.

Slight median sagittal elevation is also present in the parietal region of the vault and here also the bosses are less than moderately developed. Temporal fullness is submedium. The temporal and supramastoid crests show average development. Occipital curvature is pronounced and the torus of the occiput is a mound type of moderate size. The inion is average.

Suture patterns are obscured by advanced occlusion. The coronal suture, which shows advanced closure, appears to have been moderately intricate. The sagittal is so nearly obliterated that its former serration cannot be determined, and the lambdoidal, which is moderately closed, exhibits average intricacy. No Wormian bones can be defined but these may have occurred and become obliterated.

The only observations on the skull base are of a few traits on the petrous parts of the temporals. The glenoid fossae are of average size, as are the mastoids. The tympanic plates are medium in thickness and the external auditory meatuses are round.

The zygomatic fragment indicates moderate size but not enough of the face remains to describe the projection of the malars. Small suborbital fossae are demonstrated by the right maxillary bone. The remains of the nasal region show submedium nasion depression and a low nasal root. The nasal sills are rather dull and the anterior spine is small. Small subnasal grooves are present.

The palate is elliptical in shape and moderately high. The transverse suture is directed posteriorly. What remains of the right half of the mandible indicates that the jaw was moderately large although alveolar absorption has reduced the original size. The chin region is mostly missing but the remnants suggest medium development. Also average is the mylo-hyoid ridge. The gonial angles are not everted and the bony relief at the pterygoid attachment is medium.

A limited number of dental observations are possible. The

total ante-mortem tooth loss cannot be determined but, on the basis of the existing parts, probably more than half of the teeth were lost before death. The teeth that remain are of good quality though extremely worn, some of them beyond the original level of the pulp layer. Only one tooth among the ten is carious and there are no abscesses. The pronounced attrition of the molars obliterates the cusp patterns, nor can observations on possible shovel-shaped incisors be made.

Description of Burial 20

This burial was too fragmentary and fragile to warrant an attempt at reconstruction. The nature of the bone tissue is very similar to that of burial 36; it is very porous and easily crumbled. The few sex criteria suggest an adult female.

Summary of the Pre-Pottery Crania

The two crania underlying the pottery horizon of Ventana, described above, have many traits in common. Despite the unfortunate lack of several important parts, the general similarity of the remaining features moves the writer to the view that they are of the same morphological type. The most important evidence to support this opinion lies in the close affinities shown by vault conformation. Both crania are hyperdolichocranial and have moderately high vaults. The horizontal outline of each is an elongated ellipse. Pronounced slope and narrowness of the forehead are shared by the two and conspicuous postorbital constriction, small frontal bosses, and median sagittal elevation add to their mutual likeness.

The facial remains, though very incomplete, do not disturb the vault indications of physical affinity. Both, for example, share nasal features like poorly developed sills and subnasal grooves. Wherever comparison is possible, similarity is the rule, particularly for the more significant traits.

Space does not permit lengthy and detailed comparisons of the pre-ceramic skulls, but the closest resemblance to other American material is found in a series of undeformed hyperdolichocephals from the Texas Coast described by the Woodburys,[9] and these latter crania, according to the same report, compare rather closely with other Texas crania defined by Hooton[10] and Oetteking.[11] The Woodburys also point out the physical resemblance of this long-headed type with the Pericue of Lower California who are "by some considered an archaic physical variety of American Indian."[12]

COMPARISON OF VENTANA PRE-POTTERY AND POTTERY CRANIA AND MODERN PAPAGO

The cranial data considered thus far, though inadequate in quantity, cover a time period that ranges from a pre-ceramic horizon to the modern Papago inhabitants of the same area. The possibility of physical affinity between one element of the Ventana population, that is, the element represented by undeformed crania, and the modern Papago has been presented earlier in the discussion. It remains to be seen how the earliest known inhabitants of Papagueria compare with the people who occupied the same region during the Hohokam period, as well as the present day residents. Table 65 presents the metrical and indicial data available from the two fragmentary pre-pottery crania of Ventana Cave (burials 35 and 36) along with comparable

TABLE 65

MEASUREMENTS AND INDICES OF VENTANA PRE-POTTERY, HOHOKAM, AND MODERN PAPAGO CRANIA

	Pre-pottery		*Hohokam*	*Papago*
	B35	B36	B14	
Head length	196mm.	191mm.	177mm.	178.3mm.
Head breadth	130	126	137	135
Cephalic index	66.3	66.0	77.4	75.8
Auricular height	120	115	104	113
Auricular height index	61.2	60.2	58.8	62.3
Min. frontal breadth	84.0	88.0	87.0	91.2
Fronto-parietal index	64.6	67.7	63.5	67.6

★

9. G. and E. Woodbury, 1935.
10. E. A. Hooton, 1933.
11. B. Oetteking, 1930.
12. G. and E. Woodbury, 1935, p. 43.

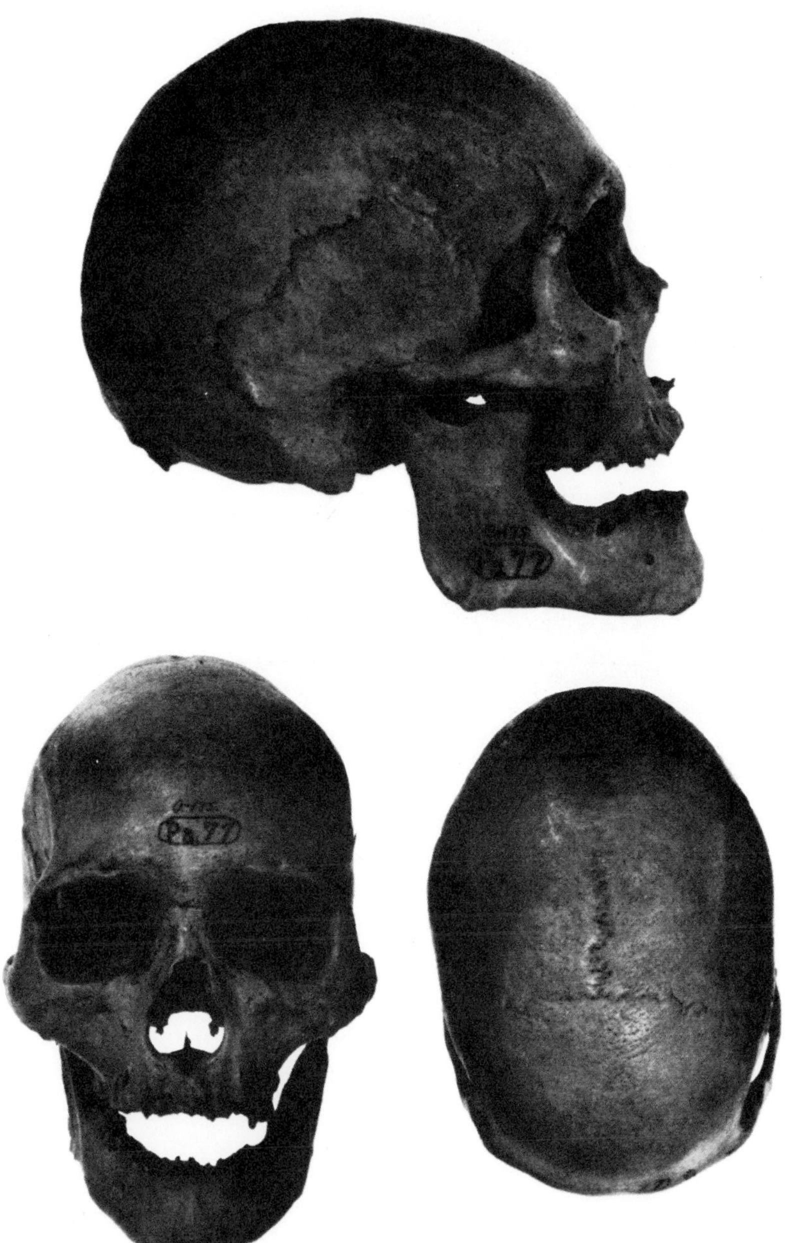

PLATE 65

Modern Papago male, undeformed.

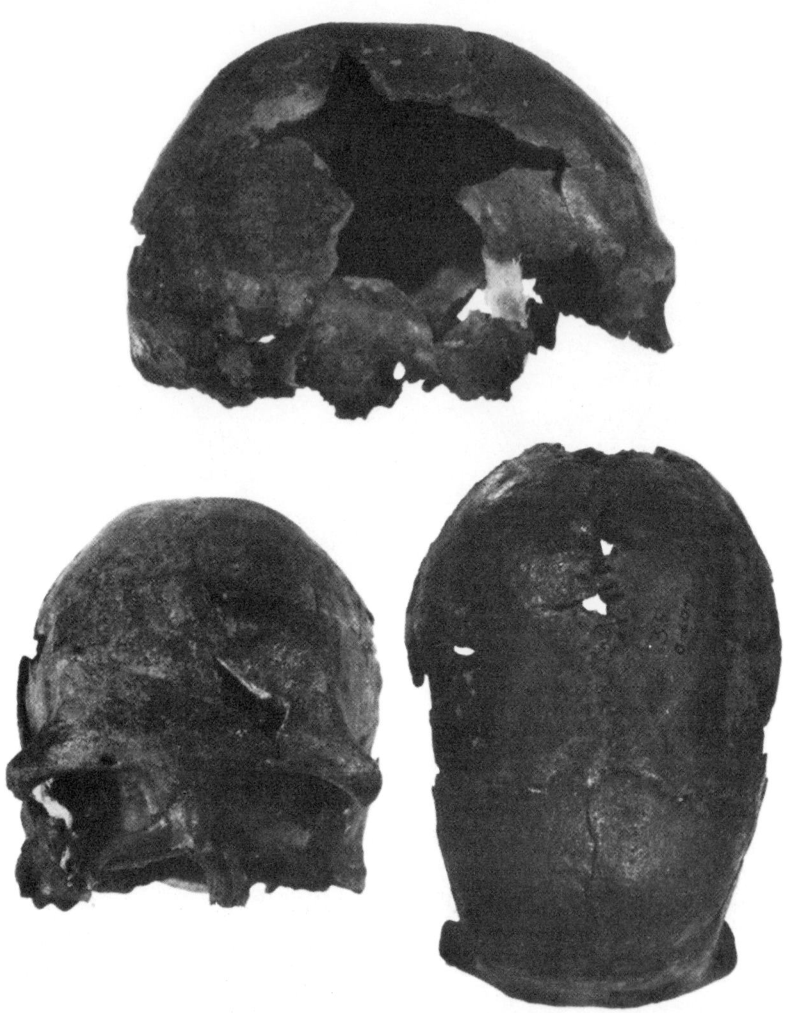

PLATE 66

Burial 35. Pre-pottery level. Undeformed male.

information on the undeformed Hohokam specimen (burial 14) and the series of modern Papago males. Since the pre-ceramic specimens are both males, females are excluded from the comparison. Also not included here are the deformed Puebloid crania from the Hohokam horizon because of their obvious lack of resemblance to any of the undeformed series, either modern or prehistoric.

The vault measurements describe the pre-pottery crania as pronouncedly longer-headed than either the Hohokam or Papago. The contrast is conspicuous both in absolute and relative values. Auricular height of the early skulls is considerably superior to that of the Hohokam male although it was suggested earlier that the latter may not be representative in that trait. Compared with modern Papago, the pre-pottery vault height excess is reduced to an insignificant difference. Relative to head length, all of the skulls considered fall into the orthocranial category, the Hohokam example at the lower, the Papago at the upper, end of the class. All of the skulls have narrow foreheads, particularly burial 35 of the pre-pottery level; in relation to maximum head breadth all of the early crania and the Hohokam example are stenometopic, while the other pre-ceramic skull and the Papago are metriometopic.

The non-measurable morphological characters (Table 66) demonstrate numerous points of likeness and several dissimilarities. The pre-pottery cranial vaults are narrower and more elliptical in outline than the later types although the difference is not marked. All of the skulls, as stated above, are undeformed and they all show moderate muscularity with the exception of burial 36, which is less rugged.

Pronounced slope of the frontal region is characteristic of all of the specimens. Burial 35 has pronounced supraorbital ridges but the others are moderately developed. Brow ridge type is more variable. General agreement between burial 36 and the more recent skulls occurs in the moderate glabella development and in the submedium forehead height. The pre-pottery crania have more marked postorbital constriction and none of

TABLE 66

MORPHOLOGICAL OBSERVATIONS OF VENTANA PRE-POTTERY, HOHOKAM, AND MODERN PAPAGO

	Pre-pottery B35	B36	*Hohokam* B14	*Papago*
GENERAL				
Vault shape	ellipse	ellipse	pentagonal	pentagonal
Age	young adult	old adult	old adult	young adult
Muscularity	+	sm	+	+
Deformation	O	O	O	O
FRONTAL REGION				
Brow ridges				
Size	++	+	+	+
Type	continuous	divided	median	median
Glabella	++	+	+	+
Frontal height	+	sm	sm	sm
Frontal slope	++	++	++	++
Postorbital constriction	++	++	+	+
Bosses	sm	sm	+	sm
Median crest	sm	sm	sm	sm
Breadth	sm	sm	+	sm
PARIETAL REGION				
Sagittal crest	sm	sm	+	+
Bosses	sm	sm	+	sm
Foramina	O	sm	sm	sm
TEMPORAL REGION				
Fullness	sm	sm	sm	sm
Crests	+	+	sm	+
Supramastoid crest	?	+	++	+
Mastoids	?	+	+	+
OCCIPITAL REGION				
Curve	++	++	+	+
Torus				
Size	+	+	+	+
Type	mound	mound	mound	crest
Inion	++	+	sm	++
BASAL REGION				
Glenoid fossa	+	+	+	+
Postglenoid process	+	O	O	O
Tympanic plate	sm	+	sm	+
Ext. auditory meatus	round	round	ellipse	ellipse
SUTURES				
Serration				
Coronal	simple	+	+	+
Sagittal	+	?	?	+
Lambdoidal	+	+	+	+

TABLE 66 (CONTINUED)

Occlusion				
Coronal	ssm	++	sm	ssm
Sagittal	O	+++	+++	O
Lambdoidal ..	O	+	++	O
ORBITAL REGION				
Suborbital fossa .	+	sm	sm	sm
MALARS				
Size	++	+	+	+
NASAL REGION				
Nasion depression	+	sm	sm	sm
Root height ...	sm	sm	+	sm
Root breadth ...	+	+	+	+
Profile	?	?	concavo-convex	concavo-convex
Bridge height ..	?	?	++	+
Bridge breadth .	?	?	+	+
Nasal sills	round	dull	dull	dull
Nasal spine	?	sm	sm	sm
Subnasal grooves	+	sm	O	O
PALATE				
Shape	?	ellipse	ellipse	ellipse
Height	?	+	+	+
Torus	?	O	O	O
MANDIBLE				
Size	?	+	sm	+
Chin form	?	?	median	median
Chin projection	?	—	+	+
Prognathism	?	?	O	O
Mylo-hyoid ridge	?	+	+	+
Gonial angles				
Pterygoid attach.	?	+	+	+
Eversion	?	sm	+	sm

the foreheads can be described as broad. Frontal bosses are small to medium and a slight median sagittal elevation is present in each.

The parietal area is also elevated in the sagittal plane and the protuberances tend to be slight. Parietal foramina are lacking in burial 35 and small in the others. All the specimens have flattened temporal areas. The temporal crests are not strongly developed nor are the mastoids and supramastoid crests large, excepting those of the Hohokam male.

The occipital portions of the pre-ceramic skulls are more strongly curved but the later crania are also well rounded in that area. Moderate occipital tori are the rule and all but the modern Papago have a mound type superior nucal crest. Depth and size of the glenoid fossae are medium in every case. The shape of the external auditory meatuses is round in the pre-pottery skulls, ellipsoidal in the later specimens. Serration of the sutures of the vault shows little difference in the various time levels.

Only a few of the facial traits can be compared. Suborbital fossae are present in each case but they are never pronounced. The malars, excepting burial 36, are moderately developed. In the region of the nose, submedium nasion depression is exhibited by all save burial 36. Root breadth is medium in every case and height is submedium, excepting that of the Hohokam male. None of the specimens have sharply defined nasal sills and small nasal spines are also the rule. The pre-pottery crania show some development of subnasal grooves; the Hohokam and Papago do not.

Close agreement is shown in the conformation of the palate. All have an ellipsoidal outline and are of medium height. Comparisons of the mandibles are not very satisfactory because burial 35 lacks this member and that of burial 36 is incomplete; but judging from the data available, there are no important points of difference.

GENERAL SUMMARY

The general picture from the foregoing comparisons is that the earliest inhabitants of Papagueria, those represented by the pre-ceramic burials 35 and 36, were hyperdolichocranial, orthocranial, with ellipsoidal vault shape. Their foreheads were laterally constricted and sloped sharply. Slight median sagittal elevation of the vault was also characteristic and the occipital area was well curved. No impression of the general conformation of the face is possible but what fragments remain indicate slight to moderate nasion depression, low nasal root and poorly developed nasal spine and sill along with subnasal grooves. Palatal and mandibular remains are not distinctive. The resemblance of this cranial type to other early Southwestern Indians has been previously pointed out.

At a later time, during the Hohokam horizon, there is indication of greater diversity among the inhabitants. Associated with the pottery level was one type of Indian that fits the usual concept of Anasazi people. These had very broad and high heads that were artificially deformed by cradling practices. Their general facial proportions were moderate as were their nasal ratios. Broad palates, high orbits, alveolar prognathism and good chin development also characterize this physical element. This type is a rather marked departure from the earlier pre-ceramic crania; it is also quite different from some of its contemporaries.

From the same cultural level comes a morphological type that is less rugged in appearance, undeformed, mesocranial and rather low vaulted. It has a more receding, more constricted forehead, median sagittal vault elevation, and more strongly curved occiput. It shares a good deal with the conformation of the pre-pottery crania, the chief difference being increased cranial index. In other words, no great physical change is indicated between the pre-ceramic and undeformed Hohokam representatives.

Finally, the possibility of direct relationship between this latter undeformed Hohokam type and the modern Papago Indians has been presented.

Though the evidence is not conclusive, this might mean that the physical type which occupied the Ventana area of Papagueria has been rather stable for several thousand years. The presence of a Puebloid element seems to have been impermanent and conforms with the cultural evidence of dual occupation during the latter part of the Hohokam development, notably in the Gila Basin. Such an influx of Puebloid physical type could account for the increase in cranial index that the undeformed Hohokam individuals show when compared with the pre-pottery people. Archaeological data have shown that the Salado influence on the Hohokam Culture was ephemeral; now there are physical suggestions that the northern brachycephals worked no marked change on the native population. The Papago of today, like the Hohokam people, do not seem to have been strongly affected by the Indians of the north. In a word, general physical continuity is indicated for Papagueria over a time range which begins before pottery and presumably before agriculture, and which continues to the present.[13]

★

13. Since the above was written by Dr. Gabel, new evidence has come to hand which, while not conclusive, is consistent with the deduction just drawn. In 1947, Mr. Edward L. Breazeale, then with the Division of Laboratories, Arizona State Department of Health, (now Assistant Agricultural Chemist, University of Arizona), undertook blood group tests of Ventana Cave mummy tissue. Samples from ten mummies were examined by two different methods: (1) by absorption and cross agglutination studies, and (2) by extracting the tissue with normal saline and using the extracted fluid as the antigen against known type A and B cells. The results produced by these two methods are in perfect agreement. Of the ten samples analyzed, nine were type "O" (burials 2, 3, 5, 6, 8, 9, 11, 15, and 31) and one was type "AB" (burial 16). This exceptionally high incidence of type "O" is true also for the Papago Indians (93.83 per cent of a sample of 600: see E. L. Breazeale, R. A. Greene, and L. J. Kantor, 1941). Wiener (1943, pp. 297-304), in a table of racial distribution of the blood groups, shows only one Indian tribe in the United States, the Utes, with a higher incidence of type "O" (97.40 per cent), whereas the others (five tribes) run substantially lower. In the entire table of over 360 entries of world peoples there are only two groups, the Ute and the Yucatan, which exceed the Papago in the percentage of type "O" in the population, indicating further that the blood-group pattern of the Papago is a rather special one. The Papago-Ventana parallel thus has an increased probability of significance as an indicator of physical continuity in the present and early populations of Papagueria. (E. W. H.)

PART VIII

Final Discussion

We have now reached about the same position in which a little boy finds himself when he has eaten his cake, all but the frosting, and is ready for that last satisfying gulp. But unlike the boy, who knows the icing is the most toothsome part of the cake, we find that our "icing"—the generalizations derivable from the wealth of data presented—requires some real chewing to get nourishment from it. In our preoccupation with the products from the hands of these people, have we lost sight of the fact that we are still dealing with people? Can the findings of Ventana Cave be translated into human terms?

These and other questions must be coursing through the minds of the readers who have followed the report to this point. In my opinion the answer to the second question is a faint "yes," muted by the incompleteness of our knowledge of any one culture horizon and by the fact that, while the recorded succession of people in Ventana is orderly, the exact nature of the forces responsible for shaping the patterns of the lives of these people and inducing changes is about as obscure as ever. Beyond admitting the limiting effects of environment, of changing climate, and of the accident of diffusion, I doubt that these can yet be put in explicit terms, at least when affecting peoples of thousands of years ago.

The analysis made, then, of the Ventana remains has been inspired by the desire, first, to establish patterns, second, to rank them chronologically, and third, to equate them with the patterns of culture determined by other investigators to provide us with some understanding of the larger questions of Man's history in the western United States.

The first two objectives have, I believe, been met, due to the wealth of cultural material preserved in a superb succession of layers, both geological and man-made as to origin. It is admitted, of course, that the culture groupings are abstractions because, by the very nature of the evidence, they cannot be exactly defined. Yet, when other ingredients are added, notably the associated fauna and the factor of climatic change, it all adds up to a passage of time and a record, even if sketchy, of Man's long sojourn here.

To consolidate the deductions permissable with respect to the culture sequence, time, climate, and fauna of Ventana Cave, reference is made to Figure 113. Time assignments for the older deposits are based on the findings of Dr. Bryan, whose analysis is included elsewhere in this volume. The red sand (Bed 4) is given an uncertain position since there appears to be some doubt as to whether it falls within the post-glacial optimum of B. C. 5500 to 2500 or after 2500.

With respect to the internal sequence of culture patterns, it should be emphasized once again that several gaps are observable. The obvious interruption occurs between the volcanic debris and red sand layers. The disconformity, indicative of erosion and hence a dry period, and the change in fauna, attest to the passage of considerable time, but we have, at present, no means of calculating exactly how long this was. According to Bryan, this may have been as much as 5,000 years. The implement typologies from these two levels have some elements in common, but there are also differences which may be further interpreted as signifying changes within the culture of the occupants, if they were of the same ethnic group at both periods, or if not, of a new group moving in. In any case, at least one chapter in the cave's long history between the Ventana Complex and the Ventana-Amargosa I layers was torn out or was never recorded.

Following the story upward in time, Ventana-Amargosa I would appear to be the logical antecedent of Chiricahua-Amargosa II, although the older material occurred in a wind (or water?) derived layer and the latter was in man-made trash. Transitions in implement types continue smoothly in successively later horizons. The additions of pottery, agriculture, new metate and mano forms, the polishing of stone, and the manufacture of shell ornaments at about the time of Christ, would

LAYERS	BEDS (BRYAN)	TIME	CULTURE	CLIMATE	FAUNA
SURFACE		PRESENT	PAPAGO		
		1700	?		
(DRY)	1	1400	HOHOKAM		
MIDDEN (MOIST)	2	A. D. 1 ±	SAN PEDRO	DRY	MODERN
			CHIRICAHUA-AMARGOSA II		
			VENTANA-AMARGOSA I		
TALUS	3	B. C. 2,500 TO 5,500	?	POST-GLACIAL OPTIMUM MAX. WARMTH, DRY EROSION	
RED SAND	4				
		DISCONFORMITY			
VOLCANIC DEBRIS	5a		VENTANA COMPLEX		
	5b	MIN. 10,000 TO MAX. 25,000 ± YRS. AGO		MOIST, COOL	EXTINCT, AND FORMS NOT NOW IN AREA SOME MODERN SPECIES
CONGLOMERATE	6a		STERILE		
	6b				
BEDROCK					

FIGURE 113. Section of the geological and midden deposits of Ventana Cave correlated with time, culture, climate, and fauna. Age of the older deposits based on Bryan

make a cultural disconformity seem plausible. But the retention of many stone tools in unchanged form suggests rather that new elements were being taken on by an established group.

The final break in the sequence is recognizable only on the basis of the cultural remains and not in the physical composition of the debris. This was between 1400 and 1700 and is, at present, the chief obstacle in directly linking the Papago with the Hohokam.

DATING THE VENTANA DEPOSITS

Throughout these pages, frequent reference has been made to time, but these references have not always been accompanied by justifications. Further consideration of this important aspect of archaeology is now in order. The orderly succession of layers, both geological and man-made as to origin, easily permits the establishment of relative age of the various culture horizons. But can precise dates be assigned? Obviously not, because our present methods of dating cave deposits are still too imperfectly developed. Nevertheless, estimates of elapsed time may be reached which are set forth below.

The problem has two distinct facets: first, the approximate dating of the recent or higher cultures, the Neo-Indian; and second, arriving at an even more general estimate of the age of the early cultures, the Paleo-Indian. For each of these, different sets of criteria must be used. The line of separation between these two general patterns of life, insofar as Ventana is concerned, is drawn at that point when agriculture and pottery first appear. These traits, together with others which are linked with them, are considered as symbols of a higher plane of existence. It will be recalled from the preceding discussions that both of these appeared relatively high in the midden layer of the cave. Hence, only the upper third can be accredited to the Neo-Indian level while the lower midden and the preceding nature-laid layers with artifacts are assignable to the Paleo-Indian.

Fortunately there is a fixed point from which the dating of the recent occupation may be started—the present. The latest material present was left by the Papago in recent years, probably by the family which annually collected sahuaro fruit in that vicinity prior to the excavation of the cave. Items attributable to these people include modern pottery, wooden objects cut with steel knife, and material acquired from our own culture, as metal, glass, and textiles.

Older Papago material is also represented, as, for example, pottery datable to the late 18th and early 19th centuries and metal, hand-wrought knives, acquired from Whites or Mexicans possibly as early as 1800. All told, the Papago evidence constitutes a relatively thin veneer spread over the surface of the cave when found, probably not representing a span of time greater than from about 1700 to 1941.

Coming now to the highest of the prehistoric layers, including all of that part of the midden in which pottery occurred, it is necessary to employ the principle of typology to achieve an estimate of age. Cultural products of given characteristics can be used to identify a certain culture, and, within limits, they also become keys to the period of time when that particular culture flourished, especially when dated, as by tree-rings.

Turning first to pottery, we have been able to show that the main types, as represented at Snaketown, were present in Ventana. Since these two sites are not greatly distant from each other, it may be assumed that lag is of no consequence and that contemporaneity is implied. If, then, dates are established for the Snaketown horizons, these may be projected to include also the occupation at Ventana, perhaps a devious step when the dating of Snaketown itself is already once removed from a region of certain dating, namely the Flagstaff area. This was accomplished primarily by the presence in Snaketown of Flagstaff pottery types whose age was known within a century through tree-rings. This took care of the occupation there from about 700 to 1100, leaving a number of phases before 700 to be dated by estimation. The Snaketown chronology, as set forth originally, extended from about B. C. 300 to A. D. 1100.[14] More

★

14. H. S. Gladwin, E. W. Haury, E. B. Sayles, and N. Gladwin, 1937.

recently Mr. Gladwin has revised his opinion, however,[15] placing the oldest Snaketown level at A. D. 600. It seems to the writer that this view is as conservative as the first view was generous, and that the truth may lie somewhere in between. Generalizing, however, the oldest pottery from Ventana should not be much younger than A. D. 500 and may date from as early as the time of Christ. Since corn appears to have arrived at Ventana more or less simultaneously with pottery, and since, in the San Juan, corn was grown in the early centuries of the Christian Era (Basketmaker II, before A. D. 400), I favor the earlier date as marking the beginning of what may be called the Neo-Indian occupation of Ventana Cave.

One other point of light on the most recent prehistoric occupation needs to be mentioned. Out of the 31,400 sherds recovered, 35 were of a familiar Salado type, Gila Polychrome. This has been repeatedly dated in sites where it was indigenous to the 14th century. Contact between the Saladoans and the native population in Papagueria was most tenuous although this Pueblo contingent was strongly represented both north, at Casa Grande, in the Gila Valley, and east, at Tucson, in the Santa Cruz Valley, in villages occupied by relatives of the people who found refuge in Ventana. These few Gila Polychrome sherds give us thus our surest evidence of the latest prehistoric use of the cave, some time in the 1300's, and probably not later than 1400.

Summarizing, then, there was first a Papago layer ranging from the present to the inferred date of 1700, since the Papago were in the area at that time. Second, the period from 1700 to 1400 which seems not to be represented; and third, a layer with pottery, dated by somewhat devious means from about 1400 to the beginning of the Christian Era.

While most Southwesternists may agree, in the main, with the foregoing dating, the time assignments of the Paleo-Indian horizons present an altogether different set of problems in which geology, climate, and fauna are deciding factors. These are

★

15. H. S. Gladwin, 1942.

capable of an even wider range of interpretation than are tree-rings and dating by association. Because of this, conflicting correlations of the older Ventana culture levels are possible, as is brought out when relating the Ventana stratigraphy, particularly Bryan's dates for the older beds, to the geochronologies evolved by others for Arizona. Of especial interest here is the work of Antevs[16] in connection with dating the Cochise Culture, which ties in so intimately with the Ventana story and also with the work of Hack[17] for northern Arizona. The comparison shown in Figure 114 is not made with the idea of throwing discredit on the conclusions of anyone, but to emphasize the fact pointed out above, namely, that substantial differences of opinion do exist. Note should be taken of the fact that neither Antevs nor Hack has expressly endeavored to date the Ventana deposits and that the equation has been made by myself on their available published records. The talus has been omitted since it was almost sterile. The dividing line between San Pedro and Chiricahua-Amargosa II in the Hack and Bryan columns is arbitrary, and the red sand with its Ventana-Amargosa I material had to be interpolated in the Antevs column. The Sulphur Springs Stage under Antevs has also been omitted because it was not represented in Ventana Cave.

A point of agreement, or at least near agreement, is the ending date for the final substage of the last glacial during which time the conglomerate and volcanic debris of Ventana Cave, the formations containing the Sulphur Springs Stage material of southeastern Arizona and the Jeddito formation of northern Arizona, were laid down. This was approximately ten thousand years ago, although Hack[18] leans toward a more recent date, B. C. 6000 or about eight thousand years ago. The real discrepancies appear between the time of ten thousand and two thousand years ago, or between about B. C. 8000 and A. D. 1, and stem from the fact that Bryan regards the Ventana sequence as showing a long interruption—the erosion of the post-glacial

★

16. E. B. Sayles and E. Antevs, 1941, pp. 31-56.
17. John T. Hack, 1942.
18. *Ibid.*, pp. 68-69.

optimum of B. C. 5500 to 2500—thereby placing the red sand (Bed 4) and subsequent deposits after B. C. 2500 in alternate scheme A; or, if we follow the alternate scheme B (Fig. 114), the red sand might fall within the post-glacial optimum and therefore before B. C. 2500. Antevs, on the other hand, regards the Cochise Culture stages as continuous[19] and establishes boundaries of B. C. 8000 to 3000 for the Chiricahua Stage here involved. His further statement, however, that ". . . the Chiricahua sites (are) about 6000 . . ."[20] years old somewhat reduces the apparent difference. Hack finds the erosion of the Post-Glacial Optimum accompanied by the formation of dunes. If it is as assumed, that the red sand of Ventana (Bed 4) is wind-de-

19. E. B. Sayles and E. Antevs, 1941, p. 55.
20. *Ibid.*

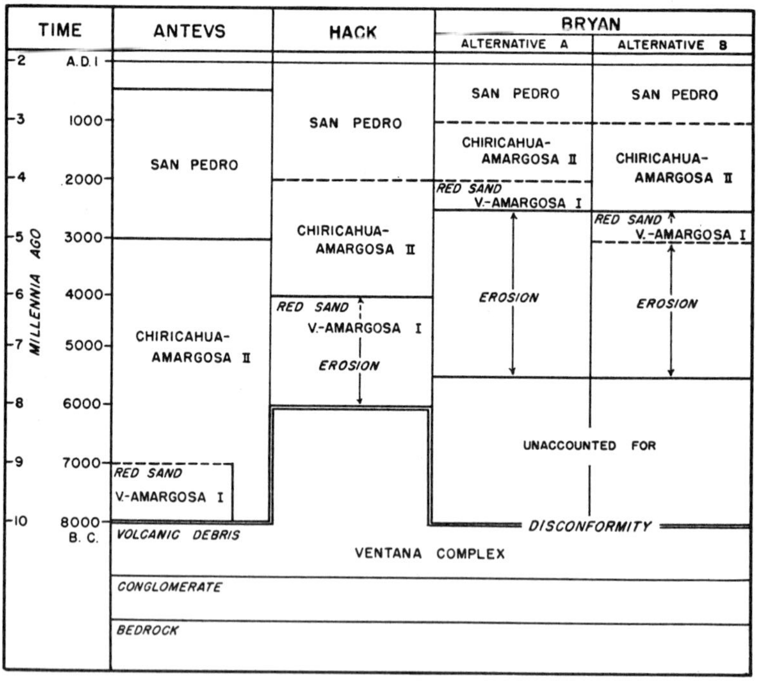

FIGURE 114. Trial correlation of the Ventana cultural sequence with the geochronologies of Antevs, Hack, and Bryan. Horizons after A.D. 1 not shown

rived, this formation might, then, fall within the same period, as has been indicated in Figure 114.

As I see it, from the archaeological point of view, the difficulties with either Bryan's or Antevs' correlation can be put as follows: Bryan's alternate possibility A calls for a compression of Ventana-Amargosa I, Chiricahua-Amargosa II, and San Pedro into the period from B. C. 2500 to the time of Christ which, in terms of the cultural changes involved, appears acceptable. His scheme B would extend the time somewhat but without materially changing the picture. Either way, a long space of time, from ten thousand years ago to B. C. 2500 or just before, is left unaccounted for culturally. If there was a continuum in the Cochise Culture, as Sayles contends, one wonders what happened during this interval of about five millennia.

Antevs' time schedule for the Cochise Culture, namely, before B. C. 8000 for the Sulphur Springs Stage, B. C. 8000 to 3000 for the Chiricahua Stage, and B. C. 3000 to 500 for the San Pedro Stage, constructs a cultural continuity but, in terms of American prehistory, assigns what appears to be too much time to the stages. To put it another way, can we believe that culture was so near static, even in a food-gathering form of economy, as to reveal so little change during such a long period of time? Further, no allowance is made in the Cochise sequence for what must have been some lapse in time during which certain animals died out and the climate was altered from sub-humid and cool to semi-arid and warm conditions.

The obvious answer is that we still have far to go in bringing the respective ideas of geochronology into agreement. Subsequently, the archaeologist may arrive at his own conclusions with respect to the rapidity of cultural change.

The preceding discussion of chronology, which has included the recognition of several cultural gaps and an attempt to assign dates to the various horizons in terms of the Christian calendar, points up what I consider to be the outstanding contributions of Ventana Cave. In recent years, with the development of new dating tools, as dendrochronology, the archaeologist has had to compress the chronology for the late or higher cultures appreciably to the period since Christ, while at the same time activities in the field of Early Man studies have led to estimates which place man farther and farther into antiquity. On several occasions warnings have been sounded that this dilemma was of such proportions as to throw doubt on the dating as a whole, unless we prefer to believe that parts of America were depopulated altogether for a good many millennia. The delineation of several stages of the Cochise Culture, and other pre-ceramic but post-glacial complexes, has done much to restore the idea that a continuous history is nearer the truth. Ventana Cave has gone far to bring the old and the recent cultures together with a series of connecting links excepting, of course, the probable interruption of early post-glacial times. It adds to the picture by confirming the order of the last two stages of the Cochise Culture and providing data on other groups, notably in the Californian desert, all falling within that period separating the early hunters of the late glacial period from the farmers after the time of Christ. Sauer[21] holds that there is ". . . an impressive development of culture to be accounted for . . . and a good deal of time is needed." Both of these qualifications have, I believe, been partly met by the evidence produced herein, excepting the fact that the actual cultural transition from late glacial to post-glacial times is not represented.

It is worth emphasizing again that we have been able to observe, in a single trash accumulation, the actual transition from a pre-agricultural to an agricultural existence, together with the appearance of pottery, not accompanied, apparently, by an ethnic upheaval.[22]

CORRELATIONS AND CONTINUITIES

An interesting fact emerges when we think of the cave in terms of people. Throughout much of its history of occupation it did not harbor a culture distinctive of the area. The human

★

21. C. O. Sauer, 1944, p. 573.
22. E. W. Haury, 1943*b*, pp. 262-263.

manifestations present, excepting the late Desert Branch of the Hohokam and the Papago, are mostly a fusion of complexes known better elsewhere. In other words, the region appears to have supported no virile and characteristically local people whose influence reached out to affect other groups. Rather, there are left the traces of people whose centers of development lay in adjacent areas. Ventana was actually marginal and consequently a receiving rather than a creating center. A plotting of the known stations of the Cochise Culture from southeastern Arizona to the west, and of the Amargosa Complex of the Lower Colorado River, to the east, shows a thinning out respectively, the two appearing in combination under the favorable environment offered by the Cave. Nowhere in Papagueria have we yet found clear and unmistakable surface or buried sites of these two groups.

The problem then boils down to the question as to what people were there rather than with whom they were affiliated. But this in no sense should be interpreted as detracting from the archaeological situation. On the contrary, it permits a much safer approach to the problem of cross-dating horizons of different people than is possible when only infrequent and sometimes not easily identifiable intrusive material is used. Implement assemblages, as outlined previously (p. 338*ff*) are the basis for the following observations.

The meeting-ground role of the Cave is seen from the very beginning of its occupancy. Elements of the far-flung but characteristically High Plains Folsom Culture and of the San Dieguito I Complex, of the Lower Colorado River Basin, met and combined to form the Ventana Complex. As far as our information goes now, this is a local situation and deserves note chiefly because Folsom and San Dieguito I are brought into chronological agreement. The geologic age of this horizon, more than ten thousand years ago, has already been amply commented on by Bryan herein. The typology of the San Dieguito tools in relation to those of the west is not only similar, but identical, while, for Folsom, it is a matter of similarity and not identity. Hence, the conclusion may be drawn that the western connections were predominant.[23]

On this same time level, the presence of marine shells in Ventana suggests contacts with a littoral group on the Gulf of California. Whether these were an extension of the San Dieguito I or a wholly new group is not known.

Moving up in the time scale, the red sand layer containing the Ventana-Amargosa I pattern so far expresses western relationships only. Although suspected heretofore by Rogers, it has not been isolated in the Lower Colorado River Basin where the elements of the pattern appear to be the strongest. Ventana Cave preserves in the red sand layer only a faint reflection of what should be more sharply defined eventually elsewhere.

The valuable data of Rogers for the western desert and of Sayles and Antevs for southeastern Arizona leave little room for misinterpreting the cultural evidence next in line from the lower third of the midden. This involves the hunting pattern of the Amargosa II, of the west, and the food-gathering pattern of the Chiricahua Stage of the Cochise Culture to the southeast. The identity of the tools of these two culture types forges strong links between Ventana and those groups. Once again it seems clear that the Cave was little more than a meeting ground and that a highly useful correlation has thereby been established between these two stages of different groups.

Still later, in the culture type from the middle third of the midden, the western connections were declining in favor of San Pedro Stage elements of the east. In fact, the inability to identify any diagnostic Amargosa III traits would make it appear that western influence had come to an end. This is best explained in terms of the fact that the Amargosa Complex faced increasingly difficult environmental conditions and its vitality was being sapped, while the makers of the San Pedro Stage tools, better

★

23. It is worth noting that highly altered tools of the San Dieguito I type have been found in Papagueria elsewhere than in Ventana Cave. Several open sites occur along Anegam Wash, and in company with Mr. Rogers the writer visited a station (Ariz. DD:2:4) near Baboquivari Mountain on an old land form. I know of no Folsom remains which have appeared under similar circumstances in the region.

situated as to habitat, were not so affected. It cannot be shown yet that the San Pedro people who pressed westward were different in any essentials from their more eastern kinsmen. It is true that the early (Chiricahua Stage) metate and mano forms survived among them whereas these had changed in the nuclear area, but this hardly seems of major significance.

By way of summarizing the history of the cave in pre-ceramic times, the situation may be best visualized by recognizing western (San Dieguito and Amargosa) and eastern (Folsom and Cochise) cultures as present, the former predominating at first and giving way finally to a preponderance of eastern (Cochise) culture elements. This is schematically shown in Figure 115. Amargosa III, included on the chart to complete the western sequence, was not represented in Ventana Cave as far as can be determined.

We now come to grips with the problem of cultural corre-

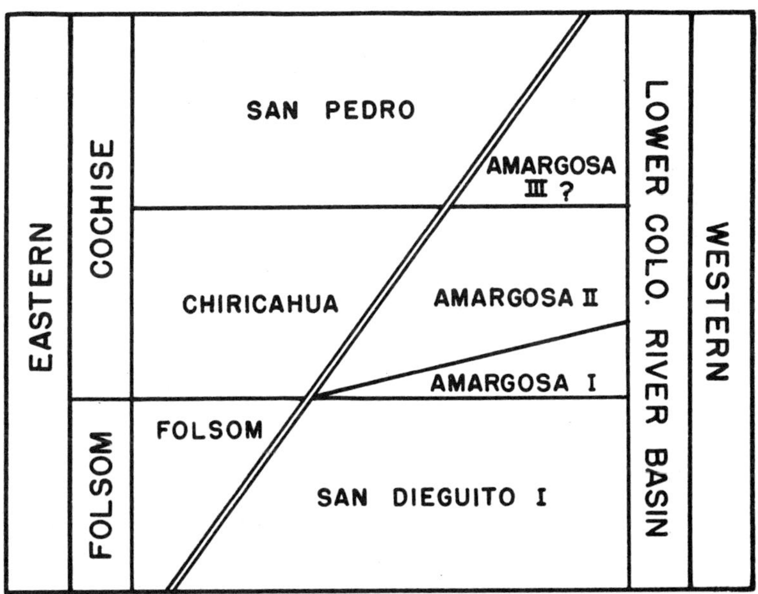

FIGURE 115. Schematic chart showing early dominance of western elements and late dominance of eastern elements prior to introduction of pottery about A.D. 1

lation on a wider base. This is a formidable task, made so because of uncertainties inherent in geological dating which have led to sharp contrasts in interpretation, and because of the difficulties of establishing cultural identities. The temporal equation of the Ventana culture history with others contributing to it, based on Bryan's dating, is presented in Figure 116. A contrasting correlation, in which Antevs' dates for the Cochise Culture are employed as the control, is shown in Figure 117.[24] Schemes of this sort probably suffer from over-simplification but I know of no better way to present the ideas.

First, with reference to Folsom in Figure 116: equating this with the Ventana Complex is done on the basis of typology, faunal association, and geological context, as previously outlined. No serious problems intrude in making this assignment

24. This chart was worked out in collaboration with M. J. Rogers.

MILLENNIA AGO	TIME	HIGH PLAINS — *FOLSOM-YUMA*	SE ARIZONA — *COCHISE*	PAPAGUERIA — *VENTANA*	LOWER COLO. RIVER BASIN — *SAN DIEGUITO-AMARGOSA*	
	PRESENT			PAPAGO	YUMA III	NEO-INDIAN
	1500			?	YUMA II	
1	1000			HOHOKAM	YUMA I	
	500		MOGOLLON		BM III - P II	
2	A. D. 1	CORN & POTTERY				
3	1000		SAN PEDRO	SAN PEDRO	AMARGOSA III	PALEO-INDIAN
4	2000		CHIRICAHUA	CHIRICAHUA-AMARGOSA II	AMARGOSA II ?	
5	3000			VENTANA-AMARGOSA I ?	AMARGOSA I	
6	4000		?	EROSION		
7	5000				SAN DIEGUITO II-III	
8	6000					
9	7000	EXTINCTION OF ANIMALS				
10	8000 B. C.	YUMA FOLSOM	SULPHUR SPRING	VENTANA COMPLEX	? SAN DIEGUITO I	

FIGURE 116. Postulated correlation of western cultures and the Ventana sequence, based on Bryan's dates

if one remembers that the correlation is not absolute, in view of the fact that the exact duration of either of the two complexes involved is not known. The Yuma[25] horizon has been added although it does not directly concern us.

Next, the San Pedro and Chiricahua Stages of the Cochise Culture can be arranged as the chronological parallels of the San Pedro and Chiricahua-Amargosa II of Ventana on the basis of typology and position within their respective sequences. The San Pedro Stage of southeastern Arizona appears to lead directly into Mogollon, while the Ventana San Pedro provides the under-

★

25. The reader is cautioned against confusing the terms Yuma and Yuman, the former being a Folsom-derived complex named from Yuma County, Colorado, and the latter referring to the developmental phases leading up to the modern Yuma Indians.

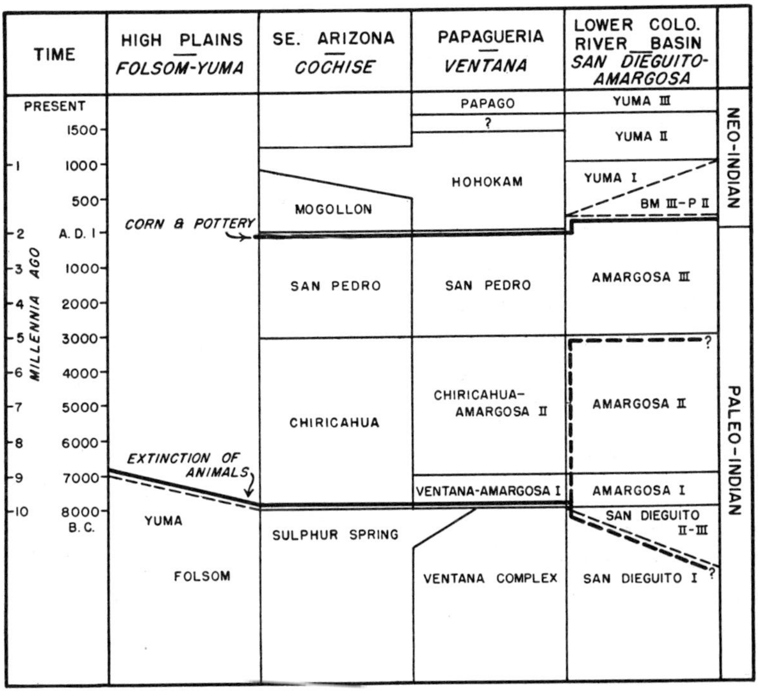

FIGURE 117. Postulated correlation of western cultures with the Ventana sequence, based on Antevs' dates for the Cochise Culture

pinning for the later Hohokam.[26] The place of the Sulphur Spring Stage is not so easily determined. Traces of this horizon, dated by Antevs[27] as older than ten thousand years ago, were not found. There are two plausible interpretations. First, that the Sulphur Spring Stage and the Ventana Complex were contemporaneous but regionally exclusive manifestations of people, the one group gatherers, the other hunters. Second, that these two horizons were not actually contemporary although both came within late glacial times. If this was the case, I would consider the Ventana Complex as the older for the following reasons: (1) its partial derivation from the Folsom hunters and *a priori* older than a gathering culture; (2) with a gathering economy so well established in the lower two-thirds of the midden (San Pedro and Chiricahua), it becomes difficult to accept the fact that the people of the locality during one or even two stages earlier would not have been similarly dependent. Therefore, on cultural grounds it appears that a substantial interruption exists in the sequence between Chiricahua-Amargosa II and the Ventana Complex. Bryan's evaluation of the geology seems to support this view. It is possible, but not probable, that the evidence of the Sulphur Spring Stage was originally contained in the cave, and washed out in the erosion of the upper part of the volcanic debris, in which case it would, of necessity, have been later than the Ventana Complex. I favor the latter of the two above stated alternatives, believing that the Sulphur Spring Stage must be interpolated in the sequence after the Ventana Complex, and have so indicated it in the chart, knowing, however, that Sayles disagrees with this interpretation. He favors the idea that the Sulphur Spring Stage and the Ventana Complex were contemporaneous. It will be quickly recognized that the projection of Ventana dates for the San Pedro and Chiricahua-Amargosa II horizons to the Cochise Culture of southeastern Arizona, as indicated in Figure 116, clashes sharply with Antevs' calculations (Fig. 117.)

★

26. E. W. Haury, 1943*b*, p. 262.
27. E. B. Sayles and E. Antevs, 1941, p. 55.

One of the outstanding contributions of Ventana Cave is the light which it sheds on the status of several Western pre-pottery cultures whose age has been variously estimated from B. C. 2000 to 15000 on the best available evidence of geology, physiography, and typology. Tricky as cave deposits are, such clues as the implement-fauna association and the relative position any given artifact complex has in a sequence, when as clearly shown as in Ventana, are to be given more weight than when the evidence has been derived from even more hazardous surface studies.

For the Lower Colorado Basin sequence, as revised (see p. 193), we have Rogers' own identification of the San Dieguito I in the Ventana Complex. San Dieguito II and III are absent. Typologically this arrangement fits well, but geologically we are up against a knotty problem. Rogers has assigned[28] San Dieguito I to the Little Pluvial, circa B. C. 2000, whereas the Ventana Complex is placed by Bryan before B. C. 8000. To reconcile this discrepancy, further field studies are called for, but I would like to voice the opinion that, since Rogers' work is based on surface material and has no associated faunal remains, his estimate appears much too conservative. His interpretation would allow altogether too little time for the succeeding phases, San Dieguito II and III, Amargosa I, II, and III, which would need to be compressed into the period from B. C. 2000 to A. D. 1. Treganza,[29] following his work in Baja, California, where San Dieguito remains occur on ancient land forms, as elevated marine terraces, river terraces, and about the margins of extinct lakes, is of the opinion that a far greater antiquity must be assigned the culture than has been placed upon it. Since Rogers has assisted in making the correlation chart shown in Figure 117, he obviously regards a greater age for San Dieguito I as a possibility. With the Amargosa III and succeeding phases we are not directly concerned.

On Figure 116 is also indicated the extinction line of animals, the position of which is uncertain in the Californian

★

28. M. J. Rogers, 1939, pp. 70-74.
29. A. E. Treganza, 1947, p. 254.

sequence. The association of extinct animals with Amargosa II (Pinto-Gypsum) in California is inferred, but none have been found either at Lake Mohave or with the Borax Lake Complex. Gypsum Cave,[30] on the other hand, does show some nonexistent forms, chiefly the sloth. In Ventana, Amargosa II is associated with an abundance of modern fauna, substantiated further in southeastern Arizona, where the Chiricahua Stage material occurs with similar life forms. To explain this it must be assumed either (1) that Amargosa II in California and Nevada were older than in Arizona and that a marginal Amargosa II culture survived in Ventana after the extinction of certain animals, if extinction was synchronous, or (2) that if Amargosa II was contemporary wherever found, the animals died out later in Nevada. Neither of these views strikes me as plausible and I can only say that something is amiss in the situation as pictured.

I favor a substantially later date assignment for Amargosa II (Pinto-Gypsum) than has heretofore been put upon it,[31] although the placement necessitated by Bryan's dates appears to be too recent. The occurrence of the California sites along former rivers and lakes, on the face of it, means a wetter climate, a fact which cannot be ignored. If, on the other hand, the Lake Mohave and Pinto Basin Cultures are as old as claimed, in the neighborhood of fifteen thousand years, and the Chiricahua-Amargosa II is accepted to be comparable in age, then the extinction of animals, for the most part, came before fifteen thousand years ago and what is of greater importance, the artifacts from the volcanic debris layer of Ventana Cave, representing a different culture type and occurring with extinct animals, would logically be pushed much farther into the past.

Such an interpretation, however, would leave an enormous gap between our Chiricahua-Amargosa II (at fifteen thousand) and San Pedro Stage (just before the time of Christ) which the

★

30. M. R. Harrington, 1933, pp. 164, *et seq.*
31. E. Antevs, 1937, pp. 45-48; D. Scharf, 1935, pp. 11-20.

Ventana or southeastern Arizona evidence simply does not support.

Figure 117 presents the problem of correlation from another point of view. Here Antevs' dates for the Cochise Culture are taken as the key and the Ventana and California sequences are adjusted accordingly. This arrangement allows more time for the levels of culture attainment before A. D. 1 and leaves no appreciable gaps.

Since both Bryan and Antevs have presented at length their respective arguments for the dates they adopt, and these dates are at variance with each other, I see no alternative for the archaeologist but to bide his time until the picture clears.

For the later cultures, the Neo-Indians of southern Arizona, little further needs be said. The equation of Mogollon, Hohokam, and Yuman is inferred on the basis of other work. All are built upon the newly acquired attributes of corn and pottery whose appearance is shown as near the time of Christ.

The foregoing correlations pass over a number of problems all too easiliy, but I do not believe that this is the place to dispose of them at greater length. The subject of inter-group relationship, both cultural and temporal, of the Paleo-Indian is worthy of an extensive report in itself.

Until now, in this report, the connections of the Ventana Culture Complexes have been viewed in terms of the western United States only. Are we to believe that this is as far as comparisons can safely be made at this time? Through the eyes of a conservative, the answer would be "yes," but one is impelled, nevertheless, to look at the problem in a larger sense. Obviously, the southwestern United States, speaking in terms of human occupancy of late glacial times, did not exist in a vacuum. Advances in the study of Early Man in America as of now make clear both the wide spread of man over the American continents and the regional diversity of his products.

Apart from the hunting tools of the Ventana Complex there are also crude choppers, usually plano-convex in section, and chipped on one face. The type persists upward in time to become especially prominent in the Chiricahua-Amargosa II and San Pedro levels. It is this emphasis on chopping tools which, for the moment, commands attention. We know that the chopper was an integral part of the tool kit of the early people throughout the southwestern desert and into northern Mexico, although the complementary artifacts are not always the same. This has been amply demonstrated by Rogers, Sayles, and others.[32] The type is also listed as present in Texas in post-pluvial horizons,[33] possibly earlier; in Baja, California,[34] coastal California;[35] in the northern Great Basin,[36] and suggestions of its presence are also seen in western Canada.[37]

Dr. Helmut de Terra's recent findings in the Valley of Mexico indicate the chopper to have been one of the basic tools of the Chalco Complex, which he assigns to a Middle Recent Age.[38] After viewing the Ventana specimens, Dr. de Terra was impressed by the similarity of the early southern Arizona lithic industries and his own material, not only as to the identities of implement types, but as to a likeness in the patterns.

In short, although I have not examined the literature thoroughly, it appears that the chopper ranges widely but continuously through western America, from Canada deep into Mexico. Were it not for the fact that Movius[39] has recently demonstrated a valid distinction in the patterns of growth of the Lower Paleolithic hand-axe and chopping-tool cultures of the Old World, one might not be inclined to give the American situation much thought. He recognizes a focus in southeastern Asia of the Lower Paleolithic industry, characterized by what he calls a chopper-chopping-tool complex, as separable from the hand-axe tradition of India, Africa, and Europe. This has

★

32. M. J. Rogers, 1939; E. B. Sayles and E. Antevs, 1941; E. W. C. and W. H. Campbell, 1935, 1937. Choppers have been observed as far south as southern Sonora, Mexico, during the course of a trip by Dr. C. O. Sauer and the writer.

33. J. C. Kelley, T. N. Campbell, and D. J. Lehmer, 1940, pp. 104, 114.

34. A. E. Treganza, 1947.

35. R. F. Heizer and E. M. Lemert, 1947; M. R. Harrington, 1948.

36. L. S. Cressman, 1942, Fig. 47.

37. F. Johnson, 1946, Pl. XXIII, 14, 19.

38. H. de Terra, 1947, pp. 42-43.

39. H. L. Movius, Jr., 1944.

two possible implications for us: (1) the eventual relating of western American culture groups into a cohesive whole on the basis of a chopping-tool tradition, and (2) a point better put as a question: Does the geographic location of chopping-tool distributions in both the Old and New Worlds mean anything at all in seeking an origin of the New World tradition? No one needs to remind me of the enormous disparity in time between the mid-Pleistocene Asiatic cultures and the late Pleistocene or early Recent New World cultures, but the implement parallel is mentioned as something to be kept in the back of one's mind.

So much then for the cultures involved. What of the people from a racial point of view? Gabel's analysis of the skeletons from Ventana Cave has shown the presence of several physical or morphological types. Briefly reviewed, these are:

(1) An undeformed hyperdolichocephalic type (two skulls), the oldest in the cave, coming from the pre-pottery zone of the midden but not clearly identifiable with either the Chiricahua-Amargosa II or San Pedro Culture patterns, although certainly representative of one or both of them.

(2) An undeformed mesocephalic type, represented by one male and seven females, from the upper dry pottery-bearing zone of the midden. The associated material culture was that of the Desert Hohokam. Physically, the crania of this type and the modern Papago have much in common.

(3) From the same level of the midden three skulls of the Puebloid type, brachycephalic and deformed, also with associated Desert Hohokam material remains. These may well indicate some racial intrusion into Desert Hohokam territory without leaving discernible cultural effects at the time of the Salado expansion into the desert after 1300.

Gabel concluded that, not counting the Puebloid type, a continuity of physical types is indicated in Papagueria. This implies some morphological changes as between the hyperdolichocephalic Paleo-Indian and the mesocephalic Neo-Indian, which may have resulted from mixtures with groups not yet defined. An overlap in the two forms is indicated by two burials recently found southeast of Tucson by the Arizona State Museum. The first of these, an adult male skeleton from Babocomari Creek, about six miles west of Fairbank, Arizona, is remarkably like the pre-pottery type from Ventana, yet this individual comes from a southern Hohokam site of the Sedentary Period, or about A. D. 1100. The second, a female, approaching the undeformed mesocephals of Ventana in type, was found in a grave put down from an old erosion surface in the Empire Valley and since covered by extensive silts. This skeleton is certainly of pre-pottery age and possibly associated with the San Pedro Stage horizon. In other words, variability as to morphological type existed and the racial elements appear to have been present from which the mesocephalic Ventana type may have emerged. Suffice it to say that the implied racial continuity is supported by the uninterrupted succession of cultural remains.

The perennial question of Papago descent has, I believe, been clarified to some extent by the Ventana excavations. The gap in the chronology from 1400 to about 1700 has retarded the acceptance of a direct Desert Hohokam-Papago relationship. Precisely the same problem exists in trying to relate the River Hohokam and the Pima. Yet, in both cases, by geographic location of the old and the modern groups, by the basic similarity in culture throughout, and by stratigraphy, a continuum can be postulated.[40]

In the pattern of existence, architecture, flood irrigation, and paddle-and-anvil pottery there is little difference between Desert Hohokam and Papago. Ventana further adds to this list (1) a morphological physical type identified as Desert Hohokam, which compares favorably with modern Papago, as brought out by Dr. Gabel; (2) the same kind of corn was grown by both, as determined by Dr. Anderson; and (3) further identities in material culture, specifically in objects of wood, basketry, and in the probable use of the horizontal loom.

It seems to me to be inconsistent with what we do know to

★

40. N. and H. S. Gladwin, 1929, pp. 129-131; E. W. Haury, 1945, pp. 211-212.

claim that no relationship exists, that after 1400 the area was depopulated only to have a new group move in with a culture that reflects so intimately that of the older occupants.

If the foregoing interpretations are acceptable, then it may be said that the modern Papago are descendants of the Desert Hohokam, who, in turn, drew from the racial and cultural reservoir of the still older people—the Cochise Culture.

CHANGES IN ECONOMY

Where direct evidence is lacking, as, for example, plant parts, the determination of a people's economy must depend mainly on the kinds of imperishable appliances used in gaining and preparing food. The presence or absence of grinding tools is helpful in establishing collecting or agricultural modes of life, but it must be remembered that an absence of stone mills does not preclude the gathering of products which were edible without grinding. Hunting tools, similarly, fail to tell the whole story because some of them serve equally well for defense. Further, we cannot be sure of the pursuits requiring only perishable equipment or possibly no specialized equipment at all. Animal bones from the refuse are a useful adjunct. In spite of the subjective element involved in determining economies archaeologically, it seems to me to be worthwhile to bring together the points already mentioned in earlier sections to indicate the trends revealed in the deep deposits of Ventana Cave.

As a starting point, we have Castetter and Bell's excellent study of Papago economy in which ratios of dependency are expressed.[41] One-fifth of the Papago food supply was drawn from cultivated products and four-fifths was derived from native plants and animal products. In the latter category, the ratio of plant and animal food was four to one. This relationship is roughly indicated in Figure 118 as a known pattern. Reading down, or backward in time, the chart shows hunting steadily on the increase, being the main source of food in the oldest cul-

★

41. 1942, pp. 57-58.

ture level which produced Ventana-Folsom tools. This interpretation seems warranted by changing proportions of grinding to chipped tools as one recedes in time and especially below the mid-part of the midden. In the basal layer of the midden, cutting, scraping, and piercing tools outnumbered those designed for grinding. In the Ventana-Amargosa I (red sand) level, no grinding tools were found and only one appeared in the Ventana Complex. Further, the kinds of animals taken by the oldest occupants of the cave, those now extinct or no longer in the area, are indicative of a well developed hunting pattern. This, however, does not mean, in my opinion, that there was no collecting although there is little direct evidence for it. Allowances have been made for this in the chart, as a weak secondary exploitation of the natural resources.

Gathering, strong in Papago economy, may be assumed to have been even more important earlier, especially prior to the introduction of corn agriculture. The marked concentration on collecting, by the Cochise Culture in southeastern Arizona, is borne out also by the evidence here during the Chiricahua

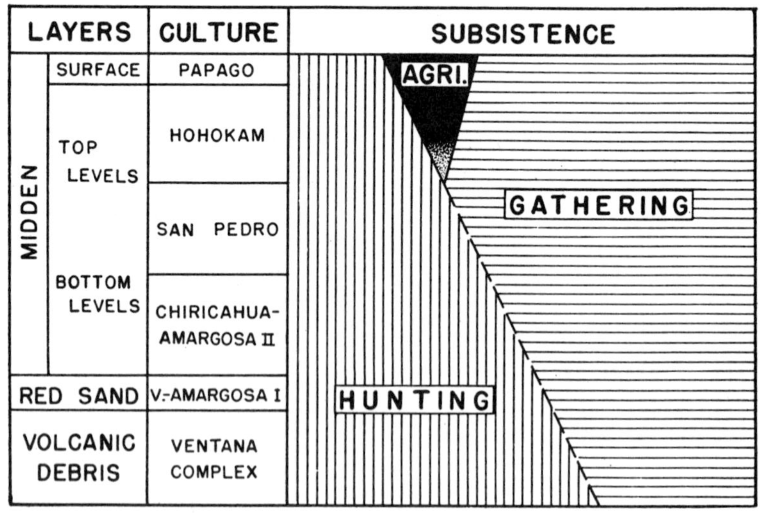

FIGURE 118. Schematic representation of changes in subsistence patterns of the Ventana Cave occupants

and San Pedro stages. While it is impossible to prove the point, the impression prevails that collecting exceeded hunting throughout the above named periods.

Agriculture, I believe, held strictly a third-rate position and certainly a late one in the combination of economies. Even the Papago depended on agriculture no more than on hunting and much less than on gathering. Among the Pima, cultivated foods provided 50 per cent to 60 per cent[42] of the supply, made possible by irrigation waters from the Gila River. And collecting overwhelmingly made up the balance. That a similar regional difference obtained for the Desert and River branches of the Hohokam of a thousand years ago is indicated. At Snaketown, for example, the rough chipped tools associated with hunting and some phases of gathering were conspicuously rare,[43] while great canal systems testify to the role played by cultivation. In Ventana Cave, the Hohokam debris yielded countless cutting, chopping, and scraping tools and the region does not permit of wholesale agriculture by irrigation. The substance of this seems to be that hunting and gathering always superceded agriculture in Papagueria, the latter having been held in check by environmental rather than cultural forces.

The appearance of maize agriculture is indicated by a change in metate form over earlier types of mills and by the presence of corn cobs in the trash. This came relatively late in the total span of time revealed by the cave's deposits and can be dated to about the beginning of the Christian Era, as an estimate. The temporal position of agriculture with respect to the more basic pursuits of hunting and collecting is probably a more significant fact than was the effect of agriculture on the cultural structure after its arrival because it was so little exploited in this marginal region.

One minor point is not brought out by the chart because it is of only passing interest. This concerns the introduction of domesticated animals which, excepting the dog, came within historic times.

★

42. *Ibid.*, pp. 56-57.
43. H. S. Gladwin, E. W. Haury, E. B. Sayles, and N. Gladwin, 1937, p. 114.

THE HOHOKAM: DESERT BRANCH

The division of people into branches on archaeological and geographical grounds is obviously a device to take account of minor differences in material cultures when a common thread nevertheless exists. The Hohokam are a case in point. The work of Scantling, Withers, and Bailey in open sites was responsible for formulating three successive phases in Papagueria, the Vamori, Topawa, and Sells, with an estimated time range of from A. D. 800 to 1400. As remarked in the Introduction, the components of these were not identical with, but were related to, equivalent phases of the Hohokam to the north.

In Ventana Cave, although the above named phases were not represented in stratigraphic order, it can be said that the same people, with essentially the same culture, inhabited it. And because older Hohokam pottery was present, not seen as yet in the open sites, it may further be concluded that the Hohokam lived in Ventana Cave possibly as early as the beginning of the Christian Era. This gives us, then, a respectable time-span for assessing the local differences of development of a single people.

For the Pioneer Period there is little more than pottery left for us to study and so far this has appeared only in Ventana Cave of the desert area. Since, on present material, this is indistinguishable from Gila Basin Hohokam ceramic products the inference may be drawn that the oldest pottery producing inhabitants of the desert were of the same order and were in a similar stage of development as those along the river. The same appears to hold true for the Tucson area where, during the Pioneer Period, remains are practically indistinguishable from those of the Gila Basin.[44]

The distinguishing qualities in Hohokam Culture of Papagueria really appear only toward the end of the Colonial Period while these become evident somewhat earlier in the Tucson area. In both sub-areas, the deviation from the Gila Basin pat-

★

44. Based on the work of Isabel Kelly in the Hodges Ruin near Tucson.

tern becomes intensified with time so that, by 1400, the ultimate had been reached (see Fig. 2 for phase correlations).

The following generalized list points out the more important differences which existed between the River and Desert branches of the Hohokam after A. D. 1000.

River Branch	*Desert Branch*
Cremation	Earth burial
Red-on-buff pottery, not polished	Red-on-brown pottery, polished
Red ware, black interiors	Red ware, red interiors
Full troughed metate, well shaped	Block metate, some shaping, not troughed as a rule
Great array of projectile points, delicate workmanship	Limited projectile point types, few in number, workmanship inferior
Well developed carved stone	Carved stone weakly represented
Few chopping, scraping, and cutting tools	Abundance of roughly chipped chopping, scraping and cutting tools
Slate palette	Slate palette, little used
Stone and shell jewelry abundant and elaborate	Stone and shell jewelry, rare and simple
Figurine complex strong	Figurines, rare
Large-scale irrigation systems, drawing water from streams	Limited irrigation canals, designed to catch surface runoff
Subsistence primarily agriculture	Subsistence primarily collecting
Heavy Salado intrusion after 1300	Little affected by Salado

It is on the strength of the above named differences that the recognition of several branches of Hohokam development seems admissible. These groups are: (1) the River Branch or People, constituting the well known and classic Hohokam as seen at Snaketown and centering on the Gila and Salt Rivers above their confluence; and closely allied members extending south along the Santa Cruz River valley toward Tucson; and (2) the Desert Branch, the people of Papagueria, limited by environment to a lower level of cultural attainment than the former group.

The dividing line geographically between these two branches is difficult to establish because of the gradual merging of the one into the other. It may be placed approximately on an east-west line drawn through Chuichu, in the northern part of the Papago Reservation. The western limits of the Desert Branch appears to have been in the vicinity of Ajo, and the eastern limit, the Avra Valley. On the south, the border roughly coincides with the present International Line where the culture change is abrupt from Desert Hohokam to the Trincheras Complex of, as yet, unknown affinities.[45] It is worth noting in passing that the area occupied by the Desert Hohokam is roughly coterminous with that held by the Papago of pre-reservation days.

Ventana Cave is distinctive among all Hohokam sites excavated thus far in that it yielded perishable culture, which, up to now, has only been suggested by occasional bits of evidence. Thus we know that the Hohokam used sewed and natural fiber sandals, made one-rod and bundle-and-rod core basketry, and had cotton textiles, incorporating such techniques as weft-wrap openwork and gauze weaves. Whether these were shared by both branches of the Hohokam or not is something we may never learn.

★

45. Studies in northern Sonora should be pushed to clear this up, along with the cultural problems. As suggested elsewhere (E. W. Haury, 1945, pp. 69-70), Trincheras-Hohokam correlations have been made and I incline to the idea that the Trincheras should be brought into the general Hohokam picture.

APPENDIX

Chemical Study of the Material from Several Horizons of the Ventana Cave Profile[1]

The geology and sequence of deposition in the profile of Ventana Cave have been presented in detail by Professor Bryan in Part III of this monograph.

Any reconstruction of the historical past of a cave from a chemical investigation of the successive strata in its profile is rendered difficult by the obvious fact that the processes involved in their deposition are in a continuous state of flux, though retarded in their rates by the general aridity of the region. Weathering under arid conditions is largely physical in nature. However, within the cave itself there are evidences of the chemical and physical action of moving water, the translocation of fine, clayey materials blown in as dust by the wind and subsequently distributed throughout the rather pervious material of the profile, and lastly, the biological processes involved in the decay of organic refuse. Soluble salts leached out by the spring water or by floods were moved from their point of origin and deposited in lower horizons, and later were drawn to the surface by capillarity, as evaporation proceeded. The component materials of the profile, whether man-made or transported by the forces of nature, or the volcanic lava out of which the cave was originally

★

1. By T. F. Buehrer, Head, Department of Agricultural Chemistry and Soils, University of Arizona.

formed, show manifest differences in their susceptibility to weathering. Stone implements, fired clay artifacts, objects made from metals, and even hard, calcined bone, are more or less stable to the changes taking place under the conditions of moisture seepage and temperature prevailing in the cave. Hence the logical difficulties involved in determining, with any degree of exactness from the present chemical composition, the true state of affairs that existed when the materials of the successive strata were originally laid down.

Nevertheless, it was deemed of interest to make a chemical study of the material sampled from certain of the horizons and to deduce therefrom significant facts that might be correlated with information derived through other channels. The determinations to be made were chosen on the basis of the inherent nature of the material. Qualitative tests had indicated that the material at each level was fairly calcareous and that a fair portion of it was water-soluble. For the purposes of this study it was deemed sufficient to make an acid extract, in which case the insoluble residue would consist of acid-resisting rock minerals, sand, organic matter, etc. The acid-soluble fraction which, incidentally, included the water-soluble salts, was then analyzed in such detail as was deemed advantageous for the purposes of this study. A separate determination of the water-soluble salts was made by simple extraction, and the ionic constituents of the extract individually determined. Since all of the samples were found to contain organic matter, an independent determination of total organic carbon was made. All analytical determinations were carried out according to standard procedures given in the following reference works:

"Official and Tentative Methods of Analysis of the Association of Official Agricultural Chemists," published by the Association, Washington, D. C., 1946.

"Diagnosis and Improvement of Saline and Alkaline Soils." Mimeographed edition of analytical methods of the Regional Salinity Laboratory, U. S. Department of Agriculture, Riverside, California, July, 1947.

The details of the methods will not be given at this point.

Among the specimens submitted by Dr. Haury for study in this connection were five samples of granular material, somewhat heterogeneous as to particle size but largely finely divided, and definitely identified by label. One sample of the caliche substratum was in the form of a dense, compact conglomerate lump, dark gray in appearance. The finely divided samples were screened to remove coarse lumps, quartered, ground, and well mixed. The author feels reasonably sure of dealing with samples representative of the respective horizons in the profile.

The analytical results are summarized in Table 1. The data are expressed in terms of percentage of constituent, on the basis of the original *dry* material. It will be observed that the data are classified under headings: Acid-Insoluble, Acid-Soluble, Water-Soluble, and Miscellaneous. The acid-soluble fraction obviously must include the water-soluble fraction, as well as soluble constituents produced by interaction with carbonates and phosphates and by ionic exchange with soil and other alumino-silicate materials. The individual constituents are expressed in terms of oxides, as is common in the analysis of rocks and minerals.

TABLE 1

CHEMICAL COMPOSITION OF MATERIAL FROM SUCCESSIVE STRATA OF THE VENTANA CAVE PROFILE, UPPER CAVE, D II

(All percentages on basis of original, dry material)

Horizon Depth *	1 0.0-0.25	2 0.25-0.50	3 0.75-1.0	4 3.0-3.25	5 3.75-4.0	6 Volcanic debris
Acid-Insol.	64.53	60.19	59.90	64.79	61.42	44.34
Acid-Soluble						
$Fe_2O_3+Al_2O_3$	9.66	11.70	11.06	10.86	9.34	11.32
CaO	12.98	14.49	11.44	11.41	12.98	22.72
MgO	3.82	3.32	0.41	0.59	0.56	9.16
K_2O	1.52	1.62	1.95	1.36	4.00	1.07
Na_2O	0.33	0.44	0.46	0.42	0.94	0.29
CO_2	8.78	7.68	8.14	7.91	6.37	13.12
P_2O_5	2.13	2.19	1.92	2.91	2.01	2.17
N_2O_5	0.81	1.01	1.04	0.91	1.01	0.80
SO_3	None	Tr	Tr	None	None	None
Totals	104.56	102.64	96.32	101.16	98.63	104.99

* In meters.

TABLE 1 (CONTINUED)

Water-Soluble						
Ca (as CaO)	0.22	1.54	0.30	0.25	0.98	0.41
Mg (as MgO)	0.06	0.59	0.22	0.13	0.83	0.24
K (as K_2O)	None	None	None	Tr	None	None
Na (as Na_2O)	0.18	0.22	0.30	0.18	0.30	0.13
NO_3 (as N_2O_5)	0.85	0.99	0.95	1.12	2.36	0.92
CO_3 (as CO_2)	0.41	0.18	0.30	0.30	0.26	0.38
Miscellaneous						
Organ. Carbon	3.17	2.55	4.05	2.68	2.43	0.26
$CaCO_3$ (from CO_2)	19.96	17.46	18.50	17.98	14.48	29.82

GENERAL NATURE OF PROFILE DEDUCIBLE FROM CHEMICAL DATA

The data in Table 1 reveal the fact that the profile is rather heterogeneous in composition and consists of mineral and organic matter from various sources. The acid-insoluble fraction is extraordinarily high in all horizons, and present in appreciable amount even in the volcanic debris substratum. It is dominantly of inorganic (mineral) composition, however. The organic portion of it, reported as "Organic Carbon" at bottom of the table, is of much smaller magnitude. This mineral fraction, which resists the solvent action of N/1 hydrochloric acid, consists of particles of lava rock which may have scaled off from the roof of the cave in the course of weathering, rock chips formed in the course of making of stone implements, fine grindings from metates, the siliceous fraction of wood ashes, and, in no small measure, of soil blown into the cave by winds. This fact is also substantiated by the magnitude of the percentages of ferric and aluminum oxides which range between 9 and 12 per cent throughout the profile and which are typical of alumino-silicate rocks like basalt and of the silt and clay fraction of all soils. To illustrate this point there are presented in Table 2 the chemical compositions of an average basalt, a typical red desert soil, and of caliche.

The data in Table 2 represent ultimate (fusion) analyses of the materials, whereas those in Table 1 are proximate. Nevertheless, it is fairly evident from the magnitude of the percentage

TABLE 2

COMPOSITION OF INDIVIDUAL MATERIALS COMPOSING THE PROFILE OF VENTANA CAVE

	Basalt[1]	Mohave Soil (0-6″)[2]	Caliche[3]
SiO_2	49.06	67.44	6.20
Fe_2O_3	5.38	5.49	1.88
Al_2O_3	15.70	14.90	2.83
FeO	6.37	—	—
CaO	8.95	2.04	47.53
MgO	6.17	1.52	1.11
K_2O	1.52	2.72	—
Na_2O	3.11	1.73	—
Co_2	—	0.20	35.68
P_2O_5	0.45	0.22	—
H_2O	1.62	—	1.20

1. From F. F. Grout: "Kemp's Handbook of Rocks," 6th Ed. D. Van Nostrand and Co. 1940, p. 264.
2. From Atlas of American Agriculture, U. S. Department of Agriculture, 1936, p. 93.
3. From W. P. Blake: Trans. Amer. Inst. Min. Engrs. 31:1901, p. 222.

of acid-soluble matter and of ferric and aluminum oxides in the acid-soluble fraction, that we are dealing with rock constituents in the Ventana profile of high relative stability against the forces of weathering. They represent the framework of rock or mineral which is not easily broken down into simpler forms under the prevailing arid conditions and not translocated to any extent by percolating water. That the material from horizons 1 to 5 could not have originated from the volcanic debris substratum is likewise indicated by the very small percentage of acid-insoluble matter which it contains, as shown by the data in Table 2. It consists dominantly of calcium and magnesium carbonates. The extent of the calcareous nature of the respective horizons is shown by the data in the last horizontal line of Table 1 in which the carbonates present are expressed as percentage of calcium carbonate, calculated from the percentage of carbon dioxide independently determined.

How much of this stable siliceous rock material was the result of inhabitation of the cave by man, or carried in by him cannot, of course, be deduced from the above data. The significant fact appears to be that the summation percentage of acid-insoluble matter and of ferric and aluminum oxides in the acid-soluble fraction is very nearly the same in all horizons from 1 to 5. The differences are too small to be significant. Doubtless the corresponding material in the caliche-like volcanic debris substratum must have become incorporated with it long before the advent of man, when it was originally laid down. There could have been penetration of materials into this layer, however, which had been solubilized by spring or rain water percolating through from above. That such penetration must have occurred is shown by the perecntage of phosphoric acid (P_2O_5), which is not usually present in caliche.

Lime and Magnesia

The percentage of lime is fairly high in all horizons. The fact that so small an amount of lime is water-soluble, argues in favor of the conclusion that it is present dominantly in the form of carbonates and in an ionically exchangeable form in the alumino-silicate complex of the acid-insoluble fraction. The origin of the lime and magnesia must be attributed to the wood ashes accumulating in the cave (See Table 3), carbonates formed by the interaction of the spring water with plant ashes, the weathering of basaltic rock, and, in no inconsiderable measure, to the fine soil blown into the cave as dust. The carbonates of lime and magnesia are soluble to a slight extent in the carbon dioxide dissolved in spring and rain water and hence could move by percolation through the profile. As indicated by the presence of considerable phosphate in every horizon, a part of the lime present originated from bone, which is the carbonato-phosphate of lime.

Water-Soluble Constituents

The composition of the water extracts is given in Table 1. The amount of the various soluble salts present is, of course, a function of the extent of water percolation. Part of the salts were contributed by the spring water, rains flooding the cave, but the larger proportion originated from the plant ashes ot the campfire. These salts consisted primarily of nitrates and bicarbonates of calcium, magnesium, and sodium. The nitrates originated from the decomposition of organic refuse, as will be described later. It is strange that potassium in soluble form should not have been present in greater amounts than mere traces. This is found to be generally true of underground waters, which rarely contain more than a mere trace of potassium. It can be accounted for in terms of the fact that potassium is firmly held by the ionic exchange complex, especially in soils. The mobility of such soluble salts is such that the amounts and kinds of cations and anions at present in the profile are no reliable criterion for judging the conditions that existed centuries ago.

PHOSPHATES

In view of the occurrence of camp refuse and, especially, of bone fragments in the profile, it was to be presumed that phosphate should be found at all levels. It will be noted in Table 1 that the phosphate content was of the order of 2 per cent P_2O_5 in all levels except the 3 to 3.25 m. level, where it approached 3 per cent.

Bone is a complex carbonato-phosphate of lime, member of the apatite family of minerals, isomorphous with the well-known fluor-apatite, and usually containing varying amounts of hydroxy-apatite and fluor-apatite according to the age of the mammal. These complex phosphates also comprise the constituents of the phosphate rock deposits, and W. T. McGeorge has advanced the hypothesis that the native phosphate in virgin desert soils is also in this form. The carbonato-phosphate of bone can be accurately represented by the apatite formula: $[Ca_3(PO_4)_2]_3 \cdot CaCO_3$ and the hydroxy-apatite:

$$[Ca_3(PO_4)_2]_3 \cdot Ca(OH)_2 \cdot xH_2O.$$

The fluor-apatite present in the enamel of teeth would have an analogous composition in which CaF_2 would take the place of $CaCO_3$ outside the coördination complex of the mineral structure.

In finely divided form these compounds are appreciably, though not very rapidly, soluble in carbonic acid solutions, while practically insoluble in water itself. The rate of solution of bone, under conditions existing in nature, is limited by the low concentration of carbon dioxide generally present in natural waters and by the inherent weakness of the acid itself. Massive as well as calcined bone also dissolves in carbonated water, though usually at a much slower rate. Intermediate organic acids formed during microbial decomposition of organic matter also act on bone. The phosphate thus solubilized would, in time, leach to lower levels, but would precipitate out again in the event of contact with alkaline substances like the carbonates of lime, magnesium, and sodium. The reactions referred to may be represented by the following equations:

$$\underset{\text{(Insoluble)}}{[Ca_3(PO_4)_2]_3 \cdot CaCO_3} + 13\,H_2CO_3 = \underset{\text{(Soluble)}}{3\,Ca(H_2PO_4)_2} + 7\,Ca(HCO_3)_2$$

Upon contact with carbonates at lower levels,

$$\underset{\text{(Soluble)}}{Ca(H_2PO_4)_2} + 2\,CaCO_3 = \underset{\text{(Insoluble)}}{2\,CaHPO_4} + Ca(HCO_3)_2$$

These reactions indicate the possibility of movement of phosphate by percolation, but the amount of carbonic acid required (See Equation 1) is quite large, a condition which is rarely fulfilled under natural conditions. Furthermore the rate of solution is governed primarily by the degree of finenss of the bone. We may, therefore, conclude that the bulk of the phosphate now existing at the various levels of the profile represents the remains of what was originally present as bone in massive or coarsely granular form. That portion of it which is now found to be intimately commingled with the finely granular material of the midden, or present in the pores of the denser caliche substratum, was most likely to have been dissolved, transported in solution, and subsequently precipitated as delineated in the foregoing equations. This would be particularly true of the phosphate found in the caliche layer, for the latter does not, under ordinary circumstances, contain considerable amounts of phosphate.

A part of the phosphate here found came into the cave as soil, blown in as dust by the winds, but this amount would generally be small, of the order of 0.2 per cent, as shown by the data in Table 2. The ash of plants, on the other hand, contains considerable amounts of phosphate, ranging from 5.5 per cent P_2O_5 in the mesquite (*Prosopis algarobillo*) to 8 per cent in the elm and as high as 14 per cent in the birch. Hence we may conclude that an appreciable amount of the phosphate found in the acid-soluble fraction of all horizons, (Table 1) may have come from the wood ashes of the campfire, but it is probable that an even larger proportion of it originated from bone, human offal, and other animal refuse.

The fact that this constituent is distributed rather uniformly throughout the profile is consistent with its solubilization by carbonic acid and its further distribution through the profile by the simple processes of leaching. Any anthropological deductions from such evidence must rather be sought in massive bone specimens present at the various levels. It has been pointed out that coarse lumps of rock or bone occurring in the material submitted for analysis were screened from the fines in order to yield a more nearly representative sample. The chemical analysis thus indicates only the result of natural forces in the form of spasmodic and limited seasonal rainstorms and the slow percolation of water from the spring through the midden underlain by a rather impervious calcareous substratum —all of which would be expected to eventuate in a more or less uniform distribution of the phosphate throughout the profile.

Potassium Nitrate Crystals

A very interesting occurrence was observed at the 4-meter level, namely, crystals of nearly pure potassium nitrate. Professor Kirk Bryan reports their occurrence at 3 meters. These crystals were very typical. They were dense, massive, slightly discolored by impurities. They were found to be completely soluble in water and gave strong qualitative tests for potassium and nitrate ions, along with certain others present in traces. A quantitative analysis of the crystals gave the following:

	K_2O	N_2O_5	Total
Ventana Cave crystals:	46.45%	53.28%	99.43%
Theoretical for KNO_3:	46.60%	53.40%	100.00

The evidence is therefore conclusive that the crystals were potassium nitrate. Soluble as this salt is in water, it is possible that the crystals were formed as a result of its translocation to lower horizons by the percolating action of the spring water, the solution gradually becoming concentrated to the point of saturation. The limited rainfall to which the region is subjected may account for the fact that the salt was not entirely washed out of the porous midden.

By what processes was this potassium nitrate formed, and how could it have accumulated in amount sufficient to separate out in the form of massive crystals? The answer to this question can be deduced from certain definite facts. First, as to the origin of the potash. This is amply accounted for by the presence of ashes in the midden, in the production of which mesquite and other desert plants growing in the vicinity must have been used as fuel. In this connection we shall cite partial analyses of the ash of several kinds of wood as given by Wise;[2] and assembled in Table 3.

The foregoing data reveal the fact that the ash of wood in general carries an unusually high content of potash, ranging from 10 to 30 per cent K_2O. It is therefore evident that the high potash content necessary to produce crystals of potassium nitrate came from the year-after-year accumulation of ash in the same place without removal except by partial leaching to lower levels by way of the ground water. Desert soils contain on the average of the order of 2 to 3 per cent K_2O, very little of which is water-soluble. It is present almost wholly in the exchangeable

★

2. From L. E. Wise: "Wood Chemistry," American Chemical Society Monograph No. 97, 1944, Reinhold Pub. Co., New York, p. 435.

TABLE 3

CHEMICAL COMPOSITION OF WOOD ASHES

	Betula alba (Birch)	*Quercus alba (Oak)*	*Pinus palustris (Long Leaf Pine)*	*Prosopis algarobillo (Mesquite)*
SiO_2	0.85	3.2	3.4	6.65
Fe_2O_3	1.3	0.5	2.7	0.8
CaO	45.8	21.2	37.2	51.0
MgO	11.6	2.43	4.2	2.5
K_2O	15.1	29.9	10.3	19.0
Na_2O	8.7	1.94	2.3	12.5
P_2O_5	14.0	6.7	2.65	5.5
SO_3	2.6	4.1	4.3	1.5
Cl	—	1.0	0.2	0.6

form, being combined with either the alumino-silicate (clay) fraction or the organic matter fraction. As shown in an earlier section, there is evidence that considerable soil came into the cave as dust, and some of the potash now there must have originated in this way. However, the bulk of it must have come by way of the plant ash from the campfire. We have made an analysis of the water-soluble potash present in the ash of mesquite *(Prosopis juliflora)* occurring in the immediate vicinity of the cave, with the following results expressed in percentage on the basis of the dry ash:

K_2CO_3	4.46%
K_2SO_4	1.49%
KCl	0.054%

Thus the ash consists of potassium carbonate primarily, with potassium sulphate and chloride in lesser amounts. It is, of course, a patent fact that wood ashes were used for centuries in the making of soap, because of the alkalinity of potassium carbonate.

It was pointed out above that the potassium nitrate crystals occurred at the 4-meter level, which would indicate that the analysis of the material from the different horizons for potash (K_2O) should show an unusual percentage of potash at that level. An examination of Table 1 shows, in fact, that the highest percentage of K_2O was found at that level in the acid-soluble fraction, but *none* was found in the water-soluble extract. This appears to be an anomaly, yet it is consistent with the fact that potassium is rarely found in highly soluble concentrations in the presence of soil and organic matter. When such soil or organic matter is treated with acid, the potassium is immediately displaced and becomes soluble. Hence its occurrence in the acid-extract. The crystals after their formation at the 4-meter level were evidently not subjected to the leaching action of water and hence may exist under dry conditions in contact with soil without being appreciably water-soluble. However, the fact that potassium readily enters the base-exchange-complex of soils and replaces other cations, gives an even more conclusive interpretation of why no water-soluble potash was found. It reacted with the base-exchange-complex immediately upon being brought in contact with water, and hence showed no water-soluble potash upon subsequent analysis.

The formation of potassium nitrate crystals under these conditions obviously necessitates the presence of a fairly abundant source of nitrate nitrogen. Elsewhere in this monograph it has been pointed out that plant, animal, and human wastes of all kinds were allowed to accumulate continuously in certain parts of the cave. Such wastes, being organic in nature, contain nitrogen in the form of protein material. Under the moist conditions resulting from the seepage of water from the spring, microbial decomposition occurs and in the ultimate, such decomposition yields nitric acid. By simple interaction of the potassium carbonate from wood ashes with the nitric acid thus formed, potassium nitrate is produced. These processes can be illustrated as follows:

$$\text{Protein N} + \text{Oxygen (Biological)} = HNO_3 + H_2CO_3 + H_2O$$

With wood ashes:

$$2\ HNO_3 + K_2CO_3 = 2\ KNO_3 + CO_2 + H_2O$$

With clay (from soil):

$$HNO_3 + \text{K-clay} = KNO_3 + \text{H-clay}$$

As may be seen from the data in Table 1, the potash percentage is substantially constant throughout the profile down to the 4-meter level, where it was found to have increased to 4.00 per cent. At this level, there was also the highest percentage of water-soluble nitrogen, present as nitrate ion, namely 2.36%, expressed as N_2O_5. At this level, conditions favored the concentration of potassium and nitrate ions to the point of saturation, and crystals separated out. It is evident that at the present level, where these crystals exist, there is no leaching action of water, nor must water have penetrated to that level for a long period of time, for the reason that, because of the high solubility of the salt, it would easily have leached out.

An interesting similar occurrence of potassium nitrate has been called to my attention by Dr. R. H. Forbes. In the Upper Nile valley in Egypt, and specifically in the vicinity of the present town of El-Fashin, there exist ruins of mud (adobe) houses dating back to ancient times. The material of these crumbling walls, which in ancient times must similarly have been impregnated with the potash from plant ashes and the nitrate formed from the disintegration of human and animal offal, is found to be fairly rich in potassium nitrate. Its value having become recognized, this material is now being crushed and spread out over the fields as fertilizer.

Organic Carbon

The question of the organic matter content of the Ventana Cave material is of interest in view of the fact that organic refuse of all kinds was left in the cave and allowed continuously to accumulate. Professor Bryan states (Part III) that in the stratum at 1-meter depth, undecomposed organic matter was present. As a matter of fact, all of the samples submitted for analysis, with possible exception of that of the volcanic debris substratum, were very dark in color, indicating the presence of organic matter in a more or less finely divided state. Preliminary qualitative tests on the material had shown that organic matter was present in both soluble and insoluble form in water. Quantitative determinations of organic carbon were accordingly made by the wet oxidation method, using chromic acid. The results are shown in Table 1, and confirm both the qualitative tests and the observations of Professor Bryan. The highest percentage of carbon was found in the top 1-meter horizon. Microscopic examination showed that part of this organic matter consisted of particles of charcoal.

It should be pointed out that the percentages of organic carbon here reported do not include the *carbonate* carbon, the latter having been determined as carbon dioxide by an independent method and reported as such. The carbonate fraction consists of the carbonates of calcium, magnesium, sodium, and potassium, and originates from various sources, chiefly wood ashes, bacterial decomposition of organic matter, and bicarbonates from the spring water.

The existence and persistence of this organic carbon within the profile centuries after inhabitation of the cave by man poses an interesting problem. Under the moist conditions maintained by flow of water from the spring and the prevailing warm temperatures, organic matter undergoes decomposition by bacteria, fungi, and protozoa which live in the soil. The constituents decompose at different rates, however, and generally in the following (decreasing) order as to ease of breakdown:

Most easily decomposed	1. Sugars and soluble proteins
	2. Starches
	3. Complex proteins
	4. Hemicelluloses
	5. Celluloses
	6. Lignins and ligno-celluloses
Most difficultly decomposed ↓	7. Oils, fats, and waxes

The soluble fraction of organic matter is necessarily the first to be acted upon by the micro-organisms, and the other less soluble constituents in decreasing order. The ultimate products of such decomposition are essentially carbonic acid, nitric, sulfuric, and phosphoric acids, though intermediate organic acids may form and persist for long periods of time. The more resistant forms may remain in the soil profile or midden, especially during long periods of drouth, during which the micro-organisms go into a dormant or inactive state. Pyrolytic products, remaining from incomplete combustion by fire, such as charcoal, are no longer amenable to bacterial decomposition and hence persist unchanged for indefinite periods of time. The higher percentages of organic carbon observed in Samples 1 and 3 suggest that they may represent residues from more recent occupation of the cave. Beyond the deductions here offered, however, it does not appear that the analytical results for organic carbon contain information of any far-reaching anthropological significance.

Bibliography

Anonymous. Stone Artifact Terminology. Notebook, Society for American
1942 Archaeology, Vol. 2, No. 4, pp. 67-69. Menasha, Wisconsin.

Albritton, C. C. Jr., and Kirk Bryan. Quaternary Stratigraphy of the Davis
1939 Mountains, Trans-Pecos, Texas. Geological Society of America, Bulletin, Vol. 50, pp. 1423-1473. New York, N.Y.

Alden, W. C. and M. M. Leighton. The Iowan Drift, a Review of the
1917 Evidences of the Iowan Stage of Glaciation. Iowa Geological Survey, Vol. 26, pp. 49-212. Des Moines, Iowa.

Allen, G. M. Dogs of the American Aborigines. Bulletin, Museum of Com-
1920 parative Zoology, Harvard College, Vol. LXIII, No. 9. Cambridge, Massachusetts.

Amsden, C. A. Navajo Weaving. Fine Arts Press, Santa Ana, California.
1934 Second edition, University of New Mexico Press, Albuquerque, New Mexico, 1949.

1935 The Pinto Basin Artifacts. *In* Campbell, E. W. C. and W. H., The Pinto Basin Site. Southwest Museum Papers, No. 9, pp. 33-51. Los Angeles, California.

1937 The Lake Mohave Artifacts. *In* The Archaeology of Pleistocene Lake Mohave. Southwest Museum Papers, No. 11, pp. 51-98. Los Angeles, California.

Anderson, E. and H. C. Cutler. Races of Zea Mays: I. Their Recognition
1942 and Classification. Annals of the Missouri Botanical Garden, Vol. 29, pp. 69-86. St. Louis, Missouri.

Antevs, E. Maps of the Pleistocene Glaciations. Geological Society of
1929 America, Bulletin, Vol. 40, pp. 631-720. New York, N.Y.

1931 Late Glacial Correlations and Ice Recession in Manitoba. Geological Survey of Canada, Memoirs, No. 168. Ottawa, Canada.

1934 Climaxes of the Last Glaciation in North America. American Journal of Science, Vol. 28, pp. 304-311. New Haven, Connecticut.

1935 Age of the Clovis Lake Clays. Academy of Natural Sciences of Philadelphia, Proceedings, Vol. 87, pp. 299-312. Philadelphia, Pennsylvania.

1937 Age of the Lake Mohave Culture. *In* The Archaeology of Pleistocene Lake Mohave. Southwest Museum Papers, No. 11, pp. 45-49. Los Angeles, California.

1938 Climatic Variations During the Last Glaciation in North America. American Meteorological Society, Bulletin, Vol. 19, pp. 172-176. Milton, Massachusetts.

1945 Correlation of Wisconsin Glacial Maxima. American Journal of Science, Vol. 243-A (Daly Vol.), pp. 1-39. New Haven, Connecticut.

Ayer, M. Y. The Archaeological and Faunal Material from Williams
1936 Cave, Guadalupe Mountains, Texas. Academy of Natural Sciences of Philadelphia, Proceedings, Vol. LXXXVIII, pp. 599-619. Philadelphia, Pennsylvania.

Bailey, V. Mammals of New Mexico. North American Fauna, No. 53, pp.
1931 1-412. Washington, D. C.

Bancroft, H. H. The Native Races. Vol. 1, Wild Tribes. San Francisco,
1883 California.

Bandelier, A. F. Final Report of the Investigations Among the Indians
1892 of the Southwestern United States, Part II. Papers of the Archaeological Institute of America, American Series, No. IV. Cambridge, Massachusetts.

Barbieri, J. A. Technique of the Implements from Lake Mohave. *In* The
1937 Archaeology of Pleistocene Lake Mohave. Southwest Museum Papers, No. 11. Los Angeles, California.

Bartlett, K. Notes Upon a Primitive Stone Industry of the Little Colo-
1942 rado Valley, Plateau, Northern Arizona Society of Science and Art, Museum of Northern Arizona, Vol. 14, No. 3, pp. 37-41. Flagstaff, Arizona.

Beals, R. L. Material Culture of the Pima, Papago and Western Apache.
1934 U. S. Department of the Interior, National Park Service, Field Division of Education. Berkeley, California.

Blackwelder, E. Pleistocene Glaciation in the Sierra Nevada and Basin
1931 Ranges. Geological Society of America, Bulletin, Vol. 42, pp. 865-922. New York, N. Y.

Bolton, H. E. Anza's California Expeditions, Vol. I, pp. 1-529. University
1930 of California Press, Berkeley, California.

1936 Rim of Christendom. Macmillan & Co., New York, N. Y.

Brand, D. D. The Distribution of Pottery Types in Northwest Mexico.
1935 American Anthropologist, n. s., Vol. 37, No. 2 (pt. 1), pp. 287-305. Menasha, Wisconsin.

Breazeale, E. L., R. A. Greene, and L. J. Kantor. Blood-Groups of the
1941 Papago Indians. The Journal of Immunology, Vol. 40, No. 2, pp. 161-162. Williams and Wilkins, Baltimore, Maryland.

Breazeale, J. F. and H. V. Smith. Caliche in Arizona. University of Arizona Agricultural Experiment Station, Bulletin No. 131. Tucson, Arizona.
1930

Bretz, J. Harlan. Keewatin End Moraines in Alberta, Canada. Geological Society of America, Bulletin, Vol. 54, pp. 31-52. New York, N. Y.
1943

Brew, J. O. Preliminary Report of the Peabody Museum Awatovi Expedition of 1939. Plateau, Northern Arizona Society of Science and Art, Museum of Northern Arizona, Vol. 13, No. 3. Flagstaff, Arizona.
1941

Brooks, C. E. P. Climate Through the Ages. 436 pp. London, England.
1926

Brues, A. M. The San Simon Branch, Excavations at Cave Creek and in the San Simon Valley II: Skeletal Material. Medallion Papers, No. XXXV. Gila Pueblo, Globe, Arizona.
1946

Bryan, Kirk. Erosion and Sedimentation in the Papago Country, Arizona, with a Sketch of the Geology. U. S. Geological Survey, Bulletin No. 730, pp. 19-90. Washington, D. C.
1923

1925*a* The Papago Country, Arizona. A Geographic, Geologic, and Hydrologic Reconnaissance with a Guide to Desert Watering Places. Water Supply Paper No. 499, U. S. Geological Survey. Washington, D. C.

1925*b* Dates of Channel Trenching (Arroyo-cutting) in the Arid Southwest. Science, n. s., Vol. 57, pp. 339-344. Washington, D. C.

1929 Geology of the Owyhee Irrigation Project, Oregon. U. S. Geological Survey, Water Supply Paper No. 597, pp. 39-72. Washington, D. C.

1941*a* Geologic Antiquity of Man in America. Science, Vol. 93, No. 2422, pp. 505-514.

1941*b* Pre-Columbian Agriculture in the Southwest, as Conditioned by Periods of Alluviation. The Association of American Geographers, Annals, Vol. 31, pp. 219-242. Albany, N. Y. Also: 8th American Scientific Congress, Vol. 2, pp. 57-74, 1942. Washington, D. C.

Bryan, Kirk and F. T. McCann. Sand Dunes and Alluvium Near Grants, New Mexico. American Antiquity, Society for American Archaeology, Vol. VIII, No. 3, pp. 281-290. Menasha, Wisconsin.
1943

Bryan, Kirk and L. L. Ray. Geologic Antiquity of the Lindenmeier Site in Colorado. Smithsonian Miscellaneous Collections, Vol. 99, No. 2. Washington, D. C.
1940

Bryan, Kirk and J. H. Toulouse, Jr. The San Jose Non-Ceramic Culture and Its Relation to a Puebloan Culture in New Mexico. American Antiquity, Society for American Archaeology, Vol. VIII, No. 3, pp. 269-280. Menasha, Wisconsin.
1943

Burchell, J. P. T. Some Pleistocene Deposits at Kirmington and Crayford.
1935 Geology Magazine, Vol. 72, pp. 327-331 (gives identifications by G. Erdtmann). London, England.

Burgess, J. T. and J. Irving. Knots, Ties and Splices. E. P. Dutton & Co.,
1941 Inc., New York, N. Y.

Cailleux, Andre. Les Actions Eolienne Periglaciaires en Europe. Societe
1942 Geologie de France, Memoirs, n. s., Vol. 21, 176 pp. Paris, France.

Campbell, E. W. C. and W. H. Campbell. The Pinto Basin Site. South-
1935 west Museum Papers, No. 9. Los Angeles, California.

Campbell, E. W. C., W. H. Campbell, E. Antevs, C. A. Amsden, J. A. Bar-
1937 bieri, and F. D. Bode. The Archaeology of Pleistocene Lake Mohave. Southwest Museum Papers, No. 11. Los Angeles, California.

Carter, G. F. Plant Geography and Cultural History in the American South-
1945 west. Viking Fund Publications in Anthropology, No. 5. New York, N. Y.

Castetter, E. F. and W. H. Bell. Ethnobiological Studies in the American
1937 Southwest, IV: The Aboriginal Utilization of the Tall Cacti in the American Southwest. The University of New Mexico Bulletin, Whole Number 307, Biological Series, Vol. 5, No. 1. Albuquerque, New Mexico.

1942 Pima and Papago Indian Agriculture. Inter-Americana Studies 1, University of New Mexico Press. Albuquerque, New Mexico.

Castetter, E. F. and Ruth M. Underhill. Ethnobiological Studies in the
1935 American Southwest, II: The Ethnobiology of the Papago Indians. The University of New Mexico Bulletin, Whole Number 275, Biological Series, Vol. 4, No. 3. Albuquerque, New Mexico.

Chesky, Jane. The Nature and Function of Papago Music. M. A. Thesis,
1943 University of Arizona, Tucson, Arizona.

Clark, E. P. Designs on the Prehistoric Pottery of Arizona. University of
1935 Arizona Social Science Bulletin No. 9, Vol. VI, No. 4. Tucson, Arizona.

Colbert, E. H. The Association of Man with Extinct Mammals in the
1942 Western Hemisphere. Proceedings, 8th American Scientific Congress, Anthropological Sciences, Vol. II, pp. 17-29. Washington, D. C.

Colton, H. S. What Can We Do About Lac? Plateau, Northern Arizona
1943*a* Society of Science and Art, Museum of Northern Arizona, Vol. 15, No. 3, pp. 46-48. Flagstaff, Arizona.

1943*b* Life History and Economic Possibilities of the American Lac Insect, *Tachardiella larrea*. Northern Arizona Society of Science and Art, Museum of Northern Arizona, Vol. 16, No. 2, pp. 21-32. Flagstaff, Arizona.

Colton, H. S. and L. L. Hargrave. Handbook of Northern Arizona Pottery Wares. Museum of Northern Arizona, Bulletin No. 11. Flagstaff, Arizona.
1937

Cosgrove, C. B. Caves of the Upper Gila and Hueco Areas in New Mexico and Texas. Papers of the Peabody Museum of American Archaeology and Ethnology, Harvard University, Vol. XXII, No. 2. Cambridge, Massachusetts.
1947

Cressman, L. S. Archaeological Researches in the Northern Great Basin. Carnegie Institution of Washington, Publication 538. Washington, D. C.
1942

Davenport, J. W. and C. Chelf. Painted Pebbles from the Lower Pecos and Big Bend Regions of Texas. Witte Memorial Museum, Bulletin V. San Antonio, Texas.
(No Date)

Denny, C. S. Glacial Geology of the Black Rock Forest (N. Y). Black Rock Forest Bulletin 8, 70 pp. Cornwall, N. Y.
1938

de Terra, H. Preliminary Note on the Discovery of Fossil Man at Tepexpan in the Valley of Mexico. American Antiquity, Vol. XIII, No. 1, pp. 40-44. Menasha, Wisconsin.
1947

Douglass, A. E. The Secret of the Southwest Solved by Talkative Tree-Rings. National Geographic Magazine, December, pp. 737-770. Washington, D. C.
1929

1935 Dating Pueblo Bonito and Other Ruins of the Southwest. National Geographic Society Technical Papers (Pueblo Bonito Series No. 1, 74 pp.). Washington, D. C.

1942 Checking the Date of Bluff Ruin, Forestdale: A Study in Technique. Tree-Ring Bulletin, Tree-Ring Society, Vol. 9, No. 2, pp. 2-7. Tucson, Arizona.

Ekholm, G. F. Excavations at Guasave, Sinaloa, Mexico. Anthropological Papers of the American Museum of Natural History, Vol. 38, Pt. 2. New York, N. Y.
1942

Evans, Glen L. and G. E. Meade. Quaternary Geology of the Texas High Plains. University of Texas Publications, No. 4401, pp. 485-507. Austin, Texas.
1945

Fewkes, J. W. Casa Grande, Arizona. Twenty-eighth Report of the Bureau of American Ethnology, pp. 25-179. Washington, D. C.
1912

Flint, R. F. The Growth of the North American Ice Sheet During the Wisconsin Age. Geological Society of America, Bulletin, Vol. 54, pp. 325-362. New York, N. Y.
1943

Glaciation of South Dakota, Preliminary Discussion, Abstract. Geological Society of America (Annual Meeting, 1947), Proceedings, 1948. New York, N. Y.

Flower, Wm. H. and Richard Lydekker. An Introduction to the Study of Mammals, Living and Extinct. Adam and Charles Black, London, England.
1891

Forde, C. D. Ethnography of the Yuma Indians. University of California
1931 Publications in American Archaeology and Ethnology, Vol. 28, No. 4, pp. 83-278. Berkeley, California.

Fraps, C. L. Tanque Verde Ruins. The Kiva, Arizona Archaeological
1935 and Historical Society, Vol. 1, No. 4. Tucson, Arizona.

Fulton, W. S. A Ceremonial Cave in the Winchester Mountains, Arizona.
1941 The Amerind Foundation, Inc., No. 2. Dragoon, Arizona.

Fulton, W. S. and C. Tuthill. An Archaeological Site near Gleeson, Ari-
1940 zona. The Amerind Foundation, Inc., No. 1. Dragoon, Arizona.

Furlong, E. L. The Pleistocene Antelope, *Stockoceros conklingi,* from San
1943 Josecito Cave, Mexico. Carnegie Institution, Publication No. 551, pp. 1-8. Washington, D. C.

Gabel, N. E. A Comparative Racial Study of the Papago. Ph.D. Thesis,
1941 Harvard University, Cambridge, Massachusetts.

1949 A Comparative Racial Study of the Papago. University of New Mexico Publications in Anthropology, No. 4, University of New Mexico Press, Albuquerque, New Mexico.

Gifford, E. W. Californian Shell Artifacts. Anthropological Records, Vol
1947 9, No. 1, University of California Press. Berkeley, California.

Gladwin, H. S. Excavations at Casa Grande, Arizona. Southwest Museum
1928 Papers, No. 2. Los Angeles, California.

1937 Excavations at Snaketown II: Comparisons and Theories. Medallion Papers, No. XXVI, Gila Pueblo. Globe, Arizona.

1942 Excavations at Snaketown III: Revisions. Medallion Papers, No. XXX, Gila Pueblo. Globe, Arizona.

Gladwin, W. and H. S. Gladwin. The Red-on-buff Culture of the Papa-
1929 gueria. Medallion Papers, No. IV, Gila Pueblo. Globe, Arizona.

1930 Some Southwestern Pottery Types, Series I. Medallion Papers, No. VIII, Gila Pueblo. Globe, Arizona.

1933 Some Southwestern Pottery Types, Series III. Medallion Papers, No. XIII, Gila Pueblo. Globe, Arizona.

Gladwin, H. S., E. W. Haury, E. B. Sayles, and N. Gladwin. Excavations
1937 at Snaketown, Material Culture. Medallion Papers, No. XXV, Gila Pueblo. Globe, Arizona.

Goddard, P. E. Indians of the Southwest. American Museum of Natural
1931 History, Handbook Series, No. 2. New York, N. Y.

Guernsey, S. J. Explorations in Northeastern Arizona: Report on the
1931 Archaeological Fieldwork of 1920-1923. Papers of the Peabody Museum of American Archaeoolgy and Ethnology, Harvard University, Vol. XII, No. 1. Cambridge, Massachusetts.

Guernsey, S. J. and A. V. Kidder. Basket Maker Caves of Northeastern
1921 Arizona. Papers of the Peabody Museum of American Archaeology and Ethnology, Harvard University, Vol. VIII, No. 2. Cambridge, Massachusetts.

Hack, John T. The Changing Physical Environment of the Hopi Indians.
1942 Peabody Museum Papers, Harvard University, Vol. 35, No. 1. Cambridge, Massachusetts.
1943 Antiquity of the Finley Site (Wyoming). American Antiquity, Vol. 8, pp. 235-241. Menasha, Wisconsin.

Handbook of South American Indians (J. H. Stewart, Editor). Smith-
1946 sonian Institution, Bureau of American Ethnology, Bulletin 143, Vol. 2. Washington, D. C.

Harrington, M. R. Gypsum Cave, Nevada. Southwest Museum Papers, No.
1933 8. Los Angeles, California.
1948 An Ancient Site at Borax Lake, California. Southwest Museum Papers, No. 16. Los Angeles, California.

Haury, E. W. The Canyon Creek Ruin and Cliff Dwellings of the Sierra
1934 Ancha. Medallion Papers, No. XIV, Gila Pueblo. Globe, Arizona.
1940 Excavations in the Forestdale Valley, East-Central Arizona. University of Arizona Social Sciences Bulletin No. 12, Vol. XI, No. 4. Tucson, Arizona.
1942 Some Implications of the Bluff Ruin Dates. Tree-Ring Bulletin, Tree-Ring Society, Vol. 9, No. 2, pp. 7-8. Tucson, Arizona.
1943*a* The Stratigraphy of Ventana Cave. American Antiquity, Vol. 8, No. 3, pp. 218-223. Menasha, Wisconsin.
1943*b* A Possible Cochise-Mogollon-Hohokam Sequence. Proceedings of the American Philosophical Society, Vol. 86, No. 2, pp. 260-263. Philadelphia, Pennsylvania.
1945 The Excavations of Los Muertos and Neighboring Ruins of the Salt River Valley, Southern Arizona. Papers of the Peabody Museum of American Archaeology and Ethnology, Harvard University, Vol. XXIV, No. 1. Cambridge, Massachusetts.

Haury, E. W. and E. B. Sayles. An Early Pit House Village of the Mogollon
1947 Culture, Forestdale Valley, Arizona. University of Arizona Social Sciences Bulletin No. 16, Vol. XVIII, No. 4. Tucson, Arizona.

Hayden, J. D. Excavations at the University Indian Ruin, 1940. Unpub-
1940 lished Ms. in the Files of the Arizona State Museum, Tucson, Arizona.

Heizer, R. F. and E. M. Lemert. Observations on Archaeological Sites
1947 in Topanga Canyon, California. University of California Publications in American Archaeology and Ethnology, Vol. 44, No. 2, pp. 237-258. Berkeley, California.

Hibben, F. C. and Kirk Bryan. Evidences of Early Occupation in Sandia
1941 Cave, New Mexico, and Other Sites in the Sandia-Manzano Region, with an Appendix; Correlation of the Deposits of Sandia Cave, New Mexico, with the Glacial Geology. Smithsonian Miscellaneous Collections, Vol. 99, No. 23. Washington, D. C.

Hobbs, W. H. The Glacial History of Iowa and Neighboring Portions
1943 of Minnesota and Missouri. *In* Glacial Studies of the Pleistocene of North America, 109 pp. Edwards Bros., Ann Arbor, Michigan.

Hodge, F. W. Hawikuk Bonework. Museum of the American Indian.
1920 Heye Foundation, Indian Notes and Monographs, Vol. III, No. 3. New York, N. Y.

Hooton, E. A. Indians of Pecos, A Study of Their Skeletal Remains.
1930 Papers of the Phillips Academy Southwestern Expeditions, No. 4. New Haven, Connecticut.

1933 Notes on Five Texas Crania. Bulletin of the Texas Archaeological and Paleontological Society, Vol. V, pp. 25-38. Abilene, Texas.

Hoover, J. W. Cerros de Trincheras of the Arizona Papagueria. The
1941 Geographical Review, Vol. XXXI, No. 2, pp. 228-239. New York, N. Y.

Hough, W. Culture of the Ancient Pueblos of the Upper Gila River Re-
1914 gion, New Mexico and Arizona. Bulletin 87, U. S. National Museum, Washington, D. C.

Howard, E. B. The Finley Site: Discovery of Yuma Points *in Situ,* near
1943 Eden, Wyoming. American Antiquity, Society for American Archaeology, Vol. VIII, No. 3, pp. 224-234. Menasha, Wisconsin.

Ives, R. L. Glacial Geology of the Monarch Valley, Grand County, Colo-
1938 rado. Geological Society of America, Bulletin, Vol. 49, pp. 1045-1066. New York, N. Y.

1942 Early Human Occupation of the Colorado Headwaters Region, An Archaeological Reconnaissance. Geographical Review, Vol. 32, pp. 448-462. New York, N. Y.

Jeancon, J. A. Excavations in the Chama Valley, New Mexico. Bulletin
1923 81, Bureau of American Ethnology. Washington, D. C.

Jessen, K. and V. Milthers. Stratigraphy and Paleontological Studies of
1928 Interglacial Fresh-water Deposits in Jutland and Northwest Germany. Denmarks Geol. Undesog., No. 48. Copenhagen, Denmark.

Johnson, F. An Archaeological Survey Along the Alaska Highway, 1944.
1946 American Antiquity, Vol. XI, No. 3, pp. 183-186. Menasha, Wisconsin.

Johnston, W. A. Frozen Ground in the Glaciated Parts of Northern
1930 Canada. Royal Society of Canada, Trans., Sect. IV, pp. 31-40. Ottawa, Canada.

Jones, V. A Summary of Data on Aboriginal Cotton of the Southwest.
1936 *In* Symposium on Prehistoric Agriculture, University of New Mexico Bulletin, Anthropological Series, Vol. 1, No. 5, Whole Number 296. Albuquerque, New Mexico.

Jones, W. R. and L. O. Quam. Glacial Land Forms in Rocky Mountain
1944 National Park, Colorado. Journal of Geology, Vol. 52, pp. 217-234. Chicago, Illinois.

Joseph, A., R. Spicer and J. Chesky. The Desert People. (Mimeographed)
1946 Sells, Arizona: or (in press) University of Chicago Press, Chicago, Illinois.

Kay, G. M. and M. M. Leighton. Eldoran Epoch of the Pleistocene Period.
1933 Geological Society of America, Bulletin, Vol. 44, pp. 669-674.

Kelley, J. C., N. T. Campbell and D. J. Lehmer. The Association of Archae-
1940 ological Materials with Geological Deposits in the Big Bend Region of Texas. Sull Ross State Teachers College Bulletin, Vol. XXI, No. 3. Alpine, Texas.

1947 The Cultural Affiliations and Chronological Position of the Clear Fork Focus. American Antiquity, Vol. 13, pp. 97-109. Menasha, Wisconsin.

Kelly, I. T. Excavations at Chametla, Sinaloa. Ibero-Americana, No. 14,
1938 University of California Press. Berkeley, California.
Unpublished Ms. on Excavations in the Hodges Ruin near Tucson, Arizona.

Kent, K. P. The Braiding of a Hopi Wedding Sash. The Plateau, North-
1940 ern Arizona Society of Science and Art, Museum of Northern Arizona, Vol. 12, No. 3, pp. 46-52. Flagstaff, Arizona.

Kerner-Marilaun, F. Palaeoklimatologie. 512 pp. Borntraeger, Berlin,
1930 Germany. (See p. 508).

Kessler, Paul. Das Eiszeitliche Klima und Seine Geologischen Wirkungen
1925 im Nichtvereisten Gebiet, 210 pp. Stuttgart.

Kesseli, J. E. Studies in the Pleistocene Glaciation of the Sierra Nevada,
1941*a* California: I. Topographic Map, etc., II. Changes in the Courses of Some Pleistocene Glaciers, etc. University of California Publications, Geography, Vol. 6, pp. 315-362. Berkeley, California.

1941*b* Rock Streams in the Sierra Nevada, California. Geographical Review, Vol. 31, pp. 203-227.

Kidder, A. V. The Artifacts of Pecos. Papers of the Phillips Academy
1932 Southwestern Expedition, No. 6. New Haven, Connecticut.

Kidder, A. V. and S. J. Guernsey. Archaeological Explorations in North-
1919 eastern Arizona. Bulletin 65, Bureau of American Ethnology. Washington, D. C.

Kissell, M. L. Basketry of the Papago and Pima. Anthropological Papers
1916 of the American Museum of Natural History, Vol. XVII, Part IV, pp. 115-273. New York, N. Y.

Kurath, W. A Brief Introduction to Papago, A Native Language of Ari-
1945 zona. University of Arizona Social Science Bulletin No. 13, Vol. XVI, No. 2. Tucson, Arizona.

Leighton, M. M. A Notable Type Pleistocene Section: The Farm Creek
1926 Exposure near Peoria, Illinois. Journal of Geology, Vol. 34, pp. 167-174. University of Chicago Press, Chicago, Illinois.
1931 The Peorian Loess and the Classification of the Glacial Drift Sheets of the Mississippi Valley. Journal of Geology, Vol. 39, pp. 48-50. University of Chicago Press, Chicago, Illinois.
1936 Geological Aspects of the Findings of Primitive Man near Abilene, Texas. Medallion Papers, No. 24. 44 pp., Gila Pueblo. Globe, Arizona.

Leverett, Frank. The Illinois Glacial Lobe. U. S. Geological Survey, Mono-
1899 graph 38. Washington, D. C.
1929 Moraines and Shore Lines of the Lake Superior Region. U. S. Geological Survey, Prof. Paper 154-A (also Prof. Paper 161, 1932).

Lidén, R. Geokronologiska Studier öfner det Finiglaciala Skedet i Anger-
1913 manland. Afhandl. Sveriges Geol. Undersökn. Ser. C. No. 9.

Lozinski, W. Über die Mechanische Verwitterung der Sandsteine im
1909 Gemässigten Klima. Acad. Sc. Cracovie Cl. Sc. Math. et Natur. Bull., pp. 1-25. Crakow, Poland.
1933 Palsenfelder und Periglaziale Bödenbildung. Neues Jahrbuch, f. Min. etc., Beil. Bd. 71, abt. B, pp. 18-47. Berlin, Germany.

Lugn, A. L. The Pleistocene Geology of Nebraska. Nebraska Geological
1935 Survey, 2nd Series, Bulletin 10. Lincoln, Nebraska.

Lull, R. S. The Remarkable Ground Sloth. Memoirs of the Peabody
1929 Museum, Yale University, Vol. III, Pt. 2, p. 8. New Haven, Connecticut.

Lumholtz, C. New Trails in Mexico. New York, N. Y.
1912

MacClintock, Paul. Interglacial Soils and the Drift Sheets of Eastern
1933 England. Sixteenth International Geological Congress, Washington, D. C. Report, pp. 1041-1053. Washington, D. C.

Mallery, T. D. Rainfall Records for the Sonoran Desert. Ecology, Vol. 17,
1936*a* pp. 110-121, Brooklyn Botanical Garden. Brooklyn, N. Y.
1936*b* Rainfall Records for the Sonoran Desert II. Ecology, Vol. 17, pp. 212-215, Brooklyn Botanical Garden. Brooklyn, N. Y.

Martin, G. C. Big Bend Basket Maker. Southwest Texas Archaeological
1933 Society, Witte Memorial Museum, Bulletin No. 3. San Antonio, Texas.

Matthes, F. E. Report Committee on Glaciers. American Geophysical
1939 Union, Trans. for 1939, pp. 518-520. Washington, D. C.
1940 Report Committee on Glaciers. American Geophysical Union, Trans. for 1940, pp. 396-403. Washington, D. C.
1942 Report Committee on Glaciers, 1941-42. American Geophysical Union, Trans. of 1942, pp. 377-384. Washington, D. C.

McGregor, J. C. Winona and Ridge Ruin, Part 1: Architecture and
1941 Material Culture. Museum of Northern Arizona, Bulletin 18. Flagstaff, Arizona.

1943 Burial of an Early American Magician. Proceedings of the American Philosophical Society, Vol. 86, No. 2, pp. 270-298. Philadelphia, Pennsylvania.

1945 Nose Plugs from Northern Arizona. American Antiquity, Society for American Archaeology, Vol. X, No. 3, pp. 303-307. Menasha, Wisconsin.

Meigs, P. The Kiliwa Indians of Lower California. Ibero-American, Vol.
1939 15, University of California Press. Berkeley, California.

Morris, E. H. An Aboriginal Salt Mine at Camp Verde, Arizona. Anthro-
1928 pological Papers of the American Museum of Natural History, Vol. XXX, Pt. III, pp. 75-97. New York, N. Y.

Morris, E. H. and R. F. Burgh. Anasazi Basketry, Basket Maker II
1941 Through Pueblo III: A Study Based on Specimens from the San Juan River Country. Carnegie Institution of Washington, Publication 533. Washington, D. C.

Movius, Hallam L., Jr. The Irish Stone Age, Its Chronology, Develop-
1942 ment, and Relationships. Harvard University Press, 339 pp. Cambridge, Massachusetts.

1944 Early Man and Pleistocene Stratigraphy in Southern and Eastern Asia. Papers of the Peabody Museum of American Archaeology and Ethnology. Harvard University, Vol. XIX, No. 3. Cambridge, Massachusetts.

Nichol, A. A. The Natural Vegetation of Arizona. University of Ari-
1937 zona, College of Agriculture, Technical Bulletin, No. 68. Tucson, Arizona.

Oetteking, B. Skeletal Remains from Texas. Notes, Museum of the Amer-
1930 ican Indian, Heye Foundation, Vol. VII, No. 3. New York, N. Y.

Pond, A. W. Primitive Methods of Working Stone, Based on Experiments
1930 of Halvor L. Skavlem. Logan Museum Bulletin, Beloit College, Vol. II, No. 1. Beloit, Wisconsin.

Powers, W. E. and George W. Ekblaw. Glaciation of the Grays Lake, Illi-
1940 nois, Quadrangle. Geological Society of America, Bulletin, Vol. 51, pp. 1329-1336. New York, N. Y.

Ray, L. L. Glacial Chronology of the Southern Rocky Mountains. Geolo-
1941 cal Society of America, Vol. 51, pp. 1851-1918. New York, N. Y.

Renaud, E. B. The First Thousand Yuma-Folsom Artifacts. University
1934 of Denver, Department of Anthropology. Denver, Colorado.

Roberts, F. H. H., Jr. Shabik'eschee Village: A Late Basket Maker Site
1929 in the Chaco Canyon, New Mexico. Bureau of American Ethnology, Bulletin 92. Washington, D. C.

1935 A Folsom Complex: Preliminary Report on Investigations at the Lindenmeier Site in Northern Colorado. Smithsonian Miscellaneous Collections, Vol. 94, No. 4. Washington, D. C.

1936 Additional Information on the Folsom Complex: Report on the Second Season's Investigations at the Lindenmeier Site in Northern Colorado. Smithsonian Miscellaneous Collections, Vol. 95, No. 10. Washington, D. C.

1937 Archaeology in the Southwest. American Antiquity, Society for American Archaeology, Vol. III, No. 1, pp. 3-33. Menasha, Wisconsin.

1940 Developments in the Problem of the North American Paleo-Indian. *In* Essays in Historical Anthropology of North America. Smithsonian Miscellaneous Collections, Vol. 100, pp. 51-116. Washington, D. C.

Rogers, M. J. Early Lithic Industries of the Lower Basin of the Colorado
1939 River and Adjacent Desert Areas. San Diego Museum Papers, No. 3. San Diego, California.

1941 Aboriginal Culture Relations Between Southern California and the Southwest. The San Diego Museum Bulletin, Vol. V, No. 3, pp. 1-6. San Diego, California.

Russell, F. The Pima Indians. Twenty-Sixth Annual Report of the Bureau
1908 of American Ethnology. Washington, D. C.

Russell, R. M. Lower Mississippi Valley Loess. Geological Society of
1944 America, Bulletin, Vol. 55, pp. 1-40. New York, N. Y.

Sauer, C. O. A Geographic Sketch of Early Man in America. The Geogra-
1944 phical Review, Vol. XXXIV, No. 4, pp. 529-573. New York, N. Y.

Sauer, C. and D. Brand. Prehistoric Settlements of Sonora with Specific
1931 Reference to Cerros de Trincheras. University of California Publications in Geography, Vol. 5, No. 3, pp. 67-148. Berkeley.

Sayles, E. B. An Archaeological Survey of Texas. Medallion Papers, No.
1935 17, Gila Pueblo. Globe, Arizona.

1936 An Archaeological Survey of Chihuahua, Mexico. Medallion Papers, No. XXII, Gila Pueblo. Globe, Arizona.

Sayles, E. B. and E. Antevs. The Cochise Culture. Medallion Papers, No.
1941 29, Gila Pueblo. Globe, Arizona.

Scantling, F. H. Jackrabbit Ruin. The Kiva, Vol. 5, No. 3, pp. 9-12, The
1939 Arizona Archaeological and Historical Society. Tucson,

1940 Excavations at the Jackrabbit Ruin, Papago Indian Reservation, Arizona. Master's Thesis, University of Arizona. Tucson, Arizona.

Scharf, D. The Quaternary History of the Pinto Basin. *In* The Pinto Basin
1935 Site, by E. W. C. and W. H. Campbell. Southwest Museum Papers, No. 9, pp. 11-20. Los Angeles, California.

Schultz, C. B. and E. B. Howard. The Fauna of Burnet Cave, Guadalupe
1935 Mountains, New Mexico. Proceedings of the Academy of

Natural Sciences, Vol. LXXXVII, pp. 273-298. Philadelphia, Pennsylvania.

Scott, Wm. B. A History of Land Mammals in the Western Hemisphere.
1929 The Macmillan Co., New York, N. Y.

Sellards, E. H. Early Man in America, Index to Localities and Selected
1940 Bibliography. Bulletin of the Geological Society of America, Vol. 51, pp. 373-432. New York, N. Y.

Sharp, R. P. Pleistocene Glaciation in the Ruby-East Humboldt Range,
1938 Northeastern Nevada. Journal of Geomorphology, Vol. 1, pp. 300-304. Columbia University Press, New York, N. Y.

1942 Multiple Pleistocene Glaciation on San Francisco Mountain, Arizona. Journal of Geology, Vol. 50, pp. 481-503. University of Chicago Press, Chicago, Illinois.

Shreve, Forrest. The Plant Life of the Sonoran Desert. Carnegie Insti-
1936 tution of Washington, Supplementary Publications, No. 22. Washington, D. C.

Shreve, Margaret B. Modern Papago Basketry. Master's Thesis, Univer-
1943 sity of Arizona. Tucson, Arizona.

Smith, H. V. The Climate of Arizona. University of Arizona, College of
1930 Agriculture Bulletin No. 130. Tucson, Arizona.

Soergel, W. Die Gliederung und Absolute Zeitrechnung des Eiszeitalters.
1925 Fortshr. Geol. und Pal., Vol. 13, 251 pp. Berlin, Germany.

Spier, L. Yuman Tribes of the Gila River. University of Chicago Press,
1933 Chicago, Illinois.

Taylor, W. P. Ecology and Life History of the Porcupine (*Erethizon*
1935 *epixanthum*) as Related to the Forests of Arizona and the Southwestern United States. University of Arizona Biological Science Bulletin No. 3, Vol. VI, No. 5. Tucson, Arizona.

Thornbury, W. D. Weathered Zones and Glacial Chronology in Southern
1940 Indiana. Journal of Geology, Vol. 48, pp. 449-475. University Chicago Press, Chicago, Illinois.

Thornthwaite, C. W., C. F. S. Sharpe, and E. F. Dosch. Climate and
1942 Accelerated Erosion in the Arid and Semi-arid Southwest With Special Reference to the Polacca Wash Drainage Basin, Arizona. U. S. Dept. of Agriculture, Tech. Bull. 808.

Thwaites, F. T. Pleistocene of Part of Northeastern Wisconsin. Geological
1943 Society of America, Bulletin, Vol. 54, pp. 87-144. New York, N. Y.

Treganza, A. E. Notes on the San Dieguito Lithic Industry of Southern
1947 California and Northern Baja California. *In* Observations on Archaeological Sites in Topanga Canyon, California. University of California Publications in American Archaeology and Ethnology, Vol. 44, No. 2, pp. 253-255. Berkeley, California.

Turney, O. A. The Land of the Stone Hoe. Privately Printed. Phoenix,
1924 Arizona.

Tuthill, Carr The Tres Alamos Site on the San Pedro River, Southeastern
1947 Arizona. The Amerind Foundation, Inc., Paper No. 4. Dragoon, Arizona.

Underhill, R. M. Social Organization of the Papago Indians. Columbia
1939 Contributions to Anthropology, Vol. XXX. New York, N. Y.

1940 The Papago Indians of Arizona and Their Relatives, the Pima. Sherman Pamphlets, No. 3, Education Division, U. S. Office of Indian Affairs. Haskell Institute, Lawrence, Kansas.

United States Naval Institute The Bluejackets' Manual. United States
1940 Naval Institute, Tenth Edition. Annapolis, Maryland.

Vaillant, G. C. Excavations at Ticoman. Anthropological Papers of the
1931 American Museum of Natural History, Vol. 32, Pt. 2. New York, N. Y.

Weltfish, G. Prehistoric North American Basketry Techniques and Mod-
1930 ern Distributions. American Anthropologist, American Anthropological Association, Vol. 32, No. 3, Pt. I, n. s., pp. 454-495. Menasha, Wisconsin.

1932 Problems in the Study of Ancient and Modern Basket Makers. American Anthropologist, American Anthropological Association, Vol. 34, No. 1, n. s., pp. 108-117. Menasha, Wisconsin.

Wheeler, S. M. Archaeology of Etna Cave, Lincoln County, Nevada.
1942 Nevada State Park Commission, Carson City, Nevada.

Wiener, A. S. Blood Groups and Blood Transfusions, 3rd Edition. Charles
1943 C. Thomas, Springfield, Illinois.

Wilson, L. R. The Two Creeks Forest Bed, Manitowoc County, Wisconsin.
1932 Trans. Wisconsin Academy of Science, Vol. 27, pp. 31-46. Madison, Wisconsin.

1945 Pebble Band Ventifacts on Iowa Till in Linn Co., Iowa. Iowa Academy of Science, Vol. 52, pp. 235-241. Des Moines, Iowa.

Withers, A. M. Excavations at Valshni Village, Papago Indian Reserva-
1941 tion. Master's Thesis, University of Arizona. Tucson, Arizona.

1944 Excavations at Valshni Village, A Site on the Papago Indian Reservation. American Antiquity, Vol. X, No. 1, pp. 33-47, Society for American Archaeology. Menasha, Wisconsin.

Woodbury, G. and Edna Woodbury Prehistoric Skeletal Remains from the
1935 Texas Coast. Medallion Papers, No. XVIII, Gila Pueblo. Globe, Arizona.

Woodward, A. A Shell Bracelet Manufactory. American Antiquity, Society
1936 for American Archaeology, Vol. II, No. 2, pp. 117-125. Menasha, Wisconsin.

Wormington, H. M. Ancient Man in North America. The Colorado Mu-
1939 seum of Natural History, Popular Series, No. 4. Denver.

Wyllys, R. K. Padre Luis Velarde's Relación of Pimería Alta, 1716. New
1931 Mexico Historical Review, Vol. 6, pp. 111-157. Albuquerque.

Zeuner, F. L. The Pleistocene Period, Its Climate, Chronology, and Faunal
1945 Successions. Royal Society, Vol. 130, 322 pp. B. Quaritch, London, England.

Index

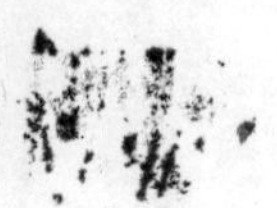